Baseball America
2022 DIRECTORY

Baseball America
2022 DIRECTORY

Editors
J.J. Cooper, Josh Norris,
Chris Hilburn-Trenkle

Assistant Editors
Matt Eddy, Carlos Collazo,
Teddy Cahill, Kyle Glaser,
Ben Badler

Contributing
Paul Trap

Design & Production
James Alworth, Leah Tyner,
Seth Mates

Cover Photo
Joseph Gareri

Distributed by: Simon & Schuster **ISBN-13:** 978-1-7355482-7-2

Baseball America

PRESIDENT Tom Dondero
EDITOR IN CHIEF J.J. Cooper @jjcoop36
EXECUTIVE EDITOR Matt Eddy @MattEddyBA
CHIEF INNOVATION OFFICER Ben Badler @benbadler
CHIEF FINANCIAL OFFICER Dan Curvelo

EDITORIAL

SENIOR EDITOR Josh Norris @jnorris427
NATIONAL WRITERS Teddy Cahill @tedcahill,
Carlos Collazo @CarlosACollazo, Kyle Glaser @KyleAGlaser
PROSPECT WRITER Geoff Pontes @GeoffPontesBA
ASSOCIATE EDITOR Chris Hilburn-Trenkle @ChrisTrenkle
STAFF WRITER Joe Healy @JoeHealyBA
WEB EDITOR Kayla Lombardo @KaylaLombardo11
CONTENT PRODUCER Savannah McCann @savjaye
SPECIAL CONTRIBUTOR Tim Newcomb @tdnewcomb

PRODUCTION

CREATIVE DIRECTOR Seth Mates

BUSINESS

TECHNOLOGY MANAGER Brent Lewis
MARKETING/OPERATIONS COORDINATOR Angela Lewis
CUSTOMER SERVICE Melissa Sunderman

STATISTICAL SERVICE

Major League Baseball Advanced Media

BASEBALL AMERICA ENTERPRISES

CHAIRMAN & CEO Gary Green
PRESIDENT Larry Botel
GENERAL COUNSEL Matthew Pace
DIRECTOR OF MARKETING Amy Heart
INVESTOR RELATIONS Michele Balfour
DIRECTOR OF OPERATIONS Joan Disalvo
PARTNERS Stephen Alepa, Craig Amazeen, Jon Ashley, Martie Cordaro,
Andrew Fox, Robert Hernreich, Glenn Isaacson, Sonny Kalsi, Peter G.
Riguardi, Ian Ritchie, Brian Rothschild, Peter Ruprecht, Beryl Snyder,
Tom Steiglehner, Dan Waldman

TABLE OF CONTENTS

WILLIAM PURNELL/ICON SPORTSWIRE VIA GETTY IMAGES

MAJOR LEAGUES

Major League Baseball	**14**
American League	**15**
National League	**15**

Arizona	**16**	Milwaukee	**46**
Atlanta	**18**	Minnesota	**48**
Baltimore	**20**	New York (NL)	**50**
Boston	**22**	New York (AL)	**52**
Chicago (NL)	**24**	Oakland	**54**
Chicago (AL)	**26**	Philadelphia	**56**
Cincinnati	**28**	Pittsburgh	**58**
Cleveland	**30**	St. Louis	**60**
Colorado	**32**	San Diego	**62**
Detroit	**34**	San Francisco	**64**
Houston	**36**	Seattle	**66**
Kansas City	**38**	Tampa Bay	**68**
Los Angeles (AL)	**40**	Texas	**70**
Los Angeles (NL)	**42**	Toronto	**72**
Miami	**44**	Washington	**74**

Media	**76**
General Information	**79**
Spring Training	**82**

MINOR LEAGUES

Minor League Baseball	**86**

Triple-A East	**87**	High-A East	**124**
Triple-A West	**97**	High-A West	**129**
Double-A NE	**103**	Low-A West	**132**
Double-A South	**109**	Low-A East	**136**
Double-A Central	**113**	Low-A Southeast	**141**
High-A Central	**118**		

MLB PARTNER LEAGUES

American Assoc.	**171**	Pecos	**187**
Atlantic	**175**	United Shore	**187**
Frontier	**179**		
Pioneer	**184**		

OTHER LEAGUES & ORGANIZATIONS

International	**188**	Summer College	**228**
College	**194**	High School	**242**
Am. International	**226**	Youth	**245**
National	**227**	Senior	**247**

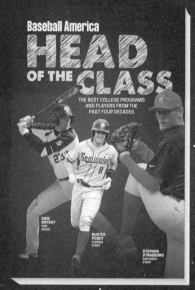

WHAT'S NEW IN 2022

The minor leagues saw the biggest shakeup in decades coming into the 2021 season. Major League Baseball took over governance and responsibility for administering the minor leagues, and minor league teams signed 10-year licenses directly with MLB. The 2022 season is the second under the current agreement.

That meant Minor League Baseball, (legally known as the National Association), wound down operations. MLB's takeover also brought with it the elimination of the league presidents and league offices that had long been a part of the minor leagues. It also meant that beginning in 2021, there were only five levels of affiliated minor league baseball in North America—the Arizona and Florida Complex Leagues as well as four full-season levels. The shuffling meant that 43 teams that were affiliated going into 2020 are no longer in affiliated baseball. Three teams that had been part of independent baseball joined affiliated baseball as well.

LEAGUE MOVEMENT

TRIPLE-A
Name Change: The Triple-A Sugar Land Skeeters have been renamed the Sugar Land Space Cowboys.

HIGH-A
Name Change: The High-A Beloit Snappers have been renamed the Beloit Sky Carp.

ATLANTIC LEAGUE
Added: Wild Health Genomes (they share the Lexington park with the Lexington Legends) and the Staten Island FerryHawks.
Name Change: The West Virginia Power have been renamed the Charleston Dirty Birds.

AMERICAN ASSOCIATION
Added: Lake Country Dockhounds.

FRONTIER LEAGUE
Added: Ottawa Titans. The Trois-Rivieres Aigles also join the league. The Aigles were slated to be part of the league in 2021, but could not play because of coronavirus restrictions.

PIONEER LEAGUE
Added: Glacier Range Riders and Northern Colorado Owlz.

Map illustrations by Paul Trap

Vancouver

Everett

Spokane

Tacoma

Tri-City

Hillsboro

Eugene

Sacramento

Reno

 A's Stockton

Modesto

 San Jose Fresno

Rancho Cucamonga Visalia

Las Vegas

LA

 Inland Empire

Lake Elsinore

SD

Salt Lake

 CR

 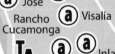

Albuquerque

El Paso

TRIPLE-A

 West

HIGH-A

 West

LOW-A

 West

Map illustrations by Paul Trap

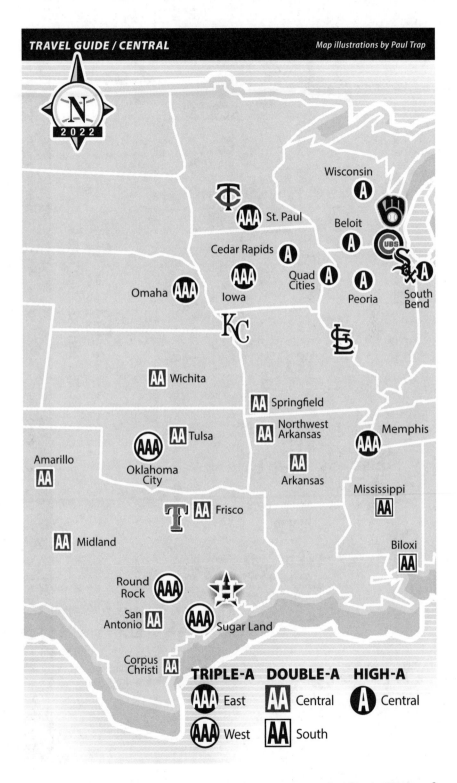

Wisconsin

St. Paul

Beloit

Cedar Rapids

Quad Cities

Omaha

Iowa

Peoria

South Bend

Wichita

Springfield

Northwest Arkansas

Tulsa

Memphis

Amarillo

Oklahoma City

Arkansas

Mississippi

Frisco

Midland

Biloxi

Round Rock

San Antonio

Sugar Land

Corpus Christi

TRIPLE-A   **DOUBLE-A**   **HIGH-A**

East   Central   Central

West   South

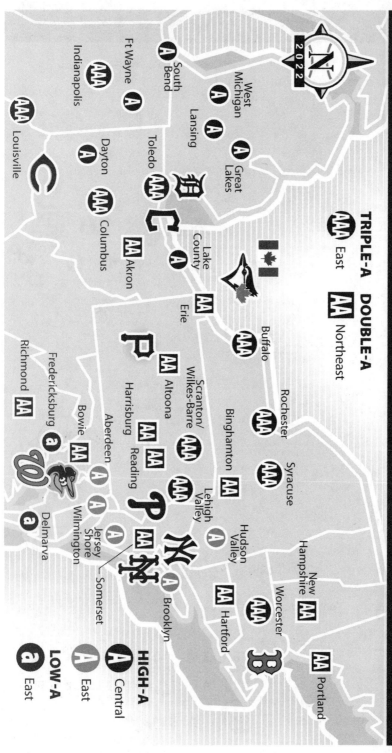

TRIPLE-A

AAA East

DOUBLE-A

AA Northeast

HIGH-A

A Central

A East

LOW-A

a East

Indianapolis — AAA
Louisville — AAA
South Bend — A
Ft Wayne — A
West Michigan — A
Lansing — A
Great Lakes — A
Dayton — A
Toledo — AAA
Columbus — AAA
Akron — AA
Lake County — A
Erie — AA
Buffalo — AAA
Rochester — AAA
Syracuse — AAA
Binghamton — AA
Scranton/Wilkes-Barre — AAA
Altoona — AA
Harrisburg — AA
Reading — AA
Lehigh Valley — AAA
Hudson Valley — A
New Hampshire — AA
Worcester — AAA
Hartford — AA
Portland — AA
Brooklyn — A
Somerset — AA
Jersey Shore — A
Wilmington — A
Aberdeen — A
Bowie — AA
Fredericksburg — a
Richmond — AA
Delmarva — a

Map illustrations by Paul Trap

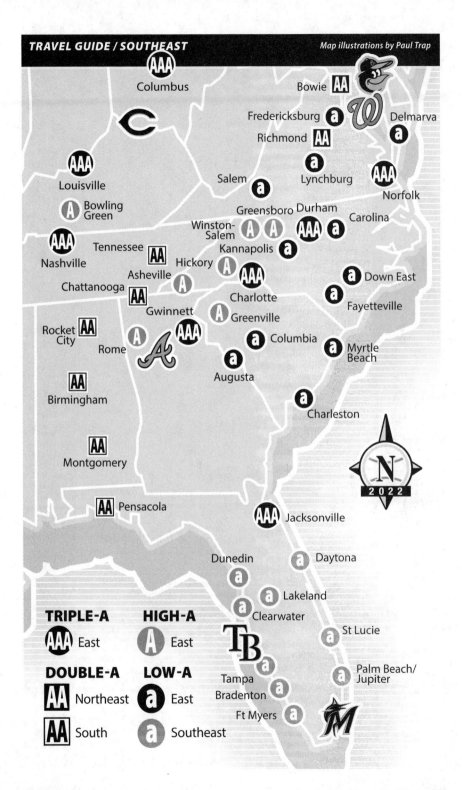

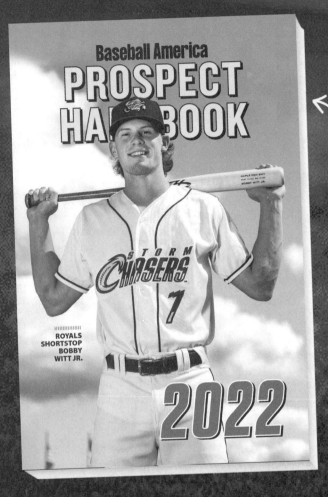

MAJOR LEAGUES

MAJOR LEAGUE BASEBALL

Mailing Address: 1271 Avenue of the Americas, New York, NY 10020.
Telephone: (212) 931-7800. **Website:** www.mlb.com.
Commissioner of Baseball: Rob Manfred.
Deputy Commissioner, Baseball Administration and Chief Legal Officer: Dan Halem.
Chief Communications Officer: Pat Courtney. **Chief Baseball Development Officer:** Tony
Reagins. **Chief Financial Officer/Sr. Advisor:** Bob Starkey. **Chief Operations & Strategy
Officer:** Chris Marinak. **Chief Revenue Officer:** Noah Garden. **Executive Vice President &
General Counsel:** Lara Pitaro Wisch. **Executive Vice President, Chief Marketing Officer:**
Karin Timpone.

Rob Manfred

ON-FIELD OPERATIONS

Executive Vice President, Baseball Operations: Morgan Sword. **Senior Vice President,
On-Field Operations:** Michael Hill. **Senior Vice President, On-Field Operations:** Raul Ibañez.
Senior VP, Minor League Operations & Development: Peter Woodfork. **Vice President,
Amateur & Medical:** John D'Angelo. **Vice President, Baseball Economics:** Reed MacPhail.
Vice President, **Head Baseball Operations Counsel:** Paul Mifsud. Vice President, **Instant Replay Operations:** Justin
Klemm. V**ice President, Umpiring Operations:** Matt McKendry. **Senior Director, On-Field Operations:** Gregor
Blanco. **Senior Director, On-Field Operations:** Rajai Davis. **Senior Director, On-Field Operations:** Dan Otero.
Senior Director, International Operations: Rebecca Seesel. **Senior Director, Player Programs:** Yenifer Fauche.
Senior Director, Baseball Operations: Jeff Pfeifer. **Senior Director, Minor League Operations & Affairs:** Freddie
Seymour. **Senior Director, On-Field Strategy:** Joe Martinez. **Senior Director, Front Office & Field Staff Diversity:**
Tyrone Brooks. **Director, Draft Operations:** Bill Francis. **Director, Umpire Development:** Rich Rieker. **Director, Sports
Medicine:** Scott Sheridan. **Director, Player Development:** Mike LaCassa. **Senior Manager, Baseball Economics:**
Cameron Barwick. **Senior Manager, Player Programs:** Ricardhy Grandoit. **Senior Manager, Umpiring Operations:**
Raquel Wagner. **Manager, Baseball Economics:** Travis Buck. **Manager, Baseball Economics:** Kyle Krueger. **Manager,
Medical & Equipment:** Kevin Ma. **Manager, Instant Replay:** Jeff Moody. **Manager, On-Field Operations:** Chris
Knettel. **Manager, Baseball Operations:** Garrett Horan. **Senior Coordinator, Umpiring Operations:** Chris Romanello.
Senior Coordinator, Video: Freddie Hernandez. **Senior Coordinator, Baseball Operations:** Gina Liento. **Senior
Coordinator, Baseball Operations:** Elizabeth Benn. **Senior Coordinator, On-Field Operations:** Danielle Monday.
Senior Coordinator, Player Programs: Carla Chalas. **Analyst, Baseball Operations:** Josh Keen. **Coordinator, Medical
Operations:** Becky Reifler. **Coordinator, Medical Operations:** Zack Tenner. **Coordinator, Draft Operations:** Jack
Clark. **Coordinator, Draft Operations:** Diego Delgado. **Coordinator, Draft Operations:** Mark Nader. **Coordinator,
International Operations:** Maritza Grillo. **Coordinator, Umpiring Operations:** Alejandro Bermudez. **Coordinator,
Baseball Operations:** Anthony Montes. **Coordinator, Baseball Economics:** Mallory Williamson. **Coordinator, Minor
League Operations:** Sabrina Warren. **Coordinator, Minor League Operations:** Gianna Finz. **Coordinator, On-Field
Operations:** Julia Hernandez.

LABOR RELATIONS

Senior Vice President, Deputy General Counsel, Labor Relations: Patrick Houlihan. **Vice President, Drug, Health
& Safety Programs:** Jon Coyles. **Director, Drug, Health & Safety Programs:** Lindsey Ingraham. **Senior Counsel:** Kasey
Sanossian. **Counsel:** Vanish Grover. **Counsel:** Justin Wiley. **Coordinator, Drug Health & Safety Programs:** Isabel Caro.

BASEBALL & SOFTBALL DEVELOPMENT

Chief Baseball Development Officer: Tony Reagins. **Vice President, Baseball & Softball Development:** David
James. **Vice President, Youth & Facility Development:** Darrell Miller. **Vice President, Baseball Development:**
Del Matthews. **Senior Director, Baseball & Softball Development:** Chris Haydock. **Senior Director, Compliance:**
Katherine Anderson. **Director, New Orleans Youth Academy:** Eddie Davis. **Senior Manager, Baseball & Softball
Development:** Chuck Fox. **Senior Manager, Play Ball & RBI:** Bennett Shields. **Senior Coordinator, Baseball
Development:** Kindu Jones. **Senior Coordinator, Softball Development and Legal:** Sarah Padove. **Senior
Coordinator, Baseball Development, RBI:** Steven Smiegocki. **Coordinator, Softball Development:** Koely Kempisty.
Coordinator, Baseball & Softball Development: Cameron Scott. **Coordinator, MLB Compton Youth Academy:**
Kenneth Landreaux.**Coordinator, MLB Compton Youth Academy Softball:** Eliza Crawford. **Senior Administrative
Assistant:** Grace Carrasco.

COMMUNICATIONS

Telephone: (212) 931-7878. **Fax:** (212) 949-5654.
Chief Communications Officer: Pat Courtney. **Senior Vice President, Communications:** Matt Bourne. **Vice
President, Communication:** John Blundell. **Vice President, Communication:** Mike Teevan. **Senior Director,
Business Communications & Youth Engagement:** Steve Arocho. **Senior Director, Business Communications:**
Ileana Peña. **Director, Communications:** Donald Muller. **Senior Manager, Communications:** Jeff Lantz. **Manager,
Communications:** Lydia Devlin. **Manager, Business Communications:** David Hochman. **Senior Coordinator,
Communications & Scheduling:** Paul Koehler. **Senior Coordinator, Communications:** Yolayna Alvarez. **Coordinator,
Business Communications:** Troy Watson. **Executive Assistant, Communications:** Ginger Dillon. **Official Historian:**
John Thorn.

AMERICAN LEAGUE

Year League Founded: 1901.
2022 Opening Date: March 31. **Closing Date:** Oct. 2.
Regular Season: 162 games.
Division Structure: East—Baltimore, Boston, New York, Tampa Bay, Toronto.
Central—Chicago, Cleveland, Detroit, Kansas City, Minnesota. **West**—Houston, Los Angeles, Oakland, Seattle, Texas.
Playoff Format: Two non-division winners with best records meet in one-game wild card. Wild card winner and three division champions meet in two best-of-five Division Series. Winners meet in best-of-seven Championship Series.
All-Star Game: July 19, Dodger Stadium, Los Angeles (American League vs. National League).
Roster Limit: 26, through Sept. 1, when rosters expand to 28. **Brand of Baseball:** Rawlings.
Statistician: MLB Advanced Media, 1271 Avenue of the Americas, New York, NY, 10020.

STADIUM INFORMATION

Team	Stadium	Dimensions			Capacity	2021 Att.
		LF	CF	RF		
Baltimore	Oriole Park at Camden Yards	333	410	318	45,971	793,229
Boston	Fenway Park	310	390	302	37,673	1,725,323
Chicago	Guaranteed Rate Field	330	400	335	40,615	1,596,385
Cleveland	Progressive Field	325	405	325	37,675	1,114,368
Detroit	Comerica Park	345	420	330	41,782	1,102,621
Houston	Minute Maid Park	315	435	326	40,976	2,068,509
Kansas City	Kauffman Stadium	330	410	330	37,903	1,159,613
Los Angeles	Angel Stadium	333	404	333	45,050	1,515,689
Minnesota	Target Field	339	404	328	39,504	1,310,199
New York	Yankee Stadium	318	408	314	50,291	1,959,854
Oakland	Oakland Coliseum	330	400	367	35,067	701,430
Seattle	T-Mobile Park	331	401	326	47,447	1,215,985
Tampa Bay	Tropicana Field	315	404	322	41,315	761,072
Texas	Globe Life Park in Arlington	332	400	325	48,114	2,110,258
Toronto	Rogers Centre	328	400	328	50,598	805,901

NATIONAL LEAGUE

Year League Founded: 1901.
2022 Opening Date: March 31. **Closing Date:** Oct. 2.
Regular Season: 162 games.
Division Structure: East—Atlanta, Miami, New York, Philadelphia, Washington. **Central**—Chicago, Cincinnati, Milwaukee, Pittsburgh, St. Louis. **West**—Arizona, Colorado, Los Angeles, San Diego, San Francisco.
Playoff Format: Two non-division winners with best records meet in one-game wild card. Wild card winner and three division champions meet in two best-of-five Division Series. Winners meet in best-of-seven Championship Series.
All-Star Game: July 19, Dodger Stadium, Los Angeles (American League vs. National League).
Roster Limit: 26, through Sept. 1, when rosters expand to 28. **Brand of Baseball:** Rawlings.
Statistician: MLB Advanced Media, 1271 Avenue of the Americas, New York, NY, 10020.

STADIUM INFORMATION

Team	Stadium	Dimensions			Capacity	2021 Att.
		LF	CF	RF		
Arizona	Chase Field	330	407	334	49,033	1,043,010
Atlanta	Truist Park	335	400	325	41,500	2,300,247
Chicago	Wrigley Field	355	400	353	41,160	1,978,934
Cincinnati	Great American Ball Park	328	404	325	42,319	1,505,024
Colorado	Coors Field	347	415	350	50,499	1,938,645
Los Angeles	Dodger Stadium	330	395	330	56,000	2,804,693
Miami	Marlins Park	344	407	335	36,742	642,617
Milwaukee	Miller Park	344	400	345	41,900	1,824,282
New York	Citi Field	335	408	330	42,200	1,511,926
Philadelphia	Citizens Bank Park	329	401	330	43,647	1,515,890
Pittsburgh	PNC Park	325	399	320	38,496	859,498
St. Louis	Busch Stadium	336	400	335	46,681	2,191,950
San Diego	Petco Park	336	396	322	42,685	1,679,484
San Francisco	Oracle Park	339	399	309	41,503	2,102,530
Washington	Nationals Park	336	402	335	41,888	1,465,543

ARIZONA DIAMONDBACKS

Office Address: Chase Field, 401 E. Jefferson St, Phoenix, AZ 85004.
Mailing Address: P.O. Box 2095, Phoenix, AZ 85001.
Telephone: (602) 462-6500. **Website:** www.dbacks.com, www.losdbacks.com.

OWNERSHIP
Managing General Partner: Ken Kendrick. **General Partners:** Mike Chipman, Jeff Royer.

BUSINESS OPERATIONS
President & CEO: Derrick Hall. **Executive Vice President & Chief Financial Officer:** Tom Harris. **Executive Vice President & General Manager:** Mike Hazen. **Executive Vice President & Chief Legal Officer:** Nona Lee. **Executive Vice President, Business Operations & Chief Revenue Officer:** Cullen Maxey.

Ken Kendrick

COMMUNITY IMPACT
Senior Vice President, Corporate/Community Impact: Debbie Castaldo. **Director, Community and Foundation Operations:** Tara Trzinski. **Director, Community Initiatives & Partner Programs:** Dustin Payne.

CONTENT & COMMUNICATIONS
Senior Vice President, Content & Communications: Jaci Brown. **Vice President, DBTV Productions & Game Ops:** Rob Weinheimer. **Vice President, Communications:** Casey Wilcox. **Senior Director, Player & Media Relations:** Patrick O'Connell.

CORPORATE PARTNERSHIPS, MEDIA & EVENTS
Senior Vice President, Corporate Partnerships, Media & Events: Steve Mullins. **Vice President, Broadcasting:** Scott Geyer. **Senior Director, Event Development & Operations:** Michael Hilburn. **Director, Corporate Partnerships:** Brendan Cunningham.

FINANCE
Vice President, Finance: Craig Bradley. **Senior Director, Financial Management & Purchasing:** Jeff Jacobs.

GOVERNMENT AFFAIRS
Vice President, Government Affairs: Amilyn Pierce.

INFORMATION TECHNOLOGY
Senior Vice President & Chief Technology Officer: Bob Zweig. **Senior Director, Business Systems:** Craig Pozen **Senior Director, Technology Infrastructure & Services:** Derek Ferguson

LEGAL
General Counsel: Caleb Jay.

MARKETING & BUSINESS ANALYTICS
Senior Vice President, Marketing & Analytics: Kenny Farrell. **Senior Director, Business Analytics:** Brandon Buser. **Senior Director, Ticket Operations:** Josh Simon. **Director, Clubhouse Creative:** Zachary Alvarez.

PEOPLE & CULTURE
Senior Vice President, People & Culture: Joe Walsh. **Director, People & Culture:** Jackie Dickerson.

TICKETING
Telephone: (602) 514-8400. **Senior Vice President, Ticket Sales & Marketing:** John Fisher. **Vice President, Ticket Sales & Services:** Mike Dellosa. **Director, Season Ticket Experience:** Jamie Roberts.

BASEBALL OPERATIONS

Executive Vice President, General Manager: Mike Hazen. **Senior Vice President, Assistant GM:** Amiel Sawdaye. **Vice President, Assistant GM:** Michael Fitzgerald. **Vice President, Latin Operations:** Junior Noboa. **Director of Pitching:** Ross Seaton. **Senior Director of Team Travel:** Roger Riley. **Director, Baseball Administration:** Kristyn Pierce. **Assistant Director, Baseball Operations:** Max Phillips. **Director, Baseball Research & Development:** Max Glick. **Senior Analyst, Baseball Research & Development:** Cody Callahan. **Analyst, Baseball Research & Development:** Carl Gonzalez. **Analysts, Research & Development:** Taylor Choe, Micah Daley-Harris. **Director, Baseball Systems:** John Krazit. **Senior Baseball Systems Developer:** Thomas Johnson. **Baseball Systems Developer:** Creagor Elsom. **Analyst, Player Personnel:** Connor Shannon. **Analyst, Player Personnel:** Chris Slivka. **Analyst, Player Personnel:** Jake Greenberg.

Mike Hazen

MAJOR LEAGUE STAFF

Manager: Torey Lovullo. **Bench Coach:** Jeff Banister. **Hitting Coach:** Joe Mather. **Pitching Coach:** Brent Strom. **First Base Coach:** Dave McKay. **Third Base Coach:** Tony Perezchica. **Assistant Hitting Coach:** Damion Easley. **Bullpen Coach:** Mike Fetters. **Bullpen Catcher:** Jose Queliz. **Coordinator, Major League Video:** Allen Campbell. **Coordinator, Major League Player Development & Instruction:** Luis Urueta. **Coordinator, Run Prevention:** Alex Cultice

MEDICAL/TRAINING

Club Physician: Dr. Gary Waslewski. **Club Physician:** Roger McCoy. **Club Physician:** Kareem Shaarawy. **Director, Sports Medicine & Performance:** Ken Crenshaw. **Head Athletic Trainer:** Ryan DiPanfilo. **Assistant Athletic Trainer:** Ryne Eubanks. **Strength & Conditioning Coordinator:** Nate Shaw. **Assistant Strength & Conditioning:** Scott Cline. **Manual Therapist:** Ben Hagar. **Physical Therapist:** Max Esposito. **Manual Therapist/Athletic Trainer:** Junko Yazawa. **Senior Analyst, Sports Medicine & Performance:** Patrick Sellas. **Director of Nutrition, Sports Medicine & Performance Team:** Michelle Riccardi

PLAYER DEVELOPMENT

Director, Player Development: Josh Barfield. **Assistant Director, Player Development:** Matt Grabowski. **Assistant Director, Minor League Administration:** Shawn Marette. **Coordinator, Baseball Developmental Technology:** Cory Swope. **Coordinator, Mental Skills:** Zach Brandon. **Field Coordinator:** Blake Lalli. **Pitching Coordinator /Assistant ML Pitching Coach:** Dan Carlson. **Pitching Coordinator /Assistant ML Pitching Coach:** Barry Enright. **Minor League Hitting Coordinator/Assistant ML Hitting Coach:** Rick Short. **Director of Minor League Hitting/Assistant ML Hitting Coach:** Drew Hedman. **Infield Coordinator/Reno Manager:** Gil Velazquez. **Outfield/Baserunning Coordinator:** Peter Bourjos. **Catching Coordinator /Reno Hitting Coach:** Mark Reed. **Rehab and Complex Pitching Coordinator:** Matt Herges. **Rehab Pitching Coordinator:** Brad Arnsberg. **Player Development Assistant:** Orlando Hudson. **Short-Season Pitching Coordinator:** Manny Garcia. **Short-Season Hitting Coordinator:** Casey Chenoweth. **Arizona Complex Coordinator:** Jaime Del Valle. **DR Complex Coordinator:** Luis Silverio. **DR Infield Coordinator:** Juan Francia. **Director, Skills Development/Strength & Conditioning Coordinator:** Vaughn Robinson. **Major League & Minor League Medical Administrator:** Jon Herzner. **Minor League Medical Coordinator:** Kelly Boyce. **Minor League Physical Therapist:** Merritt Walker. **Mental Skills Coach:** Charley Jauss. **Mental Skills Coach:** Sydney Masters. **Mental Skills Consultant:** Derin McMains.

FARM SYSTEM

Class	Club (League)	Manager	Hitting Coach	Pitching Coach
Triple-A	Reno	Gil Velazquez	Mark Reed/Nick Evans	Doug Drabek
Double-A	Amarillo	Shawn Roof	Travis Denker	Shane Loux
High-A	Hillsboro	Vince Harrison	KC Judge	Jeff Bajenaru
Low-A	Visalia	Jorge Cortes	Ty Wright	G.Hernandez
Rookie	Diamondbacks (ACL)	TBD	TBD	TBD

SCOUTING

Telephone: (602) 462-6500. **Fax:** (602) 462-6425.

Director, Amateur Scouting: Ian Rebhan. **Assistant Director, Amateur Scouting:** Kerry Jenkins. **Assistant, Amateur Scouting & Latin American Assimilation:** Chloe Medina. **Director, Pro Scouting:** Jason Parks. **Assistant Director, Player Personnel:** Cory Hahn. **Vice President, Latin American Scouting & Player Development:** Cesar Geronimo. **Director, International Scouting:** Peter Wardell. **Manager, International Baseball Operations & Scouting:** Mariana Patraca. **National Scouting Supervisor:** Greg Lonigro. **National Scouting Supervisor:** James Merriweather III. **National Pitching Supervisor:** Jeff Mousser. **Amateur Scouting Supervisor:** Steve Connelly. **Amateur Scouting Supervisor:** Frank Damas. **Amateur Scouting Supervisor:** Rick Matsko. **Amateur Scouting Supervisor:** Steve McAllister. **Amateur Scouting Supervisor:** Doyle Wilson. **Area Scouts:** Andrew Allen, Hudson Belinsky, Nathan Birtwell, Eric Cruz, Pedro Hernandez, Jeremy Kehrt, Jeremiah Luster, Rick Matsko, Matt Mercurio, Mike Meyers, Dan Ramsay, Mark Ross, JR Salinas, George Swain, Garry Templeton, Jake Williams, Stephen Baker, Jason Gallagher. **Major League Advance Scout:** Jeff Gardner. **Special Assignment Scouts:** Todd Greene, Danny Haas, Tim Wilken. **Major League Scouts:** Bill Gayton, Mike Piatnik. **Independent League Scouting Coordinator/Pro Scout:** Chris Carminucci. **Professional/International Scout:** Mack Hayashi. **Professional/International Scout, Pacific Rim Operations:** Kelvin Kondo. **Professional Scouts:** Tucker Blair, Diego Bordas, Jacob Frisaro, Matthew Hahn, Rob Leary, Alex Lorenzo, Colin Sabean, Aaron Thorn, Brett West. **International Crosschecker:** Jon Lukens. **International Crosschecker:** Hector Otero. **Crosschecker, Latin America:** Francisco Cartaya. **Supervisor, Dominican Republic:** Omar Rogers. **Coordinator, Dominican Republic:** Ronald Rivas. **Special Assignment Scout:** Mark Snipp. **International Scouts:** Luis Gonzalez Arteaga, Bradley Stuart, Pablo Arias, David Felida, Pedro Meyer, Jose Ortiz, Wilfredo Tejada, Kyle Lee, Ray Padilla, Luis Pena, Julio Sanchez, Jose Luis Santos.

ATLANTA BRAVES

Office Address: 755 Battery Avenue, SE Atlanta, GA 30339-3017.
Mailing Address: PO Box 723009, Atlanta, GA 31139-2704.
Telephone: (404) 522-7630. **Website:** www.braves.com.

OWNERSHIP

Operated/Owned By: Liberty Media. **Chairman:** Terry McGuirk. **Vice Chairman, Emeritus:** John Schuerholz.

BUSINESS OPERATIONS

President/CEO, Atlanta Braves: Derek Schiller. **President/CEO, Braves Development Company:** Mike Plant. **Executive VP/Chief Legal Officer:** Greg Heller.

MARKETING/SALES

Senior VP, Marketing and Content: Adam Zimmerman. **Senior VP, Ticket Sales:** Paul Adams. **Senior VP, Corporate & Premium Partnerships:** Jim Allen. **Executive VP, Chief Culture Officer:** DeRetta Rhodes, PhD.

FINANCE

Executive VP, Chief Financial Officer: Jill Robinson.

COMMUNICATIONS

Telephone: (404) 522-7630.

Terry McGuirk

Vice President, Communications: Beth Marshall. **Director, Baseball Communications:** Jonathan Kerber. **Manager, Baseball Communications:** Jared Burleyson. **Manager, Player Relations:** Franco García. **Coordinator, Baseball Communications:** Mitch George. **Director, Corporate Communications:** Sarit Babboni. **Senior Coordinator, Corporate Communications:** Kara Zoellner.

STADIUM OPERATIONS

Senior Vice President, Facility Operations: Eric Perestuk. **Senior Director, Field Operations:** Ed Mangan. **VP, Fan Experience:** Scott Cunningham. **PA Announcer:** Casey Motter. **Official Scorers:** Guy Curtright, Richard Musterer, Mike Stamus.

TICKETING

Telephone: (404) 577-9100. **Email:** ticketsales@braves.com.
Senior VP, Ticket Operations: Anthony Esposito.

TRAVEL/CLUBHOUSE

Director of Team Travel: Jim Lovell. **Director, Equipment & Clubhouse Service:** Calvin Minasian.
Visiting Clubhouse Manager: Fred Stone. **Assistant Equipment and Clubhouse Service Managers:** Eric Durban and Chris Hunter.

BASEBALL OPERATIONS

Telephone: (404) 522-7630. **Fax:** (404) 614-3308.

President, Baseball Operations & General Manager: Alex Anthopoulos. **VP, Scouting:** Dana Brown. **VP, Baseball Development:** Mike Fast. **Assistant GM/Research & Development:** Jason Paré. **Special Assistant to GM:** Bobby Cox. **Senior Director, Baseball Administration:** Dixie Keller. **Director, Baseball Operations:** Adam Sonabend. **Manager, Baseball Video Operations:** Rob Smith. **Executive Assistant to the President, Baseball Operations & General Manager:** Elizabeth Terán. **Director, Baseball Operations:** Adam Sonabend. **Assistant Director, Major League Operations:** Doug Wachter. **Manager, Baseball Video Operations:** Rob Smith. **Advance Scout:** Braeden Schlehuber. **Special Assistant, Major League Operations:** Tyler Flowers. **Manager, Major League Operations:** Caelan Collins. **Coordinators, Major League Operations:** Kenny Dorian, Tom O'Donnell. **Analysts, Major League Operations:** Jeremy Dorsey, Robert Sanders, Will Siskell and Matt Winn. **Manager, Baseball Systems:** Garrett Wilson. **Lead Developer, Baseball Systems:** Mike Copeland. **Developer, Baseball Systems:** Isaac Lee. **Assistant Director, Research & Development:** Josh Malek. **Coordinator, Research & Development:** Kyle Sargent. **Analysts, Research & Development:** Evan Olawsky. **Senior Data Scientist:** Evan Tucker, PhD. **Manager, Family Relations:** Rafael Becerra. **Coordinator, Family Relations:** Seth Heizer, **Bill Lucas Fellowship:** Terrence Pinkston. **Advance Scouting Trainee:** Jack Byrne. **Research and Development Trainee:** Ryan Corkrean.

Alex Anthopoulos

MAJOR LEAGUE STAFF

Manager: Brian Snitker. **Coaches: Bench**—Walt Weiss, **Pitching**—Rick Kranitz, **Hitting**—Kevin Seitzer, **Assistant Hitting Coach**—José Castro and Bobby Magallanes, **First Base**—Eric Young Sr, **Third Base**—Ron Washington. **Catching Coach:** Sal Fasano. **Bullpen Coach:** Drew French. **Coach:** Eddie Pérez. **Hitting Consultant:** Chipper Jones. **Bullpen Catchers:** Jimmy Leo & José Yépez. **Batting Practice Pitcher:** Tomás Pérez.

MEDICAL/TRAINING

Director, Player Health/Head Athletic Trainer: George C. Poulis. **Head Team Physician:** Tim Griffith. **Assistant Athletic Trainer:** Jeff Stevenson and Nick Flynn. **Head Strength & Conditioning Coach:** Brad Scott. **Assistant Strength & Conditioning Coach:** Jordan Wolf. **Head Physical Therapist:** Nick Valencia. **Assistant Physical Therapist:** Marcus Ahrens. **Physical Therapy Consultant:** Pete Cicinelli. **Massage Therapist:** Nate Leet. **Performance Nutritionist:** Patrick O'Brien.

PLAYER DEVELOPMENT

Telephone: (404) 522-7630.

Assistant GM/Player Development: Ben Sestanovich. **Director, Minor League Operations:** Ron Knight. **Manager, Video & Technology:** Kyle Clements. **Assistants:** Dylan Quantz, Ryan Taylor and Tucker Meredith. **Advisor:** Doug Mansolino. **Director, Player Development:** Kevin Hooper. **Director, Pitching Development:** Paul Davis. **Hitting Coordinator:** TBD. **Instructor:** Tom Goodwin. **Roving Coordinators:** Jay Pryor (infield), Cale Johnson (assistant pitching), Greg Walker (assistant hitting), JD Closser (catching), Eric Hrycko (medical), Toby Williams (assistant medical), Jordan Sidwell (strength & conditioning), Ryan Meehan (assistant strength & conditioning), Sean Reagan (video), Fernando Piñeres (cultural development), Zach Sorensen (mental skills). **Coordinator, Florida Operations:** Jeff Pink. **Physical Therapist:** Johnny Passarelli. **Assistant Director, Baseball Development Analytics:** Colin Wyers. **Data Scientist:** Christina Zaccardi. **Assistant, Baseball Development:** David Lee.

FARM SYSTEM

Class	Club	Manager	Hitting Coach	Pitching Coach
Triple-A	Gwinnett	Matt Tuiasosopo	Carlos Mendez	Mike Maroth
Double-A	Mississippi	Bruce Crabbe	Mike Bard	Bo Henning
High-A	Rome	Kanekoa Texeira	Danny Santiesteban	Wes McGuire
Low-A	Augusta	Michael Saunders	Connor Narron	Michael Steed
Rookie	Braves (FCL)	Chris Swauger	Einar Diaz	Elvin Nina

SCOUTING

Special Assistants to Baseball Operations: Andruw Jones, Chipper Jones, and Terry Pendleton. **Special Assistant, Scouting Operations:** Jonathan Schuerholz. **Special Assignment Scouts:** Ralph Garr, John Gibbons, Fred McGriff. **Assistant Director, Amateur Scouting Operations:** Ronit Shah. **National Crosscheckers:** Joe Jordan, Gary Rajsich. **Regional Crosscheckers: West/Southwest**—Joey Davis, **Southeast**—Reed Dunn, **Pacific Northwest**—Alan Hull, **Midwest**—Terry Tripp Jr. **Area Scouting Supervisors:** Billy Best (Holly Springs, NC), Jon Bunnell (Tampa, FL), Alan Butts (Newnan, GA), Travis Coleman (Trail Hoover, AL), Ryan Dobson (Culver City, CA), Anthony Flora (Phoenix, AZ), JD French (Kennett, MO), Jeremy Gordon (Clinton Township, MI), Ted Lekas (Brewster, MA), Cody Martin (Vancouver, WA), Kevin Martin (Los Angeles, CA), Trey McNickle (Olive Branch, MS), Will Rich (Nashville, TN), Lou Sanchez (Miami, FL), Alan Sandberg (Hopatcong, NJ), Brian Sankey (Newburyport, MA), and Darin Vaughan (Kingwood, TX). **Video Coordinators:** Trevor Andresen (Solana Beach, CA), Alex Burritt (St. Petersburg, FL), and Ryan Egdes (Naples, FL). **Manager, Latin American Operations:** Jonathan Cruz. **Manager, International Scouting Administration:** Gerald Milanes. **Manager, Dominican Republic Administration & Operations:** Lothar Schott. **Scouting Supervisors:** Orlando Covo (South America), Raul Gonzalez (Dominican Republic & Mexico), and Carlos Sequera (Venezuela). **International Scouts: Dominican Republic**—Reymond Nunez, Miguel Prestol, Luis Santos, and Victor Torres. **Venezuela**—Richard Castillo, Raphachel Colatosti, Rafael Marcano, Edison Sanchez, and Jesus Simancas. **Video Coordinator:** Jaime Gil (Dominican Republic).

BALTIMORE ORIOLES

Office Address: 333 W Camden St., Baltimore, MD 21201.
Telephone: (888) 848-BIRD. **Fax:** (410) 547-6272.
E-mail Address: birdmail@orioles.com. **Website:** www.orioles.com.

OWNERSHIP

Operated By: The Baltimore Orioles Limited Partnership Inc.
Chairman/CEO: John Angelos. **Ownership Representative:** Louis Angelos.

BUSINESS OPERATIONS

Peter Angelos

SENIOR LEADERSHIP TEAM

Executive Vice President and General Manager: Mike Elias. **Senior Vice President, Administration & Experience:** Greg Bader. **Senior Vice President, Chief Revenue Officer:** T.J. Brightman. **Senior Vice President, Community Development & Communications:** Jennifer Grondahl. **Senior Vice President, Finance:** Michael D. Hoppes, CPA. **Senior Vice President, Human Resources:** Lisa Tolson.

EXECUTIVE BUSINESS ADMINISTRATION

Vice President, Ticket Partnerships: Neil Aloise. **Vice President, Finance:** Carole Bohon. **Vice President, Creative Content:** Tyler Hoffberger. **Senior Vice President, Business Development:** Lou Kousouris. **Vice President, Ballpark Experience & Operations:** Troy Scott. **Vice President, Corporate Partnerships:** Anthony Verni. **Executive Administrative Assistant:** Colleen Gellatly.

BALLPARK OPERATIONS & EXPERIENCE

Senior Director, Ballpark Operations: Kevin Cummings. **Senior Director, Florida Operations:** Trevor Markham. **Director, Ballpark Experience:** Kristen Schultz. **Director, Field Operations:** Nicole Sherry. **Director, Hospitality:** Tom Orszulak.

COMMUNICATIONS/ALUMNI

Telephone: (410) 547-6150. **Fax:** (410) 547-6272.
Senior Vice President, Community Development & Communications: Jennifer Grondahl. **Director, Public Relations:** Katie Krause. **Senior Coordinator, Public Relations & Publications:** Kailey Adams. **Senior Coordinator, Player & Family Relations:** Jackie Harig. **Baseball Communications Assistant:** Liam Davis. **Public Relations Assistant:** Tessa Sayers. **Director, Orioles Alumni, Team Historian:** Bill Stetka. **Official Scorers:** Marc Jacobson, Ryan Eigenbrode, Dennis Hetrick, Jason Lee.

DIGITAL MARKETING AND CONTENT CREATION

Vice President, Creative Content: Tyler Hoffberger. **Director, Video Creative:** Tony Price. **Video Content Creator:** Johnny Douglas. **Coordinator, Senior Graphic Designer:** Julie Ludwig. **Social Media Coordinators:** Kevin Hargrave and Paige Hutchinson. **Director, Team Photography:** Todd Olszewski.

MARKETING/PRODUCTIONS

Senior Director, Marketing & Product Development: Jason Snapkoski. **PA Announcer:** Adrienne Roberson.

CORPORATE PARTNERSHIPS

Director, Strategy & Corporate Partner Relations: Cory Daniele. **Director, Suite Sales:** Matt Dryer. **Director, Corporate Partnership Sales:** Ray Naimoli.

INFORMATION TECHNOLOGY

Director, Information Systems: Chad Harvey.

TICKET OPERATIONS, FAN SERVICES & PARTNERSHIPS

Telephone: (888) 848-BIRD. **Fax:** (410) 547-6270.
Senior Director, Ticket Operations & Fan Services: Scott Rosier. **Director, Birdland Memberships:** Zach Brown. **Director, Group Events & Hospitality:** Mark Hromalik.

BASEBALL OPERATIONS

Telephone: (410) 547-6107. **Fax:** (410) 547-6271.
Executive Vice President and General Manager: Mike Elias. **Director, Baseball Development:** Eve Rosenbaum. **Director, Baseball Administration:** Kevin Buck. **Manager, Team Travel:** Spenser Clark.

Mike Elias

ADVANCE SCOUTING AND STRATEGY

Manager, Major League Strategy: Bill Wilkes. **Manager, Major League Video/Run Creation Strategist:** Ben Sussman-Hyde. **Manager, Pitching Strategy:** Ryan Klimek.

BASEBALL ANALYTICS

Vice President and Assistant General Manager, Analytics: Sig Mejdal.
Director, Baseball Systems: Di Zou. **Director, Baseball Strategy:** Brendan Fournie.
Senior Software Engineers: Peter Ash and Jim Daniels. **Senior Data Scientist, Pro Player Evaluation:** Ryan Hardin. **Senior Data Scientists:** James Martin III, Hugh McCreery, Michael Weis. **Developer, Special Projects:** Ryan Hallahan.

MAJOR LEAGUE STAFF

Manager: Brandon Hyde.
Co-Hitting Coach—Matt Borgschulte. **Major League Field Coordinator/Catching Instructor**—Tim Cossins. **Co-Hitting Coach**—Ryan Fuller. **Bench Coach**—Fredi González. **Major League Coach**—José Hernández. **Assistant Pitching Coach**—Darren Holmes. **Pitching Coach/Director of Pitching**—Chris Holt. **Third Base Coach**—Tony Mansolino. **First Base Coach**—Anthony Sanders. **Home Clubhouse and Equipment Manager:** Fred Tyler. **Visiting Clubhouse Manager:** Andrew Guinart. **Umpire Room Manager:** James W. Tyler. **Assistant Equipment Managers:** Irving "Bunny" German and Patrick Thomas.

MEDICAL/TRAINING

Head Team Physician: Dr. Sean Curtin.
Orthopedists: Dr. Christopher Looze, Dr. Leigh Ann Curl, Dr. Derek Papp, Dr. Dave Cohen. **Senior Consulting Orthopedist:** Dr. Michael Jacobs. **Primary Care:** Dr. Kelly Ryan, Dr. Jeff Mayer, Dr. Matt Sedgley. **Cardiologist:** Dr. Ankit Shah. **Dentist:** Dr. Gus Livaditis. **Optometrist:** Dr. Elliott Myrowitz. **Head Athletic Trainer:** Brian Ebel. **Assistant Athletic Trainers:** Mark Shires, Pat Wesley. **Assistant to Head Athletic Trainer:** Chris Poole. **Strength and Conditioning Coach:** Trey Wiedman. **Assistant Strength and Conditioning Coach:** Justin Bucko. **Massage Therapist:** Adrian Pettaway. **Major League Physical Therapist:** Kyle Corrick. **Mental Skills Coordinator:** Kathryn Rowe.

PLAYER DEVELOPMENT

Fax: (410) 547-6298.
Director, Player Development: Matt Blood. **Director, Minor League Operations:** Kent Qualls. **Senior Manager, International Administration:** J. Maria Arellano. **Coordinator, Minor League Operations:** Ramón Alarcón. **Coordinator, Technology:** Joe Botelho. **Coordinator, Intercultural Education:** Anaíma García. **Coordinator of Instruction:** Jeff Kunkel. **Upper-Level Hitting Coordinator:** Cody Asche. **Lower-Level Hitting Coordinator:** Anthony Villa. **Upper-Level Pitching Coordinator:** Justin Ramsey. **Latin American Pitching Supervisor:** Anderson Tavárez. **Latin American Field Coordinator:** Samuel Vega. **Complex Pitching and Rehab Coordinator:** Dave Schmidt. **Player Development Analyst, Hitting:** Dave Barry. **Player Development Analyst, Pitching:** Adam Schuck. **Player Development Assistant, Complexes:** Jackson McDonell. **Dominican Republic Academy Administrator:** Rancel Rosado. **Dominican Republic Facilities Superintendent:** Elvis Fernández.

FARM SYSTEM

Class	Club	Manager	Hitting Coach	Pitching Coach
Triple-A	Norfolk	Buck Britton	Tim Gibbons	Justin Ramsey
Double-A	Bowie	Kyle Moore	Branden Becker	Josh Conway
High-A	Aberdeen	Roberto Mercado	Zach Cole	Forrest Hermann
Low-A	Delmarva	Felipe Rojas Alou, Jr.	Brink Ambler	Joe Haumacher
Rookie	Orioles 1 (FCL)	Matt Packer	Josh Bunselmeyer	Adam Bleday
Rookie	Orioles 2 (FCL)	Christian Frias	Jaylen Ferguson	Andy Sadoski
Rookie	Orioles 1 (DSL)	Elbis Morel	Julian Gonzalez	Jake Witt
Rookie	Orioles 2 (DSL)	Chris Madera	Christian Poulsen	Dioni Pascual

SCOUTING

Telephone: 410-547-6107. **Fax:** 410-547-6928.
Senior Director, International Scouting: Koby Perez. **Director, Pro Scouting:** Mike Snyder. **Director, Draft Operations:** Brad Ciolek. **Coordinator, Draft Operations:** Chandler Couch. **Analysts, Scouting:** Hendrik Herz, Alex Tarandek, Chad Tatum. **Analysts, Pro Scouting:** Kevin Carter, Ben MacLean, Will Robertson. **Scouting Analyst Consultant:** Luke Siler. **Area Scouts:** Rich Amaral, David Blume, Quincy Boyd, Ryan Carlson, Thom Dreier, Dan Drullinger, Trent Friedrich, Ken Guthrie, David Jennings, Donovan O'Dowd, Jim Richardson, Eric Robinson, Logan Schuemann, Brandon Verley, Scott Walter. **Pro Scouting Consultants:** John Pierson and Jake Tillinghast. **Puerto Rico Scouting Consultant:** Anibal Zayas. **Dominican Republic—Latin American Supervisor:** Gerardo Cabrera. **D.R. Scouting Assistant:** Michael Cruz. **Scouts:** Rafael Belen, Luis Noel, Francisco Rosario. **Venezuela—Scout:** Oscar Alvarado, Adel Granadillo. **Dominican Republic Scouting Supervisor:** Geraldo Cabrera. **Area Scouts:** Rafael Belen, Michael Cruz, Luis Noel, Francisco Rosario. **Area Scout, Venezuela:** Adel Granadillo (Barquisimeto).

BOSTON RED SOX

Office Address: Fenway Park, 4 Jersey Street, Boston, MA 02215.
Telephone: (617) 226-6000. **Fax:** (617) 226-6416. **Website:** www.redsox.com

OWNERSHIP
Principal Owner: John Henry. **Chairman:** Thomas C. Werner. **President/CEO:** Sam Kennedy. **President/CEO Emeritus:** Larry Lucchino.

BUSINESS OPERATIONS
EVP/COO: Jonathan Gilula. **SVP/Ballpark Operations:** Peter Nesbit. **SVP/Fan Services & Entertainment:** Sarah McKenna. **VP/Red Sox Productions:** John Carter. **VP/Fenway Park Tours:** Marcita Thompson. **VP/Facilities Management:** Jonathan Lister.

Sam Kennedy

STRATEGY & BUSINESS DEVELOPMENT / FINANCE & ANALYTICS
EVP/Chief Strategy Officer: Dave Beeston. **EVP/Chief Financial Officer:** Tim Zue. **SVP/Finance:** Ryan Oremus. **VP/Strategy & Growth:** Samantha Barkowski. **VP/Financial Planning & Operations:** Ryan Scafidi. **VP/ Data, Intelligence & Analytics:** Jonathan Hay.

HUMAN RESOURCES / INFORMATION TECHNOLOGY
EVP/Chief Human Resources Officer: Amy Waryas. **VP/Human Resources:** Mike Danubio. **SVP/Information Technology:** Brian Shield. **VP/IT Operations:** Randy George. **VP/Software Engineering:** Dan White.

LEGAL
EVP, FSG Corporate Strategy and General Counsel: Ed Weiss. **EVP/ Legal & Gov. Affairs Chief Compliance Officer:** David Friedman. **VP/Senior Club Counsel:** Elaine Weddington Steward.

MARKETING/COMMUNICATIONS
EVP/Chief Marketing Officer: Adam Grossman. **SVP/Chief Communications Officer:** Zineb Curran. **SVP/Marketing & Broadcasting:** Colin Burch. **VP/Creative Services & Content:** Tim Heintzelman.

PARTNERSHIPS / CLIENT SERVICES
EVP/Partnerships: Troup Parkinson. **SVP/Client & Sponsor Services:** Marcell Bhangoo. **SVP/Community, Alumni & Player Relations:** Pam Kenn.

TICKETING / SALES / EVENTS
EVP/Ticketing, Concerts, & Events: Ron Bumgarner. **SVP/Fenway Concerts & Entertainment:** Larry Cancro. **SVP/Ticketing:** Richard Beaton. **SVP/Ticket Services & Operations:** Naomi Calder. **SVP/Ticket Sales:** William Droste. **SVP/Fenway Park Events:** Carrie Campbell.

RED SOX FOUNDATION
EVP/Social Impact & Executive Director, Red Sox Foundation: Rebekah Salwasser. **Honorary Chairman:** Tim Wakefield.

SPORTS MEDICINE SERVICE
Director, Sports Medicine Service/Head Athletic Trainer: Brad Pearson. **Medical Director:** Dr. Larry Ronan. **Head Team Orthopedist:** Dr. Peter Asnis. **Senior Physical Therapist/Clinical Specialist:** Jamie Creps. **Associate Head Athletic Trainer:** Brandon Henry. **Major League Assistant Athletic Trainers:** Masai Takahashi, Anthony Cerundolo. **Athletic Trainer/Major League Rehab Coordinator:** Jon Jochim. **Strength/Conditioning Coach:** Kiyoshi Momose, Chris Messina. **Coordinator, Minor League S&C:** Kirby Retzer. **Sports Science Coordinator:** Mike Cianciosi. **Sports Scientist:** Shaun Owen. **Biomechanist:** Donna Scarborough; **Massage Therapists:** Russell Nua, Shinichiro Uchikubo. **Head Minor League Physician:** Dr. Brian Busconi. **Minor League Rehab Coordinator:** Kevin Avilla. **Minor League Rehab Strength & Conditioning Coach:** Jeffrey Dolan. **Minor League AT Coordinator:** Joel Harris. **Director, Behavioral Health Program:** Dr. Richard Ginsburg. **Mental Skills Coordinators:** Rey Fuentes, Dan Abroms, Jake Chaplin, Jonathan Jenkins. **Latin American Mental Skills Coordinator:** Adan Severino. **Team Nutritionist, Major League:** Allen Tran. **Minor League Sports Dietitian:** Gabriela Alfonso. **Sports Medicine Administrative Manager:** Elana Webb.

BASEBALL OPERATIONS

Chief Baseball Officer: Chaim Bloom

General Manager: Brian O'Halloran. **EVP/Assistant GM:** Raquel Ferreira, Eddie Romero. **SVP, Assistant GM:** Michael Groopman. **SVP, Baseball Operations:** Ben Crockett. **Senior Director, Club Relations:** Jack McCormick. **Director, Team Travel:** Mark Cacciatore. **Director, Major League Operations:** Mike Regan. **Manager, Major League Operations:** Alex Gimenez. **Executive Assistant/Manager, Staff Support:** Erin Cox. **Director, Baseball Analytics:** Joe McDonald. **Director, Education & Process Analysis:** Greg Rybarczyk. **Manager, Major League Strategic Information:** Dave Miller. **Manager, Baseball Analytics:** Brad Alberts, Spencer Bingol, Daniel Meyer. **Analyst, Baseball Analytics:** Tyler Burch, Sam Larson, Katy McKeough, Jonathan Waring. **Assistant, Baseball Analytics:** Kayla Mei, Jimmy O'Donnell, Scott Steinberg. **Coordinator, Major League Strategic Information:** Mark Heil. **Analyst, ML Strategic Information:** Jeb Clarke. **Director, Baseball Systems:** Mike Ganley. **Sr. Developer, Baseball Systems:** Eric Edvalson, Fred Hubert, Connor McCann, Kim Eskew. **Data Architect, Baseball Systems:** Bill Letson. **Developer, Baseball Systems:** Deven Swiergiel. **Data Engineer, Baseball Systems:** Kameron Wells. **Major League Assistant, Baseball Systems:** Tyler Forgione. **Minor League Assistant, Baseball Systems:** Sam Denomme. **Home Clubhouse Manager:** Tom McLaughlin. **Assistant Home Clubhouse Manager:** Josh Liebenow. **Visiting Clubhouse Manager:** Pookie Jackson. **Special Assistants:** Pedro Martinez, David Ortiz, Tim Wakefield.

Chaim Bloom

BILLIE WEISS/BOSTON RED SOX

MAJOR LEAGUE STAFF

Manager: Alex Cora

Coaches: Bench—Will Venable; **Pitching**—Dave Bush; **Hitting**—Peter Fatse; **Assistant Hitting**—Luis Ortiz, Ben Rosenthal; **Assistant Pitching**—Kevin Walker; **First Base**—Ramon Vazquez; **Third Base**—Carlos Febles; **Game Planning Coordinator:** Jason Varitek; **Field Coordinator:** Andy Fox; **Major League Staff Assistant:** Michael Brenly; **Bullpen Catcher:** Mani Martinez; **BP Pitcher:** Matt Noone; **Interpreter:** Yutaro Yamaguchi.

PLAYER DEVELOPMENT

Director, Player Development: Brian Abraham. **Assistant Director, Player Development:** Chris Stasio. **Manager, Minor League Operations:** Patrick McLaughlin. **Coordinator, Player Development:** Harry Roberson. **Assistant, Florida Baseball Operations:** Stephen Aluko. **Minor League Field Coordinator:** Ryan Jackson. **Infield Coordinator:** Darren Fenster. **Senior Coordinator, Hitting:** Anthony Iapoce. **Outfield/Baserunning Coordinator:** Corey Wimberly. **Senior Coordinator, Pitching:** Shawn Haviland. **Pitching Coordinator, Upper Level:** Julio Rangel. **Pitching Coordinator, Lower Level:** Chris Mears. **Hitting Coordinator, Upper Level:** Lance Zawadzki. **Hitting Coordinator, Lower Level:** Reed Gragnani. **Latin American Pitching Coordinator:** Walter Miranda. **Latin American Field Coordinator:** Jose Zapata. **PD Pitching Advisor:** Goose Gregson, Ralph Treuel. **Coordinator, Baseball Development:** Jordan Elkary. **Coach/Interpreter:** Mickey Jiang. **Minor League Equipment Manager:** Mike Stelmach.

FARM SYSTEM

Class	Club	Manager	Hitting Coach	Pitching Coach	Position Coach
Triple-A	Worcester	Chad Tracy	Rich Gedman	Paul Abbott	Jose Flores
Double-A	Portland	Chad Epperson	Doug Clark	Lance Carter	Katie Krall
High-A	Greenville	Iggy Suarez	Nate Spears	Bob Kipper	Joe Cronin
Low-A	Salem	Luke Montz	Nelson Paulino	Nick Green	
Rookie	Red Sox (FCL)	Tom Kotchman	Junior Zamora	Brett Merritt	Bianca Smith
Rookie		Jimmy Gonzalez	Josh Prince	Jason Blanton	
Rookie	Red Sox (DSL)	Ozzie Chavez	Danny Ortega	Oscar Lira	Leonel Vasquez
Rookie	Red Sox (DSL)	Sandy Madera	Eider Torres	Humberto Sanchez	Claudio Sanchez

SCOUTING

VP/ Scouting Development & Integration: Gus Quattlebaum. **VP/Scouting:** Mike Rikard. **Director, Professional Scouting:** Harrison Slutsky. **Director, Amateur Scouting:** Paul Toboni. **Assistant Director, Amateur Scouting:** Devin Pearson. **Assistant Director, Professional Scouting:** Andrew Mack. **Assistant Director, Latin American Operations:** Alberto Mejia. **Manager, International Scouting:** Marcus Cuellar. **Coordinator, Amateur Scouting:** Jake Bruml. **Assistant, Amateur Scouting:** Mark Sluys. **Amateur Scouts:** Spencer Brown, Greg Morhardt. **Special Assistant, Amateur Scouting:** Justin Horowitz. **Special Assignment Scout:** Steve Peck. **Special Assistant, Player Personnel:** Mark Wasinger. **Professional Scouts:** Chris Calciano, Nate Field, Blair Henry, Mark Kiefer, Steve Langone, Dana LeVangie, Matt Mahoney, Donovan May, Josh Tobias, Anthony Turco, Kyri Washington, JT Watkins. **Professional/Advance Scout:** James Cuthbert. **Crosscheckers:** Chris Becerra (Special Assistant International & Amateur), Dan Madsen (National), John Booher (Hitting), Paul Fryer (Hitting), Fred Petersen (National Supervisor), Jim Robinson (National Supervisor), Tom Kotchman (Florida), Stephen Hargett. **Area Scouts:** JJ Altobelli, Lee Bryant, Matt Davis, Lane Decker, Raymond Fagnant, Kirk Fredriksson, Todd Gold, Josh Labandeira, , Brian Moehler, Carl Moesche, Wallace Rios, Chris Reilly, Dante Ricciardi, Willie Romay, Danny Watkins, Vaughn Williams, Alonzo Wright. **Part Time Scouts:** Joey Casey, Rob English, Tim Martin, David Scrivines, Dick Sorkin, Terry Sullivan. **Co-Directors, International Scouting:** Todd Claus, Ronaldo Pino. **International Crosscheckers:** Jason Karegeannes, Greg Schilz. **Latin American Crosschecker:** Hector Rincones. **Coordinator, Pacific Rim Operations:** Brett Ward. **Manager, DR Academy:** Javier Hernandez. **Coordinator, DR Academy:** Martin Rodriguez. **Scouting Supervisor, Latin America:** Manny Nanita. **Assistant Supervisor, Dominican Republic:** Jonathan Cruz. **International Scouts:** Juan Carlos Calderon, Alfredo Castellon, Cris Garibaldo, Ernesto Gomez, John Kim, Matias Laureano, Louie Lin, Wilder Lobo, Esau Medina, Rafael Mendoza, Ramon Mora, Jorge Moreno, Cesar Morillo, Rafael Motooka, Dennis Neuman, Carlos Ocando, Alex Requena, Rene Saggiadi, Sotero Torres, Carlos Vasquez. **International Pro Scouts:** Won Lee (Korea), Kento Matsumoto (Japan).

CHICAGO CUBS

Office Address: Wrigley Field, 1060 W. Addison St., Chicago, IL 60613.
Telephone: (773) 404-2827. **Website:** www.cubs.com.

OWNERSHIP

Executive Chairman: Tom Ricketts. **Board of Directors:** Laura Ricketts, Todd Ricketts.

BUSINESS OPERATIONS

President, Business Operations: Crane Kenney. **Executive Assistant to Chairman:** Lorraine Swiatly. **EVP, Business Operations and Chief Strategy Officer:** Alex Sugarman. **EVP and CFO:** Jon Greifenkamp

BALLPARK/EVENT OPERATIONS

Senior Vice President, Operations: David Cromwell. **Director, Event Operations &Security:** Morgan Bucciferro. **Vice President, Facility & Supply Chain Operations:** Patrick Meenan. **Director, Facilities:** Ryan Egan.

LEGAL

EVP, Community & Gov't Affairs, Chief Legal Officer: Michael Lufrano. **Senior Vice President, General Counsel:** Brett Scharback. **Counsel:** Amy Timm. **Counsel:** Shameeka Quallo. **Executive Director, Community Affairs:** Alicia Gonzalez.

Tom Ricketts

TICKET SALES/SALES & PARTNERSHIPS

Executive Vice President, Sales & Marketing: Colin Faulkner. **Senior Vice President, Marquee 360:** Cale Vennum. **Vice President, Partnerships, Marquee 360:** Alex Seyferth. **Vice President, Partnership Development:** Andy Blackburn.

COMMUNICATIONS

Senior Vice President, Communications: Julian Green

MEDIA RELATIONS

Director, Media Relations: Jason Carr. **Media Relations Manager:** Joanna Schimmel. **Media Relations Representative:** William Nadal.

BASEBALL OPERATIONS

Telephone: (773) 404-2827. **Fax:** (773) 404-4147.

President, Baseball Operations: Jed Hoyer. **General Manager:** Carter Hawkins. **Assistant GMs:** Jeff Greenberg, Ehsan Bokhari. **Assistant GM/Vice President, Pitching:** Craig Breslow. **Vice President, Player Personnel:** Matt Dorey. **Vice President, Research & Development:** Chris Moore. **Senior Advisor:** Randy Bush. **Special Assistant, Innovation:** Bobby Basham. **Director, Baseball Operations:** Greg Davey. **Director, Team Travel and Clubhouse Operations:** Vijay Tekchandani. **Director, Strategic Modeling:** Jeremy Greenhouse. **Director, Research and Development:** Chris Jones. **Director, Pro Analytics:** Garrett Chiado. **Assistant Director, Baseball Operations Administration and Strategic Initiatives:** Meghan Jones. **Assistant Director, Research & Development /Performance Science:** Jacob Eisenberg. **Architect, Baseball Systems:** Dan Codos. **Analysts, Research & Development:** Bryan Cole, Jennifer Gossels, Ben Martin, Troy Mulholland. **Analyst, Pro Personnel/ Research & Development:** Jasmine Horan. **Manager, Baseball Systems & Technology:** Kyle Chin. **Senior Software Engineer/Analyst, Research & Development:** Eli Shayer. **Software Engineers, Baseball Systems:** Zack Brusso, Shingo Murata, Sami Williams.

Jed Hoyer

MAJOR LEAGUE STAFF

Manager: David Ross. **Coaches: Bench**—Andy Green, **Pitching**—Tommy Hottovy, **Hitting**—Greg Brown, **Assistant Pitching**—Daniel Moskos, **Assistant Hitting**—Johnny Washington, **Third Base**—Willie Harris, **Game Strategist/Catching**—Craig Driver, **First Base/Baserunning**—Mike Napoli, **Bullpen**—Chris Young. **Staff Assistants:** Juan Cabreja, Jonathan Mota. **Bullpen Catcher:** Garrett Lloyd. **Assistant Director, Major League Data & Development:** Alex Smith. **Assistant Director, Run Production:** Jim Adduci. **Major League Pitching Strategist:** Danny Hultzen. **Coordinator, Major League Video/Pacific Rim Liaison:** Nao Masamoto.

MEDICAL/TRAINING

Team Physician: Dr. Stephen Adams. **Team Orthopedist:** Dr. Stephen Gryzlo. **Major League Head Athletic Trainer:** P.J. Mainville. **Major League Assistant Head Athletic Trainer:** Nick Frangella. **Major League Assistant Athletic Trainer:** Chuck Baughman. **Major League Head S&C Coach:** Quentin Eberhardt. **Major League Assistant S&C Coach:** Keegan Knoll. **Major League Physical Therapist:** Nate Whitney. **Major League Massage Therapist:** Aaron Witz.

PLAYER DEVELOPMENT

Telephone: (773) 404-2827. **Fax:** (773) 404-4147.

Vice President, Player Development: Jared Banner. **Senior Director, International Player Development:** Alex Suarez. **Director, Hitting:** Justin Stone. **Head S&C and Performance Science:** Cory Kennedy. **Assistant Director, Pitching Initiatives:** Ryan Otero. **Assistant Director, Minor League Operations:** Adam Unes. **Coordinator, Minor League Operations and Player Support:** Allyson Darragh. **Manager, Mesa Administration:** Gil Passarella. **Equipment Manager:** Dana Noeltner. **Minor League Coordinators:** Dustin Kelly (hitting), Casey Jacobson (pitching development), James Ogden (pitching performance), Mark Johnson (catching), Doug Dascenzo (outfield & baserunning), Dave Keller (Latin America field), Paul Serena (infield), Tom Beyers (asst. hitting development), Steven Pollakov (DSL/ACL hitting), Will Remillard (hitting initiatives), Mike Mason (asst. pitching performance), Carlos Chantres (asst. pitching development), Josh Zeid (rehab pitching). **Minor League Medical Coordinator:** James Edwards. **Minor League Medical Administrator:** Jeremy Clipperton. **Minor League Physical Therapist:** Logan Nordquist.

FARM SYSTEM

Class	Club (League)	Manager	Hitting Coach	Pitching Coach
Triple-A	Iowa	Marty Pevey	Desi Wilson	Ron Villone
Double-A	Tennessee	Michael Ryan	Rick Strickland	Jamie Vermilyea
High-A	South Bend	Lance Rymel	Dan Puente	Tony Cougoule
Low-A	Myrtle Beach	Buddy Bailey	Steven Pollakov	Clayton Mortensen
Rookie	Cubs (ACL)	Edgar Perez	R. Folden/E. Patterson	D. Willey/A. Gabino
Rookie	Cubs 1 (DSL)	Carlos Ramirez	Enrique Wilson	Jose Zapata
Rookie	Cubs 2 (DSL)	Chris Pieters	Jhonny Bethencourt	Luis Hernandez

SCOUTING

Director, Pro Scouting/Special Assistant to President & GM: Andrew Bassett. **Coordinator, Pro Scouting:** Sam Abrams. **Senior Pro Personnel Specialist:** Steve Boros. **Senior Pro Personnel Specialist/Supervisor, Pacific Rim Scouting:** Jason Cooper. **Special Assignment Scouts:** Jake Ciarrachi, Kyle Phillips, Mitchell Webb. **Pro Personnel Specialists:** Nate Halm, Thad Weber. **Pro Scouts:** Steve Nagy, Max Brill, Andrew Ahn. **Part-Time Pro Scouts:** Robert Lofrano, Adam Wogan. **Vice President, Scouting:** Dan Kantrovitz. **Coordinator, Amateur Scouting:** Scottie Munson. **Assistant, Amateur Scouting:** Ben Kullavanijaya. **National Supervisors:** Ron Tostenson, Jaron Madison, Marti Wolever. **Crosscheckers: West** — Alex Lontayo, **Central** — Daniel Carte, **Southeast** — Bobby Filotei, **Northeast** — Matt Sherman. **Area Scouts:** Tom Clark, M'Lynn Dease, Trey Forkerway, Todd George, Greg Gerard, Edwards Guzman, Evan Kauffman, Alex McClure, Steve McFarland, Ty Nichols, John Pedrotty, Ralph Reyes, Billy Swoope, Jacob Williams, Jim Woodward, Gabe Zappin, Zach Zielinski. **Amateur Video Scout:** Garrett Tolivar. **Part-Time Area Scout:** Keronn Walker. **Vice President, International Scouting:** Louie Eljaua. **Coordinator, International Scouting:** Kenny Socorro. **Director, Dominican Scouting:** Gian Guzman. **International/Global Crosschecker:** Pete Vuckovich Jr. **Coordinator, D.R. Scouting:** Miguel Diaz. **Scouting Supervisor, Central and South America:** Cirilo Cumberbatch. **Supervisor, Mexico:** Sergio Hernandez. **Coordinator, Colombian Operations:** Manny Esquivia. **International Scouts:** Hansel Izquierdo, Jaime McFarland, Brent Phelan. **Latin America Scouts: D.R.**—Alejandro Pena, Valerio Heredia, **Venezuela**—Julio Figueroa, Carlos Figueroa, **Mexico**—Salvador Hernandez, **Taiwan**—Po-chun Chang.

CHICAGO WHITE SOX

Office Address: Guaranteed Rate Field, 333 W. 35th St., Chicago, IL 60616.
Telephone: (312) 674-1000. **Fax:** (312) 674-5116.
Website: whitesox.com, loswhitesox.com.

OWNERSHIP
Chairman: Jerry Reinsdorf.
Board of Directors: Robert Judelson, Judd Malkin, Allan Muchin, Jay Pinsky, Lee Stern, Burton Ury. **Special Assistant to Chairman:** Dennis Gilbert. **Assistant to Chairman:** Katie Hermle. **Manager, Investor Relations/Special Projects:** Elizabeth Anderson.

BUSINESS OPERATIONS
Senior Executive Vice President: Howard Pizer. **Senior Systems Analyst:** Stan Czyzewski.
Vice President, Human Resources: Moira Foy. **Senior Coordinator, Human Resources:** Leslie Gaggiano.

Jerry Reinsdorf

FINANCE
Senior VP, Administration/Finance: Tim Buzard. **VP, Finance:** Bill Waters. **Director of Accounting:** Mallory Penn.

MARKETING/SALES
Senior VP, Chief Revenue and Marketing Officer: Brooks Boyer. **Director, Game Presentation:** Cris Quintana. **Sr. Manager, Scoreboard Operations/Production:** Jeff Szynal. **Sr. Manager, Game Operations:** Dan Mielke. **Sr. Director, Corporate Partnerships Sales Development:** George McDoniel. **Sr. Director, Corporate Partnerships Activation:** Gail Tucker. **Sr. Manager, Corporate Partnerships Development:** Jeff Floerke. **VP of Sales and Service:** Jim Willits. **Sr. Manager, Ticket Sales:** Rich Kuchar.

MEDIA RELATIONS/PUBLIC RELATIONS
Telephone: (312) 674-5300. **Fax:** (312) 674-5116.
Senior VP, Communications: Scott Reifert. **Senior Director, Media Relations:** Bob Beghtol. **Director, Public Relations:** Sheena Quinn. **Assistant Director, Media Relations:** Ray Garcia. **Coordinator, Public Relations:** Colin McGauley. **Coordinators, Media Relations/Services:** Joe Roti, Hannah Sundwall. **VP, Community Relations/Executive Director/CWS Charities:** Christine O'Reilly-Riordan. **Director, Community Relations:** Lindsey Jordan. **Manager, Youth Baseball Initiatives:** Anthony Olivo. **Manager of Social Media:** Jordan Doyle.

STADIUM OPERATIONS
Senior VP, Stadium Operations: Terry Savarise. **Senior Director, Park Operations:** Jonathan Vasquez.
Senior Director, Guest Services/Diamond Suite Operations: Julie Taylor. **Head Groundskeeper:** Roger Bossard. **PA Announcer:** Gene Honda. **Official Scorers:** Don Friske, Allan Spear, Bill Sieple, Randy Liss.

TICKETING
Senior Director, Ticket Operations: Mike Mazza. **Manager, Ticket Operations:** Pete Catizone.

TRAVEL/CLUBHOUSE
Director, Team Travel: Ed Cassin. **Manager, White Sox Clubhouse:** Rob Warren. **Manager, Visiting Clubhouse:** Jason Gilliam. **Manager, Umpires Clubhouse:** Joe McNamara Jr.

BASEBALL OPERATIONS

Executive Vice President: Ken Williams. **Senior VP/General Manager:** Rick Hahn. **Assistant General Manager:** Jeremy Haber. **Special Assistants:** Bill Scherrer, Marco Paddy, Jim Thome, Nick Hostetler, Jose Contreras, Todd Steverson. **Executive Assistant to GM:** Nancy Nesnidal. **Senior Director, Baseball Operations:** Dan Fabian. **Director, Baseball Analytics:** Matt Koenig. **Director, Baseball Operations:** Daniel Zien. **Assistant Director, Baseball Operations:** Rod Larson. **Manager, Baseball Operations:** Zach Jones.

Rick Hahn

MAJOR LEAGUE STAFF

Manager: Tony La Russa. **Coaches: Bench**—Miguel Cairo; **Pitching**—Ethan Katz; **Hitting**—Frank Menechino; **Assistant Hitting Coach**—Howie Clark; **First Base**—Daryl Boston; **Third Base**—Joe McEwing; **Bullpen**—Curt Hasler. **Bullpen Catcher:** Miguel Gonzalez. **Mgr. of Cultural Development/Bullpen Catcher:** Luis Sierra. **Instructor:** Jerry Narron. **Analytics Coordinator:** Shelley Duncan.

MEDICAL/TRAINING

Senior Team Physician: Dr. Nikhil Verma. **Head Athletic Trainer Emeritus:** Herm Schneider. **Head Athletic Trainer:** James Kruk. **Director of Rehabilitation:** Brett Walker. **Assistant Athletic Trainer:** Josh Fallin. **Director, Strength & Conditioning:** Goldy Simmons. **Assistant Director, Strength & Conditioning:** Ibrahim Rivera..

PLAYER DEVELOPMENT

Assistant General Manager/Player Development: Chris Getz. **Director, Minor League Operations:** Jasmine Dunston. **Assistant Director, Player Development:** Kenny Williams, Jr. **Assistant Director, Baseball Operations:** Graham Harboe. **Assistant, PD/Latin Education:** Grant Flick. **Assistant, PD/Video:** Jack Larimer. **Manager, Minor League Administration:** Kathy Potoski. **Education Coordinator:** Erin Santana. **Sports Psychologist:** Rob Seifer. **Dietitians:** Danielle Mach, Christine Jordhamo. **Field Coordinator:** Doug Sisson. **Pitching Coordinator:** Everett Teaford. **Assistant Pitching Coordinator:** J.R. Perdew. **Hitting Coordinator:** Andy Barkett. **Assistant Hitting Coordinator:** Ryan Johansen. **Infield Coordinator:** Ryan Newman. **Catching Coordinator:** Julio Mosquera. **Rehab Pitching Coach:** Donnie Veal. **Assistant OF/Baserunning Coach:** Mike Daniel. **Development Coach:** Danny Gonzalez. **Minor League Performance Coordinator:** Gage Cosgrove. **Medical Coordinator:** Scott Takao. **Physical Therapist Coordinator:** Brooks Klein. **Minor League Physical Therapist:** Katie Stone. **Minor League ATC:** Evan Jurjevic.

ARIZONA OPERATIONS

Facility Manager: Joe Lachcik. **Minor League Clubhouse and Equipment Manager:** Dan Flood. **Assistant Minor League Clubhouse Manager:** Bryant Biasotti.

FARM SYSTEM

Class	Club (League)	Manager	Hitting Coach	Pitching Coach
Triple-A	Charlotte	Wes Helms	Chris Johnson	Matt Zaleski
Double-A	Birmingham	Justin Jirschele	Charlie Romero	Richard Dotson
High-A	Winston-Salem	Lorenzo Bundy	Nicky Delmonico	Danny Farquhar
Low-A	Kannapolis	Guillermo Quiroz	Cam Seltzer	John Ely
Rookie	White Sox (ACL)	Pat Leland	Devin DeYoung	Drew Hasler
Rookie	White Sox (DSL)	Angel Rosario	Gerardo Olivares	Leo Hernandez

SCOUTING

Telephone: (312) 674-1000.

Pro Scouts: Bruce Benedict (Atlanta, GA), Joe Butler (Long Beach, CA), Toney Howell (Darien, IL), Daraka Shaheed (Vallejo, CA), Joe Siers (Wesley Chapel, FL), Keith Staab (College Station, TX), Chris Walker (Katy, TX), Bill Young (Scottsdale, AZ).

Director, Amateur Scouting: Mike Shirley. **Senior Advisor, Scouting Operations:** Doug Laumann. **Assistant Director, Amateur Scouting:** Garrett Guest. **National Crosschecker:** Nathan Durst (Sycamore, IL). **National Pitching Crosschecker:** Kirk Champion. **Regional Crosscheckers: West**—Derek Valenzuela (Temecula, CA), **Southeast**—Juan Alvarez (Miami, FL), **Midwest**—Rob Cummings (Chicago, IL). **Area Scouts:** Mike Baker (Santa Ana, CA), Kevin Burrell (Sharpsburg, GA), Ryan Dorsey (Dallas, TX), Abe Fernandez (Miami, FL), Mike Gange (Portland, OR), Phil Gulley (Morehead, KY), Warren Hughes (Mobile, AL), JJ Lally (Denison, IA), John Kazanas (Phoenix, AZ), Carlos Muniz (Harbor City, NY), Stephen Octave (New Windsor, NY), Steffan Segui (St. Petersburg, FL), John Stott (Charlotte, NC), Adam Virchis (Modesto, CA), Justin Wechsler (Niles, MI), Tyler Wilt (Willis, TX), Torreon Woods (Overland Park, KS)

International Scouts: Venezuela Supervisor: Amador Arias (Maracay, Venezuela). Marino DeLeon (Yamasa, Dominican Republic), Tomas Herrera (Saltillo, Mexico), Reydel Hernandez (Puerto La Cruz, Venezuela), Luis Moncada (Valencia, Venezuela). **Latin America Supervisor:** Ruddy Moreta (Santo Domingo, Dominican Republic), Miguel Peguero (Santo Domingo, Dominican Republic), Guillermo Peralta (Santiago, Dominican Republic), Fermin Ubri (Bani, Dominican Republic). Ricardo Ortiz (Colon, Panama).

CINCINNATI REDS

Office Address: 100 Joe Nuxhall Way, Cincinnati, OH 45202.
Telephone: (513) 765-7000. **Fax:** (513) 765-7342. **Website:** www.reds.com.

OWNERSHIP

Operated by: The Cincinnati Reds LLC. **Chief Executive Officer:** Robert H. Castellini. **Chairman:** W. Joseph Williams Jr. **Vice Chairman:** Thomas L. Williams. **President & Chief Operating Officer:** Phillip J. Castellini. **Sr. Advisor to President/COO:** Barry Larkin. **Executive Operations Manager:** Shellie Petrey. **Executive Advisor to the CEO:** Walt Jocketty. **Secretary & Treasurer:** Christopher L. Fister.

BUSINESS OPERATIONS

Senior Vice President, Business Operations: Karen Forgus. **Business Operations Assistant:** Emily Mahle.

FINANCE/ADMINISTRATION

Sr. Vice President of Finance and CFO: Doug Healy. **Chief Legal Counsel:** James A. Marx, Esq. **Executive Assistant to CFO/CLO:** Teena Schweier.

TICKETING/BUSINESS DEVELOPMENT

Senior Director of Ticket Sales & Service: Mark Schueler. **Director of Ticketing New Business:** Patrick Montague. **Director of Season Ticket Membership:** Shelley Volpenhein. **Director of Premium Sales & Service:** Chris Bausano. **Director of Group Sales & Development:** Carmen Alberini Zerhusen. **Season Sales Manager:** Chris Herrell. **Sr. Account Executive, New Business Dev.:** Blake Williams. **Account Executive, New Business Dev.:** Jake Eby. **Sr. Account Executive, Retention and Sales:** Eric Keller. **Account Executive, Retention and Sales:** Angel Gonzalez, Tori Priest, Nick Fedders, Tiffany Huffman. **Premium Sales Manager:** Ryan Rizzo. **Sr. Premium Sales/Ownrshp Svcs. Exec.:** Megan Stuerenberg. **Suites and Premium Service Executive:** Kory Hetzer. **Premium Service Executive:** Craig Sample. **Group Account Executives:** Cardell Carter, Reilly Burns, Nick Geraci.

Bob Castellini

MEDIA RELATIONS

Vice President, Media Relations: Rob Butcher. **Director, Media Relations:** Larry Herms. **Director, Media Relations/Digital Content:** Jamie Ramsey. **Spanish Translator/Media Relations Assistant:** Jorge Merlos. **Japanese Interpretor/Media Relations Coordinator:** Luke Shinoda.

COMMUNICATIONS/MARKETING

Vice President of Communications & Marketing: Ralph Mitchell. **Director of Digitial Media:** Lisa Braun. **Director of Marketing:** Audra Sordyl. **Director of Communications:** Jarrod Rollins. **Public Relations Manager:** Michael Anderson. **Promotional Purchasing/Broadcasting Admin.:** Lori Watt. **Communications Manager:** Brendan Hader. **Social Media Manager:** Chadwick Fischer. **Director of Creative Operations:** Jansen Dell. **Creative Services Manager:** Amy Calo. **Senior Designer:** Michael King. **Graphic Designer:** Sara Green. **Social Media Design Coordinator:** Carter Kennedy.

COMMUNITY RELATIONS

Director, Community Relations: Lindsey Dingeldein. **Diversity & Community Relations Coordinator:** Adriana Pons.

BALLPARK OPERATIONS

Senior Vice President, Ballpark Operations: Tim O'Connell. **Vice President, Ballpark Operations:** Sean Brown.

BASEBALL OPERATIONS

Vice President & General Manager: Nick Krall. **Executive Assistant to Pres. of Baseball Ops:** Sarah Vedder. **Vice President, Assistant General Manager:** Sam Grossman. **Vice President, Player Personnel:** Chris Buckley. **Senior Director, Player Acquisition & Strategy:** Jeff Graupe. **Manager, Baseball Operations:** Mark Edwards. **Director of Data Systems & Development:** Michael Mentzer. **Sr. System Architect, Baseball Systems:** Brett Elkins. **Data Scientist:** Chris Jackson. **Major League Analytics Coordinator:** James Brand. **Data Quality Engineer, Baseball Systems:** Andrew Kyne. **Baseball Systems Developer:** Joe Delia. **Data Engineer, Baseball Systems:** Bryce Dugar. **Manager, Advance Scouting:** Bo Thompson. **Coordinator, Major League Video & Technology:** Gary Hall. **Baseball Operations Analysts:** Cameron LeBlanc, Nick Perez. **Senior Director, Team Travel:** Gary Wahoff. **Data Architect:** Steven Wyant. **Senior Director, Clubhouse Operations:** Rick Stowe. **Visiting Clubhouse Manager:** Josh Stewart. **Clubhouse Assistant:** Mark Stowe.

Nick Krall

MEDICAL/TRAINING

Senior Director, Health & Performance: Geoff Head. **Major League Applied Sports Scientist:** Dan Adams. **Coordinator, Mental Skills:** Tyler Klein. **Coordinator, Minor League Nutrition:** Leah Reitmayer. **Minor League Rehabilitation Coordinator:** Marcus Ahrens. **Major League Physical Therapist:** Alexander Plum. **Minor League Physical Therapist:** Eric Gonzalez. **Director, Sports Science Initiatives:** Charles Leddon. **Director, Strength & Conditioning:** Rob Fumagalli. **Coordinator, Strength & Conditioning:** Will Gilmore. **Manager, Wellness & Education:** Becky Schnakenberg. **Wellness Coach, Latin America:** Rafael Castillo. **Director, Athletic Training:** Patrick Serbus.

MAJOR LEAGUE STAFF

Manager: David Bell. **Coaches: Bench**—Freddie Benavides, **Hitting**—Alan Zinter, **Pitching**— Derek Johnson, **First Base**—Delino DeShields, **Third Base/Catching**—J.R. House, **Bullpen**—Lee Tunnell, **Game Planning/Outfield**—Jeff Pickler, **Assistant Hitting**—Joel McKeithan, **Assistant Pitching:** Eric Jagers, **Assistant Coaches:** Rolando Valles, Kyle Arnsberg. **Advance Scouting Coach:** Cristian Pérez. **Bullpen Catchers:** Jose Duarte.

MEDICAL STAFF

Medical Director: Dr. Timothy Kremchek. **Head Athletic Trainer, PT, DPT, ATC:** Sean McQueeney. **Assistant Athletic Trainer, ATC:** Tomas Vera. **Health & Performance Specialist:** Takeshi Yamamoto. **Director, Strength & Conditioning:** Rob Fumagalli. **Assistant Director, Str. & Cond.:** Aaron Reis. **Director, Physical Therapy and Rehab:** Brad Epstein. **Major League Sports Dietician:** Ashley Meuser.

PLAYER DEVELOPMENT

Vice President, Player Development: Shawn Pender. **Director, Player Development:** Jeremy Farrell. **Special Assistant, Player Performance:** Eric Davis, Bill Doran, Mario Soto. **Coordinator, Baseball Administration:** Melissa Hill. **Coordinator, Minor League Video & Technology:** Mitchell Bonds. **Manager, Arizona Operations:** Mike Saverino. **Specialist, Player Development & Arizona Operations:** Branden Croteau. **Manager, Minor League Equipment:** Jon Snyder. **Minor League Clubhouse Assistant:** John Bryk. **Field Coordinator:** Chris Tremie. **Catching Coordinator:** Corky Miller. **Hitting Coordinators:** Jim Rickon, Dave Hansen. **Academies Coordinator:** Luis Bolivar. **Latin American Field Coordinator:** Joel Noboa. **Infield Coordinator:** Jose Nieves. **Pitching Coordinators:** Bryan Conger, Casey Weathers.

FARM SYSTEM

Class	Club (League)	Manager	Hitting Coach	Pitching Coach
Triple-A	Louisville	Pat Kelly	Alex Pelaez	Seth Etherton
Double-A	Chattanooga	Jose Moreno	Eric Richardson	Rob Wooten
High-A	Dayton	Bryan LaHair	Daryle Ward	Brian Garman
Low-A	Daytona	Gookie Dawkins	Darryl Brinkley	Todd Naskedov
Rookie	Reds (ACL)	Julio Morillo	Jason Broussard	Elmer Dessens/Fred Corral
Rookie	Reds (DSL)	Gustavo Molina	José León	TBD

SCOUTING

Senior Director, Professional Scouting: Rob Coughlin. **Special Assistant to GM, Player Personnel:** Cam Bonifay. **Special Assistants to the General Manager:** "J" Harrison, Marty Maier, John Morris, Jeff Schugel. **Pro Scouts:** Gary Glover, Joe Jocketty, Ben Jones, Mick Mattaliano, Jeff Morris, Steve Roadcap. **Analyst, Pro Scouting:** Daniel Beattie. **Director, Amateur Scouting:** Brad Meador. **Assistant Director, Amateur Scouting:** Paul Pierson. **National Crosscheckers:** Jerry Flowers, Mark McKnight, Will Harford. **Regional Crosschecker: East Coast/Canada**—Bill Byckowski, **West Coast**—Rex De La Nuez, **Midwest**—Paul Pierson, **Southeast**—Greg Zunino. **Scouting Supervisors:** Charlie Aliano, Rich Bordi, Jeff Brookens, Sean Buckley, John Ceprini, Dan Cholowsky, Andrew Fabian, Tyler Gibbons, Jerel Johnson, Mike Keenan, Brandon Marr, Mike Misuraca, Jimmy Moran, Mike Partida, Jonathan Reynolds, Paul Scott, Juan Silva, Andy Stack. **Senior Director, International Scouting:** Trey Hendricks. **Assistant Director, Player Development and International Scouting:** Greg McMillin. **Director, South American Scouting:** Hernan Albornoz. **Director, Caribbean Scouting:** Enmanuel Cartagena. **International Crosscheckers:** David Espinosa, Matt Gaski, Boomer Prinstein, Phil Stringer. **Caribbean Crosschecker:** Dargello Lodowica. **Supervisor, Venezuela:** Ricardo Quintero. **Coordinator, D.R.:** Jose Diaz. **Scouts, Australia:** Matt Everingham, Donald Lutz. **Scout, Bahamas:** Brian Armbrister. **Scout, Brazil:** Jean Tome. **Scout, Colombia:** Jose Valdelamar. **Video Scout, D.R.:** Luis Aguero. **Scouts, D.R.:** Edgar Melo, Victor Nova, Samuel Pimentel, Jenfry Del Rosario. **Scout, Europe:** Ryan Schurman. **Scout, Mexico:** Alex Ahumada. **Scout, Netherlands:** Evert-Jan't Hoen. **Scout, Nicaragua:** Gustavo Martinez. **Scout, Panama:** Concepcion Rodriguez. **Scout, South Korea:** Dan Kim. **Scouting Assistant, Venezuela:** German Arteaga. **Scouts, Venezuela:** Aguido Gonzalez, Ivan Mora, Victor Serrano. **Video Scout, Venezuela:** Miguel Montero.

CLEVELAND GUARDIANS

Office Address: Progressive Field, 2401 Ontario St., Cleveland, OH 44115.
Telephone: (216) 420-4200. **Fax:** (216) 420-4396.
Website: www.indians.com.

OWNERSHIP
Owner: Larry Dolan. **Chairman/Chief Executive Officer:** Paul Dolan.

BUSINESS OPERATIONS
President, Business Operations: Brian Barren. **Senior Vice President, Marketing/ Strategy:** Alex King. **Executive Assistant, Ownership & Business Operations:** Dru Kosik. **Administrative Assistant:** Kim Scott.

CORPORATE PARTNERSHIPS/FINANCE
Vice President, Corporate Partnership: Ted Baugh. **Senior Director, Corporate Partnership & Premium Hospitality:** Dom Polito. **Director, Corporate Partnership & Premium Hospitality:** Kevin Murphy. **Senior Sales Manager, Corporate Partnerships:** Bryan Hoffart and Joe Sullivan. **Manager, Corporate Partnerships & Premium Hospitality:** Bridget Sullivan. **Sr. Account Manager, Corporate Partnerships & Premium Hospitality:** Julie Weaver. **VP/General Counsel:** Joe Znidarsic. **Deputy Counsel:** Max Kosman. **Vice President, Finance & Chief Financial Officer:** Rich Dorffer. **Controller:** Erica Chambers. **Manager, Accounting:** Karen Menzing. **Assistant Director, Payroll and Payables Accounting:** Mary Forkapa. **Concessions Accounting Manager:** Diane Turner. **Senior Staff Accountant:** Kim Haist.

Larry Dolan

HUMAN RESOURCES
VP, Human Resources/Chief Diversity Officer: Sara Lehrke. **Head of Diversity, Equity & Inclusion:** Matt Grimes. **Director, Human Resources Operations:** Jennifer Gibson. **Director, Talent Acquisition:** Mailynh Vu Nguyen. **Manager, Talent Acquisition:** Colleen Lynch. **Asst. Director, Organizational Development:** Nate Daymut. **Coordinator, Benefits:** Andrea Jirousek. **Coordinator, Training & Development:** George Hill.

MARKETING
VP, Marketing/Brand Management: Nicole Schmidt. **Director, Brand Management:** Jason Wiedemann. **Manager, Advertising/Promotions:** Anne Madzelan.

COMMUNICATIONS/BASEBALL INFORMATION
Telephone: (216) 420-4380. **Fax:** (216) 420-4430.
Senior VP, Public Affairs: Bob DiBiasio. **Vice President, Communications and Community Impact:** Curtis Danburg. **Director, Baseball Information & Player Relations:** Bart Swain. **Director, Communications & Player Relations:** Court Berry-Tripp. **Manager, Communications:** Austin Controulis. **Coordinator, Player Engagement & Family Relations:** Megan Ganser. **Team Photographer:** Dan Mendlik. **Coordinator, Communications & Team Historian:** Jeremy Feador. **Content Creation Specialist:** Olivia Lavelle. **Content Creation Specialist:** Brian Havrilla.

BALLPARK OPERATIONS
VP, Ballpark Improvements: Jim Folk. **Senior Director, Ballpark Operations:** Jerry Crabb. **Senior Director, Facility Operations:** Seth Cooper. **Senior Director, Security:** Jonathan Wilham. **Head Groundskeeper:** Brandon Koehnke. **Director, Facility Maintenance:** Ron Miller. **Manager, Ballpark Operations:** Steve Walters. **Manager, Ballpark Operations:** Tyler Cochran. **Manager, Safety Policy and Training:** David Bonacci. **Manager, Facility Operations:** Rosalie Morrison. **Manager, Gameday Staff:** Anna Powell.

TICKETING
Telephone: (216) 420-4487. **Fax:** (216) 420-4481.
Director, Ticket Services: Matt Coppo. **Ticket Services Manager:** Becky Emery. **Ticket Office Manager:** Eric Fronczek. **Manager, Ticket Operations:** Paige Selle.

TEAM OPERATIONS/CLUBHOUSE
Director, Team Travel: Mike Seghi. **Director, Team Travel and Logistics:** Jared Jones. **Home Clubhouse Manager:** Tony Amato. **Asst. Home Clubhouse Manager:** Brandon Biller. **Director, Video Operations:** Bob Chester. **Goodyear Facility Manager:** Amiro Santana. **Manager, Visiting Clubhouse:** Willie Jenks.

BASEBALL OPERATIONS

President, Baseball Operations: Chris Antonetti. **General Manager:** Mike Chernoff. **Executive Vice President & Assistant General Manager:** Matt Forman. **Assistant General Managers:** Sky Andrecheck, James Harris. **Senior Vice President, Scouting:** Paul Gillispie. **Senior Vice President, Player Acquisitions:** Victor Wang. **Vice President, Baseball Operations—Development:** Alex Merberg. **Vice President, Baseball Operations, Strategy & Administration:** Brad Grant. **Vice President, Baseball Learning & Development:** Jay Hennessey. **Vice President, Baseball Learning & Development:** Josh Gibson. **Vice President, Hitting:** Alex Eckelman. **Director, Research and Development:** Kevin Tenenbaum. **Director, Baseball Operations—Technology:** Sam Giller. **Director, Baseball Operations—Systems:** Will Landess.

Chris Antonetti

MAJOR LEAGUE STAFF

Manager: Terry Francona. **Coaches: Bench**—DeMarlo Hale. **Pitching**—Carl Willis. **Hitting**—Chris Valaika. **First Base**—Sandy Alomar Jr. **Third Base**—Mike Sarbaugh. **Bullpen**—Brian Sweeney. **Assistant Hitting Coach**—Victor Rodriguez. **Assistant Pitching Coach**—Joe Torres. **Assistants, Major League Staff:** Mike Barnett, Armando Camacaro, Justin Toole, Kyle Hudson, Ricky Pacione.

MEDICAL/TRAINING

Senior Vice President, Medical Services: Lonnie Soloff. **Head Team Physician:** Dr. Mark Schickendantz. **Head Athletic Trainer:** James Quinlan. **Assistant Athletic Trainers:** Jeff Desjardins, Chad Wolfe. **Performance Coach (Triple-A/Major League):** Brian Miles. **Director of Sport Science:** Jonathan Freeston. **Director of Sport Psychology:** Dr. Lindsay Shaw.

PLAYER DEVELOPMENT

Director, Player Development: Rob Cerfolio. **Director, Hitting Development:** Nate Freiman. **Director, Pitching Development:** Stephen Osterer. **Director, Physical Development:** Andrew Bahnert. **Asst. Director, Player Development:** Ilana Mishkin. **Asst. Director, Player Development—Education:** Anna Bolton. **Asst. Director, Player Development—Life Skills:** Jen Wolf. **Administrative Assistant, Player Development—**Nilda Taffanelli. **Special Assistant to President of Baseball Operations/GM: Fundamental Coordinators:** Tom Wiedenbauer. **Coordinators:** John McDonald (Field), Anthony Medrano (Assistant Field), Joel Mangrum (Pitching), Luke Carlin (Catching), Larry Day (Arizona Player Programs), Jose Mejia (Dominican Republic Academy), JT Maguire (OF/Baserunning), JB Eary (Infield), Grant Fink (Hitting), Josh Tubbs (Hitting Resource), Ben Johnson (Pitching Resource), Hasani Torres (S/C). **Asst. Director, Medical Services:** Jeremy Harris. **AZ Hitting Development Coach:** Ian Forster. **AZ Pitching Development Coaches:** Anderson Polanco, Brad Goldberg. **Clubhouse Manager (AZ):** Fletcher Wilkes.

FARM SYSTEM

Class	Club	Manager	Hitting Coach	Pitching Coach
Triple-A	Columbus	Andy Tracy	Jason Esposito	Rigo Beltran
Double-A	Akron	Rouglas Odor	Junior Betances	Owen Dew
High-A	Lake County	Greg DiCenzo	Chris Smith	Caleb Longshore
Low-A	Lynchburg	Omir Santos	Craig Massoni	Kevin Erminio
Rookie	Guardians (ACL)	Jordan Smith	Danny-David Linahan	Tony Arnold
Rookie	Guardians Blue (DSL)	Jesus Tavarez	Ordomar Valdez	Jesus Sanchez
Rookie	Guardians Red (DSL)	Carlos Fermin	Cole Nieto	Carlos Yan

SCOUTING

Amateur Scouting Director: Scott Barnsby. **Assistant Director, Amateur Scouting:** Ethan Purser. **Assistant, Amateur Scouting:** Matthew Czechanski. **Amateur Scouting Coordinators:** Jonathan Heuerman, David Compton, Andrew Krause. **Area Scouts:** Kyle Bamberger, Gustavo Benzan, Alexander Botts, Garrick Chaffee, Michael Cuva, Aaron Etchison, Conor Glassey, Andrew Kelly, Matthew Linder, Chirag Nanavati. **International Scouting Director:** Richard Conway. **Assistant Director, Latin American Scouting/Player Development:** Alex DeMoya. **International Scouting Coordinator:** Eugenio Melendez. **Senior Vice President, Scouting:** Paul Gillispie. **Senior Vice President, Player Acquisitions:** Victor Wang. **Director of Acquisitions:** Clint Longenecker. **Special Assistants to the Vice President and General Manager:** David Malpass, Steven Lubratich. **Director, Player Evaluations:** Chris Gale. **Special Assignment Scouts:** David Miller, Scott Meaney, Doug Carpenter. **Sr. Player Acquisition Scouts:** Lukas McKnight, Kevin Cullen. **Player Acquisition Scout:** Ryan Perry.

COLORADO ROCKIES

Office Address: 2001 Blake St., Denver, CO 80205.
Telephone: (303) 292-0200. **Fax:** (303) 312-2116.
Website: www.Rockies.com.

OWNERSHIP

Operated by: Colorado Rockies Baseball Club Ltd.
Owner/Chairman & Chief Executive Officer: Richard L. Monfort. **Executive Assistant to the Owner/Chairman & Chief Executive Officer:** Terry Douglass. **Owner/General Partner:** Charles K. Monfort.

BUSINESS OPERATIONS

President/Chief Operating Officer: Greg Feasel. **Assistant to President/Chief Operating Officer:** Kim Olson. **VP, Human Resources:** Kimberly Molina. **Director, Diversity, Equity, Inclusion & Recruiting, Human Resources:** Dallas Davis.

FINANCE

Assistant to the Executive Vice President: Tammy Vergara. **VP/CFO:** Michael Kent. **VP/General Counsel:** Brian Gaffney. **Senior Director, Procurement:** Gary Lawrence. **Coordinator, Purchasing:** Robert Wilkinson. **Senior Director, Accounting:** Phil Emerson. **Accountants:** Joel Binfet, Laine Campbell.

Richard Monfort

CORPORATE PARTNERSHIPS

VP, Corporate Partnerships: Walker Monfort. **Assistant to VP, Corporate Partnerships:** Nicole Scheller. **Senior Director, Client Services & Promotions:** Kari Anderson. **Director, Corporate Partnerships:** Nate VanderWal. **Senior Account Executive, Corporate Partnerships:** Chris Zumbrennen. **Senior Director, In-Game Entertainment & Event Operations:** Kent Krosbakken. **Public Address Announcer:** Reed Saunders.

COMMUNITY/RETAIL OPERATIONS

VP, Community & Retail Operations: James P. Kellogg. **Assistant to the VP, Community & Retail Operations:** Kelly Hall. **Senior Director, Retail Operations:** Aaron Heinrich.

MARKETING/COMMUNICATIONS

Director, Communications: Cory Little. **Supervisor: Communications:** Shelby Cravens. **Assistants, Communications:** Kevin Collins, Robert Livingston. **Manager, Digital Communications/Social Media:** Erin Hodges. **Assistants, Social Media:** Madison Casiano, David Saunders. **Editor/Designer, Communications & Marketing:** Sarah Topf. **Team Photographer:** Kyle Cooper.

BALLPARK OPERATIONS

VP/Chief Customer Officer, Ballpark Operations: Kevin Kahn. **Assistant to the VP/Chief Customer Officer, Ballpark Operations:** Lenus Lucero. **Senior Director, Food Service Operations/Development:** Albert Valdes. **Senior Director, Guest Services:** Steven Burke. **Head Groundskeeper:** Mark Razum. **Assistant Head Groundskeeper:** Doug Zabinsky. **Senior Director, Engineering & Facilities:** Allyson Gutierrez.

TICKETING

Telephone: (303) 762-5437, (800) 388-7625. **Fax:** (303) 312-2115.
VP, Ticket Operations, Sales & Services: Sue Ann McClaren.

TRAVEL/CLUBHOUSE

Senior Director, Major League Operations: Paul Egins. **Manager, Major League Clubhouse:** Mike Pontarelli. **Manager, Clubhouse Purchasing/Visiting Clubhouse:** Alan Bossart.

BASEBALL OPERATIONS

Senior VP/General Manager: Bill Schmidt. **Assistant to Senior VP/GM:** Irma Castañeda. **VP, Asst GM/BB Ops and Assistant General Counsel:** Zack Rosenthal. **Director, Baseball Operations:** Al Gilbert. **Director: Research & Development:** Scott Van Lenten. **Full Stack Developer: R&D:** Isaac Gerhart-Hines. **Data Architect-R&D:** Ryan Kelley. **Data Engineer:** Tae Hwa Hong. **Manager-BB Research:** Brittany Haby. **Analyst-R&D:** Ethan Moore. **Baseball Operations Fellow:** Julianna Rubin.

Bill Schmidt

MAJOR LEAGUE STAFF

Manager: Bud Black. **Coaches: Bench**—Mike Redmond, **Pitching**—Darryl Scott, **Hitting**—David Magadan. **Assistant Hitting Coaches**—Andy Gonzalez, P.J. Pilittere. **Third Base**—Stu Cole, **First Base**—Ron Gideon, **Bullpen**—Reid Cornelius, **Bullpen Catcher**—Aaron Munoz, **Director, Physical Performance**—Gabe Bauer. **Coordinator, ML Performance:** Mike Jasperson. **Video**—Brian Jones.

MEDICAL/TRAINING

Senior Director, Medical Operations/Special Projects: Tom Probst. **Medical Director:** Dr. Thomas Noonan. **Club Physicians:** Dr. Allen Schreiber, Dr. Douglas Wyland. **Head Trainer:** Keith Dugger. **Assistant Head Athletic Trainer:** Heath Townsend. **ML Assistant Athletic Trainer:** Andy Stover.

PLAYER DEVELOPMENT

Director: Chris Forbes. **Assistant Director:** Jesse Stender. **Coordinator, Minor League Operations:** Tim Batesole. **PD & Pro Scouting Assistant:** Avery Griggs. **Director Pitching Operations:** Steve Foster. **Coordinator of Pitching Strategies:** Flint Wallace. **Pitching Coordinator:** Doug Linton. **Hitting Coordinator:** Darin Everson. **Latin American Hitting Coordinator:** Michael Ramirez. **Field & Catching Coordinator:** Mark Strittmatter. **Defensive Coordinator:** Doug Bernier. **Latin America Field & Pitching Coordinator:** Edison Lora. **Physical Performance Coordinator:** Trevor Swartz. **Assistant Rehab Coordinator:** Arnaldo Gomez. **Director, Mental Skills Development:** Doug Chadwick. **Coordinators, Mental Skills:** Jerry Amador, Colt Olson. **Coordinator, Cultural Education:** Angel Amparo. **Video and Technology Assistant:** Chris Bonk. **Minor League Clubhouse & Equipment Manager/Manager Salt River Fields:** Daniel Kleinholz. **Dominican Republic Complex Administrator:** Ana Espiñal. **Special Assistant to the GM:** Clint Hurdle. **Special Assistant, PD:** Rick Mathews. **Special Assistant, PD & Scouting:** Jerry Weinstein.

FARM SYSTEM

Class	Club (League)	Manager	Hitting Coach	Pitching Coach
Triple-A	Albuquerque	Warren Schaeffer	Jordan Pacheco	Frank Gonzales
Double-A	Hartford	Chris Denorfia	Tom Sutaris	Blaine Beatty
High-A	Spokane	Scott Little	Zach Osborne	Ryan Kibler
Low-A	Fresno	Robinson Cancel	Nic Wilson	Mark Brewer
Rookie	Rockies (ACL)	Fred Ocasio	Trevor Burmeister	D. Burba/H. Rodriguez
Rookie	Rockies 1 (DSL)	M. Gonzalez/E. Jose	F. Rosario/F. Nunez	Sam Deduno

SCOUTING

VP / Assistant General Manager Scouting: Danny Montgomery. **Sr. Director, Scouting Operations:** Marc Gustafson. **Scout/Scouting Ops Administrator:** Emily Glass. **Assistant Scouting Director:** Damon Iannelli. **Advance Scouts:** Joe Little (Arvada, CO), Alan Regier (Gilbert, AZ). **Director, Pro Scouting:** Sterling Monfort. **Special Assistant, Player Personnel:** Ty Coslow (Louisville, KY). **Major League Scouts:** Kevin Bootay (Elk Grove, CA), Steve Fleming (Louisa, VA), Will George (Milford, DE), Jack Gillis (Sarasota, FL), Mark Germann (Denver, CO), Joe Housey (Hollywood, FL), John Corbin (Savannah, GA). **National Crosscheckers:** Mike Ericson (Phoenix, AZ), Jay Matthews (Concord, NC). **Area Scouts:** Scott Alves (Phoenix, AZ), Brett Baldwin (Kansas City, MO), Julio Campos (Guaynabo, PR) John Cedarburg (Fort Myers, FL), Jermaine Clark (Fresno, CA) Scott Corman (Lexington, KY), Jordan Czarniecki (Greenville, SC), Jeff Edwards (Fresno, TX), Sean Gamble (Atlanta, GA), Mike Garlatti (Edison, NJ), Matt Hattabaugh (Westminster, CA), Tim McDonnell (Olinda, CA) Matt Pignataro (Seattle, WA), Jesse Retzlaff (Dallas, TX), Rafael Reyes (Miami, FL), Ed Santa (Powell, OH), Zack Zulli (Hammond, LA). **Part-Time Scouts:** Dave McQueen (Bossier City, LA), Greg Pullia (Plymouth, MA). **VP, International Scouting/Player Development:** Rolando Fernandez. **Dominican Scouting/Development Coordinator:** Enmanuel Frias. **International Crosschecker:** Marc Russo. **Supervisor, Latin America Scouting:** Orlando Medina. **International Scouting:** Martin Cabrera (Dominican Republic), Carlos Gomez (Venezuela), Alving Mejias (Mexico), Frank Roa (Dominican Republic), Rogers Figueroa (Colombia).

DETROIT TIGERS

Office Address: 2100 Woodward Ave, Detroit, MI 48201.
Telephone: (313) 471-2000. **Fax:** (313) 471-2138. **Website:** www.tigers.com

OWNERSHIP

Operated By: Detroit Tigers Inc. **Chairman & CEO, Detroit Tigers:** Christopher Ilitch. **President & CEO, Ilitch Sports and Entertainment:** Chris McGowan.

BUSINESS OPERATIONS

Chris Ilitch

BUSINESS OPERATIONS LEADERSHIP

Senior Vice President, Operations and Development: Keith Bradford. **Senior Vice President, Finance:** Russ Borrows. **Senior Vice President, Legal Affairs:** Robert E. Carr. **Senior Vice President, Corporate Sales:** Chris Coffman. **Senior Vice President & Chief Marketing Officer:** Emily Neenan. **Vice President, Finance:** Bobby Hoekstra. **Vice President, Human Resources:** Michele Bartos. **Vice President, Communications:** Ron Colangelo. **Vice President, Venue Security:** Mike Hartnett. **Vice President, Park Operations:** Chris Lawrence. **Vice President, Ticket Sales & Service:** Joe Schiavi. **Vice President, Premium Sales & Special Events:** Michael Leinert. **Vice President, Partnership Activation:** Molly Wurdack. **Vice President, Marketing:** Ellen Hill Zeringue.

FINANCE/ADMINISTRATION

Senior Director, Human Resources: Karen Gruca. **Director, Finance:** Katelyn Haas. **Director, Purchasing:** McKenzie Reeves. **Accounting Manager & Treasury Analyst:** Sheila Robine. **Manager, Payroll:** Mark Cebelak.

CORPORATE PARTNERSHIPS/TICKET SALES & SERVICES

Director, Corporate Partnership Activation: Tiffany Harrington. **Director, Corporate Partnership Business Strategy and Solutions:** Mike Singer. **Activation Managers, Corporate Partnerships:** Ian Fontenot, Michael Holley, Riley McCord. **Solutions Managers, Corporate Partnerships:** Max Klepper, Jacob Pnakovich. **Sales Managers, Corporate Partnerships:** Cameron Close, Megan Garlow, Matt Gay, Tina Genitti, Donovan Powell, John Wolski.

TICKET SALES & SERVICES

Senior Director, Ticket Services: Grant Anderson. **Director, Ticket Sales:** Allen Jabaro. **Director, Client Services:** Brian Jemison. **Director, Business Analytics:** Jeff Lutz. **Manager, Group Sales:** Marc Lopez. **CRM & Database Manager:** Kevin Sucher. **Manager, Ticket Services:** Adam Klein.

MARKETING/COMMUNICATIONS/COMMUNITY IMPACT

Director, Promotions & Special Events: Haley Kolff. **Director, Player Relations & Authentics:** Jordan Field. **Director, Communications:** Chad Crunk. **Director, Broadcasting & In-Game Entertainment:** Stan Fracker. **Director, Community Impact:** Kevin Brown. **Manager, Communications:** Ben Fidelman. **Manager, Promotions & Special Events:** Evan Novak. **Project Manager:** Taylor Olson. **Social Media Manager:** Greg Garno. **Manager, Fantasy Camp, Alumni & Player Engagement:** Ashley Robinson. **Community Impact Manager, Fundraiser and Development:** Kelsey Stewart. **Senior Producer & Scoreboard Production Manager:** Alex Lovachis.

PARK OPERATIONS

Director, Event Operations: Mike Bauer. **Director, Park Operations:** Shaun O'Brien. **Director, Security:** Sean Furlong. **Head Groundskeeper:** Heather Nabozny. **Event Services Manager:** Caitlin Kelly. **Operations Managers:** Steve Burrows, Mike Kiefer, Dana Smith.

BASEBALL OPERATIONS

Telephone: (313) 471-2000. **Fax:** (313) 471-2099.

Executive Vice President, Baseball Operations/General Manager: Al Avila. **Vice President/Assistant General Managers:** David Chadd, Sam Menzin, Jay Sartori. **Vice President, Player Personnel:** Scott Bream. **Vice President, Player Development:** Ryan Garko. **Special Assistants to the GM:** Kirk Gibson, Willie Horton, Jim Leyland, Lance Parrish, Mike Russell, Alan Trammell. **Director, Baseball Analytics:** Jim Logue. **Director, Team Travel:** Brian Britten. **Associate Counsel, Baseball Operations:** Alan Avila. **Executive Assistant to the Executive Vice President, Baseball Operations/General Manager:** Marty Lyon.

MAJOR LEAGUE STAFF

Manager: A.J. Hinch. **Coaches: Pitching**—Chris Fetter, **Hitting** —Scott Coolbaugh, **First Base**—Gary Jones, **Third Base**—Ramon Santiago, **Assistant Pitching**—Juan Nieves, **Bench**—George Lombard, **Assisting Hitting**—Mike Hessman, **Quality Control**—Josh Paul.

MEDICAL/TRAINING

Senior Director, Medical Services: Kevin Rand. **Head Athletic Trainer:** Doug Teter. **Assistant Athletic Trainers:** Chris McDonald, Matt Rankin. **Strength/Conditioning Coordinator:** Steve Chase. **Assistant Strength/Conditioning Coordinator:** Matt Rosenhamer. **Team Physicians:** Dr. Michael Workings, Dr. Stephen Lemos, Dr. Louis Saco (Florida). **Coordinator, Medical Services:** Gwen Keating.

PLAYER DEVELOPMENT

Vice President, Player Development: Ryan Garko. **Director, Minor League Operations:** Dan Lunetta. **Director, Player Development:** Kenny Graham. **Assistant Director, Player Development:** Peter Bransfield. **Director, Pitching:** Gabe Ribas. **Director, Coaching/Field Coordinator:** Ryan Sienko. **Director, Performance Science:** Dr. Georgia Giblin. **Director, Minor League/Scouting Administration:** Cheryl Evans. **Director, International Operations:** Tom Moore. **Director, Latin American Operations:** Miguel Garcia. **Director, Latin American Player Development:** Euclides Rojas. **Administrators, Dominican Academy:** Wilfredo Crespo, Jimmy Ortiz. **Manager, Player Development:** David Allende. **Manager, International Operations:** Rafael Gonzalez. **Coordinators, Player Development:** Daniel Crago, Jose Sajour. **Coordinator, Minor League Complex:** Kevin Guthrie. **Coordinator, Cultural Assimilation:** Sharon Lockwood. **Minor League Medical Coordinator:** Corey Tremble. **Minor League Strength/Conditioning Coordinators:** Ryan Maedel, Francisco Rivas. **Medical Coordinator —International:** Manny Pena. **Assistant Medical Coordinator—International:** Gabe Garcia. **Physical Therapist:** Duncan Evans. **Minor League Video Coordinators:** Correy Erickson, Zach Monash. **Minor League Clubhouse Manager:** Patrick Saenz. **Minor League Clubhouse Assistant Manager:** Pete Mancuso. **Roving Instructors:** Jeff Branson (hitting), Max Gordon (hitting), Steve Smith (pitching), Stephanos Stroop (pitching), Jorge Cordova (assistant pitching), Billy Boyer (infield), Angel Berroa (Latin American infield), Arnie Beyeler (base running/outfield), Brian Peterson (performance enhancement coach), Brian Taggett (Latin American performance coach).

FARM SYSTEM

Class	Club	Manager	Hitting Coach	Pitching Coach
Triple-A	Toledo	Lloyd McClendon	Adam Melhuse	Doug Bochtler
Double-A	Erie	Gabe Alvarez	John Murrian	Dan Ricabal
High-A	West Michigan	Brayan Pena	CJ Wamsley	Dean Stiles
Low-A	Lakeland	Andrew Graham	Francisco Contreras	Juan Pimentel
Rookie	Tigers (FCL)	Mike Alvarez	Rafael Gil	Carlos Bohorquez
Rookie	Tigers 1 (DSL)	Marcos Yepez	Francisco Martinez	Luis Marte
Rookie	Tigers 2 (DSL)	Salvador Paniagua	Luis Mateo	Wilian Moreno

SCOUTING

Vice President, Assistant General Manager: David Chadd, Sam Menzin. **Vice President, Player Personnel:** Scott Bream. **Special Assistant to the GM:** Mike Russell. **Director, Amateur Scouting:** Scott Pleis. **Director, Minor League & Scouting Administration:** Cheryl Evans. **Assistant Director, Amateur Scouting:** Eric Nieto. **Amateur Scouting Video Coordinator:** Greg Bundrage. **Major League Scouts:** Ray Crone, Jim Elliott, Kevin Ellis, Joe Ferrone, P.J. Jones, Dave Littlefield, Paul Mirocke, Jim Olander, Jim Rough, John Stockstill, Bruce Tanner, Josh Wilson. **National Crosscheckers:** Justin Henry, Steve Hinton, James Orr. **Regional Crosscheckers: East**—Taylor Black, **Midwest**—Tim Grieve, **Central**—Bryson Barber, **West**—Dave Lottsfeldt. **Area Scouts:** Nick Avila, Jim Bretz, Donald Brown, RJ Burgess, Austin Cousino, Ryan Johnson, Joey Lothrop, Tim McWilliam, Steve Pack, Daniel Sabatino, George Schaefer, Mike Smith, Steve Taylor, Cal Towey, Matt Zmuda, Harold Zonder. **Part-Time Scouts:** German Geigel, Deryl Horton, Mark Monahan, Clyde Weir. **Director, International Operations:** Tom Moore. **Director, Latin American Operations:** Miguel Garcia. Manager, **International Operations:** Rafael Gonzalez. Coordinator, **Pacific Rim Scouting:** Kevin Hooker. **International Crosscheckers:** Alejandro Rodriguez, Jeff Wetherby. **Dominican Republic Special Assignment Scout:** Oliver Arias. **Venezuelan Scouting Supervisor:** Jesus Mendoza. **Venezuelan Academy Administrator/Area Scout:** Oscar Garcia. **International Area Scouts:** Rodolfo Penalo, Aldo Perez, Miguel Rodriguez, Carlos Santana, Rudy Garcia, Raul Leiva, Jose Zambrano, Pedro Vivas, Pedro Castellano, Luis Molina, Michael Hsieh, Kan Ikeda, Ho-Kyun Im.

Al Avila

HOUSTON ASTROS

Office Address: Minute Maid Park, Union Station, 501 Crawford, Suite 400, Houston, TX 77002.
Mailing Address: PO Box 288, Houston, TX 77001. **Telephone:** (713) 259-8000. **Fax:** (713) 259-8981.
Email Address: fanfeedback@astros.mlb.com. **Website:** www.astros.com.

OWNERSHIP
Owner/Chairman: Jim Crane.

BUSINESS OPERATIONS

Jim Crane

Executive Assistant: Eileen Colgin. **Administrative Assistant:** Brittany Redeaux. **Senior VP, Affiliate Business Operations:** Creighton Kahoalii. **Senior VP, Business Operations:** Marcel Braithwaite. **Senior VP, Chief Financial Officer:** Michael Slaughter. **Senior VP, Community Relations/Executive Director, Astros Foundation:** Paula Harris. **Senior VP/ General Counsel:** Giles Kibbe. **Senior VP, Marketing/Communications:** Anita Sehgal. **VP, Tax:** Vito Ciminello. **VP, Communications:** Gene Dias. **VP, Stadium Operations:** Bobby Forrest. **VP, Information Technology:** Chris Hanz. **VP, Foundation Development:** Marian Harper. **VP, Merchandising/Retail Operations:** Tom Jennings. **VP, Human Resources:** Jennifer Springs. **VP, Finance:** Doug Seckel. **VP, Event Sales/Operations:** Stephanie Stegall. **VP, Marketing:** Jason Wooden. **VP, Ticket Sales and Service:** P.J. Keene. **VP, Corporate Partnerships:** Jeff Stewart. **VP, Accounting:** Abby Brantley. **VP, Affiliate Operations:** Thomas Bell. **VP, Business Strategy and Analytics:** Jay Verrill.

COMMUNICATIONS/COMMUNITY RELATIONS
Senior Manager, Communications: Steve Grande. **Manager, Business Communications:** Rachel Caton. **Coordinator, Communications:** Meshach Sullivan. **Manager, Broadcasting:** Ginny Gotcher Grande. **Director, Astros Youth Academy:** Daryl Wade. **Manager, Astros Youth Academy:** Duane Stelly. **Coordinators, Community Relations/ Astros Foundation:** Andrew McMullin, Hugo Mojica. **Coordinator, Astros Youth Academy:** Megan Hays.

MARKETING/ANALYTICS
Senior Directors, Fan Experience: Chris E. Garcia. **Director, Content:** Alex Herko. **Senior Managers, Marketing Entertainment:** Kyle Hamsher, Richard Tapia. **Senior Manager, Promotions & Events:** Daniel Klimpel. **Senior Manager, Graphic & Marketing Projects:** Larry Provitt. **Manager, Digital Marketing:** Catie Willis Guidry. **Manager, Photo & Video Content:** Cato Cataldo. **Manager, Production:** Garret Young. **Team Photographer:** Evan Triplett. **Graphic and Design Media Designers:** Kim Rogers, Clint Self and Ruben Valdez. **Content Producers:** Matt Blum and Matt Rewis. **Coordinator, Digital Marketing:** Luke Hooten. **Coordinator, Entertainment:** Oscar Liendo. **Coordinator, Grassroots Marketing:** Meehee Kim. **Coordinators, Promotions and Events:** Liz Sherman and Hannah Kirsch. **Coordinator, Social Media:** Riley Milhon.

CORPORATE PARTNERSHIPS
Sponsorship Advisor: Matt Brand. **Senior Director, Corporate Sponsorship Sales:** Matt Richardson. **Directors, Corporate Partnerships:** Melissa Hahn, Keshia Henderson, Jimmy Comerota. **Account Managers, Corporate Partnerships:** Ashley Sciambra, Cam Copeland, Chris Leahy, Lauren Hill, Haleigh Sanders.

STADIUM OPERATIONS
Director, Security: Ben Williams. **Manager, Security:** Roy Pippin. **Senior Manager, Stadium Operations:** William Connaught. **Manager, Parking:** Gary Rowberry. **Head Groundskeeper:** Izzy Hinojosa. **Assistant Groundskeeper:** James Vaughn.

TICKETING
Director, Group Sales: Mariza Lerma. **Director, Season Ticket Sales:** Adam Martelli. **Director, Ticket Operations:** Mark Cole. **Senior Manager, Box Office and Ticket Services:** Marcus Barefield. **Senior Manager, Ticket Technology and Solutions:** Trevor Purvis.

BASEBALL OPERATIONS

General Manager: James Click. **Assistant GMs:** Andrew Ball, Scott Powers, Pete Putila. **Special Assistants:** Craig Biggio, Jeff Bagwell, Enos Cabell. **Sr. Director, Baseball Operations:** Bill Firkus. **Sr. Director, Player Evaluation:** Charles Cook. **Special Advisor, Baseball Operations:** Will Sharp. **Director, Performance Science:** Jacob Buffa. **Director, Player Development:** Sara Goodrum. **Director, Amateur Scouting:** Kris Gross. **Director, Player Personnel:** Matt Hogan. **Director, Minor League Operations:** Derrick Fong. **Director, Research/Development:** Sarah Gelles. **Director, Latin American Operations:** Caridad Cabrera.

James Click

MAJOR LEAGUE STAFF

Manager: Dusty Baker. **Coaches: Bench**—Joe Espada, **Pitching**—Josh Miller. **Pitching**—Bill Murphy. **Hitting**— Alex Cintron. **Second Hitting**—Troy Snitker. **First Base**—Omar Lopez. **Third Base**—Gary Pettis. **Quality Control**—Dan Firova. **Major League Coach**—Jason Kanzler. **Coach**—Michael Collins.

TEAM OPERATIONS/CLUBHOUSE

Manager, Team Travel: Juan Huitron. **Coordinator, Major League Advance Information:** Tommy Kawamura. **Clubhouse Manager:** Carl Schneider. **Visiting Clubhouse Manager:** Steve Perry.

MEDICAL/TRAINING

Head Team Physician: Dr. David Lintner. **Team Physicians:** Dr. Thomas Mehlhoff, Dr. James Muntz, Dr. Pat McCulloch, Dr. Vijay Jotwani. **Head Athletic Trainer and Head Physical Therapist:** Jeremiah Randall. **Massage Therapist:** Katsumi Oka. **Major League Strength/Conditioning Coach:** Taylor Rhoades.

PLAYER DEVELOPMENT

Director, Player Development: Sara Goodrum. **Director, Minor League Operations:** Derrick Fong. **Minor League Coordinators:** Jason Bell (fundamentals).

FARM SYSTEM

Class	Club	Manager	Hitting Coach	Pitching Coach
Triple-A	Sugar Land	Mickey Storey	Rafael Pena	Erick Abreu
Double-A	Corpus Christi	Gregorio Petit	Aaron Westlake	Thomas Whitsett
High-A	Asheville	Nate Shaver	Rene Rojas	Jose Rada
Low-A	Fayetteville	Joe Thon	Jose Puentes	John Kovalik
Rookie	Astros (FCL)	Ricky Rivera	Bryan Muniz	Sean Buchanan
Rookie		Carlos Lugo	L. Reynoso/A. Cresci	TBD
Rookie	Astros 1 (DSL)	Marcelo Alfonsin	Elvis Rodriguez	Starlyng Sanchez
Rookie		Alejandro Martinez	Kyle Brennan	Rick Aponte

SCOUTING

Director, Amateur Scouting: Kris Gross. **Assistant Director, Scouting:** Evan Brannon. **Special Assistants, Scouts:** Gavin Dickey and Charlie Gonzalez. **Domestic Crosschecker:** Ryan Leake. **Domestic Scouts:** Tim Costic (Los Angeles, CA), Ryan Courville (South Texas), Steven DiPuglia (Bradenton, FL), Joe Dunigan (Phoenix, AZ), Andrew Johnson (Raleigh, NC), Kevin Mello (Richmond, CA), Scott Oberhelman (Columbus, OH), Steve Payne (Barrington, RI), Drew Pearson (Milwaukee, WI), Freddy Perez (Nashville, TN), Bobby St. Pierre (Atlanta, GA), Jim Stevenson (Tulsa, OK), Landon Townsley (Baton Rouge, LA), Eli Tupuola (San Diego, CA).

Scouting Analyst: Cam Pendino. **Scouting Coordinator:** TJ Tulis. **Assistant Director, International Scouting:** Brian Rodgers. **Supervisors:** Alfredo Ulloa, Jose Palacios. **Scouts, Dominican Republic:** Leocadio Guevara, Jose Lima, Hassan Wessin, Jose Torres, Alfred Ramirez. **Mexico:** Miguel Pintor. **Venezuela:** Enrique Brito. **Assistant Scouts, Dominican Republic:** Francisco Navarro, Omar Frias and Oriana Gonzalez. **Venezuela:** Carlos Freiaas.

VIDEO & TECHNOLOGY

Coordinator, Video: Kyle Connell.

KANSAS CITY ROYALS

OWNERSHIP

Operated By: Kansas City Royals Baseball Club, LLC. **Chairman & CEO:** John Sherman.

EXECUTIVE LEADERSHIP

President, Baseball Operations: Dayton Moore. **Sr. Vice President/Chief Operating Officer:** Brooks Sherman. **Sr. Vice President/Chief Revenue & Innovation Officer:** Sarah Tourville. **Sr. Vice President/Chief Legal Officer:** Adam Sachs.

BUSINESS OPERATIONS

FINANCE/ADMINISTRATION

VP, Chief Financial Officer: Whitney Beaver. **VP, Ticket Operations:** Anthony Blue. **VP, People & Culture:** Iris Edelin. **Director, Accounting/Risk Management:** Patrick Fleischmann. **Director, Payroll:** Jodi Parsons. **Director, Ticket Ops:** Chris Darr.

GITTINGS PHOTOGRAPHY

John Sherman

TECHNOLOGY

VP, Technology & Business Analytics: Brian Himstedt. **Director, Business Analytics:** Daniel Sommerhauser. **Director, Business Data Architecture:** Collin Brody. **Director, Technology Infra/Ops:** Mitchell McDaniel.

COMMUNICATIONS

VP, Communications: Sam Mellinger. **Director, Media Relations:** Nick Kappel. **Assistant Director, Media Relations:** Ian Kraft. **Manager, Communications:** Logan Jones.

COMMUNITY IMPACT & URBAN YOUTH ACADEMY

VP, Community Impact: Kyle Vena. **Sr. Director, Community Investments & Exec. Director, Royals Charities:** Amanda Grosdidier. **Director, Community Partnerships & Events:** Chris Major. **Director, Community Investments/ Alumni:** Dina Blevins. **Director, Royals Hall of Fame:** Curt Nelson. **Sr. Director, Professional and Community Development:** Jeff Diskin.

BALLPARK OPERATIONS

VP, Ballpark Operations: Isaac Riffel. **Sr. Director, Landscaping:** Trevor Vance. **Sr. Director, Stadium Engineering:** Todd Burrow. **Director, Ballpark Services:** Johnny Williams. **Director, Guest Experience:** Nick Pieroni. **Director, Event Operations:** Bryan Ross.

PINE TAR COLLECTIVE

VP, Pine Tar Collective: Tony Snethen. **Group Director, Branded Content & Innovation:** Scott Lichtenauer. **Sr. Director, Content Strategy & Emerging Tech:** Erin Sleddens. **Sr. Director, Scoreboard Operations:** Steven Funke. **Director, Event Presentation:** Nicole Averso. **Director, Creative Services:** Caitlin Wienck.

CORPORATE PARTNERSHIPS & TICKET SALES

VP, Corporate Partnerships: Alex Schulte. **Director, Corporate Partnership Sales:** Jason Kramer. **Director, Corporate Partnership Solutions:** Steve Garvey. **Director, New Sales & Development:** Adam Cain. **Director, Premium** & **Retention Sales:** Kayla Shively.

BASEBALL OPERATIONS

Telephone: (816) 921-8000. **Fax:** (816) 924-0347.

President, Baseball Operations: Dayton Moore. **Executive Asst. to the President:** Emily Penning. **Sr. VP/GM:** J.J. Picollo. **SVP/Asst., GM:** Major League/International Operations: Rene Francisco. **Baseball Operations:** Scott Sharp. **VP, Asst. GM:** Baseball Administration: Jin Wong. **VP, Player Personnel:** Lonnie Goldberg. **Research & Development:** Dr. Daniel Mack. **Special Asst. to Baseball Ops/Leadership:** Willie Aikens, Blaine Boyer, Reggie Sanders, Mike Sweeney. **Sr. Directors: Leadership & Cultural Dev:** Matt Marasco. **Performance Science:** Austin Driggers. **Behavioral Science:** Dr. Ryan Maid. **Professional & Community Dev:** Jeff Diskin. **Director, Arizona Ops:** Nick Leto. **Asst. Director, Behavioral Science:** Melissa Lambert. **Lead Developer:** Paul Turner. **Sr. Developer:** Joseph San Diego. **Developer,** Jenny Segelke. **Manager, Baseball Administration:** Kristin Lock. **Analysts:** Brandon Nelson, Rob Sorge, Robyn Wampler. **Baseball Operations Admin. Asst.:** Jared Hinton.

Dayton Moore

TRAVEL/CLUBHOUSE

Vice President, Major League Team Operations: Jeff Davenport. **Sr. Director, Clubhouse Operations:** Chuck Hawke. **Manager, Equipment:** Patrick Gorman. **Manager, Culinary Service:** T.J. Stack. **Manager, Clubhouse & Umpire Services:** Tom Walsh.

MAJOR LEAGUE STAFF

Manager: Mike Matheny. **Coaches: Bench**—Pedro Grifol, **Pitching**—Cal Eldred, **Hitting**—Terry Bradshaw, **Asst. Hitting**—Keoni DeRenne, **First Base**—Damon Hollins, **Third Base**—Vance Wilson, **Bullpen**—Larry Carter. **Major League Coach:** John Mabry. **Replay/Advance Scouting Coordinator:** Bill Duplissea. **Bullpen Catchers:** Parker Morin, Allan de San Miguel. **Video:** Jason Nicols. **Advanced Scouting Analyst:** Andy Ferguson. **Batting Practice Pitcher:** Miguel Garcia.

MEDICAL/TRAINING

Team Physician: Dr. Vincent Key. **Director Medical Services:** Nick Kenney. **Head Athletic Trainer:** Kyle Turner. **Asst. Athletic Trainers:** Chris Delucia, Dave Iannicca. **Strength & Conditioning:** Ryan Stoneberg. **Asst. Strength & Conditioning:** Luis Perez. **Physical Therapist:** Jeff Blum. **Registered Sports Dietitian:** Erika Wincheski.

PLAYER DEVELOPMENT

Sr. Directors: Player Development/Hitting Performance: Alec Zumwalt. **Pitching Performance:** Paul Gibson. **Directors: Player Development/Field Coordinator:** Mitch Maier. **Performance Science:** John Wagle. **Medical Services/Physical Therapist:** Justin Hahn. **Asst. Director, Player Development:** Malcom Culver. **Manager, Pitching Performance/Strategist**—Mitch Stetter. **Special Asst. to the GM/Player Development:** Rafael Belliard, Chino Cadahia. **Field Coordinator:** Victor Baez (DSL). **Special Asst., Player Development:** John Wathan, Harry Spilman. **Special Assignment Hitting Coach:** Mike Tosar. **Coordinators:** Jason Simontacchi (Pitching), Drew Saylor (Hitting), Eddie Rodriguez (Infield), J.C. Boscan (Catching), Logan Gudde (Physical Therapy), Justin Kemp (Medical), Jarret Abell (Strength/Conditioning). **Assistant Coordinators:** Nic Jackson (hitting), Derrick Robinson (Outfield, Bunting, Baserunning), Tony Medina (Medical/Latin America), Phil Falco (Strength/Conditioning), Jeff Suppan (Pitching Rover). **Support Staff:** Will Simon (Equipment), Monica Ramirez (Ed/ESL & Latin American Initiatives).

FARM SYSTEM

Class	Club (League)	Manager	Hitting Coach	Pitching Coach
Triple-A	Omaha	Scott Thorman	Brian Buchanan	Dane Johnson
Double-A	Northwest Arkansas	Chris Widger	Abraham Nunez	Derrick Lewis
High-A	Quad Cities	Brooks Conrad	Andy LaRoche	Steve Luebber
Low-A	Columbia	Tony Pena Jr	Jesus Azuaje	John Habyan
Rookie	Royals (ACL)	Omar Ramirez	Ramon Castro	C. Martinez/M. Davis
Rookie	Royals (DSL1)	Ramon Martinez	Wilson Betemit	Rafael Feliz
Rookie	Royals (DSL2)	Sergio de Luna	Fernando Martinez	Jose Veras

SCOUTING

Telephone: (816) 921-8000. **Fax:** (816) 924-0347. **Director, Amateur Scouting:** Danny Ontiveros. **Pro Scouting:** Michael Cifuentes. **Baseball Ops—Scouting/PD:** Jack Monahan. **Sr. Advisors:** Mike Arbuckle, Roy Clark, Gene Lamont, Donnie Williams. **Special Assts to the Pres/GM:** Tim Conroy, Tom McNamara, Louie Medina, Don Poplin. **Special Assignment Scouts:** Mitch Webster, Dale Sveum. **Pro Scouts:** Nate Adcock, Dennis Cardoza, Brad Kelley, Mark Leavitt, John McMichen, Terry Wetzel, Jon Williams. **Part-Time Pro Scout:** Rene Lachemann. **Advance Scout:** Tony Tijerina. **Special Asst to Amateur Scouting:** Darwin Pennye. **National Pitching Supervisor:** Gary Wilson. **Regional Supervisors: Midwest**—Gregg Miller, **Northeast**—Keith Connolly, **Southeast**—Sean Gibbs, **West**— Colin Gonzales. **Area Supervisors:** Joe Barbera, Tim Bittner, Cody Clark, Mike Farrell, Abe Flores, Buddy Gouldsmith, Daniel Guerrero, Todd Guggiana, Josh Hallgren, Nick Hamilton, Will Howard, Scott Melvin, Ken Munoz, Matt Price, Joe Ross, Bobby Shore. **Underclass Scouts:** Tim Bavester, Travis Ezi, Vance Vizcaino. **Part-Time Scouts:** Brett Bailey, Rick Clendenin, Louis Collier, Jeremy Jones, Howard McCullough, Brittan Motley, Johnny Ramos, Mike Ranson, Chris Reitsma, Lloyd Simmons, Adam Stern. **Asst. GM/Int'l Operations:** Albert Gonzalez. **Coordinators: Latin America:** Richard Castro. **Pacific Rim:** Phil Dale. **Manager, International Ops:** Fabio Herrera. **International Supervisor:** Orlando Estevez. Luis Ortiz. **International Scouts:** Roberto Aquino (D.R.) Nicolas Bautista (D.R.), Neil Burke (Australia), Elias Despardel (D.R.), Francis Feliciano (D.R.), Alberto Garcia (VZ), Joelvis Gonzalez (VZ), Jose Gualdron (VZ), Djionny Joubert (Curacao), Edson Kelly (Aruba), Hyunsung Kim (S. Korea), Nathan Miller (Taiwan), Rafael Miranda (Colombia), Fausto Morel (D.R.), Hiroyuki Oya (Japan), Edis Perez (D.R), Manuel Samaniego (Mexico), Rafael Vasquez (D.R.).

LOS ANGELES ANGELS

Office Address: 2000 Gene Autry Way, Anaheim, CA 92806.
Mailing Address: 2000 Gene Autry Way, Anaheim, CA 92803.
Telephone: (714) 940-2000. **Fax:** (714) 940-2205. **Website:** www.angels.com.

OWNERSHIP

Owners: Arte & Carole Moreno. **Chairman:** Dennis Kuhl. **President:** John Carpino. **Senior Vice President, Finance/Administration:** Molly Jolly. **Executive Vice President:** Dana Wells.

BUSINESS OPERATIONS

Senior Director of Finance: Doug Mylowe. **Controller:** Sue Bassett. **Assistant Controller:** Jennifer Whynott. **Financial Operations Manager:** Jennifer Jeanblanc. **Payroll Manager:** Lorelei Schlitz. **Accountants:** Kylie McManus and Matt Asato. **Accounts Payable Specialist:** Sarah Talamonte. **Senior Director, Human Resources:** Deborah Johnston. **Director, Human Resources:** Mayra Castro. **Benefits Manager:** Cecilia Schneider. **Human Resources Coordinator:** Reyna Mancilla. **Senior Director, Information Services:** Al Castro. **Director Network Infrastructure:** Neil Fariss. **Senior Network Engineer:** James Sheu. **Manager, Technical Services:** Josh Schnoor. **Desktop Support Analyst:** Dennis De Jesus.

Arte and Carole Moreno

CORPORATE SALES

Senior Director, Corporate Partnerships/Business Development: Mike Fach. **Director, Partnership Services:** Bobby Kowan. **Director, Corporate & Community Partnerships:** Nicole Provansal. **Senior Account Executive, Corporate Partnerships:** Drew Zinser. **Account Executives, Corporate Partnerships:** Jared Florin and Jonathan Chodzko. **Senior Manager, Partnership Services:** Andie Mitsuda.

ENTERTAINMENT

Director, Entertainment/Production: Peter Bull. **Coordinator:** Cole Dragon. **Engineer:** Zac Applegate. **Marketing and Entertainment Coordinator:** Mandi Ortiz.

MARKETING

Director, Ticket Marketing and Business Analytics: Ryan Vance. **Senior Marketing Managers:** Alex Tinyo and Vanessa Vega. **Graphic Designers:** Tricia Kami and Dominic Mitrano. **Manager, Business Analytics:** JJ Evans. **Business Analyst:** Nicole Yamasaki.

PUBLIC/MEDIA RELATIONS/COMMUNICATIONS

Telephone: (714) 940-2014.
Director, Communications: Adam Chodzko. **Senior Manager, Communications:** Matt Birch. **Manager, Communications:** Grace McNamee. **Manager, Digital Communications:** Hannah Stange. **Senior Coordinator, Digital Communications:** Ricardo Zapata. **Team Photographer:** Blaine Ohigashi.

COMMUNITY RELATIONS

Director, Corporate & Community Partnerships: Nicole Provansal. **Manager, Foundation and Community Initiatives:** Adam Cali. **Scholarship Programs and Marketing Coordinator:** Lillea Acasio.

SALES, CLIENT SERVICES & TICKETING

Senior Director, Ticket Sales & Service: Jim Panetta. **Director, Premium & Business Development Sales & Service:** Aaron Dragomir. **Senior Director, Ticket Operations/Service:** Tom DeTemple. **Senior Manager, Ticket Operations:** Sheila Brazelton. **Ticket Operations Manager:** Armando Reyna. **Sr. Ticket Sales Manager:** David Neumann. **Client Services Manager:** Jennifer Moran. **Business Development Manager:** Jeff Leuenberger. **Premium Sales Manager:** Eddie Gomez. **Premium Sales Account Manager:** Nick Andre. **Business Development Account Managers:** Chris Young and Robert Foster. **Business Development Account Executive:** Eduardo Inarra. **Group Sales Supervisor:** Phil Gurule. **Sr. Group Account Specialist:** Angel Rodriguez. **Group Sales Account Executives:** Melissa Fombona, Keegan Forbes, Mary Myers, Tucker McGarrity, Luis Martinez, Randy Rigali, Clare Weehan and Jon Leachman. **Sr. Client Services Representative:** Abbi Newton.

BALLPARK OPERATIONS/FACILITIES

Vice President, Ballpark Operations: Brian Sanders. **Director, Ballpark Operations and Development:** Nathan Bautista. **Director Stadium Facilities:** Calvin Ching. **Senior Manager, Stadium Operations and Security:** Carlos Campos. **Senior Manager, Housekeeping Facilities:** Jose Padilla. **Manager, Ballpark Operations and Events:** Shanelle Stephens. **Manager, Ballpark Operations:** Jacqueline Urbanus. **Assistant Manager, Security:** JB Jaso. **Manager, Special Events Sales and Service:** Eileen Prescott. **Special Events Sales and Service:** An Pham and Brett Halstead. **Custodial Supervisors:** Robert Iglesias, Ray Nells. **Purchasing Manager:** Suzanne Peters. **Senior Supervisor, Stadium Facilities:** Pedro Del Castillo. **Wardrobe Supervisor:** Genero Luna.

TRAVEL/CLUBHOUSE

Traveling Secretary: Tom Taylor. **Director, Equipment and Clubhouse Operations:** Guy Gallagher. **Assistant Clubhouse Manager:** Shane Demmitt. **Visiting Clubhouse Manager:** Brett Crane. **Assistant Clubhouse Manager:** Aaron Wiedeman. **Manager, Major League Video:** Ryan Dundee.

BASEBALL OPERATIONS

General Manager: Perry Minasian. **Assistant GM:** Alex Tamin. **Special Assistants to the GM:** Ben Francisco. **Senior Advisors:** Bill Stoneman. **Director, Player Procurement:** David Haynes. **Senior Director, R&D:** Michael Lord. **Director, Advance Scouting:** John Pratt. **Senior Coordinator, Baseball Administration:** Amanda Kropp. **Coordinator, Baseball Administration:** Peggy Berroa-Morales. **Coordinator, Pitching Analysis:** Jared Hughes. **Sr. Analyst, Research and Development:** Chet Gutwein. **Analyst, Research and Development:** Matt Johnson and Connor Moffatt. **Analyst, Baseball Operations:** Joe Chernak, Dylan Mortimer, Jake Sauberman, Matt Spring and Andrew Zenner. **Pitching Analyst, Baseball Operations:** Connor Hinchliffe. **Lead Data Architect, Baseball Systems:** Neeketh Sheth. **Sr. Developer, Baseball Systems:** Josh Krowiorz. **Baseball Systems Developer:** Nick Usoff and Patrick Seminatore. **MLB Advance Scout:** Ben Rowen.

Perry Minasian

MAJOR LEAGUE STAFF

Manager: Joe Maddon. **Bench Coach:** Ray Montgomery. **Field Coordinator:** Mike Gallego. **Pitching Coach:** Matt Wise. **Hitting Coach:** Jeremy Reed. **First Base Coach:** TBD. **Third Base Coach:** Phil Nevin. **Catching Coach:** Bill Haselman. **Assistant Pitching Coach:** Dom Chiti. **Assistant Hitting Coach:** John Mallee. **Hitting Instructor:** Paul Sorrento. **Quality Assurance Coach:** Benji Gil. **Batting Practice Pitcher:** Mike Ashman. **Staff Assistants:** Jason Brown, Tim Buss and Ali Modami. **Bullpen Catcher:** Manny Del Campo. **Interpreter:** Ippei Mizuhara.

MEDICAL/TRAINING

Team Physician: Dr. Craig Milhouse. **Team Orthopedic Physicians:** Dr. Brian Schulz, Dr. Steve Yoon, Dr. John Itamura and Dr. Carlos Uquillas. **Director, Performance Integration:** Kenneth Smale. **Director Sports Medicine & Head Athletic Trainer:** Mike Frostad. **Assistant Athletic Trainers:** Eric Munson and Matt Biancuzzo. **Athletic Training Services Coordinator:** Rick Smith. **Head Strength/Conditioning Coach:** Matt Tenney. **Assistant Strength and Conditioning Coach:** Adam Auer. **Head Physical Therapist:** Marc Oceguera. **Assistant Physical Therapist:** Robbie Williams. **Massage Therapist:** Yoichi Terada. **Registered Dietician:** Rebecca Twombley.

PLAYER DEVELOPMENT

Director, Player Development: Joey Prebynski. **Assistant Director, Player Development:** Tony Ferreira. **Assistant, Player Development:** Luis Barranco. **Field Coordinator:** Joe Kruzel. **Manager, Minor League Equipment:** Louie Raya. **Minor League Video Coordinator:** Alexandria Woody. **Roving Instructors:** Tony Jaramillo (Hitting Coordinator), Rudy Jaramillo (Assistant Hitting Coordinators), Buddy Carlyle (Pitching Coordinator), Dylan Axelrod (Pitching Performance Coordinator), Chris Carpenter (Pitching Consultant), Bill Lachemann (Pitching Instructor), Jayson Nix (Assistant Field Coordinator), Damon Mashore (Outfield/Baserunning Coordinator), Hainley Statia (Infield Coordinator), Rod Barajas (Catching Coordinator), Kernan Ronan (Rehab Coach), Joseph Skrzypek (Minor League Rehab Coordinator), Matt Morrell (Medical Coordinator), Dylan Cintula (Strength & Conditioning Coordinator), Doug Jarrow (Return to Performance Strength & Conditioning Coordinator), Humberto Miranda (Latin America Field Coordinator), Erick Salcedo (Arizona Field Coordinator), Trey Hillman (Player Development Staff Coach), Keith Kocher (Physical Therapist), Michael Noboa (Latin America Operations Coordinator), Fausto Betances (Coordinator, DR Academy Administration) and Pietro Oliva (Assistant, DR Academy Administration).

FARM SYSTEM

Class	Club	Manager	Hitting Coach	Pitching Coach
Triple-A	Salt Lake	Lou Marson	Brian Betancourth	Jairo Cuevas
Double-A	Rocket City	Andy Schatzley	Kenny Hook	Michael Wuertz
High-A	Tri-City	Jack Howell	TBD	Doug Henry
Low-A	Inland Empire	Ever Magallanes	Ryan Sebra	Bo Martino
Rookie	Angels (ACL)	Dave Stapleton	Sean Kazmar	G.Heredia/D.Ebert
Rookie	Angels (DSL)	Hector De La Cruz	R. Gomez/A. De los Santos	J.Marte/E.Gonzalez

SCOUTING

Director, Pro Scouting: Derek Watson. **Special Assignment Scout:** Ric Wilson. **Professional Scouts:** Jeff Cirillo, Jim Miller, Andrew Schmidt, Bobby Williams and Rick Williams. **Director, Amateur Scouting:** Timothy McIlvaine. **Assistant Director of Amateur Scouting:** Jeremy Schied. **Special Assistant to Scouting:** Matt Swanson. **Coordinator, Amateur Scouting:** Aidan Donovan. **National Crosscheckers:** Jason Smith, Steffan Wilson. **Crosscheckers:** Jason Baker, Jayson Durocher, Scott Richardson, Nick Gorneault, Brandon McArthur and Doug Witt. **Area Supervisors:** KJ Hendricks, Bo Hughes, Billy Lipari, John Burden, Drew Dominguez, Brian Gordon, Chris McAlpin, Joel Murrie and Ross Vecchio. **Senior Director, International Scouting:** Brian Parker. **Asst. Director, International Scouting:** Brian Cruz. **Administrator, International Scouting:** Grace Mercedes. **Latin American Crosschecker:** Jean Carlos Alvarez. **Amateur & International Crosschecker:** Matt Bishoff. **DR Supervisor:** Felix Feliz. **VZ Supervisor:** Marlon Urdaneta. **DR Crosschecker:** Frank Tejeda. **DR Area Scouts:** Jochy Cabrera, Rusbell Cabrera, Domingo Garcia and Jonathan Genao. **VZ Area Scouts:** Joel Chicarelli, Melvin Dorta, Ender Gonzalez and Vicente Lupo. **Panama Area Scout:** Raul Gonzalez. **Mexico Area Scout:** Cosme Valle. **Curacao Area Scout:** Rubylin Nicasia. **Video Scout—DR:** Rafael Reyes. **Video Scout— VZ:** Jesus Colina.

LOS ANGELES DODGERS

Office Address: 1000 Vin Scully Ave., Los Angeles, CA 90012.
Telephone: (323) 224-1500. Fax: (323) 224-1269. **Website:** www.dodgers.com.

OWNERSHIP/EXECUTIVE OFFICE

Chairman: Mark Walter. **Partners:** Earvin 'Magic' Johnson, Peter Guber, Todd Boehly, Robert 'Bobby' Patton, Jr, Billie Jean King, Ilana Kloss, Robert L. Plummer, Alan Smolinisky. **President/CEO:** Stan Kasten.

BUSINESS OPERATIONS

EMMA MCINTYRE/GETTY IMAGES

Mark Walter

Executive Vice President/COO: Bob Wolfe. **Executive VP/Chief Marketing Officer:** Lon Rosen. **Executive VP/General Counsel:** Sam Fernandez. **Executive VP, Planning/ Development:** Janet Marie Smith. **Senior VP, Marketing, Communications and Broadcaster:** Erik Braverman. **Senior VP, Ticket and Premium Sales & Service:** Antonio Morici. **Senior VP, Stadium Operations:** Joe Crowley. **VP, Security/Guest Services:** Shahram Ariane. **Senior VP, Information Technology:** Ralph Esquibel.

FINANCE AND BUSINESS ANALYTICS

Senior VP, Finance: Eric Hernandez. **Senior Director, Financial Planning/Analysis:** Gregory Buonaccorsi. **Controller:** Sara Curran. **Director, Purchasing:** Lisa McShane. **VP, Business Development & Analytics:** Royce Cohen. **Director, Business Analytics:** Michael Spetner.

GLOBAL PARTNERSHIPS

Senior VP, Global Partnerships: Corey Norkin. **Senior Director, Global Partnership Administration & Services:** Jenny Oh. **Senior Director, Marketing Solutions:** Matt Grable. **Director, Global Partnership Services:** Corey Schimmel, Kirsten Jareck.

MARKETING/BROADCASTING AND COMMUNICATIONS

Senior VP, Marketing/Broadcasting Communications: Erik Braverman. **Vice President, Digital Strategy:** Caroline Morgan. **Senior Director, Public Relations:** Joe Jareck. **Executive Producer, Los Angeles Dodgers Productions:** Greg Taylor. **Senior Director, Graphic Design:** Ross Yoshida. **Senior Director, Broadcast Engineering:** Tom Darin. **Director, Player Relations & Publicity:** Juan Dorado. **Director, Social Media:** Sue Jo. **Director, Motion Graphics:** Kevin Cook.

HUMAN RESOURCES/LEGAL

VP, Human Resources: Marilyn Davis. **Senior Director, Human Resources:** Leonor Romero. **Vice President, Deputy General Counsel:** Daniel Martens. **Associate General Counsel:** Chad Gunderson. **Vice President, Risk Management:** Michelle Darringer.

LOS ANGELES DODGERS FOUNDATION AND COMMUNITY AFFAIRS

Chief Executive Officer, Los Angeles Dodgers Foundation: Nichol Whiteman. **VP, External Affairs/Community Relations:** Naomi Rodriguez. **COO, Los Angeles Dodgers Foundation:** Chaitali Gala Mehta.

TICKETING

Telephone: (323) 224-1471. **Fax:** (323) 224-2609.
Senior Vice President, Ticket Sales & Premium Sales & Services: Antonio Morici. **VP, Ticket Operations:** Seth Bluman. **VP, Premium Sales & Services:** Craig Sindici.
Director, Premium Services: Justin Treibel. **Director, Ticket Operations:** Dan Gilmore. **Director, Ticket Operations:** Steven Zymkowitz.

BASEBALL OPERATIONS

Telephone: (323) 224-1500. **Fax:** (323) 224-1463.

Andrew Friedman

President: Andrew Friedman. **Executive Vice President & General Manager:** Brandon Gomes. **Senior Vice President, Baseball Operations:** Josh Byrnes. **Vice President & Assistant General Manager:** Jeffrey Kingston. **Vice President & Assistant General Manager:** Alex Slater. **Vice President, Assistant General Manager & Baseball Legal Counsel:** Damon Jones. **Vice Presidents:** Dave Finley (Scouting), Galen Carr (Player Personnel), Ismael Cruz (International Scouting), Billy Gasparino (Amateur Scouting). **Senior Directors:** Ellen Harrigan (Baseball Administration), Scott Akasaki (Team Travel), Duncan Webb (Baseball Resources). **Directors:** Megan Schroeder (Performance Science), Eric Potterat (Specialized Performance Programs), John Focht (Baseball Systems Platform), Brian McBurney (Baseball Systems Applications), Michael Voltmer (Baseball Strategy & Information). **Senior Advisors & Special Assistants:** Thomas Allison, Pat Corrales, Joel Peralta, Ron Roenicke, Chase Utley, Jose Vizcaino.

MAJOR LEAGUE STAFF

Manager: Dave Roberts. **Coaches:** Bob Geren (Bench), Mark Prior (Pitching), Robert Van Scoyoc & Brant Brown (Hitting), Clayton McCullough (First Base), Dino Ebel (Third Base), Josh Bard (Bullpen), Aaron Bates (Assistant Hitting), Connor McGuiness (Assistant Pitching). **Coordinator, Game Planning/Communications Coach:** Danny Lehmann. **Bullpen Catcher:** Steve Cilladi. **Director, Player Health:** Ron Porterfield. **Head Athletic Trainer:** Thomas Albert. **Major League Assistant Athletic Trainer:** Yosuke Nakajima. **Major League Athletic Trainer:** Nathan Lucero. **VP, Player Performance:** Brandon McDaniel. **Director, Clubhouse Operations:** Alex Torres. **Major League Head Strength & Conditioning Coach:** Travis Smith. **Physical Therapists:** Johnathan Erb, Bernard Li. **Manager, Performance Nutrition:** Tyrone Hall. **Head Performance Chef:** Kristen DeCesare. **Head Team Physician:** Dr. Neal ElAttrache. **Manager, Medical Administrator and Billing:** Andy Otovic.

PLAYER DEVELOPMENT

Telephone: (323) 224-1500. **Fax:** (323) 224-1359.

Director, Player Development: Will Rhymes. **Assistant Director, Player Development:** Matt McGrath. **Manager, Minor League Administration:** Adriana Urzua. **Manager, Arizona Operations:** Matt Peabody. **Manager, Player Development:** Andrea La Pointe. **Coordinator, Player Development:** James Weilbrenner. **Assistant, Baseball Operations:** Mark Kozhaya. **Field Coordinator:** Shaun Larkin. **Assistant Field Coordinator:** Keith Beauregard.

Directors: Rob Hill (Minor League Pitching), Brian Stoneberg (MiLB Player Performance), Leo Ruiz (Strong Mind Cultural Development). **Coordinators:** Don Alexander (Pitching, Logistics), Brent Minta (Pitching, Analytics), Ian Walsh (Minor League Pitching Development Assistant), Rocky Gale (Catching), Louis Iannotti (Hitting Analytics), Tim Laker (Hitting), Jeff Salazar (Hitting), Mark Kertenian (Strategy and Communication), AJ LaLonde (Strong Mind), Charles Wagner (Video), Cole Finnegan (Assistant Video). **Minor League Medical Coordinator:** Victor Scarpone. **Assistant Minor League Medical Coordinator:** James Southard. **MiLB Strength and Conditioning Coordinator:** Carl Kochan. **International Athletics Coordinator:** Chris Dunaway. **Return-to-Competition Coordinator:** Jeff Taylor. **Special Assistants:** Bobby Cuellar, Charlie Hough, Placido Polanco, Jamey Wright.

CAMPO LOS PALMAS

Sr. Facility Manager: Jesus Negrette. **Manager:** Marian Vasquez. **Operations Coordinator:** Jose Vargas. **Manager, Clubhouse:** Julio Martinez. **Latin American Field Coordinator:** Keyter Collado. **Latin American Pitching Coordinator:** Luis Meza. **Latin American Hitting Coordinator:** Carlos Asuaje. **Latin American Defensive Coordinator:** Pedro Mega. **Latin American Medical Coordinator:** Jorge Gonzalez.

CAMELBACK RANCH

Manager, Arizona Operations: Matt Peabody. **Minor League Equipment Manager:** Troy Timney.

FARM SYSTEM

Class	Club (League)	Manager	Hitting Coach	Pitching Coach
Triple-A	Oklahoma City (PCL)	Travis Barbary	Emmanuel Burriss	Dave Borkowski
Double-A	Tulsa (TL)	Scott Hennessey	Brett Pill	TBA
High-A	Great Lakes (MWL)	Austin Chubb	TBA	TBA
Low-A	Rancho Cucamonga (CAL)	John Shoemaker	O'Koyea Dickson	R. Trancoso//D. O'Linger
Rookie	Dodgers (ACL)	TBA	TBA	TBA
Rookie	Dodgers (DSL)	TBA	TBA	TBA

SCOUTING

VP, Amateur/International Scouting: David Finley. **VP, Director, Amateur Scouting:** Billy Gasparino. **VP, International Scouting:** Ismael Cruz. **Assistant Director, Amateur Scouting:** Zach Fitzpatrick. **Assistant Director, International Scouting:** Matthew Doppelt. **Manager, Amateur Scouting:** Jalen Phillips. **Manager, International Scouting:** Javier Camps. **Special Advisor:** Paul Cogan. **Athleticism Development Coordinator:** Tyler Norton. **Global Crosschecker:** John Green. **National Crosscheckers:** Brian Stephenson, Rob St. Julien. **National Pitching Crosschecker:** Jack Cressend. **Regional Crosscheckers:** Jon Adkins, Brian Compton, Stephen Head, Brian Kraft, Alan Matthews. **Area Scouts:** Tim Adkins, Garrett Ball, Clint Bowers, Tom Kunis, Marty Lamb, Benny Latino, Brent Mayne, Paul Murphy, Tom Myers, John Pyle, Jonah Rosenthal, Wes Sargent, Mitch Schulewitz, Jeffrey Stevens. **Junior Area Scouts:** Logan Crook, Dean Kim. **Part-Time Scout:** Luis Faccio. **VP, Player Personnel:** Galen Carr. **Manager, Pro Scouting:** Luke Geoghegan. **Special Assistant to Pro Scouting:** Jeff McAvoy. **Special Assignment Scouts:** Vance Lovelace, Matt Smith. **Professional Scouts:** Tydus Meadows, Scott Groot, Peter Bergeron, Jason Lynn, Franco Frias, Lee Tackett, Jack Murphy, Greg Golson, Stephen Lyons, Sam Ray, Carlos Jose Lugo, Tim Schmidt. **Advisor, Pacific Rim:** Yogo Suzuki.

MIAMI MARLINS

Office Address: Marlins Park, 501 Marlins Way, Miami, FL 33125
Telephone: (305) 480-1300. **Fax:** (305) 480-3012.
Website: www.marlins.com.

OWNERSHIP
Chairman & Principal Owner: Bruce Sherman.

BUSINESS OPERATIONS
Chief Executive Officer: Derek Jeter. **General Manager:** Kim Ng. **Chief Strategy Officer:** Adam Jones. **Chief Operating Officer:** Caroline O'Connor.

ADMINISTRATIVE SERVICES
Executive Assistant, Executive Office: Alyssa Perez. **Executive Assistant, Business Operations:** Kristen Keane. **Executive Assistant:** Ivette Rosado.

FINANCE
Vice President, Financial Planning & Accounting: Fred Koczwara. **Senior Director, Financial Planning & Accounting:** Michael Mullane. **Director, Compensation & Benefits:** Carolina Calderon. **Manager, Compensation & Benefits:** Edgar Perez. **Manager, Finance:** Veronica Vega. **Senior Accountant:** Jarred Smith. **Supervisor, Accounts Payable:** Anthony Paneque.

Derek Jeter

MARKETING
Director, Digital Marketing: Karry Pomes. **Manager, Social Media:** Sarah Penalver. **Manager, Fan Programs:** Jessica Lee.

LEGAL & RISK MANAGEMENT
Vice President and General Counsel: Ashwin Krishnan. **Associate Counsel:** Benjamin Lash. **Staff Counsel:** Amanda Bethel. **Manager, Risk Management:** Will Moy.

SALES/TICKETING
Vice President, Sales & Service: Andre Luck. **Manager, Inside Sales:** Jason Arellano. **Senior Premium Sales Executive:** Chema Sanchez. **Director, Membership Sales:** Matt Hernandez. **Senior Membership Sales Executive:** Isaac Paladino. **Membership Sales Executive:** Jennifer Owston. **Membership Sales Executive:** Christian Jablonski. **Membership Sales Executive:** John Franchi. **Director, Group Sales & Service:** Kyle Brant. **Manager, Group Sales:** Brandon Grengs. **Senior Group Sales & Service Executive:** Antonio Diz. **Group Sales & Service Executive:** Brad Johnson. **Group Sales & Service Executive:** Ernesto Penton. **Group Sales & Service Executive:** Jessica Crosson. **Group Sales & Service Executive:** David Garcia. **Groups Sales Coordinator:** Lucas Terwilliger.

COMMUNICATIONS/MEDIA RELATIONS
Senior Vice President, Communications & Outreach: Jason Latimer. **Director, Communications:** Jon Erik Alvarez. **Manager, Broadcasting:** Kyle Sielaff. **Player Relations & Spanish Media Liaison:** Luis Dorante. **Sr. Coordinator, Corporate Communications & Employee Engagement:** Dorilys Miralles. **Coordinator, Media Relations:** Daniel Kurish. **Broadcaster, Radio:** Glenn Geffner.

TRAVEL/CLUBHOUSE
Director, Team Travel: Max Thomas. **Equipment Manager:** John Silverman. **Visiting Clubhouse Manager:** Rock Hughes. **Assistant Clubhouse Manager:** Michael Diaz.

BASEBALL OPERATIONS

Telephone: (305) 480-1300. **Fax:** (305) 480-3032.

General Manager: Kim Ng. **Assistant General Managers:** Brian Chattin, Daniel Greenlee. **Director, Team Travel:** Max Thomas. **Assistant Director, Baseball Operations:** Joseph Nero. **Senior Director, International Operations:** Adrian Lorenzo. **Senior Director, Amateur Scouting:** DJ Svihlik.

Kim Ng

JON SOOHOO/LA DODGERS

MAJOR LEAGUE STAFF

Manager: Don Mattingly. **Pitching Coach:** Mel Stottlemyre Jr. **Hitting Coach:** Marcus Thames. **Assistant Hitting Coach:** Edwar Gonzalez. **Bench Coach:** James Rowson. **First Base Coach:** Keith Johnson. **Third Base Coach:** Al Pedrique. **Bullpen Coordinator:** Robert Flippo. **Bullpen Coach:** Wellington Cepeda. **Catching Coach:** Eddy Rodriguez. **Bullpen Catcher:** Michael Hernandez. **Massage Therapist:** Koji Tanaka. **Quality Control Coach:** Eric Duncan.

MEDICAL/TRAINING

Medical Director: Dr. Lee Kaplan. **Senior Director Medical Services:** Stan Conte. **Head Athletic Trainer:** Lee Meyer. **Strength and Conditioning Coach:** Lee Tressel. **Equipment Manager:** John Silverman. **Visiting Clubhouse Manager:** Rock Hughes. **Assistant Home Clubhouse Manager:** Michael Diaz.

PLAYER DEVELOPMENT

Vice President, Player Development and Scouting: Gary Denbo. **Senior Director, Amateur Scouting:** DJ Svihlik. **Director, Pro Scouting:** Hadi Raad. **Senior Director, International Scouting:** Adrian Lorenzo. **Director, Player Development Minor League Operations:** Geoffrey DeGroot. **Director, Minor League Operations:** Hector Crespo. **Manager Baseball Operations:** Jordan Jackson. **Manager, Pro Scouting:** Alexandria Rigoli. **Manager, International Scouting:** David-Hernandez-Beayne. **Manager, Amateur Scouting:** Joshua Kapiloff. **Assistant Director, Minor League Operations:** Danny M. Henriquez. **Amateur Scouting Analyst:** Justin Brands. **Manager Video:** Julio Jauregui. **Coordinator Video Production:** Victor Martinez.

FARM SYSTEM

Class	Club (League)	Manager	Hitting Coach	Pitching Coach
Triple-A	Jacksonville	Daren Brown	Phil Plantier	Jeremy Powell
Double-A	Pensacola	Kevin Randel	Scott Seabol	Dave Eiland
High-A	Beloit	Jorge Hernandez	Matt Snyder	Bruce Walton
Low-A	Jupiter	Angel Espada	Ty Hawkins	Jason Erickson
Rookie	Marlins (FCL)	Luis Dorante	Jesus Merchan	Justin Pope
Rookie	Marlins (DSL)	Rigo Silverio	Esmerling De La Rosa	Nelson Prada/Emilio Linares

SCOUTING

Senior Director, Amateur Scouting: DJ Svihlik. **Manager, Amateur Scouting:** Josh Kapiloff. **National Crosschecker:** Eric Valent. **Amateur Scouting Analyst:** Justin Brands. **West Supervisor:** Scott Goldby. **Central Supervisor:** Ryan Wardinsky. **South Supervisor:** Carmen Carcone. **East Supervisor:** Mike Soper. **Amateur Crosschecker:** T.R. Lewis. **Area Scouts:** Eric Brock, Hunter Jarmon, Scott Stanley, Scott Fairbanks, Eric Wordekemper, Ryan Cisterna, Chris Joblin, Brett Bittiger, JT Zink, Brad Tyler, Hank LaRue, Shaeffer Hall, Blake Newsome, Alex Smith. **Part-Time Scouts:** Bob Oldis, Omar Rosado.

Director, Professional Scouting: Hadi Raad. **Manager, Professional Scouting:** Alexandria Rigoli. **Special Assignment Scouts:** Joe Caro, Bill Masse, Joe Lisewski. **Professional Scouting Crosscheckers:** Jim Howard, Chris Pelekoudas. **Professional Scouts:** Johnny Almaraz, Jose Almonte, Jared Barnes, Jordan Bley, John Eshleman, Jalal Leach, Alexander Noel, Alvin Rittman, Phil Rossi, Tony Russo, Brian Sikorski. **Part-Time Scouts:** Paul Ricciarini.

Senior Director, International Operations: Adrian Lorenzo. **Director, International Scouting:** Roman Ocumarez. **Manager, International Scouting:** David Hernandez Beayne. **International Crosschecker:** Manny Padron. **International Crosschecker:** Adrian Puig. **Scouts, Dominican Republic:** Domingo Ortega, Angel Izquierdo, Sahir Fersobe, Miguel Beltre. **Venezuela Administration Coordinator:** Clifford Nuitter. **Scouts, Venezuela:** Tibaldo Hernandez, Nestor Moreno, Aly Gonzalez. **Scout, Mexico:** Andres Guzman. **Video Coordinator, Dominican Republic:** Shamir Arias. **Manager, Dominican Operations:** Ismael Granadillo. **DR Academy Secretary:** Leidy Mercado

MILWAUKEE BREWERS

Office Address: American Family Field, One Brewers Way, Milwaukee, WI 53214.
Telephone: (414) 902-4400. **Fax:** (414) 902-4053. **Website:** www.brewers.com.

OWNERSHIP
Operated By: Milwaukee Brewers Baseball Club.
Chairman/Principal Owner: Mark Attanasio.

BUSINESS OPERATIONS
President, Business Operations: Rick Schlesinger. **Senior Vice President, Communications & Affiliate Operations:** Tyler Barnes. **Senior Vice President, Stadium Operations:** Steve Ethier. **Chief Financial Officer:** Daniel Fumai. **Chief Revenue Officer:** Jason Hartlund. **Senior Vice President, Brand Experience:** Teddy Werner. **General Counsel & Senior Vice President, Administration:** Marti Wronski. **Executive Assistant, Ownership Group:** Samantha Ernest. **Executive Assistant, General Manager:** Nichole Kinateder. **Executive Assistant, Paralegal:** Kate Rock. **Executive Assistant, Revenue:** Lisa Brzeski. **Executive Assistant:** Adela Reeve. **Executive Assistant:** Kate Stempski.

Mark Attanasio

FINANCE/ACCOUNTING
VP, Finance/Accounting: Jamie Norton. **Accounting Director:** Vicki Wise. **Disbursements Director:** Erica Umbach. **Senior Payroll Administrator:** Corrine Wolff. **Senior Financial Analysts:** Cory Loppnow, Mike Anheuser, Kristin Hahn. **Financial Analyst:** Pat Fennell. **Senior Accounts Payable Specialist:** Taikana Bentley. **Workday Systems Analyst:** Tara Ali. **Consultant:** Bob Quinn.

HUMAN RESOURCES
VP, Human Resources: Cas Castro. **Senior Director, Human Resources, Diversity, Equity & Inclusion:** Brenda Best. **Manager, Employee Benefits & HRIS:** Heather Schreiner. **Human Resources Business Partners:** Genevieve Hayes, Kristin Rutter, Kelly Rosenquist.

MARKETING
VP, Marketing: Sharon McNally. **Art Director:** Jeff Harding. **Director, Digital Marketing:** Becky Imig. **Director, Video Production:** Matt Gompper. **Productions Manager:** Caitlin Walter. **Manager, Content Marketing:** Ezra Siegel. **Manager, Social Media:** Bradly Ford. **Manager, Motion Graphics:** Steven Armendariz. **Graphic Designer:** Alex Pera. **Videographer:** Collin Schroeder. **Editors:** Lucas Seidel, Cody Oasen. **Senior Coordinator, Marketing:** Gina Moretti. **Marketing Administrator:** Brittany Luznicky.

ENTERTAINMENT
Executive Producer, Entertainment & Event Production: Taylor Goldman. **Director, Audio/Video Production:** Deron Anderson. **Manager, Entertainment & Event Production:** Hannah Creighton. **Coordinators, Entertainment:** Amanda Beierle, Zak Nye.

BUSINESS ANALYTICS
VP, Business Analytics & Strategic Support: Sam Mahjub. **Senior Manager, Data Science:** Mike Dairyko. **Senior Business Intelligence Analyst:** Danny Henken. **Analyst, Strategy & Analytics:** Evan Alvarez.

MEDIA RELATIONS/PUBLICATIONS
Senior Director, Media Relations: Mike Vassallo. **Senior Director, Business Communications:** Leslie Stachowiak. **Senior Coordinator, Media Relations:** Andrew Gruman.

MILLER PARK OPERATIONS
Senior Director, Security: Randy Olewinski. **Senior Director, Event Services:** Matt Lehmann. **Senior Director, Facility Services:** Mike Brockman. **Director, Grounds:** Ryan Woodley. **Senior Manager, Event Services:** Scott Quade. **Manager, Guest Experience:** Jonelle Johnson. **Manager, Grounds:** Zak Peterson. **Manager, Fields:** Tyler Tschetter. **Manager, Warehouse:** John Weyer. **Lead, Fields:** Taitum Priewe. **Lead, Game & Event:** Trace Blomberg.

TICKET SALES
Telephone: (414) 902-4000. **Fax:** (414) 902-4056.
VP, Ticket Sales: Jim Bathey. **Sr. Director, Ticket Sales:** Billy Friess. **Sr. Director, Ticket Services & Technology:** Jess Brown. **Director, Group Sales:** Chris Kimball.

BASEBALL OPERATIONS

Telephone: (414) 902-4400. **Fax:** (414) 902-4515.

President, Baseball Operations: David Stearns. **SVP/GM:** Matt Arnold. **Special Asst., President of Baseball Operations:** Doug Melvin. **VP, Baseball Projects:** Gord Ash. **SVP, Player Personnel:** Karl Mueller. **Special Asst. to GM, Player Development:** Carlos Villanueva. **VP, Baseball Operations:** Matt Kleine. **Vice President, Baseball Product and Strategy:** Will Hudgins. **VP, Baseball R&D:** Dan Turkenkopf. **Asst. Director, Baseball R&D:** Andrew Fox. **Asst., Major League Video/Spanish Translator:** Carlos Brizuela. **Special Asst., Baseball Research and Development:** Nick Davis. **Special Assignment Scout:** Scott Campbell. **Senior Manager, Technology Operations:** Matt Kerls. **Sr. Analyst, Baseball R&D:** Ethan Bein. **Senior Analyst, Baseball Research and Development:** Michael Harper. **Senior Manager, Data Engineering:** Matt Culhane. **Data Architect:** Phil Hauser. **Data Engineers:** Charles Clark, Harrison Jacobs. **Manager, Application Development:** Andy Acosta. **Senior Developer:** DJ Michalski. **Developers, Baseball Systems:** Scott Molling, Dan Yang. **Coordinator, Baseball Operations:** Kevin Ottsen. **Coordinator, Major League Video and Technology:** August Sandri. **Development Scouts:** Davis Knapp, Kevin O'Sullivan.

David Stearns

MAJOR LEAGUE STAFF

Manager: Craig Counsell. **Coaches: Bench**—Pat Murphy, **Pitching**—Chris Hook, **Hitting**—Connor Dawson, Ozzie Timmons, **First Base**—Quintin Berry, **Third Base**—Jason Lane, **Bullpen**—Jim Henderson, **Infield/Asst. Hitting Coach**—Matt Erickson, **Bullpen Catchers**—Néstor Corredor, Adam Weisenburger, **Associate Pitching, Catching and Strategy Coach**—Walker McKinven.

MEDICAL/TRAINING

Vice President, Medical Operations, Health and Safety: Roger Caplinger. **Head Team Physician:** Dr. William Raasch. **Team Physicians:** Dr. Mark Niedfeldt, Dr. Craig Young. **Director, Player Health:** Blair Bundy. **Major League Sports Psychologist:** Matt Krug. **Head Athletic Trainer:** Scott Barringer. **Asst. Athletic Trainer:** Dave Yeager. **Asst. Athletic Trainer/Physical Therapist:** Theresa Lau. **S&C Specialist:** Josh Seligman. **Asst. Strength and Conditioning Specialist:** Daniel Vega. **Rehabilitation Strength and Conditioning Coach:** Jason Meredith. **Rehabilitation Coach:** Scott Schneider. **Asst. Director, Psychological Services:** Blake Pindyck. **Consulting Orthopedic Physician, Phoenix:** Dr. Evan Lederman. **Consulting Team Physician, Phoenix:** Dr. Carlton Richie.

PLAYER DEVELOPMENT

Vice President, Minor League Operations: Tom Flanagan.

General Manager, Player Development: Eduardo Brizuela. **Vice President, Player Development:** Jake McKinley. **Asst. Director, Player Development/Information:** August Fagerstrom. **Sr. Manager, Baseball Administration:** Mark Mueller. **Minor League Clubhouse Manager:** Travis Voss. **Special Asst., Baseball Operations/Player Development:** Quinton McCracken. **Coordinator, Baseball Diversity Initiatives:** Junior Spivey. **Coordinator, Hitting Development:** Brenton Del Chairo. **Field Coordinator & Catching Instructor:** Charlie Greene. **Infield Coordinator:** Bob Miscik. **Asst. Hitting Coordinator:** Eric Theisen. **Asst. Pitching Coordinator:** Bryan Leslie. **Coordinator, Minor League Medical:** Nick Jensen. **Assistant Director, Player Health:** Frank Neville. **Senior Analyst, Performance Science:** Eric Crispell. **Coordinator, Education:** Adela Marquez. **Coordinator, Latin America Operations:** Manuel Vargas.

FARM SYSTEM

Class	Club (League)	Manager	Hitting Coach	Pitching Coach
Triple-A	Nashville	Rick Sweet	Al LeBoeuf	Jeremy Accardo
Double-A	Biloxi	Mike Guerrero	Chuckie Caufield	Nick Childs
High-A	Wisconsin	Joe Ayrault	Nick Stanley	Will Schierholz
Low-A	Carolina	Victor Estevez	Ken Joyce	Drew Thomas
Rookie	Brewers Blue (ACL)	Rafael Neda	Hiram Burgos	C.J. Retherford
Rookie	Brewers Gold (ACL)	David Tufo	Paul Moeller	Mike Habas
Rookie	Brewers Blue (DSL)	Fidel Pena	Juan Sandoval	Austin Turner
Rookie	Brewers Blue (DSL)	Natanael Mejia	Jesus Hernandez	Luis De Los Santos

SCOUTING

Vice President, Domestic Scouting: Tod Johnson. **Special Assignment Scout:** Scott Campbell. **Manager, Advance Scouting:** Brian Powalish. **Coordinator, Domestic and International Scouting Operations:** Oscar Garcia. **Coordinator, Scouting Operations:** Matt Roffe. **Asst. Baseball Operations/Player Development:** Pedro Alvarez. **Assistant, Player Development:** Rickie Weeks. **Special Assistant, Scouting:** Bryan Gale. **Asst. Director, International Scouting:** Luis Pérez. **Asst. Director, Scouting/International Player Development:** Taylor Green. **Special Assistant, Scouting:** Mike Berger. **Pro Scout:** Lary Aaron. **National Supervisor, Scouting:** Doug Reynolds. **Supervisor, Scout Teams/West Coast Special Assignment Scout:** Corey Rodriguez. **Regional Supervisors, Scouting:** Drew Anderson, Wynn Pelzer, Dan Nellum, Mike Serbalik. **Area Scouts:** Riley Bandelow, Mike Burns, Daniel Cho, Steve Ditrolio, James Fisher, Taylor Frederick, Joe Graham, Adam Hayes, Lazaro Llanes, Mark Muzzi, Scott Nichols, Pete Orr, Ginger Poulson, Jeff Simpson, Craig Smajstrla, Steve Smith, Shawn Whalen. **Latin American Crosschecker/Venezuelan Operations:** Fernando Veracierto. **Regional Crosschecker, Dominican Republic:** Rodolfo Rosario. **Supervisor, Dominican Republic:** Gary Peralta. **Supervisor, Venezuela:** José Rodriguez. **Scouts:** Trino Aguilar, Salvador Ayestas, José Barraza, Esteban Castillo, Javier Castillo, Julio de la Cruz, Diego Flores, Kenji Galavis, Jesús Garces, Teofilo Gutierrez, Jonas Lantigua, Fabian Mendez, Mario Mendoza, Javier Meza, José Morales, Kevin Ramos, Jean Carlos Reynoso, Pedro Robles, Luis Rosario, Miguel Vásquez.

MINNESOTA TWINS

Office Address: Target Field, 1 Twins Way, Minneapolis, MN 55403.
Telephone: (612) 659-3400. **Fax:** 612-659-4025. **Website:** www.twinsbaseball.com.

OWNERSHIP

Operated By: The Minnesota Twins. **Executive Chair:** Jim Pohlad. **Executive Board:** Jim Pohlad, Bob Pohlad, Bill Pohlad, Dave St. Peter.

BUSINESS OPERATIONS

Jim Pohlad

President/Chief Executive Officer, Minnesota Twins: Dave St. Peter. **Executive Vice President/Chief Business Officer:** Laura Day. **Executive Vice President/Chief Administrative Officer/Chief Financial Officer:** Kip Elliott. **Executive Vice President/Chief Revenue Officer:** Meka Morris. **Executive Vice President/Brand Strategy & Growth:** Joe Pohlad. **Senior Vice President, Technology:** John Avenson. **Senior Vice President, Ticket Sales & Brand Partnerships:** Mike Clough. **Senior Vice President, General Counsel:** Mary Giesler. **Senior Vice President, Operations:** Matt Hoy. **Senior Vice President, Chief Strategy Officer:** Jason Lee. **Senior Vice President, Human Resources:** Leticia Silva. **Deputy General Counsel:** Mari Guttman. **Executive Legal Assistant:** Mel Yackley. **Senior Executive Assistant:** Danielle Berg. **Executive Assistants:** Rachel Snyder, Tina Flowers.

HUMAN RESOURCES/FINANCE/TECHNOLOGY

Senior Vice President, Human Resources: Leticia Silva. **Senior Vice President, Technology:** John Avenson. **Vice President, Finance:** Andy Weinstein. **Senior Director, Compensation & Benefits:** Lori Beasley. **Sr. Director, Business Systems:** Wade Navratil. **Director, Accounting:** Lori Windschitl. **Director, Information Security:** Robert Jacoby. **Director, Technology Infrastructure:** Tony Persio. **Sr. Manager, Accounting:** Matt Fernholz. **Sr. Manager, Financial Planning & Analysis:** Mike Kramer. **Sr. Manager, Ticket Accounting:** Jerry McLaughlin. **Manager, Business Systems:** Shelley Andrew. **Manager, Technology Services:** Ryan Schmit.

MARKETING

Vice President, Brand Marketing: Heather Hinkel. **Senior Director, Brand Experience & Innovation:** Chris Iles. **Director, Broadcast:** Andrew Halverson. **Senior Manager, Project Lead:** Corrina Wertzberger. **Senior Manager, Digital Content:** Brea Hinegardner. **Senior Manager, Special Events & Promotions:** Heather Rajeski. **Senior Manager, Authentics:** Venika Streeter. **Manager, Digital Experience:** Mac Slavin. **Senior Coordinator, Brand Marketing:** Abby Martinson. **Coordinator, Social Media:** Kassie Dunnihoo.

COMMUNICATIONS

Vice President, Communications & Content: Dustin Morse. **Creative Director:** Kevin Hughes. **Director, Game Day Experience:** Sam Henschen. **Senior Manager, Baseball Communications:** Mitch Hestad. **Senior Manager, Business Communications:** Matt Hodson. **Manager, Video:** Jim Diehl. **Manager, Scoreboard Operations:** Jeremy Loosbrock. **Team Curator:** Clyde Doepner. **Coordinator, Communications/Interpreter:** Elvis Martinez. **Senior Photographer, Baseball Content:** Brace Hemmelgarn. **Senior Video Producer:** Peter Nelson. **Senior Motion Graphics Producer:** Matt Semke. **Creative Content Producer:** Dalton Browne. **Graphic Designer:** Rachel Haselhorst. **Assistant, Communications:** Nina Zimmerman.

COMMUNITY RELATIONS

Vice President, Community Engagement: Nancy O'Brien. **Senior Director, Diversity & Inclusion:** Miguel Ramos. **Senior Director, Community Engagement & Executive Director, Minnesota Twins Community Fund:** Kristen Rortvedt. **Director, Community Engagement & Events:** Julie Vavruska. **Manager, Youth Engagement:** Chelsey Falzone. **Manager, Community Relations:** Sondra Ciesielski. **Mascot Supervisor:** Blair Kelly. **Coordinator, Youth Baseball & Softball:** Kobi Allen. **Coordinator, Community Engagement:** Mackenzie Bongard.

TICKETING

Vice President, Ticket Operations: Paul Froehle. **Senior Director, Ticket Service & Retention:** Eric Hudson. **Senior Director, Ticket Strategy & New Business:** Rob Malec. **Senior Director, Ticket Operations:** Mike Stiles. **Director, Suites & Premium Seating:** P.J. Williams. **Senior Manager, Ticket Operations:** Ashley Geldert. **Senior Manager, Season Retention & Service:** Craig Gumz. **Senior Manager, Group Sales & Service:** Phil McMullen. **Manager, Florida Business Operations:** Mark Weber. **Manager, New Business Development:** Bryan Van Den Bosch. **Assistant Manager, Ticket Operations:** Colleen Seeker. **Senior Group Ticket Sales & Service Executive:** Luis Breazeale. **Senior Premium Sales & Service Executives:** Alex Hover, Cory Johnson. **Senior Premium & Suite Sales Executive:** Todd Krulewich.

BALLPARK OPERATIONS

Senior Vice President, Operations: Matt Hoy. **Vice President, Ballpark Operations:** Dave Horsman. **Senior Director, Ballpark Development & Planning:** Dan Starkey. **Senior Director, Facilities:** Gary Glawe. **Senior Director, Guest Experience:** Patrick Forsland. **Senior Director, Security:** Jeff Beahen. **Director, Team Security:** Charles Adams III. **Director, Guest Services:** Katie Rock. **Director, Ballpark Maintenance:** Dana Minion. **Head Groundskeeper:** Larry DiVito. **Senior Manager, Target Field Events:** Quinn Handahl. **Senior Manager, Guest Services:** Bryan Johnson. **Manager, Field Maintenance:** Jared Alley. **Manager, Building Security:** Jeff Reardon. **Manager, Event Security:** Scott Larson. **Manager, Tours & Event Support:** Ivan Cardona. **Manager, Ballpark Operations:** Ryan Heither.

BASEBALL OPERATIONS

President, Baseball Operations: Derek Falvey. **Senior Vice President/General Manager:** Thad Levine. **Vice President/Special Assistant to Baseball Operations:** Rob Antony. **Vice President, Assistant GM:** Daniel Adler. **Vice President, Assistant GM:** Jeremy Zoll. **Vice President, Baseball Operations Strategy & Innovation:** Josh Kalk. **Senior Director, Team Travel:** Mike Herman. **Senior Director, Baseball Systems:** Jeremy Raadt. **Director, Baseball Administration:** Kate Townley. **Director, Baseball Research:** Dane Sorensen. **Director, Baseball Technology:** Sean Harlin. **Director, Professional Player Procurement:** Brad Steil. **Assistant Director, Professional Player Procurement:** Navery Moore. **Assistant Director, Baseball Operations:** Nick Beauchamp. **Special Assistants:** Michael Cuddyer, LaTroy Hawkins, Torii Hunter, Justin Morneau. **Manager, Baseball Technology:** Tyler Schmitz. **Manager, Player Development Research:** Josh Ruffin. **Manager, Baseball Technology (Major League):** David Jeffrey. **Coordinator, Baseball Technology (Major League):** Ryan Wolfson. **Coordinator, Baseball Technology:** Kevin Marable. **Coordinators, Professional Player Procurement:** Zane McPhee, Chris Mitchell. **Analyst, Pro Scouting:** Sam Isenberg. **Analysts, Baseball Research:** Jake Bensky, Santiago Caride, Andrew Ettel, Holden Bridge, Grey Wilburn. **Analyst, Major League Operations:** Hailey Leviton. **Analyst, Player Development:** Chad Raines. **Coordinator, Amateur Scouting R&D:** Ezra Wise. **Coordinator, Run Creation:** Frankie Padulo. **Coordinator, Run Prevention:** Colby Suggs. **Senior Data Engineers, Baseball Systems:** Brad Ankrom, Jerad Parish, Hans Van Slooten. **Developers, Baseball Systems:** Anthony Metcalfe, Nick Winegar. **Data Quality Engineer:** John Edman. **Assistant Director, Sports Science:** Martijn Verhoeven. **Analysts, Sports Science:** James, Barber, Colin Robertson. **Biomechanist:** Chris Curran.

Derek Falvey

MAJOR LEAGUE STAFF

Manager: Rocco Baldelli. **Coaches: Bench**—Jayce Tingler, **Assistant Bench/Infield**—Tony Diaz, **Pitching**—Wes Johnson, **Hitting**—Rudy Hernandez, **Hitting**—David Popkins, **First Base/Catching**—Hank Conger, **Third Base/Outfield**—Tommy Watkins, **Bullpen Coach**—Pete Maki, **Assistant Pitching**—Luis Ramirez, **Quality Control**—Nate Dammann, **Bullpen Catcher**—Connor Olson. **Equipment Manager:** Rod McCormick.

MEDICAL/TRAINING

Director, Medical High Performance: Dr. Christopher Camp. **Medical Director Emeritus:** Dr. John Steubs. **Club Physicians:** Dr. Rahul Kapur, Dr. Dave Olson, Dr. Corey Wulf, Dr. Amy Beacom. **Head Athletic Trainer:** Michael Salazar. **Assistant Trainers:** Masamichi Abe, Jason Kirkman. **Physical Therapist:** Adam Diamond. **Director, Strength & Conditioning:** Ian Kadish. **Strength & Conditioning Coaches:** Chuck Bradway, Aaron Rhodes. **Massage Therapist:** Kelli Bergheim.

PLAYER DEVELOPMENT

Telephone: (612) 659-3480. **Fax:** (612) 659-4026.

Director, Player Development: Alex Hassan. **Assistant Directors, Player Development:** Drew MacPhail, Tommy Bergjans. **Senior Manager, Minor League Operations:** Brian Maloney. **Manager, Florida Operations:** Victor Gonzalez. **Assistant Manager, Florida Operations:** Jason Davila. **Director, Performance Nutrition:** Kara Lynch. **Supervisor, Language and Cultural Development:** Linda Merlo. **Minor League Coordinators:** Kevin Morgan (field), Edgar Varela (Instruction), Justin Willard (pitching), Zach Bove (assistant pitching), Nat Ballenberg (special projects pitching), Bryce Berg (hitting), Tucker Frawley (Infield and catching), Mike Quade (outfield).

FARM SYSTEM

Class	Club (League)	Manager	Hitting Coach	Pitching Coach
Triple-A	St. Paul	Toby Gardenhire	Ryan Smith	Cibney Bello/Virgil Vasquez
Double-A	Pensacola	Ramon Borrego	Derek Shomon	Peter Larson/Dan Urbina
High-A	Cedar Rapids	Brian Dinkelman	Jairo Rodriguez	Mark Moriarty/Richard Salazar
Low-A	Fort Myers	Brian Meyer	Rayden Sierra	Jared Gaynor/Carlos Hernandez
Rookie	Twins (FCL)	Seth Feldman	A. DiTullio/E.Guerrero	B. Hearn/E. Julio/C. Maduro
Rookie	Twins (DSL)	Rafael Martinez	Ricardo Nanita	Kevin Rodriguez/DJ Engle

SCOUTING

Vice President, Amateur Scouting: Sean Johnson. **Vice President, Player Personnel:** Mike Radcliff. **Senior Advisor, Scouting:** Deron Johnson. **Director, Latin American Scouting & US Integration:** Fred Guerrero. **Assistant Director, Scouting:** Tim O'Neil. **Manager, Amateur Scouting Research:** Ezra Wise. **Manager, Baseball Technology/International Scouting:** Anthony Liriano. **National Crosschecker:** Billy Corrigan. **Amateur Crosschecker:** Freddie Thon. **Senior Manager, International Administration and Education:** Amanda Daley. **Coordinator, Amateur Scouting:** Annika Mau. **Coordinator, International Scouting:** Iván Verástica Mora. **Scouting Supervisors: East**—Mark Quimuyog, **Mideast**—Derrick Dunbar, **Midwest**—Mike Ruth, **West**—Elliott Strankman. **Area Scouts:** Andrew Ayers, Joe Bisenius, Kyle Blackwell, Trevor Brown, Walt Burrows, Ty Dawson, J.R. DiMercurio, Brett Dowdy, John Leavitt, Mitch Morales, Jeff Pohl, Jack Powell, Brian Tripp, Kyle Van Hook, Nick Venuto, Chandler Wagoner, Matt Williams, John Wilson. **Coordinator, Dominican Republic Scouting:** Eduardo Soriano. **Dominican Republic:** Luis Lajara, Manuel Luciano, Daniel Sanchez. **Coordinator, Venezuela Scouting:** Jose Leon. **Venezuela:** Edgar Guerra, Marlon Nava, Oswaldo Troconis. **Colombia:** Andres Garcia. **Pacific Rim:** David Kim. **Pro Scouts:** Ken Compton, Earl Frishman, John Manuel, Jose Marzan, Bill Milos, Jason Pennini, Keith Stohr, Wesley Wright, Rafael Yanez.

NEW YORK METS

Office Address: Citi Field, 41 Seaver Way, Flushing, NY 11368.
Telephone: (718) 507-6387. **Fax:** (718) 507-6395.
Website: www.mets.com. **Twitter:** @mets.

OWNERSHIP

Owner, Chairman and CEO: Steven A. Cohen. **Owner & President, Amazin' Mets Foundation:** Alexandra M. Cohen.
Vice Chairman: Andrew B. Cohen. **Chairman Emeritus:** Fred Wilpon. **Board of Directors:** Jeanne Melino, Chris Christie.

BUSINESS OPERATIONS

President: Sandy Alderson. **Senior Executive Assistant, President:** June Napoli. **Chief Financial Officer & Treasurer:** Steve Canna. **Chief Technology Officer:** Mark Brubaker. **Chief Revenue Officer:** Jeff Deline. **Executive Vice President & Chief Marketing, Content & Communications Officer:** David Newman. **Executive Vice President, Operations:** Jeffrey White. **Senior Vice President Foundation and Community Engagement:** Jeanne Melino. **Senior Vice President & Chief of Staff:** John Ricco. **Vice President, Guest Experience & Venue Services:** Chris Brown. **Senior Vice President, Mets Events & Venue Services:** Heather Collamore. **Vice President, Alumni Public Relations & Team Historian:** Jay Horwitz. **Vice President, Technology Solutions:** Oscar Fernandez. **Vice President, Corporate Partnerships:** Brian Fling. **Vice President, Strategy:** Neal Kaplan. **Vice President, Communications:** Harold Kaufman. **Vice President, Ticket Sales & Services:** Kenny Koperda. **Vice President, Ballpark Operations:** Sue Lucchi. **Vice President, Security:** John McKay. **Vice President, Technology Infrastructure:** Sean Olsen. **Vice President, Financial Planning & Analysis:** Peter Woll. **Vice President, Financial Planning & Analysis:** Peter Woll. **Vice President, Employee Relations & Co-General Counsel:** Jessica Villanella. **Head of Human Resources:** Ariel Speicher.

Steve Cohen

MEDIA RELATIONS

Telephone: (718) 565-4330. **Fax:** (718) 639-3619.
Vice President, Communications: Harold Kaufman. **Senior Director, Communications:** Ethan Wilson. **Director, Communications & Publications:** Zach Weber. **Coordinator, Communications:** Zack Becker. **Coordinator, Communications/Translator:** Alan Suriel. **Assistant, Communications:** Josh Lederman.

TRAVEL/CLUBHOUSE

Director, Team Travel: Brian Small. **Equipment Manager:** Kevin Kierst. **Visiting Clubhouse Manager:** Dave Berni. **Coordinator, Clubhouse Operations:** Scott Keltner.

BASEBALL OPERATIONS

Telephone: (718) 803-4013, (718) 565-4339. **Fax:** (718) 507-6391.
General Manager: Billy Eppler. **Assistant General Manager, Pro Player Evaluation &
Personnel:** Bryn Alderson. **Assistant General Manager, Baseball Operations:** Ian Levin.
Assistant General Manager, Baseball Analytics: Ben Zauzmer. **Vice President, Amateur
& International Scouting:** Thomas Tanous. **Director, Baseball Development:** Bryan Hayes.
Coordinator, Baseball Administration: Brooklyn Covell. **Coordinator, Baseball Operations:**
John Madsen.

Billy Eppler

COURTESY OF NEW YORK METS

MAJOR LEAGUE STAFF

Manager: Buck Showalter. **Bench Coach:** Glenn Sherlock. **Pitching Coach:** Jeremy Hefner.
Hitting Coach: Eric Chavez. **Assistant Hitting Coach:** Jeremy Barnes. **First Base Coach:** Wayne
Kirby. **Third Base Coach:** Joey Cora. **Bullpen Coach:** Craig Bjornson. **Bullpen Catcher:** Dave
Racaniello. **Bullpen Catcher:** Eric Langill.

PLAYER DEVELOPMENT

Telephone: (718) 565-4302. **Fax:** (718) 205-7920.
Director, Player Development: Kevin Howard. **Coordinator, Coaching Development and Instruction:** Dick Scott.
Director, Hitting Development: Hugh Quattlebaum. **Hitting, Coordinator:** Tim Lamonte. **Pitching Coordinator:**
Jono Armold. **Infield Coordinator:** Tim Teufel. **Catching Coordinator:** Bob Natal. **Outfield/Baserunning Coordinator:**
Matt den Dekker. **Coordinator, Throwing Projects:** Ken Knutson. **Roving Instructor:** Jemile Weeks. **Roving Catching
Instructor:** Hector Alvarez. **Senior Advisor, Pitching Development:** Phil Regan. **Senior Advisor, Player Development
& Scouting:** Tony DeFrancesco. **Manager, Player Development Initiatives:** Kevin Walsh. **Coordinator, Player
Development Initiatives:** Andrew Christie. **Senior Advisor, Player Development Initiatives:** Bobby Floyd.

RESEARCH AND DEVELOPMENT

Assistant General Manager, Baseball Analytics: Ben Zauzmer. **Director, Baseball Analytics:** Joseph Lefkowitz.
Coordinator, Major League Strategy: Jared Faust. **Coordinator, Pitching Analytics:** David Lang. **Coordinator, Minor
League Analytics:** Daniel Schoenfeld. **Manager, Video Operations:** Joseph Scarola. **Senior Coordinator, Video
Operations:** Sean Haggans. **Analyst, Major League Strategy:** Jack Bredeson. **Analyst, Major League Strategy:** Joey
Keating. **Analyst, Major League Strategy:** Natalie Maurice. **Replay Analyst:** Harrison Friedland. **Senior Analyst, Baseball
Analytics:** Michael Jerman. **Biomechanical Analyst, Baseball Analytics:** Siddhartha Thakur. **Affiliate Analyst, Minor
League Analytics:** Max Vogel-Freedman. **Analyst, Baseball Analytics:** Desmond McGowan. **Analyst, Baseball Analytics:**
Tatiana DeRouen. **Analyst, Baseball Analytics:** Sam Saskin. **Analyst, Baseball Analytics:** Jake Toffler. **Analyst, Baseball
Analytics:** Kuan-Cheng Fu. **Analyst, Baseball Analytics:** Tim Wise. **Director, Baseball Systems:** Kevin Meehan.

MINOR LEAGUE PERFORMANCE

Medical Coordinator: Matt Hunter. **Athletic Training Coordinator:** Bob Tarpey. **Rehab and Reconditioning
Co-Coordinator:** Alanna Salituro. **Rehab and Reconditioning Co-Coordinator:** Luke Novosel. **Performance Coaching
Coordinator:** Luke Passman. **Sport Science Coordinator:** Jackson Bertoli. **Mental Performance Coordinator:**
Samantha Gilmore. **Performance Dietitian:** Geordan Stapleton

FARM SYSTEM

Class	Club	Manager	Hitting Coach	Pitching Coach
Triple-A	Syracuse	Kevin Boles	Joel Chimelis	Steve Schrenk
Double-A	Binghamton	Reid Brignac	Tommy Joseph	Jerome Williams
High-A	Brooklyn	Luis Rivera	Richie Benes	AJ Sager
Low-A	St. Lucie	Robbie Robinson	Victor Burgos	Victor Ramos
Rookie	Mets (FCL)	David Davalillo	Eduardo Nunez	Miguel Bonilla
Rookie	Mets (DSL)	Manny Martinez	Leo Hernandez	Christian Martinez

SCOUTING

Telephone: (718) 565-4311. **Fax:** (718) 205-7920.
Assistant General Manager, Pro Player Evaluation & Personnel: Bryn Alderson. **Director, Pro Player Evaluation:**
Jeff Lebow. **Senior Manager, Pro Player Personnel:** Jason Stein. **Senior Advisor, Pro Player Personnel:** Joseph
Kowal. **Special Advisor, Pro Player Personnel/Manager, Pacific Rim:** Conor Brooks. **Special Advisor, Pro Player
Personnel/International/Amateur Special Assignments:** David Keller. **Pro Player Evaluators:** Jaymie Bane, Jason
Davis, Pat Jones, Jim Kelly, Ash Lawson, Chad MacDonald, Shaun McNamara, Andy Pratt, Roy Smith, Rudy Terrasas, Ernie
Young. **Pacific Rim Evaluators:** Bon Kim, Jeffrey Kusumoto. **VP, Amateur and International Scouting:** Thomas Tanous.
Director, Amateur Scouting: Marc Tramuta. **Assistant Director, Amateur & International Scouting:** Drew Toussaint.
Coordinator, Amateur & International Scouting: Tom Fleischman. **Regional Supervisor, SE:** Cesar Aranguren. **Senior
Advisor, Amateur Scouting:** Eddie Bane. **Regional Supervisor, MW:** Nathan Beuster. **Underclass Supervisor:** Tom
Clark. **National Pitching Crosschecker:** Chris Hervey. **Regional Supervisor, W:** Tyler Holmes. **Senior Advisor, Amateur
Scouting:** Ron Hopkins. **Regional Supervisor, NE:** Mike Ledna. **National Crosschecker:** Doug Thurman. **Area Scouts:**
Gary Brown, Jet Butler, Daniel Coles, Jarrett England, Chris Heidt, John Kosciak, Rusty McNamara, Marlin McPhail, Nelson
Mompierre, Rich Morales, Joe Raccuia, Brian Reid, Harry Shelton, Scott Thomas, Jon Updike, Glenn Walker. **Director,
International Scouting:** Steve Barningham. **Supervisor, Latin America:** Moises de la Mota. **Supervisor, Venezuela:**
Ismael Perez. **Supervisor, Dominican Republic:** Oliver Dominguez. **Coordinator, Latin America:** Harold Herrera.
Coordinator, Dominican Republic: Felix Romero. **Coordinator, Mexico:** Martin Arvizu. **Caribbean Crosschecker:** Luis
Scheker. **Scouts, Dominican Republic:** Kelvin Dominguez, Wilson Peralta. **Scouts, Venezuela:** Robert Espejo, Manuel
López, Andres Nunez, Carlos Perez. **Scout, Panama:** Elvis Rios. **Video Coordinator, Dominican Republic:** Jose Luis de
Leon. **Video/Area Scout:** Carlos Pellerano. **Video Coordinator, Venezuela:** Miguel Chang.

NEW YORK YANKEES

Office Address: Yankee Stadium, One East 161st St., Bronx, NY 10451.
Telephone: (718) 293-4300.
Website: www.yankees.com, www.yankeesbeisbol.com.
Twitter: @Yankees, @YankeesPR, @LosYankees, @LosYankeesPR.

OWNERSHIP

Managing General Partner/Chairperson: Harold Z. (Hal) Steinbrenner. **General Partner/Vice Chairperson:** Jennifer Steinbrenner Swindal. **General Partner/Vice Chairperson:** Jessica Steinbrenner.

BUSINESS OPERATIONS

Harold Z.
Steinbrenner

President: Randy Levine, Esq.
Chief Operating Officer: Lonn A. Trost, Esq.
Senior VP, Strategic Ventures: Marty Greenspun. **Senior VP, Chief Security Officer:** Sonny Hight. **Senior VP, Yankee Global Enterprises/Chief Financial Officer:** Anthony Bruno. **Chief Financial Officer/Senior VP, Financial Operations:** Scott M. Krug. **Senior VP, Corporate/Community Relations:** Brian E. Smith. **Senior VP, Partnerships:** Michael J. Tusiani. **Senior VP, Marketing:** Deborah A. Tymon. **Senior VP, Stadium Operations:** Doug Behar. **Senior VP & General Counsel:** Alan Chang, Esq. **Senior VP, Chief Information Officer:** Mike Lane. **Vice President, Human Resources, Employment & Labor Law:** Aryn Sobo, Esq. **Sr. Vice President, Chief Legal Officer:** Michael Mellis, Esq. **Vice President, Non-Baseball Sports Events:** Mark Holtzman.

COMMUNICATIONS/MEDIA RELATIONS

Telephone: (718) 579-4460. **Email:** media@yankees.com.
Vice President, Communications/Media Relations: Jason Zillo. **Senior Director, Communications/Media Relations:** Michael Margolis. **Manager, Communications/Media Relations:** Kaitlyn Brennan. **Assistant, Communications/Media Relations:** Jon Butensky. **Assistant, Communications/Media Relations:** Dan Laverde. **Bilingual Media Relations Coordinator:** Marlon Abreu. **Administrative Assistant, Communications/Media Relations:** Germania Dolores Hernandez-Simonetti.

TICKET OPERATIONS

Telephone: (718) 293-6000.
VP, Ticket Sales/Service/Operations: Kevin Dart. **Vice President, Partnership Sales:** Danny Gallivan.

BASEBALL OPERATIONS

Senior VP/General Manager: Brian Cashman.
Senior VP/Assistant GM: Jean Afterman, Esq. **VP/Assistant GM:** Michael Fishman. **VP, Baseball Operations:** Tim Naehring. **Director, Team Travel & Player Services:** Ben Tuliebitz. **Director, Quantitative Analysis:** David Grabiner. **Director, Baseball Operations:** Matt Ferry. **Director, Mental Conditioning:** Chad Bohling. **Director, Baseball Systems:** Brian Nicosia.

Brian Cashman

MAJOR LEAGUE STAFF

Manager: Aaron Boone.
Coaches: Pitching—Matt Blake, **Hitting**—Dillon Lawson. **Assistant Pitching**—Desi Druschel. **Assistant Hitting**—Casey Dykes. **First Base/Infield**—Travis Chapman. **Third Base/ Outfield**—Luis Rojas. **Bench**—Carlos Mendoza. **Quality Control/Catching**—Tanner Swanson. **Bullpen**—Mike Harkey. **Bullpen Catchers**—Aaron Barnett, Collin Theroux. **Coaching Assistant/Replay Coordinator**—Brett Weber.

MEDICAL/TRAINING

Head Team Physician: Dr. Christopher Ahmad. **Senior Advisor, Orthopedics:** Stuart Hershon, M.D. **Head Team Internist:** Paul Lee, M.D. **Director, Player Health/Performance:** Eric Cressey. **Director, Sports Medicine/Rehab:** Michael Schuk. **Director, Medical Services:** Steve Donohue. **Head Athletic Trainer:** Tim Lentych. **Asst. Athletic Trainer:** Alfonso Malaguti. **Major League Physical Therapist:** Joe Bello. **Major League Strength & Conditioning Coach:** Brett McCabe. **Assistant Major League Strength & Conditioning Coach:** Matt Rutledge. **Massage Therapist:** Doug Cecil. **Major League Dietitian:** Drew Weisberg.

PLAYER DEVELOPMENT

Vice President, Player Development: Kevin Reese.
Director, Player Development: Eric Schmitt. **Assistant Director, Player Development:** Stephen Swindal Jr. **Director, Minor League Operations:** Nick Avanzato. **Manager, International Operations:** Victor Roldan. **Manager, Player Development Analytics:** Dan Walco. **Analyst, Player Development:** Matt Reiland. **Assistant, Minor League Operations:** Nick Leon. **Assistant, International Operations:** Giuliano Montanez. **Assistant, Player Development:** Austin Zieg. **Player Development Advisor:** Pat McMahon. **Coordinator, Baseball Development:** Mario Garza. **Director of Pitching:** Sam Briend. **Rehab Pitching Coordinator:** John Kremer. **Complex Pitching Coordinator:** Ben Buck. **Minor League Hitting Coordinator:** Joe Migliaccio. **Asst. Minor League Hitting Coordinator:** Aaron Leanhardt. **Complex Coordinator/Minor League Manager:** David Adams. **Director of Speed Development & Baserunning/Roving Hitting Coach:** Matt Talarico. **Defensive Coordinator:** Aaron Gershenfeld. **Roving Upper-Level IF/OF Instructor:** Dan Fiorito. **Roving Lower-Level IF/OF Instructor:** Ryan Hunt. **Asst. Director, Player Health & Performance:** Donovan Santas. **Medical Coordinator:** Mark Littlefield. **Asst. Medical Coordinator:** Greg Spratt. **Rehabilitation Coordinator:** David Colvin. **Asst. Rehab Coordinator:** Charlie Domnisch. **Rehab Strength Coach:** Ty Hill. **Manual Therapy & Corrective Exercise Coordinator:** Mike Wickland. **Minor League Nutrition Coordinator:** Sydney Boehnlein. **Minor League Dietitian:** Chandler Falcon. **PD, Equipment & Clubhouse Operations Manager:** Ryan Ornstein. **Education Coordinator:** Joe Perez. **Baseball Solutions Engineer:** Rob Owens. **Minor League Video Coordinator:** Zach Iannarelli. **Asst. Minor League Video Coordinators:** Paul Henshaw, Luke Morris. **Associate Director, Mental Conditioning:** Chris Passarella. **Coordinator, Cultural Development:** Héctor González. **Video Coord./Mental Conditioning Coach:** David Schnabel. **Mental Conditioning Coach:** Noel Garcia. **Director, Performance Science:** David Whiteside. **Senior Biomechanist:** Gillian Weir. **Performance Science Coordinator:** Joe Siara. **Sport Scientist:** Patrick Hipes. **Senior Analyst, Performance Science:** Christina Williamson. **Director, D.R. Baseball Operations:** Andrew Wright. **Director, Latin Baseball Academy:** Joel Lithgow. **DR Academy Complex Coordinator:** Rainiero Coa. **Assistants, Int'l Baseball Operations:** Manuel Castillo, J.T. Hernandez.

FARM SYSTEM

Yankees minor league managers were unavailable at time of press.

SCOUTING

Telephone: (813) 875-7569. **Fax:** (813) 873-2302.
VP, Domestic Amateur Scouting: Damon Oppenheimer. **Director, Professional Scouting:** Matt Daley. **Assistant Director, Professional Scouting:** Adam Charnin-Aker. **Special Assignment Scout:** Jim Hendry. **Pro Scouts:** Scott Atchison, Kendall Carter, Jay Darnell, Marc DelPiano, Jonathan Diaz, Brandon Duckworth, Tyler Greene, Shawn Hill, Cory Melvin, Pat Murtaugh, Jaylon Pimentel, Jose Ravelo, Jimmy Stokes, JT Stotts, Alex Sunderland, Dennis Twombley, Aron Weston, Tom Wilson. **Assistant Director, Domestic Amateur Scouting, Operations:** Mitch Colahan. **Assistant Director, Domestic Amateur Scouting, Analytics:** Scott Benecke. **National Crosscheckers:** Sam Hughes, Tim Kelly, Steve Kmetko, Jeff Patterson, Mike Wagner. **Amateur Scouting Video & Administration Coordinator:** Joe Wielbruda. **Amateur Scouting & Affiliate Pitching Analyst:** Scott Lovekamp. **Hitting Analyst:** Jeff Deardorff. **Amateur Scouts:** Troy Afenir, Tim Alexander, Chuck Bartlett, Denis Boucher, Ricky Castle, Bobby DeJardin, Mike Gibbons, Matt Hyde, Brian Jeroloman, David Keith, Steve Lemke, Mike Leuzinger, Ronnie Merrill, Darryl Monroe, Bill Pintard, Matt Ranson, Brian Rhees, Tyler Robertson, Stewart Smothers, Mike Thurman. **Director, International Scouting:** Donny Rowland. **Asst. Director, International Scouting:** Brady LaRuffa. **Asst. to Director, Latin America:** Edgar Mateo. **Asst. to Director, Quality Control:** Ethan Sander. **Crosscheckers, International Scouting:** Steve Wilson, Dennis Woody, Ricardo Finol. **Crosscheckers, Latin America:** Victor Mata, Juan Rosario, Jose Gavidia. **Video Coordinator, International Scouting:** Kurt Bathelt. **Video Assistant, Dominican Republic:** Carlos Ravelo. **Manager, Data/Technology, International Scouting:** Vianco Martinez. **Technology/Data Analyst, D.R.:** Kevin Valera. **Technology/Data Analyst, Venezuela:** Victor Deyan. **International Scouts:** Doug Skiles, John Wadsworth, Alvaro Noriega, Luis Sierra, Esdras Abreu, Luis Brito, R. Arturo Peña, Juan Piron, Luis Rodriguez, Jose Sabino, Troy Williams, Rudy Gomez, Lee Sigman, Edgard Rodriguez, Carlos Levy, Chi Lee, Peng Pu Lee, Alan Atacho, Darwin Bracho, Roney Calderon, Cesar Suarez, Jesus Taico, Luis Tinoco.

OAKLAND ATHLETICS

Office Address: 7000 Coliseum Way, Oakland, CA 94621.
Telephone: (510) 638-4900. **Fax:** (510) 562-1633. **Website:** www.athletics.com.

OWNERSHIP
Owner/Managing Partner: John Fisher. **Chairman Emeritus:** Lew Wolff. **Board Members:** Sandy Dean, Bill Gurtin, Keith Wolff.

BUSINESS OPERATIONS
President: David Kaval. **Chief of Staff:** Miguel Duarte. **VP, Government Affairs:** Taj Tashombe. **Director, Special Projects:** Dash Davidson. **Senior Coordinator, Operations:** Colette Lucas-Conwell. **Executive Assistant & Board Liaison:** Curtis Wiggington. **Director, Alumni & Family Relations:** Detra Paige. **Senior Coordinator, Alumni & Family Relations:** Melissa Guzman.

FINANCE/ADMINISTRATION
Controller: Adam Tyhurst. **Senior Director, Finance:** Kasey Jarcik. **Director, Accounting:** John Anki. **Senior Payroll Manager:** Rose Dancil. **Senior Accountants:** Danna Mouat. Jr. **Accountant:** Carlos Hidalgo. **GL Accountant:** Naima Peterson. **Director, People Operations and Talent:** Adam Scoggan. **People Operations Business Partner & Benefits Specialist:** Mari Rodriguez. **Director, Information Technology:** Jody Johnson. **Senior Systems Administrator:** Kevin Lowe. **Lead IT Support Administrator:** Dave Cramer.

David Kaval

MARKETING/BROADCASTING
VP, Marketing & Communications: Catherine Aker. **Director, Marketing:** Lisa Bullard. **Manager, Marketing & Advertising:** Alissa Persichetti. **Team Photographer:** Michael Zagaris. **Senior Broadcast Producer & Host:** Chris Townsend. **Coordinating Producer, Broadcasting:** D'Aulaire Louwerse. **Multimedia Producer:** Cody Elias.

PUBLIC RELATIONS/COMMUNICATIONS
Director, Baseball Communications: Mark Ling. **Director, Communications & Content:** Erica George. **Social Media Manager:** Madison Campos. **Senior Video Producer:** Kit Karutz. **Baseball Information Manager:** Mike Selleck. **Baseball Communications Manager:** Olivia Hummer. **Baseball Communications Coordinator:** Greg Korn.

STADIUM OPERATIONS
VP, Stadium Operations: David Rinetti. **Senior Director, Stadium Operations:** Paul La Veau. **Director, Concessions & Merchandise:** Nicole Morgan. **Senior Manager, Stadium Operations Events:** Kristy Ledbetter. **Senior Manager, Stadium Services:** Randy Duran. **Senior Manager, Guest Services:** Elisabeth Aydelotte. **Senior Manager, Stadium Operations:** Matt Van Norton. **Stadium Operations Systems Manager:** Jason Silva. **Head Groundskeeper:** Clay Wood.

TICKET SALES/OPERATIONS/SERVICES
VP, Ticket Sales & Analytics: Steve Fanelli. **Director, Ticket Operations:** David Adame. **Senior Director, Service/Retention:** Josh Ziegenbusch. **Senior Manager, Ticket Solutions:** Austin Redman. **Ticket Operations Coordinator:** Allie Guido.

TRAVEL/CLUBHOUSE
Director, Team Travel: Mickey Morabito. **Equipment Manager:** Steve Vucinich. **Visiting Clubhouse Manager:** Mike Thalblum. **Manager, Clubhouse & Equipment Operations:** Brian Davis. **Director, Clubhouse & Equipment Operations:** Matt Weiss. **Arizona Senior Facility Manager:** James Gibson. **Oakland Clubhouse Staff & Umpire Attendant:** Chad Yaconetti.

BASEBALL OPERATIONS

Executive VP, Baseball Operations: Billy Beane.
General Manager: David Forst. **Assistant General Manager, Major League & International Operations:** Dan Feinstein. **Assistant General Manager/Director of Player Personnel:** Billy Owens. **Assistant General Manager, Baseball Development and Technology:** Rob Naberhaus. **Special Assistant to General Manager:** Grady Fuson. **Special Assistant to General Manager:** Chris Pittaro. **Special Assistant to Baseball Operations:** Scott Hatteberg. **Director of Baseball Administration:** Pamela Pitts. **Director of Team Travel:** Mickey Morabito. **Research Scientist:** David Jackson-Hanen. **Assistant Directors, Research and Analytics:** Pike Goldschmidt, Ben Lowry. **Assistant Director, Scouting and Baseball Operations:** Haley Alvarez. **Coordinator, Scouting and Baseball Operations:** Greg Ledford **Analyst, Baseball Operations:** Samantha Schultz. **Video Coordinator:** Adam Rhoden.

Billy Beane

MAJOR LEAGUE STAFF

Manager: Mark Kotsay.
Coaches: Bench—Brad Ausmus. **Pitching**— Scott Emerson. **Hitting**—Tommy Everidge. **Asst. Hitting**—Chris Cron. **First Base**—Eric Martins. **Third Base**—Darren Bush. **Bullpen**—Marcus Jensen.

MEDICAL/TRAINING

Head Athletic Trainer: Nick Paparesta. **Assistant Athletic Trainers:** Jeff Collins, Brian Schulman. **Sport Performance Coach:** Josh Cuffe. **Assistant Sport Performance Coach:** Steven Candelaria. **Major League Massage Therapist:** Ozzie Lyles. **Head Team Physician:** Dr. Allan Pont. **Team Physician:** Dr. Grant Wang. **Chief Team Orthopedists:** Dr. Will Workman. **Team Orthopedists:** Dr. Michael T Freehill, Dr. Keith Chan. **Arizona Team Physician:** Dr. Fred Dicke. **Arizona Team Orthopedist:** Dr. Douglas Freedberg.

PLAYER DEVELOPMENT

Telephone: (480) 387-5800. **Fax:** (480) 387-5830.
Director, Player Development: Ed Sprague. Director, **Latin American Operations:** Raymond Abreu. **Special Advisor, Player Development:** Keith Lieppman. **Minor League Hitting Coordinator:** Jim Eppard. **Minor League Pitching Coordinator:** Gil Patterson. **Minor League Infield Coordinator:** Juan Navarrete. **Minor League Outfield and Baserunning Coordinator:** Steve Scarsone. **Minor League Catching Coordinator:** Gabe Ortiz. **Throwing Performance Coach:** Casey Upperman. **Hitting Performance Coach:** Scott Steinmann. **Hitting Technology Coach:** Lloyd Turner. **Minor League Pitching Rehab Coordinator:** Craig Lefferts. **Assistant Pitching Rehab Coordinator:** Rick Rodriguez. **Latin America Field Coordinator:** Eddie Menchaca. **Senior Coordinator of Medical Services:** Larry Davis. **Minor League Medical Coordinator:** Nate Brooks. **Latin America Medical Coordinator:** Javier Alvidrez. **Minor League Sport Performance Coordinator:** J.D. Howell. **Assistant Minor League Sport Performance Coordinator:** Scott Smith. **Sport Performance Rehab Coordinator:** Derek Clovis. **Minor League Technology and Development Manager:** Ed Gitlitz Coordinator, **Minor League Technology and Development:** Taylor Schmid. **Senior Coordinator of Educational and Cultural Programs:** Kelvin Todd. **Coordinator of Educational and Cultural Programs:** Leo Bejarán-Specht. Senior Facility Manager, **Arizona:** James Gibson. Manager, Minor League Equipment & **Clubhouse Operations:** Thomas Miller. Manager, **Minor League Operations:** Nancy Moriuchi. **Minor League Operations Coordinator:** Luis Victoria. Assistants, **Arizona Clubhouse Operations:** Dylan Ruth, Alex Haas. **Interpreter:** Yen Po Wang. **Arizona Head Groundskeeper:** Chad Huss. **Arizona Assistant Groundskeeper:** Greg Hofer. **Arizona Groundskeepers:** Jose Delgado, James Folk, Chris Gracia, Rodolfo Lopez.

FARM SYSTEM

Class	Club (League)	Manager	Hitting Coach	Pitching Coach
Triple-A	Las Vegas	Fran Riordan	Brian McArn	Steve Connelly
Double-A	Midland	Bobby Crosby	Todd Takayoshi	Chris Smith
High-A	Lansing	Phil Pohl	Javier Godard	Don Schulze
Low-A	Stockton	Anthony Phillips	Kevin Kouzmanoff	Bryan Corey
Rookie	Athletics (ACL)	Adam Rosales	Francisco Santana	Gabriel Ozuna
Rookie			Ruben Escalera	
Rookie	Athletics (DSL)	TBD	TBD	TBD

SCOUTING

Director of Scouting: Eric Kubota. **Assistant Director of Scouting:** Sean Rooney. **Special Assistant to Scouting & International Operations:** Steve Sharpe. **Professional Scouts:** Shooty Babitt, Jeff Bittiger, Grant Brittain, Dan Freed, Will Schock, Steve Springer, Tom Thomas, Mike Ziegler. **West Coast Supervisor:** Scott Kidd. **Midwest Supervisors:** Mark Adair, Armann Brown. **East Coast Supervisor:** Marc Sauer. **Master Pitching Scout:** John Hughes. **Area Scouts:** Steve Abney, Anthony Aliotti, Neil Avent, Chris Botsoe, Fletcher Byrd, Jim Coffman, Ruben Escalera, Tripp Faulk, Julio Franco, Matt Higginson, Derek Lee, Kelcey Mucker, Trevor Schaffer, Rich Sparks, Jemel Spearman, Troy Stewart, Dillon Tung, Jeff Urlaub, Ron Vaughn. **Latin American Scouting Supervisor:** Juan Mosquera. **Dominican Republic Scouts:** Yendri Bachelor, Juan Carlos De La Cruz, Angel Eusebio, Wilfredo Magallanes, Amaurys Reyes. **Venezuela Scouts:** Jose Barradas, Andri Garcia, Kevin Garcia, Argenis Paez, Oswaldo Troconis. **Australia Scout:** Dan Betreen. **Colombia Scouts:** Tito Quintero, Oswaldo Garcia. **Japan Scout:** Toshiyuki Tomizuka. **South Korea Scout:** Lewis Kim. Taiwan Scout/ Coordinator, **Pacific Rim:** Adam Hislop. **Mexico Scout:** Javier Agelvis.

PHILADELPHIA PHILLIES

Office Address: Citizens Bank Park, One Citizens Bank Way, Philadelphia, PA 19148.
Telephone: (215) 463-6000. **Website:** www.phillies.com.

OWNERSHIP
Operated By: The Phillies. **Managing Partner:** John Middleton. **Chairman Emeritus:** Bill Giles.

BUSINESS OPERATIONS

EXECUTIVE MANAGEMENT
Executive VP: David Buck. **VP/General Counsel:** Leslie Safran. **Director, Human Resources:** Jon Madden. **VP, Administration:** Kathy Killian. **VP, Chief Technology Officer:** Sean Walker. **Director, Technology Services:** Matt Bryan. **Director, Technology Systems Architect:** Kevin Donahue. **Director, Information Technology:** Bob Tonnon.

David Montgomery

BUSINESS AFFAIRS
VP, Business Affairs: Howard Smith. **Director, Operations/Facility:** Mike DiMuzio. **Director, Operations/Security:** Sal DeAngelis. **Director, Field Operations:** Mike Boekholder.

COMMUNICATIONS
Telephone: (215) 463-6000. **Fax:** (215) 389-3050
VP, Communications: Bonnie Clark. **VP, Baseball Communications:** Kevin Gregg. **Director, Publications:** Christine Negley. **Director, Player Relations and Phillies Charities:** Sophie Riegel. **PA Announcer:** Dan Baker. **Official Scorers:** Mark Gola, Mike Maconi, Dick Shute.

FINANCE
Sr. VP/CFO: John Nickolas. **Director, Business Analytics:** Josh Barbieri. **Director, Business Analytics Strategy:** Blake Summerfield. **Director, Finance and Controller:** Shannon Snellman. **Director, Payroll:** Bryan Humphreys.

BROADCAST/VIDEO SERVICES
Director, Broadcasting/Video Services: Mark DiNardo. **Director, Video Production:** Sean Rainey. **Director, Video Engineering:** Martin Otremsky.

MARKETING/PROMOTIONS
VP, Partnership Sales and Corporate Marketing: Jacqueline Cuddeback. **VP, Marketing Programs & Events:** Kurt Funk. **VP, Marketing & New Media:** Michael Harris. **Director, Promotions:** Scott Brandreth. **Director, Relationship Marketing:** John Brazer. **Director, Community and Charity Events:** Michele DeVicaris. **Director, Youth Baseball Development:** Jon Joaquin. **Director, Partnership Sales & Corporate Marketing:** Rob MacPherson. **Director, Community Initiatives:** Mary Ann Moyer. **Director, Corporate Sales:** Scott Nickle. **Director, Entertainment:** Teresa Harris. **Director, Marketing Events & Special Projects:** James Trout.

SALES/TICKETS
Telephone: (215) 463-1000. **Fax:** (215) 463-9878.
Sr. VP, Ticket Operations & Projects: John Weber. **Director, Ticket Technology & Development:** Chris Pohl. **Director, Sales:** Derek Schuster. **Director, Suite Sales & Business Ventures:** Kevin Beale. **Director, Group Sales:** Vanessa Mapson. **Director, Season Ticket Services:** Mike Holdren. **Director, Premium Sales & Services:** Matt Kessler. **Director, Ticket Operations:** Ken Duffy.

TRAVEL/CLUBHOUSE
Director, Clubhouse Services: Phil Sheridan. **Manager, Team Travel:** Jameson Hall. **Manager, Equipment/Umpire Services:** Dan O'Rourke. **Manager, Visiting Clubhouse:** Kevin Steinhour.

BASEBALL OPERATIONS

President, Baseball Operations: David Dombrowski. **VP/General Manager:** Sam Fuld. **Assistant GM:** Ani Kilambi. **Assistant GM:** Ned Rice. **Assistant GM:** Jorge Velandia. **Senior Advisor:** Pat Gillick. **Senior Advisors, GM:** Larry Bowa, Charlie Manuel. **Director, Player Development:** Preston Mattingly. **Director, International Scouting:** Sal Agostinelli. **Director, Amateur Scouting:** Brian Barber. **Director, Professional Scouting:** Mike Ondo. **Director, Research and Development:** Alex Nakahara. **Director, Integrative Baseball Performance:** Rob Segedin. **Director, Amateur Scouting Administration:** Rob Holiday. **Director, Minor League Operations:** Lee McDaniel. **Director, Mental Performance:** Ceci Craft.

BILLIE WEISS/BOSTON RED SOX

Dave Dombrowski

MAJOR LEAGUE STAFF

Manager: Joe Girardi. **Coaches: Bench**—Rob Thomson, **Pitching**—Caleb Cotham, **Hitting**—Kevin Long, **First Base**—Paco Figueroa, **Third Base**—Dusty Wathan, **Infield**—Bobby Dickerson, **Bullpen**—Dave Lundquist, **Coaching Assistant**— Bobby Meacham, **Assistant Pitching Coach/Director of Pitching Development:** Brian Kaplan. **Assistant Hitting Coach:** Jason Camilli, **Bullpen Catchers:** Brad Flanders, Hector Rabago. **Quality Assurance Coach:** Mike Calitri.

MEDICAL/TRAINING

Director, Medical Services: Dr. Michael Ciccotti. **Head Athletic Trainer:** Paul Buchheit. **Assistant Athletic Trainers:** Aaron Hoback. **Director, Strength and Conditioning and Nutrition:** Morgan Gregory. **Assistant Strength & Conditioning Coach:** Furey Leva. **Major League Physical Therapist:** Joe Rauch.

PLAYER DEVELOPMENT

Director, Player Development: Preston Mattingly. **Director, Minor League Operations:** Lee McDaniel. **Field Coordinator:** Kevin Bradshaw. **Coordinator, DR Academy:** Manny Amador. **Pitching Coordinator:** Travis Hergert. **Pitching Development Analyst:** Mark Lowy. **Hitting Coordinator:** Jason Ochart. **Asst. Hitting Coordinator:** Chris Heintz. **Offensive Development Analyst:** Kevin Mahala. **Catching Coordinator:** Bob Stumpo. **Infield Coordinator:** Adam Everett. **Outfield/BR Coordinator:** Andy Abad. **Medical & Athletic Training Coord.:** Alex Rodriguez. **Minor Lg Rehab Coord.:** Justin Tallard. **S&C Coordinator:** Pat Trainor. **Asst. S&C Coordinator:** Jose Salas. **Minor Lg. Nutrition Coordinator:** Stephanie MacNeill. **Mental Performance Coordinator:** Todd Dilbeck. **Video Coordinator:** Connor Carroll. **Asst. Video Coordinator:** Thomas Knauss. **Man. Lang. Ed. & Cultural Assim.:** Kiah Villamán. **Minor League Physical Therapist:** Brittany Gooch. **Mental Performance Coach:** Frances Cardenas. **Mental Performance Coach:** Brea Hapken. **Pitching Strategist:** Pat Robles. **Director, Florida Operations/GM, Clearwater Threshers:** John Timberlake. **Assistant Director, Minor League Operations/Florida:** Joe Cynar. **Assistant Director, International Operations:** Ray Robles. **Assistant Director, Player Development:** Dana Parks.

FARM SYSTEM

Class	Club (League)	Manager	Hitting Coach	Pitching Coach
Triple-A	Lehigh Valley	Anthony Contreras	Joe Thurston	Cesar Ramos
Double-A	Reading	Shawn Williams	Tyler Henson	Matt Hockenberry
High-A	Jersey Shore	Keith Werman	Ari Adut	Brad Bergesen
Low-A	Clearwater	Marty Malloy	Jake Elmore	Vic Diaz
Rookie	Phillies (FCL)	Roly DeArmas	Rafael DeLima	Tyler Anderson
Rookie		Chris Adamson		
Rookie	Phillies 1 (DSL)	Nerluis Martinez	Zack Jones	Alex Concepcion
Rookie	Phillies 2 (DSL)	TBA	Samuel Hiciano	Les Straker

SCOUTING

Director, Amateur Scouting: Brian Barber. **Director, Amateur Scouting Administration:** Rob Holiday. **National Scouting Coordinators:** David Crowson, Darrell Conner. **Coordinator, Amateur Scouting:** Connor Betbeze. **Regional Supervisors:** Alex Agostino, Shane Bowers, Buddy Hernandez, Brad Holland, Brian Kohlscheen. **Special Assignment Scouts:** Dean Albany, Craig Colbert, Charley Kerfeld, Mike Koplove, Dan Wright. **Director, Professional Scouting:** Mike Ondo. **Professional Scouts:** Erick Dalton, Todd Donovan, Jon Mercurio. **Area Scouts:** Chris Duffy, Tommy Field, Zach Friedman, Ralph Garr Jr., Victor Gomez, Bryce Harman, Aaron Jersild, Tim Kissner, Kellan McKeon, Timi Moni, Justin Morgenstern, Justin Munson, Demerius Pittman, Hilton Richardson, Derrick Ross, Mike Stauffer, Jason Waugh, Jeff Zona Jr. **Director, International Scouting:** Sal Agostinelli. **International Scouting Coordinator:** Derrick Chung. **Latin America Coordinator:** Jesús Méndez. **Latin America Supervisor:** Carlos Salas. **International Crosscheckers:** Oneri Fleita, Alex Mesa. **Crosschecker, Dominican Republic:** Andres Hiraldo. **Crosschecker, Dominican Republic:** Luis Garcia. **International Scouts:** Alvaro Blanco (Colombia), Jesus Blanco (Venezuela), Alex Choi (South Korea), Elvis García (Venezuela), Luis García (Dominican Republic), Charlie Gastelum (Mexico), Gene Grimaldi (Associate Scout), Jose Guzman (Dominican Republic), Jonatan Hernandez (Venezuela), William Mota (Venezuela), Howard Norsetter (Australia), Bernardo Pérez (Dominican Republic), Abdiel Ramos (Panama), Franklin Rojas (Venezuela), Claudio Scerrato (Italy), Ebert Velásquez (Venezuela), Youngster Wang (Taiwan). **Video Assiants:** Jean Montalvo (Dominican Republic), Gustavo Mogollon (Venezuela).

PITTSBURGH PIRATES

Office Address: PNC Park at North Shore, 115 Federal St., Pittsburgh, PA, 15212.
Mailing Address: PO Box 7000, Pittsburgh, PA 15212.
Telephone: (412) 323-5000. **Fax:** (412) 325-4412.
Website: www.pirates.com. **Twitter:** @Pirates.

BUSINESS OPERATIONS

OWNERSHIP
Chairman of the Board: Bob Nutting.
President: Travis Williams. **Associate General Counsel:** Drew Singer.

Travis Williams

COMMUNICATIONS
Senior VP, Communications/Broadcasting: Brian Warecki. **Director, Baseball Communications:** Jim Trdinich. **Director, Broadcasting:** Marc Garda. **Director, Media Relations:** Dan Hart. **Director, Communications:** Terry Rodgers.

MARKETING/CORPORATE SPONSORSHIPS
Director, Alumni Affairs/Promotions/Licensing: Joe Billetdeaux. **Director, Special Events:** Christine Serkoch. **Director,PNC Park Events:** Ann Regan. **Manager, Advertising/Digital Marketing:** Haley Artayet. **Manager, Ballpark Presentation:** Emilie Matson. **Director, Corporate & Premium Partnership Sales:** Chris Stevens. **Director, Corporate Partnership Activation:** Katie Shockey. **Director, Corporate & Premium Partnership Sales:** Dave Shinsky.

STADIUM OPERATIONS
Executive VP/General Manager, PNC Park: Dennis DaPra. **Vice President, Ballpark Operations:** Chris Hunter. **Senior VP, Florida and Dominican Operations:** Jeff Podobnik. **Director, Field Operations:** Matt Brown. **Director, PNC Park Operations:** J.J. McGraw. **Director, Facility Operations and Strategy:** Jackie Riggleman.

TRAVEL/CLUBHOUSE
Home Clubhouse Manager: Scott Bonnett. **Visiting Clubhouse Manager:** Kevin Conrad. **Assistant Equipment Manager:** Kiere Bulls. **Manager, Team Travel:** Ryan Denlinger.

BASEBALL OPERATIONS

Executive Vice President, General Manager: Ben Cherington. **Senior Vice President, Baseball Development:** Bryan Stroh. **Assistant General Manager:** Kevan Graves. **Assistant General Manager:** Steve Sanders. **Director, Baseball Operations and Pro Scouting:** Will Lawton. **Assistant Director, Baseball Operations:** Trey Rose. **Assistant, Baseball Operations:** Zach Aldrich. **Manager, Team Travel:** Ryan Denlinger. **Business Manager, Baseball Operations:** Sarah Steinberg

Ben Cherington

MAJOR LEAGUE STAFF

Manager: Derek Shelton. **Bench Coach:** Don Kelly. **Hitting Coach:** Andy Haines. **Pitching Coach:** Oscar Marin. **Assistant Hitting Coach:** Christian Marrero. **Major League Field Coordinator and 3rd Base Coach:** Mike Rabelo. **First Base Coach:** Tarrik Brock. **Bullpen Coach:** Justin Meccage. **Coaching Assistant:** Heberto Andrade. **Major League Run Prevention & Game Planning Coach:** Radley Haddad. **Bullpen Catcher:** Jordan Comadena. **Coordinator, ML Pitching Operations:** Jeremy Bleich. **Coordinator, ML Hitting Operations:** Tim McKeithan. **Major League Assistant:** Jake Mencacci.

MEDICAL/TRAINING

Director, Sports Medicine: Todd Tomczyk. **Director, Sports Performance:** A.J. Patrick. **Head Strength and Conditioning Coach:** Terence Brannic. **Major League Strength & Conditioning Coach:** Adam Vish. **Head Major League Athletic Trainer:** Rafael Freitas. **Major League Assistant Athletic Trainer:** Tony Leo. **Strength and Conditioning Coach:** Glenn Nutting. **Strength and Conditioning Coach:** Nicholas Pressley. **Minor League Strength & Conditioning Coach:** Cory Cook. **Minor League Athletic Training Coordinator:** Dru Scott. **Major League Physical Therapist:** Seth Steinhauer. **Medical Director:** Dr. Patrick DeMeo. **Team Physicians:** Dr. Darren Frank, Dr. Dennis Phillips, Dr. Michael Scarpone, Dr. Robert Schilken, Dr. Edward Snell.

INFORMATICS

Senior Director, Baseball Informatics: Dan Fox. **Assistant Director, R&D:** Sean Ahmed. **Senior Quantitative Analyst:** Justin Newman. **Senior Developer, Baseball Informatics:** Brian Hulick. **Data Architect, Baseball Systems:** Matthew Reiersgaard. **Developer, Baseball Informatics:** Frank Wolverton. **Software Developer, Baseball Informatics:** Nichols Siefken. **Data Engineer:** Andrew Gibon. **Performance Analyst:** Justin Perline. **Major League Advance Coordinator:** Aaron Razum. **Data Scientist, R&D:** Dan Gustafson

PLAYER DEVELOPMENT

Senior Director, Player Personnel: Steve Williams. **Special Assistant, Player Personnel:** Oz Ocampo. **Assistant Director, Player Personnel:** Max Kwan.

Assistant Director, Pro Player Valuation: Joe Douglas. **Pro Evaluation Team Leaders:** Sean McNally, Rodney Henderson, Larry Broadway. **Player Valuation Analyst:** Grant Jones. **Player Evaluation Analyst:** Joe Hultzen. **Player Valuation Analyst:** Christine Harris. **Pro Scouts:** Kinza Baad, Ricky Bennett, Carlos Berroa, Jim Dedrick, Michael Landestoy, Andrew Lorraine, Matt Ruebel, Everett Russell. **Special Assignment Scout:** Doug Strange

FARM SYSTEM

Class	Club (League)	Manager	Hitting Coach	Pitching Coach
Triple-A	Indianapolis	Miguel Perez	Eric Munson	Dan Meyer
Double-A	Altoona	Kieran Mattison	Jon Nunnally	Drew Benes
High-A	Greensboro	Callix Crabbe	Ruben Gotay	Fernando Nieve
Low-A	Bradenton	Jonathan Johnston	Mendy Lopez	TBA
Rookie	Pirates (FCL)	TBA	TBA	TBA
Rookie	Pirates (DSL)	TBA	TBA	TBA

SCOUTING

Fax: (412) 325-4414.

Senior Director, Amateur Scouting: Joe DelliCarri. **Director, International Scouting:** Junior Vizcaino. **Assistant Director, Amateur Scouting:** Mike Mangan. **Assistant Director, Amateur Scouting Operations:** Matt Skirving. **Coordinator, International Operations:** Matt Benedict.

National Supervisors: Jimmy Lester, Jack Bowen. **Regional Supervisors:** Trevor Haley, Sean Heffernan. **Area Supervisors:** Richard Allen, Matt Bimeal, Adam Bourassa, Michael Bradford, Eddie Charles, Brett Evert, John Lombardo, Wayne Mathis, Darren Mazeroski, Cam Murphy, Nick Presto, Dan Radcliff, Mike Sansoe, Brian Tracy, Derrick Van Dusen, Anthony Wycklendt

Major League Scouts: Ricky Bennett, Jim Dedrick. **Special Assignment Scout:** Doug Strange. **Pro Scouts:** Kinza Baad, Ricky Bennett, Carlos Berroa, Jim Dedrick, Michael Landestoy, Andrew Lorraine, Matt Ruebel, Everett Russell. **International Crosschecker:** Jesus Lantigua. **International Supervisors:** Saul Torres (Venezuela); Emmanuel Gomez (D.R.); Raul Lopez (Mexico); Tony Harris (International/Australia); Fu-Chun Chiang (Far East); Tom Gillespie (Europe/Africa). **International Scouts:** Esteban Alvarez, Daurys Nin, Leudy Castro, Cristino Valdez, Omelbis Corporan (D.R.); Victor Alvarez, Gregory Bolivar (Colombia), Pedro Avila, Omar Gonzalez, Jesus Morelli, Jessie Nava, Jose Partidas Dirimo Chavez (Venezuela); Roberto Saucedo (Mexico); Marcos Guimaraes (Brazil); Eugene Helder (Aruba); Mark Van Zanten (Curacao); Jose Pineda (Panama).

ST. LOUIS CARDINALS

Office Address: 700 Clark Street, St. Louis MO 63102.
Telephone: (314) 345-9600. **Fax:** (314) 345-9523. **Website:** www.cardinals.com.

OWNERSHIP

Operated By: St. Louis Cardinals, LLC. **Chairman/Chief Executive Officer:** William DeWitt, Jr. **President:** Bill DeWitt III. **Senior Administrative Assistant to Chairman:** Grace Pak. **Senior Administrative Assistant to President:** Julie Laningham. **Sr. VP & General Counsel:** Mike Whittle. **Associate Counsel:** Nick Garzia.

BUSINESS OPERATIONS

FINANCE

Fax: (314) 345-9520.
Senior VP/Chief Financial Officer: Brad Wood. **Director, Risk Management:** Rex Carter. **VP, Human Resources:** Ann Seeney. **VP, Event Services/Merchandising:** Vicki Bryant.

MARKETING/SALES/COMMUNITY RELATIONS

Fax: (314) 345-9529.
Senior VP, Sales & Marketing: Dan Farrell. **Administrative Assistant, VP, Sales & Marketing:** Gail Ruhling. **VP, Corporate Sales & Broadcasting:** Thane Van Breusegen.

COMMUNICATIONS

Fax: (314) 345-9530.
Director, Communications: Brian Bartow. **Manager, Baseball Communications:** Michael Whitty. **Administrator, Baseball Information & Media Services:** Chris Tunno. **Spanish Interpreter:** TBD. **PA Announcer:** John Ulett. **Official Scorers:** Gary Muller, Jeff Durbin, Mike Smith.

Bill DeWitt III

STADIUM OPERATIONS

Fax: (314) 345-9535.
VP, Stadium Operations: Matt Gifford. **Director, Security:** Phil Melcher. **Director, Facility Operations & Planning:** Hosei Maruyama.

TICKETING

Fax: (314) 345-9522.
VP, Ticket Sales/Service: Joe Strohm. **Director, Marketing & Brand Execution:** Martin Coco. **Director, Ticket Sales & Retention:** Rob Fasoldt. **Director, Ticket Operations:** Kerry Emerson.

TRAVEL/CLUBHOUSE

Fax: (314) 345-9523.
Team Travel Director: Ernie Moore. **Equipment Manager:** Mark Walsh. **Visiting Clubhouse Manager:** Rip Rowan. **Video Coordinator:** Chad Blair.

BASEBALL OPERATIONS

President of Baseball Operations: John Mozeliak. **Senior Executive Assistant to the President of Baseball Operations:** Linda Brauer. **Vice President & General Manager:** Michael Girsch. **Assistant GM:** Moises Rodriguez. **Assistant GM & Director of Scouting:** Randy Flores. **Assistant GM, Director of Player Development:** Gary LaRocque. **Special Assistant to GM, Player Procurement:** Matt Slater. **Director, Baseball Administration:** John Vuch. **Manager, Player Communications:** Melody Yount. **Coordinator, Technology & Innovation:** Javier Duren

Sr. Director Analytics: Jeremy Cohen. **Project Director:** Matt Bayer. **Director, Baseball Analytics:** Kevin Seats. **Senior Data Scientist:** Alan Kessler. **Data Scientist:** Garrett Greenwood. **Amateur Scouting Analyst:** Julia Prusaczyk. **Analyst, Baseball Development:** John Kern.

Senior Systems Developer: Brian Seyfert. **Sr. Analytics Engineer:** Todd Heitmann. **Sr. Cloud Engineer:** John Weeks. **Systems Engineer II:** Isaiah Berg. **Application Developer:** Austin Lukaschewski. **Analytics Engineer:** Jack Hanley.

John Mozeliak

MAJOR LEAGUE STAFF
Telephone: (314) 345-9600.

Manager: Oliver Marmol. **Coaches: Bench**—Jared "Skip" Schumaker. **Pitching**—Mike Maddux. **Hitting**—Jeff Albert. **Assistant Hitting Coach**—Turner Ward. **First Base**—Richard "Stubby" Clapp. **Third Base**—Ron "Pop" Warner. **Bullpen**—Bryan Eversgerd. **Assistant Coach:** Willie McGee. **Assistant ML Hitting Coach:** Patrick Elkins. **Pitching Strategist:** Dusty Blake. **Bullpen Catchers**—Jamie Pogue, Kleininger Teran.

MEDICAL/PERFORMANCE
Head Orthopedist Surgeon: Dr. George Paletta. **Major League Medical Services Coordinator:** Brian Mahaffey. **Director of Medical Operations/Head Athletic Trainer:** Adam Olsen. **Director of Performance:** Robert Butler. **Assistant Athletic Trainers:** Chris Conroy. **Assistant Director, Performance:** Thomas Knox. **Performance Specialist & Physical Therapist:** Jason Shutt. **Strength & Conditioning Coach:** Lance Thomason. **Medical Adm/Asst Ath Trainer:** Keith Joynt. **Physical Therapist:** Matt Leonard.

PLAYER DEVELOPMENT
Asst. GM & Director, Player Development: Gary LaRocque. **Manager, Player Dev & Performance:** Emily Wiebe. **Coordinator, Player Development:** Antonio Mujica. **Minor League Instructors—Coordinator of Instruction:** Jose Oquendo. **Sr. Pitching Coordinator:** Tim Leveque. **Hitting Coordinator:** Russ Steinhorn. **Asst. Pitching Coordinator:** Dean Kiekhefer. **Jupiter Complex Pitching Coordinator/FCL Pitching Coach:** Rick Harig. **Asst. Hitting Coordinator:** Daniel Nicolaisen. **Special Advisors:** Ryan Ludwick & Jason Isringhausen. **Medical Coordinator:** Chris Whitman. **S&C Coordinator:** Frank Witkowski. **Rehab Coordinator:** Victor Kuri. **Technology Integration:** DC MacLea. **Performance Specialist:** Ross Hasegawa. **DR Medical Coordinator:** Pedro Betancourt. **Minor League Athletic Trainers:** Dan Martin (Memphis), Alex Wolfinger (Springfield), Paden Eveland (Peoria), Jeff Case (Palm Beach), Kiomy Martinez (FCL). **Minor League Strength & Conditioning Coaches:** Jacqueline Grover (Memphis), Dan Trapp (Springfield), Cambell Quirk (Palm Beach), Gerardo De Leon (DSL)

FARM SYSTEM

Class	Club (League)	Manager	Hitting Coach	Pitching Coach
Triple-A	Memphis	Ben Johnson	Brandon Allen	Dernier Orozco
Double-A	Springfield	Jose Leger	Tyger Pederson	Darwin Marrero
High-A	Peoria	Patrick Anderson	Willi Martin	Edwin Moreno
Low-A	Palm Beach	Gary Kendall	Kedeem Octave	Giovanni Carrara
Rookie	Cardinals (FCL)	Roberto Espinoza	Benard Gilkey	Rick Harig
Rookie	Cardinals Red (DSL)	Fray Peniche	Erick Almonte &Luis Cruz	Bill Villallanueva

SCOUTING
Fax: (314) 345-9519.

Assistant General Manager & Director of Scouting: Randy Flores. **Special Advisor to the Scouting Director:** Jamal Strong. **Amateur Manager, Domestic Scouting:** Ty Boyles. **National Crosscheckers:** Aaron Looper (Shawnee, OK), Zachary Mortimer (Pilesgrove, NJ), Jamal Strong (Surpirse, AZ). **Jabari Barnett** (Humble, TX), Aaron Krawiec (Gilbert, AZ), Clint Brown (Braselton, GA), Sean Moran (Furlong, PA) **Area Scouts:** Nick Longmire (Cumming, GA), Jason Bryans (Tecumseh, ON), TC Calhoun (Abingdon, VA), Keanan Lamb (Birmingham, AL), Josh Lopez (West Palm Beach, FL), Mike Garciaparra (Manhattan Beach, CA), Dirk Kinney (Lenexa, KS), Donnie Marbut (Olympia, WA), Jim Negrych (Phoenixville, PA), Pete Parise (Ok), Stacey Pettis (Brentwood, CA), Joe Quezada (Houston, TX), Chris Rodriguez (Los Angeles, CA), Mauricio Rubio (Tempe, AZ), Nathan Sopena (Cary, IL). **Part-Time Scouts:** Juan C Ramos (Caguas, PR), Paul Ah Yat (Hon, HI). **Manager, Pro Scouting:** Jared Odom (St. Louis, MO). **Special Assistant to Scouting Director:** Jeff Ishii (Chino, CA). **Professional Scouts:** Brian Hopkins (Holly Springs, NC), Jeff Ishii (Chino, CA), Aaron Klinic (Baltimore, MD), Deric McKamey (Cincinnati, OH), Craig Richmond (Tampa, FL) Joe Rigoli (Parsippany, NJ), Kerry Robinson (Ballwin, MO). **Assistant General Manager (International Scouting):** Moises Rodriguez. **Senior International Crosschecker:** Joe Almaraz. **International Crosschecker:** Damaso Espino. **Senior Latin American Crosschecker/DR Scouting Supervisor:** Angel Ovalles. **Latin American Crosschecker/DR Crosschecker:** Alix Martinez. **Dominican Republic Scouts:** Braly Guzman, Raymi Dicent, Filiberto Fernandez, Darluimis Almonte. **Venezuela Scouting Supervisor:** Jose Gonzalez Maestre. **Venezuela Scouts:** Estuar Ruiz, Jesus Perez, Neriel Morillo, Wilmer Castillo. **Mexico:** Ramon Garcia. **Colombia:** Carlos Balcazar

SAN DIEGO PADRES

Office and Mailing Address: Petco Park, 100 Park Blvd., San Diego, CA 92101.
Telephone: (619) 795-5000.
E-mail address: comments@padres.com. **Website:** www.padres.com. **Twitter:** @padres.
Facebook: www.facebook.com/padres. **Instagram:** www.instagram.com/padres

OWNERSHIP

Operated By: Padres LP. **Owner and Chairman:** Peter Seidler. **Vice Chairman:** Ron Fowler.

BUSINESS OPERATIONS

Chief Executive Officer: Erik Greupner. **EVP, Business Administration & General Counsel:** Caroline Perry. **SVP, People & Culture:** Sara Greenspan. **VP, Information Technology:** Ray Chan. **VP, Sports Programs:** Bill Johnston. **VP, Special Events:** Jaclyn Lash.

Ron Fowler

COMMUNITY RELATIONS/MILITARY AFFAIRS

Telephone: (619) 795-5265. **Fax:** (619) 795-5266. **SVP, Community Relations & Military Affairs:** Tom Seidler. **VP, Public Affairs:** Diana Puetz.

ENTERTAINMENT/MARKETING/COMMUNICATIONS/CREATIVE SERVICES

SVP, Chief Marketing Officer: Chris Connolly. **VP, Broadcasting & Entertainment:** Erik Meyer. **Sr. Director, Content:** Nicky Patriarca. **Director, Media Relations & Baseball Information:** Darren Feeney. **Director, Business Communications & Spanish Media Relations:** Danny Sanchez. **Director, Marketing:** Emily Wittig.

BALLPARK OPERATIONS/HOSPITALITY

VP, Ballpark Operations: Ken Kawachi. **Sr. Dir, Facility Services:** Randy McWilliams. **Sr. Director, Security/Transportation:** Kevin Dooley. **Sr. Director, Guest Experience:** Erin Sheehan. **Sr. Director, Field Operations:** Matt Balough.

TICKETING

Telephone: (619) 795-5500. **Fax:** (619) 795-5034. **SVP, Corporate Partnerships:** Sergio Del Prado. **VP, Ticket Sales and Service:** Curt Waugh. **VP, Partnership Services:** Eddie Quinn. **VP, Business Strategy & Analytics:** Scott Robish. **Sr. Director, Ticket Operations:** Jim Kiersnowski.

TRAVEL/CLUBHOUSE

Director, Player & Staff Services: TJ Lasita. **Home Clubhouse & Equipment Manager:** TJ Laidlaw. **Assistant Equipment Manager/Umpire Room Attendant:** Tony Petricca. **Visiting Clubhouse Manager:** Spencer Dallin.

BASEBALL OPERATIONS

Telephone: (619) 795-5077. **Fax:** (619) 795-5361.

President, Baseball Operations & General Manager: A.J. Preller. **VP/Assistant GM:** Josh Stein. **VP/Assistant GM:** Fred Uhlman Jr. **VP, Baseball Operations:** Nick Ennis. **Senior Advisor/Director, Player Personnel:** Logan White. **Special Assistants to the GM:** Moises Alou, Trevor Hoffman, James Keller, David Post. **Special Assistant to the GM/Field Coordinator:** Mark Conner. **Special Assistants & Advisors to Baseball Operations:** Allen Craig, A.J. Ellis, Glenn Hoffman, Ian Kinsler, Hideo Nomo, Chan Ho Park. **Senior Advisor, Scouting:** Ron Rizzi. **Director, Baseball Information Services:** Matt Klotsche. **Director, Baseball Administration & Special Assistant to the GM:** Michaelene Courtis. **Director, Baseball R&D:** Adam Esquer. **Assistant Director, Baseball R&D:** Cody Zupnick. **Manager of Amateur Analysis, Baseball R&D:** Layne Gross. **Senior Analyst, Baseball R&D:** Jeremy Muesing. **Analysts, Baseball R&D:** Mario Paciuc, Joseph Sutcliffe. **Director, Baseball Systems:** Wells Oliver. **Senior Developers, Baseball Systems:** Garret Doe, Michael Vanger. **Developer, Baseball Systems:** Gustavo Montalvo. **Director, Sports Science:** Nathan Landau. **Senior Performance Scientist:** Patrick Cherveny. **Biomechanist, Sports Science:** Jesus Ramos. **Sports Science Instructor:** Christian Wonders.

A.J. Preller

MAJOR LEAGUE STAFF

Manager: Bob Melvin. **Bench Coach:** Ryan Christenson. **Quality Control Coach:** Ryan Flaherty. **Pitching Coach:** Ruben Niebla. **Hitting Coach:** Michael Brdar. **First Base Coach:** David Macias. **Third Base Coach:** Matt Williams. **Bullpen Coach:** Ben Fritz. **Catching Coach:** Francisco Cervelli. **Senior Advisor to the Major League Coaching Staff:** Bryan Price. **Coordinator, Game Planning and Coaching Assistant:** Peter Summerville. **Bullpen Catcher:** Heberto Andrade. **Major League Batting Practice/Hitting Instructor:** Morgan Burkhart. **Major League Video Coordinator:** Joe McAlpin. **Major League Assistant Video Coordinator:** Adam Hunt. **Coordinator, Japanese Player Services:** Shingo Horie. **Coordinator, Advance Scouting:** Jim McKew. **Major League Coaching Assistant:** Justin Novak. **Korean Interpreter:** Leo Bae.

MEDICAL/TRAINING

Club Physician: UC San Diego Health—Dr. Catherine Robertson, Dr. Kenneth Taylor, Dr. Bryan Leek. **Director, Player Health & Performance:** Don Tricker. **Head Athletic Trainer:** Mark Rogow. **ML Physical Therapist:** Scott Hacker. **ML Assistant Athletic Trainers:** Ben Fraser, Ricky Huerta. **ML S&C Coach:** Jay Young. **Coordinator, Performance Nutrition & Baseball Dietician:** Whitney Milano. **Massage Therapists:** Yuji Nagahama, Atsushi Nakasone.

PLAYER DEVELOPMENT

Director, Player Development: Ryley Westman. **Assistant Director, Player Development:** Mike Daly. **Manager, Player Development:** Brett Becker. **Manager, Player Development Video Operations:** Ethan Dixon. **Manager, Player Programming & Performance:** Vinny Lopez. **Manager, Minor League Clubhouse & Equipment:** Zach Nelson. **Manager, Minor Leagues/Peoria Operations:** Todd Stephenson. **Manager, Learning, Education & Life Skills:** Kaitlyn Teske. **Special Assistant, Player Development:** Steve Finley. **Player Development Consultant:** Mike Shildt. **On-Field Coordinators & Instructors:** Rob Marcello (director of pitching development), Oscar Bernard & Mike McCoy (hitting), Ryan Barba (infield), Brian Whatley (catching), Paul Porter (minor league ATC), JoJo Tarantino (minor league medical administration), Ryo Naito (S&C). **Physical Therapists:** Aaron Wengertsman, Taylor McWilliams. **Advisor, Professional Development:** Jason Amoroso. **Coordinator, International Player Development:** Vicente Cafaro. **Coordinator, Mental Skills:** Rosa Pou. **Assistant, PD Technology & Video:** Clinton Sewell. **Clubhouse Assistant:** Kyle Ross.

FARM SYSTEM

Class	Farm Club (League)	Manager	Hitting Coach	Pitching Coach
Triple-A	El Paso	Jared Sandberg	Jonathan Mathews	Mike McCarthy
Double-A	San Antonio	Phillip Wellman	Raul Padron	Pete Zamora
High-A	Fort Wayne	Brian Esposito	Randolph Gassaway	Jimmy Jones
Low-A	Lake Elsinore	Eric Junge	Pat O'Sullivan	Leo Rosales
Rookie	Padres (ACL)	Lukas Ray	M. Del Castillo/J. Morris	C. Chavez/R. Price
Rookie	Padres (DSL)	Luis Mendez	Yunir Garcia	N. Cruz/J. Quezada

SCOUTING

Vice President, Amateur & International Scouting: Chris Kemp. **Vice President, Professional Scouting:** Pete DeYoung. **Director, Latin American Operations:** Cesar Rizik. **Director, Pacific Rim Operations:** Acey Kohrogi. **Scouting Crosschecker:** Luke Murton. **Amateur Scouting Supervisors:** Nick Brannon, Josh Emmerick, Mike Kanen, Kurt Kemp, Andrew Salvo. **Amateur Scouting Coordinators:** Max Kraust, Spencer Babcock. **Area & Amateur Scouts:** Doug Banks, Justin Baughman, Clint Harrison, Troy Hoerner, Chris Kemlo, Matthew Maloney, John Martin, John McNamara, Stephen Moritz, Tim Reynolds, Willie Ronda, Danny Sader, Matt Schaffner, Will Scott, Jack Shannon, Tyler Stubblefield, Tyler Watson. **Special Assistants, Professional Scouting:** Keith Boeck, Spencer Graham. **Professional Scouting Crosscheckers:** Mike Juhl, Chuck LaMar, Dominic Viola. **Professional Scouts:** Patrick Coghlan, Kimball Crossley, Tim Holt, Chris Kusiolek, Spike Lundberg, Mark Merila, Mac Seibert, Tyler Tufts, Mike Venafro, Cory Wade, Jacob Zweiback. **International Scouting Supervisors:** Trevor Schumm, Bill McLaughlin. **Area Scout/International Crosscheckers:** Jake Koenig, Cliff Terracuso. **Scouting Coordinator, Dominican Republic:** Alvin Duran. **Administrator, International Operations:** Franklyn Peguero. **International Scouts:** Antonio Alejos, Andres Cabadias, Emenejildo Diaz, Jhonathan Feliz, Po-Hsuan Keng, Sherman Lacrus, Richard Montenegro, Luis Prieto, Hoon Namgung, Keiji Uezono, Jose Salado, Damian Shanahan, Carlos Taveras. Administrative Assistant, International Operations: Martina Pereyra.

SAN FRANCISCO GIANTS

Office Address: Oracle Park, 24 Willie Mays Plaza, San Francisco, CA 94107.
Telephone: (415) 972-2000. **Fax:** (415) 947-2800. **Website:** sfgiants.com, sfgigantes.com.

OWNERSHIP

Operated By: San Francisco Baseball Associates L.P.

BUSINESS OPERATIONS

President/Chief Executive Officer: Laurence M. Baer. **Executive VP:** Brian R. Sabean.
Senior Executive Advisor: Staci Slaughter. **Special Assistants:** Will Clark, Willie Mays. **Special Advisors:** Barry Bonds, Bruce Bochy.

Laurence M. Baer

FINANCE/LEGAL/INFORMATION TECHNOLOGY

Executive Vice President & Chief Legal Officer: Jack F. Bair. **Senior Vice President & General Counsel:** Amy Tovar. **Senior VP/Chief Financial Officer:** Lisa Pantages. **Senior VP/ CIO:** Bill Schlough. **VP, Information Technology:** Ken Logan. **VP, Finance:** Chris Rossi.

ADMINISTRATION

Executive VP, Administration: Alfonso Felder. **Senior Vice President & Chief Venue Officer, Oracle Park:** Jorge Costa. **VP, Ballpark Operations:** Gene Telucci. **VP, Security:** Tinie Roberson. **Vice President, Guest Services:** Alexis Lustbader. **Senior Vice President & Chief People Officer:** Jose Martin. **Vice President, Human Resources:** Lan Huynh Lee. **President, Giants Enterprises:** Stephen Revetria. **VP, Giants Enterprises:** Joey Nevin. **Senior VP, Event Strategy & Services:** Sara Grauf.

COMMUNICATIONS &COMMUNITY RELATIONS

Telephone: (415) 972-2445. **Fax:** (415) 947-2800. **Senior Vice President, Communications & Community Relations:** Shana Daum. **Executive Assistant to the Senior VP, Communications & Community Relations:** Lyz Socha. **Executive Director, Giants Community Fund:** Sue Petersen. **Vice President, Media Relations:** Matt Chisholm. **Senior Director, Broadcast Communications & Media Operations:** Maria Jacinto. **Senior Manager, Hispanic Communications & Marketing:** Erwin Higueros. **Media Relations Manager:** Megan Brown. **Baseball Information Manager:** Mike Passanisi.

BUSINESS OPERATIONS

Executive VP, Business Operations: Mario Alioto. **Senior Vice President & Chief Business Development Officer:** Jason Pearl. **VP, Marketing/Advertising:** Danny Dann. **Vice President,Content & Entertainment:** Paul Hodges. **Vice President, Brand Development & Digital Media:** Bryan Srabian. **PA Announcer:** Renel Brooks-Moon.

TICKETING

Telephone: (415) 972-2000. **Fax:** (415) 972-2500.
Senior VP, Ticket Sales/Services: Russ Stanley. **Vice President, Ticket & Premium Revenue:** Jeff Tucker. **VP, Business Analytics:** Rocky Koplik.

BASEBALL OPERATIONS

President of Baseball Ops.: Farhan Zaidi. **General Manager:** Scott Harris. **Senior Advisor to President of Baseball Ops:** JP Ricciardi, John Barr. **VP/Assistant GM:** Jeremy Shelley. **VP, Baseball Resources and Development:** Yeshayah Goldfarb. **VP, Player Performance and Wellness:** Colin Cahill. **VP, Pro Scouting:** Zack Minasian. **Special Assistant, Scouting:** Craig Weissmann. **Special Assistant to Baseball Ops:** Felipe Alou. **Executive Assistant to Baseball Ops/Administration:** Karen Sweeney. **VP, Baseball Analytics:** Paul Bien. **Director of Player Personnel Administration:** Clara Ho-Frawley. **Director, Baseball Analytics:** Michael Schwartze. **Baseball Ops Analyst:** Rohanna Pacheco, Simon Ricci, Mark Ferraro, Jimmy Kerr. **Senior Data Scientist:** Greg Starek. **Data Scientist:** Brian Huey. **Staff Software Engineer, Baseball Systems:** Kevin Deggelman. **Senior Software Engineer, Baseball Systems:** Alex Case, Eddie Elliott. **Software Engineer:** Rob Bertucci, Krystine Xie, Matt Fong, Jack McGeary. **Assistant, Baseball Ops:** Josh Zimmerman.

Farhan Zaidi

MAJOR LEAGUE STAFF

Manager: Gabe Kapler. **Coaches: Bench**—Kai Correa. **Director of Pitching**—Brian Bannister. **Pitching Coach**—Andrew Bailey. **Asst Pitching Coach**—J.P. Martinez. **Hitting Coach**—Justin Viele. **Director of Hitting/ML Assistant Hitting Coach:** Dustin Lind. **Assistant Hitting Coach:** Pedro Guerrero. **Third Base Coach**—Mark Hallberg. **First Base Coach**—Antoan Richardson. **Bullpen**—Craig Albernaz. **Quality Assurance Coach:** Nick Ortiz. **Assistant Coaches:** Alyssa Nakken, Taira Uematsu. **Director, Video Coaching:** Fernando Perez. **Video Coaching Assistant:** Kit Larson. **Bullpen Catchers:** Alex Burg, Brant Whiting. **Batting Practice Pitcher:** John Yandle.

MEDICAL/TRAINING

Head Team Physician: Dr. Anthony Saglimbeni. **Head Team Orthopedist:** Dr. Ken Akizuki. **Team Physicians:** Dr. Robert Murray, Dr. Chris Chung. **Team Orthopedist:** Dr. Ben Ma. **Senior Dir. of Athletic Training:** Dave Groeschner. **Head Athletic Trainer:** Anthony Reyes. **Asst. Athletic Trainer:** LJ Petra. **Physical Therapist:** Tony Reale. **Strength & Conditioning Coach:** Brad Lawson. **Asst. Strength & Conditioning Coach/Sports Science Specialist:** Saul Martinez. **Massage Therapist:** Hiroki Sato. **Coordinator, Medical Admin.:** Chrissy Yuen. **Dir. of Performance Nutrition:** Leron Sarig. **Medical Review Analyst:** Eric Ortega.

PLAYER DEVELOPMENT

Sr. Director, Player Development: Kyle Haines. **Assistant Director, Education & Cultural Development:** Laura Nuñez. **Minor League Medical Director:** Dustin Luepker. **Director, Arizona Field Operations:** Josh Warstler. **Manager, Minor League Operations:** Gabriel Alvarez. **Field Coordinator:** Tony Diggs. **Coordinator, Latin America Development:** Hector Borg. **Assistant Field/Infield Coordinator:** Jason Wood. **Pitching Coordinator:** Justin Lehr. **Hitting Coordinator:** Ed Lucas. **Assistant Pitching Coordinator:** Clay Rapada. **Assistant Hitting Coordinator:** Jacob Cruz. **Outfield/Baserunning Coordinator:** Tim Leiper. **Catching Coordinator:** Lance Burkhart. **Rehab Pitching Coordinator:** Matt Yourkin. **Coordinator, Pitching Sciences:** Matt Daniels. **Roving Hitting Instructor:** Pat Burrell. **Roving Pitching Instructor:** Ryan Vogelsong. **Baseball Operations Analyst:** Mark Ferraro. **Minor League Clubhouse and Equipment Coordinator:** Ryan Stiles. **Minor League Operations Coordinator:** Jacob Koch. **Minor League Video and Technology Coordinator:** Nick Horning. **Minor League Medical Coordinator:** Ryo Watanabe. **Minor League S&C Coordinator:** Andy King. **Mental Health Coordinator:** Emily Cheatum. **Latin America S&C Coordinators:** Sergio Rojas, Andrea Nuñez. **Mental Skills Coaches:** Kellen Lee, Francisco Rodriguez. **Minor League Nutrition Coordinator:** Adam Rodriguez. **Manager, Minor League Field Operations:** Jeff Winsor.

FARM SYSTEM

Class	Farm Club (League)	Manager	Hitting Coach	Pitching Coach
Triple-A	Sacramento	Dave Brundage	Damon Minor	Garvin Alston
Double-A	Richmond	Dennis Pelfrey	Danny Santin	Paul Oseguera
High-A	Eugene	Carlos Valderrama	Cory Elasik	Alain Quijano
Low-A	San Jose	Lipso Nava	Travis Ishikawa	Dan Runzler
Rookie	Giants Orange (ACL)	Jose Montilla	Mike McCormack	Michael Couchee
Rookie	Giants Black (ACL)	Greg Tagart	Craig Maddox	Mario Rodriguez
Rookie	Giants 1 (DSL)	Drew Martinez	Juan Parra	Luis Pino
Rookie	Giants 2 (DSL)	Juan Ciriaco	Rob Riggins	Osiris Matos

SCOUTING

VP, Pro Scouting: Zack Minasian. **Senior Director, Amateur Scouting:** Michael Holmes. **Senior Director, International Scouting:** Joe Salermo. **Director, International Scouting:** Felix Peguero. **Director of International Operations/Baseball Administration:** Jose Bonilla. **Coordinator of Amateur Scouting:** Mike Navolio. **Pro Scouts:** Ellis Burks, Keith Champion, Jim D'Aloia, Steve Decker, Ben McDonough, Ross Pruitt, Steve Riha, Ryan Thompson, Shane Turner. **Senior Advisors to President:** JP Ricciardi, John Barr. **Special Assistant, Scouting:** Craig Weissmann. **National Crosscheckers:** Brian Bridges, John Castleberry. **National Pitching Coordinator:** Dan Murray. **Scouting Supervisors: Northeast**—Arnold Brathwaite, **Southeast**—Jim Buckley, **Midwest**—Andrew Jefferson, **West**—Matt Woodward. **Area Scouts:** Jose Alou, Ray Callari, Brad Cameron, Larry Casian, Todd Coryell, John DiCarlo, Paul Faulk, Jim Gabella, Chuck Hensley Jr., DJ Jauss, Michael Kendall, Nick Long, James Mouton, Jared Schlehuber, Tom Shafer, Keith Snider, Jeff Wood. **International Crosscheckers:** Jose Alou, Michael Silvestri, Charlie Sullivan. **Director, Venezuela Scouting:** Ciro Villalobos. **Venezuela Crosschecker:** Edgar Fernandez. **Asst. Director & Dominican Republic Crosschecker:** Jesus Stephens. **Supervisor, Dominican Republic:** Gabriel Elias. **Scouts, Dominican Republic:** Abner Abreu, Jonathan Bautista, Andrew Polonia, Michel De Jesus. **Scouting Video Coordinator:** Carlos Reyes. **Scouts, Venezuela:** Joanthan Arraiz, Jose Beyron, Carlos Leon, Juan Marquez, Oscar Montero, Robert Moron, Ciro Villalobos Jr. **Scout, Colombia:** Daniel Mavarez. **Scout, Nicaragua:** Sandy Moreno. **Scout, Panama:** Rogelio Castillo. **Scout, Pacific Rim:** Evan Hsueh.

SEATTLE MARINERS

Office Address: 1250 First Ave. South, Seattle, WA 98134.
Mailing Address: PO Box 4100, Seattle, WA 98194.
Telephone: (206) 346-4000. **Fax:** (206) 346-4400. **Website:** www.mariners.com.

OWNERSHIP
Board of Directors: John Stanton (Chairman), John Ellis, Howard Lincoln (Chairman Emeriti), Chris Larson, Jeff Raikes, Buck Ferguson, Betsy Pepper Larson. **President, Business Operations:** Catie Griggs. **Senior VP/Special Advisor to the Chairman and CEO:** Randy Adamack.

BUSINESS OPERATIONS

John Stanton

FINANCE
Executive Vice President and CFO: Tim Kornegay. **VP, Finance:** Greg Massey. **Director, Internal Audit Operations:** Connie McKay.

LEGAL & GOVERNMENTAL AFFAIRS/ COMMUNITY RELATIONS
Executive Vice President and General Counsel: Fred Rivera. **VP, Deputy General Counsel:** Melissa Robertson. **Senior VP, People and Culture:** Lisa Winsby. **VP, People and Culture:** Brooke Sullivan.

SALES
Senior VP, Sales: Frances Traisman. **VP, Corporate Partnerships:** Charles Johnson. **Senior Director, Partnerships & Strategy/Activation:** Ingrid Russell-Narcisse. **VP, Ticket Sales & Service:** Cory Carbary.

MARKETING/COMMUNICATIONS
Telephone: (206) 346-4000. **Fax:** (206) 346-4400.
Senior VP, Marketing/Communications: Kevin Martinez. **VP, Communications:** Tim Hevly. **VP, Marketing:** Gregg Greene. **Senior Director, Public Information:** Rebecca Hale. **Senior Manager, Baseball Information:** Kelly Munro. **Coordinators, Baseball Information:** Adam Gresch, Alex Mayer. **Senior Director, Mariners Productions:** Ben Mertens. **Senior Director, Marketing:** Mandy Lincoln. **Director, Graphic Design:** Carl Morton. **Director, Strategic Marketing & Sales:** Haley Durmer. **Director, Digital Marketing:** Tim Walsh.

TICKETING
Telephone: (206) 346-4001. **Fax:** (206) 346-4100.
VP, Fan Experience: Malcolm Rogel. **Senior Director, Ticket Services:** Jennifer Sweigert.

STADIUM OPERATIONS
Senior VP, Ballpark Events & Operations: Trevor Gooby. **Senior Director, Event Sales:** Alisia Anderson. **Director, Ballpark Services:** Juan Rodriguez. **Director, Security:** Michael Bogosian. **Director, Facilities:** Dave Wilke. **Senior VP, Information Technology:** Kari Escobedo. **VP, Product & Technology:** Letitia Selk. **Director, Information Systems:** Oliver Roy. **Director, Database/Applications:** Justin Stolmeier.
Senior Director, Procurement: Norma Cantu. **Head Groundskeeper:** Tim Wilson. **PA Announcer:** Tom Hutyler.

MERCHANDISING
Sr. Director, Retail Operations: Julie McGillivray. **Director, Retail Merchandising:** Renee Steyh. **Director, Retail Stores:** Mary Beeman.

TRAVEL/CLUBHOUSE
Director, Major League Operations: Jack Mosimann. **Clubhouse Managers:** Chris DeWitt and Joe Van Vleck. **Visiting Clubhouse Manager:** Jeff Bopp. **Video Coordinator:** Patrick Hafner.

BASEBALL OPERATIONS

President, Baseball Operations: Jerry Dipoto.
VP, Assistant GM: Justin Hollander **Director, Major League Operations:** Jack Mosimann. **Director, Baseball Operations:** Tim Stanton. **Director, Baseball Projects:** David Hesslink. **Coordinator, Advance Scouting:** Sam Reinertsen. **Director, Data Strategy:** Skylar Shibayama. **Senior Director, Analytics:** Jesse Smith. **Director, Analytics:** Joel Firman. **Manager, Analytics:** John Choiniere.

Jerry Dipoto

MAJOR LEAGUE STAFF
Manager: Scott Servais. **Pitching**—Pete Woodworth. **Hitting**—Jarret DeHart. **Hitting**—Tony Arnerich. **First Base**—Kristopher Negrón. **Third Base**—Manny Acta. **Bullpen**—Trent Blank. **Infield Coach**—Perry Hill. **Field Coordinator**—Carson Vitale. **ML Coach**—Andy McKay. **Bullpen Catcher**—Fleming Báez. **Batting Practice Pitcher**—Nasusel Cabrera. **Video Coordinator:** Patrick Hafner. **Video Assistant:** Dan Kaplan.

MEDICAL/TRAINING
Head Orthopedist: Dr. Jason King. **Sr. Director, High Performance:** Rob Scheidegger. **Head Athletic Trainer:** Kyle Torgerson. **Asst. Athletic Trainer:** Taylor Bennett, Kevin Orloski. **Physical Therapist:** Ryan Bitzel. **Director, Performance Training:** James Clifford. **Asst. Performance Specialist:** Derek Cantieni. **Director, Sports Science:** Kate Weiss.

PLAYER DEVELOPMENT
Telephone: (206) 346-4316. **Fax:** (206) 346-4300.
Sr. Director, Baseball Development: Andy McKay. **Director, Player Development:** Emanuel Sifuentes. **Asst. Director, Player Development:** Mat Snider. **Special Assistants, Player Development:** Alvin Davis, Dan Wilson, Mike Cameron, Franklin Gutiérrez, Hisashi Iwakuma. **Manager, Rehab and Return to Play:** John Walker. **Director, Hitting Strategy:** Jarret DeHart. **Director, Pitching Strategy:** Trent Blank. **Hitting Strategist:** Edward Paparella. **Pitching Strategist:** Ken Roberts. **Pitching Strategist and Rehab Coordinator:** Ari Ronick. **Field Coordinator:** Louis Boyd. **Hitting Coordinator:** CJ Gillman. **Pitching Coordinator:** Max Weiner. **Catching Coordinator:** Zac Livingston. **Performance Specialist Coordinator:** Jeff Mathers.

FARM SYSTEM

Class	Club (League)	Manager	Hitting Coach	Pitching Coach
Triple-A	Tacoma	Tim Federowicz	Brad Marcelino	Alon Leichman
Double-A	Arkansas	Collin Cowgill	Shawn O'Malley	Sean McGrath
High-A	Everett	Eric Farris	Ryan McLaughlin	Matt Pierpont
Low-A	Modesto	Austin Knight	Michael Fransoso	Nathan Bannister
Rookie	Peoria (ACL)	Luis Caballero	Brett Schneider	Yoel Monzon
Rookie	Mariners (DSL)	TBD	TBD	Jose Amancio

SCOUTING
Director, Amateur Scouting: Scott Hunter. **Asst. Director, Amateur Scouting:** Frankie Piliere. **Director, Player Personnel:** Brendan Domaracki. **Global Crosschecker:** Carlos Gomez (Miami, FL). **Crosscheckers:** Ben Collman (German Valley, IL), Jesse Kapellusch (Cooper City, FL), Mark Lummus (Godley, TX), Devitt Moore (Bryn Mawr, PA). **Regional Scouts:** Ty Bowman (Phoenix, AZ), Dan Holcomb (Nashville, TN), Ryan Holmes (Thousand Oaks, CA), Tyler Holub (Durham, NC), Bobby Korecky (Estero, FL), Jackson Laumann (Florence, KY), Derek Miller (Sugar Land, TX), Rob Mummau (Palm Harbor, FL), Patrick O'Grady (Dallas, TX), David Pepe (Boonton, NJ), Joe Saunders (Chicago, IL), John Wiedenbauer (Jacksonville, FL). **Coordinator, Player Personnel:** Austin Yamada. **Scouting Analysts:** Matt Ault, Matt Doughty, Tyler Warmoth. **Director, International Amateur Scouting:** Frankie Thon (Doral, FL). **Asst. Director, International Scouting:** Andrew Herrera. **International Crosschecker:** Kevin Fox (Roseville, CA). **Supervisor, Dominican Republic:** Audo Vicente (Santo Domingo, DR). **Latin America Supervisor:** David Brito (Baranquilla, CO). **Venezuela Supervisor:** Federico Hernandez (Caracas, VZ). **International Scouts:** Felipe Burin (Brazil), Alfredo Celestin (D.R.), Rodrigo Cortez (Venezuela) Franklin Diaz (D.R.) Luis Fuenmayor (Venezuela), Kenny Hart (Aruba & Curacao), Sam Kao (Taiwan), Luis Martinez (Venezuela), Rafael Mateo (D.R.), Manabu Noto (Japan), Rigoberto Rangel (Panama), Ismael Rosado (Dominican Republic), Illich Salazar (Venezuela), David Velazquez (Mexico).

TAMPA BAY RAYS

Office Address: Tropicana Field, One Tropicana Drive, St. Petersburg, FL 33705.
Telephone: (727) 825-3137. **Fax:** (727) 825-3111.

OWNERSHIP
Principal Owner: Stuart Sternberg.

BUSINESS OPERATIONS
Presidents: Brian Auld, Matt Silverman
Chief Development Officer: Melanie Lenz. **Senior Vice President, Administration/
General Counsel:** John Higgins. **President, Baseball Operations:** Erik Neander. **Chief Public
Affairs & Communications Officer:** Rafaela A. Amador. **VP/Chief Financial Officer:** Rob
Gagliardi. **Chief Technology Officer:** Juan Ramirez. **Chief People & Culture Officer:** Jenn
Tran. **Chief Business Officer:** Bill Walsh. **Chief People & Community Officer:** Bill Wiener Jr.
Senior Vice President of Baseball Operations/General Manager: Peter Bendix. **VP, Baseball
Development:** Will Cousins. **VP, Baseball Operations:** Chanda Lawdermilk, Carlos Rodriguez.
VP, Corporate Partnerships: Brian Richeson. **VP, Ticket Sales and Service:** Jeff Tanzer. **VP,
Fan Experience:** Eric Weisberg.

Stuart Sternberg

DOUG BENC/GETTY IMAGES

FINANCE
Senior Director, Controller: Patrick Smith. **Director, Financial Planning and Analysis:**
Jason Gray.

MARKETING/COMMUNITY RELATIONS
Senior Director, Creative: Warren Hypes. **Director, Marketing:** Emily Miller. **Executive Director, Rays Baseball
Foundation:** David Egles. **Director, Community Engagement:** Kim Couts.

GAME OPERATIONS
Director, Game Presentation & Production: Mike Weinman. **Director, Promotions:** Stephon Thomas.

COMMUNICATIONS/BROADCASTING
Senior Director, Broadcasting: Larry McCabe. **Director, Public Affairs & Corporate Communications:** Devin
O'Connell. **Senior Director, Diversity, Equity & Inclusion:** Stephen Thomas.

CORPORATE PARTNERSHIPS
Director, Corporate Partnerships Sales: Anthony Rioles. **Director, Corporate Partnerships Services:** Sean Liston.

STADIUM OPERATIONS
Senior Director, Building Operations: George Dowling. **Senior Director, Partner and VIP Relations:** Cass Halpin.
Senior Director, Security & Stadium Operations: Jim Previtera. **Director, Building Operations:** Chris Raineri.
Director, Stadium Operations: Mike Ferrario. **Head Groundskeeper & Director of Operations, Charlotte Sports
Park:** Dan Moeller.

STRATEGY & DEVELOPMENT/TICKET SALES & SERVICES
Director, Strategy & Development: Josh Momberg, Robbie Artz. **Director, Ticket Operations:** Robert Bennett.
Director, Ticket Sales & Service: Dan Newhart. **Director, Ticket Services & Technology:** Matt Fitzpatrick. **Assistant
Director, Ticket Operations:** Ken Mallory.

MEDICAL/TRAINING
Medical Director: Dr. James Andrews. **Orthopedic Team Physician:** Dr. Koco Eaton. **Massage Therapists:** Ray Allen,
Homare Watanabe. **ML Medical Coordinator:** Paul Harker. **Head Trainer:** Joe Benge. **First Assistant ATC:** Michael
Sandoval. **Assistant ATC:** Aaron Scott. **Special Projects:** Mark Vinson. **S&C:** Trung Cao (Head), Joey Greany (Assistant),
Bryan King (Rehab).

BASEBALL OPERATIONS

President: Erik Neander. **Senior VP Baseball Operations/GM:** Peter Bendix. **VP, Baseball Operations:** Chanda Lawdermilk, Carlos Rodriguez. **VP, Baseball Development:** Will Cousins. **Special Assistant to the President and GM:** Bobby Heck. **Special Assistant, Baseball Operations:** Denard Span. **Senior Advisor, Player Development and Baseball Operations:** Mitch Lukevics. **Senior Advisor, Scouting/Baseball Operations:** R.J. Harrison. **Senior Director, Baseball Systems:** Brian Plexico. **Senior Director, Team Travel and Logistics:** Chris Westmoreland. **Director, Baseball Operations:** Cole Figueroa, Hamilton Marx. **Director, Development Strategy:** Sandy Sternberg. **Director, Baseball Performance Science:** Joe Myers. **Director, Predictive Modeling:** Taylor Smith. **Baseball Systems:** Clayton Elger, Todd Daniels, Brandon Cordell, Daniel Nolan, Luke Fair, Avery Wilkening, Ted Lopez, Lauren Griffin. **Manager, Baseball Operations:** Samantha Bireley. **Manager, Major League Operations:** Jeremy Sowers. **Lead Analysts, R&D:** Salem Marrero, David Marshall. **Senior Analysts R&D:** Emmie Dolfi, Michael McClellan, Jason Pellettiere. **Analysts:** Vibhor Agarwal, Josh Arthurs, Bryant Davis, Michael Topol, John Williams, JJ Lamb, Jeff Sullivan, Keegan Henderson. **Junior Analysts, R&D:** Michael Model, Tim Morales, Ben Smith. Jr. **Data Technician R&D:** David Yamin. **Coordinators:** Bobby Kinne, Brad Ballew, Dani Dockx, Elly Weller, Grace Dowling, Mike Lambiaso, Vishnu Sarpeshkar. **Assistants:** Mathew Bennett, Matt Bruno, Allison DeKuiper, Max Kassan, Randell Kanemaru, Seiya Sano. **MnL Video Coordinator:** Michael O'Toole. **Lead Sports Dietician:** Courtney Ellison. **Head of Mental Performance:** Justin Su'a. **Lead Biomechanist:** Mike McNally. **Applied Biomechanist:** Jillian Hawkins.

Erik Neander

SKIP MILOS

MAJOR LEAGUE STAFF

Manager: Kevin Cash. **Coaches: Bench**—Matt Quatraro, **Pitching**—Kyle Snyder, **Assistant Pitching/Rehab**—Rick Knapp. **Hitting**—Chad Mottola, **Assistant Hitting**—Dan Dement, Brady North, **First Base**—Chris Prieto, **Third Base**—Rodney Linares, **Bullpen**—Stan Boroski, **Field Coordinator**—Paul Hoover. **Process/Analytics Coach**—Jonathan Erlichman.

PLAYER DEVELOPMENT

Director, Minor League Operations: Jeff McLerran. **Assistant Director, Minor League Operations:** George Pappas. **Assistant Director, Minor League Operations/Baseball Development:** Simon Rosenbaum. **AD, Performance Science/Player Development:** Ryan Pennell. **Sr. Administrator, International/Minor League Operations:** Giovanna Rodriguez. **Pitching Strategist:** Winston Doom. **Coordinator, Training Methods:** Brett Ebers. **Coordinator, Minor League Operations:** Wilson Made. **Coordinator, Minor League and International Operations:** Jeremy Sanders. **Assistant, Minor League/Baseball Operations:** Isha Rahman. **Minor League Equipment Manager:** Tim McKechney. **Assistant Minor League Equipment Manager:** Shane Rossetti. **Education Coordinator:** Lenore Sanchez. **Advisor, Player Education:** Milton Jamail. **EAP:** Vince Lodato. **Field Coordinators:** Alejandro Freire, Michael Johns. **Minor League Coordinators: Pitching:** Jorge Moncada, Rolando Garza. **Hitting:** Steve Livesey, Kyle Wilson. **Catching:** Tomas Francisco. **Infield:** Ivan Ochoa. **OF/Baserunning:** Chris Constantine. **Medical:** Marty Brinker. **Rehab:** Joel Smith. **Latin America Medical Admin:** Oscar Orengo. **Latin America Cultural:** Jairo De La Rosa. **S&C:** Chris Osmond. **MnL Nutrition:** Al Roth. **Mental Performance:** Josh Kozuch. **Mental Performance Coaches:** Kris Goodman, Jenny Ferriter, Carla Diaz. **Clubhouse/MnL Nutrition Asst:** Sean Jones.

FARM SYSTEM

Class	Club (League)	Manager	Hitting Coach	Pitching Coach
Triple-A	Durham	Brady Williams	Will Bradley	Brian Reith
Double-A	Montgomery	Morgan Ensberg	Wuarner Rincones	Jim Paduch
High-A	Bowling Green	Jeff Smith	Paul Rozzelle	Alberto Bastardo
Low-A	Charleston	Blake Butera	Perry Roth	R.C. Lichtenstein
Rookie	Rays (FCL)	R. Valenzuela	J.Nelson/M. Castillo	L.Romero/J.Gonzalez
Rookie	Rays (DSL)	J. Zorrilla/H. Gimenez	Omar Luna	L. Urena/J. Sanchez

SCOUTING

Sr. Director, Pro Personnel & Pro Scouting: Kevin Ibach. **Assistant Director, Pro Personnel & Pro Scouting:** Ryan Bristow. **Analyst, Pro Personnel & Pro Scouting:** Tyler Chamberlain-Simon. **Sr. Director, Amateur Scouting:** Rob Metzler. **National Crosschecker:** Chuck Ricci. **Coordinator, Amateur Scouting:** David Hamlett, Sydney Malone. **Assistant, Amateur Scouting:** Jake Girard. **Special Assignment Scout:** Jeff Cornell. **Pro Personnel Specialists:** Mike Brown, Max Cohen, Jason Cole, Jason Grey, Nate Howard, Mike Langill, Tyler Stohr. **Pro Scouts:** Ken Califano, JD Elliby, Jose Gomez, Carlos Herazo, Ken Kravec, Dave Myers, Wood Myers, Eduardo Sanchez. **Regional Crosscheckers:** Rickey Drexler (South), Kevin Elfering (Southeast), Joe Hastings (Northeast), Brian Hickman (Midwest), Jake Wilson (West). **Pitching Crosschecker:** Ryan Henderson. **Scout Supervisors:** Matt Alison, Steve Ames, James Bonnici, CT Bradford, Zach Clark, Tom Couston, Brett Foley, Tim Fortugno, Luke Harrigan, Milt Hill, Chris Hom, Jaime Jones, Landon Lassiter, Reggie Lawson, ML Morgan, Brian Oliver. **Part-Time Area Scouts:** Jose Hernandez, Josh Jackson, Dave Jorn, Gil Martinez, Casey Onaga, Jack Sharp, Marcos Tovar, Lou Wieben. **International Crosschecker/South Florida Supervisor:** Victor Rodriguez. **Director, International Scouting:** Steve Miller. **Director, International Operations:** Patrick Walters. **Assistant Director, International Operations:** Ronnie Blanco. **Coordinator, International Scouting:** Jeff Johnson. **International Crosschecker:** Brad Budzinski. **Consultant, International Operations:** John Gilmore. **Scouting Supervisor, Colombia:** Angel Contreras. **Scouting Supervisor, Dominican Republic:** Danny Santana. **Venezuela Crosschecker:** William Bergolla. **Regional Crosschecker, Dominican Republic:** Rigo De Los Santos. **International Scouts:** Miguel De La Cruz, Felix Fermin, Remmy Hernandez, Jorge Perez (Dominican Republic), Marlon Roche, Juan Francisco Castillo, Carlos Leon, Frank Tineo (Venezuela), Tiago Campos (Brazil), Karla Espinoza, Keith Hsu (Taiwan), Chairon Isenia (Curacao), Joe Park (Korea), Tateki Uchibori (Japan), Gustavo Zapata (Panama), Alex Zuniga (Colombia).

TEXAS RANGERS

Office Address: 734 Stadium Drive, Arlington, TX 76011.
Telephone: (817) 273-5222. **Website:** www.texasrangers.com. **Twitter:** @Rangers.

OWNERSHIP

Managing Partner & Majority Owner: Ray C. Davis. **Executive Committee:** Bob R. Simpson. **President, Business Operations & Chief Operating Officer:** Neil Leibman.

BUSINESS OPERATIONS

President, REV Entertainment: Sean Decker. **Executive VP, Business Operations:** Rob Matwick. **Executive VP/CFO:** Kellie Fischer. **Executive VP/General Counsel:** Katie Pothier. **Executive VP, Public Affairs:** John Blake. **Executive VP, Ballpark Entertainment/Productions:** Chuck Morgan.

HUMAN RESOURCES/LEGAL/INFORMATION TECHNOLOGY

VP, Human Resources: Jeff Miller. **VP, Info Technology:** Mike Bullock. **Sr. Corporate Counsel:** Erin Kearney. **Director, Human Resources:** Mercedes Riley. **Corporate Counsel:** Robert Fountain. **Director, IT Infrastructure & Security:** Chris Hedrick. **Senior Desktop Engineer, IT Applications & Operations:** Greg Garrison. **Senior Engineers, Infrastructure & Security:** Justin Stockdale, Robert Wiggs.

Ray Davis

FINANCE

Sr. VP/Finance: Starr Gulledge. **Senior Accountants:** Kellie Alford, Shelley Bell. **Senior Treasury Accountant:** Michael Trybul.

COMMUNICATIONS/COMMUNITY IMPACT/FOUNDATION

Telephone: (817) 273-5203
VP, Broadcasting/Communications: Angie Swint. **VP, Media Relations:** Rich Rice. **Director, Radio Operations & Network Management:** Kaylan Eastepp. **Assistant Director, Baseball Information:** Matt Mallian. **Manager, Baseball Information & Media Services:** Tyler Strachan. **Manager, Communications:** Lauren Wyatt. **Sr. Coordinator, Alumni & Public Affairs:** Ashley Quintilone. **Manager, Photography:** Ben Ludeman. **Sr. Vice President, Community Impact & Executive Director, Texas Rangers Foundation:** Karin Morris. **Director, Youth Baseball and Youth Academy Programs:** Juan Leonel Garciga. **Director, Development:** Justin Henry. **Director, Community Impact:** Reynaldo Casas.

FACILITIES/GUEST SERVICES

Sr. VP, Venue Operations & Guest Experience: Mike Healy. **Sr. Director, Parking & Security:** Mike Smith. **Director, Parking Services:** Dana Jons. **Director, Major League Grounds:** Dennis Klein. **Director, Complex Grounds:** Steve Ballard. **Director, Facility Operations:** Gabriel Saenz. **Director, Guest Services:** Craig Hodnik. **Director, Engineering Services:** Grant Phifer.

TICKET AND SPONSORSHIP SALES

Sr. VP, Partnerships & Client Services: Jim Cochrane. **Vice President, Business Analytics & Ticket Strategy:** Katie Morgan. **Vice President, Ticket Sales:** Dan Hessling. **Vice President, Ticket Retention & New Business Development:** Nick Richardson. **Vice President, Corporate Partnerships:** Chad Wynn. **Director, Group Sales:** Jamie Roberts. **Director, Suites & Premium Services:** Delia Willms. **Director Ticket Operations:** Mike Lentz. **Director, Business Partnerships:** Brian Nephew. **Director, Corporate Partnerships:** Sean Ferretti.

MARKETING/GAME PRESENTATION

VP, Marketing: Travis Dillon. **Sr. Director, Game Entertainment/Productions:** Chris DeRuyscher. **Director, Marketing & Advertising:** Kyle Bartlett. **Creative Director:** Scott Biggers. **Director, Digital & Social Media:** Kyle Smith. **Art Director:** Cole Smith.

EVENTS/REV ENTERTAINMENT

VP, Events: Jared Schrom. **Sr. Director, Marketing:** Lindsey Hopper. **Sr. Director, Communications:** Madison Pelletier. **Sr. Director, Event Operations:** Pedro Soto, Jr.

BASEBALL OPERATIONS

Telephone: (817) 273-5222. **Fax:** (817) 273-5285.

President, Baseball Operations: Jon Daniels. **Executive VP/General Manager:** Chris Young. **VP/Assistant General Manager, Scouting:** Josh Boyd. **VP/Assistant General Manager, Player Development & International Scouting:** Ross Fenstermaker. **Special Assistants to the GM:** Colby Lewis, Brandon McCarthy, Darren Oliver, Ivan Rodriguez, Michael Young. **Sr. Director, Baseball Research & Development:** Ryan Murray. **Sr. Director, Player & Family Services:** Taunee Paur Taylor. **Sr. Director, Research & Development, Applications:** Daren Willman. **Director, Baseball Operations:** Paul Kruger. **Director, Baseball Administration & Executive Assistant:** Joda Parent. **Director, Leadership, Organizational Development, & Mental Performance:** Ben Baroody. **Director, Pitching Analysis:** Todd Walther. **Director, Travel:** Josh Shelton. **Director, Team Security:** Blake Miller. **Assistant Director, Baseball Operations:** Vinesh Kanthan. **Assistant, Pitching Analysis:** Rich Birfer-Karlin. **Assistant, Baseball Operations:** Leonard Yang. **Senior Analyst:** Alexander Booth.

Jon Daniels

Analysts, Baseball Operations: Bobby Bandelow, Justin Bedard, Brett Mele, Will Melville, Randall Puffer, Shravan Ramamurthy, R.J. Walsh. **Sr. Software Engineer:** Stephen Coward. **Data Engineer:** Ryan Stoll. **Major League Video Coordinator:** Adam Brenner. **Equipment & Home Clubhouse Manager:** Brandon Boyd. **Assistant Clubhouse Manager:** Dave Bales. **Visiting Clubhouse Manager:** Mason McKenna.

MAJOR LEAGUE STAFF

Manager: Chris Woodward.

Coaches: Bench/Offensive Coordinator—Donnie Ecker. **Pitching**—Doug Mathis, Brendan Sagara. **Hitting**—Tim Hyers. **First Base**—Corey Ragsdale. **Third Base**—Tony Beasley. **Bullpen**—Brett Hayes. **Catching**—Bobby Wilson. **Assistant Hitting Coach**—Seth Conner. **Assistant, Major League Staff**—Theo Hooper.

MEDICAL/TRAINING

Sr. Director, Medical Operations/Sports Science: Jamie Reed. **Team Physician:** Dr. Keith Meister. **Team Physician, Internal Medicine:** Dr. David Hunter. **Assistant Team Physicians:** Dr. Jesse Even, Dr. Tariq Hendawi, Dr. Shane Seroyer. **Head Trainer:** Matt Lucero. **Assistant Trainer:** Jacob Newburn. **Physical Therapist:** Regan Wong. **Strength/Conditioning Coach:** José Vázquez. **Assistant Strength/Conditioning Coach:** Al Sandoval. **Mental Skills Coach:** Mike Franco. **Message Therapist:** Raul Cardenas.

PLAYER DEVELOPMENT

Director, Player Development: Josh Bonifay. **Director, Minor League Operations:** Stosh Hoover. **Assistant Directors, Player Development:** Conner Gunn, Sam Niedorf. **Coordinator, Player Development Projects:** Jesse Behr. **Coordinators:** Kenny Holmberg (Field/Infield), Danny Clark (pitching), Jordan Tiegs (pitching), Cody Atkinson (director, hitting), Garrett Kennedy (catching), Turtle Thomas (roving catching coach), Keith Comstock (rehab). **Sr. Director, Performance:** Napoleon Pichardo. **Assistant Director, Performance:** Logan Frandsen. **Medical Coordinators:** Sean Fields, Chris Olson. **Nutrition Coordinator:** Ellen Rice. **Arizona Medical Consultant:** Dr. Julie Best. **Mental Performance:** David Franco, Hannah Huesman. **Physical Therapist:** Kaita Okitsu.

FARM SYSTEM

Class	Club (League)	Manager	Hitting Coach	Pitching Coach
Triple-A	Round Rock	Matt Hagen	Matt Lawson	Bill Simas
Double-A	Frisco	Jared Goedert	Eric Dorton	Jeff Andrews
High-A	Hickory	Carlos Cardoza	Ryan Tuntland	Jon Goebel
Low-A	Down East	Steve Mintz	Collin McBride	Demetre Kokoris
Rookie	Rangers (ACL)	Carlos Maldonado	Sharnol Adriana	J. Delgado/J. Jaimes/J. Valdez
Rookie	Rangers (DSL)	Kevin Torres	E. Gonzalez/E. Orona/E. Kingsdale	R. Valencia/T. St. Clair

SCOUTING

Director, Pro Scouting: Mike Parnell. **Special Assistants:** Mike Anderson, Scot Engler, Scott Littlefield, Greg Smith. **Pro Scouts:** Elliott Blair, Jay Eddings, Jonathan George, Mike Grouse, Touré Harris, Donzell McDonald, Michael Quesada. **Special Assignment Scout:** Curtis Jung.

Senior Director, Amateur Scouting: Kip Fagg. **Director, Amateur Scouting:** Adam Lewkowicz. **National Crosscheckers: Special Assignment Crosschecker:** Bobby Crook. **West Coast Crosschecker:** Casey Harvie. **National Crosschecker:** Jake Krug. **Southeast Crosschecker:** Arthur McConnehead. **Midwest Crosschecker:** Demond Smith. **Northern Crosschecker:** Brian Williams. **Area Scouts:** Brett Campbell, Tyler Carroll, Chris Collias, Tommy Duenas, Steve Flores, Jay Heafner, Levi Lacey, Brian Matthews, Gray McGraw, Michael Medici, Brian Morrison, Patrick Perry, Takeshi Sakurayama, Gabe Sandy, Josh Simpson, Dustin Smith.

Director, International Scouting & Development: Hamilton Wise. **Senior Advisor, International Scouting:** Rafic Saab. **Assistant Director, International Scouting & Development:** Jonny Clum. **Assistant, International Scouting:** Jack Marino. **Supervisor, Dominican Republic:** Willy Espinal. **International Crosscheckers:** Jhonny Gomez, Jesus "Chu" Halabi, Yfrain Linares, Chris Roque. **International Scouts:** Christian Cabral, Rafael Cedeno, Anthony Dominguez, Jose Fernandez, Efrain Lara, Daniel Liscano, Nelson Muniz, Carlos Plaza, Carlos Plaza Jr., Jose Gabriel Rodriguez, Maikol Rojas, Juan Salazar, Hamilton Sarabia, Cesar Sarmiento, Pablo Savinon.

Senior Advisor, Major League Scouting (Hokkaido): Randy Smith. **Coordinator, Pacific Rim Operations:** Joe Furukawa. **International Scouts:** Hajime Watabe (Japan), Daniel Chang (Taiwan).

TORONTO BLUE JAYS

Office/Mailing Address: 1 Blue Jays Way, Suite 3200, Toronto, Ontario M5V 1J1.
Telephone: (416) 341-1000. **Fax:** (416) 341-1245. **Website:** www.bluejays.com.

OWNERSHIP

Operated by: Toronto Blue Jays Baseball Club. **Principal Owner:** Rogers Communications Inc. **Chairman, Toronto Blue Jays:** Edward Rogers. **Vice Chairman, Rogers Communications Inc.:** Phil Lind. **President and CEO, Rogers Communication:** Anthony Staffieri. **President, Rogers Sports & Media, Rogers Communication:** Colette Watson.

BUSINESS OPERATIONS

President and CEO: Mark A. Shapiro. **President Emeritus:** Paul Beeston. **Executive Vice President, Baseball Operations/General Manager:** Ross Atkins. **Executive Vice President, Finance:** Ben Colabrese. **Executive Vice Presidents, Business Operations:** Anuk Karunaratne. **Executive Vice President, Marketing and Business Operations:** Marnie Starkman. **Executive Assistant to the President/CEO:** Gail Ricci.

Mark Shapiro

FINANCE/ADMINISTRATION

Director, Finance: Josh Hoffman. **Senior Manager, Blue Jays US Payroll & Benefits:** Sharon Dykstra. **Senior Manager, Finance:** Mark Murray. **Manager, Finance:** Leslie Galant-Gardiner. **Manager, Treasury & Vault Operations:** Garrett Mercer. **Senior Financial Analysts:** Melissa Patterson, Troy Mercuri. **Senior Payroll Analyst:** Joyce Chan. **Senior Payroll Analyst:** Joy Baybayan. **Finance Associate:** Marisa Paine

MARKETING/COMMUNITY RELATIONS

Vice President, Brand & Digital Marketing: Christine DesJardine. **Director, Creative Services & Marketing Management:** Sherry Oosterhuis. **Content Director:** George Skoutakis. **Director, Game Entertainment & Production:** Stefanie Wright. **Senior Manager, Player Relations & Community Marketing:** Shannon Curley. **Content Producer:** John Woo. **Program Manager, Amateur Baseball:** T.J. Burton. **Manager, Creative Services:** Maureen Kinghorn. **Marketing Department Manager & Alumni Relations:** Maria Cresswell. **Senior Motion Graphics Designer:** Michael Campbell. **Motion Graphics Designer:** Ben Simpson. **Social Community Manager:** Alykhan Ravjiani. **Social Content Specialist:** Nico Canavo. **Program Specialist, Amateur Baseball:** Jeff Holloway. **Authentics Specialist:** Mike Ferguson. **Program Assistant, Amateur Baseball:** Lucas McKernan. **Coordinator, Community Marketing:** Erinn White. **Coordinator, In-Game Entertainment & Production:** Shaina Gibson.

BASEBALL MEDIA

Communications Advisor & Liaison: Richard Griffin. **Director, Communications:** Jessica Beard. **Manager, Communications:** Madeleine Davidson. **Coordinators, Communications:** Adam Felton, Rodney Hiemstra.

TRAVEL/CLUBHOUSE

Director, Team Travel/Clubhouse Operations: Mike Shaw. **Senior Manager, Visiting Clubhouse:** Kevin Malloy. **Senior Manager, Clubhouse Operations:** Scott Blinn. **Manager, Home Clubhouse Operations:** Mustafa Hassan.

BASEBALL OPERATIONS

Senior Vice President, Player Personnel: Tony Lacava. **Vice President, International Scouting:** Andrew Tinnish. **Assistant General Manager:** Joe Sheehan. **Assistant General Manager:** Michael Murov. **Director, Team Travel & Clubhouse Operations:** Michael Shaw. **Director, Baseball Research:** Sanjay Choudhury. **Director, Baseball Operations:** Jeremy Reesor. **Director, Baseball Systems:** Peter Saunders. **Manager, Baseball Research:** Graydon Carruthers. **Coordinator, Baseball Research & Development:** Spencer Estey. **Coordinator, Baseball Research:** Adam Yudelman. **Coordinator, Game Planning:** Theron Simpson. **Coordinator, Baseball Research:** Liam Stevenson. **Coordinator, Baseball Operations:** Bryan Lee. **Player Personnel Analyst:** John Babocsi. **Assistant, Pro Scouting & Baseball Operations:** Megan Evans. **Major League Video Coordinator:** Eric Slotter. **Assistant, Advance Scouting:** Anthony Lucchese. **Executive Assistant to the General Manager:** Anna Coppola. **Bilingual Player Interpreter:** Hector Lebron. **Analytics Developer:** John Meloche. **Research Analyst:** Dan Goldberg. **Baseball Systems Engineer:** Alex Robson. **Assistant, Baseball Research & Development:** Gabrielle Campos. **Video Advisor:** Robert Baumander.

Ross Atkins

MAJOR LEAGUE STAFF

Manager: Charlie Montoyo. **Coaches: Bench—** John Schneider, **Pitching—**Pete Walker, **Hitting—**Guillermo Martinez, **First Base—**Mark Budzinski, **Third Base—**Luis Rivera, **Bullpen—**Matt Buschmann. **Major League Field Coordinator —** Gil Kim. **Major League Hitting Strategist—**Dave Hudgens. **Assistant Hitting Coach—**Hunter Mense. **Major League Pitching Strategist—**David Howell. **Major League Process Coach—**Adam Yudelman. **Bullpen Catchers:** Alex Andreopoulos, Luis Hurtado.

HIGH PERFORMANCE/MEDICAL STAFF

Assistant Director, High Performance Operations: Steve Rassel. **Assistant Director, High Performance Applied Performance Research:** Dehra Harris. **MiLB S&C Coordinator:** Aaron Spano. **S&C Latin American Coordinator:** Omar Aguilar. **ML Head S&C:** Scott Weberg. **ML Assistant S&C:** Jeremy Trach. **Rehab S&C:** Taylor Haslinger. **Dietitian Coordinator:** Kat Mangieri. **ML Dietitian:** Jeremy Chiang. **Mental Performance Coordinator:** Rob DiBernardo. **ML Mental Performance Coach:** Jimmy VanOstrand.

PLAYER DEVELOPMENT

Telephone: (727) 734-8007. **Fax:** (727) 734-8162.

Director, Player Development: Joe Sclafani. **Director, Minor League Operations:** Charlie Wilson. **Director, Pitching Development:** Matt Buschmann. **Director, Latin America Operations:** Sandy Rosario. **Field Coordinator:** Casey Candaele. **Short-Season Field Coordinator:** John Tamargo Jr. **Defense Coordinator:** Dallas McPherson. **Hitting Coordinator:** Hunter Mense. **Infield Coordinator:** Danny Solano. **Pitching Coordinator:** Cory Popham. **Pitching Coordinator:** Matt Tracy. **Coordinator, Player Development & HP Operations:** Will Habib. **Coordinator, Player Development & Amateur Scouting:** Reed Kienle. **Business Manager, Minor League Operations:** Michelle Rodgers. **Assistant, Player Development:** Michael Rivera. **MiLB Pitching Analyst:** Evan Short. **Coordinator, Technology Operations:** Matt von Roemer. **Assistant, Player Development Technology:** Jordan Eaddy. **Special Assistant to Player Development:** Tim Raines. **Swing Consultant & Affiliate Hitting Coach:** Matt Hague. **Rehab Pitching Coach:** Greg Vogt. **Rehab Position Player Coach:** Luis Silva.

FARM SYSTEM

Class	Club (League)	Manager	Hitting Coach	Pitching Coach	Position Coach
Triple-A	Buffalo	Casey Candaele	Corey Hart	Jeff Ware	Devon White
Double-A	New Hampshire	Cesar Martin	Matt Hague	Jim Czajkowski	Chris Schaeffer
High-A	Vancouver	Brent Lavallee	Ryan Wright	Phil Cundari	TBD
Low-A	Dunedin	Donnie Murphy	Matt Young	Drew Hayes	Danny Canellas
Rookie	Blue Jays (FCL)	Jose Mayorga	Paul Elliott	Cory Riordan	D. Holmberg
			Justin Echevarria	Antonio Caceres	Petr Strbicky
			Jaime Vieira	Robelin Bautista	
Rookie	Blue Jays (DSL)	Andy Fermin	Fred Landers	Yoel Hernandez	Barreto/Mateo

SCOUTING

Director, Pro Scouting: Ryan Mittleman. **Pro Scouting Analyst:** Tommy Farah. **Special Assignment Scout:** Russ Bove. **Special Assignment Scout:** Dean Decillis. **Major League Scouts:** Sal Butera, Jim Skaalen. **Professional Scouts:** Matt Anderson, Kevin Briand, Blake Bentley, Justin Coleman, David May Jr., Marc Lippman, Tim Rooney, Stephen Yoo. **Pacific Rim Scout:** Hideaki Sato. **Player Personnel Coordinators:** Carson Cistulli, Jon Lalonde, Nick Manno, Brent Urcheck. **Pro Scouting Fellow:** Dean Steinman. **Director, Amateur Scouting:** Shane Farrell. **Manager, Amateur & International Scouting:** Harry Einbinder. **Manager, Amateur Scouting:** Kory Lafreniere. **Amateur Scouting Analyst:** Chris Weikel. **Assistant, Scouting:** Matt McCue. **National Supervisor:** Blake Crosby. **Regional Crosscheckers:** CJ Ebarb, Jamie Lehman, Greg Runser, Noah St. Urbain, Michael Youngberg. **Crosscheckers:** Brian Johnston, Paul Tinnell. **Area Scouts:** Adam Arnold, Joey Aversa, Coulson Barbiche, Brandon Bishoff, Tom Burns, Adrian Casanova, Chris Curtis, Ryan Fox, Pete Holmes, Matt Huck, Randy Kramer, Jim Lentine, Nate Murrie, Don Norris, Matt O'Brien, Wes Penick, Max Semler, Bud Smith, Mike Tidick. **Scouts:** Chris Lionetti, Roberto Santana. **Development Scout:** Tony Cho. **Canadian Scouting:** Patrick Griffin, Jay Lapp, Jasmin Roy, Rene Tosoni. **Director, Latin American Operations:** Sandy Rosario. **Scouting Supervisors:** Aaron Acosta, Jose Contreras, Lorenzo Perez. **Scouting Coordinator, South America:** Francisco Plasencia. **Assistant, International Scouting:** Julio Ramirez. **Assistant, International Operations:** Tyler Baldwin. **International Scouting:** Franklin Briceno, Alexis de la Cruz, Luciano del Rosario, Oscar Delgado, Enrique Falcon, Jhoan Gomez, Miguel Leal, Alirio Ledezma, Jose Natera, Luis Natera, Enmanuel Rojo, Daniel Sotelo, Alex Zapata.

WASHINGTON NATIONALS

Office Address: 1500 South Capitol Street SE, Washington, DC 20003.
Telephone: (202) 640-7000. **Fax:** (202) 547-0025.
Website: www.nationals.com.

OWNERSHIP

Managing Principal Owner: Mark D. Lerner. **Founding Principal Owner:** Theodore N. Lerner.
Principal Owners: Annette M. Lerner, Marla Lerner Tanenbaum, Debra Lerner Cohen, Robert K. Tanenbaum, Edward L. Cohen, Judy Lenkin Lerner.

EXECUTIVE MANAGEMENT

Chief Operating Officer, Lerner Sports: Alan H. Gottlieb. **Chief Financial Officer:** Lori Creasy. **Senior Vice President:** Elise Holman.

Mark Lerner

BALLPARK ENTERPRISES

Executive Director, Ballpark Enterprises: Keely O'Brien

LEGAL

Vice President & General Counsel: Betsy Philpott. **Deputy General Counsel:** John Bramlette

HUMAN RESOURCES

Senior Vice President & Chief People Officer: Bob Frost. **Senior Director, Human Resources:** Tatiana Diener. **Director, Benefits:** Stephanie Giroux.

COMMUNICATIONS

Executive Director, Communications: Valerie Krebs. **Director, Communications:** Kyle Brostowitz. **Manager, Communications:** Melissa Strozza. **Senior Manager, Communications:** Christopher Browne. **Coordinator, Communications:** Devon Bridges.

COMMUNITY RELATIONS

Senior Vice President, Community Engagement: Gregory McCarthy. **Executive Director, Player & Community Relations:** Shawn Bertani. **Director, Community Relations:** Nicole Murray. **Director, Community Relations:** Alex Robbins.

BROADCASTING/GAME PRESENTATION

Senior Vice President, Marketing, Broadcasting & Game Presentation: Jacqueline Coleman. **Director, Promotions & Events:** Lindsey Norris. **Vice President, Production & Broadcasting:** Dave Lundin. **Director, Game Production:** Michael Masino. **Director, Video & Broadcast Engineering:** Benjamin Smith.

BUSINESS STRATEGY & ANALYTICS

Senior Vice President, Business Strategy & Operations: Mike Carney. **Vice President, Business Strategy & Analytics:** John Choi. **Vice President, Strategic Partnerships:** Missy Jenkins

TICKETING

Vice President, Ticket Sales & Service: Ryan Bringger. **Executive Director, Ticket Services & Operations:** Thomas Kildahl. **Director, Ticket Sales:** Zach Henderson

BALLPARK OPERATIONS

Senior Vice President & General Manager of Nationals Park: Frank Gambino. **Senior Vice President, Ballpark Operations:** Lisa Marie Czop

EXPERIENCE AND HOSPITALITY

Vice President, Experience and Hospitality: Jonathan Stahl.

CORPORATE PARTNERSHIPS

Vice President, Corporate Partnerships: Matt Lemire.

BASEBALL OPERATIONS

President of Baseball Operations and General Manager: Mike Rizzo. **Assistant General Manager & Vice President, Scouting Operations:** Kris Kline. **Assistant General Manager & Vice President, Finance:** Ted Towne. **Assistant General Manager & Vice President, International Operations:** Johnny DiPuglia. **Vice President & Assistant General Manager, Baseball Operations:** Michael DeBartolo. **Assistant General Manager, Player Personnel:** Mark Scialabba. **Special Assistant to the General Manager:** Jon Weil. **Senior Advisor to the General Manager:** Jack McKeon. **Special Assistant, Major League Administration:** Harolyn Cardozo. **Assistant, Major League Administration:** Jordan Missal. **Assistant Director, Baseball Operations:** James Badas. **Quality Assurance Coordinator:** Jonathan Tosches. **Manager, Advance Scouting:** Greg Ferguson. **Coordinator, Major League Video/Technology:** Kenny Diaz.

Mike Rizzo

BASEBALL RESEARCH AND DEVELOPMENT

Senior Director, Baseball Research & Development: Lee Mendelowitz. **Assistant Director, Baseball R&D:** Max Ehrman, Scott Van Lenten. **Manager, Major League Strategy:** David Higgins. **Lead Analyst, Baseball Research & Development:** Michael Schatz. **Analysts, Baseball R&D:** David Gagnon, Omar Taveras. **Coordinator, Player Development Analytics:** Jordan Rassman. **Data Engineer, Baseball R&D:** Chris Jordan. **Senior Developers, Baseball R&D:** Jason Holt, Jay Liu.

MAJOR LEAGUE OPERATIONS

Vice President, Clubhouse Operations & Team Travel: Rob McDonald. **Clubhouse & Equipment Manager:** Mike Wallace. **Visiting Clubhouse Manager:** Matt Rosenthal. **Equipment Manager:** Dan Wallin. **Clubhouse Assistants:** Mike Gordon, Andrew Melnick, Gregory Melnick.

MAJOR LEAGUE STAFF

Manager: Dave Martinez. **Coaches: Bench—** Tim Bogar. **Pitching—**Jim Hickey. **Hitting—** Darnell Coles. **First Base—** Eric Young Jr.. **Third Base—**Gary DiSarcina. **Bullpen—** Ricky Bones. **Catching & Strategy Coach—**Henry Blanco **Assistant Hitting Coach:** Pat Roessler.

MEDICAL/TRAINING

Executive Director, Medical Services: Harvey Sharman. **Lead Team Physician:** Dr. Robin West. **Director, Athletic Training:** Paul Lessard. **Head Athletic Trainer:** Dale Gilbert.

PLAYER DEVELOPMENT

Director, Player Development: De Jon Watson. **Senior Advisor, Player Development:** Dave Jauss. **Senior Advisor, Player Development:** Spin Williams. **Director, Minor League and Florida Operations:** Ryan Thomas. **Director, Player Development Technology & Strategy:** David Longley. **Assistant Director, Player Development:** John Wulf. **Assistant Director, Minor League Operations:** JJ Estevez. **Manager, Florida Operations:** Dianne Wiebe. **Player Education and Cultural Development Coordinator:** Andrew Scarlata. **Minor League Clubhouse & Equipment Coordinator:** Carlos Felix. **Minor League Clubhouse Operations:** Scott Paquin. **DSL Academy Administrator:** Eduardo Castro. **DSL Clubhouse Assistant:** Edniel Rouancourt. **DSL Academy Administrative Assistant:** Lorena Rosario. **Field Coordinator:** Bob Henley. **Assistant Field Coordinator:** Jeff Garber. **Hitting Coordinator:** Joe Dillon. **Lower Level Hitting Coordinator:** Troy Gingrich. **Pitching Coordinator:** Sam Narron. **Lower Level Pitching Coordinator:** Michael Tejera. **Outfield/Baserunning Coordinator:** Coco Crisp. **Infield Coordinator:** José Aguacil. **Catching Coordinator:** Randy Knorr. **Quality Control Coordinator:** Bill Mueller. **Rehabilitation Pitching Coordinator:** Mark Grater. **Medical Rehab Coordinator:** Gene Basham. **Assistant Medical Rehab Coordinator:** Jeff Allred. **Strength and Conditioning Coordinator:** Gabe Torres. **Athletic Trainer:** Cesar Roman. **Mental Skills Coordinator:** Dana Sinclair. **Nutritionist:** Emily Kaley

FARM SYSTEM

Class	Club	Manager	Hitting Coach	Pitching Coach
Triple-A	Rochester	Matt LeCroy	Brian Daubach	Rafael Chaves
Double-A	Harrisburg	Tripp Keister	Brian Rupp	Justin Lord
High-A	Wilmington	Mario Lisson	Tim Doherty	Mark DiFelice
Low-A	Fredericksburg	Jake Lowery	Delwyn Young	Joel Hanrahan
Rookie	Nationals (FCL)	Luis Ordaz	Ender Chávez	F. Bravo/D. Hood
Rookie	Nationals (DSL)	Sandy Martinez	Freddy Guzman	Edwin Hurtado

SCOUTING

Director, Scouting Operations: Eddie Longosz. **Director, Player Procurement:** Kasey McKeon. **Director, Pitching Evaluation & Special Asst. to the President of Baseball Ops & GM:** Jeff Zona. **Assistant Director, Amateur Scouting:** Mark Baca. **Special Assistants to the President of Baseball Operations & GM:** Steve Arnieri, Mike Daughtry, Willie Fraser, Jeff Harris, Greg Hunter, Dan Jennings, John Mirabelli, Mike Pagliarulo, Jay Robertson, Bob Schaefer. **East Crosschecker:** Alan Marr. **Midwest Crosschecker:** Jimmy Gonzales. **West Crosschecker:** Fred Costello. **Southeast Crosschecker and Area Supervisor:** Alex Morales. **Area Supervisors:** Bryan Byrne, Brian Cleary, Ben Diggins, James Goodwin, Kevin Ham, Bob Hamelin, Tommy Jackson, Steve Leavitt, John Malzone, Bobby Myrick, Scott Ramsay, Mitch Sokol, Cody Staab. **Director, International Operations:** Mike Cadahia. **Director, Latin American Scouting:** Fausto Severino. **Assistant, International Scouting:** Taisuke Sato. **Crosscheckers:** Alex Rodriguez, Modesto Ulloa, Riki Vasquez. **Coordinator, Venezuela:** German Robles. **Colombia:** Eduardo Cabrera. **Curacao and Aruba:** David Leer. **Dominican Republic:** Abraham Despradel, Oscar Disla, Fernando Encarnacion, Virgilio De Leon, Bolivar Pelletier. **Panama:** Miguel Ruiz. **Venezuela:** Salvador Donadelli, Juan Indriago, Ronald Morillo, Juan Munoz.

MEDIA
INFORMATION

LOCAL MEDIA INFORMATION

AMERICAN LEAGUE

BALTIMORE ORIOLES
Radio Announcers: Kevin Brown, Geoff Arnold, Melanie Newman, Brett Hollander, Rob Long. **Flagship Station:** WJZ-FM 105.7 The Fan.
TV Announcers: Geoff Arnold, Kevin Brown, Scott Garceau, Ben McDonald, Melanie Newman, Jim Palmer. **Flagship Station:** Mid-Atlantic Sports Network.

BOSTON RED SOX
Radio Announcers: Joe Castiglione, Will Flemming. **Flagship Station:** WEEI (93.7 FM).
TV Announcers: Dave O'Brien, Dennis Eckersley, Tom Caron, Mike Monaco, Steve Lyons, Jim Rice, Tim Wakefield, Lenny Dinardo, Manny Delcarmen, Guerin Austin, Jahmai Webster, Adam Pellerin. **Flagship Station:** NESN.

CHICAGO WHITE SOX
Radio Announcers: Len Kasper, Darrin Jackson. **Flagship Station:** WLS-AM 720. **Spanish Language:** Hector Molina, Billy Russo. **TV Announcers:** Steve Stone, Jason Benetti. **Flagship Stations:** WGN TV-9, WPWR-TV, NBC Sports Chicago (regional cable).

CLEVELAND GUARDIANS
Radio Announcers: Tom Hamilton, Jim Rosenhaus. **Flagship Station:** WTAM 1000-AM.
TV Announcers: Rick Manning, Matt Underwood, Andre Knott. **Flagship Station:** Bally Sports Ohio.

DETROIT TIGERS
Radio Announcers: Dan Dickerson, Jim Price. **Flagship Station:** WXYT 97.1 FM and AM 1270.
TV Announcers: Jack Morris, Kirk Gibson, Matt Shepard, Craig Monroe, John Keating, Dan Petry. **Flagship Station:** Bally Sports Detroit (regional cable).

HOUSTON ASTROS
Radio Announcers: Steve Sparks, Robert Ford. **Spanish:** Alex Trevino, Francisco Romero. **Flagship Stations:** KBME 790-AM, KLAT 1010-AM (Spanish).
TV Announcers: Todd Kalas, Geoff Blum, Julia Morales. **Flagship Station:** AT&T Sports Net Southwest.

KANSAS CITY ROYALS
Radio Announcers: Denny Matthews, Steve Physioc, Steve Stewart. **Kansas City Affiliate:** KCSP 610-AM.
TV Announcers: Ryan Lefebvre, Rex Hudler, Joel Goldberg, Steve Physioc, Jeff Montgomery (pregame). **Flagship Station:** Bally Sports Kansas City.

LOS ANGELES ANGELS
Radio Announcers: Terry Smith, Mark Langston, Jose Tolentino (Spanish). **Flagship Station:** AM 830, 1330 KWKW (Spanish).
TV Announcers: Matt Vasgersian, Mark Gubicza, Jose Mota. **Flagship TV Station:** Bally Sports West (regional cable).

MINNESOTA TWINS
Radio Announcers: Cory Provus, Dan Gladden. **Radio Network Studio Host:** Kris Atteberry. **Spanish Radio:** Alfonso Fernandez, Tony Oliva. **Flagship Station:** WCCO-AM 830. **TV Announcers:** Dick Bremer, Roy Smalley, LaTroy Hawkins, Justin Morneau. **Flagship Station:** Bally Sports North.

NEW YORK YANKEES
Radio Announcers: John Sterling, Suzyn Waldman. **Flagship Station:** WFAN 660-AM, WADO 1280-AM. **Spanish Radio Announcers:** Francisco Rivera, Rickie Ricardo.
TV Announcers: David Cone, Jack Curry, John Flaherty, Michael Kay, Ryan Ruocco, Meredith Marakovits, Paul O'Neill. **Flagship Station:** YES Network (Yankees Entertainment & Sports).

OAKLAND ATHLETICS
Radio Announcers: Vince Cotroneo, Ken Korach. **Flagship Station:** KTRB 860 AM.
TV Announcers: Glen Kuiper, Dallas Braden. **Flagship Stations:** NBC Sports California.

SEATTLE MARINERS
Radio Announcers: Rick Rizzs, Aaron Goldsmith. **Flagship Station:** 710 ESPN Seattle (KIRO-AM 710).
TV Announcers: Mike Blowers, Dave Sims, Aaron Goldsmith, Alex Rivera. **Flagship Station:** ROOT Sports Northwest.

TAMPA BAY RAYS
Radio Announcers: Andy Freed, Dave Wills. **Flagship Station:** WDAE 620 AM/95.3 FM Tampa/St. Petersburg **TV Announcers:** Brian Anderson, Dewayne Staats, Tricia Whitaker. **Flagship Station:** Bally Sports Sun.

TEXAS RANGERS
Radio Announcers: Eric Nadel, Matt Hicks. **Spanish:** Eleno Ornelas, Jose Guzman. **Flagship Station:** 105.3 The FAN FM, KFLC 1270 AM (Spanish).
TV Announcers: Dave Raymond, Tom Grieve, C.J. Nitkowski, David Murphy, Emily Jones. **Flagship Station:** Bally Sports Southwest (regional cable).

TORONTO BLUE JAYS
Radio Announcers: Ben Wagner. **Flagship Station:** SportsNet Radio Fan 590-AM.
TV Announcers: Buck Martinez, Dan Shulman, Hazel Mae. **Flagship Station:** Rogers Sportsnet.

NATIONAL LEAGUE

ARIZONA DIAMONDBACKS
Radio Announcers: Greg Schulte, Tom Candiotti, Rodrigo Lopez (Spanish), Oscar Soria (Spanish), Richard Saenz (Spanish). **Flagship Stations:** Arizona Sports 98.7 FM, TUDN 105.1 (Spanish).
TV Announcers: Steve Berthiaume, Bob Brenly. **Flagship Stations:** Bally Sports Arizona (regional cable).

ATLANTA BRAVES
Radio Announcers: Jim Powell, Ben Ingram. **Flagship Stations:** WCNN-AM 680 The Fan.
TV Announcers: Chip Caray, Joe Simpson, Tom Glavine, Jeff Francoeur. **Flagship Stations:** Bally Sports South/Southeast (regional cable).

CHICAGO CUBS
Radio Announcers: Pat Hughes, Ron Coomer. **Flagship Station:** WSCR-670 The Score.
TV Announcers: Jon Sciambi, Jim Deshaies. **Flagship Stations:** Marquee Sports Network.

CINCINNATI REDS
Radio Announcers: Jeff Brantley, Tommy Thrall. **Flagship Station:** WLW 700-AM.
TV Announcers: Chris Welsh, Jeff Brantley, John Sadak, Barry Larkin, Jim Day. **Flagship Station:** Bally Sports Ohio.

COLORADO ROCKIES
Radio Announcers: Jack Corrigan, Mike Rice, Salvador Hernandez (Spanish), Carlos Valdez (Spanish), Hector Salazar (Spanish) **Flagship Station:** KOA 850-AM & 94.1 FM, Rockies Spanish Radio 1150 AM.
TV Announcers: Drew Goodman, Jeff Huson, Ryan Spilborghs. **Flagship Station:** AT&T SportsNet.

LOS ANGELES DODGERS
Radio Announcers: Rick Monday, Charley Steiner, Tim Neverett. **Spanish:** Jaime Jarrín. **Flagship Stations:** AM570 Bally Sports LA, KTNQ 1020-AM (Spanish).
TV Announcers: Joe Davis, Orel Hershiser, Nomar Garciaparra, Kirsten Watson, Tim Neverett. **Spanish:** Pepe Yniguez, Fernando Valenzuela. **Flagship Stations:** SportsNet LA (regional cable).

MIAMI MARLINS
Radio Announcers: Dave Van Horne, Glenn Geffner. **Flagship Stations:** WINZ 940-AM.
TV Announcers: Paul Severino, Todd Hollandsworth. **Flagship Stations:** FSN Florida (regional cable).

MILWAUKEE BREWERS
Radio Announcers: Bob Uecker, Jeff Levering, Josh Maurer, Lane Grindle. **Flagship Station:** WTMJ 620-AM.
TV Announcers: Brian Anderson, Bill Schroeder, Matt Lepay, Sophia Minnaert. **Flagship Station:** Bally Sports Wisconsin.

NEW YORK METS
Radio Announcers: Howie Rose, Ed Coleman and Wayne Randazzo. **Flagship Station:** WCBS 880-AM.
TV Announcers: Gary Cohen, Keith Hernandez, Ron Darling, Steve Gelbs, Todd Zeile. **Flagship Stations:** Sports Net New York (regional cable), PIX11-TV.

PHILADELPHIA PHILLIES
Radio Announcers: Scott Franzke, Larry Andersen, Bill Kulik (Spanish Radio). **Flagship Station:** SportsRadio 94WIP (94.1 FM).
TV Announcers: Tom McCarthy, Ben Davis, John Kruk, Gregg Murphy, Mike Schmidt, Ruben Amaro Jr. **Flagship Stations:** NBC 10 (regional cable).

PITTSBURGH PIRATES
Radio Announcers: Joe Block, Matt Capps, Kevin Young, Michael McKenry, Greg Brown, Bob Walk, John Wehner. **Flagship Station:** Sports Radio 93.7 FM The Fan.
TV Announcers: Joe Block, Matt Capps, Kevin Young, Michael McKenry, Greg Brown, Bob Walk, John Wehner. **Flagship Station:** AT&T SportsNet Pittsburgh (regional cable).

ST. LOUIS CARDINALS
Radio Announcers: John Rooney, Ricky Horton, Mike Claiborne. **Flagship Station:** KMOX 1120 AM. **Spanish Radio Announcers:** Polo Ascencio, Bengie Molina. **Flagship Station:** WJIR 880
TV Announcers: Dan McLaughlin, Ricky Horton, Al Hrabosky, Brad Thompson, Jim Edmonds, Tim McCarver, Jim Hayes, Erica Weston, Scott Warmann. **Flagship Station:** Bally Sports Midwest.

SAN DIEGO PADRES
Radio Announcers: Jesse Agler, Tony Gwynn Jr. **Flagship Stations:** 97.3 The Fan.
TV Announcers: Don Orsillo, Mark Grant. **Flagship Station:** Bally Sports San Diego. **Spanish Announcers:** Eduardo Ortega, Carlos Hernandez on XEMO-860-AM.

SAN FRANCISCO GIANTS
Radio Announcers: Mike Krukow, Duane Kuiper, Jon Miller, Dave Flemming.
Spanish: Tito Fuentes, Erwin Higueros. **Flagship Station:** KNBR 680-AM (English); ESPN Deportes-860AM (Spanish).
TV Announcers: Mike Krukow, Duane Kuiper, Jon Miller, Dave Flemming. **Flagship Stations:** KNTV-NBC 11, CSN Bay Area (regional cable).

WASHINGTON NATIONALS
Radio Announcers: Charlie Slowes, Dave Jageler. **Flagship Station:** WJFK 106.7 FM.
TV Announcers: Bob Carpenter, Kevin Frandsen. **Flagship Station:** Mid-Atlantic Sports Network.

NATIONAL MEDIA INFORMATION

BASEBALL STATISTICS

ELIAS SPORTS BUREAU INC. NATIONAL MEDIA BASEBALL STATISTICS
Official Major League Statistician Mailing Address: 500 Fifth Ave., Suite 2140, New York, NY 10110.
Telephone: (212) 869-1530. **Fax:** (212) 354-0980. **Website:** esb.com.
President: Joe Gilston.
Vice President: Chris Thorn. **Email Address:** Chris.Thorn@ESB.com
Manager, Baseball Operations: John Labombarda. **Email Address:** John.Labombarda@ESB.com

MLB ADVANCED MEDIA
Official Minor League Statistician Mailing Address: 1271 Avenue of the Americas, New York, NY, 10020.
Telephone: (212) 485-3444. **Fax:** (212) 485-3456.
Director, Stats: Chris Lentine. **Senior Manager, Stats:** Shawn Geraghty.
Senior Stats Supervisors: Jason Rigatti, Ian Schwartz. **Stats Supervisors:** Lawrence Fischer, Jake Fox, Dominic French, Kelvin Lee.

MILB.COM OFFICIAL WEBSITE OF MINOR LEAGUE BASEBALL
Mailing Address: 1271 Avenue of the Americas, New York, NY, 10020.
Telephone: (212) 485-3444. **Fax:** (212) 485-3456. **Website:** MiLB.com.
Director, Minor League Club Initiatives: Nathan Blackmon. **Sr. Producer, MiLB.com:** Dan Marinis.

STATS PERFORM
Mailing Address: 203 N. LaSalle St. Chicago, IL, 60601.
Telephone: (866) 221-1426. **Fax:** (847) 470-9140. **Website:** statsperform.com.
Email: sales@stats.com. **Twitter:** @STATSBiznews; @STATS_MLB. **CEO:** Carl Mergale. **Chief Operating Officer:** Mike Perez. **Chief Revenue Officer:** Steve Xeller. **Chief Financial Officer:** Ashley Milton. **Chief Technology Officer:** Dr. Helen Sun. **Advanced Analytics Coordinatior:** Micah Parshall.

GENERAL INFORMATION

SCOUTING

SCOUT OF THE YEAR FOUNDATION
Mailing Address: P.O. Box 211585, West Palm Beach, FL 33421.
Telephone: (561) 798-5897, (561) 818-4329. **E-mail Address:** bertmazur@aol.com.
President: Roberta Mazur. **Vice President:** Tracy Ringolsby. **Treasurer:** Ron Mazur II. **Board of Advisers:** Pat Gillick, .
Scout of the Year Program Advisory Board: Grady Fuson, Dan Jennings, Linda Pereira, Gene Watson.

MUSEUMS

NATIONAL BASEBALL HALL OF FAME AND MUSEUM
Address: 25 Main St., Cooperstown, NY 13326.
Telephone: (888) 425-5633, (607) 547-7200. **Fax:** (607) 547-2044. **E-mail Address:** info@baseballhall.org. **Website:** www.baseballhall.org.
Year Founded: 1939.
Chairman: Jane Forbes Clark. **President:** Josh Rawitch.
Museum Hours: Open daily, year-round, closed only Thanksgiving, Christmas and New Year's Day. 9 a.m.-5 p.m. Summer hours, 9 a.m.-9 p.m. (Memorial Day weekend through the day before Labor Day.)
2022 Hall of Fame Induction Weekend: July 24.

NEGRO LEAGUES BASEBALL MUSEUM
Mailing Address: 1616 E. 18th St., Kansas City, MO 64108.
Telephone: (816) 221-1920. **Fax:** (816) 221-8424.
E-mail Address: bkendrick@nlbm.com. **Website:** www.nlbm.com.
Year Founded: 1990.
President: Bob Kendrick.
Museum Hours: Tues.-Sat. 9 a.m.-6 p.m.; Sun. noon-6 p.m.

RESEARCH

SOCIETY FOR AMERICAN BASEBALL RESEARCH
Mailing Address: Cronkite School at ASU, 555 N Central Ave., #416 , Phoenix, AZ 85004.
Website: www.sabr.org. **Year Founded:** 1971.
President: Mark Armour. **Executive Vice President:** Scott Carter. **Vice President:** Leslie Heaphy. **Secretary:** Todd Lebowitz. **Treasurer:** Daniel R. Levitt. **Directors:** Dan Evans, Tara Krieger, Allison Levin, Bill Nowlin. **CEO:** Scott Bush. **Director of Editorial Content:** Jacob Pomrenke.

ALUMNI ASSOCIATIONS

MAJOR LEAGUE BASEBALL PLAYERS ALUMNI ASSOCIATION

Mailing Address: 1631 Mesa Ave., Copper Building, Suite D, Colorado Springs, CO 80906.
Telephone: (719) 477-1870. **Fax:** (719) 477-1875.
E-mail Address: postoffice@mlbpaa.com. **Website:** www.baseballalumni.com.
Facebook: facebook.com/majorleaguebaseballplayersalumniassociation. **Twitter:** @MLBPAA.
Chief Executive Officer: Dan Foster (dan@mlbpaa.com). **Chief Operating Officer:** Geoffrey Hixson (geoff@mlbpaa
.com). **Vice President, Operations:** Mike Groll (mikeg@mlbpaa.com). **Director, Communications:** Nikki Warner (nikki
@mlbpaa.com). **Vice President, Membership/Content:** Kate Tyo (Kate@mlbpaa.com). **Director, Memorabilia
Operations:** Greg Thomas (greg@mlbpaa.com). **Database Manager:** Chris Burkeen (cburkeen@mlbpaa.com).

BASEBALL ASSISTANCE TEAM (B.A.T.)

Mailing Address: 1271 Avenue of the Americas, New York, NY 10020
Telephone: (212) 931-7822, **Fax:** (212) 949-5433.
Website: www.baseballassistanceteam.com.

MINISTRY

BASEBALL CHAPEL

Mailing Address: P.O. Box 10102, Largo FL 33773.
Telephone: (610) 999-3600.
E-mail Address: office@baseballchapel.org. **Website:** www.baseballchapel.org.
Year Founded: 1973.
President: Vince Nauss. **Hispanic Ministry:** Cali Magallanes, Gio Llerena. **Ministry Operations:** Rob Crose, Steve
Sisco. **Board of Directors:** Don Christensen, Greg Groh, Dave Howard, Vince Nauss, Walt Wiley.

CATHOLIC ATHLETES FOR CHRIST

Mailing Address: 3703 Cameron Mills Road, Alexandria, VA 22305.
Telephone: (703) 239-3070.
E-mail Address: info@catholicathletesforchrist.org. **Website:** www.catholicathletesforchrist.org.
Year Founded: 2006.
President: Ray McKenna. **MLB Ministry Coordinator:** Kevin O'Malley. **MLB Athlete Advisory Board Members:**
Mike Sweeney (Chairman), Jeff Suppan (Vice Chairman), Sal Bando, Lauren Bauer, David Eckstein, Terry Kennedy, Jack
McKeon, Darrell Miller, Mike Piazza, Vinny Rottino, Craig Stammen.

TRADE/EMPLOYMENT

BASEBALL WINTER MEETINGS

E-Mail Address: BaseballWinterMeetings@milb.com. **Website:** www.baseballwintermeetings.com.
2022 Convention: Dec. 5-7/8, San Diego.

BASEBALL TRADE SHOW

E-Mail Address: TradeShow@MiLB.com. **Website:** www.BaseballTradeShow.com.
Contact: Noreen Brantner, Sr. Asst. Director, Exhibition Services & Sponsorships.
2022 Convention: Dec. 5-7/8, San Diego.

REVIVING BASEBALL IN INNER CITIES

Mailing Address: 1271 Avenue of the Americas, New York, NY 10020
Telephone: (212) 931-7800. **Fax:** (212) 949-5695
Year Founded: 1989
Executive Vice President, Baseball & Softball Development: Tony Reagins (Tony.Reagins@mlb.com). **Vice
President, Baseball & Softball Development:** David James (David.James@mlb.com). **E-mail:** rbi@mlb.com. **Website:**
www.mlb.com/rbi

MLB YOUTH ACADEMIES

CINCINNATI REDS YOUTH ACADEMY

Director: Jerome Wright
Asst. Director: Jeremy Hamilton
Mailing Address: 2026 E. Seymour Avenue. Cincinnati, OH 45327
Phone Number: 513-765-5000

COMPTON YOUTH ACADEMY

Vice President: Darrell Miller
Mailing Address: 901 East Artesia Blvd. Compton, CA

HOUSTON ASTROS YOUTH ACADEMY

Director: Daryl Wade
Mailing Address: 2801 South Victory Drive. Houston, TX 77088.
Email: uya@astros.com

KANSAS CITY ROYALS URBAN YOUTH ACADEMY

Executive Director: Darwin Pennye
Email: Darwin.Pennye@royals.com

NEW ORLEANS YOUTH ACADEMY

Director: Eddie Anthony Davis III
Mailing Address: 6403 Press Drive. New Orleans, LA 70126
Phone Number: 504-282-0443

PHILADELPHIA PHILLIES YOUTH ACADEMY

Director: Jon Joaquin
Phone Number: 215-218-5634
Director: Rob Holiday
Phone Number: 215-218-5204

PUERTO RICO BASEBALL ACADEMY AND HIGH SCHOOL

Phone Number: 787-712-0700
Lucy Batista: Headmaster
Phone Number: 787-531-1768

TEXAS RANGERS YOUTH ACADEMY

Director: Juan Leonel Garciga
Mailing Address: 1000 Ballpark Way, Arlington, TX 76011
Phone Number: 817-273-5297

WASHINGTON NATIONALS YOUTH ACADEMY

Executive Director: Tal Alter
Mailing Address: 3675 Ely Place SE. Washington, DC 20019
Phone Number: 202-827-8960

SPRING TRAINING

CACTUS LEAGUE

ARIZONA DIAMONDBACKS

MAJOR LEAGUE

Complex Address: Salt River Fields at Talking Stick, 7555 North Pima Road, Scottsdale, AZ 85256. **Telephone:** (480) 270-5000. **Seating Capacity:** 11,000 (7,000 fixed seats, 4,000 lawn seats). **Location:** From Loop-101, use exit 44 (Indian Bend Road) and proceed west for approximately one-half mile; turn right at Pima Road to travel north and proceed one-quarter mile; three entrances to Salt River Fields will be available on the right-hand side.

MINOR LEAGUE

Complex Address: Same as major league club.

CHICAGO CUBS

MAJOR LEAGUE

Complex Address: Sloan Park, 2330 West Rio Salado Parkway, Mesa, AZ 85201. **Telephone:** (480) 668-0500. **Seating Capacity:** 15,000. **Location:** on the land of the former Riverview Golf Course, bordered by the 101 and 202 interchange in Mesa.

MINOR LEAGUE

Complex Address: 2510 W. Rio Salado Parkway, Mesa, AZ 85201. **Telephone:** (480) 668-0500

CHICAGO WHITE SOX

MAJOR LEAGUE

Complex Address: Camelback Ranch-Glendale, 10710 West Camelback Road, Phoenix, AZ 85037. **Telephone:** (623) 302-5000. **Seating Capacity:** 13,000. **Hotel Address:** Residence Inn Phoenix Glendale Sports and Entertainment District, 7350 N Zanjero Blvd, Glendale, AZ 85305, **Telephone:** (623) 772-8900. **Hotel Address:** Renaissance Glendale Hotel & Spa, 9495 W Coyotes Blvd, Glendale, AZ 85305. **Telephone:** 629-937-3700.

MINOR LEAGUE

Complex/Hotel Address: Same as major league club.

CINCINNATI REDS

MAJOR LEAGUE

Complex Address: Cincinnati Reds Player Development Complex, 3125 S Wood Blvd, Goodyear, AZ 85338. **Telephone:** (623) 932-6590. **Ballpark Address:** Goodyear Ballpark, 1933 S Ballpark Way, Goodyear, AZ 85338. **Telephone:** (623) 882-3120. **Hotel Address:** Marriott Residence Inn, 7350 N Zanjero Blvd, Glendale, AZ 85305. **Telephone:** (623) 772-8900. **Fax:** (623) 772-8905.

MINOR LEAGUE

Complex/Hotel Address: Same as major league club.

CLEVELAND GUARDIANS

MAJOR LEAGUE

Complex Address: Cleveland Guardians Player Development Complex 2601 S Wood Blvd, Goodyear, AZ 85338; Goodyear Ballpark 1933 S Ballpark Way, Goodyear, AZ 85338. **Telephone:** (623) 882-3120. **Location: From Downtown Phoenix/East Valley:** West on I-10 to

Exit 127, Bullard Avenue and proceed south (left off exit), Bullard Avenue turns into West Lower Buckeye Road. Turn left onto Wood Blvd. **Hotel Address:** (Media) Hampton Inn and Suites, 2000 N Litchfield Rd, Goodyear, AZ 85395. **Telephone:** (623) 536-1313. **Hotel Address:** Holiday Inn Express, 1313 N Litchfield Rd, Goodyear, AZ 85395. **Telephone:** (623) 535-1313. **Hotel Address:** TownePlace Suites, 13971 West Celebrate Life Way, Goodyear, AZ 85338. **Telephone:** (623) 535-5009. **Hotel Address:** Residence Inn by Marriott, 2020 N Litchfield Rd, Goodyear, AZ 85395. **Telephone:** (623) 866-1313.

MINOR LEAGUE

Complex Address: Same as major league club.

COLORADO ROCKIES

MAJOR LEAGUE

Complex Address: Salt River Fields at Talking Stick, 7555 North Pima Rd, Scottsdale, AZ 85258. **Telephone:** (480) 270-5800. **Seating Capacity:** 11,000 (7,000 fixed seats, 4,000 lawn seats). **Location:** From Loop-101, use exit 44 (Indian Bend Road Talking Stick Way) and proceed west for approximately one-half mile; turn right at Pima Road to travel north and proceed one-quarter mile; three entrances to Salt River Fields will be available on the right-hand side. **Visiting Team Hotel:** The Scottsdale Plaza Resort, 7200 North Scottsdale Road, Scottsdale, AZ 85253. **Telephone:** (480) 948-5000. **Fax:** (480) 951-5100.

MINOR LEAGUE

Complex/Hotel Address: Same as major league club.

KANSAS CITY ROYALS

MAJOR LEAGUE

Complex Address: Surprise Stadium, 15850 North Bullard Ave, Surprise, AZ 85374. **Telephone:** (623) 222-2000. **Seating Capacity:** 10,700. **Location:** I-10 West to Route 101 North, 101 North to Bell Road, left on Bell for five miles, stadium on left. **Hotel Address:** Wigwam Resort, 300 East Wigwam Blvd, Litchfield Park, Arizona 85340. **Telephone:** (623) 935-3811.

MINOR LEAGUE

Complex Address: Same as major league club. **Hotel Address:** Comfort Hotel and Suites, 13337 W Grand Ave, Surprise, AZ 85374. **Telephone:** (623) 583-3500.

LOS ANGELES ANGELS

MAJOR LEAGUE

Complex Address: Tempe Diablo Stadium, 2200 West Alameda Drive, Tempe, AZ 85282. **Telephone:** (480) 858-7500. **Fax:** (480) 438-7583. **Seating Capacity:** 9,558. **Location:** I-10 to exit 153B (48th Street), south one mile on 48th Street to Alameda Drive, left on Alameda.

MINOR LEAGUE

Complex Address: Tempe Diablo Minor League Complex, 2225 W Westcourt Way, Tempe, AZ 85282. **Telephone:** (480) 858-7558.

LOS ANGELES DODGERS

MAJOR LEAGUE
Complex Address: Camelback Ranch, 10710 West Camelback Rd, Phoenix, AZ 85037. **Seating Capacity:** 13,000, plus standing room. **Location:** I-10 or I-17 to Loop 101 West or North, Take Exit 5, Camelback Road West to ballpark. **Telephone:** (623) 302-5000. **Hotel:** Unavailable.

MINOR LEAGUE
Complex/Hotel Address: Same as major league club.

MILWAUKEE BREWERS

MAJOR LEAGUE
Complex Address: Maryvale Baseball Park, 3600 N 51st Ave, Phoenix, AZ 85031. **Telephone:** (623) 245-5555. **Seating Capacity:** 9,000. **Location:** I-10 to 51st Ave, north on 51st Ave. **Hotel Address:** Unavailable.

MINOR LEAGUE
Complex Address: Maryvale Baseball Complex, 3805 N 53rd Ave, Phoenix, AZ 85031. **Telephone:** (623) 245-5600. **Hotel Address:** Unavailable.

OAKLAND ATHLETICS

MAJOR LEAGUE
Complex Address: Hohokam Stadium, 1235 North Center Street, Mesa, AZ 85201. **Telephone:** 480-907-5489. **Seating Capacity:** 10,000.

MINOR LEAGUE
Complex Address: Fitch Park, 160 East 6th Place, Mesa, AZ 85201. **Telephone:** 480-387-5800. **Hotel Address:** Unavailable.

SAN DIEGO PADRES

MAJOR LEAGUE
Complex Address: Peoria Sports Complex, 8131 West Paradise Lane, Peoria, AZ 85382. **Telephone:** (619) 795-5720. **Fax:** (623) 486-7154. **Seating Capacity:** 12,000. **Location:** I-17 to Bell Road exit, west on Bell to 83rd Ave. **Hotel Address:** La Quinta Inn & Suites (623) 487-1900, 16321 N 83rd Avenue, Peoria, AZ 85382.

MINOR LEAGUE
Complex/Hotel: Country Inn and Suites (623) 879-9000, 20221 N 29th Avenue, Phoenix, AZ 85027.

SAN FRANCISCO GIANTS

MAJOR LEAGUE
Complex Address: Scottsdale Stadium, 7408 East Osborn Rd, Scottsdale, AZ 85251. **Telephone:** (480) 990-7972. **Fax:** (480) 990-2643. **Seating Capacity:** 11,500. **Location:** Scottsdale Road to Osborne Road, east on Osborne for a 1/2 mile. **Hotel Address:** Hilton Garden Inn Scottsdale Old Town, 7324 East Indian School Rd, Scottsdale, AZ 85251. **Telephone:** (480) 481-0400.

MINOR LEAGUE
Complex Address: Giants Minor League Complex 8045 E Camelback Road, Scottsdale, AZ 85251. **Telephone:** (480) 990-0052. **Fax:** (480) 990-2349.

SEATTLE MARINERS

MAJOR LEAGUE
Complex Address: Seattle Mariners, 15707 North 83rd Street, Peoria, AZ 85382. **Telephone:** (623) 776-4800. **Fax:** (623) 776-4829. **Seating Capacity:** 12,339. **Location:** Hwy 101 to Bell Road exit, east on Bell to 83rd Ave, south on 83rd Ave. **Hotel Address:** La Quinta Inn & Suites, 16321 N 83rd Ave, Peoria, AZ 85382. **Telephone:** (623) 487-1900.

MINOR LEAGUE
Complex Address: Peoria Sports Complex (1993), 15707 N 83rd Ave, Peoria, AZ 85382. **Telephone:** (623) 776-4800. **Fax:** (623) 776-4828. **Hotel Address:** Hampton Inn, 8408 W Paradise Lane, Peoria, AZ 85382. **Telephone:** (623) 486-9918.

TEXAS RANGERS

MAJOR LEAGUE
Complex Address: Surprise Stadium, 15754 North Bullard Ave, Surprise, AZ 85374. **Telephone:** (623) 266-8100. **Seating Capacity:** 10,714. **Location:** I-10 West to Route 101 North, 101 North to Bell Road, left at Bell for seven miles, stadium on left. **Hotel Address:** Residence Inn Surprise, 16418 N Bullard Ave, Surprise, AZ 85374. **Telephone:** (623) 249-6333.

MINOR LEAGUE
Complex Address: Same as major league club. **Hotel Address:** Holiday Inn Express and Suites Surprise, 16549 North Bullard Ave, Surprise AZ 85374. **Telephone:** (800) 939-4249.

GRAPEFRUIT LEAGUE

ATLANTA BRAVES

MAJOR LEAGUE

Complex Address: Cool Today Park, 18800 South West Villages Pkwy Venice, FL 34293. **Telephone:** (941) 413-5000. **Seating Capacity:** 8,000. **Location:** From **I-75S:** Take Exit 191 (River Rd Englewood/North Port). Keep Right onto River Road for 3.9 miles. Turn Right onto US 41/Tamiami Trail. In 1.5 miles take a left onto W. Villages Pkwy. Continue on W. Villages Pkwy for .75 miles.

From **I-75N:** Take Exit 191 (River Rd Englewood/North Port). Turn left onto River Road. Continue for 3.9 miles. Turn Right onto US 41/Tamiami Trail. In 1.5 miles take a left onto W. Villages Pkwy. Continue on W. Villages Pkwy for .75 miles.

Hotel Address: Unavailable.

MINOR LEAGUE

Complex Address: Same as major league club. **Telephone:** (407) 939-2232. **Fax:** (407) 939-2225. **Hotel Address:** Marriot Village at Lake Buena Vista, 8623 Vineland Ave, Orlando, FL 32821. **Telephone:** (407) 938-9001.

BALTIMORE ORIOLES

MAJOR LEAGUE

Complex Address: Ed Smith Stadium, 2700 12th Street, Sarasota, FL 34237. **Telephone:** (941) 893-6300. **Fax:** (941) 893-6377. **Seating Capacity:** 7,500. **Location:** I-75 to exit 210, West on Fruitville Road, right on Tuttle Avenue.

MINOR LEAGUE

Complex Address: Buck O'Neil Baseball Complex at Twin Lakes Park, 6700 Clark Rd, Sarasota, FL 34241. **Telephone:** (941) 923-1996.

BOSTON RED SOX

MAJOR LEAGUE

Complex Address: JetBlue Park at Fenway South, 11500 Fenway South Drive, Fort Myers, FL 33913. **Telephone:** (239) 334-4700. **Directions: From the North:** Take I-75 South to Exit 131 (Daniels Parkway); Make a left off the exit and go east for approximately two miles; JetBlue Park will be on your left. **From the South:** Take I-75 North to Exit 131 (Daniels Parkway); Make a right off exit and go east for approximately two miles; JetBlue Park will be on your left.

MINOR LEAGUE

Complex/Hotel Address: Fenway South, 11500 Fenway South Drive, Fort Myers, FL 33913.

DETROIT TIGERS

MAJOR LEAGUE

Complex Address: Joker Marchant Stadium, 2301 Lakeland Hills Blvd, Lakeland, FL 33805. **Telephone:** (863) 686-8075. **Seating Capacity:** 9,568. **Location:** I-4 to exit 33 (Lakeland Hills Boulevard).

MINOR LEAGUE

Complex Address: Tigertown, 2125 N Lake Ave, Lakeland, FL 33805. **Telephone:** (863) 686-8075.

HOUSTON ASTROS

MAJOR LEAGUE

Complex Address: The Ballpark of the Palm Beaches, 5444 Haverhill Road, West Palm Beach, FL 33407. **Telephone:** (844) 676-2017. **Seating Capacity:** 7,838. **Location:** Exit Florida's Turnpike onto Okeechobee Blvd. Proceed east to Haverhill Road turning left onto Haverhill Road. On game days, all vehicles may park in one of two grass parking areas. Proceed toward the stadium for disabled parking or drop-off. The North entrance on Haverhill Road will be right-out only. **Hotel Address:** Unavailable.

MINOR LEAGUE

Complex Information: Same as major league club. **Hotel Address:** Unavailable.

MIAMI MARLINS

MAJOR LEAGUE

Complex Address: Roger Dean Stadium, 4751 Main Street, Jupiter, FL 33458. **Telephone:** (561) 775-1818. **Telephone:** (561) 799-1346. **Seating Capacity:** 7,000. **Location:** I-95 to exit 83, east on Donald Ross Road for one mile to Central Blvd, left at light, follow Central Boulevard to circle and take Main Street to Roger Dean Stadium. **Hotel Address:** Palm Beach Gardens Marriott, 4000 RCA Boulevard, Palm Beach Gardens, FL 33410. **Telephone:** (561) 622-8888. **Fax:** (561) 622-0052.

MINOR LEAGUE

Complex/Hotel Address: Same as major league club.

MINNESOTA TWINS

MAJOR LEAGUE

Complex Address: Centurylink Sports Complex/Hammond Stadium, 14100 Six Mile Cypress Parkway, Fort Myers, FL 33912. **Telephone:** (239) 533-7610. **Seating Capacity:** 8,100. **Location:** Exit 21 off I-75, west on Daniels Parkway, left on Six Mile Cypress Parkway. **Hotel Address:** Four Points by Sheraton, 13600 Treeline Avenue South, Ft. Myers, FL 33913. **Telephone:** (800) 338-9467.

MINOR LEAGUE

Complex/Hotel Address: Same as major league club.

NEW YORK METS

MAJOR LEAGUE

Complex Address: Tradition Field, 525 NW Peacock Blvd, Port St. Lucie, FL 34986. **Telephone:** (772) 871-2100. **Seating Capacity:** 7,000. **Location:** Exit 121C (St Lucie West Blvd) off I-95, east 1/4 mile, left onto NW Peacock. **Hotel Address:** Hilton Hotel, 8542 Commerce Centre Drive, Port St. Lucie, FL 34986. **Telephone:** (772) 871-6850.

MINOR LEAGUE

Complex Address: Same as major league club. **Hotel Address:** Main Stay Suites, 8501 Champions Way, Port St. Lucie, FL 34986. **Telephone:** (772) 460-8882.

NEW YORK YANKEES

MAJOR LEAGUE

Complex Address: George M. Steinbrenner Field, One Steinbrenner Drive, Tampa, FL 33614. **Telephone:** (813) 875-7753. **Hotel:** Unavailable.

MINOR LEAGUE

Complex Address: Yankees Player Development/ Scouting Complex, 3102 N Himes Ave, Tampa, FL 33607. **Telephone:** (813) 875-7569. **Hotel:** Unavailable.

PHILADELPHIA PHILLIES

MAJOR LEAGUE

Complex Address: BayCare Ballpark, 601 N Old Coachman Road, Clearwater, FL 33765. **Telephone:** (727) 467-4457. **Fax:** (727) 712-4498. **Seating Capacity:** 8,500. **Location:** Route 60 West, right on Old Coachman Road, ballpark on right after Drew Street. **Hotel Address:** Holiday Inn Express, 2580 Gulf to Bay Blvd, Clearwater, FL 33765. **Telephone:** (727) 797-6300. **Hotel Address:** La Quinta Inn, 21338 US 19 North, Clearwater, FL 33765. **Telephone:** (727) 799-1565.

MINOR LEAGUE

Complex Address: Carpenter Complex, 651 N Old Coachman Rd, Clearwater, FL 33765. **Telephone:** (727) 799-0503. **Fax:** (727) 726-1793. **Hotel Addresses:** Hampton Inn, 21030 US Highway 19 North, Clearwater, FL 34625. **Telephone:** (727) 797-8173. **Hotel Address:** Econolodge, 21252 US Hwy 19, Clearwater, FL 34625. **Telephone:** (727) 799-1569.

PITTSBURGH PIRATES

MAJOR LEAGUE

Stadium Address: 17th Ave West and Ninth Street West, Bradenton, FL 34205. **Seating Capacity:** 8,500. **Location:** US 41 to 17th Ave, west to 9th Street. **Telephone:** (941) 747-3031. **Fax:** (941) 747-9549.

MINOR LEAGUE

Complex: Pirate City, 1701 27th St E, Bradenton, FL 34208.

ST. LOUIS CARDINALS

MAJOR LEAGUE

Complex Address: Roger Dean Stadium, 4751 Main Street, Jupiter, FL 33458. **Telephone:** (561) 775-1818. **Fax:** (561) 799-1380. **Seating Capacity:** 7,000. **Location:** I-95 to exit 58, east on Donald Ross Road for 1/4 mile. **Hotel Address:** Embassy Suites, 4350 PGA Blvd, Palm Beach Gardens, FL 33410. **Telephone:** (561) 622-1000.

MINOR LEAGUE

Complex: Same as major league club. **Hotel:** Double Tree Palm Beach Gardens. **Telephone:** (561) 622-2260.

TAMPA BAY RAYS

MAJOR LEAGUE

Stadium Address: Charlotte Sports Park, 2300 El Jobean Road, Port Charlotte, FL 33948. **Telephone:** (941) 206-4487. **Seating Capacity:** 6,823 (5,028 fixed seats). **Location:** I-75 to US-17 to US-41, turn left onto El Jobean Rd. **Hotel Address:** None.

MINOR LEAGUE

Complex: Same as major league club.

TORONTO BLUE JAYS

MAJOR LEAGUE

Stadium Address: Florida Auto Exchange Stadium, 373 Douglas Ave, Dunedin, FL 34698. **Telephone:** (727) 733-9302. **Seating Capacity:** 5,509. **Location:** US 19 North to Sunset Point; west on Sunset Point to Douglas Avenue; north on Douglas to Stadium; ballpark is on the southeast corner of Douglas and Beltrees.

MINOR LEAGUE

Complex Address: Bobby Mattick Training Center at Englebert Complex, 1700 Solon Ave, Dunedin, FL 34698. **Telephone:** (727) 734-8007. **Hotel Address:** Clarion Inn & Suites, 20967 US Highway 19 North Clearwater, FL 33765. **Telephone:** (727) 799-1181.

WASHINGTON NATIONALS

MAJOR LEAGUE

Stadium Address: The Ballpark of the Palm Beaches, 5444 N. Haverhill Road, West Palm Beach, FL 33407. **Telephone:** (844) 676-2017.

MINOR LEAGUE

Complex: Same as major league club.

MINOR
LEAGUES

TRIPLE-A EAST

STADIUM INFORMATION

Club	Stadium	Opened	LF	CF	RF	Capacity	2021 Att.
Buffalo	Sahlen Field	1988	325	404	325	18,025	200,752
Charlotte	BB&T Ballpark	2015	325	400	315	10,002	345,305
Columbus	Huntington Park	2009	325	400	318	10,100	393,879
Durham	Durham Bulls Athletic Park	1995	305	400	327	10,000	320,873
Gwinnett	Coolray Field	2009	335	400	335	10,427	162,494
Indianapolis	Victory Field	1996	320	402	320	14,500	353,729
Iowa	Principal Park	1992	335	400	335	11,000	314,749
Jacksonville	Baseball Grounds of Jacksonville	2003	321	420	317	11,000	242,667
Lehigh Valley	Coca-Cola Park	2008	336	400	325	10,000	356,355
Louisville	Louisville Slugger Field	2000	325	400	340	13,131	269,338
Memphis	AutoZone Park	2000	319	400	322	10,000	183,217
Nashville	First Tennessee Park	2015	330	405	310	10,000	436,868
Norfolk	Harbor Park	1993	333	400	318	12,067	262,496
Omaha	Werner Park	2011	310	402	315	9,023	245,170
Rochester	Frontier Field	1997	335	402	325	10,840	219,941
St. Paul	CHS Field	2015	330	396	320	7,140	393,394
Scranton/WB	PNC Field	2013	330	408	330	10,000	236,559
Syracuse	NBT Bank Stadium	1997	330	400	330	11,671	215,336
Toledo	Fifth Third Field	2002	320	408	315	10,300	300,063
Worcester	Polar Park	2021	330	403	320	9,508	362,559

BUFFALO BISONS

Address: Sahlen Field, One James D. Griffin Plaza, Buffalo, NY 14203.
Telephone: (716) 846-2000. **Fax:** (716) 852-6530.
E-Mail Address: info@bisons.com. **Website:** www.bisons.com.
Affiliation (first year): Toronto Blue Jays (2013). **Years in League:** 2021-

OWNERSHIP/MANAGEMENT

Operated By: Rich Products Corp. **Principal Owner/President:** Robert Rich Jr. **President, Rich Entertainment Group:** Melinda Rich. **Vice President/Chief Operating Officer, Rich Entertainment Group:** Joseph Segarra. **President, Rich Baseball Operations:** Mike Buczkowski. **VP/Secretary:** William Gisel. **Corporate Counsel:** Jill Bond, William Grieshober. **VP/Operations & Finance:** Kevin Parkinson. **VP/Food Service Operations:** Robert Free. **General Manager:** Anthony Sprague. **Assistant General Manager/Marketing & PR:** Brad Bisbing. **Director, Stadium Operations:** Brian Phillips. **Senior Accountants:** Chas Fiscella. **Accountants:** Amy Delaney, Tori Dwyer. **Director, Ticket Operations:** Mike Poreda. **Director, Corporate Sales:** Jim Harrington. **Director, Sales:** Geoff Lundquist. **Account Executives:** Mark Gordon, Kim Milleville, Shaun O'Lay. **Manager, Merchandise:** Theresa Cerabone. **Executive Assistant:** Tina Lesher. **Community Relations:** Gail Hodges. **Director, Food & Beverage Operations:** Sean Regan. **Food Service Operations Supervisor:** Curt Anderson. **Chief Engineer:** Gerald Hamilton. **Home Clubhouse/Baseball Operations Coordinator:** Scott Lesher. **Visiting Clubhouse Manager:** Steve Morris. **Graphic Designer:** Allison Marcano.

FIELD STAFF

Manager: Casey Candaele. **Pitching Coach:** Jeff Ware. **Hitting Coach:** Corey Hart. **Defensive Coach:** Devon White. **Development Coach:** Jake McGuiggan. **Athletic Trainer:** Caleb Daniel. **Strength/Conditioning Coach:** Justin Batcher.

GAME INFORMATION

Radio Announcers: Pat Malacaro, Duke McGuire. **No. of Games Broadcast:** 150. **Flagship Station:** ESPN 1520. **PA Announcer:** Jerry Reo, Tom Burns. **Official Scorers:** Kevin Lester, Jon Dare.
Stadium Name: Sahlen Field. **Location:** From north, take I-190 to Elm Street exit, left onto Swan Street; From east, take I-190 West to exit 51 (Route 33) to end, exit at Oak Street, right onto Swan Street; From west, take I-190 East, exit 53 to I-90 North, exit at Elm Street, left onto Swan Street. **Standard Game Times:** 7:05 pm, Sun. 1:05. **Ticket Price Range:** TBA.

CHARLOTTE KNIGHTS

Address: Truist Field, 324 S. Mint St., Charlotte, NC 28202.
Telephone: (704) 274-8300. **Fax:** 704-274-8330.
E-Mail Address: knights@charlotteknights.com. **Website:** charlotteknights.com.

MINOR LEAGUES

Affiliation (first year): Chicago White Sox (1999). **Years in League:** 2021-

OWNERSHIP/MANAGEMENT

Operated by: Knights Baseball, LLC. **Principal Owners:** Don Beaver, Bill Allen. **Chief Operating Officer:** Dan Rajkowski. **General Manager:** Rob Egan. **Director, Special Projects:** Julie Clark. **Finance/HR Manager:** Sara Maple. **VP, Communications:** Tommy Viola. **VP, Sponsorship Sales:** Marty Steele. **VP, Marketing:** Matt DuBois. **VP, Stadium Operations:** Tom Gorter. **VP, Ticket Sales:** Matt Harper. **Senior Director of Game Entertainment & Creative Services:** Will Adams. **Director, Field Operations:** Matt Parrott. **Director, Broadcasting/Team Travel:** Matt Swierad. **Director, Community Relations:** Megan Smithers. **Director, Video Production:** Cameron Moist. **Director, Special Events:** Grace Eng. **Business Development Executive:** Josh Otterline. **Business Development Liaison:** Laura Little. **Client Services Manager:** Taylor Fike. **Group Sales Manager:** Carter Buffkin. **Ticket Operations Manager:** Leighton Foster. **Season Memberships Manager:** Alex Michel. **Ticket Sales and Service Representative:** Jack Doran. **Ticket Sales Account Executives:** Kelsey Kandil, T.J. King, Cooper Kinsey, Colin Kirby, Ryan Sorrow. **Director, Merchandise/Retail Operations:** Matt Strader. **Creative/IT Director:** Bill Walker. **Promotions Manager:** Chris Dillon. **Community & Promotions Coordinator:** Abbey Miller. **Digital Media and Graphic Design Manager:** Jason Furst. **Special Events Manager:** Troy Rodrigues. **Mascot/Entertainment Coordinator:** Diego Davila. **Operations Manager:** Matt Fisher. **Assistant Groundskeeper:** Julian Brown. **Assistant Manager, Clubhouse/Ballpark Operations:** Corbin Balzer. **Front Desk Receptionist/Administrative Assistant:** Victoria Liefert.

FIELD STAFF

Manager: Wes Helms. **Pitching Coach:** Matt Zaleski. **Hitting Coach:** Chris Johnson. **Trainer:** Cory Barton. **Performance Coach:** Shawn Powell.

GAME INFORMATION

Radio Announcers: Matt Swierad, Mike Pacheco. **No. of Games Broadcast:** 150. **Flagship Station:** 730 The Game ESPN Charlotte. **PA Announcer:** Ken Conrad. **Official Scorers:** Dave Friedman, Jim Morrison, Richard Walker. **Stadium Name:** Truist Field. **Location:** Exit 10 off Interstate 77. **Ticket Price Range:** $11-$23. **Visiting Club Hotel:** DoubleTree by Hilton Charlotte, 895 W. Trade St., Charlotte, NC 28202.

COLUMBUS CLIPPERS

Address: 330 Huntington Park Lane, Columbus, OH 43215.
Telephone: (614) 462-5250. **Fax:** (614) 462-3271. **Tickets:** (614) 462-2757.
E-Mail Address: info@clippersbaseball.com. **Website:** www.clippersbaseball.com.
Affiliation (first year): Cleveland Guardians (2009). **Years in League:** 2021-

OWNERSHIP/MANAGEMENT

President & General Manager: Ken Schnacke. **Vice-President, Assistant GM:** Mark Galuska. **Vice-President, Business:** Mark Warren. **Vice-President, Tickets:** Scott Ziegler. **Executive Assistant:** Ashley Held. **Team Historian:** Joe Santry. **Director, Merchandising:** Krista Oberlander. **Director, Ticket Operations:** Eddie Langhenry. **Director, Ticket Services:** Chris Sprague. **Director, Ticket Sales:** Kevin Daniels. **Assistant Director, Ticket Sales:** Matt Harrison. **Director, Group Sales:** Jacob Fleming. **Director, Finance & Administration:** Ashley Ramirez. **Director, Administration & Travel:** Shelby White. **Director, Multimedia:** Larry Mitchell. **Assistant Director, Multimedia:** Pat Welch.

Director, Marketing/In-Game Entertainment: Steve Kuilder. **Director, Game Ops/Creative Services:** Yoshi Ando. **Director, Pressbox Operations:** Anthony Slosser.

Director, Sales: Austin Smith. **Director, Corporate Sales:** Jason Hillyer. **Director, Ballpark Ops:** Tom Rinto. **Assistant Director, Ballpark Ops:** Spencer Harrison.

Director, Community Relatons: Emily Poynter. **Director, Special Projects:** Aaliyah Phounsavath. **Director, Website/Media Relations:** Matt Leininger. **Director, Social Media:** Don Hawkins. **Ballpark Superintendent:** Gary Delozier. **Maintenance Supervisor:** Curt Marcum. **Director, Event Planning:** Micki Shier. **Director, Broadcasting:** Ryan Mitchell. **Assistant Director, Broadcasting:** Scott Leo. **Director, Field Operations:** Wes Ganobcik. **Manager, Field Operations:** Connor Smith. **GM, Levy Food & Beverage:** Jeff Roberts. **Support Services:** Marvin Dill, Beth Morris. **Home Clubhouse:** John McCausland. **Visiting Clubhouse:** Adam Meader.

FIELD STAFF

Field Manager: Andy Tracy. **Pitching Coach:** Rigo Beltran. **Pitching Strategist:** Cody Buckel. **Hitting Coach:** Jason Esposito. **Bench Coach:** Kyle Lindquist. **Trainer:** Jeremy Heller. **Strength/Conditioning Coach:** Trent Kaltenbach.

GAME INFORMATION

Stadium Name: Huntington Park. **No. of Games Broadcast:** 150. **Location: From North:** South on I-71 to I-670 west, exit at Neil Avenue, turn left at intersection onto Neil Avenue. **From South:** North on I-71, exit at Front Street (#100A); turn left at intersection onto Front Street, turn left onto Nationwide Blvd. **From East:** West on I-70, exit at Fourth Street, continue on Fulton Street to Front Street, turn right onto Front Street, turn left onto Nationwide Blvd. **From West:** East on I-70, exit at Fourth Street, continue on Fulton Street to Front Street, turn right onto Front Street, turn left onto Nationwide Blvd. **Ticket Price Range:** $6-21. **Visiting Club Hotel:** Sonesta Columbus Downtown (formerly Crowne Plaza), 33 East Nationwide Blvd, Columbus, OH 43215. **Telephone:** (614) 461-4100. **Visiting Club Hotel:** Drury Hotels Columbus Convention Center, 88 East Nationwide Blvd, Columbus, OH 43215. **Telephone:** (614) 221-7008. **Visiting Club Hotel:** Hyatt Regency Downtown, 350 North High Street, Columbus, OH 43215. **Telephone:** (614) 463-1234. **Visiting Club Hotel:** Red Roof Inn, 111 East Nationwide Blvd., Columbus Ohio 43215. **Telephone:** 614-224-6539.

DURHAM BULLS

Office Address: 409 Blackwell St., Durham, NC 27701. **Mailing Address:** PO Box 507, Durham, NC 27702
Telephone: (919) 687-6500. **Fax:** (919) 687-6560
Website: durhambulls.com. **Twitter:** @DurhamBulls
Affiliation (first year): Tampa Bay Rays (1998). **Years in League:** 2021-

OWNERSHIP/MANAGEMENT

Operated by: Capitol Broadcasting Company, Inc. **President/COO:** Jimmy Goodmon. **Vice President of Baseball Operations:** Mike Birling. **Assistant General Manager, Sales:** Chip Allen. **Assistant General Manager, Operations:** Scott Strickland. **Business Manager:** Theresa Stocking. **Senior Accountant:** Jordan Tucker. **Senior & Special Projects Accountant:** Nick Bornhoft. **Senior Sponsorship Account Executive:** Andrew Ferrier. **Sponsorship Account Executive:** Kathleen Dwulet. **Head Groundskeeper:** Cameron Brendle. **Head Groundskeeper, Durham Athletic Park:** Joe Stumpo. **Stadium Operations Manager:** Will Bender. **Facility Operations Supervisor:** Tex Law. **Director, Marketing/Communications:** Michael Ward. **Director, Promotions:** Leslie Martin. **Video & Digital Production Manager:** Patrick Norwood. **Digital & Social Content Manager:** Andrew Green. **Production Designer:** Paxton Rembis. **Mascot & Community Relations Coordinator:** Eric Topolewski. **Director, Ticket Operations:** Peter Wallace. **Group Ticket Sales Manager:** Cassie Fowler. **Corporate Sales Account Executive:** Fulton Beasley. **Group Sales Account Executive:** Andy Benson. **Manager, Membership Services:** Timothy Troy. **Inside Ticket Sales Representative:** Erin Thompson. **Inside Ticket Sales Representative:** Andre Jackson. **Director of Merchandising and Team Travel:** Bryan Wilson. **Assistant Director of Merchandise, E-Commerce:** Emily Goddard. **Director of Food and Beverage:** Dave Levey. **Assistant Director of Food and Beverage:** Todd Feneley. **Concessions Manager:** Andrew Houston. **Hospitality Executive Chef:** Derek Crayton.

FIELD STAFF

Manager: Brady Williams. **Pitching Coach:** Brian Reith. **Hitting Coach:** Will Bradley. **Bench Coach:** Reinaldo Ruiz. **Athletic Trainers:** Scott Thurston/Kris Russell. **Strength Coach:** Carlos Gonzalez.

GAME INFORMATION

Broadcasters: Patrick Kinas, Scott Pose. **No. of Games Broadcast:** 150. **Flagship Station:** 96.5 FM and 99.3 FM. **PA Announcer:** Tony Riggsbee. **Official Scorer:** Brent Belvin. **Stadium Name:** Durham Bulls Athletic Park. **Location:** From Raleigh, I-40 West to Highway 147 North, exit 12B to Willard, two blocks on Willard to stadium; From I-85, Gregson Street exit to downtown, left on Chapel Hill Street, right on Mangum Street. **Standard Game Times:** 7:05 pm, Sat. 6:35 pm, Sun. 5:05 pm. **Ticket Price Range:** $7-14. **Visiting Club Hotel:** TBA. **Telephone:** TBA.

GWINNETT STRIPERS

Office Address: 2500 Buford Drive, Lawrenceville, GA 30043.
Mailing Address: P.O. Box 490310, Lawrenceville, GA 30049.
Telephone: (678) 277-0300. **Fax:** (678) 277-0338.
E-Mail Address: stripersinfo@braves.com. **Website:** www.gostripers.com.
Affiliation (first year): Atlanta Braves (1966). **Years in League:** 2021-

OWNERSHIP/MANAGEMENT

Ownership: Diamond Baseball Holdings, LLC. **Vice President & General Manager:** Erin McCormick. **Senior Director of Operations:** Ryan Stoltenberg. **Senior Director of Ticket Sales:** Peter Billups. **Office Manager:** Tyra Williams. **Ticket Sales Manager:** Zack Mandelblatt. **Account Executives:** Ansley Mitchell, Carlos Ortiz, Virginia Nelle Reid, Taylor Roach. **Ticket Operations Coordinator:** Richard Moseley. **Manager of Corporate Partnerships:** Robbie Burnstein. **Partnership Activation Coordinator:** Katie McDermott. **Media Relations Manager & Broadcaster:** Dave Lezotte. **Creative Services Manager:** Nick Gosen. **Marketing Manager:** Kyle Kamerbeek. **Director of Fun (Non-Game Events):** Nino Dandan. **Stadium Operations Manager:** Rick Fultz. **Facilities Engineer:** Gary Hoopaugh. **Director of Sports Turf Management:** McClain Murphy. **Sports Turf Coordinator:** Kiley Coursey. **Home Clubhouse Manager:** Nick Dixon. **Merchandise Coordinator:** Malik Perkins. **Director of Operations, Professional Sports Catering:** Chiara Perkins.

FIELD STAFF

Manager: Matt Tuiasosopo. **Hitting Coach:** Carlos Mendez. **Pitching Coach:** Mike Maroth. **Coach:** TBD. **Athletic Trainer:** TBD

GAME INFORMATION

Radio Announcer: Dave Lezotte. **No. of Games Broadcast:** 150. **Flagship Station:** My Country 99.3 WCON (streaming online only at MyCountry993.com). **PA Announcer:** Kevin Kraus. **Official Scorers:** Jack Woodard, Guy Curtright, Stan Awtrey, Phil Engel. **Stadium Name:** Coolray Field. **Location:** I-85 (at Exit 115, State Road 20 West) and I-985 (at Exit 4); follow signs to park. **Ticket Price Range:** $8-30 (advance) or $11-33 (day-of-game). **Visiting Club Hotels:** Courtyard by Marriott Buford/Mall of Georgia, 1405 Mall of Georgia Boulevard, Buford, GA 30519. **Telephone:** (678) 745-3380. Fairfield Inn & Suites Atlanta Buford/Mall of Georgia, 1355 Mall of Georgia Boulevard, Buford, GA 30519. **Telephone:** (678) 714-0248.

INDIANAPOLIS INDIANS

Address: 501 W. Maryland Street, Indianapolis, IN 46225.
Telephone: (317) 269-3542. **Fax:** (317) 269-3541.
E-Mail Address: Indians@IndyIndians.com. **Website:** www.indyindians.com.
Affiliation (first year): Pittsburgh Pirates (2005). **Years in League:** 2021-

OWNERSHIP/MANAGEMENT

Chairman of the Board & Chief Executive Officer: Bruce Schumacher. **President & General Manager:** Randy Lewandowski. **Chairman Emeritus:** Max Schumacher. **Assistant General Manager, Corporate Sales & Marketing:** Joel Zawacki. **Assistant General Manager, Tickets & Operations:** Matt Guay. **Director, Business Systems & Talent:** Bryan Spisak. **Business Intelligence Analyst:** Bill Fulton. **Business Operations Manager:** Sarah Haynes. **Guest Relations Coordinator:** Michelle Trevino. **Director, Communications:** Cheyne Reiter. **Baseball Communications Coordinator:** Anna Kayser. **Social Media Coordinator:** Katie Bostic. **Voice of the Indians:** Howard Kellman. **Director, Creative:** Adam Pintar. **Videographer:** Alex Leachman. **Director, Corporate Sales:** Christina Toler. **Senior Corporate Sales Account Executive:** Mike McClure. **Partnership Activation Manager:** Kylie Kinder. **Partnership Activation Coordinators:** Ben Kayser, Chandler McKinney. **Senior Director, Facilities:** Tim Hughes. **Senior Facilities Manager:** Allan Danehy. **Facilities Maintenance Tech:** Kyle Winters. **Director, Field Operations:** Joey Stevenson. **Field Operations Manager:** Adam Basinger. **Director, Marketing:** Kim Stoebick. **Marketing Manager:** Hayden Barnack. **Digital Marketing Manager:** Max Freeman. **Marketing Project Manager:** Heidi Gahm. **Director, Merchandise:** Mark Schumacher. **Merchandise Manager:** Patrick Westrick. **Stadium Operations Manager:** Kim Duplak. **Operations Support:** Ki Hubbard, Sandra Reaves. **Home Clubhouse Manager:** Bobby Martin. **Visiting Clubhouse Manager:** Jeremy Martin. **Director, Ticket Sales:** Chad Bohm. **Director of Tickets, Premium Services & Events:** Kerry Vick. **Stadium Events Manager:** Paige McClung. **Premium & Ticket Services Manager:** Kathryn Bobel. **Ticket Services Manager:** Cara Carrion. **Senior Ticket Sales Account Executives:** Jonathan Howard, Garrett Rosh. **Ticket Sales Account Executives:** Jack Becker, Ty Eaton, Matt Marencik, Nathan Watson. **ARAMARK General Manager:** Chris Scherrer. **Concession Manager:** Jamie Nicholson.

FIELD STAFF

Manager: Miguel Perez. **Pitching Coach:** Dan Meyer. **Hitting Coach:** Eric Munson. **Bench Coach:** Gary Green. **Integrated Performance Coach:** Brady Conlan. **Athletic Trainer:** Tyler Brooks. **Strength & Conditioning Coach:** Alan Burr.

GAME INFORMATION

Radio Announcers: Howard Kellman, Andrew Kappes, Joel Godett, Cheyne Reiter. **Flagship Station:** CBS 1430 AM.
PA Announcer: David Pygman. **Official Scorers:** Ed Holdaway, Kim Rogers, Will Roleson, Geoff Sherman, Jeff Williams.
Stadium Name: Victory Field. **Location:** I-70 to West Street exit, north on West Street to ballpark; I-65 to Martin Luther King and West Street exit, south on West Street to ballpark. **Standard Game Times:** 7:05 pm; 6:35 (Sat in April/May/Sept.); 1:35 (Wed/Sun.). **Ticket Price Range:** $12-18. **Visiting Club Hotel:** Fairfield Indianapolis Downtown, 501 W. Washington Street, Indianapolis, IN 46204. **Telephone:** (317) 636-7678.

IOWA CUBS

Address: One Line Drive, Des Moines IA 50309.
Telephone: (515) 243-6111. **Fax:** (515) 243-5152.
Website: www.iowacubs.com.
Affiliation (first year): Chicago Cubs (1981). **Years in League:** 2021-

OWNERSHIP/MANAGEMENT

Owner: Diamond Baseball Holdings. **Executive Chairman:** Pat Battle. **Chief Executive Officer:** Peter B. Freund. **President/General Manager:** Sam Bernabe. **VP/Assistant GM:** Randy Wehofer. **VP/CFO:** Sue Tollefson. **Manager, Media Relations:** Colin Connolly. **Director, Video and Multimedia Arts:** Justin Walters. **Director, Ticket Operations:** Clayton Grandquist. **Director, Broadcasting:** Alex Cohen. **Director, Group Outings/Senior Account Executive:** Jason Gellis. **VP/Director, Premium Seating/Corporate Marketing:** Brent Conkel. **VP/Director, Stadium Operations:** Jeff Tilley. **Managers, Stadium Operations:** Andrew Quillin, Dustin Halderson. **Supervisor, Stadium Operations:** Josh Stephens. **Account Executive:** John Rodgers. **Manager, Marketing:** Beth Kneeskern. **VP/Manager, Sports Turf:** Chris Schlosser. **Assistant Sports Turf Manager:** Brooks Montange. **Assistant Grounds Crew/Outside Grounds:** Bridger Claassen. **Director, Merchandise:** Lisa Hufford. **Accounts Payable & Receivable:** Lori Auten. **Chief Technology Officer:** Ryan Clutter. **Manager, Digital Media/Graphic Design:** Matt Evers. **Special Events:** Scott Sailor. **Landscape Coordinator:** Shari Kramer.

FIELD STAFF

Manager: Marty Pevey. **Hitting Coach:** Desi Wilson. **Pitching Coach:** Ron Villone. **Coach:** Griffin Benedict. **Athletic Trainers:** TBD. **Strength/Conditioning:** TBD.

GAME INFORMATION

Radio Announcer: Alex Cohen. **No. of Games Broadcast:** 150. **Flagship Station:** AM 940 KPSZ. **PA Announcers:** Mark Pierce, Corey Coon, Rick Stageman, Joe Hammen. **Official Scorers:** Michael Pecina, James Hilchen, Steve Mohr. **Stadium Name:** Principal Park. **Location:** I-80 or I-35 to I-235, to Third Street exit, south on Third Street, left on Line

Drive. **Standard Game Times:** Tues.-Thurs. 6:38, Fri. 7:08, Sat. 6:08, Sun. 1:08. **Ticket Price Range:** $5-35. **Visiting Hotel:** Hampton Inn and Suites Downtown, 120 SW Water Street, Des Moines IA 50309. **Telephone:** (515) 244-1650.

JACKSONVILLE JUMBO SHRIMP

Office Address: 301 A. Philip Randolph Blvd, Jacksonville, FL 32202.
Telephone: (904) 358-2846. **Fax:** (904) 358-2845.
E-Mail Address: info@jaxshrimp.com. **Website:** www.jaxshrimp.com.
Affiliation (first year): Miami Marlins (2009). **Years In League:** 2021-

OWNERSHIP/MANAGEMENT
Operated by: Jacksonville Baseball LLC.
Owner & Chief Executive Officer: Ken Babby. **Executive Assistant to Ken Babby:** Jill Popov. **President, Fast Forward Sports Group:** Jim Pfander. **Chief Human Resources Office:** Leatrice Buck. **Chief Financial Officer:** Shawn Carlson. **Executive Vice President/General Manager:** Harold Craw. **Vice President, Marketing and Media:** Noel Blaha. **Senior Vice President, Sales:** Linda McNabb. **Assistant General Manager:** Matt Goudreau. **Director, Field Operations:** Christian Galen. **Director, Promotions & Special Events:** David Ratz. **Director of Corporate Partnerships:** Terry O'Grady. **Director of Ticket Operations:** Peter Ercey. **Director of Broadcasting and Media Relations:** Scott Kornberg. **Assistant Director, Food & Beverage:** Nevious Love. **Stadium Operations Manager:** Tom Snyder. **Creative Services Manager:** Brian DeLettre. **Merchandise Manager:** Brennan Earley. **Community Relations Manager:** Miranda Rossum. **Accounting Manager:** Bryson Lenderman. **Box Office Manager:** Cody Davis. **Partner Services Coordinator:** Holden Hitchcock. **Chef, Food & Beverage:** Travis Bosche. **Account Executives:** Damon Aultman, Kacie Jevic, Jenna Smith, Devin Walker. **Stadium Operations Assistant:** Matthew Maynard. **Field Operations Assistant:** Chris Campbell. **Finance Assistant:** Patrick Jordan. **Travel Coordinator/Office Administrator:** Christine Collins. **Broadcast & Media Relations Assistant:** Matt Present. **Payroll Coordinator:** Teresa Lively-Hall.

FIELD STAFF
Manager: Daren Brown. **Pitching Coach:** Jeremy Powell. **Hitting Coach:** Phil Plantier. **Defensive Coach:** Jose Ceballos. **Athletic Trainer:** Greg Harrel. **Strength/Conditioning Coach:** TBA.

GAME INFORMATION
Radio Announcers: Scott Kornberg & Matt Present. **No. of Games Broadcast:** 150. **Flagship Station:** ESPN 690.
PA Announcer: John Leard. **Official Scorer:** Jason Eliopulos. **Stadium Name:** 121 Financial Ballpark. **Location:** I-95 South to Martin Luther King Parkway exit, follow Gator Bowl Blvd around TIAA Bank Field; I-95 North to Exit 347 (Emerson Street), go right to Hart Bridge Expressway, take Sports Complex exit, left at light to stop sign, take left and follow around TIAA Bank Field; From Mathews Bridge, take A Philip Randolph exit, right on A Philip Randolph, straight to ballpark. **Standard Game Times:** 7:05 pm, Sat. 6:35 pm, Sun. 3:05 pm. **Ticket Price Range:** $5-$28. **Visiting Club Hotel:** Doubletree by Hilton Hotel Jacksonville Riverfront, 1201 Riverplace Blvd., Jacksonville, FL 32207. **Telephone:** (904) 398-8800.

LEHIGH VALLEY IRONPIGS

Address: 1050 IronPigs Way, Allentown, PA 18109
Telephone: (610) 841-7447. **Fax:** (610) 841-1509
E-Mail Address: info@ironpigsbaseball.com. **Website:** www.ironpigsbaseball.com.
Affiliation (first year): Philadelphia Phillies (2008). **Years in League:** 2021-

OWNERSHIP/MANAGEMENT
Ownership: LV Baseball LP. **President & General Manager:** Kurt Landes. **Vice President, Ticket Sales:** Andy Beuster. **Senior Director, Marketing and Entertainment:** Matthew Bari. **Manager, Media Relations:** Mike Ventola. **Director, Digital Media & Communications:** Matthew Stratton. **Director, Multimedia Design:** Kevin Whitehead. **Manager, Multimedia Design:** Michael Raineri. **Director, Promotions/Entertainment:** Rachel Novotny. **Manager, IronPigs Charities:** Matthew Sommers. **Manager, Community Relations:** Mike Ianniello. **Vice President, Food & Beverage:** Alex Rivera. **Director, Food & Beverage:** Brock Hartranft. **Director, Special Events:** Allison Valentine. **Executive Chef:** Wael Samaan. **Senior Director, Corporate Partnerships:** Erik Hoffman. **Manager, Sponsorship Services:** Peter Schiffert. **Administrative Assistant:** Pat Golden. **Director, Field Operations:** Andy Gossel. **Manager, Field Operations:** Tom Klich. **Vice President, Stadium Operations:** Jason Kiesel. **Managers, Stadium Operations:** Derrike Mason. **Vice President, Administration:** Michelle Perl. **Manager, Corporate Partnerships:** Ray Bleam, Jordan Perrine, Molly Pyne. **Director, Guest Experience:** Brad Ludwig. **Director, Group Sales:** Ryan Hines. **Managers, Group Sales:** Daniel Sterenberg, Zach Groover, Nikki Homanick, Chad Mazepa. **Senior Manager, Corporate Ticket Sales:** Cody Hallman. **Director, Ticket Operations:** Brittany Balonis. **Senior Manager, Ticket Operations & Analytics:** Collin DeJong. **Managers, Ticket Coordinator:** David Reynolds, Chris DeSpirito. **Manager, Corporate Ticket Sales:** Erik Kerns, Dante Strella. **Director, Merchandise:** Mike Luciano.

FIELD STAFF
Manager: Anthony Contreras. **Pitching Coach:** Cesar Ramos. **Hitting Coach:** Joe Thurston. **Bench Coach:** Greg Brodzinski. **Athletic Trainers:** Elliot Diehl, Meaghan Flaherty. **Strength/Conditioning Coach:** Mike Lidge

GAME INFORMATION

Radio Announcers: Pat McCarthy and Mike Ventola. **No. of Games Broadcast:** 150. **Flagship Radio Station:** FOX Sports Radio 1230 AM & 94.7 FM. **Television Station:** Service Electric Network. **Television Announcers:** Mike Zambelli, Steve Degler, Doug Heater. **No. of Games Televised:** 75 (all home games). **PA Announcer:** Justin Choate. **Official Scorers:** Mike Falk, Jack Logic, David Sheriff, Dick Shute. **Stadium Name:** Coca-Cola Park. **Location:** Take US 22 to exit for Airport Road South, head south, make right on American Parkway, left into stadium. **Standard Game Times:** 7:05 pm, Sat. 6:35, Sun. 1:35.

LOUISVILLE BATS

Address: 401 E Main St, Louisville, KY 40202.
Telephone: (502) 212-2287. **Fax:** (502) 515-2255.
E-Mail Address: info@batsbaseball.com. **Website:** www.batsbaseball.com.
Affiliation (first year): Cincinnati Reds (2000). **Years in League:** 2021-

OWNERSHIP/MANAGEMENT

Chairman: Stuart and Jerry Katzoff (MC Sports)
President: Greg Galliete. **Vice President of Finance, Controller:** Michele Anderson. **Vice President of Stadium Operations:** Brett Myers. **Vice President of Business Development:** Claudia Padgett. **Vice President of Marketing:** Tony Brown. **Director of Ticket Sales:** David Barry. **Director of Communications:** Chris Robinson. **Head Clubhouse Manager:** TBD. **Club Physicians:** Walter Badenhausen, M.D.; John A. Lach, Jr., M.D. **Club Dentist:** Pat Carroll, D.M.D. **Chaplains:** Jose Castillo.

FIELD STAFF

Manager: Pat Kelly. **Pitching Coach:** Seth Etherton. **Hitting Coach:** Alex Pelaez. **Bench Coach:** Dick Schofield. **Game Planning/Outfield Coach:** Mike Jacobs. **Athletic Trainer:** Steve Gober. **Strength/Conditioning Coach:** Kenny Matanane.

GAME INFORMATION

Radio Announcers: Nick Curran. **No. of Games Broadcast:** 150. **Flagship Station:** WXVW 1450 AM and 96.1 FM. **PA Announcer:** Charles Gazaway. **Official Scorers:** Nick Evans, Neil Rohrer, Ryan Ritchey, Jeff Kopple. **Stadium Name:** Louisville Slugger Field. **Location:** I-64 and I-71 to I-65 South/North to Brook Street exit, right on Market Street, left on Jackson Street; stadium on Main Street between Jackson and Preston. **Ticket Price Range:** $9-55. **Visiting Club Hotel:** Omni Hotel, 400 South 2nd Street, Louisville, KY 40202. **Telephone:** (502) 313-6664.

MEMPHIS REDBIRDS

Office Address: 198 Union, Memphis, TN 38103.
Stadium Address: 198 Union Ave, Memphis, TN 38103.
Telephone: (901) 721-6000. **Fax:** (901) 328-1102. **Website:** www.memphisredbirds.com.
Affiliation (first year): St. Louis Cardinals (1998). **Years in League:** 2021-

OWNERSHIP/MANAGEMENT

Ownership: Peter B. Freund.
President/General Manager: Craig Unger. **Vice President, Stadium and Baseball Operations:** Mike Voutsinas. **Manager, Group Sales:** Dylan Powers. **Director, Field Operations:** Eric Taylor. **Manager, Ticket Operations:** Nate Deavers. **Manager, Corporate Sales:** Tyler Gilles. **Coordinator, Integrated Marketing:** Sarah Jent. **Graphic Designer:** John Privitera. **Manager, Retail Operations:** Kyle Nekoloff. **Accounting Manager:** Cindy Neal. **Facilities Manager:** Spencer Shields.

FIELD STAFF

Manager: Ben Johnson. **Hitting Coach:** Brandon Allen. **Pitching Coach:** Dernier Orozco. **Trainer:** Dan Martin. **Strength & Conditioning:** Jacqueline Grover.

GAME INFORMATION

Radio Announcer: TBA **No. of Games Broadcast:** 150. **Flagship Station:** online. **PA Announcer:** Greg Ratliff. **Official Scorers:** TBA. **Stadium Name:** AutoZone Park. **Location:** North on I-240, exit at Union Avenue West, one and half miles to park. **Standard Game Times:** Mon-Wed. 6:45, Thu-Fri. 7:10, Sat. 6:**35**, Sun 2:05. **Ticket Price Range:** $9-24. **Visiting Club Hotel:** TBA.

NASHVILLE SOUNDS

Address: 19 Junior Gilliam Way, Nashville, TN 37219.
Telephone: (615) 690-HITS. **Fax:** (615) 256-5684.
E-Mail address: info@nashvillesounds.com. **Website:** www.nashvillesounds.com.
Affiliation (first year): Milwaukee Brewers (2021). **Years in League:** 2021-

OWNERSHIP/MANAGEMENT

Operated By: MFP Baseball. **Owners:** Frank Ward, Masahiro Honzawa.

GM/Chief Operating Officer: Adam English. **Asst. GM/VP, Operations:** Doug Scopel. **VP, Corporate Partnerships:** Danielle Gaw. **VP, Ticket Sales and Service:** Taylor Fisher. **Director, Finance:** Barb Walker. **Director, Accounting:** Katie Sigman. **Director, Communications:** Chad Seely. **Director, Marketing:** Abby Holman. **Director, Broadcasting:** Jeff Hem. **Director, Stadium Operations:** Jeremy Wells. **Director, Ticket Sales:** Kevin Kurowski. **Director, Ticket Operations:** Kyle Hargrove. **Director, Retail:** Wade Becker. **Director, Special Events:** Sierra Siegel. **Manager, Fan Services:** Travis Williams. **Manager, Business Development:** Jon Brownfield. **Manager, Entertainment and Promotions:** Karly Deland. **Manager, Community Relations:** Jade Dugdale. **Manager, Video & Production:** Neil Rosan. **Manager, Stadium Operations:** Caleb Yorks and Hannah Onken. **Account Executive:** Kelsen Adeni, Jay Evans, Jacob Friehauf, Ben Whalin, Kelsey Wisner. **Coordinator, Ticket Operations:** Lyndsey Tarver. **Coordinator, Mascot:** Buddy Yelton. **Coordinator, Production Events:** Stephen Hart. **Coordinator, Digital Marketing:** Griffin Westbrook. **Assistant, Marketing:** Chris Daniels. **Assistant, Graphic Design:** Katelyn Fleming. **Assistant, Video Production:** Kelly Teseny. **Ticket Sales Representatives:** Luke Povolny and Wesley Rose. **Head Groundskeeper:** Thomas Trotter. **Assistant Groundskeepers:** Shay Adams and McKinley Griggs. **Clubhouse & Equipment Manager:** Matt Gallant. **Visiting Clubhouse Manager:** Patrick King. **Team Photographer:** Casey Gower.

FIELD STAFF

Manager: Rick Sweet. **Hitting Coach:** Al LeBoeuf. **Pitching Coach:** TBD. **Coach:** Ned Yost IV. **Development Coach:** Sean Isaac. **Athletic Trainer:** Jeff Paxson. **Assistant Athletic Trainer:** Myles Fish. **Strength & Conditioning Specialist:** Andrew Emmick.

GAME INFORMATION

Radio Announcer: Jeff Hem. **No. of Games Broadcast:** 150. **Flagship Station:** 94.9 ESPN. **Official Scorers:** Eric Jones, Cody Bush, Eric Moyer. **Stadium Name:** First Horizon Park. **Location:** I-65 to exit 85 (Rosa L Parks Blvd) and head south; Turn left on Jefferson St, then turn right onto Rep. John Lewis Way, then turn left on Jackson St. **Standard Game Times:** 7:05, 6:35, 6:05, 2:05. **Ticket Price Range:** $10-35. **Visiting Club Hotel:** Sonesta Nashville. 600 Marriott Drive, Nashville, TN 37214.

NORFOLK TIDES

Address: 150 Park Ave, Norfolk, VA 23510.
Telephone: (757) 622-2222. **Fax:** (757) 624-9090.
E-Mail Address: receptionist@norfolktides.com. **Website:** www.norfolktides.com.
Affiliation (first year): Baltimore Orioles (2007). **Years in League:** 2021-

OWNERSHIP/MANAGEMENT

Operated By: Tides Baseball Club Inc.
President: Ken Young. **General Manager:** Joe Gregory.
Assistant General Managers: Mike Watkins, Mike Zeman. **Director, Ticket Operations:** Sze Fong. **Director, Ticket Sales:** John Muszkewycz. **Business Manager:** Dawn Coutts. **Head Groundskeeper:** Kenny Magner. **Home Clubhouse Manager:** Adam Sehlmeyer. **Visiting Clubhouse Manager:** Jack Brenner.

FIELD STAFF

Manager: Buck Britton. **Pitching Coach:** Justin Ramsey. **Hitting Coach:** Tim Gibbons. **Fundamentals Coach:** Ramon Sambo. **Development Coach:** Joshua Rodrigues. **Strength Coach:** Jon Medici. **Trainer:** Alan Rail.

GAME INFORMATION

Radio Announcer: Pete Michaud. **No. of Games Broadcast:** 150. **Flagship Station:** ESPN 94.1 FM. **PA Announcer:** Jack Ankerson. **Official Scorers:** Mike Holtzclaw, Jim Hodges. **Stadium Name:** Harbor Park. **Location:** Exit 9, 11A or 11B off I-264, adjacent to the Elizabeth River in downtown Norfolk. **Standard Game Times:** 6:35 pm Monday-Thursday and Saturday, Friday 7:05 pm, Sun 1:05 pm (first half of season); 4:05 pm (second half of season). **Ticket Price Range:** $12-15. **Visiting Club Hotel:** Sheraton Waterside, 777 Waterside Dr, Norfolk, VA 23510. **Telephone:** (757) 622-6664.

OMAHA STORM CHASERS

Address: Werner Park, 12356 Ballpark Way, Papillion, NE 68046.
Administrative Office Phone: (402) 734-2550. **Ticket Office Phone:** (402) 738-5100. **Fax:** (402) 734-7166.
E-mail Address: info@omahastormchasers.com. **Website:** www.omahastormchasers.com.
Affiliation (first year): Kansas City Royals (1969). **Years in League:** 2021-

OWNERSHIP/MANAGEMENT

Operated By: Alliance Baseball Managing Partners. **Owners:** Gary Green, Larry Botel, Brian Callaghan, Eric Foss, Stephen Alepa, Peter Huff, Evan Friend. **CEO:** Gary Green. **President:** Martie Cordaro. **Vice President/General Manager:** Laurie Schlender. **Human Resources Manager:** Aniya Tate. **Director of Sales:** Marcus Sabata. **Director/Operations:** Steve Farrens. **Head Groundskeeper:** Zach Ricketts. **Director of Marketing & Communications:** Justin Rolfes. **Broadcaster:** Jake Eisenberg. **Promotions/Game Operations Manager:** Emily Hintz. **Client Services Manager:** Mackenzie Parker. **Media/Public Relations Manager:** Justin Rolfes. **Video/Multimedia Coordinator:** Lexi Gross.

Graphic Design Coordinator: Alex Seder. **Social Media Manager:** Nina Sobotka. **Director/Ticket Operations:** Jeremy Ramey. **Director of Group Sales:** Zach Ziler. **Sales Executive:** Blake Paris. **Sales Executive:** Tyler St. Denny. **Sales Executive:** Dru Sauer. **Retail Operations Manager:** Mitch Cunningham. **Bookkeepers:** Pennie Martindale. **Grounds Manager:** Tom Walter. **Home Clubhouse Manager:** Mike Brown. **Front Office Assistants:** Donna Kostal, Michelle VanBemmelen.

FIELD STAFF

Manager: Scott Thorman. **Hitting Coach:** Brian Buchanan. **Pitching Coach:** Dane Johnson. **Athletic Trainer:** James Stone. **Strength Coach:** Yannick Plante.

GAME INFORMATION

Radio Announcers: Jake Eisenberg. **No. of Games Broadcast:** 150. **Flagship Station:** KZOT-AM 1180.
PA Announcer: Craig Evans. **Official Scorers:** Gary Sharp & Ryan White. **Stadium Name:** Werner Park. **Location:** Highway 370, just east of I-80 (exit 439). **Standard Game Times:** 6:35 pm (April-May), 7:05 (June-Sept), Fri./Sat. 7:05, Sun. 2:05. **Visiting Club Hotel:** Courtyard Omaha La Vista, 12560 Westport Parkway, La Vista, NE 68128. **Telephone:** (402) 339-4900. **Fax:** (402) 339-4901.

ROCHESTER RED WINGS

Address: One Morrie Silver Way, Rochester, NY 14608.
Telephone: (585) 454-1001. **Fax:** (585) 454-1056.
E-Mail: info@redwingsbaseball.com. **Website:** RedWingsBaseball.com.
Affiliation (first year): Washington Nationals (2021). **Years in League:** 2021-

OWNERSHIP/MANAGEMENT

Operated by: Rochester Community Baseball, Inc.
President/CEO/COO: Naomi Silver.
Chairman: Gary Larder. **General Manager:** Dan Mason. **Assistant GM:** Will Rumbold. **Assistant GM, Sales:** Bob Craig. **Senior Director, Tickets & Group Sales:** Eric Friedman. **Director, Communications:** Nate Rowan. **Director, Corporate Development:** Nick Sciarratta. **Manager, Promotions:** Tim Doohan. **Director, Video Production:** John Blotzer. **Director, Ticket Operations:** Mike Ewing. **Director, Merchandising:** Nicole Boyle. **Director, Ballpark Operations:** Cam Mason. **Director, Gameday Operations:** Morrie Silver. **Coordinator, Digital Media:** Stephen Lasnick. **Head Groundskepper:** Gene Buonomo. **Assistant Groundskeeper:** Geno Buonomo. **Office Manager:** Amber Johnson. **Assistant, Merchandising:** Ava Kohut. **Controller:** Michelle Schiefer. **Director, Human Resources:** Paula LoVerde. **Ticket Office Mgr. & Business Coordinator:** Dave Welker.
GM, Food & Beverage: Jeff DeSantis. **Business Manager, F&B:** Dave Bills. **Director, Catering & Hospitality:** Megan Ridings. **Manager, Catering Sales:** Emily Chard. **Kitchen Manager:** Cheryl Jefferson.

FIELD STAFF

Manager: Matthew LeCroy. **Hitting Coach:** Brian Daubach. **Pitching Coach:** Rafael Chaves. **Development Coach:** Billy McMillon. **Athletic Trainer:** Eric Montague. **Strength & Conditioning Coach:** Mike Warren.

GAME INFORMATION

Radio Announcer: Josh Whetzel. **No. of Games Broadcast:** 150. **Flagship Stations:** WHTK 1280-AM.
PA Announcers: Kevin Spears, Rocky Perrotta. **Official Scorers:** Warren Kozireski, Nicole Harrington, Craig Bodensteiner, Bob Simms. **Stadium Name:** Frontier Field. **Location:** I-490 East to exit 12 (Brown/Broad Street) and follow signs; I-490 West to exit 14 (Plymouth Ave) and follow signs. **Standard Game Times:** 7:05 pm, Sun 1:05. **Ticket Price Range:** $13-19. **Visiting Club Hotel:** Hyatt Regency Rochester, 125 E Main St, Rochester, NY 14604. **Telephone:** (585) 546-1234

ST. PAUL SAINTS

Office Address: 360 Broadway Street, St. Paul, MN 55101.
Telephone: (651) 644-3517. **Fax:** (651) 644-1627.
Email Address: funisgood@saintsbaseball.com.
Website: saintsbaseball.com.
Affiliation: Minnesota Twins (2021). **Years in League:** 2021-

OWNERSHIP/MANAGEMENT

Chairman of the Board: Marvin Goldklang. **President:** Mike Veeck. **Executive VP/General Manager:** Derek Sharrer. **Executive VP/Business Development:** Tom Whaley. **Executive Vice President, Sales and Operations:** Chris Schwab. **Vice President, Director of Media Relations/Broadcasting:** Sean Aronson. **Vice President/Assistant General Manager:** Zane Heinselman. **Vice President, Brand Marketing & Experience:** Sierra Bailey. **Director, Community Partnerships and Fan Services:** Eddie Coblentz. **Director, Ticket Operations:** Shana McGlynn. **Director of Creative Services:** Rob Thompson. **Multi-Media Content Producer:** Joey Skare. **Digital Media Specialist:** Aly May. **Ticket Sales Manager:** Michael Villafana. **Senior Account Executive:** Luke Mericle. **Ticket Sales Executives:** Kailyn Johnson, Eric Simon. **CHS Field Events Coordinator:** Grace Hall. **Business Manager/Community Relations:** Krista Schnelle. **Office Manager:** Gina Kray. **Director, Ballpark Operations:** Curtis Nachtsheim. **Head Groundskeeper, Sports Turf Manager:** Marcus Campbell. **Vice President of Operations, Professional Sports Catering:** Justin Grandstaff. **Director**

of Operations, Professional Sports Catering: Gregg Kraly. Assistant Director of Operations: Daniel Franklyn. Sr. Business Manager: Amy Schroer. Executive Chef: James Cross. Premium Manager: Sarah Spires.

FIELD STAFF

Manager: Toby Gardenhire. Pitching Coaches: Cibney Bello and Virgil Vasquez. Hitting Coach: Ryan Smith. Infield Coach: Tyler Smarslok. Athletic Trainer: Ben Myers.

GAME INFORMATION

Radio Announcer: Sean Aronson. Games Broadcast: 150. Flagship Station: KFAN+ 96.7 FM. Webcast Address: www.saintsbaseball.com. Stadium Name: CHS Field. Location: From the west take I-94 to the 7th St. Exit and head south to 5th & Broadway. From the east take I-94 to the Mounds Blvd/US-61N exit. Turn left on Kellogg and a right on Broadway until you reach 5th St. Standard Game Times: (Games through May 8) Tue.- Fri.: 6:37 pm, Sat: 2:07 p.m., Sun.: 2:07 pm. (Games from May 24-September 28): Tue-Sat: 7:07 p.m., Sun: 2:07 p.m.

SCRANTON/WILKES-BARRE
RAILRIDERS

Address: 235 Montage Mountain Rd., Moosic, PA 18507.
Telephone: (570) 969-2255. Fax: (570) 963-6564.
E-Mail Address: info@swbrailriders.com.
Website: www.swbrailriders.com.
Affiliation (first year): New York Yankees (2007). Years in League: 2021-

OWNERSHIP/MANAGEMENT

Ownership: Diamond Baseball Holdings. Executive Chairman: Pat Battle. CEO: Peter Freund. Team President: John Adams. General Manager: Katie Beekman. VP, Ticket Sales: Chris Hutson. VP, Corporate Partnerships: Matt Hamilton. Director, Communications/Broadcaster: Adam Marco. Director, Community Relations: Jordan Maydole. Corporate Partnerships Manager: Josh Klein. Director, Corporate Services & Design: Kristina Knight. Corporate Services Manager: Katie Mummert. Senior Accountant: Holly Gumble. Director, Marketing: Jordan Calvey. Marketing Manager: Katherine Arata. Social Media/ Special Events Manager: Kirsten Peters. Video Production Manager: Taylor Moy. Director of Ticket Operations: Felicia Adamus. Director, Season Ticket Sales & Service: Kelly Cusick. Account Executives, Season Tickets: Kyle Davis & Devin Dunsing. Director, Group Sales: Mike Harvey. Group Sales Executives: Anthony D'Andrea & Chris Kunzmann. Director, Youth Baseball & Sports Sales: Robby Judge. Premium Sales Manager: Tim Duggan. Premium Sales Executive: Mike Phipps. Director, Field Operations: Steve Horne. Assistant Groundskeeper: Dustin Spiegel. Director, Facility Operations: Ryan Long. Stadium Operations Manager: Brandon Brzenski.

FIELD STAFF

Manager: TBA. Pitching Coach: TBA. Hitting Coach: TBA. Defensive Coach: TBA. Athletic Trainer: TBA. Strength/ Conditioning Coach: TBA.

GAME INFORMATION

Radio Announcer: Adam Marco. No. of Games Broadcast: 150. Flagship Stations: 1340 WYCK-AM, 1400 WICK-AM, 1440 WCDL-AM. Television Announcer: Adam Marco. No. of Games Broadcast: TBA. Flagship Station: TBA. PA Announcers: Unavailable. Official Scorers: Dean Corwin, Dick Devans, Mark Ligi & Armand Rosamilia. Stadium Name: PNC Field. Location: Exit 182 off Interstate 81; stadium is on Montage Mountain Road. Standard Game Times: Mon.- Sat. 6:35 pm (April/May) 7:05 pm (June-August); Sun. 1:05 pm. Ticket Price Range: $10-$16. Visiting Club Hotel: Hilton Scranton & Conference Center. Telephone: (570) 343-3000.

SYRACUSE METS

Address: One Tex Simone Drive, Syracuse NY, 13208
Telephone: 315-474-7833. Fax: 315-474-2658.
E-Mail Address: baseball@syracusemets.com. website: syracusemets.com
Affiliation (First year): New York Mets (2019). Years in league: 2021-

OWNERSHIP/MANAGEMENT

Operated by: NY Mets. General Manager: Jason Smorol. Assistant GM, Business Development: Katie Stewart. Assistant GM, Stadium/Business Ops: Brian Paupeck. Director, Sales/Marketing: Kathleen McCormick. Manager, Corporate Sales: Julie Cardinali. Senior Accountant: Patrick Taylor. Director, Finance: Frank Santoro. Director, Broadcasting/Media Relations: Michael Tricarico. Director, Ticket Operations: Will Commisso. Director, Multimedia Production: Anthony Cianchetta. Manager, Suites/Hospitality: Bill Ryan. Manager, Equipment/Clubhouse Operations: Craig Nielsen. Head Groundskeeper/Director, Turf Management: John Stewart.

FIELD STAFF

Manager: Kevin Boles. Pitching Coach: Steve Schrenk. Hitting Coach: Joel Chimelis. Bench Coach: Jay Pecci.

GAME INFORMATION
Radio Announcer: Michael Tricarico. **No. of Games Broadcast:** 150. **Flagship Station:** The Score 1260 AM. **PA Announcer:** Nick Aversa. **Official Scorer:** Dom Leo. **Stadium Name:** NBT Bank Stadium. **Location:** New York State Thruway to exit 36 (I-81 South); to 7th North Street exit, left on 7th North, right on Hiawatha Boulevard. **Standard Game Times:** 6:35 pm, Sun. 1:05 pm. **Ticket Price Range:** $10-18. **Visiting Club Hotel:** Embassy Suites @ Destiny USA.

TOLEDO MUD HENS

Address: 406 Washington St., Toledo, OH 43604.
Telephone: (419) 725-4367. **Fax:** (419) 725-4368.
E-Mail Address: mudhens@mudhens.com. **Website:** www.mudhens.com.
Affiliation (first year): Detroit Tigers (1987). **Years in League:** 2021-

OWNERSHIP/MANAGEMENT
Operated By: Toledo Mud Hens Baseball Club, Inc. **Chairman of the Board:** Michael Miller. **Vice President:** David Huey. **Secretary/Treasurer:** Charles Bracken. **President/CEO:** Joseph Napoli. **GM/Executive Vice President:** Erik Ibsen. **President, CFO:** Brian Leverenz. **Assistant Controller:** Tom Mitchell. **Social Media Coordinator:** Amanda Jerzykowski. **Director Corporate Partnerships:** Ed Sintic. **Director Ticket Sales:** Kyle Moll. **Game Plan Consultants:** Becky Fitts, Adam Haman, Rita Natter. **Manager, Box Office Sales:** Jennifer Hill. **Game Day Coordinator:** Tyler Clark. **Director, Merchandise & Licensing:** Craig Katz. **Turf Manager:** Kyle Leppelmeier. **Clubhouse Manager:** Joe Sarkisian.

FIELD STAFF
Manager: Lloyd McClendon. **Hitting Coach:** Adam Melhuse. **Pitching Coach:** Doug Bochtler. **Bench Coach:** Tony Cappucilli. **Athletic Trainer:** Jason Schwartzman. **Strength Coach:** Phill Hartt.

GAME INFORMATION
Radio Announcer: Jim Weber. **No. of Games Broadcast:** 150. **Flagship Station:** WCWA 1230-AM. **TV Announcers:** Jim Weber, Matt Melzak. **No. of Games Broadcast:** 72 (all home games). **TV Flagship:** Buckeye Cable Sports Network (BCSN). **PA Announcer:** Mason. **Official Scorers:** Jeff Businger, Ron Kleinfelter, John Malkoski Jr., Jack Malkoski, Lee Schuh. **Stadium Name:** Fifth Third Field. **Location:** From Ohio Turnpike 80/90, exit 54 (4A) to I-75 North, follow I-75 North to exit 201-B, left onto Erie Street, right onto Washington Street; From Detroit, I-75 South to exit 202-A, right onto Washington Street; From Dayton, I-75 North to exit 201-B, left onto Erie Street, right on Washington Street; From Ann Arbor, Route 23 South to I-475 East, I-475 east to I-75 South, I-75 South to exit 202-A, right onto Washington Street. **Ticket Price Range:** $12. **Visiting Club Hotel:** Park Inn, 101 North Summit, Toledo, OH 43604. **Telephone:** (419) 241-3000.

WORCESTER RED SOX

Office Address: Polar Park, 100 Madison St., Worcester, MA 01608.
Mailing Address: PO Box 3180, Worcester, MA 01613.
Telephone: (508) 500-8888 and (508) 500-1000
E-Mail Address: info@woosox.com. **Website:** www.woosox.com.
Affiliation (first year): Boston Red Sox (2021). **Years in League:** 2021-

OWNERSHIP/MANAGEMENT
Principal Owner & Chairman: Larry Lucchino. **Vice Chairman:** Mike Tamburro. **President:** Dr. Charles Steinberg. **Ballpark Design Advisor:** Janet Marie Smith. **Executive Vice President-General Manager/Business and Real Estate:** Dan Rea III. **Executive Vice President/General Counsel:** Kim Miner, Esq. **Senior Vice President/Communications:** Bill Wanless. **Senior Vice President/Corporate Partnerships:** Michael Gwynn. **Vice President/Corporate Partnerships:** Jack Verducci. **Vice President/Marketing:** Brooke Cooper. **Vice President/Baseball Operations & Community Relations:** Joe Bradlee. **Executive Assistant to the Chairman:** Fay Scheer. **Special Assistant to the President & Intern Coordinator:** Jackie Wilkes. **Ballpark Concessions Consultant:** Jason Emmett. **Chief Ambassador:** Rick Medeiros. **Senior Director of Ticket Operations:** Samantha Saccoia-Beggs. **Senior Director of Client Services:** Bernadette Provost. **Senior Director of Marketing Programs:** Steve Oliveira. **Senior Director of Ballpark Operations:** Robert Malone. **Director of Graphic Design:** Courtney Cowsill Capparelle. **Director of Polar Park Events:** Hannah Butler. **Office Manager:** Carol Krushnowski. **Corporate & Community Partnerships:** Mike Lyons. **Director of Ticket Sales & Strategy:** Anthony Cahill. **Director of Security:** Lee Boykin. **Director of Facilities Management:** Jeff Caster. **Director of Merchandising:** Kat Burns. **Corporate Event Manager:** Jim Cain. **Group Event Managers:** Ryan Nesbit & Dalton Boudreau. **Manager of Accounting:** Dan Fontaine. **Manager of Ballpark & Community Relations Assistant:** Alex Richardson. **Radio/TV Broadcasters:** Jim Cain, Mike Antonellis, Jay Burnham.

FIELD STAFF
Field Manager: Chad Tracy. **Hitting Coach:** Rich Gedman. **Pitching Coach:** Paul Abbott. **Coaches:** Jose Flores & Mike Montville. **Trainers:** David Herrera & Scott Gallon. **Strength & Conditioning Coach:** Ben Chadwick.

GAME INFORMATION
Radio Announcers: Jim Cain. **No. of Games Broadcast:** 150. **Flagship Station:** NASH Icon 98.9-FM. **PA Announcer:** Ben DeCastro. **Official Scorer:** Bruce Guindon. **Stadium Name:** Polar Park. **Location:** Canal District, **Worcester, MA** **Standard Game Times:** 6:45 pm, Sat. 4:05, Sun 1:05. **Ticket Price Range:** $8-21. **Visiting Club Hotel:** Hilton Gardens, Worcester, MA.

TRIPLE-A WEST

STADIUM INFORMATION

Club	Stadium	Opened	LF	CF	RF	Capacity	2021 Att.
Albuquerque	Isotopes Park	2003	340	400	340	13,500	329,295
El Paso	Southwest University Park	2014	322	406	322	8,018	403,657
Las Vegas	Las Vegas Ballpark	2019	340	415	340	8,196	428,369
Oklahoma City	Chickasaw Bricktown Ballpark	1998	325	400	325	9,000	305,290
Reno	Aces Ballpark	2009	339	410	340	9,100	233,961
Round Rock	Dell Diamond	2000	330	405	325	8,722	305,742
Sacramento	Raley Field	2000	330	403	325	14,014	259,640
Salt Lake	Smith's Ballpark	1994	345	420	315	14,511	300,535
Sugar Land	Constellation Field	2012	348	405	325	7,500	211,560
Tacoma	Cheney Stadium	1960	325	425	325	6,500	245,706

ALBUQUERQUE ISOTOPES

Address: 1601 Avenida Cesar Chavez SE, Albuquerque, NM 87106
Telephone: (505) 924-2255. **Fax:** (505) 242-8899.
E-Mail Address: info@abqisotopes.com. **Website:** www.abqisotopes.com.
Affiliation (first year): Colorado Rockies (2015). **Years in League:** 2021-

OWNERSHIP/MANAGEMENT

President: Ken Young. **Vice President/Secretary/Treasurer:** Emmett Hammond. **VP/GM:** John Traub. **Assistant GM, Business Operations:** Chrissy Baines. **Assistant GM, Sales/Marketing:** Adam Beggs. **Media Relations Manager:** Forest Stulting. **Communications Associate:** Joe Traub. **Director, Retail Operations:** Michael Malgieri. **Director, Stadium Operations:** Bobby Atencio. **Director, Accounting/Human Resources:** Cynthia DiFrancesco. **Box Office/Administration Manager:** Mark Otero. **Director, Community Relations:** Michelle Montoya. **Marketing/Promotions Manager:** Dylan Storm. **Director of Game Production:** Kris Shepard. **Front Office Assistant:** Alexia Gutierrez. **Suite Relations Manager:** TBD. **Travel Coordinator/Home Clubhouse Manager:** Ryan Maxwell. **Season Ticket, Group Sales Manager:** CJ Scroger. **Ticket Sales Executives:** Brandon Begley, Marcus Castle. **Graphic Designer:** Rebecca Zook. **Event Operations Coordinator:** Summer Noelle. **Head Groundskeeper:** Clint Belau. **Assistant Groundskeeper:** Thomas Gallegos. **GM, Spectra:** TBD. **Executive Chef, Spectra:** Ryan Kagimoto.

FIELD STAFF

Manager: Warren Schaeffer. **Hitting Coach:** Jordan Pacheco. **Pitching Coach:** Frank Gonzales. **Bench Coach:** Pedro Lopez. **Athletic Trainer:** Hoshi Mizutani. **Physical Performance Coach:** Phil Bailey.

GAME INFORMATION

Radio Announcer: TBD. **No. of Games Broadcast:** 150. **Flagship Station:** KNML 95.9-FM & 610-AM. **PA Announcer:** Francina Walker. **Official Scorers:** Gary Herron, Brent Carey, John Miller, Frank Mercogliano. **Stadium Name:** Isotopes Park. **Location:** From I-25, exit east on Avenida Cesar Chavez SE to University Boulevard; From I-40, exit south on UniversityBoulevard SE to Avenida Cesar Chavez. **Standard Game Times:** 6:35 pm/7:05 pm. Sun 1:35/6:05 pm. **Ticket Price Range:** $8-$27. **Visiting Club Hotel:** Sheraton Albuquerque Airport Hotel, 2910 Yale Blvd SE, Albuquerque, NM 87106. **Telephone:** (505) 843-7000.

EL PASO CHIHUAHUAS

Address: 1 Ballpark Plaza, El Paso, TX 79901.
Telephone: (915) 533-2273. **Fax:** (915) 242-2031.
E-Mail Address: info@epchihuahuas.com. **Website:** www.epchihuahuas.com.
Affiliation (first year): San Diego Padres (2014). **Years in League:** 2021-

OWNERSHIP/MANAGEMENT

Owner/Chairman of the Board: Josh Hunt. **Owners:** Alejandra de la Vega Foster, Woody Hunt, Josh Hunt, Paul Foster. **President:** Alan Ledford. **Senior Vice President/General Manager:** Brad Taylor. **Senior Director, Finance & Administration:** Pamela De La O. **Senior Accounting Manager:** Heather Hagerty. **Accounts Payable/Accounts Receivable Supervisor and Payroll Coordinator:** Pamela Nieto. **Staff Accountant:** Jasmine Alcantara. **Director, Corporate Partnerships & Suites:** Judge Scott. **Senior Account Executive, Corporate Partnership:** Cole Buck. **Senior Director, Ticket Sales & Service:** Nick Seckerson. **Manager, Season Seat Sales:** Primo Martinez. **Senior Director, Strategy & Analytics:** Ross Rotwein. **Manager, Group Sales:** Brittany Morgan. **Senior Account Executive, Ticket Sales:** Matt Heiligenberg. **Account Executives, Ticket Sales:** Ethan Andersen, Jake Spitz. **Senior Account Executives, Group Sales:** Janine Quiroz, Austin Weber. **Account Executive, Group Sales:** Joshalyn Estrada. **Senior Manager, Ticket Operations:** Ruben Armendariz. **Senior Director, Marketing & Communications:** Angela Olivas. **Senior Manager, Video & Digital Production:** Juan Gutierrez. **Senior Manager, Broadcast & Media Relations:** Tim Hagerty. **Director,**

Promotions & Community Relations: Andy Imfeld. **Production & Social Media Coordinator:** Gage Freeman. **Community Relations & Promotions Supervisor:** Kate Lewis. **Creative Services & Digital Marketing Coordinator:** Ilene Serna. **Senior Director, Guest Services & Baseball Operations:** Lizette Espinosa. **Director, Grounds & Building Operations:** Travis Howard. **Assistant Groundskeeper:** Andrew Faust. **Assistant Groundskeepers:** Bryan Shira, Tony Tafoya. **Manager, Facilities:** Michael Raymundo. **Manager, Baseball Operations & Guest Services:** Latoya Wright. **Manager, Retail & Merchandise Operations:** David Apodaca. **Director, Special Events:** Gina Roe-Davis.

FIELD STAFF

Manager: Jared Sandberg. **Hitting Coach:** Jon Mathews. **Pitching Coach:** Mike McCarthy. **Bench Coach:** Robby Hammock.

GAME INFORMATION

Broadcaster: Tim Hagerty. **No. of Games Broadcast:** 150. **Flagship Station:** ESPN 600 AM El Paso. **PA Announcer:** TBA. **Official Scorer:** Bernie Ricono. **Stadium Name:** Southwest University Park. **Standard Game Times:** TBD. **Ticket Price Range:** $5-10.50. **Visiting Club Hotel:** TBD

LAS VEGAS AVIATORS

Address: 1650 S. Pavilion Center Drive, Las Vegas, NV 89135.
Telephone: (702) 943-7200. **Fax:** (702) 943-7214.
E-Mail Address: info@aviatorslv.com. **Website:** www.aviatorslv.com.
Affiliation (first year): Oakland Athletics (2019). **Years in League:** 2021-

OWNERSHIP/MANAGEMENT

President/COO: Don Logan. **General Manager/Vice President, Sales/Marketing:** Chuck Johnson. **Vice President, Ticket Sales:** Erik Eisenberg. **Vice President/Ballpark Operations & Merchandise:** Jason Weber. **Vice President/Ticket Operations:** Siobhan Steiermann. **Vice President/Public Safety:** Bill Corder. **Director, Sponsorships:** James Jensen. **Director/Team Operations:** Steve Dwyer. **Director, Ticket Sales:** Bryan Frey. **Director, Broadcasting:** Russ Langer. **Director, Business Development:** Larry Brown. **Media Relations Director:** Jim Gemma. **Director/Game Entertainment:** Gary Arlitz. **Director, Retail Operations:** Edward Dorville. **Senior Account Executive:** Nathan Erbach. **Account Executives, Ticket Sales:** Daniel Crawford, Rickie Ritchie, Brock Shively. **Controller:** Brian Winslow. **Senior Accountant:** Danniel Recinos. **Stadium Operations Manager:** Deonte Hawkins. **Ballpark Support Manager:** Chip Vespe. **Marketing & Social Media Manager:** Elsye Jones. **Box Office Manager:** Annette Evans. **Ticket Operations Coordinator:** Michelle Taggart. **Ticket Services Coordinator:** Jessica Becerra. **Special Events Manager:** Jenna Potter. **Special Events Coordinator:** Olivia Perry. **Premium Ticket Services Coordinator:** Katie Greener. **Executive Administrative Assistant:** Jan Dillard. **Administrative Support Specialist:** Kirsten Sheff. **Retail Coordinator:** Tom Brazile. **Retail Sales Associates:** Andrew Lockhart, Daymian Yohner. **Engineering Manager:** Ronnie Cabrera. **Facility Maintenance Engineer:** Michael Hoyes. **IT Las Vegas Ballpark Support:** Reko Pinson. **Head Groundskeeper:** Isaiah Lienau

FIELD STAFF

Manager: Fran Riordan. **Hitting Coach:** TBA. **Pitching Coach:** Rick Rodriguez. **Assistant Hitting Coach:** Brian McArn. **Head Athletic Trainer:** TBA. **Sport Performance Coach:** TBA.

GAME INFORMATION

Radio Announcer: Russ Langer. **No. of Games Broadcast:** 150. **Flagship Station:** Raider Nation Radio 920 AM **PA Announcer:** Dan Bickmore. **Official Scorer:** Peter Legner. **Stadium Name:** Las Vegas Ballpark. **Location:** I 215 North Beltway to Sahara Avenue (exit east), left on Pavilion Center Drive; 1 215 South Beltway to Charleston Blvd. (exit east), right on Pavilion Center Drive. **Standard Game Time:** 7:05 pm. **Ticket Price Range:** $13-60. **Visiting Club Hotel:** Red Rock Casino Resort & Spa, 11011 W. Charleston Blvd. Las Vegas, NV 89135. **Telephone:** (702) 797-7777.

OKLAHOMA CITY DODGERS

Address: 2 S Mickey Mantle Dr., Oklahoma City, OK 73104.
Telephone: (405) 218-1000. **Fax:** (405) 218-1011.
E-Mail Address: info@okcdodgers.com. **Website:** www.okcdodgers.com.
Affiliation (first year): Los Angeles Dodgers (2015). **Years in League:** 2021-

OWNERSHIP/MANAGEMENT

Operated By: Diamond Baseball Holdings, LLC. **Principal Owner:** Diamond Baseball Holdings, LLC.
President/General Manager: Michael Byrnes. **Senior Vice President:** Jenna Byrnes. **Vice President, Ticket Sales:** Kyle Daugherty. **Vice President, Finance/Accounting:** John MacDonald. **Vice President, Operations:** Mitch Stubenhofer. **Vice President, Marketing/Communications:** Ben Beecken. **Director, Business Intelligence:** Kyle Logan. **Director, Corporate Partnerships:** Ryan Vanlow. **Director, Communications/Broadcasting:** Alex Freedman. **Director, Food Service Operations:** Will Fenwick. **Director, Game Presentation & Video:** A.J. Navarro. **Executive Director, OKC Dodgers Baseball Foundation:** Carol Herrick. **Director, Special Events:** Shelby Kirkes. **Communications Manager:** Lisa Johnson. **Baseball Operations Coordinator:** Billy Maloney. **Merchandise Manager:** Jasmine Buchanan. **Office Administrator:** Travis Hunter. **Head Groundskeeper:** Jeff Jackson. **Clubhouse Manager:** TBA.

FIELD STAFF

Manager: Travis Barbary. **Hitting Coach:** Emmanuel Burriss. **Pitching Coach:** Dave Borkowski. **Bench Coach:** Daniel Nava. **Bullpen Coach:** Justin DeFratus. **Athletic Trainers:** Chelsea Willette & Yuya Mukaihara. **Performance Coach:** Noah Huff.

GAME INFORMATION

Radio Announcer: Alex Freedman. **No. of Games Broadcast:** 150. **Station:** KGHM-AM 1340 (www.1340thegame.com). **PA Announcer:** TBA. **Official Scorers:** Jim Byers, Mark Heusman, Rich Tortorelli. **Stadium Name:** Chickasaw Bricktown Ballpark. **Location:** Bricktown area in downtown Oklahoma City, near interchange of I-235 and I-40, off I-235 take Sheridan exit to Bricktown; off I-40 take Shields exit, north to Bricktown. **Standard Game Times: 705 pm, Sun 2:**05 (April-June; Sept.), 6:05 (July-Aug). **Ticket Price Range:** $9-28. **Visiting Club Hotel:** Courtyard Oklahoma City Downtown, 2 West Reno Ave., Oklahoma City, OK 73102. **Telephone:** (405) 232-2290.

RENO ACES

Address: 250 Evans Ave, Reno, NV 89501.
Telephone: (775) 334-4700. **Fax:** (775) 334-4701.
Website: www.renoaces.com.
Affiliation (first year): Arizona Diamondbacks (2009). **Years in League:** 2021-

OWNERSHIP/MANAGEMENT

President: Eric Edelstein.
Chief Operations Officer: Chris Phillips. **Chief Commercial Officer:** Mike Murray. **Chief Financial Officer:** Stacey Bowman. **VP of Business Development:** Brian Moss. **VP of Event Experience:** Sarah Bliss. **Accounting Director:** Adam Hyde. **VP of Marketing and Communications:** Vince Ruffino. **Digital Media Manager:** AJ Grimm. **VP of Ticket Sales:** Alex Strathearn. **Event Production and Partnership Development Manager:** Devin Levan-Galang. **Ticket Operations Director:** Kristina Solis. **Facilities Manager:** Maurice Lewis. **Creative Manager:** Blake O'Brien. **VP of Corporate Partnerships:** Max Margulies. **Communications Manager:** Kevin Bass. **Corporate Partnerships Services Manager:** Hannah Jurgens. **Corporate Partnerships Services Coordinator:** Olivia Reese. **Senior Director of Ticket Services & Operations:** Laura Raymond. **Stadium Operations Manager:** Myles Fresquez. **Head Groundskeeper:** Leah Withrow. **Visiting Clubhouse Manager:** TBA.

FIELD STAFF

Manager: Gil Velazquez. **Hitting Coach:** Nick Evans/Mark Reed. **Pitching Coach:** Doug Drabek.

GAME INFORMATION

Radio Announcer: Zack Bayrouty. **No. of Games Broadcast:** 150. **PA Announcers:** Cory Smith, Chris Payne. **Official Scorers:** Alan Means, Greg Erny, Gregg Zive. **Stadium Name:** Greater Nevada Field. **Location: From north, south and east:** I-80 West, Exit 14 (Wells Ave.), left on Wells, right at Kuenzil St., field on right; From West, I-80 East to Exit 13 (Virginia St.), right on Virginia, left on Second, field on left. **Standard Game Times:** 7:05 p.m., 6:35 p.m., 1:05 p.m. **Ticket Price Range:** $8-35.

ROUND ROCK EXPRESS

Address: 3400 East Palm Valley Blvd, Round Rock, TX 78665.
Telephone: (512) 255-2255. **Fax:** (512) 255-1558.
E-Mail Address: info@rrexpress.com. **Website:** www.RRExpress.com.
Affiliation (first year): Texas Rangers (2011). **Year in League:** 2021-

OWNERSHIP/MANAGEMENT

Operated By: Ryan Sanders Sports & Entertainment. **Principal Owners:** Nolan Ryan, Don Sanders. **Owners:** Reid Ryan, Reese Ryan, Bret Sanders, Brad Sanders, Eddie Maloney. Chief Executive Officer, **Ryan Sanders Sports & Entertainment:** Reid Ryan. **Chief Operating Officer, Ryan Sanders Sports & Entertainment:** JJ Gottsch. **Chief Financial Officer, Ryan Sanders Sports & Entertainment:** Jonathan Germer. **Executive Assistant, Ryan Sanders Sports & Entertainment:** Debbie Bowman. **Administrative Assistant, Ryan Sanders Sports & Entertainment:** Jacqueline Bowman. **President:** Chris Almendarez. **General Manager:** Tim Jackson. **Executive Advisor to President & General Manager:** Dave Fendrick. **Senior Vice President, Marketing:** Laura Fragoso. **Vice President, Administration & Accounting:** Debbie Coughlin. **Assistant General Manager, Sales:** Stuart Scally. **Senior Director, Corporate Partnerships:** Elisa Fogle. **Senior Director, Stadium Operations & Security:** Gene Kropff. **Senior Director, United Heritage Conference Center:** Scott Allen. **Director, Ballpark Entertainment:** Steve Richards. **Director, Broadcasting:** Mike Capps. **Director, Express Select:** Chris Godwin. **Director, Information Technology:** Mark Ramos. **Director, Retail Operations:** Joe Belger. **Director, Sales:** Oscar Rodriguez. **Director, Stadium Maintenance:** Aurelio Martinez. **Director, Ticket Operations:** Aschley Carvalho. **Manager, Clubhouse Operations:** Kenny Bufton. **Manager, Digital Content:** Taylor Shipp. **Manager, Nolan Ryan Foundation:** Mary Conley Thompson. **Manager, Office:** Wendy Abrahamsen. **Manager, Post-Event Cleaning:** Mark Maloney. **Manager, PR & Communications:** Andrew Felts. **Manager, Promotional Events:** Casey Wright. **Manager, Venue Operations:** Alex Blair. **Coordinator, Brand Marketing:** Karlie Dyer. **Coordinator, Communications & Travel:** Aubrey Losack. **Specialist, Information Technology:** Anthony Newell. **Specialist, Ticket Operations:** Garrett Smith. **Account Executives:** Anthony Pollo, Connor Truitt, John Watts. **Head**

Groundskeeper: Nick Rozdilski. **Housekeeping Staff:** Ofelia Gonzalez. **Electrician/HVAC Maintenance Staff:** Leslie Hitt. **Consultant, Human Resources:** Missy Martin.

FIELD STAFF

Manager: Matt Hagen. **Hitting Coach:** Matt Lawson. **Pitching Coach:** Bill Simas. **Bench Coach:** Chase Lambin. **Development Coach:** Josh Johnson. **Athletic Trainer:** Carlos Olivas. **Strength and Conditioning Coach:** Wade Lamont.

GAME INFORMATION

Radio Announcer: Mike Capps. **No. of Games Broadcast:** 150. **Flagship Station:** AM 1300 The Zone. **PA Announcer:** Glen Norman. **Official Scorer:** Andrew Haynes.

Stadium Name: Dell Diamond. **Location:** US Highway 79, 3.5 miles east of Interstate 35 (exit 253) or 1.5 miles west of Texas Tollway 130. **Standard Game Times:** 7:05 pm, 6:35, 6:05, 1:05, 12:05. **Ticket Price Range:** $7-$30.

Visiting Club Hotel: LaQuinta Inn & Suites by Wyndham Round Rock East, 3900 East Palm Valley Blvd., Round Rock, TX 78665. **Telephone:** (737) 346-6652.

SACRAMENTO RIVER CATS

Address: Sutter Health Park - 400 Ballpark Drive, West Sacramento, CA 95691
Telephone: (916) 376-4700. **Fax:** (916) 376-4710.
E-Mail Address: reception@rivercats.com. **Website:** www.rivercats.com
Affiliation (first year): San Francisco Giants (2015). **Years in League:** 2021-

OWNERSHIP/MANAGEMENT

Majority Owner: Susan Savage. **CEO:** Jeff Savage. **President/COO:** Chip Maxson. **Executive Vice President, Finance:** Maddie Strika. **Vice President, Partner Services:** Greg Coletti. **Vice President, Ticket Sales & Marketing:** Troy Loparco. **Director, Human Resources:** Isabella Guedes. **Sr. Coordinator, Human Resources:** Vanessa Villanueva. **Assistant, Executive:** Kathryn Mullins. **Assistant, Administrative:** Bailey Metcalf. **Accountant:** Darcy Kooman. **Director, Business Development:** Jack Barbour. **Manager, Partnership Activation:** Krystal Jones. **Assistant, Corporate Partnerships:** Natalie Torres. **Director, Marketing:** Sarah Hebel. **Sr. Coordinator, Promotions & Production:** Carolyn Scherpe. **Coordinator, Social Media & Marketing:** Travis Hall. **Coordinator, Marketing:** Haley Cyr. **Coordinator, Graphic Design:** Jay Rivett. **Coordinator, Mascot:** Matthew Francis. **Radio Broadcaster:** Johnny Doskow. **Coordinator, Baseball Operations:** N/A. **Coordinator, Communications:** Maverick Pallack. **Director, Ticket Operations:** Joe Carlucci. **Director, Ticket Sales:** Justice Hoyt. **Coordinator, Membership & Suite Services:** Gabriela Salazar. **Membership Experience Specialist:** Jared Rebensdorf. **Account Executive, Corporate Sales:** Timothy Williams. **Account Executive, Group Sales:** Jack Miller. **Account Executive, Group Sales:** Corey Takiguchi. **Account Executive, Inside Sales:** Henry Weiss. **Representative, Inside Sales:** Tyler Pon. **Sr. Manager, Merchandise Marketing & Online Sales:** Erin Kilby. **Director, Events/Entertainment:** Brittney Nizuk. **Coordinator, Events/Entertainment:** Micaela Brewer. **Assistant, Events & Entertainment:** Evelyn Chavez. **Director, Stadium Operations:** Matt Singer. **Director, Field Operations:** Chris Shastid. **Manager, Security:** Darrell Graham. **Supervisor, Facilities:** Anthony Hernandez. **Supervisor, Stadium Operations:** Mike Correa. **Coordinator, Field Operations:** Marcello Clamar. **Director, Food & Beverage:** Steve De La Rosa. **Executive Chef:** Brad Morris. **Manager, Concessions:** Colene Groth. **Manager, Premium Hospitality:** Timothy Steele. **Office Coordinator, Food & Beverage:** Leticia Perez.

FIELD STAFF

Manager: Dave Brundage. **Hitting Coach:** Damon Minor. **Pitching Coach:** Garvin Alston. **Fundamentals Coach:** Jolbert Cabrera. **Bullpen Coach:** TBD. **Athletic Trainers:** David Getsoff, TBD. **Strength & Conditioning Coach:** TBD.

GAME INFORMATION

Radio Broadcaster: Johnny Doskow. **No. of Games Broadcast:** 150. **PA Announcer:** TBD. **Official Scorers:** TBD. **Stadium Name:** Sutter Health Park. **Location:** I-5 to Business-80 West, exit at Jefferson Boulevard. **Standard Game Time:** 6:35 p.m. **Ticket Price Range:** $10-$80.

SALT LAKE BEES

Address: 77 W 1300 South, Salt Lake City, UT 84115.
Telephone: (801) 325-2337. **Fax:** (801) 485-6818.
E-Mail Address: info@slbees.com. **Website:** www.slbees.com.
Affiliation (first year): Los Angeles Angels (2001). **Years in League:** 2021-.

OWNERSHIP/MANAGEMENT

Principal Owner: Gail Miller. **President/General Manager:** Marc Amicone. **President, Smith Entertainment Group & Utah Jazz:** Jim Olson. **Chief Revenue Officer:** Chris Barney. **Chief Financial Officer:** John Larson. **Chief Communications Officer:** Frank Zang. **Chief Marketing Officer:** Bart Sharp. **General Counsel:** Sam Harkness. **Assistant GM:** Bryan Kinneberg. **Director, Broadcasting:** Steve Klauke. **VP Ticket Sales:** Trevor Haws. **Director, Ticket Sales:** Brad Jacoway. **Director, Ticket Sales:** Koy Pruitt. **Sr. Director, Corporate Partnership Activation:** Kim Brown. **Director, Corporate Partnerships:** Jackson Brown. **Director, Marketing:** Brady Brown. **Manager, Game Operations:** Carlos Avila. **Graphic Designer:** Cassidy Heaton. **Director, Ticket Operations:** Derrek DeGraaff. **Box Office Manager:** Duane Sartori. **Director, Communications:** Kraig Williams. **Youth Programs Coordinator:** Nate Martinez. **Home

Clubhouse Manager: Cole Filosa. **Visiting Clubhouse Manager:** Chris Simonsen. **Head Groundskeeper:** Brian Soukup. **Asst. Head Groundskeeper:** Paul Sheffield.

FIELD STAFF
Manager: Lou Marson. **Pitching Coach:** Jairo Cuevas. **Hitting Coach:** Brian Betancourth.

GAME INFORMATION
Radio Announcer: Steve Klauke. **No. of Games Broadcast:** 150. **Flagship Station:** 1280 AM. **PA Announcer:** Jeff Reeves. **Official Scorers:** Jeff Cluff, Brooke Frederickson, Randy Upton. **Stadium Name:** Smith's Ballpark. **Location:** I-15 North/South to 1300 South exit, east to ballpark at West Temple. **Standard Game Times:** 6:35 (Night games), 1:05 Sunday day games. **Ticket Price Range:** $10-24.

SUGAR LAND SPACE COWBOYS

Office Address: 1 Stadium Drive, Sugar Land, Texas, 77498.
Telephone: (281) 240-4487.
Affiliation (first year): Houston Astros (2021). **Years in League:** 2021-

OWNERSHIP/MANAGEMENT
Owner: Jim Crane. **Senior Vice President, Affiliate Business Operations:** Creighton Kahoalii. **Vice President Affiliate Operations:** Thomas Bell. **General Manager:** Tyler Stamm. **Assistant General Manager:** Chris Parsons. **Special Assistant:** Deacon Jones. **Senior Director of Finance:** Greg Hodges. **Office Administrator:** Ashley Richter. **Retail Manager:** Shamaine St. Julien. **Affiliate Business Operations Coordinator:** Philip Raven. **Vice President of Tickets:** Jennifer Schwarz. **Box Office Manager:** Matt Blum. **Senior Sales Manager:** Sunny Okpon. **Director of Special Projects:** Teneisha Richardson. **Director of Ticket Sales:** Aaron Johnson. **Director of Corporate Partnerships:** Zach Kaddatz. **Account Executive:** Alex Rodriguez. **Account Executive:** Samuel Stubbs. **Account Executive:** Tyler Tumbleson. **Community Relations Coordinator:** Megan Brown. **Community Relations Manager:** Sallie Ferris. **Graphic Design Coordinator:** Michael Kloska. **Marketing and Digital Media Coordinator:** Megan Murnane. **Media Relations Manager:** Ryan Posner. **Marketing Coordinator:** Erin Williams. **Director of Special Events:** Eddy Juarez. **Event Operations Manager:** Russell Wohldman. **Director of Field Operations:** Brad Detmore. **Clubhouse Manager:** DJ Pirson.

FIELD STAFF
Manager: Mickey Storey. **Pitching Coach:** Erick Abreu. **Hitting Coach:** TBA. **Athletic Trainer:** TBA. **Strength and Conditioning Coach:** TBA.

GAME INFORMATION
Radio Announcer: Gerald Sanchez. **No. of Games Broadcast:** 150. **Flagship Streaming Station:** MiLBTV. **Standard Game Times:** Mon.-Fri., 7:05 pm, Sat-Sun.: 6:05 pm. **Visiting Club Hotel:** Sugar Land Marriott Town Square. **Telephone:** (281) 275-8400.

TACOMA RAINIERS

Address: 2502 South Tyler St, Tacoma, WA 98405.
Telephone: (253) 752-7707. **Fax:** (253) 752-7135.
Website: www.tacomarainiers.com
Affiliation (first year): Seattle Mariners (1995). **Years in League:** 2021-

OWNERSHIP/MANAGEMENT
Owners: The Baseball Club of Tacoma. **President:** Aaron Artman. **CFO:** Brian Coombe. **Assistant General Manager:** Nick Cherniske. **Vice President, Sales:** Shane Santman. **Director of Administration and Assistant to the President:** Patti Stacy. **Senior Director, Ticket Sales:** Tim O'Hollaren. **Director, Business Development:** Ben Nelson. **Senior Manager, Corporate Sales:** Kevin Drugge. **Manager, Corporate Sales:** Devon Barker. **Director, Group Sales and Event Marketing:** Caitlin Calnan. **Senior Manager, Group Sales:** Chris Aubertin. **Premium Experience and Events Manager:** Cassidy Larson. **Director, Ticket Operations:** Alexa Covarrubias. **Manager, Box Office:** Necia Borba. **Coordinator, Group Events:** Hayley Hacker. **Vice President, Marketing:** Megan Mead. **Director, Creative:** Casey Catherwood. **Director, Media Relations and Baseball Information:** Paul Braverman. **Graphic Designer:** Delaney Saul. **Graphic Designer:** Erin Fogerty. **Director, Technical:** Anthony Phinney. **Specialist, Multimedia:** Branson Gustafson. **Broadcaster:** Mike Curto. **Manager, Partner Services:** Hannah McArthur. **Coordinator, Partner Services:** Ceciley Weinmann. **Director, Baseball Ops and Merchandise:** Ashley Schutt. **Manager, Team Store:** Kyle McGilvray. **Staff Accountant:** Amy Tucci. **Head Groundskeeper:** Michael Kerns. **Manager, Stadium Operations:** Zack Armstrong. **Front Office Coordinator:** Megan Elliott.

FIELD STAFF
Manager: Tim Federowicz. **Hitting Coach:** Brad Marcelino. **Pitching Coach:** Alon Leichman. **Coach:** Zach Vincej. **Trainers:** TBA.

GAME INFORMATION
Radio Broadcaster: Mike Curto. **No. of Games Broadcast:** 150. **Flagship Station:** TBA. **PA Announcer:** Randy McNair. **Official Scorers:** Kevin Kalal, Gary Brooks, Jon Gilbert, Scott Hauter. **Stadium Name:** Cheney Stadium.

Location: From I-5, take exit 132 (Highway 16 West) for 1.2 miles to 19th Street East exit, merge right onto 19th Street, right onto Clay Huntington Way and follow into parking lot of ballpark. **Standard Game Times:** 7:05, Sun. 1:05. (Monday–**Wednesday games start at 6:**05pm in April–**June, Saturday at 5:**05pm in April, May, June & September.) **Ticket Price Range:** $7.50-$25.50. **Visiting Club Hotel:** Hotel Murano, 1320 Broadway Plaza, Tacoma, WA 98402. **Telephone:** (253) 238-8000.

DOUBLE-A NORTHEAST

STADIUM INFORMATION

| | | | Dimensions | | | | |
Club	Stadium	Opened	LF	CF	RF	Capacity	2021 Att.
Akron	Canal Park	1997	331	400	337	7,630	208,162
Altoona	Peoples Natural Gas Field	1999	325	405	325	7,210	213,686
Binghamton	Mirabito Stadium	1992	330	400	330	6,012	107,803
Bowie	Prince George's Stadium	1994	309	405	309	10,000	128,467
Erie	UPMC Park	1995	317	400	328	6,000	145,445
Harrisburg	Metro Bank Park	1987	325	400	325	6,300	167,810
Hartford	Dunkin' Donuts Park	2018	325	400	325	6,146	287,752
New Hampshire	Northeast Delta Dental Stadium	2005	326	400	306	6,500	183,730
Portland	Hadlock Field	1994	315	400	330	7,368	210,211
Reading	FirstEnergy Stadium	1951	330	400	330	9,000	226,667
Richmond	The Diamond	1985	330	402	330	9,560	275,169
Somerset	TD Bank Ballpark	1999	317	402	315	6,100	205,246

AKRON RUBBERDUCKS

Address: 300 S Main St, Akron, OH 44308.
Telephone: (330) 253-5151. (855) 97-QUACK. **Fax:** (330) 253-3300.
E-Mail Address: information@akronrubberducks.com.
Website: www.akronrubberducks.com.
Affiliation (first year): Cleveland Guardians (1989). **Years in League:** 2021-

OWNERSHIP/MANAGEMENT
Operated by: Fast Forward Sports Group/Akron Baseball, LLC. **Principal Owner/CEO:** Ken Babby. **President:** Jim Pfander. **CFO:** Shawn Carlson. **Chief Human Resource Officer:** Leatrice Buck. **Executive Assistant to Ken Babby:** Jill Popov. **General Manager/COO:** Jim Pfander. **Assistant GM/Director, Corporate Sales:** Anthony Chadwick. **Vice President, Sales and Operations:** Dave Burke. **Vice President, Premium Experience:** Sam Dankoff. **Office Manager:** Missy Dies. **Senior Director, Ballpark Operations:** Adam Horner. **Director, Ballpark Operations:** James Parsons. **Head Groundskeeper:** Chris Walsh. **Assistant Groundskeeper:** Colt Boxler. **Director, Player Facilities:** Shad Gross. **Coordinator, Community Relations:** Austin Stephens. **Art Director:** Scott Watkins. **Coordinator, Creative Services:** Jack Haines. **Coordinator, Media Relations:** Jimmy Farmer. **Lead Broadcaster:** Marco LaNave. **Manager, Corporate Partnerships and Special Events:** Brian Lobban. **Manager, Accounting:** Trevor Burk. **Finance Assistant:** Breana Burkhart. **Director, Food and Beverage:** Dave Dreher. **Assistant Director, Food and Beverage:** Maddie Smith. **Manager, Culinary Operations:** Louis Willmon-Holland. **Coordinator, Merchandise:** Jamie Vanaman. **Director, Marketing and Promotions:** Kyle Hixenbaugh. **Director, Amateur Baseball Development/RubberDucks Baseball Academy:** Roy Jacobs. **Manager, Season Ticket Service and Sales:** Trevor McGuire. **Coordinator, Ticket Operations:** Luke Farmer. **Ticket Sales Executives:** Ethan Graham, Kyle Magovac, Noah Finley, Austin Havekost.

FIELD STAFF
Manager: Rouglas Odor. **Hitting Coach:** Junior Betances. **Assistant Hitting Coach:** Mike Mergenthaler. **Pitching Coach:** Owen Dew. **Bench Coach:** Juan De La Cruz. **Trainer:** Jake Legan. **Strength and Conditioning Coach:** Tyler Grisdale.

GAME INFORMATION
Radio Announcers: Marco LaNave, Jim Clark. **No. of Games Broadcast:** 138. **Flagship Station:** WHLO 640-AM. **PA Announcer:** Ethan Graham. **Official Scorer:** Chuck Murr. **Stadium Name:** Canal Park. **Location:** From I-76 East or I-77 South, exit onto Route 59 East, exit at Exchange/Cedar, right onto Cedar, left at Main Street; From I-76 West or I-77 North, exit at Main Street/Downtown, follow exit onto Broadway Street, left onto Exchange Street, right at Main Street. **Standard Game Time:** 6:35 (non-fireworks game); 7:05 pm (fireworks games), Sun 2:05. **Ticket Price Range:** $5-25. **Visiting Club Hotel:** Fairfield Inn & Suites by Marriott Akron Fairlawn. **Telephone:** (330) 665-0641.

ALTOONA CURVE

Address: Peoples Natural Gas Field, 1000 Park Avenue, Altoona, PA 16602
Telephone: (814) 943-5400. **Fax:** (814) 942-9132
E-Mail Address: frontoffice@altoonacurve.com. **Website:** www.altoonacurve.com
Affiliation (first year): Pittsburgh Pirates (1999). **Years in League:** 2021-

OWNERSHIP/MANAGEMENT
Operated By: Lozinak Professional Baseball.
Managing Members: Bob and Joan Lozinak. **COO:** David Lozinak. **CFO:** Mike Lozinak. **General Manager:** Nate Bowen. **Senior Advisor:** Sal Baglieri, Derek Martin. **Director of Finance:** Mary Lamb. **Administrative Assistant:**

Michelle Anna. **Director of Communications & Broadcasting:** Jon Mozes. **Communications & Broadcasting Assistant:** Preston Shoemaker. **Director of Ticketing:** Ed Moffett. **Box Office Manager:** Austin Finochio. **Ticket Account Manager:** Madison Shetrom. **Ticket Account Manager:** Rebekah Grainer. **Ticket Account Manager:** Reagan McKeon. **Director of Community Relations & Social Media:** Annie Choiniere. **Director of Ballpark Operations:** Doug Mattern. **Operations Assistant:** Corbin Padgett. **Head Groundskeeper:** James Petrella. **Assistant Groundskeeper:** Matt Clark. **Director of Concessions:** Glenn McComas. **Assistant Director of Concessions:** Ryan Long. **Mascot Coordinator & Graphic Design Assistant:** Jordan Bunce. **Director of Creative Services:** Jon Weaver. **Creative Services Assistant:** Reid Pohland. **Director of Marketing, Promotions & Special Events:** Mike Kessling. **Director of Merchandise:** Michelle Gravert.

FIELD STAFF

Manager: Kieran Mattison. **Hitting Coach:** Jon Nunnally. **Pitching Coach:** Drew Benes. **Integrated Baseball Performance Coach:** Blake Butler. **Development Coach:** Stephan Morales. **Athletic Trainer:** Victor Silva. **Strength & Conditioning Coach:** Henry Torres.

GAME INFORMATION

Radio Announcers: TBD. **No. of Games Broadcast:** 138. **Flagship Station:** WRTA 98.5 FM and 1240 AM. **PA Announcer:** Rich DeLeo. **Official Scorers:** Ted Beam, Dick Wagner. **Stadium Name:** Peoples Natural Gas Field. **Location:** Located just off the Frankstown Road Exit off I-99. **Standard Game Times:** TBD. (Weekdays, April-May); TBD. (Weekdays, June-August); Fri TBD.; Sat. TBD. and TBD.; Sun TBD and TBD. **Ticket Price Range:** $8-17. **Visiting Club Hotel:** Microtel Inn & Suites Altoona.

BINGHAMTON RUMBLE PONIES

Office Address: 211 Henry St., Binghamton, NY 13901.
Mailing Address: PO Box 598, Binghamton, NY 13902.
Telephone: (607) 722-3866. **Fax:** (607) 723-7779.
E-Mail Address: info@bingrp.com. **Website:** www.bingrp.com.
Affiliation (first year): New York Mets (1992). **Years in League:** 2021-

OWNERSHIP/MANAGEMENT

President: David Sobotka. **General Manager:** John Bayne. **Creative Director:** Karen Sobotka. **Director of Business Operations:** Kelly Hust. **Director of Broadcasting & Media Relations:** Jacob Wilkins. **Director of Video Production:** Clemente Rufo Director of Stadium Operations: Craig Baker. **Scholastic Programs Coordinator:** Lou Ferraro.

FIELD STAFF

Manager: Reid Brignac. **Hitting Coach:** Tommy Joseph. **Pitching Coach:** Jerome Williams. **Bench Coach:** Mariano Duncan.

GAME INFORMATION

Radio Announcer: Jacob Wilkins. **No. of Games Broadcast:** 138. **PA Announcer:** Frank Perney. **Official Scorer:** TBD. **Stadium Name:** Mirabito Stadium. **Stadium Location:** I-81 to exit 4S (Binghamton), Route 11 exit to Henry Street. **Standard Game Times:** 6:35, 7:05 (Fri), 1:05 (Day Games). **Ticket Price Range:** $8-$14. **Visiting Club Hotel:** Holiday Inn Downtown.

BOWIE BAYSOX

Address: Prince George's Stadium, 4101 Crain Hwy, Bowie, MD 20716.
Telephone: (301) 805-6000. **Fax:** (301) 464-4911.
E-Mail Address: info@baysox.com. **Website:** www.baysox.com.
Affiliation (first year): Baltimore Orioles (1993). **Years in League:** 2021-

OWNERSHIP/MANAGEMENT

Owned By: Attain Sports and Entertainment Bowie Baysox. **President:** Greg Baroni. **General Manager:** Brian Shallcross. **Assistant GM:** Phil Wrye. **Business Manager:** Landon Ferrell. **Director, Ticket Operations:** Charlene Fewer. **Director, Sponsorships:** Matt McLaughlin. **Communications Manager:** TBD. **Group Events Manager:** Vinny Lewis. **Lead Broadcaster:** Adam Pohl. **Box Office Manager:** TBD. **Marketing & Promotions Coordinator:** Dani Fox. **Head Groundskeeper:** TBD. **Stadium Operations Manager:** TBD. **Director, Gameday Personnel:** Darlene Mingioli. **Clubhouse Manager:** Jon Weinberg.

FIELD STAFF

Manager: Kyle Moore. **Hitting Coach:** Branden Becker. **Pitching Coach:** Josh Conway. **Fundamentals Coach:** Tim DeJohn. **Development Coach:** Billy Facteau. **Athletic Trainer:** William Kelly. **Strength & Conditioning:** Chandler Geller.

GAME INFORMATION

Radio Broadcaster: Adam Pohl. **No. of Games Broadcast:** 138. **PA Announcer:** Adrienne Roberson & Tom DeGroff. **Official Scorers:** Dan Gretz, Patrick Stevens. **Stadium Name:** Prince George's Stadium. **Location:** 1/4 mile south of US 50/Route 301 Interchange in Bowie. **Standard Game Times:** Mon-Thu, Sat. 6:35 pm, Fri 7:05 pm, Sun 1:35 pm. **Ticket Price Range:** $8-$18. **Visiting Club Hotel:** Crowne Plaza Annapolis, 173 Jennifer Rd, Annapolis, MD 21401; **Telephone:** (410) 266-3131.

ERIE SEAWOLVES

Address: 831 French St, Erie, PA 16501.
Telephone: (814) 456-1300.
E-Mail Address: seawolves@seawolves.com. **Website:** www.seawolves.com.
Affiliation (first year): Detroit Tigers (2001). **Years in League:** 2021-

OWNERSHIP/MANAGEMENT
Principal Owners: At Bat Group, LLC.
CEO: Fernando Aguirre. **President:** Greg Coleman. **Assistant GM, Communications:** Greg Gania. **Assistant GM, Sales:** Mark Pirrello. **Director, Accounting/Finance:** Amy McArdle. **Director, Operations:** Mike Lockhart. **Director, Entertainment:** David Micik. **Community Engagement Manager:** Christopher McDonald. **Director, Merchandise:** Christy Buchar. **Director, Food/Beverage:** Jeff Burgess. **Director of Ticket Sales:** Tom Barnes.

FIELD STAFF
Manager: Gabe Alvarez. **Hitting Coach:** John Murrian. **Pitching Coach:** Dan Ricabal. **Developmental Coach:** Ollie Kadey. **Trainer:** Chris Vick. **Strength/Conditioning Coach:** Andres Rodriguez.

GAME INFORMATION
Radio Announcer: Greg Gania. **No. of Games Broadcast:** 138. **Flagship Station:** Fox Sports Radio WFNN 1330-AM. **PA Announcer:** TBA. **Official Scorer:** Bob Shreve. **Stadium Name:** UPMC Park. **Location:** US 79 North to East 12th Street exit, left on State Street, right on 10th Street. **Standard Game Times:** 6:05 p.m., Sun 1:35 p.m. **Ticket Price Range:** TBA. **Visiting Club Hotel:** Baymont Inn & Suites, 8170 Perry Hwy., Erie, PA 16509. **Telephone:** (814) 866-8808.

HARRISBURG SENATORS

Office Address: FNB Field, City Island, Harrisburg, PA 17101.
Mailing Address: PO Box 15757, Harrisburg, PA 17105.
Telephone: (717) 231-4444. **Fax:** (717) 231-4445.
E-Mail address: information@senatorsbaseball.com. **Website:** www.senatorsbaseball.com.
Affiliation (first year): Washington Nationals (2005). **Years in League:** 2021-

OWNERSHIP/MANAGEMENT
President: Kevin Kulp. **Vice President/General Manager:** Randy Whitaker. **Assistant General Manager, Marketing:** Ashley Grotte. **Vice President of Stadium Operations:** Tim Foreman. **Accounting Manager:** Donna Demczak. **Sr. Corporate Sales Executive:** Todd Matthews. **Corporate Sales Executive:** Nathan Rovenolt. **Director of Ticket Operations:** Matt McGrady. **Group Event Coordinator:** Alyssa Kimmel. **Group Event Coordinator:** Cole Single. **Radio Broadcaster:** Terry Byrom. **Director of Merchandise:** Ann Marie Naumes. **Director of Community Relations:** JK McKay. **Director of Game Entertainment:** Jess Knaster. **Video Production Manager:** Troy Matthews. **Digital Marketing Coordinator:** Casey Saussaman. **Head Groundskeeper:** Brandon Forsburg.

FIELD STAFF
Manager: Tripp Keister. **Hitting Coach:** Micah Franklin. **Pitching Coach:** Justin Lord. **Developmental Coach:** Oscar Salazar. **Trainer:** T.D. Swinford. **Strength Coach:** R.J. Guyer.

GAME INFORMATION
Radio Announcers: Terry Byrom & Frankie Vernouski. **No. of Games Broadcast:** 138. **Flagship Station:** CBS Sports Radio Harrisburg. **PA Announcer:** TBD. **Official Scorers:** Andy Linker and Mick Reinhard. **Stadium Name:** FNB Field. **Location:** I-83, exit 23 (Second Street) to Market Street, bridge to City Island. **Ticket Price Range:** $9-35. **Visiting Club Hotel:** Comfort Inn and Suites Harrisburg Airport, 1589 W. Harrisburg Pike, Middletown, PA 17057. **Telephone:** (717) 857-8776. **Visiting Team Workout Facility:** TBD.

HARTFORD YARD GOATS

Address: Dunkin' Donuts Park, 1214 Main Street, Hartford CT 06103
Telephone: (860) 246-4628. **Fax:** (860) 247-4628
E-Mail Address: info@yardgoatsbaseball.com. **Website:** www.YardGoatsBaseball.com
Affiliation (first year): Colorado Rockies (2015). **Years in League:** 2021-

OWNERSHIP/MANAGEMENT
President: Tim Restall. **General Manager:** Mike Abramson.
Assistant General Manager, Sales: Josh Montinieri. **Assistant General Manager, Operations:** Dean Zappalorti. **Controller:** Jim Bonfiglio. **Director, Broadcasting & Media Relations:** Jeff Dooley. **Executive Director of Business Development:** Steve Given. **Executive Director, Yard Goats Foundation:** Tiffany Young. **Director of Ticket Sales:** Steve Mekkelsen. **Director of Stadium Events:** Jessica Skelly. **Director of Stadium Operations:** Andrew Girard. **Director of Production and Creative Services:** Mike Delgado. **Hospitality Manager:** Matt DiBona. **Sports Turf Manager:** Kyle Calhoon. **Marketing Manager:** Lynette Perez. **Promotions Manager:** Isabelle Meckfessel. **Stadium**

Events Coordinator: Alyssa Pelosi. Senior Account Executive: Shawn Perry. Senior Account Executive: Jacob Michney. Ticket Sales Account Executive: Kofi Reid. Ticket Sales Account Executive: Matt Johnson. Operations Assistant: Anthony Marcel. Front Office Receptionist: Shirelle Buie. Professional Sports Catering, Regional Vice President: Scott Gustafson. Director of Operations: Jenny Nelson. Concessions Manager: Andrew Labov. Business Manager: Kevin Molde. Executive Chef: Joe Bartlett.

FIELD STAFF

Manager: Chris Denorfia. Bench Coach: Luis Lopez. Pitching Coach: Blaine Beatty. Hitting Coach: Tom Sutaris. Trainer: Kelsey Branstetter. Physical Performance Coach: Mason Rook.

GAME INFORMATION

Radio Announcers: Jeff Dooley, Dan Lovallo. No. of Games Broadcast: 138. Flagship Station: News Radio 1410 AM/100.9 FM Spanish AM 1120 Danny Rodriguez, Derik Rodriguez. PA Announcer: Jared Doyon. Official Scorer: Jim Keener. Stadium Name: Dunkin' Donuts Park. Directions: From the West: Take 84 East to Exit 50 (Main Street). Take Exit 50 toward Main St. Use the left lane to merge onto Chapel St S. Turn left onto Trumbull St. Use the middle lane to turn left onto Main St. From the East: Take 84 West to Exit 50 (US-44 W/Morgan Street). Follow I-91 S/Main St. Take a slight right onto Main St. From the North: Take 91 South to Exit 32A - 32B (Trumbull St). Turn left onto Market St. Turn right onto Morgan St. Take a slight right onto Main St. From the South: Take 91 North to Exit 32A - 32B (Market St). Use the left lane to take Exit 32A-32B for Trumbull St. Use the middle lane to turn left onto Market St. Turn right onto Morgan St. Take a slight right onto Main St. Ticket Price Range: $6-22. Visiting Club Hotel: Holiday Inn Express, 2553 Berlin Turnpike, Newington, CT 06111. Telephone: (860) 372-4000.

NEW HAMPSHIRE
FISHER CATS

Address: 1 Line Dr, Manchester, NH 03101.
Telephone: (603) 641-2005. Fax: (603) 641-2055.
E-Mail Address: info@nhfishercats.com. Website: www.nhfishercats.com.
Affiliation (first year): Toronto Blue Jays (2004). Years in League: 2021-

OWNERSHIP/MANAGEMENT

Operated By: DSF Sports Group & NHSC LLC. Partner: Art Solomon. Partner: Rick Brenner. Partner: Tom Silvia. President: Mike Ramshaw. Senior VP, Sales: Jeff Tagliaferro. VP, Business Development: Erik Lesniak. VP, Marketing and Communications: Tyler Murray. Executive Director of Facilities: Shawn Greenough. Executive Director, Hospitality and Special Events: Stephanie Fournier. Senior Account Executive: Nate Newcombe. Box Office Manager: Tara Leeth. Graphic Design & Production Manager: Amy Cecil. Marketing and Promotions Manager: Maddie Saines. Merchandise Manager: Jacob Madsen. Stadium Operations Manager: D.J. Peer. Facility Operations Manager: Kevin Matthews. Special Assistant to the Team President & Front Office Manager: Aubrey Smith. Corporate Sales and Promotions Coordinator: Andrew Marais. Corporate Sales Coordinator: Courtney Williams. Ticket Sales Account Executive: Andrew Larson. Ticket Sales Account Executive: Caleb Baum. Ticket Sales Account Executive: Darrin Messier. Professional Sports Catering, Director, Food & Beverage: Steve Kelly.

FIELD STAFF

Manager: Cesar Martin. Hitting Coach: Matt Hague. Pitching Coach: Jim Czajkowski. Position Coach: Chris Schaeffer. Athletic Trainer: Luke Greene. Strength Coach: Casey Callison.

GAME INFORMATION

Radio Announcers: Tyler Murray, Bob Lipman. No. of Games Broadcast: 138. Flagship Station: WGIR 610-AM. PA Announcer: Ben Altsher. Official Scorers: Chick Smith, Lenny Parker. Stadium Name: Delta Dental Stadium. Location: From I-93 North, take I-293 North to exit 5 (Granite Street), right on Granite Street, right on South Commercial Street, right on Line Drive. Ticket Price Range: $8-$14. Visiting Club Hotel: Tru by Hilton Manchester Downtown 135 Spring St, Manchester, NH 03101. Telephone: (603) 669-3000.

PORTLAND SEA DOGS

Office Address: 271 Park Ave, Portland, ME 04102.
Mailing Address: PO Box 636, Portland, ME 04104.
Telephone: (207) 874-9300. Fax: (207) 780-0317.
E-Mail address: seadogs@seadogs.com. Website: www.seadogs.com.
Affiliation (first year): Boston Red Sox (2003). Years in League: 2021-

OWNERSHIP/MANAGEMENT

Operated By: Portland, Maine Baseball, Inc.
Chairman: Bill Burke. Treasurer: Sally McNamara. President/General Manager: Geoff Iacuessa. Senior VP: John Kameisha. VP/Financial Affairs & Game Operations: Jim Heffley. VP/Communications & Fan Experience: Chris Cameron. Assistant General Manager/Sales: Dennis Meehan. Director, Corporate Sales: Justin Phillips. Director of Ticket Operations: Jesse Scaglion. Director of Promotions: Allison Casiles. Director, Creative Services: Ted

Seavey. **Mascot Coordinator:** Tim Jorn. **Director, Media Relations & Broadcasting:** Emma Tiedemann. **Director, Food Services:** Mike Scorza. **Assistant Director, Food Services:** Greg Moyes. **Ticket Office Coordinator:** Alan Barker. **Account Executive:** Melissa Mayhew. **Senior Advisor:** Charlie Eshbach. **Clubhouse Manager:** Mike Coziahr. **Head Groundskeeper:** Jason Cooke.

FIELD STAFF

Manager: Chad Epperson. **Hitting Coach:** Doug Clark. **Pitching Coach:** Lance Carter. **Development Coach:** Katie Krall. **Athletic Trainer:** Nick Kuchwara. **Strength & Conditioning Coach:** Joe Hudson.

GAME INFORMATION

Radio Announcer: Emma Tiedemann. **No. of Games Broadcast:** 138. **Flagship Station:** WPEI 95.9 FM. **PA Announcer:** Paul Coughlin. **Official Scorer:** Thom Hinton. **Stadium Name:** Hadlock Field. **Location:** From South, I-295 to exit 5, merge onto Congress Street, left at St John Street, merge right onto Park Ave; From North, I-295 to exit 6A, right onto Park Ave. **Ticket Price Range:** $8-13. **Visiting Club Hotel:** Holiday Inn Express, 303 Sable Oaks Dr., South Portland, ME 04106. **Telephone:** (207) 775-3900.

READING FIGHTIN PHILS

Office Address: Route 61 South/1900 Centre Ave, Reading, PA 19605. **Mailing Address:** PO Box 15050, Reading, PA 19612.
Telephone: (610) 370-2255. **Fax:** (610) 373-5868.
E-Mail Address: info@fightins.com. **Website:** www.fightins.com.
Affiliation: Philadelphia Phillies (1967). **Years in League:** 2021-

OWNERSHIP/MANAGEMENT

Operated By: E&J Baseball Club, Inc. **Principal Owner:** Reading Baseball LP. **Managing Partner:** Craig Stein.
General Manager: Scott Hunsicker. **Assistant General Manager:** Matt Hoffmaster. **Exec. Director, Sales:** Joe Bialek. **Exec. Director, BaseballOperations:** Kevin Sklenarik. **Exec. Director, Tickets & Groups:** Mike Becker. **Exec. Director, Community & FanDevelopment:** Mike Robinson. **Exec.Director, Business Development:** Anthony Pignetti. **Exec. Director, Promotions, Entertainment & Education:** Todd Hunsicker. **Controller:** Kris Haver. **Head Groundskeeper:** Dan Douglas. **Director, Marketing & Exec. Director, Baseballtown Charities:** Tonya Petrunak. **Video Director:** Andy Kauffman. **Director, Food &Beverage:** Travis Hart. **Office Manager:** Deneen Giesen. **Director, Groups:** Jon Nally. **Director, Client Fulfillment/Clubhouse Operations:** Andrew Nelson. **Director, Graphic Arts/Merchandise:** Ryan Springborn. **Account Executive:** Nick Helber. **Account Executive:** Mara Fulmer. **Media Relations/Broadcasting Manager:** Emily Messina. **Account Executive:** Matt Koch. **Stadium Operations Manager:** Ricky Bruno.

FIELD STAFF

Manager: Shawn Williams. **Hitting Coach:** Tyler Henson. **Pitching Coach:** Matt Hockenberry. **Coach:** Mycal Jones. **Athletic Trainer:** Andrew Dodgson. **Strength and Conditioning Coach:** Bruce Peditto.

GAME INFORMATION

Radio Announcer: Emily Messina. **No. of Games Broadcast:** 138. Internet Stream. **Official Scorers:** Kyle Matschke, Brian Kopetsky, Josh Leiboff, Dick Shute. **Stadium Name:** FirstEnergy Stadium. **Location:** From east, take Pennsylvania Turnpike West to Morgantown exit, to 176 North, to 422 West, to Route 12 East, to Route 61 South exit; From west, take 422 East to Route 12 East, to Route 61 South exit; From north, take 222 South to Route 12 exit, to Route 61 South exit; From south, take 222 North to 422 West, to Route 12 East exit at Route 61 South. **Standard Game Times:** 6:45 or 7:00pm, **Sundays** 3:15 or 5:15. **Ticket Price Range:** $7-13. **Visiting Club Hotel:** DoubleTree by Hilton Hotel Reading, 701 Penn St., Reading, PA 19601. **Telephone:** (610) 375-8000.

RICHMOND FLYING SQUIRRELS

Address: 3001 N Arthur Ashe Boulevard, Richmond, VA 23230.
Telephone: (804) 359-3866. **Fax:** (804) 359-1373.
E-Mail Address: info@squirrelsbaseball.com. **Website:** www.squirrelsbaseball.com.
Affiliation: San Francisco Giants (2010). **Years in League:** 2021-

OWNERSHIP/MANAGEMENT

Operated By: Navigators Baseball LP. **President/Managing Partner:** Lou DiBella.
CEO: Todd "Parney" Parnell. **Vice President/General Manager:** Ben Rothrock. **Assistant General Manager:** Ben Terry.
Controller: Faith Casey-Harriss. **Assistant Director of Corporate Partnerships:** Jamie Gordon. **Corporate Sales Associate:** Clayton Cotner. **Director of Group Sales:** Garrett Erwin. **Box Office Manager:** Derrick McCabe. **Box Office Ticket Representative:** Deja King. **Group Sales Executive:** Marquez Goode. **Group Sales Executive:** Wesley Donald. **Group Sales Executive:** Daniel Mumphery. **Group Hospitality Manager:** Carnie Bragg. **Group Sales & Box Office Associate:** James Dillard. **Director of Communications & Broadcasting:** Trey Wilson. **Communications & Broadcasting Assistant:** Blaine McCormick. **Director of Entertainment:** Caroline Phipps. **Special Events & Flying Squirrels Charities Manager:** Hannah DeFrank. **Creative Services & Production Director:** Nick Elder. **Graphic Design & Creative Services Manager:** Hunter Glotz. **Community Relations Manager:** Bailey Johnson. **Marketing & Social Media Manager:** Samantha McCloskey. **Mascot & Performance Manager:** Jack Caldwell. **Community Relations**

& Promotions Associate: Janell Armstead. **Director of Stadium Operations:** Evan Smith. **Facility Supervisor & Baseball Operations:** Joe Tarnowski. **Stadium Operations Assistant:** Chris Lasher. **Director of Food & Beverage:** Steve Bales. **Director of Merchandising:** Jackson Hairfield.

FIELD STAFF

Manager: TBA. **Hitting Coach:** TBA. **Pitching Coach:** TBA. **Fundamentals Coach:** TBA. **Athletic Trainer:** TBA. **Strength Coach:** TBA.

GAME INFORMATION

Radio Announcers: Trey Wilson & Blaine McCormick. **No. of Games Broadcast:** 138. **Flagship Station:** Sports Radio 910 The Fan WRNL. **PA Announcer:** Bianca Bryan. **Official Scorer:** Bob Flynn. **Stadium Name:** The Diamond. **Location:** Right off I-64 at the Boulevard exit. **Standard Game Times:** 6:35 pm, Fri., 7:05, Sat. 6:05, Sun. 1:05. **Ticket Price Range:** $10-14. **Visiting Club Hotel:** Fairfield Inn & Suites by Marriott Richmond Short Pump/1-64. **Telephone:** (804) 545-4200.

SOMERSET PATRIOTS

Office Address: One Patriots Park, Bridgewater, NJ 08807.
Telephone: (908) 252-0700. **Fax:** (908) 252-0776.
Website: somersetpatriots.com.
Affiliation: New York Yankees (2021). **Years in League:** 2021-

OWNERSHIP/MANAGEMENT

Operated by: Somerset Baseball Partners, LLC. **Ownership:** Jonathan Kalafer and Josh Kalafer. **Co-Chairmen:** Jonathan Kalafer and Josh Kalafer. **President/GM:** Patrick McVerry. **Senior VP, Marketing:** Dave Marek. **VP, Communications & Media Relations:** Marc Russinoff. **VP, Operations:** Bryan Iwicki. **VP, Ticket Operations:** Matt Kopas. **Senior Director, Merchandise:** Rob Crossman. **Director, Tickets:** Nick Cherrillo. **Director, Marketing:** Hal Hansen. **Director, Business Development:** Ken Smith. **Director, Administration:** Michele DaCosta. **Manager, Media Relations & Broadcasting:** Steven Cusumano. **Account Executives:** Justin King, Mike Katims, Stephen Goldsmith, Molly Swayne, Jacob Unger. **Controller:** Suzanne Colon. **Accountant:** Stephanie DePass. **Head Groundskeeper:** Dan Purner. **Homeplate Catering and Hospitality VP/General Manager:** Mike McDermott. **Assistant General Manager of Homeplate Catering and Hospitality:** Jimmy Search. **Director, Operations of HomePlate Catering:** Aly McGrath.

FIELD STAFF

Manager: TBA. **Hitting Coach:** TBA. **Pitching Coach:** TBA. **Fundamentals Coach:** TBA. **Athletic Trainer:** TBA. **Strength Coach:** TBA.

GAME INFORMATION

Lead Play-By-Play: Steven Cusumano. **No. of Games Broadcast:** 138. **Flagship Station:** FOX Sports New Jersey 93.5 FM/ 1450 AM . **Video Streams:** MiLB.tv. **Ballpark Name:** TD Bank Ballpark. **Standard Game Times:** Mon.- Thurs. 6:05 pm/ 6:35 pm/ 7:05 pm, Fri & Sat., 6:35 pm / 7:05 pm, Sun., 1:05 pm/ 5:05 pm.

DOUBLE-A SOUTH

STADIUM INFORMATION

| Club | Stadium | Opened | Dimensions | | | Capacity | 2021 Att. |
			LF	CF	RF		
Biloxi	MGM Park	2015	335	400	335	6,000	114,276
Birmingham	Regions Field	2013	320	400	325	8,500	231,365
Chattanooga	AT&T Field	2000	325	400	330	6,362	131,322
Mississippi	Trustmark Park	2005	335	402	332	7,416	118,776
Montgomery	Riverwalk Stadium	2004	314	380	332	7,000	137,709
Pensacola	Blue Wahoos Stadium	2012	325	400	335	6,000	235,948
Rocket City	Toyota Field	2021	326	400	326	7,500	274,858
Tennessee	Smokies Stadium	2000	330	400	330	6,000	245,821

BILOXI SHUCKERS

Address: 105 Caillavet Street, Biloxi, MS 39530
Telephone: (228) 233-3465
E-Mail Address: info@biloxishuckers.com. **Website:** www.biloxishuckers.com.
Affiliation (first year): Milwaukee Brewers (2015). **Years in League:** 2021-.

OWNERSHIP/MANAGEMENT

Operated By: Biloxi Baseball LLC.
President: Ken Young. **General Manager:** Hunter Reed. **Assistant General Manager:** Trevor Matifes. **Ticket Operations Coordinator:** Johnny Tribbett. **Ballpark Entertainment Manager:** Daniel Clapper. **Media Relations Manager and Broadcaster:** Garrett Greene. **Community Relations Manager:** Allyson Staton. **Stadium Operations Manager:** Diana Garber-Dovenspike. **Marketing Coordinator:** Paige Bell. **Accounting Manager:** Pam Hendrickson.

FIELD STAFF

Manager: Mike Guerrero. **Hitting Coach:** Chuckie Caufield. **Pitching Coach:** Nick Childs. **Athletic Trainer:** Matt Deal.

GAME INFORMATION

PA Announcer: Kyle Curley. **Official Scorer:** Scotty Berkowitz. **No. of Games Broadcast:** 138. **Stadium Name:** MGM Park. **Location:** I-10 to I-110 South toward beach, take Ocean Springs exit onto US 90 (Beach Blvd), travel east one block, turn left on Caillavet Street, stadium is on the left. **Ticket Price Range:** $7-$24. **Visiting Club Hotel:** DoubleTree by Hilton Biloxi on Beach Blvd.

BIRMINGHAM BARONS

Office Address: 1401 1st Ave South, Birmingham, AL, 35233. **Mailing Address:** PO Box 877, Birmingham, AL, 35201.
Telephone: (205) 988-3200. **Fax:** (205) 988-9698.
E-Mail Address: barons@barons.com. **Website:** www.barons.com.
Affiliation (first year): Chicago White Sox (1986). **Years in League:** 2021-

OWNERSHIP/MANAGEMENT

Principal Owners: Don Logan, Jeff Logan, Stan Logan. **President/General Manager:** Jonathan Nelson. **Vice President of Business Development & Entertainment:** John Cook. **CFO:** Randy Prince. **Assistant Controller:** Cary Southerland. **Inventory Control Accountant:** Jonathan Judge. **Director of Group Sales:** Richard Coats. **Director of Corporate Sponsorships:** Rich Smyth. **Group Sales Manager:** Brett Tornow. **Group Sales Manager:** Kevin Piotrzkowski. **Group Sales Manager:** Makenzie Warren. **Creative Services Coordinator:** DeAnna Scarpelli. **Ticket Sales & Operations Manager:** Josh Freund. **Ticket Sales Manager:** Savion Hill, Jennifer McGee. **Director of Broadcasting:** Curt Bloom. **Director of Retail Sales:** Will Larsen. **Head Groundskeeper:** Caleb Paullus. **Director of Stadium Operations:** Corey Johnson. **Director of Customer Service:** George Chavous. **Receptionist & Data Clerk:** Ashlee Bryan. **Operations Assistant:** Roderick Smith. **Director of Food & Beverage:** Gus Stoudemire. **Concessions Manager:** Tametrius Motley. **Assistant Catering Manager:** Bo Gaston. **Premium Services Manager & Sponsorship Sales Coordinator:** Austyn Eldridge. **Executive Chef:** Nick Tittle. **Sous Chef:** Vic Arnold.

FIELD STAFF

Manager: Justin Jirschele. **Hitting Coach:** Charlie Romero. **Pitching Coach:** Richard Dotson. **Head Athletic Trainer:** TBD. **Performance Coach:** TBD

GAME INFORMATION

Radio Announcer: Curt Bloom. **No of Games Broadcast:** 69. **Flagship Station:** JOX 94.5-WJOX-FM. **PA Announcers:** Derek Scudder, Andy Parish. **Official Scorers:** Jeff Allison, David Tompkins. **Stadium Name:** Regions Field. **Location:** I-65 (exit 259B) in Birmingham. **Standard Game Times:** 7:05 pm, Sat. 6:30, Sun 4:00. **Ticket Price Range:** $10-23. **Visiting Club Hotel:** Hyatt Regency Birmingham - The Wynfrey Hotel, 1000 Riverchase Galleria, Birmingham, AL 35244. **Telephone:** (205) 988-3200

CHATTANOOGA LOOKOUTS

Office Address: 201 Power Alley, Chattanooga, TN 37402.
Mailing Address: PO Box 11002, Chattanooga, TN 37401.
Telephone: (423) 267-2208. **Fax:** (423) 267-4258.
E-Mail Address: lookouts@lookouts.com. **Website:** www.lookouts.com.
Affiliation (first year): Cincinnati Reds (2019). **Years in League:** 2021-

OWNERSHIP/MANAGEMENT

Operated By: Chattanooga Lookouts, LLC.
Principal Owner: Hardball Capital. **Managing Partner:** Jason Freier. **President:** Rich Mozingo. **Public/Media Relations Manager:** Dan Kopf. **Head Groundskeeper:** Casey Kyle. **Marketing & Promotions Manager:** Alex Tanish. **Director of Broadcasting:** Larry Ward. **Operations Manager:** Michael Matheson. **Vice President:** Andrew Zito. **Ticket Partnership Manager:** Jennifer Crum. **Ticket Partnership Manager:** Mark Curtis. **Ticket Partnership Manager:** Jarrah Vella-Wright. **Ticket Operations Manager:** Sidney Hooper. **Concessions Manager:** William Marr.

FIELD STAFF

Manager: Jose Moreno. **Hitting Coach:** Eric Richardson. **Pitching Coach:** Rob Wooten. **Coach:** Nate Irving.

GAME INFORMATION

Radio Announcers: Larry Ward. **No. of Games Broadcast:** 138. **Flagship Station:** 98.1 The LAKE. **PA Announcer:** Ron Hall. **Official Scorers:** Adam Belford, Andrew Mindeman. **Stadium Name:** AT&T Field. **Location:** From I-24, take US 27 North to exit 1C (4th Street), first left onto Chestnut Street, left onto Third Street. **Ticket Price Range:** TBD. **Visiting Club Hotel:** Holiday Inn, 2232 Center Street, Chattanooga, TN 37421. **Telephone:** (423) 485-1185.

MISSISSIPPI BRAVES

Office Address: Trustmark Park, 1 Braves Way, Pearl, MS 39208.
Mailing Address: PO Box 97389, Pearl, MS 39288.
Telephone: (601) 932-8788. **Fax:** (601) 936-3567.
E-Mail Address: mississippibraves@braves.com. **Web site:** www.mississippibraves.com.
Affiliation (first year): Atlanta Braves (2005). **Years in League:** 2021-

OWNERSHIP/MANAGEMENT

Ownership: Diamond Baseball Holdings, LLC.
Vice President & General Manager: Pete Laven. **Assistant General Manager/Director of Sales:** Tim Mueller. **Office Manager:** Christy Shaw. **Ticket Manager:** Jeff Olson. **Account Executive:** Garrett Butler. **Head Groundskeeper:** Tyler Seibert. **Director of Group Sales:** David Kerr. **Director of Stadium Operations:** Zach Evans. **Director of Communications, Media & Broadcasting:** Chris Harris. **Food & Beverage Director:** Mike Kardamis.

FIELD STAFF

Manager: Bruce Crabbe. **Hitting Coach:** Mike Bard. **Pitching Coach:** Bo Henning. **Trainer:** TBD. **Coach:** TBD.

GAME INFORMATION

Radio Announcer: Chris Harris. **No. of Games Broadcast:** 138. **Flagship Station:** TBA
PA Announcer: Greg Flynn. **Official Scorer:** Mark Beason.
Stadium Name: Trustmark Park. **Location:** I-20 to exit 48/Pearl (Pearson Road). **Ticket Price Range:** $6-$25.
Visiting Club Hotel: Hilton Garden Inn Jackson Flowood, 118 Laurel Park Cove, Flowood, MS 39232. **Telephone:** (601) 487-0800.

MONTGOMERY BISCUITS

Address: 200 Coosa St., Montgomery, AL 36104.
Telephone: (334) 323-2255. **Fax:** (334) 323-2225.
E-Mail address: info@biscuitsbaseball.com. **Website:** www.biscuitsbaseball.com.
Affiliation (first year): Tampa Bay Rays (2004). **Years in League:** 2021-

OWNERSHIP/MANAGEMENT

Operated By: Biscuits Baseball LLC. **Chief Executive Officer:** Lou DiBella
President: Todd "Parney" Parnell. **Chief Operating Officer:** Brendon Porter. **General Manager:** Michael Murphy.

Corporate & Military Partnerships: Jay Jones. **Director of Group Sales:** Chris Walker. **Director of Entertainment & Uniforms:** I.J. Balaban. **Box Office Manager, Season Ticket Coordinator:** Justin Ross. **Marketing & Creative Services:** Jared McCarthy. **Broadcaster, Media Relations:** Chris Adams-Wall. **Retail Manager:** Ashley Williams. **Director, Food & Beverage:** Risa Juliano. **Assistant Director of Food & Beverage:** Michael Parham. **Director, Stadium Operations:** Steve Blackwell. **Assistant Director of Stadium Operations/Head Groundskeeper:** Alex English. **Business Manager:** Tracy Mims. **Executive Administrator:** Jeannie Burke.

FIELD STAFF
Manager: Morgan Ensberg. **Pitching Coach:** Jim Paduch. **Hitting Coach:** Wuarnner Rincones. **Bench Coach:** Sean Smedley. **Athletic Trainer:** James Ramsdell. **Conditioning Coach:** James McCallie

GAME INFORMATION
Radio Announcer: Chris Adams-Wall. **No of Games Broadcast:** 138. **Flagship Station:** WMSP 740-AM. **PA Announcer:** Rick Hendrick. **Official Scorer:** Brian Wilson. **Stadium Name:** Montgomery Riverwalk Stadium. **Location:** I-65 to exit 172, east on Herron Street, left on Coosa Street. **Ticket Price Range:** $8-16. **Visiting Club Hotel:** TBA.

PENSACOLA BLUE WAHOOS

Telephone: (850) 934-8444. **Fax:** (850) 791-6256.
E-Mail Address: info@bluewahoos.com. **Website:** www.bluewahoos.com
Affiliation (first year): Miami Marlins (2021). **Years in League:** 2021-

OWNERSHIP/MANAGEMENT
Operated by: Northwest Florida Professional Baseball LLC. **Principal Owners:** Quint Studer, Rishy Studer. **Minority Owners:** Bubba Watson, Derrick Brooks, Randall Wells, John List, Dana Suskind. **President:** Jonathan Griffith. **Vice President, Operations:** Donna Kirby. **Vice President, Sales:** Alex Sides. **Vice President, Media & Entertainment:** Daniel Venn. **Receptionist:** Tori Perkins. **Executive Assistant:** TJ Johnson. **Facilities Manager:** Mike Crenshaw, Mike Fitzgerald. **Head Groundskeeper:** Dustin Hannah. **Director, Human Relations:** Candice Miller. **Senior Writer:** Bill Vilona. **Broadcaster:** Erik Bremer. **Merchandise and Community Relations Manager:** Anna Striano. **Ticket Operations Manager:** JP Stanzell. **Group Sales Executives:** Greg Liebbe, Jordan Newman. **Corporate Sales Executive:** Steven Unser. **Hospitality & Sales Coordinator:** Jordan Morrow. **CFO:** Kathy Cadwell. **Accounts Payable:** Lea Howard

FIELD STAFF
Manager: Kevin Randel. **Pitching Coach:** Dave Eiland. **Hitting Coach:** Scott Seabol. **Defensive Coach:** Frank Moore. **Trainer:** Melissa Hampton

GAME INFORMATION
Radio Announcer: Erik Bremer. **No. of Games Broadcast:** 138. **Flagship Station:** ESPN Pensacola. **PA Announcer:** Josh Gay, Kevin Peterson, Chris James, Shane Tucker. **Official Scorer:** Craig Cooper, Don Burns. **Stadium Name:** Blue Wahoos Stadium. **Field Name:** Admiral Fetterman Field. **Standard Game Times:** 6:35 pm, Sat. 6:05, Sun. 4:05. **Ticket Price Range:** $5-$19

ROCKET CITY TRASH PANDAS

Address: 1 Trash Pandas Way. Madison, AL 35758.
Telephone: (256) 325-1403.
E-Mail Address: Info@trashpandasbaseball.com. **Website:** trashpandasbaseball.com.
Affiliation (first year): Los Angeles Angels (2017). **Years in League:** 2021.

OWNERSHIP/MANAGEMENT
Owned and Operated by: BallCorps, LLC. **Executive Vice President and General Manager:** Garrett Fahrmann. **Executive Vice President, Marketing, Promotions and Entertainment:** Lindsey Knupp. **Senior Director, Finance:** Angy Blailock. **Senior Director, Operations:** Ken Clary. **Director, Food and Beverage Operations:** Garien Shelby. **Groundskeeper:** Charlie Weaver.

FIELD STAFF
Manager: Andy Schatzley. **Hitting Coach:** Kenny Hook. **Pitching Coach:** Michael Wuertz. **Bench Coach:** Dann Bilardello. **Team Trainer:** TBA. **Strength and Conditioning Coach:** Henry Aleck.

GAME INFORMATION
Director, Broadcasting and Baseball Information: Josh Caray. **No. of Games Broadcast:** 138. **Radio:** WUMP-FM 103.9. **Website:** www.umpsports.com. **PA Announcer:** Antonio MacBeath. **Stadium Name:** Toyota Field. **Location:** I-565 to Toyota Field Exit. **Standard Game Times:** 6:35 pm (Monday-Saturday) 2:35 pm (Sundays). **Ticket Price Range:** $8-$50. **Visiting Club Hotel:** AVID Hotel 125 Graphics Dr, Madison, AL 35758. **Telephone:** (256) 325-1800.

TENNESSEE SMOKIES

Address: 3540 Line Drive, Kodak, TN 37764.
Telephone: (865) 286-2300. **Fax:** (865) 523-9913.
E-Mail Address: info@smokiesbaseball.com. **Website:** www.smokiesbaseball.com.
Affiliation (first year): Chicago Cubs (2007-). **Years in League:** 2021-

OWNERSHIP/MANAGEMENT

Owners: Randy and Jenny Boyd.
CEO: Doug Kirchhofer. **President/COO:** Chris Allen. **Vice President:** Jeremy Boler. **General Manager:** Tim Volk. **Assistant General Manager, Stadium Operations:** Bryan Webster. **Assistant General Manager, Hospitality:** Chris Franklin. **Director of Broadcasting:** Mick Gillispie. **Director of Marketing & Entertainment:** Aris M Theofanopoulos. **Director of Retail Operations:** Leslie Soffa. **Director of Outside Events:** Morgan Messick. **Director of Corporate Partnerships:** Steve Brice. **Assistant Director of Corporate Partnerships:** Baylor Love. **Corporate Sales Executive:** Matt Martin. **Administrative Assistant:** Tolena Trout. **Director of Finance:** Paul Makres. **Admin/Finance Assistant:** Michelle Conway. **Accounting/HR Specialist:** Cheryl Brown. **Hospitality Manager:** David Branam. **Concessions Manager:** Tyler Kennedy. **Concessions Manager:** Caleb Mills. **Director of Ticket & Group Sales:** Emily White. **Box Office Manager:** Brett Adams. **Account Executive:** Stephen Haselton. **Account Executive:** Trey Hinton. **Account Executive:** Ben Bond. **Stadium Operations:** Jonathan Jennings. **Head Groundskeeper:** Duncan Long.

FIELD STAFF

Manager: Michael Ryan. **Hitting Coach:** Ryan Strickland. **Pitching Coach:** Jamie Vermilyea. **Coach:** TBD. **Strength Coach:** TBD. **Athletic Trainer:** TBD.

GAME INFORMATION

Radio Announcer: Mick Gillispie. **No. of Games Broadcast:** 138. **Flagship Station:** WNML 99.1-FM/990-AM.
PA Announcer: George Yardley. **Official Scorer:** Wade Mitchell. **Stadium Name:** Smokies Stadium. **Location:** I-40 to exit 407, Highway 66 North. **Standard Game Times:** 7:00 pm, Sat. 7:00 pm, Sun. 2:00 pm. **Ticket Price Range:** $10-$14.
Visiting Club Hotel: Hampton Inn & Suites Sevierville, 105 Stadium Drive, Kodak, TN 37764. **Telephone:** (865) 465-0590.

DOUBLE-A CENTRAL

STADIUM INFORMATION

Club	Stadium	Opened	Dimensions			Capacity	2021 Att.
			LF	CF	RF		
Amarillo	Hodgetown	2019	325	405	325	7,300	316,288
Arkansas	Dickey-Stephens Park	2007	332	413	330	5,842	215,050
Corpus Christi	Whataburger Field	2005	325	400	315	5,362	206,847
Frisco	Dr Pepper Ballpark	2003	335	409	335	10,216	275,169
Midland	Security Bank Ballpark	2002	330	410	322	4,669	186,134
NW Arkansas	Arvest Ballpark	2008	325	400	325	6,500	150,473
San Antonio	Wolff Stadium	1994	310	402	340	9,200	184,167
Springfield	John Q. Hammons Field	2003	315	400	330	6,750	172,134
Tulsa	ONEOK Field	2010	330	400	307	7,833	300,270
Wichita	Riverfront Stadium	2021	340	400	325	10,000	241,230

AMARILLO SOD POODLES

Ballpark Address: 715 S. Buchanan Street, Amarillo, TX 79101
Mailing Address: 715 S. Buchanan Street, Amarillo, TX 79101
Main Phone: (806) 803-7762
Stadium Name: HODGETOWN. **Estimated Capacity:** 7,300
Affiliation (first year): Arizona Diamondbacks (2021). **Years in League:** 2021-

OWNERSHIP/MANAGEMENT

Owners: Elmore Sports Group. **President & General Manager:** Tony Ensor. **Assistant General Manager, Director of Ticket Sales:** Jeff Turner. **Director of Finance:** Ben Knowles. **Merchandise Director:** Lynn Ensor. **Manager of Public Relations and Baseball Operations:** Cory Hilborne. **Director of Broadcasting:** Sam Levitt. **Community Relations & Mascot Coordinator:** Austin Jackson. **Video Production Manager:** Adrian Garcia. **Creative Services Coordinator:** Jordan Lank. **Director of Corporate Partnerships:** Grant Norman. **Corporate Partnerships Manager:** Winston Reeves. **Promotions & Corporate Partnerships Manager:** Sierra Todd. **Corporate Partnerships Activation & Fulfillment Specialist:** Isaac Galan. **Director of Group Sales:** Dustin True. **Ticket Operations Manager:** Samantha Cook. **Group Sales & Special Events Coordinator:** Zak McGrath. **Senior Tickets & Groups Account Executive:** Matt Sutherland. **Account Executive:** Adam Padgett. **Director of Stadium Operations:** Eric Walker. **Assistant Director of Stadium Operations & Events:** Koby Hood. **Head Groundskeeper:** Jason Floyd. **Director of Food and Beverage:** Mike Lindal. **Catering & Bar Manager:** Nicole Lamontagne. **Executive Chef:** Mary Wood.

FIELD STAFF

Manager: Shawn Roof. **Hitting Coach:** Travis Denker. **Pitching Coach:** Shane Loux. **Coach:** Javier Colina. **Strength & Conditioning Coach:** Logan Jones. **Athletic Trainer:** Damon Reel.

GAME INFORMATION

Radio Announcer: Sam Levitt. **No. of Games Broadcast:** 138. **Flagship Station:** KIXZ 940 AM (Townsquare Media Amarillo). **PA Announcer:** N/A. **Official Scorer:** N/A. **Stadium Name:** HODGETOWN. **Standard Game Times:** 1:05 p.m., 6:05 p.m., 7:05 p.m. CT. **Ticket Price Range:** $6-18. **Visiting Club Hotel:** Four Points by Sheraton

ARKANSAS TRAVELERS

Office Address: Dickey-Stephens Park, 400 West Broadway, North Little Rock, AR 72114.
Mailing Address: PO Box 3177, Little Rock, AR 72203.
Telephone: (501) 664-1555. **Ticket Office:** (501) 664-7559
E-Mail address: travs@travs.com. **Website:** www.travs.com.
Affiliation (first year): Seattle Mariners (2017). **Years in League:** 2021-

OWNERSHIP/MANAGEMENT

Ownership: Arkansas Travelers Baseball Club, Inc.
President: Russ Meeks.
Executive Vice President/Chief Executive Officer: Rusty Meeks. **Chief Financial Officer:** Brad Eagle. **General Manager:** Sophie Ozier. **Assistant General Manager:** Ben Hornbrook. **Assistant General Manager:** John Sjobek. **Director of Finance/Corporate Assistant Secretary:** Patti Clark. **Director of Group Sales:** Montag Genser. **Director of Charities and Community Support:** Lance Restum. **Broadcaster/Baseball Operations Director:** Steven Davis. **Park Superintendent:** Greg Johnston. **Assistant Park Superintendent:** Reggie Temple. **Assistant Grounds Manager:** Austin Paradis. **Assistant Director of Food and Beverage:** Hunter Johnston. **Creative Services Manager:** Bradley Field. **Suite and Ticket Sales Manager:** Megan Girton. **Creative Services and Merchandise Coordinator:** Tori Heck. **Corporate Event Planners:** Cameron Jefferson, Ramsey Purvis.

FIELD STAFF

Manager: Collin Cowgill. **Hitting Coach:** Shawn O'Malley. **Pitching Coach:** Sean McGrath. **Coach:** Geoff Jimenez.

GAME INFORMATION

Radio Announcer: Steven Davis. **No. of Games Broadcast:** All. **Flagship Station:** KARN 920 AM.
PA Announcer: Various. **Official Scorer:** Various. **Stadium Name:** Dickey-Stephens Park. **Location:** I-30 to Broadway exit, proceed west to ballpark, located at Broadway Avenue and the Broadway Bridge. **Standard Game Time:** 6:35 p.m. Tue-Thu; 7:05 p.m. Fri-Sat; 1:35 p.m. Sun. **Ticket Price Range:** $5-13. **Visiting Club Hotel:** TBD

CORPUS CHRISTI HOOKS

Address: 734 East Port Ave, Corpus Christi, TX 78401.
Telephone: (361) 561-4665. **Fax:** (361) 561-4666.
E-Mail Address: info@cchooks.com. **Website:** www.cchooks.com.
Affiliation (first year): Houston Astros (2005). **Years in League:** 2021-

OWNERSHIP/MANAGEMENT

Owned/Operated By: Houston Astros. **General Manager:** Brady Ballard. **Director, Business Development:** Maggie Freeborn. **Account Executive, Corporate Partnerships:** Kaleb Womack. **Community Outreach Coordinator:** Emily Carney. **Director, Sales:** Pat McCarthy. **Manager, Tickets:** Liz Adams. **Account Executive:** Agustin Brizuela. **Account Executive:** Cassie Reyna; **Account Executive:** Veronica Hartman. **Director, Media Relations/Broadcasting:** Michael Coffin. **Director, Marketing & Entertainment:** Amy Johnson. **Manager, Creative Services:** Courtney Merritt. **Manager, Marketing:** Dustin Fishman. **Manager, Ballpark Entertainment:** Travis Pettis. **Video Editor:** Val Chapa. **Director, Operations:** Brett Howsley. **Manager, Home Clubhouse:** Marcus Tramp. **Coordinator, Special Events/Operations:** Jorden Klaevemann. **Stadium Operations:** Mike Shedd. **Stadium Operations:** Mike Hoffman. **Maintenance Assistant:** Jay Conerly. **Head Groundskeeper:** Taylor Balhoff. **Assistant Groundskeeper:** Anthony Hernandez. **Director, Accounting:** Jessica Fearn. **Operations Manager/Store Supervisor:** Eric Suniga. **Receptionist:** Denise Perez.

FIELD STAFF

Manager: Gregorio Petit. **Hitting Coach:** Aaron Westlake. **Pitching Coach:** Thomas Whitsett. **Fundamentals Coach:** TBA. **Athletic Trainer:** TBA. **Strength Coach:** TBA.

GAME INFORMATION

Radio Announcers: Michael Coffin, Gene Kasprzyk. **No. of Games Broadcast:** 138. **Flagship Station:** KKTX-AM 1360. **PA Announcer:** Amy Montez Frye. **Stadium Name:** Whataburger Field. **Location:** 734 E. Port Ave: I-37 to end of interstate, left at Chaparral, left at Hirsh Ave. **Ticket Price Range:** $6-20. **Visiting Club Hotel:** Best Western Corpus Christi; 300 N Shoreline Blvd, Corpus Christi, TX 78401; (361) 883-5111.

FRISCO ROUGHRIDERS

Address: 7300 RoughRiders Trail, Frisco, TX 75034.
Telephone: (972) 731-9200. **Fax:** (972) 731-5355.
E-Mail Address: info@ridersbaseball.com. **Website:** www.ridersbaseball.com.
Affiliation (first year): Texas Rangers (2003). **Years in League:** 2021-

OWNERSHIP/MANAGEMENT

Operated by: Frisco RoughRiders LP. **Chairman/CEO/General Partner:** Chuck Greenberg. **President & General Manager:** Victor Rojas. **Assistant General Manager/Chief Operating Officer:** Scott Burchett. **Assistant General Manager/Vice President, Ticket Sales:** Skip Wallace. **Director, Business Partnerships:** Jeff Brown. **Director, Partner Services:** Eric Moore. **Customer Service Agents:** Claudia Kipp, Vicki Sohn. **Vice President, Sales:** Ross Lanford. **Director of Ticket Operations:** Jesse Evans. **Manager, Sales:** Tom Baker. **Senior Sales Executive:** Alex Sandborn. **Sales Executives:** Sydney Peterson, Toufie J. Mazzawy, Adelina Rodriguez. **Inside Sales Executives:** Sydney Blackburn, Natalie Brown, Jackson Burgess, Nestor Diaz, Sam Jochimsen, Ryan Wooten. **Sales and Service Executives:** Jacob Gibson, Adam Graham. **Box Office Coordinator:** Chris Donawho. **Director of Finance:** Rick Maddox. **Merchandise Manager:** Lorraine Spencer. **VP, Community Development:** Breon Dennis, Jr. **Marketing Manager:** Krystin King. **Manager, Ballpark Entertainment:** Tommy Bean. **Manager of Media Development/Broadcaster:** Zach Bigley. **Senior Director, Sports Turf & Grounds Manager:** David Bicknell. **Team Dog:** Brooks.

FIELD STAFF

Manager: Jared Goedert. **Hitting Coach:** Eric Dorton. **Pitching Coach:** Jeff Andrews. **Developmental Coaches:** Chad Comer, Avery Sullivan. **Athletic Trainer:** Yuichi Takizawa. **Strength & Conditioning Coach:** Jon Nazarko.

GAME INFORMATION

Broadcaster: Zach Bigley. **No. of Games Broadcast:** 138. **Flagship Station:** www.RidersBaseball.com. **Stadium Name:** Riders Field. **Location:** Intersection of Dallas North Tollway & State Highway 121. **Standard Game Times:** 6:35 PM (April-May, September), 7:05 PM (June-August), **Sunday 4:**05 PM (April-May, September), 6:05 PM (June-August). **Visiting Club Hotel:** Drury Inn and Suites, Dallas Frisco (2880 Dallas Parkway, Frisco, Texas 75034). **Visiting Club Hotel Phone:** (972) 668-9700. **Visiting Club Hotel Fax:** (972) 668-9701.

MIDLAND ROCKHOUNDS

Address: Momentum Bank Ballpark, 5514 Champions Drive, Midland, TX 79706.
Telephone: (432) 520-2255. **Fax:** (432) 520-8326.
Website: www.midlandrockhounds.org.
Affiliation (first year): Oakland Athletics (1999). **Years in League:** 2021-

OWNERSHIP/MANAGEMENT
Operated By: Midland Sports, Inc. **Principal Owners:** Miles Prentice, Bob Richmond. **President:** Miles Prentice. **Executive Vice President:** Bob Richmond. **General Manager:** Monty Hoppel. **Assistant GM:** Jeff VonHolle. **Assistant GM, Operations:** Ray Fieldhouse. **Director, Broadcasting/Publications:** Bob Hards. **Director, Business Operations:** Eloisa Galvan. **Director, Ticketing:** Ryan Artzer. **Director, Client Services/ Marketing:** Shelly Haenggi. **Director, Community and Media Relations:** Rachael DiLeonardo. **Director, Operations:** Dan Knapinski. **Sales Executive:** Jonathan Simmons. **Sales Executive:** Sam Page. **Sales Executive:** Joshua Selaya. **Head Groundskeeper:** Brian Mitchell. **Director, Game Entertainment/Video Board:** Peyton Wilkins. **Operations Assistant:** Mitch Riddle. **Assistant Concessions Manager:** Al Melville. **Office Manager:** Vanessa Redman-Bynum. **Home Clubhouse Manager:** TBA. **Visiting Clubhouse Manager:** TBA.

FIELD STAFF
Manager: TBA. **Hitting Coach:** TBA. **Pitching Coach:** TBA. **Fundamentals Coach:** TBA. **Athletic Trainer:** TBA. **Strength Coach:** TBA.

GAME INFORMATION
Radio Announcer: Bob Hards. **No. of Games Broadcast:** 138. **Flagship Station:** Streamed on Website. **PA Announcer:** Wes Coles. **Official Scorer:** TBA. **Stadium Name:** Momentum Bank Ballpark. **Location:** From I-20, exit Loop 250 North to Highway 191 intersection. **Standard Game Times: Sunday:** 2:00 pm, **Monday-Wednesday:** 6:30 pm, **Thursday-Saturday:** 7:00 pm. **Ticket Price Range:** $8-16. **Visiting Club Hotel:** Sleep Inn& Suites, 5612 Deauville Blvd, Midland, TX 79706. **Telephone:** (432) 694-4200.

NORTHWEST ARKANSAS
NATURALS

Address: 3000 Gene George Blvd, Springdale, AR 72762.
Telephone: (479) 927-4900. **Fax:** (479) 756-8088.
E-Mail Address: tickets@nwanaturals.com. **Website:** www.nwanaturals.com.
Affiliation (first year): Kansas City Royals (1995). **Years in League:** 2021-

OWNERSHIP/MANAGEMENT
Principal Owner: Rich Products Corp. **Owner/President:** Robert Rich Jr. **President, Rich Entertainment Group:** Melinda Rich. **Chief Operating Officer, Rich Entertainment Group:** Joseph Segarra. **President, Rich Baseball Operations:** Mike Buczkowski. **Vice President/General Manager:** Justin Cole. **Assistant General Manager:** Mark Zaiger. **Director, Business:** Morgan Helmer. **Director, Marketing/PR:** Dustin Dethlefs. **Director, Ballpark Operations:** Brock White. **Head Groundskeeper:** Stephen Crockett. **Ballpark Operations Manager:** Brad Ziegler. **Ticket Office Manager:** Matt Fanning. **Creative Services Coordinator:** Adam Annaratone. **Account Executive:** Spencer Lundquist. **Account Executive:** Amber McCarthy. **Account Executive:** Tim Morrissey. **Clubhouse Coordinator:** Danny Helmer.

FIELD STAFF
Manager: Chris Widger. **Pitching Coach:** Derrick Lewis. **Hitting Coach:** Abraham Nunez. **Assistant Hitting Coach:** Christian Colón. **Bench Coach:** Mike Jirschele.

GAME INFORMATION
Radio Announcer: Nicholas Badders. **No. of Games Broadcast:** 138. **Flagship Station:** Streamed Online. **PA Announcer:** TBA. **Official Scorers:** Kyle Stiles, Walter Woodie & Ken Foxx. **Stadium Name:** Arvest Ballpark. **Location:** I-49 to US 412 West (Sunset Ave), Left on Gene George Blvd. **Standard Game Times:** 7:05 pm, 6:05 pm (Saturday), 2:05 pm (Sunday). **Visiting Club Hotel:** Holiday Inn Springdale, 1500 S 48th St, Springdale, AR 72762. **Telephone:** (479) 751-8300.

SAN ANTONIO MISSIONS

Address: 5757 Highway 90 W, San Antonio, TX 78227
Telephone: 210-675-7275 | **Fax:** 210-670-0001
Email Address: sainfo@samissions.com. **Website:** www.samissions.com
Affiliation (First Year): San Diego Padres (2021). **Years in League:** 2021-

OWNERSHIP/MANAGEMENT

Operated by: Elmore Sports Group. **Principal Owner:** David Elmore. **President:** Burl Yarbrough. **General Manager:** David Gasaway. **Assistant GMs:** Mickey Holt, Jeff Long, Bill Gerlt. **GM, Diamond Concessions:** Deanna Mierzwa. **Controller:** Eric Olivarez. **Office Manager:** Delia Rodriguez. **Director of Ticketing:** JJ Jimenez. **Director of Public Relations:** Jeremy Sneed.

FIELD STAFF

Manager: Phillip Wellman. **Pitching Coach:** Pete Zamora. **Hitting Coach:** Raul Padron. **Bench Coach:** Shane Robinson. **Athletic Trainer:** Nick Coberly. **Strength and Conditioning Coach:** Mark Spadavecchia. **Clubhouse Manager:** Nash Opperman.

GAME INFORMATION

No. of Games: 138. **Flagship Station:** 93.3 FM. **PA Announcer:** Roland Ruiz. **Official Scorer:** David Humphrey. **Stadium Name:** Nelson Wolff Stadium. **Location:** From I-10, I-35 or I-37, take US Hwy 90 West to Callaghan Road exit. **Standard Game Times:** 7:05 p.m., **Sunday 2:**05 p.m./6:05 p.m. **Visiting Club Hotel:** TBA.

SPRINGFIELD CARDINALS

Address: 955 East Trafficway, Springfield, MO 65802.
Telephone: (417) 863-0395. **Fax:** (417) 832-3004.
E-Mail Address: springfield@cardinals.com. **Website:** springfieldcardinals.com.
Affiliation (first year): St. Louis Cardinals (2005). **Years in League:** 2021-

OWNERSHIP/MANAGEMENT

Operated By: St. Louis Cardinals.
Vice President/General Manager: Dan Reiter. **VP, Baseball/Business Operations:** Scott Smulczenski. **Director, Market Development:** Brad Beattie. **Senior Director, Ticket Technology & Operations:** Angela Deke. **Director, Branding & Communications/Broadcaster:** Andrew Buchbinder. **Public Relations/Digital Media Specialist:** Matt Turer. **Manager, Fan Engagement & Special Events:** Regina Norris. **Manager, Production:** Tysen Hathcock. **Graphic Designer:** T.J. Patton. **Director, Ticket Sales & Marketing Operations:** Zack Pemberton. **Manager, Ticket Sales:** Eric Tomb. **VP, Stadium Operations:** Aaron Lowrey. **Manager, Field & Stadium Operations:** Derek Edwards.

FIELD STAFF

Manager: Jose Leger. **Hitting Coach:** Tyger Pederson. **Pitching Coach:** Darwin Marrero. **Fundamentals Coach:** TBA. **Athletic Trainer:** TBA. **Strength Coach:** TBA.

GAME INFORMATION

Radio Announcer: Andrew Buchbinder. **No. of Games Broadcast:** 138. **Flagship Station:** TBA. **PA Announcer:** Eric Tomb. **Official Scorers:** TBA. **Stadium Name:** Hammons Field. **Location:** Highway 65 to Chestnut Expressway exit, west to National, south on National, west on Trafficway. **Standard Game Time:** 7:10 pm. **Ticket Price Range:** $8-50. **Visiting Club Hotel:** University Plaza Hotel, 333 John Q Hammons Parkway, Springfield, MO 65806. **Telephone:** (417) 864-7333.

TULSA DRILLERS

Address: 201 N. Elgin Ave, Tulsa, OK 74120.
Telephone: (918) 744-5998. **Fax:** (918) 747-3267.
E-Mail Address: mail@tulsadrillers.com. **Website:** www.tulsadrillers.com.
Affiliation (first year): Los Angeles Dodgers (2015). **Years in League:** 2021-

OWNERSHIP/MANAGEMENT

Operated By: Tulsa Baseball Inc.
Co-Chairman: Dale Hubbard. **Co-Chairman:** Jeff Hubbard. **President & General Manager:** Mike Melega. **Assistant General Manager & Vice President of Public Relations & Baseball Operations:** Brian Carroll. **Assistant General Manager & Vice President of Marketing:** Justin Gorski. **Vice President, Ticket Sales:** Andrew Aldenderfer. **Vice President, Stadium Operations:** Mark Hilliard. **Director, Ticket Operations:** Joanna Hubbard. **Director of Stadium Operations:** Marshall Schellhardt. **Director of Community Relations:** Taylor Levacy. **Director of Food & Beverage:** Christopher Bullis. **Director of Food & Beverage:** Amanda Coe. **Director of Corporate Sales:** Jennifer Carthel. **Director of Promotions & Merchandise:** Alex Kossakoski. **Director, Video & Game Day Production:** Madison Brophy. **Manager, Corporate Partnerships & Premium Services:** Cameron Gordon. **Senior Corporate Sales Executive:** Justin Perkins. **Creative Services Manager:** Mikki Shaw. **Office & Special Events Manager/ Assistant Director of Merchandise:** Kelsie Tulk. **Maintenance Manager:** Micah Wade. **Business Manager of F&B:** Belinda Shepherd. **Concessions Manager:** Mike Phipps. **Account Executive & Marketing Coordinator:** Brianna Root. **Video Production Assistant:** Blake Mathews. **Public Relations Assistant:** Brandon Hawkins. **Chief Financial Officer:** Jenna Savill. **Accounting Assistant:** Terry Jenner. **Head Groundskeeper:** Gary Shepherd. **Radio Broadcaster:** Dennis Higgins. **Team Photographer:** Rich Crimi. **Team Photographer:** Tim Campbell.

FIELD STAFF

Manager: Scott Hennessey. **Hitting Coach:** Brett Pill. **Pitching Coach:** TBA. **Coach:** Chris Gutierrez. **Performance Coach:** TBA. **Athletic Trainer:** TBA. **Video Associate:** TBA.

GAME INFORMATION

Radio Announcer: Dennis Higgins. **No. of Games Broadcast:** 138. **Flagship Station:** KTBZ 1430-AM.
PA Announcer: Kirk McAnany. **Official Scorers:** Bruce Howard, Duane DaPron, Larry Lewis, Barry Lewis, Greg Stanzak. **Stadium Name:** ONEOK Field. **Location:** I-244 to Cincinnati/Detroit Exit (6A), north on Detroit Ave, right onto John Hope Franklin Blvd, right on Elgin Ave. **Standard Game Times:** 7:05 pm (Monday-Saturday), Sun. 1:05. **Visiting Club Hotel:** Marriott Tulsa Hotel Southern Hills, 1902 E 71st Street, Tulsa, OK 74136. **Telephone:** (918) 493-7000.

WICHITA WIND SURGE

Address: 275 S. McLean Blvd, Wichita KS 67213
Telephone: (316) 221-8000. **Fax:** TBD
E-Mail Address: info@windsurge.com. **Website:** www.windsurge.com
Affiliation (first year): Minnesota Twins (2021). **Years in League:** 2021-

OWNERSHIP/MANAGEMENT

General Partner: Jane Schwechheimer. **General Partner:** Dan Carney. **Partner/CEO:** Jordan Kobritz. **General Partner/Chief Operating Officer/Chief Financial Officer:** Matt White. **Director of Sales:** Brian Turner. **Director of Marketing and Community Engagement:** Katie Woods. **Director of Fan Experience:** Bob Moullette. **Director of Ticket Operations:** Jason Gavigan. **Director of Broadcasting & Team Travel:** Tim Grubbs. **Digital Marketing Specialist:** Ryan Jacobs. **Marketing Coordinator:** Jenn Schwechheimer. **Community Engagement Coordinator:** Hannah Jasinski. **Account Executive:** Nick DiPaola. **Account Executive:** Austin Chippeaux. **Account Executive:** Nick Nelson. **Account Executive:** Christian Newell. **Corporate Sales & Services Coordinator:** Jacob Koch. **Ticket Sales Coordinator:** Megan Overmann. **Promotions Coordinator:** Alvin Garcia. **Video Production Coordinator:** Chance Fernandez. **Merchandise Manager:** Jake Cassidy. **Head Groundskeeper:** Ben Hartman. **Director of Food & Beverage:** Jason Wilson. **Concessions Manager:** Justin Thomas. **Hospitality Manager:** Maggie McLaughlin. **Consultant:** Eric Petterson.

FIELD STAFF

Manager: Ramon Borrego. **Hitting Coach:** Derek Shomon. **Pitching Coach:** Dan Urbina. **Pitching Coach:** Peter Larson. **Defensive Coach:** Joe Mangiameli. **Strength Coach:** John Gentile. **Athletic Trainer:** Tyler Blair. **Asst. Athletic Trainer:** Taylor Carpenter.

GAME INFORMATION

Radio Announcers: Tim Grubbs. **No. of Games Broadcast:** 138. **Flagship Station:** KKGQ 92.3 FM ESPN Radio.
PA Announcer: Derek Aalders Official Scorer: TBD. **Stadium Name:** Riverfront Stadium. **Location: From Airport:** US-400 E/US-54 E from Eisenhower Airport Pkwy, Take the Seneca/Sycamore exit from US-400 E/US-54 E, Continue on S Sycamore St to your destination. **Standard Game Times: M-F 7:**05; Sat. 6:05; Sun. 1:05. **Ticket Price Range:** $8-15. **Visiting Club Hotel:** Hyatt Regency Wichita, 400 W Waterman Street, Wichita, KS 67202. **Telephone:** (316) 293-1234.

HIGH-A CENTRAL

STADIUM INFORMATION

Club	Stadium	Opened	Dimensions			Capacity	2021 Att.
			LF	CF	RF		
Beloit	ABC Supply Stadium	2021	345	400	325	3,850	46,746
Cedar Rapids	Veterans Memorial Stadium	2002	315	400	325	5,300	100,161
Dayton	Day Air Ballpark	2000	338	402	338	6,830	344,167
Fort Wayne	Parkview Field	2009	336	400	318	8,100	219,044
Great Lakes	Dow Diamond	2007	332	400	325	5,200	124,896
Lake County	Classic Park	2003	320	400	320	6,157	126,191
Lansing	Cooley Law School Stadium	1996	305	412	305	11,000	198,878
Peoria	Dozer Park	2002	310	400	310	7,000	69,725
Quad Cities	Modern Woodmen Park	1931	343	400	318	7,140	163,263
South Bend	Four Winds Fields	1987	336	405	336	5,000	217,066
West Michigan	Fifth Third Ballpark	1994	317	402	327	9,281	228,071
Wisconsin	Neuroscience Group Field	1995	325	400	325	5,170	156,646

BELOIT SKY CARP

Office Address: 217 Shirland Ave., Beloit, WI 53511 (ABC Supply Stadium)
Mailing Address: P.O. Box 855, Beloit, WI 53512. **Telephone:** (608) 362-2272.
E-Mail: info@skycarp.com. **Website:** www.skycarp.com.
Affiliation (first year): Miami Marlins (2021). **Years in League:** 2021-

OWNERSHIP/MANAGEMENT

President: TBD. **VP, Entertainment:** Maria Valentyn. **VP, Sales:** Drew Olstead. **Box Office Manager:** Dan Gill. **Merchandise Manager:** Bob Villarreal. **Media & Public Relations Manager:** TBD. **Head Groundskeeper:** Jaymeso Wilcox. **Events Manager:** Gracey McDonald. **Operations Manager:** Ben St. Peter. **Sales Executive:** Nathan Freiberg. **GM of Food & Beverage:** Blair Schmitz. **Executive Chef:** Matthew A. Austin.

FIELD STAFF

Manager: Jorge Hernandez. **Pitching Coach:** Bruce Walton. **Hitting Coach:** Matt Snyder. **Defensive Coach:** TBD. **Trainer:** Melissa Hampton. **Strength Coach:** TBD.

GAME INFORMATION

Radio Announcer: Larry Larson. **No. of Games Broadcast:** 132. **Flagship Station:** Iron Country 101.9FM/1490AM. **Stadium Name:** ABC Supply Stadium. **Standard Game Times:** Mon.-Sat. 6:35pm, Sun 1:05pm. **Ticket Price Range:** $8-22. **Visiting Club Hotel:** Home2 Suites by Hilton. 2750 Cranston Road. Beloit, WI 53511. **Telephone:** (608) 467-5500.

CEDAR RAPIDS KERNELS

Office Address: 950 Rockford Road SW, Cedar Rapids, IA 52404.
Mailing Address: PO Box 2001, Cedar Rapids, IA 52406.
Telephone: (319) 363-3887. **Fax:** (319) 363-5631.
E-Mail: kernels@kernels.com. **Website:** www.kernels.com.
Affiliation (first year): Minnesota Twins (2013). **Years in League:** 2021-

OWNERSHIP/MANAGEMENT

President: Greg Churchill. **Chief Executive Officer:** Doug Nelson. **General Manager:** Scott Wilson. **Senior Director of Corporate Sales & Marketing:** Jessica Fergesen. **Senior Director of Ticket/Group Sales:** Andrea Brommelkamp. **Director of Food and Beverage:** Dan McAlpine. **Controller:** Josh Morris. **Assistant Director of Food and Beverage:** Tyler Benton. **Food & Beverage Staffing Manager:** Allie Mormann. **Marketing & Entertainment Manager:** Tyler Roach. **Baseball Operations Manager:** Logan Larson. **Stadium Operations Manager:** Patrick Kelly. **Box Office Manager:** Jack Denten. **Sports Turf Manager:** Jesse Roeder. **Radio Broadcaster:** Thomas Breach. **Mascot Coordinator:** Noah Layne. **Clubhouse Manager:** Nate Sinnott.

FIELD STAFF

Manager: Brian Dinkelman. **Hitting Coaches:** Shawn Schlechter, Jairo Rodriguez. **Pitching Coaches:** Richard Salazar, Mark Moriarty. **Trainers:** Matt Smith, Randy Yang. **Strength Coach:** Jake Needham.

GAME INFORMATION

Radio Announcer: Thomas Breach. **No. of Games Broadcast:** 120. Streaming Internet Only. **PA Announcer:** TBD. **Official Scorers:** TBD. **Stadium Name:** Perfect Game Field at Veterans Memorial Stadium. **Directions to Stadium:** From I-380 North, take the Wilson Ave exit, turn left on Wilson Ave, after the railroad tracks, turn right on Rockford Road, proceed .8 miles, stadium is on left; from I-380 South, exit at First Avenue West (exit 19b), Go west to 15th Street, and turn left. Turn left onto 8th Ave, then right onto Kurt Warner Way (tennis courts). **Standard Game Times:** Mon.-Sat., 6:35 pm, Sun. 2:05 pm. **Ticket Price Range:** $10-16. **Visiting Club Hotel:** Comfort Inn & Suites, 2025 Werner Ave NE, Cedar Rapids, IA 52402. **Telephone:** (319) 378-8888.

DAYTON DRAGONS

Office Address: Day Air Ballpark, 220 N. Patterson Blvd., Dayton, OH 45402.
Mailing Address: PO Box 2107, Dayton, OH 45401.
Telephone: (937) 228-2287. **Fax:** (937) 228-2284.
E-Mail Address: dragons@daytondragons.com. **Website:** www.daytondragons.com.
Affiliation (first year): Cincinnati Reds (2000). **Years in League:** 2021-

OWNERSHIP/MANAGEMENT

Operated By: Palisades Arcadia Baseball LLC.
President & General Manager: Robert Murphy. **Executive Vice President:** Eric Deutsch. **VP, Assistant General Manager:** Brandy Guinaugh. **VP, Accounting/Finance:** Mark Schlein. **VP, Corporate Partnerships:** Brad Eaton. **Director, Media Relations & Broadcasting:** Tom Nichols. **Senior Director, Operations:** John Wallace. **Director, Facility Operations:** Jason Fleenor. **Senior Director, Entertainment:** Kaitlin Rohrer. **Director, Entertainment:** Katrina Gibbs. **Director, Ticket Operations:** Stefanie Mitchell. **Director, Ticket Sales:** Andrew Hayes. **Director, Group Sales:** Carl Hertzberg. **Entertainment Administrative Manager:** Jamie Penwell. **Senior Inside Sales Manager:** Mandy Roselli. **Business Development Managers:** Travis Chittum, Auston Hottinger, Travis Prater, Andrew Zellers. **Corporate Partnerships Managers:** Jake Arthur, Megan Norkunas, Brittany Snyder, Jack Twomey. **Motion Graphics Designer & Production Manager:** David Luehring. **Digital Content Manager:** Alexa Sandler. **Ticket Operations Manager:** Jordyn Lewis. **Group Sales Managers:** Cassie Collins, Andrew Majzan, Roman Rothwell. **Operations Manager:** Leighton Mohr. **Operations Assistant:** Nick Hall. **Corporate Partnerships Assistant:** Kaylie Marshall. **Media Relations Assistant:** Lyle Goldstein. **Administrative Assistant to the President:** Mary Cleveland.

FIELD STAFF

Manager: Bryan LaHair. **Hitting Coach:** Daryle Ward. **Pitching Coach:** Brian Garman. **Bench Coach:** Juan Samuel. **Trainer:** Andrew Cleves. **Strength/Conditioning:** Dan Donahue.

GAME INFORMATION

Radio Announcers: Tom Nichols and Lyle Goldstein. **No. of Games Broadcast:** 132. **Flagship Station:** WONE 980 AM. **Television Announcer:** Tom Nichols and Jack Pohl. **No. of Games Broadcast:** Home-25. **Flagship Station:** WBDT Channel 26. **Official Scorers:** Matt Lindsay, Mike Lucas, Mark Miller. **Stadium Name:** Day Air Ballpark. **Location:** I-75 South to downtown Dayton, left at First Street; I-75 North, right at First Street exit. **Ticket Price Range:** $10-$20. **Visiting Club Hotel:** Courtyard by Marriott, 100 Prestige Place, Miamisburg, OH 45342. **Telephone:** 937-433-3131. **Fax:** 937-433-0285.

FORT WAYNE TINCAPS

Address: 1301 Ewing St., Fort Wayne, IN 46802.
Telephone: (260) 482-6400. **Fax:** (260) 471-4678.
E-Mail Address: info@tincaps.com. **Website:** www.tincaps.com.
Affiliation (first year): San Diego Padres (1999). **Years in League:** 2021-

OWNERSHIP/MANAGEMENT

Operated By: Hardball Capital. **Owner:** Jason Freier. **President:** Mike Nutter. **Vice President, Corporate Partnerships:** David Lorenz. **VP, Finance:** Brian Schackow. **VP, Marketing & Promotions:** Michael Limmer. **Creative Director:** Tony DesPlaines. **Director of Video Production:** Melissa Darby. **Assistant Video Production Manager:** Jared Law. **Broadcasting/Media Relations Manager:** John Nolan. **Assistant Director of Marketing & Promotions:** Morgan Olson. **Community & Fan Engagement Manager:** Brenda Feasby. **Merchandise Manager:** Emma Reese. **Group Sales Director:** Brent Harring. **Senior Ticket Account Manager:** Austin Allen. **Ticket Account Manager:** Dalton McGill. **Ticket & Corporate Account Manager:** Jenn Sylvester. **Ticketing Director:** Kade Zvokel. **Reading Program Director/ Assistant Director of Ticketing:** Blaine Jerome. **Special Events Coordinator:** Holly Raney. **Banquet Event Manager:** Alexis Strabala. **Food/Beverage Director:** Bill Lehn. **Executive Chef/Culinary Director:** Pisarn Amornarthakij. **Commissary Manager:** Michael Shidler. **Food/Beverage Operations Manager:** Kyle Hoffman. **Assistant Food/ Beverage Operations Manager:** Alec Bayman. **VIP Services Manager:** Kelly Kalsch. **Head Groundskeeper:** Keith Winter. **Facilities Director:** Tim Burkhart. **Accounting Manager/Facilities Manager:** Erik Lose. **Groundskeeping/ Ballpark Operations Assistant:** Jake Sperry. **Groundskeeping Assistant:** Dakota Steele. **Human Resources/Office Manager:** Cathy Tinney.

FIELD STAFF

Manager: Brian Esposito. **Pitching Coach:** Jimmy Jones. **Hitting Coach:** Randolph Gassaway. **Bench Coach:** Jhonaldo Pozo. **Athletic Trainer:** David Bryan. **Strength Coach:** Jim Buckley. **Clubhouse Manager:** Sam Lewis. **Video:** Nick Borbor. **Sports Science:** Gregory Bender.

GAME INFORMATION

Radio Announcers: John Nolan, Mike Maahs, Ben Shulman. **No. of Games Broadcast:** 132. **Flagship Station:** WKJG

1380-AM/100.9-FM. **TV Announcers:** John Nolan, Brett Rump, Tracy Coffman. **No. of TV Games Broadcast:** Home–66. **Flagship Station:** Comcast Network 81. **PA Announcer:** Jared Parcell. **Official Scorers:** Rich Tavierne, Bill Scott, Dan Watson. **Stadium Name:** Parkview Field. **Location:** 1301 Ewing St., Fort Wayne, IN, 46802. **Ticket Price Range:** $7-$14.

GREAT LAKES LOONS

Address: 825 East Main St., Midland, MI 48640.
Telephone: (989) 837-2255. **Fax:** (989) 837-8780.
E-MailAddress: info@loons.com. **Website:** www.loons.com.
Affiliation (first year): Los Angeles Dodgers (2007). **Years in League:** 2021-

OWNERSHIP/MANAGEMENT

Stadium Ownership: Michigan Baseball Foundation. **Founder, CEO:** William Stavropoulos. **President, GM:** Chris Mundhenk. **Vice President, CFO:** Jana Chotivkova. **Vice President, COO:** Eric Ramseyer. **Director, Entertainment & Community Outreach:** Cameron Bloch. **Coordinator, Creative & Services and Content:** Elizabeth Getzinger. **Executive Administrative Assistant/HR Assistant:** Jessica Gillespie. **General Manager, Dow Diamond Events:** Dave Gomola. **Ticket Account Executive:** Tyler Harlan. **Director, ESPN100.9-FM Sales:** Rich Juday. **Assistant GM, Business Development:** Tyler Kring. **Director, Corporate Partnerships:** Brandon Loker. **Manager, Video Production:** Jimmy Metiva. **Executive Chef:** Andrea Noonan. **Manager, Merchandise and Business:** Lauren Ouellette. **Director, ESPN 100.9-FM Production & Operations:** Jerry O'Donnell. **Director, Ticket Sales:** Sam PeLong. **Head Groundskeeper:** Jeff Ross. **Assistant Director, Ticket Sales:** Ivy Schaff. **Director, Accounting:** Jamie Start. **Assistant GM, Facility Operations:** Dan Straley. **Coordinator, Catering:** Stephanie Tithof. **Manager, ESPN 100.9-FM Programming & Play-by-Play Broadcaster:** Brad Tunney. **Executive Chef:** Carlos Valles. **Corporate Account Executive:** Joe Volk. **Vice President, Baseball Operations & Gameday Experience:** Tiffany Wardynski.

FIELD STAFF

Manager: Austin Chubb. **Hitting Coach:** TBD. **Pitching Coach:** TBD. **Bench Coach:** TBD. **Athletic Trainer:** TBD. **Strength & Conditioning Coach:** TBD.

GAME INFORMATION

Play-by-Play Broadcaster: Brad Tunney. **No. of Games Broadcast:** 132. **Flagship Station:** WLUN, ESPN 100.9-FM (ESPN1009.com). **PA Announcer:** Jerry O'Donnell. **Official Scorers:** Steve Robb, Jason Wirtz. **Stadium Name:** Dow Diamond. **Location:** I-75 to US-10 W, Take the M-20/US-10 Business exit on the left toward downtown Midland, Merge onto US-10 W/MI-20 W (also known as Indian Street), Turn left onto State Street, the entrance to the stadium is at the intersection of Ellsworth and State Streets. **Standard Game Times:** Mon.-Sat., 6:05 pm (April & May), 7:05 pm (May-Sept), Sun. 1:05 pm. **Ticket Price Range:** $9-18. **Visiting Club Hotel:** Fairfield Inn & Suites by Mariott; 506 Buttles Street, Midland, MI 48640. 989-631-7100.

LAKE COUNTY CAPTAINS

Address: 35300 Vine St., Eastlake, OH 44095-3142.
Telephone: (440) 975-8085. **Fax:** (440) 975-8958.
E-Mail Address: jyorko@captainsbaseball.com
Website: www.captainsbaseball.com.
Affiliation (first year): Cleveland Guardians (2003). **Years in League:** 2021-

OWNERSHIP/MANAGEMENT

Operated By: Cascia LLC. **Owners:** Peter and Rita Carfagna, Ray and Katie Murphy. **Chairman/Secretary/Treasurer:** Peter Carfagna. **Vice Chairman:** Rita Carfagna. **Vice President:** Ray Murphy. **General Manager:** Jen Yorko. **Assistant General Manager:** Drew LaFollette. **Director, Turf Operations:** Drew Maskey. **Director, Finance:** Morgan Rowe. **Manager, Stadium Operations:** Jason Schwab. **Manager, Ticket Sales:** Chris Scruggs. **Manager, Ticket Operations & Community Events:** Evan O'Donnell. **Manager, Events:** Ian Pertz. **Manager, Merchandise:** Jakob Hites. **Manager, Food & Beverage:** Nathan Richard. **Manager, Food & Beverage:** Tyler Allison.

FIELD STAFF

Field Manager: Greg DiCenzo. **Hitting Coach:** Chris Smith. **Pitching Coach:** Caleb Longshore. **Bench Coach:** Yan Rivera. **Athletic Trainer:** Matt Beauregard. **Strength & Conditioning Coach:** TBD.

GAME INFORMATION

Radio Announcer: Brian McLaughlin. **No. of Games Broadcast:** 132. **PA Announcer:** Jasen Sokol, Wayne Blankenship. **Official Scorers:** Mike Mohner, Ken Krsolovic, Chuck Murr. **Location:** From Ohio State Route 2 East, exit at Ohio 91, go left and the stadium is 1/4 mile north on your right; From Ohio State Route 90 East, exit at Ohio 91, go right and the stadium is approximately five miles north on your right. **Standard Game Times:** Mon.-Sat. 6:35 pm, Sun. at 1 pm, Mon.-Sat. in June and July at 7 pm. **Visiting Club Hotel:** Four Points by Sheraton Cleveland-Eastlake, 35000 Curtis Blvd, Eastlake, OH 44095. **Telephone:** (440) 953-8000.

LANSING LUGNUTS

Address: 505 E. Michigan Ave., Lansing, MI 48912.
Telephone: (517) 485-4500. **Fax:** (517) 485-4518.
E-Mail Address: info@lansinglugnuts.com. **Website:** www.lansinglugnuts.com.
Affiliation (first year): Oakland Athletics (2021). **Years in League:** 2021-

OWNERSHIP/MANAGEMENT

Operated By: Take Me Out to the Ballgame LLC. **Principal Owners:** Tom Dickson, Sherrie Myers. **General Manager:** Tyler Parsons. **Assistant General Manager, Sales:** Zac Clark. **Assistant General Manager, Stadium Events & Operations:** Greg Kigar. **Director of Creative Services:** Terry Alapert. **Director of Finance:** Rebecca Pensyl. **Director of Food and Beverage:** Sarah Metsky. **Director of Human Resource and Business Operations:** Angela Sees. **Director of Retail:** Matt Hicks. **Assistant Food and Beverage Director:** April Landon. **Corporate Sales Manager:** Dylan Meyer. **Corporate Account Manager:** Nick Bertoia. **Group Sales Account Executive:** Marcos Martinez. **Corporate Partnerships Manager:** Ashley Loudan. **Head Groundskeeper:** Paul Kuhna. **Manager of Stadium Operations:** Jake Warren-Kraatz. **Ticket Operations Manager:** Nicholas Lalama.

FIELD STAFF

Manager: Phil Pohl. **Hitting Coach:** Javier Godard. **Pitching Coach:** Don Schulze. **Assistant Hitting Coach:** Craig Conklin. **Athletic Trainer:** Jake Routhier. **Strength & Conditioning Coach:.** Kevin Guild.

GAME INFORMATION

Radio Announcers: Jesse Goldberg-Strassler, Adam Jaksa. **No. of Games Broadcast:** 132. **Flagship Station:** N/A. **PA Announcers:** Erik Love, Chris Snyder. **Official Scorer:** Timothy Zeko. **Stadium Name:** Jackson Field. **Location:** I-96 East/West to US 496, exit at Larch Street, north of Larch, stadium on left. **Ticket Price Range:** $8-$36. **Visiting Club Hotel:** Radisson Hotel.

PEORIA CHIEFS

Address: 730 SW Jefferson, Peoria, IL 61605.
Telephone: (309) 680-4000. **Fax:** (309) 680-4080.
E-Mail Address: feedback@chiefsnet.com. **Website:** www.peoriachiefs.com.
Affiliation (first year): St. Louis Cardinals (2013). **Years in League:** 2021-

OWNERSHIP/MANAGEMENT

Operated By: Peoria Chiefs Community Baseball Club LLC.
General Manager: Jason Mott. **Assistant General Manager:** Gary Olson. **Social and Marketing Manager:** Edward Schullo. **Director of Ticket Operations:** Matthew Vetter. **Director of Operations:** Dan Busch. **Manger of Community Relations:** Payton Leverton. **Manager of Media Relations:** Cody Schindler. **Head Groundskeeper:** Mike Reno.

FIELD STAFF

Manager: Patrick Anderson. **Hitting Coach:** Willi Martin. **Pitching Coach:** Edwin Moreno. **Trainer:** TBD. **Strength Coach:** TBD.

GAME INFORMATION

Radio Announcer: Cody Schinder. **No. of Games Broadcast:** 132. **Flagship Station:** www.peoriachiefs.com, Tune-In Radio. **PA Announcer:** Dustin Fitzpatrick. **Official Scorers:** Cody Schindler & TBA. **Stadium Name:** Dozer Park. **Location:** From South/East, I-74 to exit 93 (Jefferson St), continue one mile, stadium is one block on left; From North/West, I-74 to Glen Oak Exit, turn right on Glendale, which turns into Kumpf Blvd, turn right on Jefferson, stadium on left. **Standard Game Times:** Mon.-Sat., 6:35 p.m. Sun., 1:35 pm. **Ticket Price Range:** $9-16. **Visiting Club Hotel:** Holiday Inn Express and Suites, 1100 Bass Pro Drive East Peoria, IL 61611. **Telephone:** (309) 694-9800.

QUAD CITIES RIVER BANDITS

Address: 209 S. Gaines St., Davenport, IA 52802.
Telephone: (563) 324-3000. **Fax:** (563) 324-3109.
E-Mail Address: bandit@riverbandits.com. **Website:** www.riverbandits.com.
Affiliation (first year): Kansas City Royals (2013). **Years in League:** 2021-

OWNERSHIP/MANAGEMENT

Operated by: Main Street Iowa LLC, Dave Heller, Roby Smith and Ken Croken. **General Manager:** Joe Kubly. **Vice President, Sales:** Shawn Brown. **Executive Director, Special Events and Human Resources:** Taylor Kubly. **Assistant GM, Ballpark Operations:** Seth Reeve. **Assistant GM, Baseball Operations:** Paul Kleinhans-Schulz. **Assistant GM, Marketing:** Josh Michalsen. **Assistant GM, Amusements:** Rick Norton. **Senior Director, Ticketing and Fulfillment:** Julia McNeil. **Director, Finance:** Julie James. **Director, Marketing:** Dan Straney. **Director, Production and Creative Services:** Justin Hodge. **Director, Field Services/Head Groundskeeper:** Easton Williams. **Director, Food and**

Beverage: Joey Kaye. **Manager, Media Relations and Season Tickets:** Kyle Kercheval. **Box Office Manager:** Tyler Phillips. **Office and Merchandise Manager:** Haleigh Carnes.

FIELD STAFF

Manager: Brooks Conrad. **Hitting Coach:** Andy LaRoche. **Pitching Coach:** Steve Luebber. **Assistant Hitting Coach:** David Noworyta. **Assistant Coach:** Kevin Kuntz. **Athletic Trainer:** Brad Groleau.

GAME INFORMATION

Broadcaster: Kyle Kercheval. **No. of Games Broadcast:** 132. **Flagship Station:** MiLB.TV and audio stream at river-bandits.com. **Stadium Name:** Modern Woodmen Park. **Location:** From I-74, take Grant Street exit left, west onto River Drive, left on South Gaines Street; from I-80, take Brady Street exit south, right on River Drive, left on S. Gaines Street. **Standard Game Times:** 6:30 pm CT. **Ticket Price Range:** $8-$20.

SOUTH BEND CUBS

Office Address: 501 W. South St., South Bend, IN 46601.
Mailing Address: PO Box 4218, South Bend, IN 46634.
Telephone: (574) 235-9988. **Fax:** (574) 235-9950.
E-Mail Address: cubs@southbendcubs.com. **Website:** www.southbendcubs.com
Affiliation (first year): Chicago Cubs (2015). **Years in League:** 2021-

OWNERSHIP/MANAGEMENT

Owner: Andrew Berlin. **President:** Joe Hart. **General Manager & V.P., Corporate Partnerships:** Nick Brown. **Assistant General Manager, Marketing/Media:** Chris Hagstrom-Jones. **Assistant General Manager, Operations:** Peter Argueta. **Assistant General Manager, Tickets:** Andy Francis. **Box Office Manager:** Steve Horstmann. **Merchandise Manager:** Mary Lou Pallo. **Account Executives:** Kyle Cavanaugh, Tessa Schrager, Kyle Vincent. **Director of Finance & Administration:** Melissa Christlieb. **Finance & Administrative Assistant:** Amber Hayes. **Head Groundskeeper:** Jairo Rubio. **Assistant Groundskeeper:** Jace Coppoc. **Stadium Operations Assistant:** Dustin Saunders. **Director of Food and Beverage:** Nick Barkley. **Business and Catering Manager:** Chloe Greenboam. **Executive Chef:** Scott Craig. **Concessions Manager:** Ethan Ganger. **Radio Broadcasters:** Brendan King, Max Thoma. **Production Assistant:** Kayleigh Sedlacek.

FIELD STAFF

Manager: Lance Rymel. **Hitting Coach:** Dan Puente. **Pitching Coach:** Tony Cougoule. **Coach:** D'Angelo Jimenez.

GAME INFORMATION

Radio Announcers: Brendan King & Max Thoma. **Flagship Station:** Sports Radio 960 AM WSBT. **PA Announcer:** Gregg Sims, Jon Thompson. **Official Scorer:** Peter Yarbro. **Stadium Name:** Four Winds Field. **Location:** I-80/90 toll road to exit 77, take US 31/33 south to South Bend to downtown (Main Street), to Western Ave., right on Western, left on Taylor. **Standard Game Times:** Mon.-Sat., 7:05 pm, Sun. 2:05 pm. **Ticket Price Range:** Advance $12-15, Day of Game $13-15. **Visiting Club Hotel:** Aloft South Bend. **Hotel Telephone:** (574) 288-8000.

WEST MICHIGAN WHITECAPS

Office Address: 4500 West River Dr., Comstock Park, MI 49321.
Mailing Address: PO Box 428, Comstock Park, MI 49321.
Telephone: (616) 784-4131. **Fax:** (616) 784-4911.
E-Mail Address: playball@whitecapsbaseball.com.
Website: www.whitecapsbaseball.com.
Affiliation (first year): Detroit Tigers (1997). **Years in League:** 2021-

OWNERSHIP/MANAGEMENT

Chairmen and Founders: Lew Chamberlin/Denny Baxter. **CEO:** Joe Chamberlin. **President:** Steve McCarthy. **Vice President/General Manager:** Jim Jarecki. **Vice President, Sales:** Dan Morrison. **Director of Marketing and Media Relations:** Steve Van Wagoner. **Director of Ticket Sales:** Shaun Pynnonen. **Director of Food and Beverage:** Matt Timon. **Creative and Digital Design Manager:** Elaine Boonenberg. **MultiMedia Specialist:** Jack Powers. **Promotions and Fan Entertainment Manager:** Ben Love. **Social Media and Digital Marketing Coordinator:** Alex Brodsky. **Ticket Sales Manager:** Mike Epstein. **Box Office Manager:** Kaitlyn Silvey. **Ticket Operations Coordinator:** Emily Milne. **Ticket Sales Account Executives:** Riley Paulus, Nick Bradshaw, Brandon Olson. **Corporate Partner Sales Executives:** Brittney Behrens, JD Triemstra, Ernie McCallum. **Corporate Partnership Coordinator:** Leah Austin. **Community Relations Manager:** Jenny Garone. **Merchandising Manager:** Lori Ashcroft. **Hospitality Manager:** Amanda Stephan. **Food and Beverage Operations Manager:** Danielle O'Connor. **Event Chef:** Matt Schumaker. **Operations Manager:** Brett Frieze. **Facility Maintenance Manager:** Kipp Jelinski. **Facility Maintenance Assistant:** Matt Richardson. **Head Groundskeeper:** Mitch Hooten. **Special Events Manager:** April Butler. **Director of People:** Courtney Lutz. **Controller:** Dave Rozema. **Accounts Receivable Coordinator:** Zack Harvey. **IT Administrator:** Scott Lutz. **IT Assistant:** Kyle Willacker. **Administrative Assistants:** Martha Beals, Melanie Lonsway, Chris Parsons. **Radio Play-by-Play:** Dan Hasty.

FIELD STAFF

Manager: Brayan Peña. **Hitting Coach:** C.J. Wamsley. **Pitching Coach:** Dean Stiles. **Developmental Coach:** Nick Bredeson. **Athletic Trainer:** Sean McFarland. **Strength Coach:** Tyler Gniadek. **Baseball Information Assistant:** Quinn Smith.

GAME INFORMATION

Radio Announcers: Dan Hasty. **No. of Games Broadcast:** 132. **Flagship Station:** The TICKET 106.1FM Grand Rapids. **PA Announcers:** Mike Newell, Bob Wells. **Official Scorers:** Aaron Sagraves, Joey Sutherlin. **Stadium Name:** LMCU Ballpark. **Location:** US 131 North from Grand Rapids to exit 91 (West River Drive). **Ticket Price Range:** $9-18. **Visiting Club Hotel:** Hampton Inn, 500 Center Dr NW, Grand Rapids, MI 49544 . **Telephone:** (616) 647-1000.

WISCONSIN TIMBER RATTLERS

Office Address: 2400 N. Casaloma Dr., Appleton, WI 54913.
Mailing Address: PO Box 7464, Appleton, WI 54912.
Telephone: (920) 733-4152. **Fax:** (920) 733-8032.
E-Mail Address: info@timberrattlers.com. **Website:** www.timberrattlers.com.
Affiliation (first year): Milwaukee Brewers (2009). **Years in League:** 2021-

OWNERSHIP/MANAGEMENT

Owned by: Third Base Ventures, LLC
Principal Owner: Craig Dickman. **President/CEO:** Rob Zerjav. **Vice President/Assistant GM:** Aaron Hahn. **Vice President, Business Operations:** Ryan Moede. **Vice President, Marketing/ Assistant GM:** Hilary Bauer. **Director, Food/Beverage:** Ryan Grossman. **Director, Security:** Scott Hoelzel. **Director, Community Relations:** Dayna Baitinger. **Director, Corporate Partnerships:** Ryan Cunniff. **Director, Media Relations:** Chris Mehring. **Senior Manager, Ticket Sales & Service:** Kyle Fargen. **Ticket Account Executives:** Jon Bellis, Noah Feinstein. **Director, Business Development:** Seth Merrill. **Box Office Manager:** Tyler Van Rossum. **Controller:** Eric Dresang. **Banquet Sales & Event Manager:** Mackenzie Liedtky. **Wedding Sales & Events Manager:** Alycia Stephan. **Executive Chef:** Charles Behrmann. **Executive Sous Chef:** Chris Prentice. **Assistant, Food/Beverage Director:** Megan Andrews. **Director, Stadium Operations:** Justin Peterson. **Entertainment Coordinator:** Jacob Jirschele. **Senior Graphic Designer:** Nick Guenther. **Graphic Designer:** Jared Klein. **Accounting/Human Resources Manager:** Brooke Brefczynski. **Production Manager:** Cam Leung. **Social Media Manager:** Jessica Amo. **Clubhouse Manager:** TBA. **Office Manager:** Mary Robinson.

FIELD STAFF

Manager: Joe Ayrault. **Hitting Coach:** Nick Stanley. **Pitching Coach:** Will Schierholtz. **Coach:** Liu Rodriguez. **Trainer:** Andrew Staehling. **Strength Coach:** Connor McCarthy.

GAME INFORMATION

Radio Announcer: Chris Mehring. **No. of Games Broadcast:** All. **Flagship Station:** WNAM 1280-AM. **Television Announcer:** Chris Mehring (Radio Simulcast). **Television Affiliates:** TBA. **No. of Games Broadcast:** TBA. **PA Announcer:** Joey D. **Official Scorer:** Jay Grusznski. **Stadium Name:** Neuroscience Group Field at Fox Cities Stadium. **Location:** Highway 41 to Highway 15 (00) exit, west to Casaloma Drive, left to stadium. **Standard Game Times:** Mon.-Fri., 6:35 pm (April-May), 7:05 pm (June-Sept.), Sat., 6:35 pm, Sun., 1:05 pm. **Ticket Price Range:** $8-31. **Visiting Club Hotel:** AmericInn by Wyndham 132 N. Mall Drive, Appleton, WI 54913

HIGH-A EAST

STADIUM INFORMATION

Club	Stadium	Opened	Dimensions			Capacity	2021 Att.
			LF	CF	RF		
Aberdeen	Ripken Stadium	2002	310	400	310	6,000	104,665
Asheville	McCormick Field	1992	326	373	297	4,000	130,435
Bowling Green	Bowling Green Ballpark	2009	318	400	326	4,559	125,738
Brooklyn	MCU Park	2001	315	412	325	7,500	103,874
Greensboro	First National Bank Field	2005	322	400	320	7,599	225,905
Greenville	Fluor Field at the West End	2006	310	400	302	5,000	243,362
Hudson Valley	Dutchess Stadium	1994	325	400	325	4,494	88,453
Hickory	L.P. Frans Stadium	1993	330	401	330	5,062	125,599
Jersey Shore	FirstEnergy Park	2001	325	400	325	6,588	150,873
Rome	State Mutual Stadium	2003	335	400	330	5,100	78,538
Wilmington	Frawley Stadium	1993	325	400	325	6,532	78,690
Winston-Salem	BB&T Ballpark	2010	315	399	323	5,500	206,333

ABERDEEN IRONBIRDS

Address: 873 Long Drive, Aberdeen, MD 21001
Telephone: (410) 297-9292. **Fax:** (210) 297-6653
E-Mail Address: Info@ironbirdsbaseball.com. **Website:** ironbirdsbaseball.com
Affiliation (first year): Baltimore Orioles (2002). **Years in league:** 2021-

OWNERSHIP/MANAGEMENT

Operated By: Ripken Professional Baseball LLC. **Principal Owner:** Cal Ripken Jr. **Co-Owner/Executive Vice President:** Bill Ripken. **General Manager:** Jack Graham. **Director, Ticketing:** Justin Gentilcore. **Director, Creative Services:** Kevin Jimenez. **Director, Communications:** Tyler Weigandt. **Director, Corporate Partnerships:** Brekke Autry. **Manager, Facilities:** Larry Gluch. **Sports Turf Superintendent:** Todd Bradley. **Manager, Merchandise and Operations:** Skye Truss. **Manager, Accounting and Administration:** Sam Pugh. **Coordinator, Partnership Activation:** Mattie Wilson. **Facilities Assistant:** David Dawson. **Box Office Manager:** Daniel Carey. **Sr. Account Executive:** Andrew Spanos. **Account Executive:** Jessica Benson. **Manager, Non-Gameday Events:** Becca Ashman.

FIELD STAFF

Manager: Roberto Mercado. **Hitting Coach:** Zach Cole. **Pitching Coach:** Forrest Hermann. **Fundamentals Coach:** Isaiah Page. **Development Coach:** Ryan Goll. **Athletic Trainer:** Allyse Kramer. **Strength & Conditioning:** Michael Thomson.

GAME INFORMATION

No. of Games Broadcast on MiLB.tv: 66. **PA Announcer:** Ray Atkinson. **Official Scorer:** Jason King. **Stadium Name:** Leidos Field at Ripken Stadium. **Location:** I-95 to exit 85 (route 22), west on 22, right onto long drive. **Ticket Price Range:** $5-$40.

ASHEVILLE TOURISTS

Address: McCormick Field, 30 Buchanan Place, Asheville, NC 28801.
Telephone: (828) 258-0428. **E-Mail Address:** info@theashevilletourists.com.
Website: www.theashevilletourists.com.
Affiliation (first year): Houston Astros 1982-1993, 2021-. **Years in League:** 2021-

OWNERSHIP/MANAGEMENT

Operated By: DeWine Seeds-Silver Dollar Baseball, LLC. **President:** Brian DeWine. **General Manager:** Larry Hawkins. **Assistant General Manager:** Hannah Martin. **Director of Broadcasting/Media Relations:** Doug Maurer. **Stadium Operations Director:** Michael Mueller. **Director of Food & Beverage:** Tyler Holt. **Promotions Manager:** Alyssa Quirk. **Director of Ticket Operations:** Boston Brice IV. **Merchandise Manager:** Kali DeWine.

FIELD STAFF

Manager: Nate Shaver. **Hitting Coach:** Rene Rojas. **Pitching Coach:** Jose Rada.

GAME INFORMATION

Radio Announcer: Doug Maurer. **No. of Games Broadcast:** TBA. **Flagship Station:** Asheville Tourists Online Radio Network. **PA Announcer:** Tim Lolley. **Official Scorer:** Steven Grady, Bob Rose. **Stadium Name:** McCormick Field. **Location:** I-240 to Charlotte Street South exit, south one mile on Charlotte, left on McCormick Place. **Ticket Price Range:** $8.00-$15.00.

BOWLING GREEN HOT RODS

Address: Bowling Green Ballpark, 300 8th Avenue, Bowling Green, KY 42101.
Telephone: (270) 901-2121. **Fax:** (270) 901-2165.
E-Mail Address: fun@bghotrods.com. **Website:** www.bghotrods.com.
Affiliation (first year): Tampa Bay Rays (2009). **Years in League:** 2021-

OWNERSHIP/MANAGEMENT

Operated By: BG SKY, LLC.
President/Managing Partner: Jack Blackstock. **General Manager/COO:** Eric C. Leach. **Assistant General Manager:** Kyle Wolz. **Manager, Ticket Sales:** Taylor Dunn. **Assistant, Stadium Operations:** Jeff Ciocco. **Assistant, Stadium Operations:** Garret Browning. **Head Groundskeeper:** Matt Hill. **Manager, Broadcasting & Media Relations:** Shawn Murnin. **Assistant, Social Media and Marketing:** N/A. **Director, Marketing and Corporate Partnerships:** Ashlee Wilson. **Account Executive & Retail Store Manager:** Amber Mingus. **Account Executive:** Alex Meyers. **Manager, Graphic Design:** Christian Aguiar. **Manager, Video Production:** Blake Forshee. **Bookkeeper:** Kim Myers.

FIELD STAFF

Manager: Jeff Smith. **Pitching Coach:** Jim Paduch. **Hitting Coach:** Brady North. **Assistant Coach:** Skeeter Barnes. **Athletic Trainer:** Brian Newman. **Strength & Conditioning Coach:** Jordan Brown.

GAME INFORMATION

Radio Announcer: TBD. **No. of Games Broadcast:** 132. **Flagship Station:** TBD.
PA Announcer: Unavailable. **Official Scorer:** Unavailable. **Stadium Name:** Bowling Green Ballpark. **Location:** From I-65, take Exit 26 (KY-234/Cemetery Road) into Bowling Green for 3 miles, left onto College Street for .2 miles, right onto 8th Avenue. **Standard Game Times:** Mon.-Sat., 6:35 pm, Sun., 2:05/5:05 pm. **Ticket Price Range:** $8-24. **Visiting Club Hotel:** Tru by Hilton. **Telephone:** (270) 904-2260.

BROOKLYN CYCLONES

Address: 1904 Surf Ave, Brooklyn, NY 11224.
Telephone: (718) 372-5596. **Fax:** (718) 449-6368.
E-Mail Address: info@brooklyncyclones.com. **Website:** www.brooklyncyclones.com.
Affiliation (first year): New York Mets (2001). **Years in League:** 2021-

OWNERSHIP/MANAGEMENT

Owner, Chairman & CEO: Steven A. Cohen. **Owner & President, Amazin Mets Foundation:** Alexandra M. Cohen. **Vice Chariman & Owner:** Andrew B. Cohen. **Chairman Emeritus:** Fred Wilpon.
Vice President: Steve Cohen. **General Manager:** Kevin Mahoney. **Assistant GM:** Billy Harner. **Operations Manager:** Vladimir Lipsman. **Director, Ticket Sales & Operations:** Michael Charyn. **Marketing Manager:** Kiana Steinauer. **Director, Community Relations:** Christina Moore. **Manager, Corporate Partnerships & Development:** Jennifer Reilly. **Director, Partnership Development:** Tommy Cardona. **Manager, Special Events:** Bryan Wynne. **Account Executives:** Ryan Dougherty, Keith Raad, Mordechai Twersky, Ricky Viola. **Senior Accountant:** Tatiana Isdith. **Administrative Assistant, Community Relations:** Sharon Lundy. **Clubhouse Manager:** Max Colten.

FIELD STAFF

Manager: Luis Rivera. **Hitting Coach:** Richie Benes. **Pitching Coach:** AJ Sager. **Bench Coach:** Chris Newell. **Athletic Trainer:** Austin Dayton. **Performance Coach:** Drew Skrocki.

GAME INFORMATION

Radio Announcer: Keith Raad. **No. of Games Broadcast:** 132. **Flagship Station:** Web Streaming Only. **PA Announcer:** Mark Fratto. **Official Scorer:** Patrick McCormack & TBD. **Stadium Name:** Maimonides Park. **Location:** Belt Parkway to Cropsey Ave South, continue on Cropsey until it becomes West 17th St, continue to Surf Ave, stadium on south side of Surf Ave; By subway, west/south to Stillwell Ave./Coney Island station. **Ticket Price Range:** $10-18. **Visiting Club Hotel:** Unavailable.

GREENSBORO GRASSHOPPERS

Address: 408 Bellemeade St, Greensboro, NC 27401.
Telephone: (336) 268-2255. **Fax:** (336) 273-7350.
E-Mail Address: info@gsohoppers.com. **Website:** www.gsohoppers.com.
Affiliation (first year): Pittsburgh Pirates (2019). **Years in League:** 2021-

OWNERSHIP/MANAGEMENT

Operated By: Temerity Baseball. **Principal Owner:** Andy Sandler.
President/General Manager: Donald Moore. **Vice President, Baseball Operations:** Katie Dannemiller. **Assistant General Manager:** Tim Vangel. **Chief Financial Officer:** Brad Falkiewicz. **Director of Sales:** Todd Olson. **Director, Ticket Sales/Services:** Erich Dietz. **Director, Creative Services:** Amanda Williams. **Manager, Promotions/Community**

Relations: Stephen Johnson. **Manager, Video Production:** TBD. **Concessions Manager:** Brian Candler. **Stadium Operations:** Cody Grube. **Groundskeeper:** Anthony Alejo.

FIELD STAFF

Manager: Callix Crabbe. **Hitting Coach:** Ruben Gotay. **Pitching Coach:** Fernando Nieve. **Performance Coach:** Justin Orton. **Athletic Trainer:** Matt McNamee. **Strength & Conditioning Coach:** Glenn Nutting.

GAME INFORMATION

Announcer: Stuart Barefoot. **Official Scorer:** Jeff Mills. **Stadium Name:** First National Bank Field. **Location:** From I-85, take Highway 220 South (exit 36) to Coliseum Blvd, continue on Edgeworth Street, ballpark at corner of Edgeworth and Bellemeade Streets. **Standard Game Times:** 6:30 pm. **Ticket Price Range:** $7-11. **Visiting Club Hotel:** LaQuinta Inn @ **Greensboro Airport—**7905 Triad Center Drive, Greensboro, NC 27409. **Telephone:** (336) 840.1550.

GREENVILLE DRIVE

Mailing Address: 935 South Main St, Suite 202, Greenville, SC 29601.
Stadium Address: 945 South Main St. Greenville, SC 29601.
Telephone: (864) 240-4500. **E-Mail Address:** info@greenvilledrive.com.
Website: www.greenvilledrive.com.
Affiliation (first year): Boston Red Sox (2005). **Years in League:** 2021-

OWNERSHIP/MANAGEMENT

Owner/President: Craig Brown. **General Manager:** Eric Jarinko. **VP, Marketing:** Jeff Brown. **VP, Finance/Administration:** Jordan Smith. **VP, Ticketing:** Phil Bargardi. **VP, Grounds/Operations:** Greg Burgess. **VP, Sponsorships/Community Engagement:** Katie Batista. **VP, Business Development:** Suzanne Foody. **Director, Game Entertainment:** Alex Guest. **Director, Media/Creative Services:** TBD. **Director, Merchandise:** Jenny Burgdorfer. **Director, Video Production:** Lance Fowler. **Director, Facility Operations:** Timmy Hinds. **Director, Food & Beverage:** Preston Madill. **Director, Ticket Operations:** Elise Parish. **Senior Ticket Account Executive:** Houghton Flanagan. **Executive Chef:** Wilbert Sauceda. **Account Manager:** Daniel Baker. **Office Manager:** Allison Roedell. **Premium Hospitality Services Manager:** Logan McLaughlin. **Ticket Account Executive:** Brenden Campbell. **Ticket Account Executive:** Nathan Fenters. **Ticket Account Executive:** Caden Risen. **Assistant Groundskeeper:** Jed Huth. **Inside Sales Manager:** Sydney Richardson. **Partner Activations Manager:** Emily Peeler. **Clubhouse Manager:** Brady Andrews. **West End Events at Fluor Field Manager:** Dayna Mercer. **West End Events at Fluor Field Manager:** Elizabeth Stoffelen.

FIELD STAFF

Manager: Iggy Suarez. **Pitching Coach:** Bob Kipper. **Hitting Coach:** Nate Spears. **Development Coach:** Joe Cronin. **Coach:** Matt Wheeler. **ATC:** Bobby Stachura. **S/C Coach:** Donny Gress.

GAME INFORMATION

Radio Announcer: Dan Scott & Tom Van Hoy. **Flagship Station:** GreenvilleDrive.com. **PA Announcer:** Chuck Hussion, William Qualkinbush. **Official Scorer:** Jordan Caskey. Scott Keeler. Chandler Simpson. **Stadium Name:** Fluor Field at the West End. **Location:** I-385 into Downtown Greenville; Left onto Augusta Street; Right onto University Ridge; Right onto Augusta Street; Left onto Field Street. **Standard Game Times:** Mon.-Sat., 7:05 p.m., Sun. 3:05 p.m. **Ticket Price Range:** Advance $8-$12, Day of Game $9-13. **Visiting Club Hotel:** Wingate by Wyndham. **Hotel Telephone:** (864) 281-1281.

HUDSON VALLEY RENEGADES

Office Address: Dutchess Stadium, 1500 Route 9D, Wappingers Falls, NY 12590.
Mailing Address: PO Box 661, Fishkill, NY 12524.
Telephone: (845) 838-0094. **Fax:** (845) 838-0014.
E-Mail Address: info@hvrenegades.com. **Website:** www.hvrenegades.com.
Affiliation (first year): New York Yankees (2021). **Years in League:** 2021-

OWNERSHIP/MANAGEMENT

Operated by: Diamond Baseball Holdings, LLC. **Principal Owner:** Diamond Baseball Holdings, LLC. **President/General Manager:** Steve Gliner. **Vice President/Assistant General Manager:** Tyson Jeffers. **Vice President:** Rick Zolzer. **Director of Stadium Events:** Tom Hubmaster. **Director of Corporate Partnerships:** Zach Betkowski. **Director of Digital Media & Video Production:** Zach Neubauer. **Director of Media Relations:** Joe Vasile. **Director of Ticket Sales:** Will Young. **Community Partnerships & Guest Services Manager:** Marcella Costello. **Merchandise Manager & Ticket Sales Executive:** Luis Flores. **Ticket Sales Executive:** Mariah Tlougan. **Ticket Sales Executive:** Isaac Hennen. **Graphic Designer:** Adam Baycora.

FIELD STAFF

TBD

GAME INFORMATION

Radio Announcer: Joe Vasile. **No. of Games Broadcast:** All home and road games broadcast on hvrenegades.com. **PA Announcer:** Rick Zolzer. **Official Scorer:** Mike Ferraro. **Stadium Name:** Dutchess Stadium. **Location:** I-84 to exit 41 (Route 9D North), north one mile to stadium. **Standard Game Times:** Mon.-Fri., 7:05 pm, Sat, 6:05 pm, Sun., 4:35 pm. **Visiting Club Hotel:** Courtyard By Marriott Fishkill, 17 Westage Drive, Fishkill, NY, 12524. **Telephone:** (845) 897-2400.

HICKORY CRAWDADS

Office Address: 2500 Clement Blvd. NW, Hickory, NC 28601.
Mailing Address: 2500 Clement Blvd. NW, Hickory, NC 28601.
Telephone: (828) 322-3000.
E-Mail Address: crawdad@hickorycrawdads.com.
Website: www.hickorycrawdads.com.
Affiliation (first year): Texas Rangers (2009). **Years in League:** 2021-

OWNERSHIP/MANAGEMENT

Operated by: Hickory Baseball Inc. **Principal Owners:** Texas Rangers.
President: Neil Leibman. **General Manager:** Douglas Locascio. **Business Manager:** Donna White. **Assistant General Manager of Marketing:** Ashley Salinas. **Assistant General Manager of Sales:** Robby Willis. **Director of Operations & Special Events:** Daniel Barkley. **Director of Ticket Operations:** Kristen Buynar. **Head Groundskeeper:** Caleb Bryan. **Director of Promotions and Community Relations:** Karly Vollgrebe. **Group Sales Executives:** Emily Mitchell, Joey Norris. **Stadium Operations Manager:** Alex Cook. **General Manager of Food and Beverage:** Jim Ragin.

FIELD STAFF

Manager: Carlos Cardoza. **Hitting Coach:** Ryan Tuntland. **Pitching Coach:** Jon Goebel. **Coaches:** Jay Sullenger, Kawika Emsley-Pai. **Athletic Trainer:** Derrick Decker. **Strength and Conditioning Coach:** Andy Earp.

GAME INFORMATION

PA Announcers: Rob Eastwood, Rodney Pyatt. **Official Scorers:** Mark Parker. **Stadium Name:** LP Frans Stadium. **Location:** I-40 to exit 123 (Lenoir North), 321 North to Clement Blvd, left for 1/2 mile. **Standard Game Times:** Mon.-Sat., 7 pm, Sun., 5 pm. **Visiting Club Hotel:** Crowne Plaza, 1385 Lenior-Rhyne Boulevard SE, Hickory, NC 28602. **Telephone:** (828) 323-1000.

JERSEY SHORE BLUECLAWS

Address: 2 Stadium Way, Lakewood, NJ 08701.
Telephone: (732) 901-7000. **Fax:** (732) 901-3967.
E-Mail Address: info@blueclaws.com. **Website:** www.blueclaws.com
Affiliation (first year): Philadelphia Phillies (2001). **Years in League:** 2021-

OWNERSHIP/MANAGEMENT

Managing Partner, Shore Town Baseball: Art Matin. **President/General Manager:** Joe Ricciutti. **Assistant General Manager:** Kevin Fenstermacher. **Senior VP, Ticket Sales:** Bob McLane. **VP, Finance:** Don Rodgers. **VP, Ticket Sales:** Jim McNamara. **VP, Promotions & Entertainment:** Jamie Bertram. **Sr. Director, Corporate Partnerships:** Rob Vota. **Director, Communications:** Greg Giombarrese. **Director, Events & Operations:** Kayla Reilly. **Director, Regional Outreach:** Rob McGillick. **Director, Ticket Operations:** Garrett Herr. **Director, Partnership Services:** Zack Nicol. **Director, Grounds:** Mike Morvay. **Director, Merchandise & Ticket Sales:** Jamie Wagner. **Senior Sales Executive:** Craig Ebinger. **Ticket Membership Manager:** Joel Podos. **Manager, Accounting:** Phil Armstrong. **Manager, Food & Beverage:** Greg Witt. **Manager, Hospitality:** Susan Wallace. **Manager, Promotions:** Gianna Fiocco. **Manager, Digital Marketing:** Jess Szewczyk. **Manager, Ticket Service & Strategy:** Brendan Earls. **Manager, Partnership Services:** Ben Wilson. **Manager, Group Tickets:** Killian Vallieu. **Manager, Events & Operations:** Ryan Mead. **Manager, Operations:** Shane Eldridge. **Account Executive:** Eric Rugen. **Account Executive:** Tori Boughton.

FIELD STAFF

Manager: Keith Werman. **Pitching Coach:** Brad Bergesen. **Hitting Coach:** Ari Adut. **Bench Coach:** Pat Listach. **Trainer:** TBA. **Strength & Conditioning Coach:** TBA.

GAME INFORMATION

Radio Announcers: Greg Giombarrese. **No. of Games Broadcast:** 66. **Flagship Station:** BlueClaws.com. **PA Announcers:** Jeff Fromm. **Official Scorers:** Joe Bellina. **Stadium Name:** FirstEnergy Park. **Location:** Route 70 to New Hampshire Avenue, North on New Hampshire for 2.5 miles to ballpark. **Standard Game Times:** 7:05 pm, 6:35 pm (April-May); Sun 1:05. **Ticket Price Range:** $9-18. **Visiting Team Hotel:** Clarion Hotel & Conference Center, 815 Rt. 37 West | Toms River, NJ 08755.

ROME BRAVES

Office Address: State Mutual Stadium, 755 Braves Blvd, Rome, GA 30161.
Mailing Address: PO Box 1915, Rome, GA 30162-1915.
Telephone: (706) 378-5100. **Fax:** (706) 368-6525.
E-Mail Address: romebraves@braves.com. **Website:** www.romebraves.com.
Affiliation (first year): Atlanta Braves (2003). **Years in League:** 2021-

OWNERSHIP MANAGEMENT

Operated By: Diamond Baseball Holdings, LLC. **VP and General Manager:** David Cross. **Director, Business Operations:** Bob Askin. **Director, Stadium Operations:** Morgan McPherson. **Director, Sales:** TBD. **Ticket**

Manager: Jackie O'Reilly. **Marketing Manager:** Anna Winstead. **Graphic Design Manager:** Drew Gibby. **Account Representative:** Katie Aspin. **Account Representative:** TBD. **Field Turf Manager:** Joseph Brooks. **Retail Manager:** Starla Roden. **Food and Beverage Director:** Jonathan Jackson. **Culinary Director:** TBD.

FIELD STAFF
Manager: Kanekoa Texeira. **Hitting Coach:** Danny Santiesteban. **Pitching Coach:** Wes McGuire.

GAME INFORMATION
Radio Announcer: TBD. **No. of Games Broadcast:** 66 (Home only). **Flagship Station:** TBD, RomeBraves.com (home games). **PA Announcer:** Anthony McIntosh, Sr. **Official Scorers:** Jim O'Hara, Lyndon Huckaby. **Stadium Name:** TBA. **Location:** I-75 North to exit 190 (Rome/Canton), left off exit and follow Highway 411/Highway 20 to Rome, right at intersection on Highway 411 and Highway 1 (Veterans Memorial Highway), stadium is at intersection of Veterans Memorial Highway and Riverside Parkway. **Ticket Price Range:** $7-20. (purchased in advance). **Visiting Club Hotel:** Holiday Inn Express & Suites, 35 Hobson Way, Rome, GA 30161. **Telephone:** (706) 232-0021.

WILMINGTON BLUE ROCKS

Address: 801 Shipyard Drive, Wilmington, DE 19801.
Telephone: (302) 888-2015. **Fax:** (302) 888-2032.
E-Mail Address: info@bluerocks.com. **Website:** www.bluerocks.com.
Affiliation (first year): Washington Nationals (2021). **Years in League:** 2021-

OWNERSHIP/MANAGEMENT
Operated by: Wilmington Blue Rocks LP. **Honorary President:** Matt Minker. **Club President:** Clark Minker. **Owners:** Main Street Baseball. **Managing Partner/League Director & CEO, Main Street Baseball:** Dave Heller. **General Manager:** Vince Bulik. **Director of Web and Creative Services:** Mike Galayda. **VP, Business Devlopment:** Robert Ford. **Box Office Manager:** Ian Porter. **Director, Groups & Groups Experiences:** Bill Levy. **Director, Marketing/ Fulfillment:** Liz Welch. **Director, Stadium Operations:** Sean Mason. **Director, Field Operations:** Steve Gold. **Controller:** Seleta Harrison. **Director, Community Affairs:** Kevin Linton.

FIELD STAFF
Manager: Mario Lisson. **Hitting Coach:** Tim Doherty. **Developmental Coach:** Mark Harris. **Athletic Trainer:** Don Neidig. **Strength Coach:** Brandon Pentheny.

GAME INFORMATION
Radio Announcer: TBD. **No. of Games Broadcast:** 66. **Flagship Station:** WGLS 89.7 Online Stream. **PA Announcer:** Kevin Linton. **Official Scorer:** Dick Shute. **Stadium Name:** Judy Johnson Field at Daniel S. Frawley Stadium. **Location:** I-95 North to Maryland Ave (exit 6), right on Maryland Ave, and through traffic light onto Martin Luther King Blvd, right at traffic light on Justison St, follow to Shipyard Dr; I-95 South to Maryland Ave (exit 6), left at fourth light on Martin Luther King Blvd, right at fourth light on Justison St, follow to Shipyard Drive. **Standard Game Times:** 6:35 pm, (Mon-Sat) Sun. 1:05 p.m. **Ticket Price Range:** $13-$17. **Visiting Club Hotel:** TBD.

WINSTON-SALEM DASH

Office Address: 926 Brookstown Ave, Winston-Salem, NC 27101.
Stadium Address: 951 Ballpark Way, Winston-Salem, NC 27101.
Telephone: (336) 714-2287. **Fax:** (336) 714-2288.
E-Mail Address: info@wsdash.com. **Website:** www.wsdash.com.
Affiliation (first year): Chicago White Sox (1997). **Years in League:** 2021-

OWNERSHIP/MANAGEMENT
Operated by: W-S Dash. **Principal Owner:** Billy Prim.
President & General Manager: Brian DeAngelis. **VP, Chief Financial Officer:** Kurt Gehsmann. **Accounting Manager:** Diane Pitts. **VP, Baseball Operations:** Ryan Manuel. **Director of Facility Management:** Jeff Kelly. **Director of Grounds:** Corey Church. **VP:** Corey Bugno. **Ticket Operations & Inside Sales Manager:** Erin McGregor. **VP, Ballpark Experience and Branding:** Jessica Aveyard. **Creative Services Manager:** Mark Lavis. **Social Media & Marketing Coordinator:** Amanda Weaver. **VP, Corporate Partnerships:** Josh Strickland. **VP, Corporate Partnership Services:** Morgan Clausel. **Partner Services Coordinator:** Amanda Dove. **Director of Food and Beverage:** Kit Edwards. **Catering Manager:** Beverly Becker. **Concessions Manager:** Zachary Mounce.

FIELD STAFF
Manager: Lorenzo Bundy. **Hitting Coach:** Nicky Delmonico. **Pitching Coach:** Danny Farquhar. **Trainer:** Carson Wooten. **Performance Coach:** Michael Rheese.

GAME INFORMATION
Radio Announcer/Media Relations: Andrew Murphy. **No. of Games Broadcast:** All Home (66) and Select Road. **Flagship Station:** Audio feed available on wsdash.com. **PA Announcer:** Jeffrey Griffin. **Official Scorer:** Andy Hindman. **Stadium Name:** Truist Stadium. **Location:** Salem Parkway to Peters Creek Parkway exit. **Standard Game Times:** T-F 7 p.m., Sat. 6 p.m., Sun. 1 p.m. **Visiting Club Hotel:** Best Western Plus- University Inn.

HIGH-A WEST

STADIUM INFORMATION

Club	Stadium	Opened	Dimensions			Capacity	2021 Att.
			LF	CF	RF		
Eugene	PK Park	2010	335	400	325	4,000	91,315
Everett	Everett Memorial Stadium	1984	324	380	330	3,682	102,423
Hillsboro	Hillsboro Ballpark	2013	325	400	325	4,500	110,384
Spokane	Avista Stadium	1958	335	398	335	7,162	140,623
Tri-City	Dust Devils Stadium	1995	335	400	335	3,700	61,245
Vancouver	Nat Bailey Stadium	1951	335	395	335	6,500	15,822

EUGENE EMERALDS

Office Address: 2760 Martin Luther King Jr. Blvd, Eugene, OR 97401.
Mailing Address: PO Box 10911, Eugene, OR 97440.
Telephone: (541) 342-5367. **Fax:** (541) 342-6089.
E-Mail Address: info@emeraldsbaseball.com. **Website:** www.emeraldsbaseball.com.
Affiliation (first year): San Francisco Giants (2021). **Years in League:** 2021-

OWNERSHIP/MANAGEMENT
Operated By: Elmore Sports Group Ltd. **Principal Owner:** David Elmore.
General Manager: Allan Benavides. **Assistant GM:** Matt Dompe. **Director, Food/Beverage:** Turner Elmore.
Director, Tickets: Kennedy Schull. **Event Managers:** Chris Bowers and Max Mennemeier. **Graphic Designer:** Danny Cowley. **Director, Community Affairs:** Anne Culhane. **Sponsorship Sales:** Pat Zajac. **Home Radio:** Matt Dompe. **Away Radio:** Alex Naveja.

FIELD STAFF
Manager: Carlos Valderrama. **Hitting Coach:** Cory Elasik. **Pitching Coach:** Alain Quijano. **Fundamentals Coach:** Eliezer Zambrano. **Athletic Trainer:** Tim Vigue. **Strength Coach:** Nick Fajardo.

GAME INFORMATION
Radio Announcer: Matt Dompe. **No. of Games Broadcast:** 132. **Flagship Station:** 95.3-FM The Score. **PA Announcer:** Ted Welker. **Official Scorer:** George McPherson. **Stadium Name:** PK Park. **Standard Game Time:** Mon.-Sat., TBD, Sun., TBD. **Ticket Price Range:** $13-$22. **Visiting Club Hotel:** Couryard by Marriott, Eugene Springfield.

EVERETT AQUASOX

Mailing Address: 3802 Broadway, Everett, WA 98201.
Telephone: (425) 258-3673. **Fax:** (425) 258-3675.
E-Mail Address: info@aquasox.com. **Website:** www.aquasox.com.
Affiliation (first year): Seattle Mariners (1995). **Years in League:** 2021-

OWNERSHIP/MANAGEMENT
Operated by: 7th Inning Stretch, LLC.
Directors: Chad Volpe, Pat Filippone. **General Manager:** Danny Tetzlaff. **Director of Broadcasting:** Pat Dillon.
Director of Finance: Justin Waslaski. **Director of Corporate Partnerships:** Mike MacCulloch. **Director of Tickets:** Bryan Martin. **Corporate Partnership Manager:** Bailey Walsh. **Director of Community Relations & Merchandise:** Nellie Kemp. **Account Executives:** Scott Brownlee, Conner Grant, Peyton Kelley.

FIELD STAFF
Manager: Eric Farris. **Hitting Coach:** Ryan McLaughlin. **Pitching Coach:** Matt Pierpont. **Coach:** Jose Umbria.

GAME INFORMATION
Radio Announcer: Pat Dillon. **No. of Games Broadcast:** 132. **Flagship Station:** KRKO 1380-AM, 95.3-FM. **PA Announcer:** Tom Lafferty. **Official Scorer:** Patrick Lafferty. **Stadium Name:** Funko Field at Everett Memorial Stadium. **Location:** I-5, exit 192. **Standard Game Times:** Mon.-Sat., 7:05 pm, Sun., 4:05 pm. **Ticket Price Range:** $10-22. **Visiting Club Hotel:** Courtyard by Marriott, 3003 Colby Ave, Everett, WA 98201. **Telephone:** (425) 259-2200.

HILLSBORO HOPS

Address: 4460 NE Century Blvd., Hillsboro, OR, 97124. **Telephone:** (503) 640-0887.
E-Mail Address: info@hillsborohops.com. **Website:** www.hillsborohops.com.
Affiliation (first year): Arizona Diamondbacks (2001). **Years in League:** 2021-

OWNERSHIP/MANAGEMENT

Operated by: Short Season LLC. **Managing Partners:** Mike McMurray, Josh Weinman, Myron Levin. **Chairman and CEO:** Mike McMurray. **President and General Manager:** K.L. Wombacher. **Chief Financial Officer:** Laura McMurray. **Vice President Corporate Partnerships:** Matt Kolasinski. **Vice President, Tickets:** Brett Breece. **Director, Merchandise:** Hannah August. **Director, Marketing and Communications:** Casey Sawyer. **Director, Broadcasting:** Rich Burk.

FIELD STAFF

Manager: Vince Harrison. **Hitting Coach:** K.C Judge. **Pitching Coach:** Jeff Bajenaru. **Coach:** TBD.

GAME INFORMATION

PA Announcer: Jason Swygard. **Official Scorer:** Blair Cash. **Stadium Name:** Ron Tonkin Field. **Location:** 4460 NE Century Blvd., Hillsboro, OR. 97124. **Standard Game Times:** Mon.-Sat., 7:05 pm, Sun., 1:05 pm. **Ticket Price Range:** $7-$22. **Visiting Club Hotel:** Aloft by Marriott, Hillsboro, OR. **Telephone:** (503) 277-1900.

SPOKANE INDIANS

Office Address: Avista Stadium, 602 N Havana, Spokane, WA 99202.
Mailing Address: PO Box 4758, Spokane, WA 99220.
Telephone: (509) 535-2922. **Fax:** (509) 534-5368.
E-Mail Address: mail@spokaneindians.com. **Website:** www.spokaneindians.com.
Affiliation (first year): Colorado Rockies (2021). **Years in League:** 2021-

OWNERSHIP/MANAGEMENT

Operated By: Longball Inc. **Principal Owner:** Bobby Brett. **CEO:** Andrew Billig. **President:** Chris Duff. **Senior Vice President:** Otto Klein. **VP, Concessions & Hospitality:** Josh Roys. **VP, Business Operations:** Lesley DeHart. **VP, General Manager:** Kyle Day. **VP, Ticket Services:** Nick Gaebe. **Director of Stadium Operations:** Chris Ackerman. **Director of Public Relations:** Bud Bareither. **Director of Corporate Partnerships:** Sean Dorsey. **Director of Grounds:** Tony Lee. **Director of Hospitality & Stadium Events:** Darby Moore. **Director of Employee Development & Culture:** MacKenzie White. **Partner Services Manager:** Gina Giesseman. **Group Ticket Manager:** Jamie Isaacson. **Concessions & Hospitality Manager:** Chayton Roberts. **Ticket Services Manager:** Ryan Songey. **Partner Services Coordinator:** Aaron Croom. **Ticket Services Coordinator:** Nick Oyen. **Ticket Services Coordinator:** Justus Reimer. **Partner Services Coordinator:** Emily Shields. **Group Ticket Coordinator:** Sammy Simpson. **Group Ticket Coordinator:** Nash Thompson. **Ticket Services Coordinator:** Ben Wintringer.

FIELD STAFF

Manager: Scott Little. **Pitching Coach:** Ryan Kibler. **Hitting Coach:** Zach Osborne. **Bench Coach:** Julio Camos. **Trainer:** Coy Coker.

GAME INFORMATION

Radio Announcer: Mike Boyle. **Flagship Station:** 1510 AM/103.5 FM. **PA Announcer:** Chadron Hazelbaker. **Official Scorer:** Todd Gilkey. **Stadium Name:** Avista Stadium. **Location:** From west, I-90 to exit 283B (Thor/Freya), east on Third Avenue, left onto Havana; From east, I-90 to Broadway exit, right onto Broadway, left onto Havana. **Standard Game Time:** Mon.-Sat., 6:30 pm, Sun., 5:09 pm. **Ticket Price Range:** $5-24. **Visiting Club Hotel:** Mirabeau Park Hotel & Convention Center, 1100 N. Sullivan Rd, Spokane, WA 99037. **Telephone:** (509) 343-6886.

TRI-CITY DUST DEVILS

Address: 6200 Burden Blvd, Pasco, WA 99301.
Telephone: (509) 544-8789. **Fax:** (509) 547-9570.
E-Mail Address: info@dustdevilsbaseball.com.
Website: dustdevilsbaseball.com.
Affiliation (first year): Los Angeles Angels (2021). **Years in League:** 2021-

OWNERSHIP/MANAGEMENT

Operated by: Northwest Baseball Ventures. **Principal Owners:** George Brett, Yoshi Okamoto, Brent Miles. **President:** Brent Miles. **Vice President/General Manager:** Derrel Ebert. **Assistant General Manager, Business Operations:** Trevor Shively. **Assistant General Manager, Sponsorships:** Ann Shively. **Assistant General Manager, Tickets:** Riley Shintaffer. **Ticket Sales Account Executives:** Duncan Sanders, Jordan Ranum. **Sponsorship Operations Manager:** Brennan McIntire. **Promotions Coordinator:** Austen Serrata. **Head Groundskeeper:** Michael Angel.

FIELD STAFF

Manager: Jack Howell. **Hitting Coach:** TBD. **Pitching Coach:** Doug Henry. **Defensive Coach:** Jack Santora. **Trainer:** Will Whitehead. **Strength Coach:** TBD.

GAME INFORMATION

Radio Announcer: TBD. **No. of Games Broadcast:** 120. **Flagship Station:** 870-AM KFLD. **PA Announcer:** Patrick Harvey. **Official Scorers:** Tony Wise, Shane Kelley, Scott Tylinski. **Stadium Name:** Gesa Stadium. **Location:** I-182 to exit 9 (Road 68), north to Burden Blvd, right to stadium. **Standard Game Time:** Varies. **Ticket Price Range:** $9-15. **Visiting Club Hotel:** Hampton Inn & Suites Pasco/Tri-Cities, 6826 Burden Blvd., Pasco, WA 99301. **Telephone:** (509) 792-1660.

VANCOUVER CANADIANS

Address: Scotiabank Field at Nat Bailey Stadium, 4601 Ontario St, Vancouver, B.C. V5V 3H4.

Telephone: (604) 872-5232. **Fax:** (604) 872-1714.

E-Mail Address: staff@canadiansbaseball.com.

Website: www.canadiansbaseball.com.

Affiliation (first year): Toronto Blue Jays (2011). **Years in League:** 2021-

OWNERSHIP/MANAGEMENT

Operated by: Vancouver Canadians Professional Baseball LLP.

Managing General Partner: Jake Kerr. **Co-Owner:** Jeff Mooney. **President:** Andy Dunn. **Executive Vice President:** Tom Backemeyer. **General Manager:** Allan Bailey. **Assistant General Manager:** Stephani Ellis. **Financial Controller:** Brenda Chmiliar. **Vice President Sales & Marketing:** Walter Cosman. **Manager, Ticket Operations:** Steven Maisey. **Manager, Stadium Operations:** Charles O'Neill. **Coordinator, Marketing Services:** Kendra Chin. **Assistant Financial Controller:** Charlene Shamku.

FIELD STAFF

Manager: Brent Lavallee. **Hitting Coach:** Ryan Wright. **Pitching Coach:** Phil Cundari. **Assistant Pitching Coach:** Joel Bonnett. **Coaching Assistant:** Ashley Ponce.

GAME INFORMATION

Radio/TV Announcer: Tyler Zickel. **No. of Games Broadcast:** 132. **Flagship Station:** Sportsnet 650 AM. **PA Announcer:** Niall O'Donohoe. **Official Scorer:** Mike Hanafin. **Stadium Name:** Nat Bailey Stadium. **Location:** From downtown, take Cambie Street Bridge, left on East 29th Ave., left on Ontario St. to stadium; From south, take Highway 99 to Oak Street, right on 41st Ave, left on Cambie St. right on East 29th Ave., left on Ontario St to stadium. **Standard Game Times:** Mon.-Sat., 7:05 pm, Sun., 1:05 pm. **Ticket Price Range:** $20-32. **Visiting Club Hotel:** Sandman Hotel Vancouver Airport, 3233 St. Edwards Dr., Richmond, B.C., V6X 1N4. **Telephone:** (604) 303-8888.

LOW-A WEST

STADIUM INFORMATION

			Dimensions				
Club	Stadium	Opened	LF	CF	RF	Capacity	2021 Att.
Fresno	Chukchansi Park	2002	324	400	335	12,500	176,395
Inland Empire	San Manuel Stadium	1996	330	410	330	5,000	90,587
Lake Elsinore	The Diamond	1994	330	400	310	7,866	103,758
Modesto	John Thurman Field	1952	312	400	319	4,000	42,200
Rancho Cucamo.	LoanMart Field	1993	335	400	335	6,615	76,493
San Jose	Municipal Stadium	1942	320	390	320	5,208	62,569
Stockton	Banner Island Ballpark	2005	300	399	326	5,200	73,410
Visalia	Recreation Ballpark	1946	320	405	320	2,468	79,625

FRESNO GRIZZLIES

Address: 1800 Tulare St, Fresno, CA 93721.
Telephone: (559) 320-4487. **Fax:** (559) 264-0795.
E-Mail Address: info@fresnogrizzlies.com. **Website:** www.FresnoGrizzlies.com.
Affiliation (first year): Colorado Rockies (2021). **Years in League:** 2021-

OWNERSHIP/MANAGEMENT

Operated By: Fresno Sports & Events. **Managing Partner:** Michael Baker. **Chief Financial Officer:** Michael Moran. **President:** Derek Franks. **Assistant General Manager:** Andrew Milios. **Controller:** Allison Farrell.

FIELD STAFF

Manager: Robinson Cancel. **Hitting Coach:** Nic Wilson. **Pitching Coach:** Marc Brewer. **Bench Coach:** Steve Soliz.

GAME INFORMATION

No. of Games Broadcast: 132. **Stadium Name:** Chukchansi Park. **Location:** 1800 Tulare St, Fresno, CA 93721. **Directions:** From 99 North, take Fresno Street exit, left on Fresno Street, left on Inyo or Tulare to stadium. From 99 South, take Fresno Street exit, left on Fresno Street, right on Broadway to H Street. From 41 North, take Van Ness exit toward Fresno, left on Van Ness, left on Inyo or Tulare, stadium is straight ahead. From 41 South, take Tulare exit, stadium is located at Tulare and H Streets, or take Van Ness exit, right on Van Ness, left on Inyo or Tulare, stadium is straight ahead. **Ticket Price Range:** TBD.

INLAND EMPIRE 66ERS

Address: 280 South E St., San Bernardino, CA 92401.
Telephone: (909) 888-9922. **Fax:** (909) 888-5251. **Website:** www.66ers.com.
Affiliation (first year): Los Angeles Angels (2011). **Years in League:** 2021-

OWNERSHIP/MANAGEMENT

Operated by: Inland Empire 66ers Baseball Club of San Bernardino. **Principal Owners:** David Elmore, Donna Tuttle. **President:** David Elmore. **Chairman:** Donna Tuttle. **General Manager:** Joe Hudson. **Assistant GM:** Daniel Vazquez. **Director, Broadcasting:** Steve Wendt. **Director, Community Relations:** Stephanie O'Quinn. **Director, Group Sales:** Hollee Haines. **Sr. Director, Ticketing and Ballpark Operations:** Sean Peterson. **Manager, Creative Services:** Dusty Ferguson. **Manager, Promotions:** Mary Grinnan. **Account Executives:** Jarrett Stark, Joe Lopez, Alex Rolland, **Manager, Facility:** Richard Morales. **Head Groundskeeper:** Steven McBride. **Accountant:** Karly Strahl. **Director, Food & Beverage (Diamond Creations):** Jacob DeJong.

FIELD STAFF

Manager: Ever Magallanes. **Hitting Coach:** Ryan Sebra. **Pitching Coach:** Bo Martino. **Coach:** Trevor Nyp. **Athletic Trainer:** TBD. **Strength and Conditioning Coach:** TBD.

GAME INFORMATION

Radio Announcer: Steve Wendt. **Flagship Station:** 66ers.com. **PA Announcer:** Renaldo Gonzales. **Official Scorer:** Bill Maury-Holmes. **Stadium Name:** San Manuel Stadium. **Location:** From south, I-215 to 2nd Street exit, east on 2nd, right on G Street; from north, I-215 to 3rd Street exit, left on Rialto, right on G Street. **Standard Game Times:** Mon.-Sat. 7:05 pm; Sun. 2:05 pm (1st Half) 5:35 pm (2nd Half). **Ticket Price Range:** $9-$28. **Visiting Club Hotel:** TBD. **Telephone:** TBD.

LAKE ELSINORE STORM

Address: 500 Diamond Drive, Lake Elsinore, CA 92530
Telephone: (951) 245-4487. **Fax:** (951) 245-0305.
E-Mail Address: info@stormbaseball.com. **Website:** www.stormbaseball.com.
Affiliation (first year): San Diego Padres (2001). **Years in League:** 2021-

OWNERSHIP/MANAGEMENT

Owners: Gary Jacobs, Len Simon. **CEO/Co-General Manager:** Shaun Brock. **CFO/Co-General Manager:** Christine Kavic. **General Manager of Game Presentation and Events:** Mark Beskid. **Assistant General Manager of Baseball:** Terrance Tucker. **Assistant CFO:** Andres Pagan. **Box Office Manager:** Krista Williams. **Director of Hospitality:** Natalie Gates. **Emcee and Manager of Entertainment:** Kaz Egan. **Production Manager:** Jon Gripe. **Head Groundskeeper:** Anthony Anaya. **Operations and Facilities Manager:** Jason Natale. **Director of Food and Beverage:** Jason Wozniak. **Executive Chef:** Luciano Mulito. **Corporate Sales Executive:** Janelle Metzger. **HR Generalist:** Katherine Strehlow. **Content Strategist:** Justin Jett Pickard. **Assistant Box Office Manager:** Caleb Brock. **Brand Ambassador:** Althea Wagoner.

FIELD STAFF

Manager: Eric Junge. **Hitting Coach:** Pat O'Sullivan. **Pitching Coach:** Leo Rosales.

GAME INFORMATION

Radio Announcer: Jason Swartz. **No. of Games Broadcast:** 66. **Flagship Station:** MilB.com. **PA Announcer:** Dave McCrory. **Official Scorer:** Lloyd Nixon. **Stadium Name:** The Lake Elsinore Diamond Stadium. **Location:** From I-15, exit at Diamond Drive, west one mile to stadium. **Standard Game Times:** TBD. **Ticket Price Range:** $8-$30. **Visiting Club Hotel:** TBD.

MODESTO NUTS

Office Address: 601 Neece Dr, Modesto, CA 95351. **Mailing Address:** PO Box 883, Modesto, CA 95353.
Telephone: (209) 572-4487. **Fax:** (209) 572-4490
E-Mail Address: fun@modestonuts.com. **Website:** www.modestonuts.com.
Affiliation (first year): Seattle Mariners (2017). **Years in League:** 2021-

OWNERSHIP/MANAGEMENT

Operated by: Seattle Mariners.
General Manager: Zach Brockman. **Assistant General Manager:** Veronica Hernandez. **Head Groundskeeper:** Alan Jones. **Director of Ticket Sales:** Chris Fleischmann. **Director of Corporate Partnerships:** Corey Gales. **Box Office Manager:** Kyler Brown. **Office Manager:** Rita McCay. **Food and Beverage Manager:** Shayla Parker. **In-Game Entertainment Manager:** Charles Yutkowitz. **Community Relations Manager:** Lesley Cantu. **Stadium Operations Manager:** Connor Skustad.

FIELD STAFF

Manager: Austin Knight. **Hitting Coach:** Michael Fransoso. **Pitching Coach:** Nathan Bannister. **Coach:** Ryan Scott.

GAME INFORMATION

Radio Announcer: TBD. **PA Announcer:** Unavailable. **Official Scorer:** Unavailable. **Stadium Name:** John Thurman Field. **Location:** Highway 99 in southwest Modesto to Tuolumne Boulevard exit, west on Tuolumne for one block to Neece Drive, left for 1/4 mile to stadium. **Standard Game Times:** 7:05 pm, Sun. 2:05pm/6:05 pm. **Ticket Price Range:** $8-14. **Visiting Club Hotel:** DoubleTree Modesto.

RANCHO CUCAMONGA
QUAKES

Office Address: 8408 Rochester Ave., Rancho Cucamonga, CA 91730.
Mailing Address: P.O. Box 4139, Rancho Cucamonga, CA 91729.
Telephone: (909) 481-5000. **Fax:** (909) 481-5005.
E-Mail Address: info@rcquakes.com. **Website:** www.rcquakes.com.
Affiliation (first year): Los Angeles Dodgers (2011). **Years in League:** 2021-

OWNERSHIP/MANAGEMENT

Operated By: Bobby Brett. **Principal Owner:** Bobby Brett.
President: Brent Miles. **Vice President/General Manager:** Grant Riddle. **Vice President/Tickets:** Monica Ortega. **Vice President/Groups:** Kyle Burleson. **Vice President/Sponsorships:** Chris Pope. **Assistant General Manager/ Sponsorships:** David Fields. **Assistant General Manager/Fan Engagement:** Bobbi Salcido. **Director, Assistant**

General Manager/Season Tickets/Operations: Eric Jensen. **Director, Accounting:** Denise Vasquez. **Director, Public Relations/Voice of the Quakes:** Mike Lindskog. **Director of Operations, Food Service:** Mark Campbell. **Group Sales/ Ticket Office Manager:** Alec Maldonado. **Group Sales Coordinators:** Jake Briones, Kyle Olmstead. **Sponsorship Service Coordinator:** Madison Smeathers. **Fan Engagement Coordinator:** Grace Mikuriya. **Office Manager:** Shelley Scebbi.

FIELD STAFF
Manager: John Shoemaker. **Hitting Coach:** O'Koyea Dickson. **Pitching Coaches:** Ramon Trancoso, Durin O'Linger. **Bench Coach:** Johan Garcia.

GAME INFORMATION
Radio Announcer: Mike Lindskog. **No. of Games Broadcast:** 132. **Flagship Station:** iHeart Radio App / Tune-In Radio App. **PA Announcer:** Chris Albaugh. **Official Scorer:** Steve Wishek. **Stadium Name:** LoanMart Field. **Location:** I-10 to I-15 North, exit at Foothill Boulevard, left on Foothill, left on Rochester to Stadium. **Standard Game Times:** 6:30 pm; First Half Sundays (April through June) and Sept.11th at 2:00 pm; Second Half Sundays (July through August) 5:05 pm. **Visiting Club Hotel:** Best Western Heritage Inn, 8179 Spruce Ave, Rancho Cucamonga, CA 91730. **Telephone:** (909) 466-1111.

SAN JOSE GIANTS

Office Address: 588 E Alma Ave, San Jose, CA 95112.
Mailing Address: PO Box 21727, San Jose, CA 95151.
Telephone: (408) 297-1435. **Fax:** (408) 297-1453.
E-Mail Address: info@sjgiants.com. **Website:** www.sjgiants.com.
Affiliation (first year): San Francisco Giants (1988). **Years in League:** 2021-

OWNERSHIP/MANAGEMENT
Operated by: Diamond Baseball Holdings
Principal Owner: Diamond Baseball Holdings
President/CEO: Daniel Orum. **Chief Operating Officer:** Ben Taylor. **VP, Game Day Operations and Human Resources:** Tara Tallman. **VP, Sales:** Jeff Di Giorgio. **VP, Marketing:** Matt Alongi. **Director, Broadcasting:** Joe Ritzo. **Director, Finance:** Dave Satterfield. **Manager, Ticketing:** Ryan Anthony. **Senior Manager, Retail/Marketing:** Sierra Hanley. **Manager, Food and Beverage:** Ramiro Mijares. **Manager, Marketing and Community Relations:** David Baez. **Coordinator, Business Development:** Cecily Mitchell. **Coordinator, Digital Media:** Sam Barasch. **Groundskeeper:** Roman Ornelas. **Assistant Groundskeeper:** Kevin Tallman.

FIELD STAFF
Manager: Lipso Nava. **Hitting Coach:** Travis Ishikawa. **Pitching Coach:** Dan Runzler. **Fundamentals Coach:** Jeremiah Knackstedt. **Athletic Trainer:** Isaiah Yoder. **Strength & Conditioning Coach:** Chris Harms.

GAME INFORMATION
Radio Announcers: Joe Ritzo, Justin Allegri. **No. of Games Broadcast:** 132
Flagship: sjgiants.com. **Television Announcers:** Joe Ritzo, All home games on MiLB.TV. **PA Announcer:** Russ Call. **Official Scorer:** Mike Hohler. **Stadium Name:** Excite Ballpark. **Location:** South on I-280, Take 10th/11th Street Exit, turn right on 10th Street, turn left on Alma Ave. North on I-280, Take the 10th/11th Street Exit, Turn left on 10th Street, turn left on Alma Ave. **Standard Game Times:** Tue-Fri. 6:30 p.m, Sat. 5 p.m (6 p.m. after June 1, Sun 1 p.m. (5 p.m. after June 1). **Ticket Price Range:** $5-27.

STOCKTON PORTS

Address: 404 W Fremont St, Stockton, CA 95203.
Telephone: (209) 644-1900. **Fax:** (209) 644-1931.
E-Mail Address: info@stocktonports.com. **Website:** www.stocktonports.com.
Affiliation (first year): Oakland Athletics (2005). **Years in League:** 2021-

OWNERSHIP/MANAGEMENT
Operated By: 7th Inning Stretch LLC. **Chairman/CEO:** Tom Volpe.
President: Pat Filippone. **General Manager:** Kieran McMahon. **Assistant General Manager:** Luke Johnson. **Director of Tickets:** Richard Haifley. **Corporate Partnerships Manager:** Jordy Feneck. **Group Sales Manager:** Dora Cantu. **Ticket Sales and Media Executive:** Chris Zavaglia. **Front Office and Merchandise Manager:** Christa Leri.

FIELD STAFF
Manager: Anthony Phillips. **Pitching Coach:** Bryan Corey. **Hitting Coach:** Kevin Kouzmanoff. **Asst. Hitting Coach:** Franklin Font. **Trainer:** Eric Fasth.

GAME INFORMATION

Radio Announcer: Alex Jensen. **No of Games Broadcast:** 132. **Flagship Station:** TBD. **PA Announcer:** TBD. **Official Scorer:** Paul Muyskens. **Stadium Name:** Banner Island Ballpark. **Location:** From I-5/99, take Crosstown Freeway (Highway 4) exit El Dorado Street, north on El Dorado to Fremont Street, left on Fremont. **Standard Game Times:** 7:05 pm. **Ticket Price Range:** $10-$20.

VISALIA RAWHIDE

Address: 300 N Giddings St, Visalia, CA 93291.
Telephone: (559) 732-4433. **Fax:** (559) 739-7732.
E-Mail Address: info@rawhidebaseball.com.
Website: www.rawhidebaseball.com.
Affiliation (first year): Arizona Diamondbacks (2007). **Years in League:** 2021-

OWNERSHIP/MANAGEMENT

Ownership: First Pitch Entertainment. **Team President:** Sam Sigal. **Co-General Managers:** Mike Candela and Julian Rifkind. **Assistant General Managers:** Brady Hochhalter and Markus Hagglund. **Director of Broadcasting & Media Relations:** Jill Gearin. **Director of Facilities & Grounds:** James Templeton. **Director of Entertainment and Community:** Joe Ross. **Ballpark Operations Assistant:** Robert Skipper. **Director of Marketing and Promotions:** Marina Rojas.

FIELD STAFF

Manager: Jorge Cortes. **Hitting Coach:** Ty Wright. **Pitching Coach:** Gabriel Hernandez. **Coach:** Cody Ransom. **Trainer:** Haruki Mukohchi. **Strength & Conditioning Coach:** Ryan Harrel.

GAME INFORMATION

Radio Announcers: Jill Gearin. **Broadcasts all home and road games Flagship Station:** MiLB.com.
PA Announcer: Brian Anthony. **Official Scorer:** Harry Kargenian and Mark "Scooter" Cossentine. **Stadium Name:** Valley Strong Ballpark. **Location:** From Highway 99, take 198 East to Mooney Boulevard exit, left at second signal on Giddings; four blocks to ballpark. **Standard Game Times:** 6:30pm, Sun. 1pm April-June and 6pm July-September. **Ticket Price Range:** $13-30. **Visiting Club Hotel:** Quality Inn, 1010 E Prosperity Ave, Tulare, CA 93274.

LOW-A EAST

STADIUM INFORMATION

Club	Stadium	Opened	Dimensions			Capacity	2021 Att.
			LF	CF	RF		
Augusta	SRP Park	2018	330	395	318	4,782	211,561
Carolina	Five County Stadium	1991	330	400	309	6,500	98,976
Charleston	Joseph P. Riley, Jr. Ballpark	1997	306	386	336	5,800	208,641
Columbia	Segra Park	2016	319	400	330	7,501	153,547
Delmarva	Arthur W. Perdue Stadium	1996	309	402	309	5,200	110,281
Down East	Grainger Stadium	1949	335	390	335	4,100	85,586
Fayetteville	SEGRA Stadium	2019	319	400	330	4,786	173,243
Fredericksburg	FredNats Ballpark	2020	326	402	327	7,000	199,071
Kannapolis	Atrium Health Ballpark	2020	325	400	315	4,930	162,031
Lynchburg	City Stadium	1939	325	390	325	4,000	68,032
Myrtle Beach	TicketReturn.com Field	1999	308	400	328	5,200	199,704
Salem	Salem Memorial Stadium	1995	325	401	325	6,415	128,769

AUGUSTA GREENJACKETS

Office Address: 187 Railroad Ave. North Augusta, SC 29841.
Mailing Address: 187 Railroad Ave. North Augusta, SC 29841.
Telephone: (803) 349-9467. **Fax:** (803) 349-9434.
E-Mail Address: info@greenjacketsbaseball.com. **Website:** www.greenjacketsbaseball.com.
Affiliation (first year): Atlanta Braves (2021). **Years in League:** 2021-

OWNERSHIP/MANAGEMENT

Ownership Group: Diamond Baseball Holdings, LLC.
President: Jeff Eiseman. **VP of Business Operations:** Missy Martin. **Vice President:** Tom Denlinger. **General Manager:** Brandon Greene. **Director of Ticket Sales:** Troy Pakusch. **Accounting:** Debbie Brown. **Director of Stadium Operations:** Andrew Crawford. **Director of Marketing & Community Relations:** Catie Jagodzinski. **Corporate Partnerships Manager:** Austin Lowndes. **Director of Group Sales:** Yari Natal. **Assistant Group Sales Manager:** James Mullins. **Ticket & Events Sales Executive:** Jamie Martin. **Ticket Sales Executive:** Jake Brock. **Multimedia Video & Creative Services Specialist:** Hannah McIlree. **Stadium Operations Coordinator:** Adam Pinckard. **Stadium & Event Operations Coordinator:** Mitch Harrington. **Ticket Operations Manager:** Tyler Henderson. **Retail & Merchandise Specialist:** Adam Latta. **Director of Food & Beverage:** John Schow. **Food & Beverage Manager:** David Hutto. **Hospitality Specialist & Cook:** Gerald Fickling. **Groundskeeper:** Darrell Lemmer.

FIELD STAFF

Manager: Michael Bard. **Hitting Coach:** Connor Narron. **Pitching Coach:** Michael Steed.

GAME INFORMATION

PA Announcer: Scott Skaden. **Stadium Name:** SRP Park. **Standard Game Times:** Mon.-Fri., 7:05 pm, Sat., 6:05 pm, Sun., 1:35 pm through July 3rd, Sun., 5:05 pm after July 3. **Ticket Price Range:** $9-$28. **Visiting Club Hotel:** Comfort Suites, 2911 Riverwest Dr, Augusta, GA. **Telephone:** (706) 434-2540.

CAROLINA MUDCATS

Office Address: 1501 NC Hwy 39, Zebulon, NC 27597.
Mailing Address: PO Drawer 1218, Zebulon, NC 27597.
Telephone: (919) 269-2287. **Fax:** (919) 269-4910.
E-Mail Address: muddy@carolinamudcats.com.
Website: www.carolinamudcats.com.
Affiliation (first year): Milwaukee Brewers (2017-). **Years in League:** 2021-

OWNERSHIP/MANAGEMENT

Ownership: Milwaukee Brewers Baseball Club
Operated by: Milwaukee Brewers Baseball Club
General Manager, Baseball & Stadium Operations: Eric Gardner. **General Manager, Business Development & Brand Marketing:** David Lawrence. **Manager, Tickets & Business Development:** Mitchell Lister. **Senior Associate, Group Sales:** Megan Bloyd. **Associate, Ticket & Group Sales:** Ryder Barrett. **Coordinator, Box Office:** Jason Leone. **Director, Marketing & Broadcast Media:** Greg Young. **Manager, Multimedia:** Evan Moesta. **Coordinator, Social Media/Marketing/Graphics:** Aaron Bayles. **Manager, Club Level:** Kate Furiness. **Personnel Manager, Food & Beverage:** Edith Crudup. **Coordinator, Stadium Operations:** Logan Clark. **Coordinator, Stadium Operations:** Justin Bose. **Manager, Grounds:** John Packer.

FIELD STAFF
　　Manager: TBD. **Pitching Coach:** TBD. **Hitting Coach:** TBD. **Coach:** TBD. **Athletic Trainer:** TBD. **Strength Coach:** TBD.

GAME INFORMATION
　　Radio Announcer: Greg Young. **No. of Games Broadcast:** 132. **Flagship Station:** carolinamudcats.com. **PA Announcer:** Hayes Permar. **Official Scorer:** Bill Woodward. **Stadium Name:** Five County Stadium.
　　Location: From Raleigh, US 64 East to 264 East, exit at Highway 39 in Zebulon. **Standard Game Times:** 7:00 pm(Mon-Fri), 5:00 pm (Sat), 1:00 PM (Sun). **Ticket Price Range:** $12-16. **Visiting Club Hotel:** Doubletree by Hilton Midtown, 2805 Highwoods Blvd, Raleigh, NC, 27604.

CHARLESTON RIVERDOGS

　　Office Address: 360 Fishburne St, Charleston, SC 29403.
　　Mailing Address: PO Box 20849, Charleston, SC 29403.
　　Telephone: (843) 723-7241. **Fax:** (843) 723-2641.
　　E-Mail Address: admin@riverdogs.com. **Website:** www.riverdogs.com.
　　Affiliation (first year): Tampa Bay Rays (2021). **Years in League:** 2021-

OWNERSHIP/MANAGEMENT
　　Operated by: The Goldklang Group/South Carolina Baseball Club LP.
　　Chairman: Marv Goldklang. **President:** Jeff Goldklang. **Club President/General Manager:** Dave Echols. **Executive Advisor to the Chairman:** Mike Veeck. **Director, Fun:** Bill Murray. **Co-Owners:** Peter Freund, Al Phillips. **Senior Vice President:** Ben Abzug. **VP, Corporate Sales:** Andy Lange. **Assistant GM:** Garret Randle. **Director, Marketing and Entertainment:** Ryan Perry. **VP, Food/Beverage:** Josh Shea. **Director, Broadcasting and Media Relations:** Jason Kempf. **Director Community Outreach:** Chris Singleton. **Director, Operations:** Brandon Dunnam. **Director, Merchandise:** Cynthia Linhart. **Business Manager:** Dale Stickney. **Head Groundskeeper:** Kevin Coyne.

FIELD STAFF
　　Manager: Blake Butera. **Hitting Coach:** Perry Roth. **Pitching Coach:** R.C. Lichtenstein. **Bench Coach:** Frank Jagoda.

GAME INFORMATION
　　Radio Announcer: Jason Kempf. **No. of Games Broadcast:** 132. **Flagship Station:** TBD. **PA Announcer:** Ken Carrington. **Official Scorer:** Mike Hoffman. **Stadium Name:** Joseph P. Riley, Jr. **Location:** 360 Fishburne St, Charleston, SC 29403, From US 17, take Lockwood Dr. North, right on Fishburne St. **Standard Game Times:** Mon.-Fri., 7:05pm, Sat. 6:05 pm, Sun. 5:05 pm. **Ticket Price Range:** $8-20. **Visiting Club Hotel:** Aloft Charleston Airport.

COLUMBIA FIREFLIES

　　Office Address: 1640 Freed Street, Columbia, SC 29201.
　　Mailing Address: 1640 Freed Street, Columbia, SC 29201.
　　Telephone: (803) 726-4487.
　　E-Mail Address: info@columbiafireflies.com. **Website:** www.columbiafireflies.com.
　　Affiliation (first year): Kansas City Royals (2021). **Years in League:** 2021-

OWNERSHIP/MANAGEMENT
　　Operated By: Columbia Fireflies Baseball, LLC.
　　President: Brad Shank. **Chief Revenue Officer:** Kevin Duplaga. **Senior Vice President/Food & Beverage:** Scott Burton. **Director, Accounting & Baseball Operations:** Jonathan Mercier. **Director, Marketing:** Ashlie DeCarlo. **Office Manager:** Katie Maroney. **Director, Ticketing:** Joe Shepard. **Director, Group Sales:** Nick Spano. **Ticket Account Manager:** Austin Blevins, Claire Edwards, Aydan Fields and Conor Mitchum. **Graphics Manager:** Casey Vecchio. **Promotions/Community Relations Manager:** Halle Wade. **Video Production Manager:** Zach Branham. **Merchandise Manager:** Mallory Turnbull. **Executive Chef:** Bobby Hunter. **Food & Beverage Manager:** Michael Bolt. **Director of Stadium Operations:** Matt Lundquist. **Assistant Director of Stadium Operations:** Tyler Restrepo. **Head Groundskeeper:** Morgan Hunter. **Corporate Partnerships Account Executive:** Jason Haller. **Director of Special Events:** Alyssa Stein.

FIELD STAFF
　　Manager: Tony Pena Jr. **Hitting Coach:** Jesus Azuaje. **Pitching Coach:** John Habyan. **Bench Coach:** Glenn Hubbard.

GAME INFORMATION
　　Radio Announcer: John Kocsis Jr. **No. of Games Broadcast:** 70. **Flagship Station:** Unavailable. **PA Announcer:** Bryan Vacchio. **Official Scorer:** Bond Nickels. **Stadium Name:** Segra Park. **Location:** 1640 Freed Street, Columbia, SC 29201. **Standard Game Times:** Mon.-Fri., 7:05pm, Sat. 6:05pm, Sun. 5:05. **Ticket Price Range:** $5-$12. **Visiting Club Hotel:** Hyatt Place Columbia/Harbison, 1130 Kinley Road, Irmo, SC 29063.

DELMARVA SHOREBIRDS

Office Address: 6400 Hobbs Rd, Salisbury, MD 21804.
Mailing Address: PO Box 1557, Salisbury, MD 21802.
Telephone: (410) 219-3112. **Fax:** (410) 219-9164.
E-Mail Address: info@theshorebirds.com. **Website:** www.theshorebirds.com.
Affiliation (first year): Baltimore Orioles (1997). **Years in League:** 2021-

OWNERSHIP/MANAGEMENT

Operated By: 7th Inning Stretch, LP. **Owner:** Tom Volpe. **President:** Pat Filippone. **General Manager:** Chris Bitters. **Assistant GM:** Jimmy Sweet. **Director of Marketing:** Ben Vigliarolo. **Director of Broadcasting & Communications:** Sam Jellinek. **Community Relations Manager:** Sam Lehman. **Director of Tickets:** Brandon Harms. **Director of Ticket & Merchandise Operations:** Benjamin Posner. **Ticket Sales Account Executive:** Joe DeLucia. **Group Event Coordinator:** Jennifer Atkinson. **Director of Stadium Operations:** Billy Blackwell. **Head Groundskeeper:** Caroline Beauchamp. **Accounting Manager:** Matt Figard.

FIELD STAFF

Manager: Felipe Alou, Jr. **Pitching Coach:** Joe Haumacher. **Hitting Coach:** Brink Ambler. **Fundamentals Coach:** Daniel Fajardo. **Development Coach:** Collin Murray. **Athletic Trainer:** Julio Ibarra. **Strength & Conditioning Coach:** Liz Pardo.

GAME INFORMATION

Radio: TBD. **No. of Games Broadcast:** TBD. **Flagship Station:** TBD. **Stadium Name:** Arthur W. Perdue Stadium. **Location:** From US 50 East, right on Hobbs Rd; From US 50 West, left on Hobbs Road. **Standard Game Time:** 7:05 pm. **Ticket Price Range:** $10-$15. **Visiting Club Hotel:** TBD.

DOWN EAST WOOD DUCKS

Address: 400 East Grainger Avenue, Kinston, NC 28502
Telephone: (252) 686-5165
E-Mail Address: jbullock@woodducksbaseball.com. **Website:** woodducksbaseball.com
Affiliation (first year): Texas Rangers (2017). **Years in League:** 2021-

OWNERSHIP/MANAGEMENT

Operated By: Texas Rangers, LLC.
Chief Operating Officer & Chairman, Ownership Committee: Neil Leibman. **Executive Vice President, Sports & Entertainment for the Texas Rangers & President of REV Entertainment:** Sean Decker. **Vice President:** Wade Howell. **General Manager:** Jon Clemmons. **Assistant GM of Operations:** Janell Fitch. **Creative Services Director:** TBD. **Director of Marketing:** TBD. **Group Sales Executive & Broadcaster:** Matt Davis. **Account Executive, Group Sales:** Mark Warren. **Head Groundskeeper:** Stephen Watson.

FIELD STAFF

Manager: Steve Mintz. **Hitting Coach:** Collin McBride. **Pitching Coach:** Demetre Kokoris. **Development Coaches:** Guilder Rodriguez & Justin Jacobs. **Trainer:** Rachel Purcell. **Strength & Conditioning Coach:** Kevin Varitek.

GAME INFORMATION

Radio Announcer: Matt Davis. **PA Announcer:** Bryan Hanks. **Stadium Name:** Grainger Stadium. **Standard Game Times:** 7:00 (weekdays), 5:00 (Saturdays), 1:00 (Sundays). **Ticket Price Range:** $7-$14 **Visiting Club Hotel:** Mother Earth Motor Lodge, 501 N Heritage St., Kinston, NC 28501.

FAYETTEVILLE WOODPECKERS

Address: 460 Hay St., Fayetteville, NC 28301
Telephone: 910-339-1989.
E-Mail Address: Woodpeckers@astros.com. **Website:** fayettevillewoodpeckers.com.
Affiliation (first year): Houston Astros (2019). **Years in League:** 2021-

OWNERSHIP/MANAGEMENT

Principal Owner: Houston Astros.
General Manager: Steve Pelle. **Assistant General Manager:** Pete Subsara. **Director, Finance:** Jennifer Carpenter. **Director, Field Operations:** Alpha Jones. **Director, Ticket Sales & Service:** Gabe Evans. **Manager, Marketing & Communications:** Danyel Beaver. **Manager, Sponsorship Strategy & Activation:** Brittany Tschida. **Manager, Baseball Operations:** Mike Montesino. **Manager, Events:** Rachel Smith. **Manager, Creative Services:** Ryan LeFevre. **Manager, Community Relations & Media Relations:** Kristen Nett. **Account Executive, Ticketing:** Maurice Spagatner. **Account Executive, Sponsorships:** Kevin Hughes. **Account Manager, Season Ticket Sales:** Jackson Bingham. **Manager, Retail:** Victoria Lark. **Manager, Operations:** Matt Chappell. **Coordinator, Ballpark Entertainment:** Brian Barber. **Coordinator, Field Operations:** Eli Laney.

FIELD STAFF

Manager: Joe Thon. **Hitting Coach:** Jose Puentes. **Pitching Coach:** John Kovalik.

GAME INFORMATION

Radio Announcer: Andrew Chapman. **No. of Games Broadcast:** 132. **Flagship Station:** N/A. **PA Announcer:** Ray Thomas. **Official Scorer:** TBD. **Stadium Name:** Segra Stadium. **Standard Game Times:** M-F 7:05pm, Sat. 5:05pm, Sun. 2:05pm. **Visiting Club Hotel:** Fairfield Inn. **Telephone:** 910-223-7867.

FREDERICKSBURG NATIONALS

Office Address: 42 Jackie Robinson Way, Fredericksburg, VA 22401
Mailing Address: 42 Jackie Robinson Way, Fredericksburg, VA 22401
Telephone: (540) 858-4242. **E-Mail Address:** info@frednats.com.
Website: www.frednats.com.
Affiliation (first year): Washington Nationals (2005). **Years in League:** 2021—

OWNERSHIP/MANAGEMENT

Operated By: SAJ Baseball LLC. **Principal Owner:** Art Silber.
President: Lani Silber Weiss. **Executive VP/General Manager:** Nick Hall. **Director of Partnerships:** Tory Goodman. **Manager of Partnership Fulfillment:** Gibson Stoffer. **Director of Ticketing:** David Woodard. **Ticket Sales Account Executive:** Jimmy Burns. **Ticket Sales Account Executive:** Chris Borysewicz. **Ticket Sales Account Executive:** Brian Lehman. **Box Office Manager:** Rich Crosslin. **Ticket Operations Coordinator:** Trey Pearsall. **Special Events and Hospitality Manager:** Ally Chism. **Vice President of Operations:** Eliot Williams. **Manager of Stadium Operations:** Zak Kerns. **Director of Merchandise:** McKenzie Goodman. **Merchandise Manager:** Bekah Haskell. **Head Groundskeeper:** Steven Guertin. **Assistant General Manager/VP of Creative Services:** Robert Perry. **Director of Design:** Alexis Deegan. **Marketing Coordinator:** Paige Honaker. **Director of Production:** Zhancheng Wu. **Manager of Broadcasting and Media Relations:** Erik Bremer. **Community Relations Manager:** Adam Flock.

FIELD STAFF

Manager: Jake Lowery. **Hitting Coach:** Delwyn Young. **Pitching Coach:** Joel Hanrahan. **Developmental Coach:** Carmelo Jaime. **Athletic Trainer:** Kirby Craft. **Strength & Conditioning Coach:** Ryan Grose.

GAME INFORMATION

Radio Announcer: TBA. **No. of Games Broadcast:** 132. **Flagship:** www.frednats.com. **PA Announcer:** Todd Pristas. **Official Scorers:** Dave McAndrew, Rick Garver, John Vagnetti, Dan Kipperman. **Stadium Name:** FredNats Ballpark. **Location:** From I-95, take exit 130B onto VA-3W/Plank Road for 0.7 miles. Turn right onto Carl D. Silver Pkwy. Stay straight for 1.8 miles until you reach stadium parking lot. **Standard Game Times:** 7:05pm. **Ticket Price Range:** $10-$16. **Visiting Club Hotel:** Country Inn and Suites.

KANNAPOLIS CANNON BALLERS

Office Address: 216 West Ave. Kannapolis, NC 28081
Mailing Address: 216 West Ave. Kannapolis, NC 28081
Telephone: (704) 932-3267
Email Address: info@kcballers.com. **Website:** kcballers.com
Affiliation (first year): Chicago White Sox (2001). **Years in League:** 2021-

OWNERSHIP/MANAGEMENT

Operated by: Temerity Baseball Club, LLC. **Operating Partner:** Scotty Brown. **General Manager:** Matt Millward. **Assistant GM:** Vince Marcucci. **Account Executive:** Walker Brooke. **Broadcasting & Baseball Operations Manager:** Trevor Wilt. **Director of Retail Operations:** TBD. **Director of Ticket Operations:** Dana Shaw. **Director of Special Events:** Rachel George. **Director of Stadium Operations:** TBD. **Director of Social Media:** Blair Jewell. **Director of Creative Services & Branding:** Caitlyn Gardner. **Head Groundskeeper:** Tim Siegel. **Director of Video Production:** Melissa Clark. **Director of Food & Beverage Operations:** Chris Beasley. **Ticket Sales Account Executive:** Patrick Hicks. **Ticket Sales Account Executive:** Cashlin Copley. **Front Office Administrator:** Morgan Howden.

FIELD STAFF

Manager: Guillermo Quiroz. **Pitching Coach:** John Ely. **Hitting Coach:** Charlie Romero. **Coach:** Patrick Leyland.

GAME INFORMATION

Radio Announcer: Trevor Wilt. **No. of Games Broadcast:** TBD. **Flagship Station:** kcballers.com/TuneIn Radio App. **PA Announcer:** Jordan Connell. **Official Scorer:** Jimmy Lewis. **Stadium Name:** Atrium Health Ballpark. **Location:** Exit 58 on I-85, turn west on to South Cannon Blvd., continue straight until left turn on Dale Earnhardt Blvd., take right on Vance, then left on West Ave. **Standard Game Times:** Mon-Sat, 7p.m./Sun, 1p.m. **Ticket Price Range:** $9-$15. **Visiting Club Hotel:** Holiday Inn Express & Suites Concord.

LYNCHBURG HILLCATS

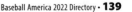

Address: Lynchburg City Stadium, 3180 Fort Ave, Lynchburg, VA 24501.
Telephone: (434) 528-1144. **Fax:** (434) 846-0768.

E-Mail Address: info@lynchburg-hillcats.com. **Website:** www.Lynchburg-hillcats.com.
Affiliation (first year): Cleveland Guardians (2015). **Years in League:** 2021-

OWNERSHIP/MANAGEMENT
Operated By: Elmore Sports Group.
President and General Manager: Chris Jones. **Vice President:** Matt Ramstead. **Assistant General Manager:** Adam Matth. **Manager of Marketing and Creative Services:** Jeff Kent. **Director of Accounting and Finance:** David Ingemi. **Director of Concessions:** Roderick Williams Jr. **Head Groundskeeper:** Tyler Bergin. **Clubhouse Manager:** Ryan Henson.

FIELD STAFF
Manager: Omir Santos. **Hitting Coach:** Craig Massoni. **Pitching Coach:** Kevin Erminio. **Bench Coach:** Daniel Robertson. **Strength & Conditioning Coach:** Juan Acevedo. **Athletic Trainer:** Franklin Sammons.

GAME INFORMATION
Radio Announcer: TBD. **No. of Games Broadcast:** 120. **Official Scorers:** TBD. **Stadium Name:** Bank of the James Stadium. **Location:** US 29 Business South to Bank of the James Stadium (exit 6); US 29 Business North to Bank of the James Stadium (exit 4). **Ticket Price Range:** $8-16. **Visiting Club Hotel:** TBD.

MYRTLE BEACH PELICANS

Mailing Address: 1251 21st Avenue N. Myrtle Beach, SC 29577.
Telephone: (843) 918-6000. **Fax:** (843) 918-6001.
E-Mail Address: info@myrtlebeachpelicans.com.
Website: www.myrtlebeachpelicans.com.
Affiliation: (first year): Chicago Cubs (2015). **Years in League:** 2021-

OWNERSHIP/MANAGEMENT
Owners, Greenberg Sports Group: Chuck Greenberg.
President: Ryan Moore. **General Manager:** Kristin Call. **Sr. Director, Finance:** Anne Frost. **Administrative Assistant:** Beth Freitas. **AGM of Sales:** Ryan Cannella. **Sports & Tourism Sales Manager:** Todd Chapman. **Corporate Sales Manager:** Eric Theiss. **Box Office Manager:** Shannon Barbee. **Sponsorship Execution Coordinator:** Samantha Parnell. **Fan Engagement:** Hunter Horenstein. **Director of Operations:** Dan Bailey. **Merchandise Manager/Pro Shop:** Dan Bailey. **Director, Food & Beverage:** Brad Leininger. **Sports Turf Manager:** Jordan Barr. **Director of Video Productions:** Ryan Nicholson. **Media Relations:** Sam Weiderhaft.

FIELD STAFF
Manager: Buddy Bailey. **Hitting Coach:** Steven Pollakov. **Pitching Coach:** Clayton Mortensen. **Coach:** Jovanny Rosario.

GAME INFORMATION
PA Announcer: TBA. **Official Scorer:** TBA. **Stadium Name:** Pelicans Ballpark. **Location:** US Highway 17 Bypass to 21st Ave. North, half mile to stadium. **Standard Game Times:** 7:05 p.m. **Ticket Price Range:** $9-$15. **Visiting Club Hotel:** Doubletree Resorts, 3200 South Ocean Blvd., Myrtle Beach, S.C., 29577. **Telephone:** (843) 315-7100.

SALEM RED SOX

Office Address: 1004 Texas St., Salem, VA 24153.
Mailing Address: PO Box 842, Salem, VA 24153.
Telephone: (540) 389-3333. **Fax:** (540) 389-9710.
E-Mail Address: info@salemsox.com. **Website:** www.salemsox.com.
Affiliation (first year): Boston Red Sox (2009). **Years in League:** 2021-

OWNERSHIP/MANAGEMENT
Operated By: Carolina Baseball LLC/Fenway Sports Group. **Managing Director:** Dave Beeston. **General Manager:** Allen Lawrence. **AGM/VP of Tickets:** Blair Hoke. **VP of Corporate Partnerships:** Steven Elovich. **Head Groundskeeper:** Joey Elmore. **Senior Ticket Operations & Analytics Manager:** Lior Bittan. **Director of Food/Beverage:** TBA. **Bookkeeper:** Barry Stephens. **Video Production Manager:** Steven Langdon. **Merchandise & Special Events Director:** Kayla Keegan. **Ticket Sales Manager:** Payton Powell. **Facilities Manager:** Weill Casey. **Promotions & Social Media Manager:** Danielle DiBenedetto. **Clubhouse Manager:** Tom Wagner.

FIELD STAFF
Manager: TBA. **Hitting Coach:** TBA. **Pitching Coach:** TBA. **Coach:** TBA. **Trainer:** TBA. **Strength & Conditioning Coach:** TBA.

GAME INFORMATION
Radio Announcer: TBD. **No. of Games Broadcast:** 120. **Flagship Station:** TBD. **PA Announcer:** TBD. **Official Scorer:** Billy Wells. **Stadium Name:** Salem Memorial Ballpark. **Location:** I-81 to exit 141 (Route 419), follow signs to Salem Civic Center Complex. **Standard Game Times:** 7:05 pm, Sat./Sun. 6:05/4:05. **Ticket Price Range:** $7-15. **Visiting Club Hotel:** Comfort Suites Ridgewood Farms, 2898 Keagy Rd., Salem, VA 24153. **Telephone:** (540) 375-4800.

LOW-A SOUTHEAST

STADIUM INFORMATION

| Club | Stadium | Opened | Dimensions | | | Capacity | 2021 Att. |
			LF	CF	RF		
Bradenton	McKechnie Field	1923	335	400	335	8,654	38,207
Clearwater	BayCare Ballpark	2004	330	400	330	8,500	108,111
Daytona	Jackie Robinson Ballpark	1930	317	400	325	4,200	79,361
Dunedin	Florida Auto Exchange Stadium	1977	335	400	327	5,509	10,043
Fort Myers	Hammond Stadium	1991	330	405	330	7,900	76,216
Jupiter	Roger Dean Chevrolet Stadium	1998	330	400	325	6,871	20,197
Lakeland	Publix Field at Joker Marchant Stadium	1966	340	420	340	7,961	26,894
Palm Beach	Roger Dean Chevrolet Stadium	1998	330	400	325	6,871	28,440
St. Lucie	First Data Field	1988	338	410	338	7,000	45,609
Tampa	Steinbrenner Field	1996	318	408	314	10,270	34,842

BRADENTON MARAUDERS

Address: 1611 9th St. W., Bradenton, FL 34205.
Telephone: (941) 747-3031.
E-Mail Address: MaraudersInfo@pirates.com
Website: bradentonmarauders.com
Affiliation (first year): Pittsburgh Pirates (2010). **Years in League:** 2021-

OWNERSHIP/MANAGEMENT
Operated By: Pittsburgh Associates of Florida
VP, Florida & Dominican Republic Operations: Jeff Podobnik. **General Manager/Director of Sales & Marketing:** Craig Warzecha. **Director, Florida Operations:** Ray Morris. **Director, Concessions & Retail:** Chuck Knapp. **Manager, Ticket Sales & Service:** Nolan Bialek. **Manager, Marketing & Game Presentation:** Rebekah Rivette. **Coordinator, LECOM Park Operations:** Tyler Skipper. **Coordinator, Fan & Community Engagement:** Megan Kottemann. **Coordinator, Ticket Operations:** Tyler Gray. **Head Groundskeeper:** Joseph Knight.

FIELD STAFF
Manager: Jonathan Johnston. **Pitching Coach:** TBD. **Hitting Coach:** Mendy Lopez. **Integrated Baseball Performance Coach:** Casey Harms. **Development Coach:** Gustavo Omaña. **Trainer:** TBD. **Strength Coach:** TBD.

GAME INFORMATION
PA Announcer: Jeff Phillips. **Official Scorer:** Dave Taylor. **Stadium Name:** LECOM Park. **Location:** I-75 to exit 220 (220B from I-75N) to SR 64 West/Manatee Ave, Left onto 9th St West, LECOM PARK on the left. **Standard Game Times:** 6:30 pm, Sun. 1:00 pm. **Ticket Price Range:** $6-10. **Visiting Club Hotel:** Holiday Inn Express West, 4450 47th St W, Bradenton, FL 34210. **Telephone:** (941) 747-3031.

CLEARWATER THRESHERS

Address: 601 N Old Coachman Road, Clearwater, FL 33765.
Telephone: (727) 712-4300. **Fax:** (727) 712-4498.
Website: www.threshersbaseball.com.
Affiliation (first year): Philadelphia Phillies (1985). **Years in League:** 2021-

OWNERSHIP/MANAGEMENT
Operated by: Philadelphia Phillies.
Director of Florida Operations: John Timberlake. **General Manager of Clearwater Threshers:** Jason Adams. **Senior Manager of Corporate Partnerships:** Dan McDonough. **Business Manager:** Dianne Gonzalez. **General Manager, BayCare Ballpark:** Doug Kemp. **Assistant GM, Clearwater Threshers:** Dan Madden. **Community Engagement/Media Manager:** Robert Stretch. **Food and Beverage Manager:** Justin Gunsaulus. **Corporate Sales Associate:** Cory Sipe. **Clubhouse Manager:** Justin Glover. **Manager, Ticket Operations:** Pat Prevelige. **Facility and Operations Coordinator:** Sean McCarthy. **Manager, Promotions and Game Entertainment:** Dominic Repper. **Merchandise Manager:** Shan Isett. **Assistant Manager, Group Sales:** Victoria Phipps. **Social Media & Entertainment Assistant:** Lindsey Settlemire. **Operations Assistant:** Will Priest. **Field Supervisor:** Ray Sayre.

FIELD STAFF
Manager: TBA. **Hitting Coach:** TBA. **Pitching Coach:** TBA.

GAME INFORMATION
PA Announcer: TBA. **Official Scorer:** Larry Wiederecht. **Stadium Name:** BayCare Ballpark. **Location:** US 19 North and Drew Street in Clearwater. **Standard Game Times:** Mon.-Sat. 6:30 pm, Sun. 12 p.m., most Wednesdays are day

games. **Ticket Price Range:** $6-11. **Visiting Club Hotel:** La Quinta Inn, 21338 US Highway 19 N, Clearwater, FL 33765. **Telephone:** (727) 799-1565.

DAYTONA TORTUGAS

Address: 110 E Orange Ave, Daytona Beach, FL 32114.
Telephone: (386) 257-3172. **Fax:** (386) 523-9490.
E-Mail Address: info@daytonatortugas.com.
Website: www.daytonatortugas.com.
Affiliation (first year): Cincinnati Reds (2015). **Years in League:** 2021-

OWNERSHIP/MANAGEMENT
Operated By: Tortugas Baseball Club LLC. **Principal Owner/President:** Reese Smith III. **Co-Owners:** Bob Fregolle, Rick French. **General Manager:** Jim Jaworski. **Finance Manager:** Dan Smith. **Director of Corporate Partnerships:** Anthony Moore. **Director of Ticket Sales:** Aly Thomas. **Ticket & Group Sales Manager:** Kristina Markus. **Community Relations Manager:** Josh McCann. **Broadcaster and Media Relations Manager:** Justin Rocke. **Director, Food and Beverage:** Angela Ford. **Stadium Operations and Grounds Manager:** TBA.

FIELD STAFF
Manager: Gookie Dawkins. **Pitching Coach:** Todd Naskedov. **Hitting Coach:** Darryl Brinkley. **Bench Coach:** Lenny Harris.

GAME INFORMATION
Radio Announcer: Justin Rocke. **No. of Games Broadcast:** 132. **Flagship Station:** MiLB First Pitch app & www.daytonatortugas.com. **PA Announcer:** Tim LeCras. **Official Scorer:** Don Roberts. **Stadium Name:** Jackie Robinson Ballpark. **Location:** I-95 to International Speedway Blvd Exit, east to Beach Street, south to Magnolia Ave east to ballpark; A1A North/South to Orange Ave west to ballpark. **Standard Game Time:** 7:05 p.m. (Mon-Sat); 5:35 p.m. (Sun). **Ticket Price Range:** $8-15. **Visiting Club Hotel:** Holiday Inn Resort Daytona Beach Oceanfront, 1615 S. Atlantic Ave Daytona Beach, FL 32118. **Telephone:** (386) 255-0921.

DUNEDIN BLUE JAYS

Address: 373 Douglas Ave Dunedin, FL 34698.
Telephone: (727) 733-9302. **Fax:** (727) 734-7661.
E-Mail Address: dunedin@bluejays.com. **Website:** dunedinbluejays.com.
Affiliation (first year): Toronto Blue Jays (1987). **Years in League:** 2021-

OWNERSHIP/MANAGEMENT
Director Florida Operations: Shelby Nelson. **Senior Manager of TD Ballpark Operations:** Zac Phelps. **Senior Manager of TD Ballpark Business Operations:** Kathi Beckman. **Accounting Manager:** Gayle Gentry. **Administrative Assistant/Receptionist:** Dea Jones. **Head Superintendent:** Patrick Skunda.

FIELD STAFF
Manager: TBA. **Hitting Coach:** TBA. **Pitching Coach:** TBA. **Position Coach:** TBA. **Strength & Conditioning Coach:** TBA. **Athletic Trainer:** TBA.

GAME INFORMATION
PA Announcer: Bradley Keville. **Official Scorer:** Steven Boychuk. **Stadium Name:** TD Ballpark. **Location:** From I-275, north on Highway 19, exit on Drew Street, right on North Keene Road, left onto Union Street. Right onto Douglas Avenue and stadium is on the right. **Standard Game Times:** 6:30 pm, Sun. noon. **Ticket Price Range:** TBD. **Visiting Club Hotel:** La Quinta, 21338 US Highway 19 North, Clearwater, FL. **Telephone:** (727) 799-1565.

FORT MYERS MIGHTY MUSSELS

Address: 14400 Six Mile Cypress Pkwy, Fort Myers, FL 33912.
Telephone: (239) 768-4210. **Fax:** (239) 768-4211.
E-Mail Address: frontdesk@mightymussels.com.
Website: www.mightymussels.com.
Affiliation (first year): Minnesota Twins (1992). **Years in League:** 2021-

OWNERSHIP/MANAGEMENT
Operated By: Kaufy Baseball, LLC. **Owner:** John Martin. **Partner:** Andrew Kaufmann. **President:** Chris Peters. **General Manager, Director of Operations:** Judd Loveland. **Vice President of Sales and Marketing:** Dan Lauer. **Director of Business Operations:** Diana Burch. **Broadcast & Media Relations Manager:** John Vittas. **Marketing Manager:** Shannon Rankin. **Operations Coordinator:** Rachel Raymer. **Director of Food & Beverage:** Loren Merrigan. **Merchandise Manager:** Lynn Izzo. **Sales Account Representatives:** Rosmy Cerdas, Austin Dutton, Gabby Miller.

FIELD STAFF

Manager: Brian Meyer. **Pitching Coaches:** Carlos Hernandez, Jared Gaynor. **Hitting Coach:** Rayden Sierra. **Bench Coach:** Takashi Miyoshi.

GAME INFORMATION

Radio Announcer: John Vittas. **No. of Games Broadcast:** 110. **Internet Broadcast:** www.mightymussels.com. **PA Announcer:** Allen Woodard. **Official Scorer:** Benn Norton. **Stadium Name:** William H. Hammond Stadium at the CenturyLink Sports Complex. **Location:** Exit 131 off I-75, west on Daniels Parkway, left on Six Mile Cypress Parkway. **Standard Game Times:** Tue-Sat 7:00 pm, Sun. 1:00 pm. **Ticket Price Range:** $10-$15. **Visiting Club Hotel:** Fairfield Inn & Suites Fort Myers Cape Coral, 7090 Cypress Terrace, Fort Myers, FL 33907.

JUPITER HAMMERHEADS

Address: 4751 Main Street, Jupiter, FL 33458.
Telephone: (561) 775-1818. **Fax:** (561) 691-6886.
E-Mail Address: PalmBeachCardinals@rogerdeanchevroletstadium.com.
Affiliation (first year): Miami Marlins (1998). **Years in League:** 2021-

OWNERSHIP/MANAGEMENT

Owned By: Miami Marlins, Jupiter Stadium, LTD.
General Manager, Jupiter Stadium, LTD: Mike Bauer. **General Manager:** Nick Bernabe. **Executive Assistant:** Lynn Besaw. **Media Relations & Promotions Coordinator:** Ryer Gardenswartz. **Media Relations Assistant:** Austin Pert. **Director of Accounting:** Pam Sartory. **Ticket Office Manager:** Amanda Seimer. **Director of Operations:** Andrew Seymour. **Corporate Partnerships Manager:** Rachel Duewer. **Marketing & Promotions Manager:** Taylor Burress. **Building Manager:** Walter Herrera. **Director, Grounds & Facilities:** Jordan Treadway. **Assistant Director, Grounds & Facilities:** Mitchell Moenster. **Event Operations Coordinator:** Justin Valverde. **Merchandise Manager:** Kimberley Emerick.

FIELD STAFF

Manager: Angel Espada. **Pitching Coach:** TBA. **Hitting Coach:** TBA. **Strength & Conditioning Coach:** TBA. **Athletic Trainer:** TBA. **Defensive Coach:** TBA.

GAME INFORMATION

PA Announcers: John Frost, Jay Zeager. **Official Scorer:** Brennan McDonald. **Stadium Name:** Roger Dean Chevrolet Stadium. **Location:** I-95 to exit 83, east on Donald Ross Road for 1/4 mile, left on Parkside Dr. **Standard Game Times:** 6:30 pm, Sat. 5:30pm, Sun. 1:00pm. **Ticket Price Range:** $7- $10. **Visiting Club Hotel:** Fairfield Inn by Marriott, 6748 Indiantown Road, Jupiter, FL 33458. **Telephone:** (561) 748-5252.

LAKELAND FLYING TIGERS

Address: 2301 Lakeland Hills Blvd., Lakeland, FL 33805.
Telephone: (863) 686-8075. **Fax:** (863) 687-4127.
Website: www.lakelandflyingtigers.com.
Affiliation (first year): Detroit Tigers (1967). **Years in League:** 2021-

OWNERSHIP/MANAGEMENT

Owned By: Detroit Tigers, Inc.
President and CEO: Ilitch Holdings, Inc. **Chairman and CEO, Detroit Tigers:** Christopher Ilitch.
Director, Florida Operations: Ron Myers. **General Manager:** Zach Burek. **Manager, Administration/Operations Manager:** Shannon Follett. **Ticket Manager:** Ryan Eason.

FIELD STAFF

Manager: Andrew Graham. **Hitting Coach:** Francisco Contreras. **Pitching Coach:** Juan Pimentel. **Developmental Coach:** Matt Malott. **Athletic Trainer:** Erick Flores. **Strength & Conditioning Coach:** Dax Fiore. **Baseball Information Assistant:** Kyle Flanagan. **Clubhouse Manager:** Pete Mancuso.

GAME INFORMATION

PA Announcer: Unavailable. **Official Scorer:** Joe Falatek. **Stadium Name:** Publix Field at Joker Marchant Stadium. **Location:** Exit 33 on I-4 to 33 South (Lakeland Hills Blvd.), 1.5 miles on left. **Standard Game Times:** M-F 630 p.m., Sat 6:00 pm, Sun 1:00 pm. **Ticket Price Range:** $6-10. **Visiting Club Hotel:** TownePlace Suites by Marriott Lakeland, 3370 US Highway 98 North, Lakeland, FL 33805, 863-680-1115.

PALM BEACH CARDINALS

Address: 4751 Main Street, Jupiter, FL 33458.
Telephone: (561) 775-1818. **Fax:** (561) 691-6886.
E-Mail Address: PalmBeachCardinals@rogerdeanchevroletstadium.com.

Affiliation (first year): St. Louis Cardinals (2003). **Years in League:** 2021-

OWNERSHIP/MANAGEMENT

Owned By: St. Louis Cardinals, Jupiter Stadium, LTD.
General Manager, Jupiter Stadium, LTD: Mike Bauer. **General Manager:** Andrew Seymour. **Executive Assistant:** Lynn Besaw. **Media Relations & Promotions Coordinator:** Ryer Gardenswartz. **Media Relations Assistant:** Austin Pert. **Director of Accounting:** Pam Sartory. **Ticket Office Manager:** Amanda Seimer. **Director of Corporate Partnerships:** Nick Bernabe. **Corporate Partnerships Manager:** Rachel Duewer. **Marketing & Promotions Manager:** Taylor Burress. **Building Manager:** Walter Herrera. **Director, Grounds & Facilities:** Jordan Treadway. **Assistant Director, Grounds & Facilities:** Mitchell Moenster. **Event Operations Coordinator:** Justin Valverde. **Merchandise Manager:** Kimberley Emerick.

FIELD STAFF

Manger: Gary Kendall. **Hitting Coach:** Kedeem Octave. **Pitching Coach:** Giovanni Carrara.

GAME INFORMATION

PA Announcers: John Frost, Jay Zeager. **Official Scorer:** Lou Villano. **Stadium Name:** Roger Dean Chevrolet Stadium. **Location:** I-95 to exit 83, east on Donald Ross Road for 1/4 mile, left on Parkside Dr. **Standard Game Times:** TBA. **Ticket Price Range:** TBA. **Visiting Club Hotel:** Fairfield Inn by Marriott, 6748 Indiantown Road, Jupiter, FL 33458. **Telephone:** (561) 748-5252.

ST. LUCIE METS

Address: 31 Piazza Drive, Port St Lucie, FL 34986.
Telephone: (772) 871-2100. **Fax:** (772) 878-9802.
Website: www.stluciemets.com.
Affiliation (first year): New York Mets (1988). **Years in League:** 2021-

OWNERSHIP/MANAGEMENT

Owner/Chairman/CEO: Steven A. Cohen. **Owner & President of Amazin' Mets Foundation:** Alexandra M. Cohen. **Vice Chairman:** Andrew B. Cohen. **President:** Sandy Alderson. **Vice President, Minor League Facilities:** Paul Taglieri. **General Manager:** Traer Van Allen. **Assistant General Manager, Team Operations & Ticketing:** Kyle Gleockler. **Assistant General Manager, Game Operations, Community Relations & Group Sales:** Kasey Blair. **Director, Sales/Corporate Partnerships:** Lauren DeAcetis. **Manager, Broadcast & Relations:** Adam MacDonald. **Manager, Group Sales & Ticketing Operations:** Josh Sexton. **Manager, Fantasy Camp & Events:** Doug Dickey. **Manager, Sales & Corporate Partnerships:** Brett Bladergroen. **Senior Accountant:** Pamela Kuhnle. **Executive Assistant:** Mary O'Brien. **Maintenance:** Jeff Montpetit.

FIELD STAFF

Manager: Robbie Robinson. **Pitching Coach:** Victor Ramos. **Hitting Coach:** Victor Burgos. **Bench Coach:** Gilbert Gomez. **Development Coach:** Bryce Wheary. **Trainer:** Kiyoshi Tada. **Performance Coach:** Kory Wan.

GAME INFORMATION

PA Announcer: Evan Nine. **Official Scorer:** Bill Whitehead. **Stadium Name:** Clover Park. **Location:** Exit 121 (St Lucie West Blvd) off I-95, east 1/2 mile, left on NW Peacock Blvd. **Standard Game Times:** Tuesday-Saturday- 6:10; Sundays-12:10. **Ticket Price Range:** $6-$14. **Visiting Club Hotel:** Holiday Inn Express & Suites, 1601 NW Courtyard Circle, Port St Lucie, FL 34986. **Telephone:** (772) 879-6565.

TAMPA TARPONS

Address: One Steinbrenner Drive, Tampa, FL 33614.
Telephone: (813) 875-7753. **Fax:** (813) 673-3186
E-Mail Address: info@tarponsbaseball.com. **Website:** tarponsbaseball.com
Affiliation (first year): New York Yankees (1994). **Years in League:** 2021-

OWNERSHIP/MANAGEMENT

Operated by: Florida Bomber Baseball LLC. **VP Business Operations and General Manager:** Vance Smith. **Assistant GM:** Jeremy Ventura. **Manager, Ticket Operations and Sales:** Jennifer Magliocchetti. **Digital/Social Media Coordinator:** TBD. **Manager, Stadium Operations:** Ralph Caputo. **Director, Grounds:** Ritchie Anderson. **Stadium Supervisor:** Ron Kaufman. **Head Groundskeeper:** Jeff Eckert.

FIELD STAFF

TBD

GAME INFORMATION

Radio: TBD. **PA Announcer:** TBD. **Official Scorer:** Unavailable. **Stadium Name:** George M. Steinbrenner Field. **Location:** I-275 to Dale Mabry Hwy, North on Dale Mabry Hwy (Facility is at corner of West Martin Luther King Blvd/ Dale Mabry Hwy). **Standard Game Times:** Mon-Sat. 6:30pm, Sun 1:00 pm. **Ticket Price Range:** $7-12. **Visiting Club Hotel:** TBD.

TEAM
SCHEDULES

Schedules are subject to change. We would suggest confirming dates and times with teams.

SCHEDULES

TRIPLE-A

TRIPLE-A WEST

ALBUQUERQUE ISOTOPES

APRIL	
5-10	at Okla. City
12-17	Tacoma
19-24	at Round Rock
26-30	Sacramento

MAY	
1	Sacramento
3-8	at Okla. City
10-15	Sugar Land
17-22	at Salt Lake
24-29	Round Rock
31	at Sugar Land

JUNE	
1-5	at Sugar Land
7-9	El Paso
10-12	at El Paso
14-19	Salt Lake
22-27	at Las Vegas
28-30	Sugar Land

JULY	
1-3	Sugar Land
4-10	at Round Rock
13-17	at Sacramento
22-24	Sugar Land
26-31	Las Vegas

AUGUST	
2-7	at El Paso
9-14	Reno
16-21	at Tacoma
23-28	Round Rock
30-31	at Sugar Land

SEPTEMBER	
1-4	at Sugar Land
6-11	El Paso
13-18	Okla. City
20-25	at Sugar Land
26-28	El Paso

EL PASO CHIHUAHUAS

APRIL	
5-10	at Round Rock
12-17	Okla. City
20-24	at Las Vegas
26-30	Reno

MAY	
1	Reno
3-8	at Sugar Land
10-15	Sacramento
17-19	at Okla. City
20-22	at Round Rock
24-29	Sugar Land
30	at Salt Lake

JUNE	
1-5	at Salt Lake
7-9	at Albuquerque
10-12	Albuquerque
14-19	Las Vegas
22-26	at Sacramento
28-30	Okla. City

JULY	
1-3	Okla. City
4-10	at Sugar Land
12-17	Round Rock
23-25	at Reno
26-31	at Tacoma

AUGUST	
2-7	Albuquerque
9-14	Sugar Land
16-21	at Round Rock
23-28	at Okla. City
30-31	Salt Lake

SEPTEMBER	
1-4	Salt Lake
6-11	at Albuquerque
13-18	Round Rock
20-25	Okla. City
26-28	at Albuquerque

LAS VEGAS AVIATORS

APRIL	
6-10	Reno
12-17	at Salt Lake
20-24	El Paso
27-30	Tacoma

MAY	
1-1	Tacoma
4-8	at Sacramento
11-15	Salt Lake
18-22	at Reno
24-29	at Tacoma

JUNE	
1-5	Sacramento
8-10	Round Rock
10-12	at Sugar Land
14-19	at El Paso
22-27	Albuquerque
28-30	at Round Rock

JULY	
2-4	Round Rock
4-9	at Okla. City
13-18	Salt Lake
22-24	at Round Rock
26-31	at Albuquerque

AUGUST	
3-8	Reno
10-14	at Tacoma
16-18	at Sacramento
20-22	Sacramento
24-29	Sugar Land
31	at Reno

SEPTEMBER	
1-5	at Reno
7-11	at Sacramento
14-18	Tacoma
20-25	Reno
26-28	at Sacramento

OKLAHOMA CITY DODGERS

APRIL	
5-10	Albuquerque
12-17	at El Paso
20-24	at Sacramento
26-30	Sugar Land

MAY	
1	Sugar Land
3-8	Albuquerque
10-15	at Round Rock
17-19	El Paso
20-22	at Sugar Land
24-29	Reno
31	at Round Rock

JUNE	
1-5	at Round Rock
7-9	Sugar Land
10-12	Salt Lake
15-19	at Reno
21-26	Round Rock
28-30	at El Paso

JULY	
1-3	at El Paso
4-9	Las Vegas
13-17	at Tacoma
22-24	Sacramento
26-31	Sugar Land

AUGUST	
2-7	at Salt Lake
9-14	Round Rock
16-21	at Sugar Land
23-28	El Paso
30-31	at Round Rock

SEPTEMBER	
1-4	at Round Rock
6-11	Tacoma
13-18	at Albuquerque
20-25	at El Paso
26-28	Salt Lake

RENO ACES

APRIL		JULY	
6-10	at Las Vegas	1	Sacramento
12-17	Sacramento	2-4	at Sacramento
19-24	Salt Lake	5-11	Tacoma
26-30	at El Paso	12-17	at Sugar Land
		23-25	El Paso
MAY		27-31	Salt Lake
1	at El Paso		
3-8	Round Rock	AUGUST	
10-15	at Tacoma	1	Salt Lake
18-22	Las Vegas	3-8	at Las Vegas
24-29	at Okla. City	9-14	at Albuquerque
		17-21	Salt Lake
JUNE		24-28	at Sacramento
1-5	Tacoma	31	Las Vegas
8-12	at Sacramento		
15-19	Okla. City	SEPTEMBER	
21-26	at Salt Lake	1-5	Las Vegas
29-29	Sacramento	6-11	at Salt Lake
		14-18	Sacramento
		20-25	at Las Vegas
		26-28	Tacoma

ROUND ROCK EXPRESS

APRIL		JULY	
5-10	El Paso	2-4	at Las Vegas
12-17	at Sugar Land	4-10	Albuquerque
19-24	Albuquerque	12-17	at El Paso
26-28	Salt Lake	22-24	Las Vegas
29-30	at Salt Lake	26-31	Sacramento
MAY		AUGUST	
1	at Salt Lake	2-7	at Sugar Land
3-8	at Reno	9-14	at Okla. City
10-15	Okla. City	16-21	El Paso
17-19	at Sugar Land	23-28	at Albuquerque
20-22	El Paso	30-31	Okla. City
24-29	at Albuquerque		
31	Okla. City	SEPTEMBER	
		1-4	Okla. City
JUNE		6-11	Sugar Land
1-5	Okla. City	13-18	at El Paso
8-10	at Las Vegas	20-25	at Tacoma
11-12	at Tacoma	26-28	Sugar Land
14-19	Sugar Land		
21-26	at Okla. City		
28-30	Las Vegas		

SACRAMENTO RIVER CATS

APRIL		JULY	
6-10	Sugar Land	1	at Reno
12-17	at Reno	2-4	Reno
20-24	Okla. City	4-10	at Salt Lake
26-30	at Albuquerque	13-17	Albuquerque
		22-24	at Okla. City
MAY		26-31	at Round Rock
1	at Albuquerque		
4-8	Las Vegas	AUGUST	
10-15	at El Paso	3-7	Tacoma
18-22	Tacoma	9-14	at Salt Lake
25-29	Salt Lake	16-18	Las Vegas
		20-22	at Las Vegas
		24-28	Reno
JUNE		31	at Tacoma
1-5	at Las Vegas		
8-12	Reno	SEPTEMBER	
15-19	at Tacoma	1-4	at Tacoma
22-26	El Paso	7-11	Las Vegas
29-29	at Reno	14-18	at Reno
		19-24	at Salt Lake
		26-28	Las Vegas

SALT LAKE BEES

APRIL		JULY	
6-10	at Tacoma	1-4	at Tacoma
12-17	Las Vegas	4-10	Sacramento
19-24	at Reno	13-18	at Las Vegas
26-28	at Round Rock	22-24	Tacoma
29-30	Round Rock	27-31	at Reno
MAY		AUGUST	
1	Round Rock	1	at Reno
3-8	Tacoma	2-7	Okla. City
11-15	at Las Vegas	9-14	Sacramento
17-22	Albuquerque	17-21	at Reno
25-29	at Sacramento	23-28	Tacoma
30	El Paso	30-31	at El Paso
JUNE		SEPTEMBER	
1-5	El Paso	1-4	at El Paso
7-9	Tacoma	6-11	Reno
10-12	at Okla. City	13-18	at Sugar Land
14-19	at Albuquerque	19-24	Sacramento
21-26	Reno	26-28	at Oklahoma City
29-30	at Tacoma		

SUGAR LAND SPACE COWBOYS

APRIL		JULY	
6-10	at Sacramento	1-3	at Albuquerque
12-17	Round Rock	4-10	El Paso
20-24	at Tacoma	12-17	Reno
26-30	at Okla. City	22-24	at Albuquerque
		26-31	at Okla. City
MAY			
1	at Okla. City	AUGUST	
3-8	El Paso	2-7	Round Rock
10-15	at Albuquerque	9-14	at El Paso
17-19	Round Rock	16-21	Okla. City
20-22	Okla. City	24-29	at Las Vegas
24-29	at El Paso	30-31	Albuquerque
31	Albuquerque		
		SEPTEMBER	
JUNE		1-4	Albuquerque
1-5	Albuquerque	6-11	at Round Rock
7-9	at Okla. City	13-18	Salt Lake
10-12	Las Vegas	20-25	Albuquerque
14-19	at Round Rock	26-28	at Round Rock
21-26	Tacoma		
28-30	at Albuquerque		

TACOMA RAINIERS

APRIL		JULY	
6-10	Salt Lake	1-4	Salt Lake
12-17	at Albuquerque	5-11	at Reno
20-24	Sugar Land	13-17	Okla. City
27-30	at Las Vegas	22-24	at Salt Lake
		26-31	El Paso
MAY			
1-1	at Las Vegas	AUGUST	
3-8	at Salt Lake	3-7	at Sacramento
10-15	Reno	10-14	Las Vegas
18-22	at Sacramento	16-21	Albuquerque
24-29	Las Vegas	23-28	at Salt Lake
		31	Sacramento
JUNE			
1-5	at Reno	SEPTEMBER	
7-9	at Salt Lake	1-4	Sacramento
11-12	Round Rock	6-11	at Okla. City
15-19	Sacramento	14-18	at Las Vegas
21-26	at Sugar Land	20-25	Round Rock
29-30	Salt Lake	26-28	at Reno

TRIPLE-A EAST

BUFFALO BISONS

APRIL	
5-10 . . . . Iowa
12-17 . . . . . at Rochester
19-24 . . . . . Scranton/WB
26-30 . . . . . at Worcester

MAY	
1 . . . . at Worcester
3-8 . . . . Durham
10-15 . . . at Lehigh Valley
17-22 . . . . . . Syracuse
24-29 . . . . . at Columbus
30 . . . . . . at Rochester

JUNE	
1-5 . . . . . . at Rochester
7-12 . . . . . . Worcester
14-19 . . . at Lehigh Valley
21-26 . . . . St. Paul
28-30 . . . . at Scranton/WB

JULY	
1-3 . . . . . . at Scranton/WB
4-10 . . . . Syracuse
12-17 . . . . at Iowa
22-24 . . . . . Rochester
26-31 . . . . . . Worcester

AUGUST	
2-7 . . . . . at Scranton/WB
9-14 . . . . . . at Syracuse
16-21 . . . . . Lehigh Valley
23-28 . . . . . . Columbus
30-31 . . . . . at Worcester

SEPTEMBER	
1-4 . . . . . . at Worcester
6-11 . . . . Gwinnett
13-18 . . . . . at Syracuse
19-24 . . . . . . Rochester
26-28 . . . . at Scranton/WB

CHARLOTTE KNIGHTS

APRIL	
5-10 . . . . at Norfolk
12-17 . . . . Memphis
19-24 . . . . . at Nashville
26-30 . . . . . Jacksonville

MAY	
1 . . . . Jacksonville
3-8 . . . . at Gwinnett
10-15 . . . . . Indianapolis
17-22 . . . . Norfolk
24-29 . . . . . at Durham
31 . . . . Memphis

JUNE	
1-5 . . . . Memphis
7-12 . . . . . at Louisville
14-19 . . . . . Jacksonville
21-26 . . . . . at Worcester
28-30 . . . . Durham

JULY	
1-3 . . . . Durham
4-10 . . . . . . at Gwinnett
12-17 . . . . . Lehigh Valley
22-24 . . . . at Jacksonville
27-31 . . . . . at Nashville

AUGUST	
2-7 . . . . Gwinnett
9-14 . . . . at Lehigh Valley
16-21 . . . . . . Syracuse
23-28 . . . . . at Memphis
30-31 . . . . Durham

SEPTEMBER	
1-4 . . . . Durham
6-11 . . . . Nashville
13-18 . . . . . at Norfolk
20-25 . . . . at Jacksonville
26-28 . . . . Durham

COLUMBUS CLIPPERS

APRIL	
5-10 . . . . at Lehigh Valley
12-17 . . . . . . Syracuse
19-24 . . . at Indianapolis
26-30 . . . . . Louisville

MAY	
1 . . . . Louisville
3-8 . . . . at Omaha
10-15 . . . . . . St. Paul
17-22 . . . . . . at Iowa
24-29 . . . . . . Buffalo
30 . . . . Toledo

JUNE	
1-5 . . . . Toledo
7-12 . . . . . at Indianapolis
14-19 . . . . St. Paul
21-26 . . . . . at Omaha
28-30 . . . . . . at Iowa

JULY	
1-3 . . . . at Iowa
4-10 . . . . Nashville
12-17 . . . . . Indianapolis
22-24 . . . . . at Toledo
26-31 . . . . . at Louisville

AUGUST	
2-7 . . . . Rochester
10-14 . . . . . at St. Paul
16-21 . . . . Toledo
23-28 . . . . . at Buffalo
30-31 . . . . Iowa

SEPTEMBER	
1-4 . . . . Iowa
6-11 . . . . . . at Louisville
13-18 . . . . Omaha
20-25 . . . . . . at Toledo
26-28 . . . . . Indianapolis

DURHAM BULLS

APRIL	
5-10 . . . . . . at Nashville
12-17 . . . . . Jacksonville
19-24 . . . . . . at Norfolk
26-30 . . . . Memphis

MAY	
1 . . . . Memphis
3-8 . . . . at Buffalo
10-15 . . . . . . Gwinnett
17-22 . . . . at Jacksonville
24-29 . . . . . . Charlotte
30 . . . . Nashville

JUNE	
1-5 . . . . Nashville
7-12 . . . . . at Memphis
14-19 . . . . . . Louisville
21-26 . . . . at Jacksonville
28-30 . . . . . at Charlotte

JULY	
1-3 . . . . at Charlotte
4-10 . . . . Memphis
12-17 . . . . . . at Gwinnett
22-24 . . . . Norfolk
26-31 . . . . . Lehigh Valley

AUGUST	
2-7 . . . . . . at Worcester
9-14 . . . . . Jacksonville
16-21 . . . . . . at Norfolk
23-28 . . . . . . Nashville
30-31 . . . . . at Charlotte

SEPTEMBER	
1-4 . . . . at Charlotte
5-11 . . . . . Scranton/WB
13-18 . . . . . at Gwinnett
20-25 . . . . Norfolk
26-28 . . . . . at Charlotte

GWINNETT STRIPERS

APRIL	
5-10 . . . . . . at Memphis
12-17 . . . . . . Nashville
19-24 . . . . at Jacksonville
26-30 . . . . Norfolk

MAY	
1 . . . . Norfolk
3-8 . . . . Charlotte
10-15 . . . . . at Durham
17-22 . . . . . . Memphis
24-29 . . . . . at Norfolk
30 . . . . Louisville

JUNE	
1-5 . . . . Louisville
7-12 . . . . at Jacksonville
14-19 . . . . . Indianapolis
22-26 . . . . . at Nashville
28-30 . . . . . . at Norfolk

JULY	
1-3 . . . . at Norfolk
4-10 . . . . Charlotte
12-17 . . . . Durham
22-24 . . . . . at Memphis
26-31 . . . . . Jacksonville

AUGUST	
2-7 . . . . at Charlotte
10-14 . . . . . at Nashville
16-21 . . . . . . Memphis
23-28 . . . at Lehigh Valley
30-31 . . . . . Jacksonville

SEPTEMBER	
1-4 . . . . Jacksonville
6-11 . . . . at Buffalo
13-18 . . . . Durham
20-25 . . . . . at Memphis
26-28 . . . . . . Louisville

INDIANAPOLIS INDIANS

APRIL	
5-10 . . . . Omaha
12-17 . . . . . . at St. Paul
19-24 . . . . . . at Columbus
26-30 . . . . . . at Iowa

MAY	
1 . . . . at Iowa
3-8 . . . . Louisville
10-15 . . . . . at Charlotte
17-22 . . . . Toledo
24-29 . . . . . at St. Paul
31 . . . . at Omaha

JUNE	
1-5 . . . . . . at Omaha
7-12 . . . . . . Columbus
14-19 . . . . . at Gwinnett
21-26 . . . . . . Memphis
29-30 . . . . . at Nashville

JULY	
1-3 . . . . at Nashville
4-10 . . . . Iowa
12-17 . . . . at Columbus
22-24 . . . . . . St. Paul
26-31 . . . . . . at Toledo

AUGUST	
2-7 . . . . Louisville
9-14 . . . . . at Memphis
16-21 . . . . Iowa
23-28 . . . . . Rochester
30-31 . . . . at Louisville

SEPTEMBER	
1-4 . . . . . . at Louisville
6-11 . . . . . . at Omaha
13-18 . . . . Toledo
19-24 . . . . . . St. Paul
26-28 . . . . at Columbus

IOWA CUBS

APRIL	
5-10	at Buffalo
12-17	Toledo
19-24	at Louisville
26-30	Indianapolis

MAY	
1	Indianapolis
3-8	at St. Paul
10-15	Omaha
17-22	Columbus
24-29	at Memphis
31	St. Paul

JUNE	
1-5	St. Paul
7-12	at Toledo
14-19	Omaha
21-26	at Louisville
28-30	Columbus

JULY	
1-3	Columbus
4-10	at Indianapolis
12-17	Buffalo
22-25	at Omaha
27-31	at St. Paul

AUGUST	
2-7	Toledo
9-14	Louisville
16-21	at Indianapolis
23-28	St. Paul
30-31	at Columbus

SEPTEMBER	
1-4	at Columbus
6-11	at Jacksonville
13-18	Memphis
20-24	at Omaha
26-28	Toledo

JACKSONVILLE JUMBO SHRIMP

APRIL	
5-10	Worcester
12-17	at Durham
19-24	Gwinnett
26-30	at Charlotte

MAY	
1	at Charlotte
3-8	at Memphis
10-15	Nashville
17-22	Durham
24-29	at Scranton/WB
31	at Norfolk

JUNE	
1-5	at Norfolk
7-12	Gwinnett
14-19	at Charlotte
21-26	Durham
28-30	at Memphis

JULY	
1-3	at Memphis
4-10	Norfolk
12-17	at Syracuse
22-24	Charlotte
26-31	at Gwinnett

AUGUST	
2-7	Memphis
9-14	at Durham
16-21	Nashville
23-28	Norfolk
30-31	at Gwinnett

SEPTEMBER	
1-4	at Gwinnett
6-11	Iowa
14-18	at Nashville
20-25	Charlotte
26-28	at Norfolk

LEHIGH VALLEY IRONPIGS

APRIL	
5-10	Columbus
12-17	at Worcester
19-24	Rochester
26-30	at Scranton/WB

MAY	
1	at Scranton/WB
3-8	at Syracuse
10-15	Buffalo
17-22	at Rochester
24-29	Worcester
31	at Scranton/WB

JUNE	
1-5	at Scranton/WB
7-12	at Omaha
14-19	Buffalo
21-26	Norfolk
28-30	at Syracuse

JULY	
1-3	at Syracuse
4-10	Rochester
12-17	at Charlotte
22-24	Scranton/WB
26-31	at Durham

AUGUST	
2-7	Syracuse
9-14	Charlotte
16-21	at Buffalo
23-28	Gwinnett
30-31	at Norfolk

SEPTEMBER	
1-4	at Norfolk
5-11	Worcester
13-18	at Rochester
20-25	Scranton/WB
26-28	at Syracuse

LOUISVILLE BATS

APRIL	
5-10	St. Paul
12-17	at Omaha
19-24	Iowa
26-30	at Columbus

MAY	
1	at Columbus
3-8	at Indianapolis
10-15	Toledo
17-22	at Nashville
24-29	Omaha
30	at Gwinnett

JUNE	
1-5	at Gwinnett
7-12	Charlotte
14-19	at Durham
21-26	Iowa
28-30	at Toledo

JULY	
1-3	at Toledo
4-10	St. Paul
12-17	at Scranton/WB
22-24	Nashville
26-31	Columbus

AUGUST	
2-7	at Indianapolis
9-14	at Iowa
16-21	Omaha
23-28	at Toledo
30-31	Indianapolis

SEPTEMBER	
1-4	Indianapolis
6-11	Columbus
14-18	at St. Paul
19-24	Nashville
26-28	at Gwinnett

MEMPHIS REDBIRDS

APRIL	
5-10	Gwinnett
12-17	at Charlotte
19-24	Omaha
26-30	at Durham

MAY	
1	at Durham
3-8	Jacksonville
10-15	at Norfolk
17-22	at Gwinnett
24-29	Iowa
31	at Charlotte

JUNE	
1-5	at Charlotte
7-12	Durham
14-19	Nashville
21-26	at Indianapolis
28-30	Jacksonville

JULY	
1-3	Jacksonville
4-10	at Durham
13-17	at Nashville
22-24	Gwinnett
26-31	Norfolk

AUGUST	
2-7	at Jacksonville
9-14	Indianapolis
16-21	at Gwinnett
23-28	Charlotte
31	at Nashville

SEPTEMBER	
1-4	at Nashville
6-11	Norfolk
13-18	at Iowa
20-25	Gwinnett
26-28	at Nashville

NASHVILLE SOUNDS

APRIL	
5-10	Durham
12-17	at Gwinnett
19-24	Charlotte
26-30	at St. Paul

MAY	
1	at St. Paul
3-8	Norfolk
10-15	at Jacksonville
17-22	Louisville
24-29	at Toledo
30	at Durham

JUNE	
1-5	at Durham
8-12	Norfolk
14-19	at Memphis
22-26	Gwinnett
29-30	Indianapolis

JULY	
1-3	Indianapolis
4-10	at Columbus
13-17	Memphis
22-24	at Louisville
27-31	Charlotte

AUGUST	
2-7	at Norfolk
10-14	Gwinnett
16-21	at Jacksonville
23-28	at Durham
31	Memphis

SEPTEMBER	
1-4	Memphis
6-11	at Charlotte
14-18	Jacksonville
19-24	at Louisville
26-28	Memphis

NORFOLK TIDES

APRIL	
5-10 . . . . Charlotte	
12-17 . . . . at Scranton/WB	
19-24 . . . . . . Durham	
26-30 . . . . . at Gwinnett	

MAY	
1 . . . . at Gwinnett	
3-8 . . . . at Nashville	
10-15 . . . . . . Memphis	
17-22 . . . . at Charlotte	
24-29 . . . . . Gwinnett	
31 . . . . . . Jacksonville	

JUNE	
1-5 . . . . Jacksonville	
8-12 . . . . at Nashville	
14-19 . . . . . . Syracuse	
21-26 . . . . at Lehigh Valley	
28-30 . . . . . Gwinnett	

JULY	
1-3 . . . . Gwinnett	
4-10 . . . . . at Jacksonville	
12-17 . . . . Worcester	
22-24 . . . . . . at Durham	
26-31 . . . . . at Memphis	

AUGUST	
2-7 . . . . .Nashville	
9-14 . . . . . . at Rochester	
16-21 . . . . Durham	
23-28 . . . . at Jacksonville	
30-31 . . . . . Lehigh Valley	

SEPTEMBER	
1-4 . . . . Lehigh Valley	
6-11 . . . . . at Memphis	
13-18 . . . . . . Charlotte	
20-25 . . . . . . at Durham	
26-28 . . . . . Jacksonville	

OMAHA STORM CHASERS

APRIL	
5-10 . . . . . at Indianapolis	
12-17 . . . . . . Louisville	
19-24 . . . . . at Memphis	
26-30 . . . . Toledo	

MAY	
1 . . . . Toledo	
3-8 . . . . Columbus	
10-15 . . . . . . at Iowa	
17-22 . . . . . . St. Paul	
24-29 . . . . . at Louisville	
31 . . . . Indianapolis	

JUNE	
1-5 . . . . .Indianapolis	
7-12 . . . . . . Lehigh Valley	
14-19 . . . . at Iowa	
21-26 . . . . Columbus	
29-29 . . . . . . at St. Paul	

JULY	
1-3 . . . . at St. Paul	
4-10 . . . . Toledo	
12-17 . . . . . at Rochester	
22-25 . . . . Iowa	
26-31 . . . . . . at Syracuse	

AUGUST	
2-7 . . . . St. Paul	
9-14 . . . . at Toledo	
16-21 . . . . . at Louisville	
23-28 . . . . . Scranton/WB	
31 . . . . at St. Paul	

SEPTEMBER	
1-4 . . . . at St. Paul	
6-11 . . . . . . Indianapolis	
13-18 . . . . . at Columbus	
20-24 . . . . Iowa	
26-28 . . . . at St. Paul	

ROCHESTER RED WINGS

APRIL	
5-10 . . . . .at Toledo	
12-17 . . . . Buffalo	
19-24 . . . . at Lehigh Valley	
26-30 . . . . Syracuse	

MAY	
1 . . . . .Syracuse	
3-8 . . . . Scranton/WB	
10-15 . . . . . at Worcester	
17-22 . . . . . Lehigh Valley	
24-29 . . . . . . at Syracuse	
30 . . . . Buffalo	

JUNE	
1-5 . . . . Buffalo	
8-12 . . . . at St. Paul	
14-19 . . . . at Scranton/WB	
21-26 . . . . Syracuse	
28-30 . . . . . . Worcester	

JULY	
1-3 . . . . . . Worcester	
4-10 . . . . . at Lehigh Valley	
12-17 . . . . Omaha	
22-24 . . . . at Buffalo	
26-31 . . . . . Scranton/WB	

AUGUST	
2-7 . . . . at Columbus	
9-14 . . . . Norfolk	
16-21 . . . . . at Worcester	
23-28 . . . . at Indianapolis	
30-31 . . . . Toledo	

SEPTEMBER	
1-4 . . . . Toledo	
6-11 . . . . . . at Syracuse	
13-18 . . . . . Lehigh Valley	
19-24 . . . . . . at Buffalo	
26-28 . . . . . . Worcester	

SCRANTON/WILKES-BARRE RAILRIDERS

APRIL	
5-10 . . . . . . at Syracuse	
12-17 . . . . Norfolk	
19-24 . . . . . . at Buffalo	
26-30 . . . . Lehigh Valley	

MAY	
1 . . . . Lehigh Valley	
3-8 . . . . . . at Rochester	
10-15 . . . . . . Syracuse	
17-22 . . . . at Worcester	
24-29 . . . . . Jacksonville	
31 . . . . . . Lehigh Valley	

JUNE	
1-5 . . . . . . Lehigh Valley	
7-12 . . . . at Syracuse	
14-19 . . . . . . Rochester	
21-26 . . . . . . at Toledo	
28-30 . . . . Buffalo	

JULY	
1-3 . . . . Buffalo	
4-10 . . . . . at Worcester	
12-17 . . . . . Louisville	
22-24 . . . at Lehigh Valley	
26-31 . . . . . at Rochester	

AUGUST	
2-7 . . . . Buffalo	
9-14 . . . . . . Worcester	
17-21 . . . . . at St. Paul	
23-28 . . . . . . at Omaha	
30-31 . . . . . . Syracuse	

SEPTEMBER	
1-4 . . . . Syracuse	
5-11 . . . . . . at Durham	
13-18 . . . . . Worcester	
20-25 . . . at Lehigh Valley	
26-28 . . . . Buffalo	

ST. PAUL SAINTS

APRIL	
5-10 . . . . . . at Louisville	
12-17 . . . . . Indianapolis	
19-24 . . . . . at Toledo	
26-30 . . . . . Nashville	

MAY	
1 . . . . .Nashville	
3-8 . . . . Iowa	
10-15 . . . . . at Columbus	
17-22 . . . . . . at Omaha	
24-29 . . . . . Indianapolis	
31 . . . . at Iowa	

JUNE	
1-5 . . . . .at Iowa	
8-12 . . . . Rochester	
14-19 . . . . . at Columbus	
21-26 . . . . . . at Buffalo	
29-29 . . . . Omaha	

JULY	
1-3 . . . . .Omaha	
4-10 . . . . . . at Louisville	
13-17 . . . . Toledo	
22-24 . . .at Indianapolis	
27-31 . . . . Iowa	

AUGUST	
2-7 . . . . at Omaha	
10-14 . . . . . . Columbus	
17-21 . . . . . Scranton/WB	
23-28 . . . . at Iowa	
31 . . . . Omaha	

SEPTEMBER	
1-4 . . . . .Omaha	
6-11 . . . . at Toledo	
14-18 . . . . . . Louisville	
19-24 . . .at Indianapolis	
26-28 . . . . Omaha	

SYRACUSE METS

APRIL	
5-10 . . . . . . Scranton/WB	
12-17 . . . . at Columbus	
19-24 . . . . Worcester	
26-30 . . . . . at Rochester	

MAY	
1 . . . . at Rochester	
3-8 . . . . . . .Lehigh Valley	
10-15 . . . at Scranton/WB	
17-22 . . . . . . at Buffalo	
24-29 . . . . . . Rochester	
31 . . . . at Worcester	

JUNE	
1-5 . . . . at Worcester	
7-12 . . . . . . Scranton/WB	
14-19 . . . . . . at Norfolk	
21-26 . . . . . at Rochester	
28-30 . . . . . Lehigh Valley	

JULY	
1-3 . . . . Lehigh Valley	
4-10 . . . . at Buffalo	
12-17 . . . . . Jacksonville	
22-24 . . . . . at Worcester	
26-31 . . . . Omaha	

AUGUST	
2-7 . . . . . at Lehigh Valley	
9-14 . . . . Buffalo	
16-21 . . . . . . at Charlotte	
23-28 . . . . Worcester	
30-31 . . . . at Scranton/WB	

SEPTEMBER	
1-4 . . . . . at Scranton/WB	
6-11 . . . . Rochester	
13-18 . . . . Buffalo	
20-25 . . . . . at Worcester	
26-28 . . . . . Lehigh Valley	

TOLEDO MUD HENS

APRIL
5-10 . . . . Rochester
12-17 . . . . at Iowa
19-24 . . . . St. Paul
26-30 . . . . at Omaha

MAY
1 . . . . at Omaha
3-8 . . . . Worcester
10-15 . . . . . . at Louisville
17-22 . . . . . at Indianapolis
24-29 . . . . Nashville
30 . . . . at Columbus

JUNE
1-5 . . . . at Columbus
7-12 . . . . Iowa
14-19 . . . . . . at Worcester
21-26 . . . . . . Scranton/WB
28-30 . . . . Louisville

JULY
1-3 . . . . Louisville
4-10 . . . . at Omaha
13-17 . . . . at St. Paul
22-24 . . . . Columbus
26-31 . . . . . . Indianapolis

AUGUST
2-7 . . . . at Iowa
9-14 . . . . Omaha
16-21 . . . . . . at Columbus
23-28 . . . . Louisville
30-31 . . . . . . at Rochester

SEPTEMBER
1-4 . . . . at Rochester
6-11 . . . . St. Paul
13-18 . . . . at Indianapolis
20-25 . . . . Columbus
26-28 . . . . at Iowa

WORCESTER RED SOX

APRIL
5-10 . . . . . at Jacksonville
12-17 . . . . . Lehigh Valley
19-24 . . . . . . at Syracuse
26-30 . . . . Buffalo

MAY
1 . . . . Buffalo
3-8 . . . . at Toledo
10-15 . . . . Rochester
17-22 . . . . . Scranton/WB
24-29 . . . . at Lehigh Valley
31 . . . . Syracuse

JUNE
1-5 . . . . Syracuse
7-12 . . . . at Buffalo
14-19 . . . . Toledo
21-26 . . . . Charlotte
28-30 . . . . . . at Rochester

JULY
1-3 . . . . at Rochester
4-10 . . . . . . Scranton/WB
12-17 . . . . at Norfolk
22-24 . . . . Syracuse
26-31 . . . . at Buffalo

AUGUST
2-7 . . . . Durham
9-14 . . . . at Scranton/WB
16-21 . . . . Rochester
23-28 . . . . . . at Syracuse
30-31 . . . . Buffalo

SEPTEMBER
1-4 . . . . Buffalo
5-11 . . . . at Lehigh Valley
13-18 . . . at Scranton/WB
20-25 . . . . Syracuse
26-28 . . . . . . at Rochester

DOUBLE-A

DOUBLE-A SOUTH

BILOXI SHUCKERS

APRIL	
8-10 . . . . . . at Pensacola	
12-17 . . . . Mississippi	
19-24 . . . . at Birmingham	
26-30 . . . . . . Pensacola	

MAY	
1 . . . . Pensacola	
3-8 . . . . . . at Montgomery	
10-15 . . . . . . Birmingham	
17-22 . . . . . at Mississippi	
24-29 . . . . . Montgomery	
31 . . . . at Pensacola	

JUNE	
1-5 . . . . at Pensacola	
7-12 . . . . Tennessee	
14-19 . . . at Chattanooga	
21-26 . . . . Pensacola	
28-30 . . . . . Mississippi	

JULY	
1-3 . . . . .Mississippi	
4-10 . . . . . at Montgomery	
12-17 . . . . . at Tennessee	
22-24 . . . . Pensacola	
26-31 . . . . . Montgomery	

AUGUST	
2-7 . . . . at Mississippi	
9-14 . . . . . . at Rocket City	
16-21 . . . . at Montgomery	
23-28 . . . . . Chattanooga	
30-31 . . . . at Rocket City	

SEPTEMBER	
1-4 . . . . . . at Rocket City	
6-11 . . . . Mississippi	
13-18 . . . . . at Pensacola	

BIRMINGHAM BARONS

APRIL	
8-10 . . . . Rocket City	
12-17 . . . at Chattanooga	
19-24 . . . . Biloxi	
26-30 . . . . at Rocket City	

MAY	
1 . . . . .at Rocket City	
3-8 . . . . Tennessee	
10-15 . . . . . . at Biloxi	
17-22 . . . . . Rocket City	
24-29 . . . at Chattanooga	
31 . . . . at Tennessee	

JUNE	
1-5 . . . . at Tennessee	
7-12 . . . . Pensacola	
14-19 . . . . . at Mississippi	
21-26 . . . . . Rocket City	
28-30 . . . . at Chattanooga	

JULY	
1-3 . . . . . at Chattanooga	
4-10 . . . . Tennessee	
12-17 . . . . . Montgomery	
22-24 . . . . at Rocket City	
26-31 . . . . . at Tennessee	

AUGUST	
2-7 . . . . Chattanooga	
9-14 . . . . . . at Pensacola	
16-21 . . . . . . Tennessee	
23-28 . . . . . . Mississippi	
30-31 . . . at Montgomery	

SEPTEMBER	
1-4 . . . . . at Montgomery	
6-11 . . . . . . Chattanooga	
13-18 . . . . at Rocket City	

CHATTANOOGA LOOKOUTS

APRIL	
8-10 . . . . at Tennessee	
12-17 . . . . . Birmingham	
19-24 . . . .at Mississippi	
26-30 . . . . . . Tennessee	

MAY	
1 . . . . .Tennessee	
3-8 . . . . . at Rocket City	
10-15 . . . . . Mississippi	
17-22 . . . . at Tennessee	
24-29 . . . . . Birmingham	
31 . . . . Rocket City	

JUNE	
1-5 . . . . . . Rocket City	
7-12 . . . . at Montgomery	
14-19 . . . . Biloxi	
21-26 . . . . . at Mississippi	
28-30 . . . . . Birmingham	

JULY	
1-3 . . . . Birmingham	
4-10 . . . . at Rocket City	
12-17 . . . . . at Pensacola	
22-24 . . . . . . Tennessee	
26-31 . . . . . . Rocket City	

AUGUST	
2-7 . . . . . .at Birmingham	
9-14 . . . . . . Montgomery	
16-21 . . . . at Rocket City	
23-28 . . . . at Biloxi	
30-31 . . . . . . Pensacola	

SEPTEMBER	
1-4 . . . . Pensacola	
6-11 . . . . at Birmingham	
13-18 . . . . . . Tennessee	

MISSISSIPPI BRAVES

APRIL	
8-10 . . . . . .Montgomery	
12-17 . . . . at Biloxi	
19-24 . . . . . Chattanooga	
26-30 . . . at Montgomery	

MAY	
1 . . . . . . at Montgomery	
3-8 . . . . Pensacola	
10-15 . . . at Chattanooga	
17-22 . . . . Biloxi	
24-29 . . . . . at Pensacola	
30 . . . . . . Montgomery	

JUNE	
1-5 . . . . . .Montgomery	
7-12 . . . . . at Rocket City	
14-19 . . . . . Birmingham	
21-26 . . . at Montgomery	
28-30 . . . . . . at Biloxi	

JULY	
1-3 . . . . at Biloxi	
4-10 . . . . Pensacola	
12-17 . . . . . Rocket City	
22-24 . . . at Montgomery	
26-31 . . . . . at Pensacola	

AUGUST	
2-7 . . . . Biloxi	
9-14 . . . . . at Tennessee	
16-21 . . . . . . Pensacola	
23-28 . . . . at Birmingham	
30-31 . . . . . . Tennessee	

SEPTEMBER	
1-4 . . . . .Tennessee	
6-11 . . . . at Biloxi	
13-18 . . . . .Montgomery	

MONTGOMERY BISCUITS

APRIL	
8-10 . . . . . .at Mississippi	
12-17 . . . . . . Tennessee	
19-24 . . . . . at Pensacola	
26-30 . . . . . . Mississippi	

MAY	
1 . . . . .Mississippi	
3-8 . . . . Biloxi	
10-15 . . . . at Tennessee	
17-22 . . . . . . Pensacola	
24-29 . . . . . . at Biloxi	
30 . . . . . . .at Mississippi	

JUNE	
1-5 . . . . . .at Mississippi	
7-12 . . . . . Chattanooga	
14-19 . . . . at Rocket City	
21-26 . . . . . . Mississippi	
28-30 . . . . . at Pensacola	

JULY	
1-3 . . . . at Pensacola	
4-10 . . . . Biloxi	
12-17 . . . at Birmingham	
22-24 . . . . . . Mississippi	
26-31 . . . . at Biloxi	

AUGUST	
2-7 . . . . Pensacola	
9-14 . . . . at Chattanooga	
16-21 . . . . Biloxi	
23-28 . . . . . at Pensacola	
30-31 . . . . . Birmingham	

SEPTEMBER	
1-4 . . . . Birmingham	
6-11 . . . . Rocket City	
13-18 . . . . .at Mississippi	

PENSACOLA BLUE WAHOOS

APRIL	
8-10 . . . . Biloxi
12-17 . . . . at Rocket City
19-24 . . . . . Montgomery
26-30 . . . . at Biloxi

MAY	
1 . . . . at Biloxi
3-8 . . . . at Mississippi
10-15 . . . . . Rocket City
17-22 . . . . at Montgomery
24-29 . . . . . . Mississippi
31 . . . . Biloxi

JUNE	
1-5 . . . . Biloxi
7-12 . . . . at Birmingham
14-19 . . . . . Tennessee
21-26 . . . . at Biloxi
28-30 . . . . . Montgomery

JULY	
1-3 . . . . Montgomery
4-10 . . . . . at Mississippi
12-17 . . . . . Chattanooga
22-24 . . . . at Biloxi
26-31 . . . . . Mississippi

AUGUST	
2-7 . . . . . at Montgomery
9-14 . . . . . . Birmingham
16-21 . . . . at Mississippi
23-28 . . . . . Montgomery
30-31 . . . . at Chattanooga

SEPTEMBER	
1-4 . . . . . at Chattanooga
6-11 . . . . . at Tennessee
13-18 . . . . Biloxi

ROCKET CITY TRASH PANDAS

APRIL	
8-10 . . . . . at Birmingham
12-17 . . . . Pensacola
19-24 . . . . . at Tennessee
26-30 . . . . . Birmingham

MAY	
1 . . . . Birmingham
3-8 . . . . Chattanooga
10-15 . . . . . at Pensacola
17-22 . . . . at Birmingham
24-29 . . . . . . Tennessee
31 . . . . . at Chattanooga

JUNE	
1-5 . . . . . at Chattanooga
7-12 . . . . Mississippi
14-19 . . . . Montgomery
21-26 . . . . at Birmingham
28-30 . . . . . at Tennessee

JULY	
1-3 . . . . at Tennessee
4-10 . . . . . Chattanooga
12-17 . . . . . at Mississippi
22-24 . . . . Birmingham
26-31 . . . . at Chattanooga

AUGUST	
2-7 . . . . Tennessee
9-14 . . . . at Biloxi
16-21 . . . . . Chattanooga
23-28 . . . . at Tennessee
30-31 . . . . Biloxi

SEPTEMBER	
1-4 . . . . Biloxi
6-11 . . . . . at Montgomery
13-18 . . . . . Birmingham

TENNESSEE SMOKIES

APRIL	
8-10 . . . . . . Chattanooga
12-17 . . . . at Montgomery
19-24 . . . . . . Rocket City
26-30 . . . . at Chattanooga

MAY	
1 . . . . at Chattanooga
3-8 . . . . . at Birmingham
10-15 . . . . . Montgomery
17-22 . . . . . Chattanooga
24-29 . . . . at Rocket City
31 . . . . Birmingham

JUNE	
1-5 . . . . Birmingham
7-12 . . . . at Biloxi
14-19 . . . . at Pensacola
21-26 . . . . . . Chattanooga
28-30 . . . . Rocket City

JULY	
1-3 . . . . Rocket City
4-10 . . . . at Birmingham
12-17 . . . . Biloxi
22-24 . . . . at Chattanooga
26-31 . . . . . Birmingham

AUGUST	
2-7 . . . . at Rocket City
9-14 . . . . Mississippi
16-21 . . . . at Birmingham
23-28 . . . . . . Rocket City
30-31 . . . . . at Mississippi

SEPTEMBER	
1-4 . . . . at Mississippi
6-11 . . . . Pensacola
13-18 . . . at Chattanooga

DOUBLE-A CENTRAL

AMARILLO SOD POODLES

APRIL	
8-10 . . . . Midland
13-16 . . . . at Tulsa
19-24 . . . . . San Antonio
26-30 . . . . at NW Arkansas

MAY	
1 . . . . . . at NW Arkansas
3-8 . . . . Midland
10-15 . . . . at Springfield
17-22 . . . . Tulsa
24-29 . . . . . . at Arkansas
31 . . . . Midland

JUNE	
1-5 . . . . Midland
7-12 . . . . Frisco
14-19 . . . . at San Antonio
21-26 . . . at Corpus Christi
28-30 . . . . . NW Arkansas

JULY	
1-3 . . . . NW Arkansas
4-10 . . . . at Wichita
12-17 . . . . . San Antonio
22-24 . . . . . . at Midland
26-31 . . . . . Corpus Christi

AUGUST	
2-7 . . . . at Frisco
9-14 . . . . Springfield
16-21 . . . . . . at Midland
23-28 . . at Corpus Christi
30-31 . . . . Frisco

SEPTEMBER	
1-4 . . . . Frisco
6-11 . . . . Arkansas
13-18 . . . . at San Antonio

ARKANSAS TRAVELERS

APRIL	
8-10 . . . . at Frisco
11-17 . . . . . . Springfield
19-24 . . . at Corpus Christi
26-30 . . . . Wichita

MAY	
1 . . . . Wichita
3-8 . . . . at Frisco
10-15 . . . . . at San Antonio
17-22 . . . . . NW Arkansas
24-29 . . . . Amarillo
31 . . . . . . at Springfield

JUNE	
1-5 . . . . at Springfield
7-12 . . . . Wichita
15-19 . . . . at NW Arkansas
21-26 . . . . Frisco
29-30 . . . . at Tulsa

JULY	
1-3 . . . . at Tulsa
4-10 . . . . Springfield
12-17 . . . . at Wichita
23-24 . . . . Frisco
27-31 . . . . at Tulsa

AUGUST	
2-7 . . . . Midland
9-14 . . . . . . NW Arkansas
16-21 . . . . at Springfield
23-28 . . . . Tulsa
30-31 . . . . . . at Midland

SEPTEMBER	
1-4 . . . . at Midland
6-11 . . . . at Amarillo
13-18 . . . . . Corpus Christi

CORPUS CHRISTI HOOKS

APRIL	
9-10 . . . . . . San Antonio
12-16 . . . . . . at Midland
19-24 . . . . Arkansas
27-30 . . . . at Tulsa

MAY	
1 . . . . at Tulsa
3-8 . . . . San Antonio
10-15 . . . . . . at Midland
17-22 . . . . at Frisco
24-29 . . . . Wichita

JUNE	
1-5 . . . . . at NW Arkansas
7-12 . . . . . . San Antonio
14-19 . . . . . at Springfield
21-26 . . . . Amarillo
28-30 . . . . at Frisco

JULY	
1-3 . . . . at Frisco
4-10 . . . . Midland
12-17 . . . . . NW Arkansas
22-24 . . . . at San Antonio
26-31 . . . . . . at Amarillo

AUGUST	
2-7 . . . . Springfield
9-14 . . . . at Wichita
16-21 . . . . Frisco
23-28 . . . . Amarillo
30-31 . . . . at San Antonio

SEPTEMBER	
1-4 . . . . . . at San Antonio
6-11 . . . . Midland
13-18 . . . . . . at Arkansas

FRISCO ROUGHRIDERS

APRIL
8-10 . . . . Arkansas
12-16 . . . . at San Antonio
19-24 . . . . . NW Arkansas
26-30 . . . . . . at Midland

MAY
1 . . . . at Midland
3-8 . . . . Arkansas
10-15 . . . . at Tulsa
17-22 . . . . Corpus Christi
24-29 . . . . . San Antonio
31 . . . . at Wichita

JUNE
1-5 . . . . at Wichita
7-12 . . . . . . at Amarillo
14-19 . . . . Midland
21-26 . . . . . at Arkansas
28-30 . . . . . Corpus Christi

JULY
1-3 . . . . . . Corpus Christi
4-10 . . . . at San Antonio
12-17 . . . . Midland
23-24 . . . . . . at Arkansas
26-31 . . . . . at Springfield

AUGUST
2-7 . . . . Amarillo
9-14 . . . . . . San Antonio
16-21 . . . at Corpus Christi
23-28 . . . . Wichita
30-31 . . . . . at Amarillo

SEPTEMBER
1-4 . . . . at Amarillo
6-11 . . . . Tulsa
14-18 . . . at NW Arkansas

MIDLAND ROCKHOUNDS

APRIL
8-10 . . . . at Amarillo
12-16 . . . . . Corpus Christi
19-24 . . . . . at Wichita
26-30 . . . . Frisco

MAY
1 . . . . Frisco
3-8 . . . . at Amarillo
10-15 . . . . Corpus Christi
17-22 . . . at San Antonio
24-29 . . . . . NW Arkansas
31 . . . . at Amarillo

JUNE
1-5 . . . . at Amarillo
7-12 . . . . . . Springfield
14-19 . . . . at Frisco
21-26 . . . . Tulsa
28-30 . . . . . San Antonio

JULY
1-3 . . . . San Antonio
4-10 . . . at Corpus Christi
12-17 . . . . at Frisco
22-24 . . . . Amarillo
26-31 . . . . . San Antonio

AUGUST
2-7 . . . . at Arkansas
10-14 . . . . . . at Tulsa
16-21 . . . . Amarillo
23-28 . . . at San Antonio
30-31 . . . . Arkansas

SEPTEMBER
1-4 . . . . Arkansas
6-11 . . . . at Corpus Christi
13-18 . . . . Wichita

NORTHWEST ARKANSAS NATURALS

APRIL
8-10 . . . . . . at Springfield
13-17 . . . . . Wichita
19-24 . . . . . . at Frisco
26-30 . . . . Amarillo

MAY
1 . . . . Amarillo
3-8 . . . . . . at Springfield
10-15 . . . . Wichita
17-22 . . . . . at Arkansas
24-29 . . . . . . at Midland

JUNE
1-5 . . . . . . Corpus Christi
8-12 . . . . at Tulsa
15-19 . . . . . . Arkansas
22-26 . . . . . . Springfield
28-30 . . . . . . at Amarillo

JULY
1-3 . . . . at Amarillo
4-10 . . . . Tulsa
12-17 . . . at Corpus Christi
23-24 . . . . . . Springfield
26-31 . . . . . at Wichita

AUGUST
3-7 . . . . Tulsa
9-14 . . . . . . at Arkansas
17-21 . . . . . San Antonio
24-28 . . . . . . Springfield
31 . . . . at Tulsa

SEPTEMBER
1-4 . . . . at Tulsa
6-11 . . . . at Wichita
14-18 . . . . Frisco

SAN ANTONIO MISSIONS

APRIL
9-10 . . . . at Corpus Christi
12-16 . . . . Frisco
19-24 . . . . . at Amarillo
26-30 . . . . . . Springfield

MAY
1 . . . . Springfield
3-8 . . . at Corpus Christi
10-15 . . . . Arkansas
17-22 . . . . Midland
24-29 . . . . . . at Frisco
31 . . . . Tulsa

JUNE
1-5 . . . . Tulsa
7-12 . . at Corpus Christi
14-19 . . . . . . Amarillo
21-26 . . . . . . at Wichita
28-30 . . . . . . at Midland

JULY
1-3 . . . . at Midland
4-10 . . . . Frisco
12-17 . . . . . at Amarillo
22-24 . . . . Corpus Christi
26-31 . . . . . . at Midland

AUGUST
2-7 . . . . Wichita
9-14 . . . . at Frisco
17-21 . . . at NW Arkansas
23-28 . . . . Midland
30-31 . . . . . Corpus Christi

SEPTEMBER
1-4 . . . . . . Corpus Christi
6-11 . . . . at Springfield
13-18 . . . . Amarillo

SPRINGFIELD CARDINALS

APRIL
8-10 . . . . . . NW Arkansas
11-17 . . . . at Arkansas
19-24 . . . . Tulsa
26-30 . . . at San Antonio

MAY
1 . . . . at San Antonio
3-8 . . . . . NW Arkansas
10-15 . . . . Amarillo
17-22 . . . . . . at Wichita
25-30 . . . . at Tulsa
31 . . . . Arkansas

JUNE
1-5 . . . . Arkansas
7-12 . . . . . . at Midland
14-19 . . . . Corpus Christi
22-26 . . . . at NW Arkansas
28-30 . . . . Wichita

JULY
1-3 . . . . Wichita
4-10 . . . . . . at Arkansas
12-17 . . . . Tulsa
23-24 . . . . at NW Arkansas
26-31 . . . . Frisco

AUGUST
2-7 . . . . . at Corpus Christi
9-14 . . . . . . at Amarillo
16-21 . . . . . . Arkansas
24-28 . . . at NW Arkansas
30-31 . . . . Wichita

SEPTEMBER
1-4 . . . . Wichita
6-11 . . . . . San Antonio
13-18 . . . . at Tulsa

TULSA DRILLERS

APRIL
8-10 . . . . at Wichita
13-16 . . . . . . Amarillo
19-24 . . . . . at Springfield
27-30 . . . . Corpus Christi

MAY
1 . . . . Corpus Christi
3-8 . . . . at Wichita
10-15 . . . . Frisco
17-22 . . . . . at Amarillo
25-30 . . . . . Springfield
31 . . . . . at San Antonio

JUNE
1-5 . . . . . at San Antonio
8-12 . . . . NW Arkansas
15-19 . . . . . . Wichita
21-26 . . . . . at Midland
29-30 . . . . . . Arkansas

JULY
1-3 . . . . Arkansas
4-10 . . . . at NW Arkansas
12-17 . . . . at Springfield
23-24 . . . . Wichita
27-31 . . . . Arkansas

AUGUST
3-7 . . . . at NW Arkansas
10-14 . . . . . . Midland
16-21 . . . . . at Wichita
23-28 . . . . at Arkansas
31 . . . . . . NW Arkansas

SEPTEMBER
1-4 . . . . . . NW Arkansas
6-11 . . . . . . at Frisco
13-18 . . . . . Springfield

WICHITA WIND SURGE

APRIL		JULY	
8-10	Tulsa	1-3	at Springfield
13-17	at NW Arkansas	4-10	Amarillo
19-24	Midland	12-17	Arkansas
26-30	at Arkansas	23-24	at Tulsa
		26-31	NW Arkansas

MAY		AUGUST	
1	at Arkansas	2-7	at San Antonio
3-8	Tulsa	9-14	Corpus Christi
10-15	at NW Arkansas	16-21	Tulsa
17-22	Springfield	23-28	at Frisco
24-29	at Corpus Christi	30-31	at Springfield
31	Frisco		

JUNE		SEPTEMBER	
1-5	Frisco	1-4	at Springfield
7-12	at Arkansas	6-11	NW Arkansas
15-19	at Tulsa	13-18	at Midland
21-26	San Antonio		
28-30	at Springfield		

DOUBLE-A NORTHEAST

AKRON RUBBERDUCKS

APRIL		JULY	
8-10	at Erie	1-3	at Erie
12-16	Reading	4-10	Altoona
19-24	at Bowie	12-17	at Bowie
26-30	Altoona	22-24	Erie
		26-31	Harrisburg

MAY		AUGUST	
1	Altoona	2-7	at Altoona
3-8	at Richmond	9-14	Bowie
10-15	Erie	16-21	at Erie
17-22	at Binghamton	23-28	Richmond
24-29	New Hampshire	30-31	at Altoona
31	Richmond		

JUNE		SEPTEMBER	
1-5	Richmond	1-4	at Altoona
7-12	at Somerset	6-11	at Harrisburg
14-19	at Hartford	13-18	Bowie
21-26	Harrisburg		
28-30	at Erie		

ALTOONA CURVE

APRIL		JULY	
8-10	Harrisburg	1-3	Harrisburg
12-17	at Richmond	4-10	at Akron
19-24	New Hampshire	12-17	Richmond
26-30	at Akron	22-24	at Harrisburg
		26-31	at Bowie

MAY		AUGUST	
1	at Akron	2-7	Akron
3-8	at Erie	9-14	at Binghamton
10-15	Somerset	16-21	Harrisburg
17-22	Richmond	23-28	at Bowie
24-29	at Harrisburg	30-31	Akron
31	Bowie		

JUNE		SEPTEMBER	
1-5	Bowie	1-4	Akron
7-12	at Reading	6-11	at Erie
14-19	Erie	13-18	Reading
21-26	at New Hampshire		
28-30	Harrisburg		

BINGHAMTON RUMBLE PONIES

APRIL		JULY	
8-10	at Hartford	1-3	at Hartford
12-17	Bowie	4-10	Portland
19-24	at Portland	12-17	at Erie
26-30	Erie	22-24	Hartford
		26-31	New Hampshire

MAY		AUGUST	
1	Erie	2-7	at Somerset
3-8	at Hartford	9-14	Altoona
10-15	at New Hampshire	16-21	at Richmond
17-22	Akron	23-28	at Reading
24-29	at Reading	30-31	Somerset
30	Somerset		

JUNE		SEPTEMBER	
1-5	Somerset	1-4	Somerset
7-12	New Hampshire	6-11	at Portland
14-19	at Bowie	13-18	Hartford
21-26	Reading		
28-30	at Hartford		

BOWIE BAYSOX

APRIL		JULY	
8-10	Richmond	1-3	Richmond
12-17	at Binghamton	4-10	at Somerset
19-24	Akron	12-17	Akron
26-30	at Richmond	22-24	at Richmond
		26-31	Altoona

MAY		AUGUST	
1	at Richmond	2-7	at Harrisburg
3-8	Harrisburg	9-14	at Akron
10-15	at Reading	16-21	Somerset
17-22	Hartford	23-28	Altoona
24-29	Erie	30-31	at Erie
31	at Altoona		

JUNE		SEPTEMBER	
1-5	at Altoona	1-4	at Erie
7-12	at Harrisburg	6-11	Richmond
14-19	Binghamton	13-18	at Akron
21-26	at Erie		
28-30	Richmond		

ERIE SEAWOLVES

APRIL		JULY	
8-10	Akron	1-3	Akron
12-17	at Somerset	4-10	at Harrisburg
19-24	Richmond	12-17	Binghamton
26-30	at Binghamton	22-24	at Akron
		26-31	Reading

MAY		AUGUST	
1	at Binghamton	2-7	at Portland
3-8	Altoona	9-14	at New Hampshire
10-15	at Akron	16-21	Akron
17-22	New Hampshire	23-28	at Harrisburg
24-29	at Bowie	30-31	Bowie
31	Harrisburg		

JUNE		SEPTEMBER	
1-5	Harrisburg	1-4	Bowie
7-12	at Richmond	6-11	Altoona
14-19	at Altoona	13-18	at Richmond
21-26	Bowie		
28-30	Akron		

HARRISBURG SENATORS

APRIL		JULY	
8-10	at Altoona	1-3	at Altoona
12-17	Portland	4-10	Erie
19-24	at Reading	12-17	at Hartford
26-30	Hartford	22-24	Altoona
		26-31	at Akron

MAY		AUGUST	
1	Hartford	2-7	Bowie
3-8	at Bowie	9-14	Reading
10-15	Richmond	16-21	at Altoona
17-22	at Portland	23-28	Erie
24-29	Altoona	30-31	at Richmond
31	at Erie		

JUNE		SEPTEMBER	
1-5	at Erie	1-4	at Richmond
7-12	Bowie	6-11	Akron
14-19	Richmond	13-18	at New Hampshire
21-26	at Akron		
28-30	at Altoona		

HARTFORD YARD GOATS

APRIL		JULY	
8-10	Binghamton	1-3	Binghamton
12-17	at New Hampshire	4-10	at New Hampshire
19-24	Somerset	12-17	Harrisburg
26-30	at Harrisburg	22-24	at Binghamton
		26-31	Portland

MAY		AUGUST	
1	at Harrisburg	2-7	at Reading
3-8	Binghamton	9-14	at Somerset
10-15	Portland	16-21	New Hampshire
17-22	at Bowie	23-28	at Portland
24-29	at Richmond	30-31	Reading
31	Reading		

JUNE		SEPTEMBER	
1-5	Reading	1-4	Reading
7-12	at Portland	6-11	Somerset
14-19	Akron	13-18	at Binghamton
21-26	at Somerset		
28-30	Binghamton		

NEW HAMPSHIRE FISHER CATS

APRIL		JULY	
8-10	at Portland	1-3	at Portland
12-17	Hartford	4-10	Hartford
19-24	at Altoona	12-17	at Reading
26-30	Reading	22-24	Portland
		26-31	at Binghamton

MAY		AUGUST	
1	Reading	2-7	Richmond
3-8	at Somerset	9-14	Erie
10-15	Binghamton	16-21	at Hartford
17-22	at Erie	23-28	at Somerset
24-29	at Akron	30-31	Portland
31	Portland		

JUNE		SEPTEMBER	
1-5	Portland	1-4	Portland
7-12	at Binghamton	6-11	at Reading
14-19	Somerset	13-18	Harrisburg
21-26	Altoona		
28-30	at Portland		

PORTLAND SEA DOGS

APRIL		JULY	
8-10	New Hampshire	1-3	New Hampshire
12-17	at Harrisburg	4-10	at Binghamton
19-24	Binghamton	12-17	Somerset
26-30	at Somerset	22-24	at New Hampshire
		26-31	at Hartford

MAY		AUGUST	
1	at Somerset	2-7	Erie
3-8	Reading	9-14	Richmond
10-15	at Hartford	16-21	at Reading
17-22	Harrisburg	23-28	Hartford
24-29	Somerset	30-31	at New Hampshire
31	at New Hampshire		

JUNE		SEPTEMBER	
1-5	at New Hampshire	1-4	at New Hampshire
7-12	Hartford	6-11	Binghamton
14-19	at Reading	13-18	at Somerset
21-26	at Richmond		
28-30	New Hampshire		

READING FIGHTIN PHILS

APRIL	
8-10	Somerset
12-16	at Akron
19-24	Harrisburg
26-30	at New Hampshire

MAY	
1	at New Hampshire
3-8	at Portland
10-15	Bowie
17-22	at Somerset
24-29	Binghamton
31	at Hartford

JUNE	
1-5	at Hartford
7-12	Altoona
14-19	Portland
21-26	at Binghamton
28-30	Somerset

JULY	
1-3	Somerset
4-10	at Richmond
12-17	New Hampshire
22-24	at Somerset
26-31	at Erie

AUGUST	
2-7	Hartford
9-14	at Harrisburg
16-21	Portland
23-28	Binghamton
30-31	at Hartford

SEPTEMBER	
1-4	at Hartford
6-11	New Hampshire
13-18	at Altoona

RICHMOND FLYING SQUIRRELS

APRIL	
8-10	at Bowie
12-17	Altoona
19-24	at Erie
26-30	Bowie

MAY	
1	Bowie
3-8	Akron
10-15	at Harrisburg
17-22	at Altoona
24-29	Hartford
31	at Akron

JUNE	
1-5	at Akron
7-12	Erie
14-19	at Harrisburg
21-26	Portland
28-30	at Bowie

JULY	
1-3	at Bowie
4-10	Reading
12-17	at Altoona
22-24	Bowie
26-31	Somerset

AUGUST	
2-7	at New Hampshire
9-14	at Portland
16-21	Binghamton
23-28	at Akron
30-31	Harrisburg

SEPTEMBER	
1-4	Harrisburg
6-11	at Bowie
13-18	Erie

SOMERSET PATRIOTS

APRIL	
8-10	at Reading
12-17	Erie
19-24	at Hartford
26-30	Portland

MAY	
1	Portland
3-8	New Hampshire
10-15	at Altoona
17-22	Reading
24-29	at Portland
30	at Binghamton

JUNE	
1-5	at Binghamton
7-12	Akron
14-19	at New Hampshire
21-26	Hartford
28-30	at Reading

JULY	
1-3	at Reading
4-10	Bowie
12-17	at Portland
22-24	Reading
26-31	at Richmond

AUGUST	
2-7	Binghamton
9-14	Hartford
16-21	at Bowie
23-28	New Hampshire
30-31	at Binghamton

SEPTEMBER	
1-4	at Binghamton
6-11	at Hartford
13-18	Portland

HIGH CLASS A

HIGH-A WEST

EUGENE EMERALDS

APRIL	
8-10	at Everett
12-17	Spokane
19-24	at Vancouver
26-30	at Tri-City

MAY	
1	at Tri-City
3-8	Hillsboro
10-15	Vancouver
17-22	at Spokane
24-29	Tri-City
31	at Everett

JUNE	
1-5	at Everett
7-12	Spokane
14-19	at Vancouver
21-26	Tri-City

28-30	Everett

JULY	
1-3	Everett
4-10	at Hillsboro
12-17	Spokane
22-24	at Everett
26-31	Hillsboro

AUGUST	
2-7	at Spokane
9-14	Vancouver
16-21	at Hillsboro
23-28	at Tri-City
30-31	Everett

SEPTEMBER	
1-4	Everett
6-11	at Vancouver

EVERETT AQUASOX

APRIL	
8-10	Eugene
12-17	at Hillsboro
19-24	Tri-City
26-30	Spokane

MAY	
1	Spokane
3-8	at Vancouver
10-15	at Tri-City
17-22	Hillsboro
24-29	at Spokane
31	Eugene

JUNE	
1-5	Eugene
7-12	at Hillsboro
14-19	Tri-City
21-26	at Spokane
28-30	at Eugene

JULY	
1-3	at Eugene
4-10	Vancouver
12-17	at Tri-City
22-24	Eugene
26-31	at Vancouver

AUGUST	
2-7	Hillsboro
9-14	at Tri-City
16-21	Vancouver
23-28	Spokane
30-31	at Eugene

SEPTEMBER	
1-4	at Eugene
6-11	Hillsboro

HILLSBORO HOPS

APRIL	
8-10	Tri-City
12-17	Everett
19-24	at Spokane
26-30	Vancouver

MAY	
1	Vancouver
3-8	at Eugene
10-15	Spokane
17-22	at Everett
24-29	Vancouver
31	at Tri-City

JUNE	
1-5	at Tri-City
7-12	Everett
14-19	at Spokane
21-26	Vancouver
28-30	at Tri-City

JULY	
1-3	at Tri-City
4-10	Eugene
12-17	at Vancouver
22-24	Tri-City
26-31	at Eugene

AUGUST	
2-7	at Everett
9-14	Spokane
16-21	Eugene
23-28	at Vancouver
30-31	Tri-City

SEPTEMBER	
1-4	Tri-City
6-11	at Everett

SPOKANE INDIANS

APRIL	
8-10	Vancouver
12-17	at Eugene
19-24	Hillsboro
26-30	at Everett

MAY	
1	at Everett
3-8	Tri-City
10-15	at Hillsboro
17-22	Eugene
24-29	Everett
31	at Vancouver

JUNE	
1-5	at Vancouver
7-12	at Eugene
14-19	Hillsboro
21-26	Everett
28-30	at Vancouver

JULY	
1-3	at Vancouver
4-10	Tri-City
12-17	at Eugene
22-24	Vancouver
26-31	at Tri-City

AUGUST	
2-7	Eugene
9-14	at Hillsboro
16-21	Tri-City
23-28	at Everett
30-31	Vancouver

SEPTEMBER	
1-4	Vancouver
6-11	at Tri-City

TRI-CITY DUST DEVILS

APRIL	
8-10	at Hillsboro
12-17	Vancouver
19-24	at Everett
26-30	Eugene

MAY	
1	Eugene
3-8	at Spokane
10-15	Everett
17-22	at Vancouver
24-29	at Eugene
31	Hillsboro

JUNE	
1-5	Hillsboro
7-12	Vancouver
14-19	at Everett
21-26	at Eugene
28-30	Hillsboro

JULY	
1-3	Hillsboro
4-10	at Spokane
12-17	Everett
22-24	at Hillsboro
26-31	Spokane

AUGUST	
2-7	at Vancouver
9-14	Everett
16-21	at Spokane
23-28	Eugene
30-31	at Hillsboro

SEPTEMBER	
1-4	at Hillsboro
6-11	Spokane

VANCOUVER CANADIANS

APRIL	
8-10	at Spokane
12-17	at Tri-City
19-24	Eugene
26-30	at Hillsboro

MAY	
1	at Hillsboro
3-8	Everett
10-15	at Eugene
17-22	Tri-City
24-29	at Hillsboro
31	Spokane

JUNE	
1-5	Spokane
7-12	at Tri-City
14-19	Eugene
21-26	at Hillsboro
28-30	Spokane

JULY	
1-3	Spokane
4-10	at Everett
12-17	Hillsboro
22-24	at Spokane
26-31	Everett

AUGUST	
2-7	Tri-City
9-14	at Eugene
16-21	at Everett
23-28	Hillsboro
30-31	at Spokane

SEPTEMBER	
1-4	at Spokane
6-11	Eugene

HIGH-A CENTRAL

BELOIT SKY CARP

APRIL		JULY	
8-10 . . . . . at Cedar Rapids		1-3 . . . . South Bend	
12-17 . . . . Wisconsin		4-10 . . . . at Peoria	
19-24 . . . . . at South Bend		12-17 . . . . . Cedar Rapids	
26-30 . . . . . Cedar Rapids		22-24 . . . . . . at Wisconsin	
		26-31 . . . . Quad Cities	

MAY		AUGUST	
1 . . . . Cedar Rapids		2-7 . . . . . at Cedar Rapids	
3-8 . . . . . . at Great Lakes		9-14 . . . . . West Michigan	
10-15 . . at West Michigan		16-21 . . . . at South Bend	
17-22 . . . . . . Peoria		23-28 . . . . Peoria	
24-29 . . . . Lansing		30-31 . . . . Quad Cities	
31 . . . . . . at Quad Cities			

JUNE		SEPTEMBER	
1-5 . . . . . . at Quad Cities		1-4 . . . . Quad Cities	
7-12 . . . . . . Wisconsin		6-11 . . . . . . at Wisconsin	
14-19 . . at Lake County			
21-26 . . . . . . at Lansing			
28-30 . . . . . South Bend			

CEDAR RAPIDS KERNELS

APRIL		JULY	
8-10 . . . . Beloit		1-3 . . . . . . at Wisconsin	
12-17 . . . . at Quad Cities		4-10 . . . . . . Quad Cities	
19-24 . . . . Peoria		12-17 . . . . . at Beloit	
26-30 . . . . at Beloit		22-24 . . . . Peoria	
		26-31 . . . . . at Wisconsin	

MAY		AUGUST	
1 . . . . at Beloit		2-7 . . . . Beloit	
3-8 . . . . Quad Cities		9-14 . . . . at Quad Cities	
10-15 . . . . . at Peoria		16-21 . . . . . Wisconsin	
17-22 . . . . . Lake County		23-28 . . . . at Lake County	
24-29 . . . . . Wisconsin		30-31 . . . . . . at Dayton	
31 . . . . at Lansing			

JUNE		SEPTEMBER	
1-5 . . . . at Lansing		1-4 . . . . at Dayton	
7-12 . . . . at South Bend		6-11 . . . . . . South Bend	
14-19 . . . . Dayton			
21-26 . . . . West Michigan			
28-30 . . . . . at Wisconsin			

DAYTON DRAGONS

APRIL		JULY	
8-10 . . . . . . Fort Wayne		1-3 . . . . . . at Great Lakes	
12-16 . . . . at Lake County		4-10 . . . . . West Michigan	
19-24 . . . West Michigan		12-17 . . . . at Lake County	
26-30 . . . . at Fort Wayne		22-24 . . . . . . Fort Wayne	
		26-31 . . . at West Michigan	

MAY		AUGUST	
1 . . . . .at Fort Wayne		2-7 . . . . Peoria	
3-8 . . . . Lake County		9-14 . . . . Lansing	
10-15 . . . . . at Lansing		16-21 . . . . at Fort Wayne	
17-22 . . . . . . Quad Cities		23-28 . . . . at Quad Cities	
24-29 . . . at West Michigan		30-31 . . . . . Cedar Rapids	
31 . . . . South Bend			

JUNE		SEPTEMBER	
1-5 . . . . South Bend		1-4 . . . . Cedar Rapids	
7-12 . . . . . . Great Lakes		6-11 . . . . at Lansing	
14-19 . . . at Cedar Rapids			
21-26 . . . . . Lake County			
28-30 . . . . at Great Lakes			

FORT WAYNE TINCAPS

APRIL		JULY	
8-10 . . . . at Dayton		1-3 . . . . at West Michigan	
12-17 . . . . . South Bend		4-10 . . . . . Lake County	
19-24 . . . . . . at Lansing		12-17 . . . . Lansing	
26-30 . . . . . . Dayton		22-24 . . . . . . at Dayton	
		26-31 . . . . at Peoria	

MAY		AUGUST	
1 . . . . .Dayton		2-7 . . . . South Bend	
3-8 . . . . . . at Wisconsin		9-14 . . . . at Lake County	
10-15 . . at South Bend		16-21 . . . . Dayton	
17-22 . . . . West Michigan		23-28 . . at Great Lakes	
24-29 . . . . . Quad Cities		30-31 . . . West Michigan	
31 . . . . . . at Great Lakes			

JUNE		SEPTEMBER	
1-5 . . . . . . at Great Lakes		1-4 . . . . . West Michigan	
7-12 . . . . . Lake County		6-11 . . . . at Lake County	
14-19 . . . . . . at Lansing			
21-26 . . . . . . Great Lakes			
28-30 . . . at West Michigan			

GREAT LAKES LOONS

APRIL		JULY	
8-10 . . . . . West Michigan		1-3 . . . . .Dayton	
12-17 . . . . at Peoria		4-10 . . . . at Lansing	
19-24 . . . . Lake County		12-17 . . . . at Quad Cities	
26-30 . . . at West Michigan		22-24 . . . . West Michigan	
		26-31 . . . . Lansing	

MAY		AUGUST	
1 . . . . . . at West Michigan		2-7 . . . . . .at Lake County	
3-8 . . . . Beloit		9-14 . . . . Peoria	
10-15 . . . . at Lake County		16-21 . . . . . . at Lansing	
17-22 . . . . Lansing		23-28 . . . . . . Fort Wayne	
24-29 . . . . at South Bend		30-31 . . . . . Lake County	
31 . . . . Fort Wayne			

JUNE		SEPTEMBER	
1-5 . . . . Fort Wayne		1-4 . . . . Lake County	
7-12 . . . . . . at Dayton		6-11 . . . at West Michigan	
14-19 . . . . Wisconsin			
21-26 . . . . . at Fort Wayne			
28-30 . . . . Dayton			

LAKE COUNTY CAPTAINS

APRIL		JULY	
8-10 . . . . .at Lansing		1-3 . . . . Lansing	
12-16 . . . . Dayton		4-10 . . . . . at Fort Wayne	
19-24 . . . . at Great Lakes		12-17 . . . . Dayton	
26-30 . . . . Lansing		22-24 . . . . . . at Lansing	
		26-31 . . . . at South Bend	

MAY		AUGUST	
1 . . . . Lansing		2-7 . . . . Great Lakes	
3-8 . . . . at Dayton		9-14 . . . . Fort Wayne	
10-15 . . . . . . Great Lakes		16-21 . . at West Michigan	
17-22 . . . at Cedar Rapids		23-28 . . . . . Cedar Rapids	
24-29 . . . . at Peoria		30-31 . . . . at Great Lakes	
31 . . . . . . West Michigan			

JUNE		SEPTEMBER	
1-5 . . . . . West Michigan		1-4 . . . . . . at Great Lakes	
7-12 . . . . . at Fort Wayne		6-11 . . . . Fort Wayne	
14-19 . . . . Beloit			
21-26 . . . . at Dayton			
28-30 . . . . Lansing			

LANSING LUGNUTS

APRIL		JULY	
8-10	Lake County	1-3	at Lake County
12-17	at West Michigan	4-10	Great Lakes
19-24	Fort Wayne	12-17	at Fort Wayne
26-30	^ at Lake County	22-24	Lake County
		26-31	at Great Lakes

MAY		AUGUST	
1	at Lake County	2-7	West Michigan
3-8	West Michigan	9-14	at Dayton
10-15	Dayton	16-21	Great Lakes
17-22	at Great Lakes	23-28	at Wisconsin
24-29	at Beloit	30-31	at South Bend
31	Cedar Rapids		

JUNE		SEPTEMBER	
1-5	Cedar Rapids	1-4	at South Bend
7-12	at West Michigan	6-11	Dayton
14-19	Fort Wayne		
21-26	Beloit		
28-30	at Lake County		

PEORIA CHIEFS

APRIL		JULY	
8-10	at Wisconsin	1-3	at Quad Cities
12-17	Great Lakes	4-10	Beloit
19-24	at Cedar Rapids	12-17	South Bend
26-30	Wisconsin	22-24	at Cedar Rapids
		26-31	Fort Wayne

MAY		AUGUST	
1	Wisconsin	2-7	at Dayton
3-8	at South Bend	9-14	at Great Lakes
10-15	Cedar Rapids	16-21	Quad Cities
17-22	at Beloit	23-28	at Beloit
24-29	Lake County	30-31	Wisconsin
31	at Wisconsin		

JUNE		SEPTEMBER	
1-5	at Wisconsin	1-4	Wisconsin
7-12	Quad Cities	6-11	at Quad Cities
14-19	West Michigan		
21-26	at South Bend		
28-30	at Quad Cities		

QUAD CITIES RIVER BANDITS

APRIL		JULY	
8-10	at South Bend	1-3	Peoria
12-17	Cedar Rapids	4-10	at Cedar Rapids
19-24	at Wisconsin	12-17	Great Lakes
26-30	South Bend	22-24	at South Bend
		26-31	at Beloit

MAY		AUGUST	
1	South Bend	2-7	Wisconsin
3-8	at Cedar Rapids	9-14	Cedar Rapids
10-15	Wisconsin	16-21	at Peoria
17-22	at Dayton	23-28	Dayton
24-29	at Fort Wayne	30-31	at Beloit
31	Beloit		

JUNE		SEPTEMBER	
1-5	Beloit	1-4	at Beloit
7-12	at Peoria	6-11	Peoria
14-19	South Bend		
21-26	at Wisconsin		
28-30	Peoria		

SOUTH BEND CUBS

APRIL		JULY	
8-10	Quad Cities	1-3	at Beloit
12-17	at Fort Wayne	4-10	Wisconsin
19-24	Beloit	12-17	at Peoria
26-30	at Quad Cities	22-24	Quad Cities
		26-31	Lake County

MAY		AUGUST	
1	at Quad Cities	2-7	at Fort Wayne
3-8	Peoria	9-14	at Wisconsin
10-15	Fort Wayne	16-21	Beloit
17-22	at Wisconsin	23-28	at West Michigan
24-29	Great Lakes	30-31	Lansing
31	at Dayton		

JUNE		SEPTEMBER	
1-5	at Dayton	1-4	Lansing
7-12	Cedar Rapids	6-11	at Cedar Rapids
14-19	at Quad Cities		
21-26	Peoria		
28-30	at Beloit		

WEST MICHIGAN WHITECAPS

APRIL		JULY	
8-10	at Great Lakes	1-3	Fort Wayne
12-17	Lansing	4-10	at Dayton
19-24	at Dayton	12-17	Wisconsin
26-30	Great Lakes	22-24	at Great Lakes
		26-31	Dayton

MAY		AUGUST	
1	Great Lakes	2-7	at Lansing
3-8	at Lansing	9-14	at Beloit
10-15	^ Beloit	16-21	Lake County
17-22	at Fort Wayne	23-28	South Bend
24-29	Dayton	30-31	at Fort Wayne
31	at Lake County		

JUNE		SEPTEMBER	
1-5	at Lake County	1-4	at Fort Wayne
7-12	Lansing	6-11	Great Lakes
14-19	at Peoria		
21-26	at Cedar Rapids		
28-30	Fort Wayne		

WISCONSIN TIMBER RATTLERS

APRIL		JULY	
8-10	Peoria	1-3	Cedar Rapids
12-17	at Beloit	4-10	at South Bend
19-24	Quad Cities	12-17	at West Michigan
26-30	at Peoria	22-24	Beloit
		26-31	Cedar Rapids

MAY		AUGUST	
1	at Peoria	2-7	at Quad Cities
3-8	Fort Wayne	9-14	South Bend
10-15	at Quad Cities	16-21	at Cedar Rapids
17-22	South Bend	23-28	Lansing
24-29	at Cedar Rapids	30-31	at Peoria
31	Peoria		

JUNE		SEPTEMBER	
1-5	Peoria	1-4	at Peoria
7-12	at Beloit	6-11	Beloit
14-19	at Great Lakes		
21-26	Quad Cities		
28-30	Cedar Rapids		

HIGH-A EAST

ASHEVILLE TOURISTS

APRIL		JULY	
8-10	at Bowling Green	1-3	Bowling Green
12-17	Greenville	4-10	at Rome
19-24	at Jersey Shore	12-17 . . .	Winston-Salem
26-30	Winston-Salem	22-24 . . .	at Bowling Green
		26-31	Aberdeen

MAY		AUGUST	
1	Winston-Salem	2-7	at Hickory
3-8	at Greensboro	9-14	Rome
10-15	Greenville	16-21	at Aberdeen
17-22 . .	at Winston-Salem	23-28 . .	at Winston-Salem
24-29	Greensboro	30-31	Bowling Green
31	Hickory		

JUNE		SEPTEMBER	
1-5	.Hickory	1-4	Bowling Green
7-12	at Greenville	6-11	at Greenville
14-19	Rome		
21-26	at Greensboro		
28-30	Bowling Green		

ABERDEEN IRONBIRDS

APRIL		JULY	
8-10	.at Jersey Shore	1-3	.Winston-Salem
12-17	Wilmington	4-10	at Brooklyn
19-24	at Greensboro	12-17 . . .	Jersey Shore
26-30	Jersey Shore	22-24	at Greenville
		26-31	at Asheville

MAY		AUGUST	
1	Jersey Shore	2-4	at Wilmington
3-8	Brooklyn	5-7	Wilmington
10-15 . .	at Hudson Valley	9-14 . . .	at Hudson Valley
17-22	Rome	16-21	Asheville
24-26	Wilmington	23-25	Wilmington
27-29	at Wilmington	26-28	at Wilmington
31	Hudson Valley	30-31	Hickory

JUNE		SEPTEMBER	
1-5	Hudson Valley	1-4	.Hickory
7-12	at Brooklyn	6-11	at Jersey Shore
14-19 . . .	at Jersey Shore		
21-23	at Wilmington		
24-26	Wilmington		
28-30	Winston-Salem		

BOWLING GREEN HOT RODS

APRIL		JULY	
8-10	.Asheville	1-3	at Asheville
12-16	at Hickory	4-10	.Hickory
19-24	Rome	12-17	at Rome
26-30	at Brooklyn	22-24	Asheville
		26-31	at Greenville

MAY		AUGUST	
1	at Brooklyn	2-7	Greensboro
3-8	at Wilmington	9-14 . . .	at Winston-Salem
10-15	Jersey Shore	16-21	Greenville
17-22	at Greensboro	23-28	Rome
24-29	Brooklyn	30-31	at Asheville
31	at Rome		

JUNE		SEPTEMBER	
1-5	at Rome	1-4	at Asheville
7-12	Hickory	6-11	Greensboro
14-19 . . .	Winston-Salem		
21-26	at Greenville		
28-30	at Asheville		

BROOKLYN CYCLONES

APRIL		JULY	
8-10	at Wilmington	1-3	.at Hudson Valley
12-17	Jersey Shore	4-10	Aberdeen
19-24 . . .	at Hudson Valley	12-17	Greensboro
26-30	Bowling Green	22-24 . . .	at Jersey Shore
		26-31 . .	at Hudson Valley

MAY		AUGUST	
1	Bowling Green	2-7	.Winston-Salem
3-8	at Aberdeen	9-14	at Wilmington
10-15	Wilmington	16-21 . . .	Hudson Valley
17-22	Hudson Valley	23-28 . . .	at Jersey Shore
24-29 . .	at Bowling Green	30-31	Wilmington
31	at Jersey Shore		

JUNE		SEPTEMBER	
1-5	.at Jersey Shore	1-4	.Wilmington
7-12	Aberdeen	6-11 . . .	at Winston-Salem
14-19	at Wilmington		
21-26	Jersey Shore		
28-30 . . .	at Hudson Valley		

GREENSBORO GRASSHOPPERS

APRIL		JULY	
8-10	Rome	1-3	at Hickory
12-17 . .	at Winston-Salem	4-10	Greenville
19-24	Aberdeen	12-17 . . .	at Brooklyn
26-30	at Rome	22-24	Hickory
		26-31	.Winston-Salem

MAY		AUGUST	
1	at Rome	2-7 . . .	at Bowling Green
3-8	Asheville	9-14	Jersey Shore
10-15	at Hickory	16-21	at Rome
17-22 . . .	Bowling Green	23-28 . . .	at Greenville
24-29 . . .	at Asheville	30-31	Winston-Salem
31	Wilmington		

JUNE		SEPTEMBER	
1-5	Wilmington	1-4	.Winston-Salem
7-12 . . .	at Winston-Salem	6-11 . . .	at Bowling Green
14-19	Hudson Valley		
21-26	Asheville		
28-30	at Hickory		

GREENVILLE DRIVE

APRIL		JULY	
8-10	Hudson Valley	1-3	.Rome
12-17	at Asheville	4-10	at Greensboro
19-24 . . .	Winston-Salem	12-17 . .	at Hudson Valley
26-30	at Hickory	22-24	Aberdeen
		26-31	Bowling Green

MAY		AUGUST	
1	at Hickory	2-7	at Rome
3-8	Rome	9-14	Hickory
10-15	at Asheville	16-21 . .	at Bowling Green
17-22	Hickory	23-28	Greensboro
24-29 . . .	at Jersey Shore	30-31	at Rome
31 . . .	at Winston-Salem		

JUNE		SEPTEMBER	
1-5 . . .	at Winston-Salem	1-4	at Rome
7-12	Asheville	6-11	.Asheville
14-19	at Hickory		
21-26 . . .	Bowling Green		
28-30	Rome		

HICKORY CRAWDADS

APRIL		JULY	
8-10 . . . . at Winston-Salem		1-3 . . . . Greensboro	
12-16 . . . . Bowling Green		4-10 . . . . at Bowling Green	
19-24 . . . at Wilmington		12-17 . . . . Wilmington	
26-30 . . . . Greenville		22-24 . . . . at Greensboro	
		26-31 . . . . Rome	

MAY		AUGUST	
1 . . . . Greenville		2-7 . . . . Asheville	
3-8 . . . . at Winston-Salem		9-14 . . . . . . at Greenville	
10-15 . . . . Greensboro		16-21 . . . . Winston-Salem	
17-22 . . . at Greenville		23-28 . . . at Hudson Valley	
24-29 . . . . Winston-Salem		30-31 . . . . . . at Aberdeen	
31 . . . . at Asheville			

JUNE		SEPTEMBER	
1-5 . . . . at Asheville		1-4 . . . . at Aberdeen	
7-12 . . . at Bowling Green		6-11 . . . . Rome	
14-19 . . . . Greenville			
21-26 . . . . at Rome			
28-30 . . . . . . Greensboro			

HUDSON VALLEY RENEGADES

APRIL		JULY	
8-10 . . . . . . at Greenville		1-3 . . . . Brooklyn	
12-17 . . . . at Rome		4-10 . . . . at Jersey Shore	
19-24 . . . . . Brooklyn		12-17 . . . . Greenville	
26-30 . . . . . Wilmington		22-24 . . . . at Wilmington	
		26-31 . . . . Brooklyn	

MAY		AUGUST	
1 . . . . Wilmington		2-7 . . . . . at Jersey Shore	
3-8 . . . . . at Jersey Shore		9-14 . . . . Aberdeen	
10-15 . . . . Aberdeen		16-21 . . . . . at Brooklyn	
17-22 . . . at Brooklyn		23-28 . . . . Hickory	
24-29 . . . . Rome		30-31 . . . . . Jersey Shore	
31 . . . . at Aberdeen			

JUNE		SEPTEMBER	
1-5 . . . . at Aberdeen		1-4 . . . . . Jersey Shore	
7-12 . . . . . . Jersey Shore		6-11 . . . . . at Wilmington	
14-19 . . . . at Greensboro			
21-26 . . . at Winston-Salem			
28-30 . . . . . . Brooklyn			

JERSEY SHORE BLUECLAWS

APRIL		JULY	
8-10 . . . . Aberdeen		1-3 . . . . . . at Wilmington	
12-17 . . . . . . at Brooklyn		4-10 . . . . . Hudson Valley	
19-24 . . . . Asheville		12-17 . . . . . at Aberdeen	
26-30 . . . . . . at Aberdeen		22-24 . . . . . . Brooklyn	
		26-31 . . . . at Wilmington	

MAY		AUGUST	
1 . . . . at Aberdeen		2-7 . . . . . . Hudson Valley	
3-8 . . . . . . Hudson Valley		9-14 . . . . . at Greensboro	
10-15 . . . at Bowling Green		16-21 . . . . . . Wilmington	
17-22 . . . . . at Wilmington		23-28 . . . . . . Brooklyn	
24-29 . . . . . Greenville		30-31 . . . at Hudson Valley	
31 . . . . Brooklyn			

JUNE		SEPTEMBER	
1-5 . . . . Brooklyn		1-4 . . . . at Hudson Valley	
7-12 . . . . at Hudson Valley		6-11 . . . . Aberdeen	
14-19 . . . . Aberdeen			
21-26 . . . . . . at Brooklyn			
28-30 . . . . . at Wilmington			

ROME BRAVES

APRIL		JULY	
8-10 . . . . . at Greensboro		1-3 . . . . at Greenville	
12-17 . . . . Hudson Valley		4-10 . . . . Asheville	
19-24 . . . at Bowling Green		12-17 . . . . Bowling Green	
26-30 . . . . Greensboro		22-24 . . . at Winston-Salem	
		26-31 . . . . at Hickory	

MAY		AUGUST	
1 . . . . Greensboro		2-7 . . . . Greenville	
3-8 . . . . at Greenville		9-14 . . . . . . at Asheville	
10-15 . . . Winston-Salem		16-21 . . . . . Greensboro	
17-22 . . . . . at Aberdeen		23-28 . . . at Bowling Green	
24-29 . . at Hudson Valley		30-31 . . . . . . Greenville	
31 . . . . . . Bowling Green			

JUNE		SEPTEMBER	
1-5 . . . . . . Bowling Green		1-4 . . . . Greenville	
7-12 . . . . Wilmington		6-11 . . . . at Hickory	
14-19 . . . . . at Asheville			
21-26 . . . . . . Hickory			
28-30 . . . . . at Greenville			

WILMINGTON BLUE ROCKS

APRIL		JULY	
8-10 . . . . Brooklyn		1-3 . . . . Jersey Shore	
12-17 . . . . at Aberdeen		4-10 . . . at Winston-Salem	
19-24 . . . . . Hickory		12-17 . . . . . at Hickory	
26-30 . . . at Hudson Valley		22-24 . . . . . Hudson Valley	
		26-31 . . . . . Jersey Shore	

MAY		AUGUST	
1 . . . . . . at Hudson Valley		2-4 . . . . Aberdeen	
3-8 . . . . . Bowling Green		5-7 . . . . at Aberdeen	
10-15 . . . . . at Brooklyn		9-14 . . . . Brooklyn	
17-22 . . . . Jersey Shore		16-21 . . . . at Jersey Shore	
24-26 . . . . . at Aberdeen		23-25 . . . . . at Aberdeen	
27-29 . . . . . . Aberdeen		26-28 . . . . Aberdeen	
31 . . . . . . at Greensboro		30-31 . . . . . at Brooklyn	

JUNE		SEPTEMBER	
1-5 . . . . . . at Greensboro		1-4 . . . . at Brooklyn	
7-12 . . . . at Rome		6-11 . . . . . Hudson Valley	
14-19 . . . . . . Brooklyn			
21-23 . . . . Aberdeen			
24-26 . . . . . at Aberdeen			
28-30 . . . . . Jersey Shore			

WINSTON-SALEM DASH

APRIL		JULY	
8-10 . . . . Hickory		1-3 . . . . at Aberdeen	
12-17 . . . . . Greensboro		4-10 . . . . . . Wilmington	
19-24 . . . . . at Greenville		12-17 . . . . . at Asheville	
26-30 . . . . . . at Asheville		22-24 . . . . Rome	
		26-31 . . . . at Greensboro	

MAY		AUGUST	
1 . . . . at Asheville		2-7 . . . . at Brooklyn	
3-8 . . . . Hickory		9-14 . . . . Bowling Green	
10-15 . . . . at Rome		16-21 . . . . at Hickory	
17-22 . . . . Asheville		23-28 . . . . Asheville	
24-29 . . . . . at Hickory		30-31 . . . . . at Greensboro	
31 . . . . Greenville			

JUNE		SEPTEMBER	
1-5 . . . . Greenville		1-4 . . . . at Greensboro	
7-12 . . . . . . Greensboro		6-11 . . . . Brooklyn	
14-19 . . at Bowling Green			
21-26 . . . Hudson Valley			
28-30 . . . . . at Aberdeen			

LOW CLASS A

LOW-A WEST

FRESNO GRIZZLIES

APRIL		JULY	
9-10	Stockton	1-3	at Stockton
13-17	at San Jose	5-11	San Jose
20-24	Lake Elsinore	12-17	at Rancho Cuca.
26-30	at Stockton	23-25	Stockton
		26-31	at Modesto

MAY		AUGUST	
1	at Stockton	3-8	San Jose
3-8	Modesto	10-15	at Inland Empire
10-15	at Visalia	16-21	at Visalia
17-22	Rancho Cuca.	24-29	Stockton
24-29	Stockton	31	Modesto
31	at Modesto		

JUNE		SEPTEMBER	
1-5	at Modesto	1-4	Modesto
8-13	Visalia	7-12	at San Jose
15-20	at San Jose		
22-27	Modesto		
28-30	at Stockton		

INLAND EMPIRE 66ERS

APRIL		JULY	
9-10	Lake Elsinore	1-3	at Lake Elsinore
12-17	at Rancho Cuca.	5-11	Rancho Cuca.
20-24	Stockton	12-17	at Stockton
26-30	at Lake Elsinore	23-25	Lake Elsinore
		27-31	Visalia

MAY		AUGUST	
1	at Lake Elsinore	1	Visalia
3-8	Visalia	2-7	at Rancho Cuca.
10-15	at Modesto	10-15	Fresno
18-22	San Jose	17-22	at San Jose
24-29	at Lake Elsinore	24-29	Lake Elsinore
31	at Visalia	31	Rancho Cuca.

JUNE		SEPTEMBER	
1-5	at Visalia	1-5	Rancho Cuca.
7-13	Modesto	6-11	at Visalia
14-19	at Rancho Cuca.		
22-27	Visalia		
28-30	at Lake Elsinore		

LAKE ELSINORE STORM

APRIL		JULY	
9-10	at Inland Empire	1-3	Inland Empire
12-17	Visalia	4-10	at Visalia
20-24	at Fresno	12-17	Modesto
26-30	Inland Empire	23-25	at Inland Empire
		26-31	Stockton

MAY		AUGUST	
1	Inland Empire	2-7	at Visalia
3-8	Rancho Cuca.	9-14	Rancho Cuca.
11-15	at San Jose	16-21	at Stockton
17-22	at Visalia	24-29	at Inland Empire
24-29	Inland Empire	30-31	Visalia
31	at Rancho Cuca.		

JUNE		SEPTEMBER	
1-5	at Rancho Cuca.	1-4	Visalia
7-12	San Jose	6-11	at Rancho Cuca.
14-19	at Modesto		
21-26	Rancho Cuca.		
28-30	Inland Empire		

MODESTO NUTS

APRIL		JULY	
8-10	San Jose	1-4	at San Jose
12-17	at Stockton	4-10	Stockton
19-24	Rancho Cuca.	12-17	at Lake Elsinore
27-30	at San Jose	22-24	San Jose
		26-31	Fresno

MAY		AUGUST	
1^	at San Jose	2-7	at Stockton
3-8	at Fresno	9-14	Visalia
10-15	Inland Empire	16-21	at Rancho Cuca.
17-22	at Stockton	23-28	San Jose
24-29	San Jose	31	at Fresno
31	Fresno		

JUNE		SEPTEMBER	
1-5	Fresno	1-4	at Fresno
7-13	at Inland Empire	6-11	Stockton
14-19	Lake Elsinore		
22-27	at Fresno		
28-30	at San Jose		

RANCHO CUCAMONGA QUAKES

APRIL		JULY	
8-10	at Visalia	1-3	Visalia
12-17	Inland Empire	5-11	at Inland Empire
19-24	at Modesto	12-17	Fresno
26-30	Visalia	22-24	at Visalia
		27-31	at San Jose

MAY		AUGUST	
1	Visalia	1	at San Jose
3-8	at Lake Elsinore	2-7	Inland Empire
10-15	Stockton	9-14	at Lake Elsinore
17-22	at Fresno	16-21	Modesto
24-29	Visalia	23-28	at Visalia
31	Lake Elsinore	31	at Inland Empire

JUNE		SEPTEMBER	
1-5	Lake Elsinore	1-5	at Inland Empire
7-12	at Stockton	6-11	Lake Elsinore
14-19	Inland Empire		
21-26	at Lake Elsinore		
28-30	Visalia		

SAN JOSE GIANTS

APRIL		JULY	
8-10	at Modesto	1-4	Modesto
13-17	Fresno	5-11	at Fresno
19-24	at Visalia	13-18	Visalia
27-30	Modesto	22-24	at Modesto
		27-31	Rancho Cuca.

MAY		AUGUST	
1	Modesto	1	Rancho Cuca.
3-8	at Stockton	3-8	at Fresno
11-15	Lake Elsinore	10-15	Stockton
18-22	at Inland Empire	17-22	Inland Empire
24-29	at Modesto	23-28	at Modesto
30	Stockton	30-31	at Stockton

JUNE		SEPTEMBER	
2-6	Stockton	1-4	at Stockton
7-12	at Lake Elsinore	7-12	Fresno
15-20	Fresno		
21-26	at Stockton		
29-29	Modesto		

STOCKTON PORTS

APRIL	
9-10	at Fresno
12-17	Modesto
20-24	at Inland Empire
26-30	Fresno

MAY	
1	Fresno
3-8	San Jose
10-15	at Rancho Cuca.
17-22	Modesto
24-29	at Fresno
30	at San Jose

JUNE	
2-6	at San Jose
7-12	Rancho Cuca.
14-19	at Visalia
21-26	San Jose
28-30	Fresno

JULY	
1-3	Fresno
4-10	at Modesto
12-17	Inland Empire
23-25	at Fresno
26-31	at Lake Elsinore

AUGUST	
2-7	Modesto
10-15	at San Jose
16-21	Lake Elsinore
24-29	at Fresno
30-31	San Jose

SEPTEMBER	
1-4	San Jose
6-11	at Modesto

VISALIA RAWHIDE

APRIL	
8-10	Rancho Cuca.
12-17	at Lake Elsinore
19-24	San Jose
26-30	at Rancho Cuca.

MAY	
1	at Rancho Cuca.
3-8	at Inland Empire
10-15	Fresno
17-22	Lake Elsinore
24-29	at Rancho Cuca.
31	Inland Empire

JUNE	
1-5	Inland Empire
8-13	at Fresno
14-19	Stockton
22-27	at Inland Empire
28-30	at Rancho Cuca.

JULY	
1-3	at Rancho Cuca.
4-10	Lake Elsinore
13-18	at San Jose
22-24	Rancho Cuca.
27-31	at Inland Empire

AUGUST	
1	at Inland Empire
2-7	Lake Elsinore
9-14	at Modesto
16-21	Fresno
23-28	Rancho Cuca.
30-31	at Lake Elsinore

SEPTEMBER	
1-4	at Lake Elsinore
6-11	Inland Empire

LOW-A EAST

AUGUSTA GREENJACKETS

APRIL	
8-10	at Columbis
12-17	at Myrtle Beach
19-24	Fayetteville
26-30	Delmarva

MAY	
1	Delmarva
3-8	at Carolina
10-15	Columbia
17-22	at Charleston
24-29	Myrtle Beach
31	Kannapolis

JUNE	
1-5	Kannapolis
7-12	at Columbia
14-19	Charleston
21-26	at Fayetteville
28-30	Columbia

JULY	
1-3	Columbia
4, 6-10	at Charleston
22-24	at Columbia
26-31	Myrtle Beach

AUGUST	
2-7	at Delmarva
9-14	at Fredericksburg
16-21	Charleston
23-28	at Myrtle Beach
30-31	Salem

SEPTEMBER	
1-4	Salem
6-11	at Kannapolis

CAROLINA MUDCATS

APRIL	
8-10	Down East
12-17	at Fredericksburg
19-24	Lynchburg
26-30	at Down East

MAY	
1	at Down East
3-8	Augusta
10-15	at Fayetteville
17-22	Down East
24-29	Kannapolis
31	at Lynchburg

JUNE	
1-5	at Lynchburg
7-12	Myrtle Beach
14-19	at Columbia
21-26	at Down East
28-30	Fayetteville

JULY	
1-3	Fayetteville
4-10	at Kannapolis
12-17	Delmarva
22-24	Down East
26-31	at Fayetteville

AUGUST	
2-7	Kannapolis
9-14	at Delmarva
16-21	Fayetteville
23-28	at Kannapolis
30-31	Columbia

SEPTEMBER	
1-4	Columbia
6-11	at Myrtle Beach

CHARLESTON RIVERDOGS

APRIL	
8-10	Myrtle Beach
12-17	Columbia
19-24	at Salem
26-30	at Fredericksburg

MAY	
1	at Fredericksburg
3-8	Fayetteville
10-15	at Myrtle Beach
17-22	Augusta
24-29	Delmarva
31	at Down East

JUNE	
1-5	at Down East
7-12	Salem
14-19	at Augusta
21-26	Columbia
28-30	at Myrtle Beach

JULY	
1-3	at Myrtle Beach
4-10	Augusta
12-17	at Lynchburg
22-24	Myrtle Beach
26-31	Down East

AUGUST	
2-7	at Columbia
9-14	Lynchburg
16-21	at Augusta
23-28	at Fayetteville
30-31	Myrtle Beach

SEPTEMBER	
1-4	Myrtle Beach
6-11	at Columbia

COLUMBIA FIREFLIES

APRIL	
8-10	Augusta
12-17	at Charleston
19-24	Down East
26-30	at Myrtle Beach

JULY	
1-3	at Augusta
4-10	Myrtle Beach
12-17	at Down East
22-24	Augusta
26-31	at Kannapolis

MAY	
1	at Myrtle Beach
3-8	Delmarva
10-15	at Augusta
17-22	Myrtle Beach
24-29	at Lynchburg
30	at Salem

AUGUST	
2-7	Charleston
9-14	at Myrtle Beach
16-21	Kannapolis
23-28	Salem
30-31	at Carolina

JUNE	
1-5	at Salem
7-12	Augusta
14-19	Carolina
21-26	at Charleston
28-30	at Augusta

SEPTEMBER	
1-4	at Carolina
6-11	Charleston

DELMARVA SHOREBIRDS

APRIL	
8-10	Fredericksburg
12-17	at Lynchburg
19-24	Myrtle Beach
26-30	at Augusta

JULY	
1-3	at Fredericksburg
4-10	Salem
12-17	at Carolina
22-24	Fredericksburg
26-31	at Lynchburg

MAY	
1	at Augusta
3-8	at Columbia
10-15	Salem
17-22	Fredericksburg
24-29	at Charleston
31	at Myrtle Beach

AUGUST	
2-7	Augusta
9-14	Carolina
16-21	at Salem
23-28	Lynchburg
30-31	at Fredericksburg

JUNE	
1-5	at Myrtle Beach
7-12	Fayetteville
14-19	at Salem
21-26	Lynchburg
28-30	at Fredericksburg

SEPTEMBER	
1-4	at Fredericksburg
6-11	Down East

DOWN EAST WOOD DUCKS

APRIL	
8-10	at Carolina
12-17	Kannapolis
19-24	at Columbia
26-30	Carolina

JULY	
1-3	Kannapolis
4-10	at Fayetteville
12-17	Columbia
22-24	at Carolina
26-31	at Charleston

MAY	
1	Carolina
3-8	at Kannapolis
10-15	Lynchburg
17-22	at Carolina
24-29	Fayetteville
31	Charleston

AUGUST	
2-7	Fredericksburg
9-14	at Fayetteville
16-21	Myrtle Beach
23-28	at Fredericksburg
30-31	Fayetteville

JUNE	
1-5	Charleston
7-12	at Kannapolis
14-19	at Lynchburg
21-26	Carolina
28-30	Kannapolis

SEPTEMBER	
1-4	Fayetteville
6-11	at Delmarva

FAYETTEVILLE WOODPECKERS

APRIL	
8-10	at Kannapolis
12-17	Salem
19-24	at Augusta
26-30	Kannapolis

JULY	
1-3	at Carolina
4-10	Down East
12-17	at Myrtle Beach
22-24	at Kannapolis
26-31	Carolina

MAY	
1	Kannapolis
3-8	at Charleston
10-15	Carolina
17-22	at Kannapolis
24-29	at Down East
31	Fredericksburg

AUGUST	
2-7	at Salem
9-14	Down East
16-21	at Carolina
23-28	Charleston
30-31	at Down East

JUNE	
1-5	Fredericksburg
7-12	at Delmarva
14-19	Kannapolis
21-26	Augusta
28-30	at Carolina

SEPTEMBER	
1-4	at Down East
6-11	Lynchburg

FREDERICKSBURG NATIONALS

APRIL	
8-10	at Delmarva
12-17	Carolina
19-24	at Kannapolis
26-30	Charleston

JULY	
1-3	Delmarva
4-10	Lynchburg
12-17	at Augusta
22-24	at Delmarva
26-31	Salem

MAY	
1	Charleston
3-8	at Lynchburg
10-15	Kannapolis
17-22	at Delmarva
24-29	Salem
31	at Fayetteville

AUGUST	
2-7	at Down East
9-14	Augusta
16-21	at Lynchburg
23-28	Down East
30-31	Delmarva

JUNE	
1-5	at Fayetteville
7-12	Lynchburg
14-19	at Myrtle Beach
21-26	at Salem
28-30	Delmarva

SEPTEMBER	
1-4	Delmarva
6-11	at Salem

KANNAPOLIS CANNON BALLERS

APRIL	
8-10	Fayetteville
12-17	at Down East
19-24	Fredericksburg
26-30	at Fayetteville

JULY	
1-3	at Down East
4-10	Carolina
12-17	at Salem
22-24	Fayetteville
26-31	Columbia

MAY	
1	at Fayetteville
3-8	Down East
10-15	at Fredericksburg
17-22	Fayetteville
24-29	at Carolina
31	at Augusta

AUGUST	
2-7	at Carolina
9-14	Salem
16-21	at Columbia
23-28	Carolina
30-31	at Lynchburg

JUNE	
1-5	at Augusta
7-12	Down East
14-19	at Fayetteville
21-26	Myrtle Beach
28-30	at Down East

SEPTEMBER	
1-4	at Lynchburg
6-11	Augusta

LYNCHBURG HILLCATS

APRIL		JULY	
		1-3 . . . . Salem
8-10 . . . . at Salem		4-10 . . . at Fredericksburg
12-17 . . . . Delmarva		12-17 . . . . Charleston
19-24 . . . . . . at Carolina		22-24 . . . . at Salem
26-30 . . . . Salem		26-31 . . . . Delmarva

MAY		AUGUST	
1 . . . . Salem		2-7 . . . . . at Myrtle Beach
3-8 . . . . . Fredericksburg		9-14 . . . . . . at Charleston
10-15 . . . . at Down East		16-21 . . . . Fredericksburg
17-22 . . . . at Salem		23-28 . . . . . at Delmarva
24-29 . . . . Columbia		30-31 . . . . . . Kannapolis
31 . . . . Carolina		

JUNE		SEPTEMBER	
		1-4 . . . . Kannapolis
1-5 . . . . Carolina		6-11 . . . . . . at Fayetteville
7-12 . . . . at Fredericksburg		
14-19 . . . . . . Down East		
21-26 . . . . at Delmarva		
28-30 . . . . Salem		

MYRTLE BEACH PELICANS

APRIL		JULY	
8-10 . . . . . at Charleston		1-3 . . . . Charleston
12-17 . . . . Augusta		4-10 . . . . . . at Columbia
19-24 . . . . . . at Delmarva		12-17 . . . . . Fayetteville
26-30 . . . . Columbia		22-24 . . . . . at Charleston
		26-31 . . . . . . at Augusta

MAY		AUGUST	
1 . . . . Columbia		2-7 . . . . Lynchburg
3-8 . . . . at Salem		9-14 . . . . Columbia
10-15 . . . . . . Charleston		16-21 . . . . at Down East
17-22 . . . . at Columbia		23-28 . . . . Augusta
24-29 . . . . . at Augusta		30-31 . . . . at Charleston
31 . . . . Delmarva		

JUNE		SEPTEMBER	
1-5 . . . . Delmarva		1-4 . . . . . . at Charleston
7-12 . . . . . at Carolina		6-11 . . . . Carolina
14-19 . . . . Fredericksburg		
21-26 . . . . . at Kannapolis		
28-30 . . . . Charleston		

SALEM RED SOX

APRIL		JULY	
8-10 . . . . Lynchburg		1-3 . . . . . . at Lynchburg
12-17 . . . . . at Fayetteville		4-10 . . . . . . at Delmarva
19-24 . . . . . . Charleston		12-17 . . . . . . Kannapolis
26-30 . . . . . at Lynchburg		22-24 . . . . Lynchburg
		26-31 . . at Fredericksburg

MAY		AUGUST	
1 . . . . at Lynchburg		2-7 . . . . Fayetteville
3-8 . . . . Myrtle Beach		9-14 . . . . . at Kannapolis
10-15 . . . . . at Delmarva		16-21 . . . . Delmarva
17-22 . . . . . . Lynchburg		23-28 . . . . . at Columbia
24-29 . . at Fredericksburg		30-31 . . . . . . at Augusta
30 . . . . Columbia		

JUNE		SEPTEMBER	
1-5 . . . . Columbia		1-4 . . . . at Augusta
7-12 . . . . . at Charleston		6-11 . . . . Fredericksburg
14-19 . . . . Delmarva		
21-26 . . . . Fredericksburg		
28-30 . . . . . at Lynchburg		

LOW-A SOUTHEAST

BRADENTON MARAUDERS

APRIL		JULY	
8-10 . . . . at Dunedin		1-3 . . . . Tampa
12-17 . . . . . . Lakeland		4-10 . . . . . . at Lakeland
19-24 . . . . . at Daytona		12-17 . . . . Jupiter
26-30 . . . . . . Dunedin		22-24 . . . at Clearwater
		26-31 . . . . . . Lakeland

MAY		AUGUST	
1 . . . . Dunedin		2-7 . . . . . . at Fort Myers
3-8 . . . . Tampa		9-14 . . . . . Palm Beach
10-15 . . . . . at Jupiter		16-21 . . . . . . at Tampa
17-22 . . . . at Palm Beach		23-28 . . . . . . Dunedin
24-29 . . . . . Fort Myers		30-31 . . . . . Fort Myers
31 . . . . at Lakeland		

JUNE		SEPTEMBER	
1-5 . . . . at Lakeland		1-4 . . . . Fort Myers
7-12 . . . . . . Clearwater		6-11 . . . . . at Clearwater
14-19 . . . . . at Fort Myers		
21-26 . . . . . at Dunedin		
28-30 . . . . Tampa		

CLEARWATER THRESHERS

APRIL		JULY	
8-10 . . . . Fort Myers		1-3 . . . . Lakeland
12-17 . . . . . at St. Lucie		4-10 . . . . . . at Dunedin
19-24 . . . . Tampa		12-17 . . . at Fort Myers
26-30 . . . at Fort Myers		22-24 . . . . . Bradenton
		26-31 . . . . . . Dunedin

MAY		AUGUST	
1 . . . . . at Fort Myers		2-7 . . . . at Tampa
3-8 . . . . at Dunedin		9-14 . . . . . . St. Lucie
10-15 . . . . . Daytona		16-21 . . . . at Daytona
17-22 . . . . . Fort Myers		23-28 . . . . Tampa
24-29 . . . . . at Jupiter		30-31 . . . . at Lakeland
31 . . . . Dunedin		

JUNE		SEPTEMBER	
1-5 . . . . Dunedin		1-4 . . . . . . at Lakeland
7-12 . . . . . at Bradenton		6-11 . . . . . . Bradenton
14-19 . . . Palm Beach		
21-26 . . . . . . at Tampa		
28-30 . . . . . . Lakeland		

DAYTONA TORTUGAS

APRIL		JULY	
8-10 . . . . St. Lucie		1-3 . . . . . at Palm Beach
12-17 . . . . at Palm Beach		4-10 . . . . St. Lucie
19-24 . . . . . Bradenton		12-17 . . . . . at Tampa
26-30 . . . . . at St. Lucie		22-24 . . . Palm Beach
		26-31 . . . . . . at Jupiter

MAY		AUGUST	
1 . . . . at St. Lucie		2-7 . . . . at St. Lucie
3-8 . . . . Jupiter		9-14 . . . . . Lakeland
10-15 . . . . at Clearwater		16-21 . . . . Clearwater
17-22 . . . . . Dunedin		23-28 . . . . . at Jupiter
24-29 . . . . . Palm Beach		30-31 . . at Palm Beach
31 . . . . . . at St. Lucie		

JUNE		SEPTEMBER	
1-5 . . . . . at St. Lucie		1-4 . . . . . at Palm Beach
7-12 . . . . . . Fort Myers		6-11 . . . . Tampa
14-19 . . . . . at Lakeland		
21-26 . . . . Jupiter		
28-30 . . . . at Palm Beach		

DUNEDIN BLUE JAYS

APRIL	
8-10	Bradenton
12-17	at Tampa
19-24	Fort Myers
26-30	at Bradenton

JULY	
1-3	at Fort Myers
4-10	Clearwater
12-17	at St. Lucie
22-24	Fort Myers
26-31	at Clearwater

MAY	
1	at Bradenton
3-8	Clearwater
10-15	Tampa
17-22	at Daytona
24-29	St. Lucie
31	at Clearwater

AUGUST	
2-7	at Lakeland
9-14	Tampa
16-21	Jupiter
23-28	at Bradenton
30-31	at Tampa

JUNE	
1-5	at Clearwater
7-12	Lakeland
14-19	at Jupiter
21-26	Bradenton
28-30	at Fort Myers

SEPTEMBER	
1-4	at Tampa
6-11	Palm Beach

FORT MYERS MIGHTY MUSSELS

APRIL	
8-10	at Clearwater
12-17	Jupiter
19-24	at Dunedin
26-30	Clearwater

JULY	
1-3	Dunedin
4-10	at Tampa
12-17	Clearwater
22-24	at Dunedin
26-31	Tampa

MAY	
1	Clearwater
3-8	at Lakeland
10-15	Palm Beach
17-22	at Clearwater
24-29	at Bradenton
31	Tampa

AUGUST	
2-7	Bradenton
9-14	at Jupiter
16-21	at Palm Beach
23-28	Lakeland
30-31	at Bradenton

JUNE	
1-5	Tampa
7-12	at Daytona
14-19	Bradenton
21-26	at Lakeland
28-30	Dunedin

SEPTEMBER	
1-4	at Bradenton
6-11	St. Lucie

JUPITER HAMMERHEADS

APRIL	
8-10	Palm Beach
12-17	at Fort Myers
19-24	St. Lucie
26-30	at Palm Beach

JULY	
1-3	at St. Lucie
4-10	Palm Beach
12-17	at Bradenton
22-24	St. Lucie
26-31	Daytona

MAY	
1	at Palm Beach
3-8	at Daytona
10-15	Bradenton
17-22	at Lakeland
24-29	Clearwater
31	at Palm Beach

AUGUST	
2-7	at Palm Beach
9-14	Fort Myers
16-21	at Dunedin
23-28	Daytona
30-31	at St. Lucie

JUNE	
1-5	at Palm Beach
7-12	St. Lucie
14-19	Dunedin
21-26	at Daytona
28-30	at St. Lucie

SEPTEMBER	
1-4	at St. Lucie
6-11	Lakeland

LAKELAND FLYING TIGERS

APRIL	
8-10	Tampa
12-17	at Bradenton
19-24	Palm Beach
26-30	at Tampa

JULY	
1-3	at Clearwater
4-10	Bradenton
12-17	at Palm Beach
22-24	Tampa
26-31	at Bradenton

MAY	
1	at Tampa
3-8	Fort Myers
10-15	at St. Lucie
17-22	Jupiter
24-26	at Tampa
27-29	Tampa
31	Bradenton

AUGUST	
2-7	Dunedin
9-14	at Daytona
16-21	St. Lucie
23-28	at Fort Myers
30-31	Clearwater

JUNE	
1-5	Bradenton
7-12	at Dunedin
14-19	Daytona
21-26	Fort Myers
28-30	at Clearwater

SEPTEMBER	
1-4	Clearwater
6-11	at Jupiter

PALM BEACH CARDINALS

APRIL	
8-10	at Jupiter
12-17	Daytona
19-24	at Lakeland
26-30	Jupiter

JULY	
1-3	Daytona
4-10	at Jupiter
12-17	Lakeland
22-24	at Daytona
26-31	at St. Lucie

MAY	
1	Jupiter
3-8	St. Lucie
10-15	at Fort Myers
17-22	Bradenton
24-29	at Daytona
31	Jupiter

AUGUST	
2-7	Jupiter
9-14	at Bradenton
16-21	Fort Myers
23-28	at St. Lucie
30-31	Daytona

JUNE	
1-5	Jupiter
7-12	at Tampa
14-19	at Clearwater
21-26	St. Lucie
28-30	Daytona

SEPTEMBER	
1-4	Daytona
6-11	at Dunedin

ST. LUCIE METS

APRIL	
8-10	at Daytona
12-17	Clearwater
19-24	at Jupiter
26-30	Daytona

JULY	
1-3	Jupiter
4-10	at Daytona
12-17	Dunedin
22-24	at Jupiter
26-31	Palm Beach

MAY	
1	Daytona
3-8	at Palm Beach
10-15	Lakeland
17-22	at Tampa
24-29	at Dunedin
31	Daytona

AUGUST	
2-7	Daytona
9-14	at Clearwater
16-21	at Lakeland
23-28	Palm Beach
30-31	Jupiter

JUNE	
1-5	Daytona
7-12	at Jupiter
14-19	Daytona
21-26	at Palm Beach
28-30	Jupiter

SEPTEMBER	
1-4	Jupiter
6-11	at Ft. Myers

TAMPA TARPONS

APRIL
8-10	at Lakeland
12-17	Dunedin
19-24	at Clearwater
26-30	Lakeland

MAY
1	Lakeland
3-8	at Bradenton
10-15	at Dunedin
17-22	St. Lucie
24-26	Lakeland
27-29	at Lakeland
31	at Fort Myers

JUNE
1-5	at Fort Myers
7-12	Palm Beach
14-19	at St. Lucie
21-26	Clearwater
28-30	at Bradenton

JULY
1-3	at Bradenton
4-10	Fort Myers
12-17	Daytona
22-24	at Lakeland
26-31	at Fort Myers

AUGUST
2-7	Clearwater
9-14	at Dunedin
16-21	Bradenton
23-28	at Clearwater
30-31	Dunedin

SEPTEMBER
1-4	Dunedin
6-11	at Daytona

PARTNER/
INDEPENDENT
LEAGUES

AMERICAN ASSOCIATION

Mailing Address: PO Box 995, Moorhead, MN 56561-0995.
Telephone: (218) 512-0380.
Email: info@aabaseball.com
Websites: aabaseball.com, aabaseball.tv
Year Founded: 2005.
Commissioner: Joshua E. Schaub. **Deputy Commissioner:** Josh Buchholz. **Director of Umpires:** Ronnie Teague.
Director of Digital Media: Jake Kranz. **Digital Content Host:** Carter Woodiel. **League Historian:** Hoffman Wolff.
Board of Directors: Jim Abel (Lincoln), Mark Brandmeyer (Kansas City), Daryn Eudaly (Cleburne), Dr. Bob Froehlich (Kane County), Shawn Hunter (Chicago), Sam Katz (Winnipeg), Tom Kelenic (Lake Country), John Roost (Sioux City), Patrick Salvi (Gary SouthShore), Brian Slipka (Sioux Falls), Bruce Thom (Fargo-Moorhead), Mike Zimmerman (Milwaukee).
Division Structure: East—Chicago Dogs, Cleburne Railroaders, Gary SouthShore RailCats, Kane County Cougars, Lake Country DockHounds, Milwaukee Milkmen. **West**—Fargo-Moorhead RedHawks, Kansas City Monarchs, Lincoln Saltdogs, Sioux City Explorers, Sioux Falls Canaries, Winnipeg Goldeyes.
Regular Season: 100 games. **Opening Date:** May 13. **Closing Date:** September 5.
Playoff Format: Top four teams in each division play in best-of-three series. Winners play in best-of-three Division Series. Winners play best-of-five American Association Finals.
Roster Limit: 25. **Player Eligibility Rule:** Minimum of five first-year players; maximum of six veterans (at least six or more years of professional service).
Brand of Baseball: Rawlings. **Statistician:** Pointstreak/Stack Sports, 5360 Legacy Drive, Suite #150, Plano, TX 75024.

STADIUM INFORMATION

Club	Stadium	Opened	LF	CF	RF	Capacity	2021 Att.
Chicago	Impact Field	2018	313	389	294	6,300	155,582
Cleburne	The Depot at Cleburne Station	2017	335	400	320	3,750	56,201
Fargo-Moorhead	Newman Outdoor Field	1996	314	408	318	4,172	145,553
Gary SouthShore	U.S. Steel Yard	2002	320	400	335	6,139	137,094
Kane County	Northwestern Medicine Field	1991	335	400	335	10,923	177,705
Kansas City	Legends Field	2003	300	396	328	6,270	102,257
Lake Country	Wisconsin Brewing Company Park	2022	325	400	325	3,641	N/A
Lincoln	Haymarket Park	2001	335	403	325	4,500	149,204
Milwaukee	Franklin Field	2019	330	407	330	4,000	79,741
Sioux City	Mercy Field at Lewis and Clark Park	1993	330	400	330	3,800	59,802
Sioux Falls	Sioux Falls Stadium	1964	313	410	312	4,462	82,932
Winnipeg	Shaw Park	1999	325	400	325	7,121	52,014

CHICAGO DOGS

Office Address: 9800 Balmoral Avenue, Rosemont, IL, 60018.
Telephone: 847.636.5450.
E-mail: info@thechicagodogs.com. **Website:** thechicagodogs.com.
Owners: Shawn Hunter, Steven Gluckstern.
Chief Operating Officer: Trish Zuro. **Baseball Operations:** Trish Zuro.
Corporate Sponsorships: Chris Lennon. **Corporate Sales Manager:** Scott Foley. **Sales and Event Manager:** Evan Gersonde. **Senior Account Executive:** Jon Ryan & Mackenzie Thomas. **Account Executive:** Robert Liable & Alec Raatz. **Corporate Sales and Event Coordinator:** Allie Grengs.
Media Relations: Alexandra Jakubiak. **Community Relations:** Daniela Barrios. **Broadcast and Media Relations Manager:** Sam Brief. **Website Design/Photographer:** Matt Zuro. **Director of Operations Food & Beverage:** Joe Costa. **Executive Chef:** A.J. Francisco.
Manager: Butch Hobson. **Pitching Coach:** Stu Cliburn. **Hitting Coach:** Joe Dominiak. **Clubhouse Manager:** Daniel Langston. **Assistant Clubhouse Manager:** David Barkan. **Head Groundskeeper:** Justin Spillman.

GAME INFORMATION

Stadium Name: Impact Field, 9850 Balmoral Avenue, Rosemont, IL 60018.
Standard Game Times: M/T/W/F, 7 pm, Thur/Sat., 6 pm, Sun., 3 pm

CLEBURNE RAILROADERS

Address: 1906 Brazzle Boulevard, Cleburne, TX 76033.
Telephone: (817) 945-8705.
Email: info@railroaderbaseball.com. **Website:** railroaderbaseball.com.
Co-Owner/General Manager: John Junker. **Co-Owner:** Daryn Eudaly. **Co-Owner:** Collide Agency. **Co-Owner:** Top Tier Sports.

Marketing Manager: Alan Miller. **Director, Business Operations:** Bill Adams. **Director, Sales:** Rory Niewenhous. **Ticket Sales Account Representatives:** Yvonne Baldwin, Jose Marroquin. **Ticket Office Manager:** Hollie Bunn. **Director, Broadcasting:** Brad Allred. **Media Relations Manager:** Taylor Robinson. **Press Box Manager:** Keaton Cordell. **Facilities Manager:** Chris Woodall. **Food and Beverage Directors:** Mike and Marshelle Langston. **Clubhouse Manager:** Gerald Morrison.

Field Manager: Logan Watkins.

GAME INFORMATION

Broadcaster: Brad Allred. **Games Broadcast:** 100. **Stadium Name:** The Depot at Cleburne Station. **Directions:** From Chisholm Trail Parkway (toll road) continue south across US HWY 67, turn left onto Cleburne Station Boulevard. From US HWY 67 South, exit Nolan River Road, turn left onto Nolan River Road, turn left onto Cleburne Station Boulevard. From US HWY 67 North, exit Nolan River Road, turn right onto Nolan River Road, turn left onto Cleburne Station Boulevard. **Standard Game Times:** Mon.-Sat., 7:06 pm, Sun., 6:00 pm.

FARGO-MOORHEAD REDHAWKS

Address: 1515 15th Ave N Fargo, ND 58102
Telephone: (701) 235-6161. **Fax:** (701) 297-9247.
Email: redhawks@fmredhawks.com, media@fmredhawks.com.
Website: fmredhawks.com
Operated by: Fargo Baseball LLC. **Chairman of the Board:** N. Bruce Thom. **President & CEO:** Brad Thom.
Vice President/General Manager: Matt Rau. **Vice President, Finance:** Rick Larson. **Assistant General Manager:** Karl Hoium. **Senior Director of Communications:** Chad Ekren. **Community Relations, Merchandise and Ticket Operations Director:** Ashley McCoy. **Stadium Superintendent/Head Groundskeeper:** Tom Drietz. **Box Office Manager:** Grant Langseth. **Group Sales Manager:** Teresa Mattson. **Food and Beverage Director:** TBD.
Field Manager: Chris Coste. **Hitting Coach:** Anthony Renz. **Pitching Coach:** Kevin McGovern. **Bullpen Coach:** Robbie Lopez. **Player Personnel Consultant:** Jeff Bittiger.

GAME INFORMATION

Radio Announcer: Jack Michaels. **Games Broadcast:** 100. **Flagship Station:** 740 THE FAN (KNFL-740AM, K297BW 107.3FM). **Stadium Name:** Newman Outdoor Field (1996). **Location:** I-29 North to exit 67, east on 19th Ave North, right on Albrecht Boulevard. **Standard Game Times:** M-F. 7:02 pm Sat.: 6:00 pm, Sun.: 1:00 pm.

GARY SOUTHSHORE RAILCATS

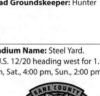

Address: One Stadium Plaza, Gary, IN 46402.
Telephone: (219) 882-2255. **Fax:** (219) 882-2259.
Email Address: info@railcatsbaseball.com. **Website:** railcatsbaseball.com.
Operated by: Salvi Sports Enterprises.
Owner/CEO: Pat Salvi. **Owner:** Lindy Salvi.
President, Salvi Sports Enterprises: Brian Lyter. **General Manager:** Anthony Giammanco. **Assistant General Manager:** Noah Simmons. **Manager, Marketing and Promotions:** Ashley Nylen. **Box Office Manager:** Matt Murphy. **Marketing Consultant:** Renee Connelly. **Manager, Stadium Operations:** Jack Stancl. **Head Groundskeeper:** Hunter Mihalic. **VP of Corporate Sponsorships, Salvi Sports Consulting:** David Kay.
Field Manager: Greg Tagert.

GAME INFORMATION

Radio Announcer: TBD. **Games Broadcast:** 100. **Flagship Station:** WEFM 95.9-FM. **Stadium Name:** Steel Yard. **Location:** Take I-65 North to end of highway at U.S. 12/20 (Dunes Highway). Turn left on U.S. 12/20 heading west for 1.5 miles (three stop lights). Stadium is on left side. **Standard Game Times:** Mon.-Fri., 6:45 pm, Sat., 4:00 pm, Sun., 2:00 pm.

KANE COUNTY COUGARS

Address: 34W002 Cherry Lane, Geneva, IL 60134.
Telephone: (630) 232-8811. **Fax:** (630) 232-8815.
Email: info@kanecountycougars.com. **Website:** www.kccougars.com.
Operated By: Cougars Baseball Partnership/American Sports Enterprises, Inc. Chairman/**Chief Executive Officer/ President:** Dr. Bob Froehlich. **Owners:** Dr. Bob Froehlich, Cheryl Froehlich. **Board of Directors:** Dr. Bob Froehlich, Cheryl Froehlich, Stephanie Froehlich, Chris Neidhart, Marianne Neidhart.
Vice President/General Manager: Curtis Haug. **Senior Director, Finance/Administration:** Douglas Czurylo. **Accounting:** Sally Sullivan. **Senior Director, Ticketing:** R. Michael Patterson. **Director, Ticket Operations:** Amy Mason. **Ticket Operations Coordinator:** Jeff Weaver. **Director, Security:** TBD. **Director, Public Relations & Promotions:** Claire Jacobi. **Design/Graphics:** TBD. **Media Placement Coordinator:** Bill Baker. **Office Manager:** Sherri Johnson. **Video Director:** Andy Cozzi. **Director, Food & Beverage:** TBD. **Director, Sales/Facilities:** Mike Klafehn. **Stadium Operations Manager:** Scott Anderson. **Director, Maintenance:** Jeff Snyder. **Head Groundskeeper:** Sean Ehlert.

Field Manager: George Tsamis. **Hitting Coach:** Matt Passarelle. **Pitching Coach:** TBD. **Bench Coach:** TBD. **Athletic Trainer:** TBD. **Strength & Conditioning Coach:** TBD. **Clubhouse Manager:** Ryan O'Brien.

GAME INFORMATION
Radio Announcer: Joe Brand. **No. of Games Broadcast:** 100. **Flagship Station:** TBD. **Official Scorer:** Mike Haase. **Stadium Name:** Northwestern Medicine Field. **Location:** From east or west, I-88 Ronald Reagan Memorial Tollway) to Farnsworth Ave. North exit, north five miles to Cherry Lane, left into stadium complex. From northwest, I-90 (Jane Addams Memorial Tollway) to Randall Rd. South exit, south 15 miles to Fabyan Parkway, east to Kirk Rd., north to Cherry Lane, left into stadium complex. **Standard Game Times:** Mon.-Sat., 6:30 pm, Sun., 1:00 pm.

KANSAS CITY MONARCHS

Address: 1800 Village West Parkway, Kansas City, KS 66111.
Telephone: (913) 328-5618.
Email: info@monarchsbaseball.com. **Web:** monarchsbaseball.com.
Operated by: Max Fun Entertainment, LLC.
Principal Owner: Mark Brandmeyer. **Partner/CEO:** Mark McKee.
President & General Manager: Jay S. Hinrichs. **Vice President, Hospitality:** Jim Cundiff. **Vice President, Sponsorships:** Jeff Foster. **Chief Financial Officer:** Tom Ross. Manager, **Sales & Special Events:** Suzi Hallas. **Manager, Group Sales:** Nick Restivo. **Manager, Ticket Operations:** Kacy Muller. **Information Technology:** David Chick. **Manager, Hospitality:** Monica Garcia. **Manager, Production & Digital Assets:** Morgan Kolenda. **Uniform and Retail Production:** Pat Bachofer. **Host Family Coordinator:** Cheryl Reitmeyer. **Facility Maintenance:** Abraham Mercado & Nick Marquez. **Business Development:** Steven Como & Tre Whittaker. **Team Physician:** Dr. Michael Dempewolf, Sanos Orthopedics. **Certified Athletic Trainer:** Jared Bashaw.
Field Manager: Joe Calfapietra. **Coaches:** Frank White, Bill Sobbe, Mike Henneman. **Equipment Manager:** John West.

GAME INFORMATION
Radio Announcer: Dan Vaughan. **Games broadcast:** 100. **Site:** www.monarchsbaseball.com. **Public Address Announcer:** Nate Herron. **Game Day Production:** Brad Zimmerman. **Stadium Name:** Legends Field. **Location:** State Avenue West off I-435 Kansas City, Kansas. **Standard Game Times:** Monday-Friday 7 p.m. **Saturday** 6:00 pm, **Sunday,** 3:00 pm.

LAKE COUNTRY DOCKHOUNDS

Address: 1011 Blue Ribbon Circle N, Oconomowoc, WI 53066.
Telephone: (262) 468-7750
Email: info@lakecountry-live.com. **Website:** dockhounds.com
Managing Partners: Tony Bryant, Sonny Bando, Tom Kelenic, Tim Neubert.
General Manager: Trish Rasberry. **Assistant General Manager:** Noelle Clarke. Director, **Marketing & Community Relations:** Lisa Kelenic.
Manager: Jim Bennett. **Pitching Coach:** Paul Wagner. **Bench/Hitting Coach:** Dave Nilsson. **Third Base Coach:** Ed Campaniello.

GAME INFORMATION
Broadcaster: Sam Metheny. **Games Broadcast:** 100. **Stadium Name:** Wisconsin Brewing Company Park. **Location:** 1011 Blue Ribbon Circle N, Oconomowoc, WI 53066. **Standard Game Times:** **Mon.-Fri** 6:35 pm, Sat. 6:05 pm, Sun. 1:35pm.

LINCOLN SALTDOGS

Address: 403 Line Drive Circle, Suite A, Lincoln, NE 68508.
Telephone: (402) 474-2255. **Fax:** (402) 474-2254.
Email Address: info@saltdogs.com. **Website:** saltdogs.com.
Chairman: Jim Abel. **President/GM:** Charlie Meyer.
Director, Broadcasting/Communications: Michael Dixon. **Director, Stadium Operations:** Dave Aschwege. **Director, Video Production:** Ty Schweer. **Assistant Director, Stadium Operations:** Brenden Gerlach. **Manager, Ticket Sales:** Colter Clarke. **Group Sales Executive:** Daniel Thomas. **Athletic Turf Manager:** Kyle Trewhitt. **Assistant Turf Manager:** Kyle Lengefeld. **Office Manager:** TBD. **Director of Operations for Concessions:** Steve Deriese. **Director of Kitchen Operations:** Katie Wilkinson.
Field Manager: Brett Jodie. **Coaches:** T.J. Zarewicz & Adam Donachie.

GAME INFORMATION
Public Address Announcer: Heath Kramer. **Broadcast Team:** Jeff Briden. **No. of Games Broadcast:** 100. **Flagship Station:** KLMS 1480AM & ESPN101.5 FM. **Stadium Name:** Haymarket Park. **Location:** I-80 to Cornhusker Highway West, left on First Street, right on Sun Valley Boulevard, left on Line Drive. **Standard Game Times:** Mon.-Sat., 7:05 pm, Sun., 1:05 pm.

MILWAUKEE MILKMEN

Address: 7044 S. Ballpark Drive, Ste 300, Franklin WI 53132
Telephone: (414) 224-9823
Website: milwaukeemilkmen.com.
Owner: Michael Zimmerman. **COO/General Manager:** Dan Kuenzi.
Director, Corporate Partnership: Joe Zimmerman. **Director, Ticket Sales:** Mike Doyle. **Director, Entertainment & Events:** Paul Cimoch. **Director, Finance:** Tom Johns. **Medical Staff:** Midwest Orthopedic Specialty Hospital.
Field Manager: Anthony Barone.

GAME INFORMATION
Stadium Name: Franklin Field. **Location:** 7035 S. Ballpark Drive, Franklin, WI 53132. **Standard Game Times:** Mon.-Fri., 6:35 pm. Sat., 6:05 pm. Sun., 1:05 pm.

SIOUX CITY EXPLORERS

Address: 3400 Line Drive, Sioux City, IA 51106.
Telephone: (712) 277-9467. **Fax:** (712) 277-9406.
Email Address: promotions@xsbaseball.com. **Website:** www.xsbaseball.com.
Owner: John Roost. **President:** Matt Adamski.
Director, Stadium Operations & Baseball Operations: Boyd Pitkin. **Director, Sales:** Michael Murphy. **Director, Media Relations/Radio Broadcaster:** Connor Ryan.
Field Manager: Steve Montgomery. **Coaches:** Bobby Post, Derek Wolfe. **Athletic Trainer:** Bruce Fischbach.
Clubhouse Manager: TBD.

GAME INFORMATION
Radio Announcer: Connor Ryan. **No. of Games Broadcast:** 100. **Flagship Station:** KSCJ 1360-AM. **Webcast Address:** www.xsbaseball.com. **Stadium Name:** Mercy Field at Lewis and Clark Park. **Location:** I-29 to Singing Hills Blvd North, right on Line Drive. **Standard Game Times:** Mon.-Fri., 7:05 pm, Sat., 6:05 pm, Sun., 4:05 pm.

SIOUX FALLS CANARIES

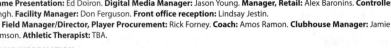

Office Address: 1001 N West Ave, Sioux Falls, SD 57104.
Telephone: (605) 336-6060.
Email Address: info@sfcanaries.com. **Website:** sfcanaries.com.
Operated by: True North Sports, LLC. **Managing Partner/Co-Owner:** Brian Slipka. **Co-Owner:** Anthony Albanese
Executive Vice President: Jack Fossand. **Vice President of Baseball and Stadium Operations:** Duell Higbe.
Director of Entertainment: John Gaskins. **Sales:** Jack Lust and Sebastian Nunuz
Field Manager: Mike Meyer.

GAME INFORMATION
Radio Announcer: Joey Zanaboni. **No. of Games Broadcast:** 100. **Flagship Station:** FOX Sports KWSN 98.1FM/1230AM. **Webcast Address:** www.kwsn.com. **Stadium Name:** Sioux Falls Stadium. **Location:** I-29 to Russell Street, east one mile, south on West Avenue. **Standard Game Times:** Mon.-Fri., 7:05 pm, Sat., 6:05 pm, Sun., 1:05 pm.

WINNIPEG GOLDEYES

Office Address: One Portage Ave E, Winnipeg, Manitoba R3B 3N3.
Telephone: (204) 982-2273. **Fax:** (204) 982-2274.
Email: contact@goldeyes.com. **Website:** www.goldeyes.com.
Operated by: Winnipeg Goldeyes Baseball Club, Inc.
Principal Owner/President: Sam Katz. **General Manager:** Andrew Collier. **Vice President & COO:** Regan Katz. **CFO:** Jason McRae-King. **Director, Sales/Marketing:** Dan Chase. **Manager, Box Office:** Paul Duque. **Coordinator, Food/Beverage:** Melissa Schlichting. **Account Executives:** Steve Schuster, Will Sutton, Sylvia Boslovitch. **Group Sales and Game Presentation:** Ed Doiron. **Digital Media Manager:** Jason Young. **Manager, Retail:** Alex Baronins. **Controller:** TJ Singh. **Facility Manager:** Don Ferguson. **Front office reception:** Lindsay Jestin.
Field Manager/Director, Player Procurement: Rick Forney. **Coach:** Amos Ramon. **Clubhouse Manager:** Jamie Samson. **Athletic Therapist:** TBA.

GAME INFORMATION
Radio Announcer: Steve Schuster. **No. of Games Broadcast:** 100. **Flagship Station:** CJNU 93.7 FM. **Stadium Name:** Shaw Park. **Location:** North on Pembina Highway to Broadway, East on Broadway to Main Street, North on Main Street to Water Avenue, East on Water Avenue to Westbrook Street, North on Westbrook Street to Lombard Avenue, East on Lombard Avenue to Mill Street, South on Mill Street to ballpark. **Standard Game Times:** Mon.-Fri., 6:30 pm, Sat., 6:00 pm, Sun., 1:00 pm.

ATLANTIC LEAGUE

Mailing Address: PO Box 5190, Lancaster, Pa., 17606.
Telephone: (303) 915-8414 or (978) 790-5421.
Email Address: suggestions@atlanticleague.com. **Website:** www.atlanticleague.com.
Year Founded: 1998.
Founder/Chairman: Frank Boulton.
Board of Directors: Brandon Bellamy, Frank Boulton, Jack Lavoie, Susan Martinelli, Andy Shea, Bill Shipley, Eric Shuffler, Coy Willard, Jr., Bob Zuckerman.
President: Rick White.
League Administrator: Emily Merrill. **Director of Communications:** Steve Shutt. **Director of Social Media:** Andrew Bandstra.
Division Structure: North—Lancaster, Long Island, Staten Island, Southern Maryland, York. **South**—Gastonia, High Point, Kentucky, Lexington, West Virginia.
Regular Season: 132 games (split-schedule).
2022 Opening Date: April 21. **Closing Date:** Sept. 18.
Playoff Format: First-half division winners meet second-half winners in best-of-five series; Winners meet in best-of-five final for league championship.
Roster Limit: 27. **Eligibility Rule:** No restrictions; MLB and MiLB suspensions honored.
Brand of Baseball: Drake. **Statistical Service:** Major League Baseball.

STADIUM INFORMATION

Club	Stadium	Opened	Dimensions LF	CF	RF	Capacity	2021 Att.
Charleston	Appalachian Power Park	2005	330	400	320	4,300	85,398
Gastonia	CaroMont Health Park	2021	315	400	325	5,000	114,416
High Point	Truist Point	2019	336	400	339	4,024	108,200
Kentucky	Wild Health Field	2001	320	401	318	6,033	N/A
Lancaster	Clipper Magazine Stadium	2005	320	400	300	6,000	182,132
Lexington	Wild Health Field	2001	320	401	318	7,800	163,798
Long Island	Fairfield Properties Ballpark	2000	325	400	325	6,002	224,120
Staten Island	Ballpark by the Ferry	2001	320	390	318	7,171	N/A
So. Maryland	Regency Furniture Stadium	2008	310	400	325	6,000	148,982
York	PeoplesBank Park	2007	300	4050	325	5,000	111,628

CHARLESTON DIRTY BIRDS

Address: 601 Morris St., Charleston, WV 25301
Telephone: (304) 344-2287
E-Mail: info@dirtybirdsbaseball.com. **Website:** www.dirtybirdsbaseball.com
Years In League: 2021-

OWNERSHIP MANAGEMENT

Operated By: Stands, LLC.
Chair: Andy Shea. **President/CEO:** Chuck Domino.
Vice President/Business Manager: Mary Nixon. **Senior Executive Director of Baseball/Stadium Operations:** Jeremy Taylor. **Executive Director of Food & Beverage:** Aaron Simmons. **Senior Account Executive:** Jay Silverman
Community Ambassador/Sales: Rod Blackstone. **Director of Ticket Operations/Digital Marketing:** Zach Kurdin.
Director of Corporate and Group Sales: George Levandoski. **Account Executive:** Andrew Trotta. **Merchandise Manager:** Jessica Swartz. **Director of Marketing/Entertainment/Media Relations:** Lindsey Webb.
Field Manager: Billy Horn. **Pitching Coach:** Joe Testa. **Hitting Coach:** Scott Kelly.

GAME INFORMATION

Flagship Station/Streaming Platform: YouTube.**com**. **Ballpark:** Appalachian Power Park. **Location:** I-77 South to Capitol Street exit, left on Lee Street, left on Brooks Street.

GASTONIA HONEY HUNTERS

Address: 800 West Franklin Blvd., Gastonia, NC 28052.
Telephone: (704) 874-1810
E-Mail: : info@gohoneyhunters.com. **Website:** www.gohoneyhunters.com.
Years In League: 2021-

OWNERSHIP MANAGEMENT

Operated by: NC Gas House Gang, LLC. **Owner:** Brandon Bellamy. **COO/GM:** David Martin.
Chief Marketing Officer: Veronica Jeon. **Assistant General Manager:** Brady Salisbury. **Box Office Manager:** Lauren

Teer. **Stadium Operations Manager:** Brian Fisher. **Director of Food & Beverage:** TBA. **Account Executives:** Blair Minton, David Traylor, Payne Yoder. **Marketing Associate/Special Asst to CMO:** Madison Welch. **Merchandise:** Morgan Day. **Venue Events Senior Manager:** Christina DeVoe.

FIELD STAFF
Manager: Mauro "Goose" Gozzo. **Hitting Coach:** Chuck Stewart. **Pitching Coach:** Reggie Harris.

GAME INFORMATION
Flagship Station/Streaming Platform: Youtube.com/honeyhuntersmedia. **Ballpark:** Caromont Health Park. **Location:** 800 W. Franklin Blvd, Gastonia.

HIGH POINT ROCKERS

Office Address: 301 N. Elm Street, High Point, NC 27262.
Telephone: (336) 888-1000. **E-Mail Address:** info@highpointrockers.com.
Website: www.HighPointRockers.com. ›**Years In League:** 2019-

OWNERSHIP MANAGEMENT
Operated by: High Point Baseball, Inc.
Chairman, Board of Directors: Coy Williard. **President:** Pete Fisch.
General Manager: Christian Heimall. **Director of Ticket Sales:** Susan Ormond. **Box Office Manager:** Abby Davis. **Facilities Operations Manager:** Shane Poling. **Sales Executive:** J.P. Rooney. **Promotions Manager:** TBA. **Director of Corporate Sales/Merchandise:** Caroline Cooling. **Business Manager:** Sherrie Poplin. **Concessions Manager:** Tyler Runyon. **Director of Communications:** Steve Shutt.

FIELD STAFF
Manager: Jamie Keefe. **Pitching Coach:** Frank Viola. **Bench Coach:** Albert Gonzalez. **Trainer:** Joe Geck

GAME INFORMATION
Radio Announcer: Kendrick Fruits. **Flagship Station/Streaming Platform:** MixlR-Highpointrockersbaseball; YouTube/High Point Rockers Baseball. **Ballpark:** Truist Point. **Location:** 301 N. Elm Street, High Point, NC 27262.

WILD HEALTH GENOMES

Address: 207 Legends Lane, Lexington, KY 40505.
Telephone: : (859) 252-4487. **Fax:** (859) 252-0747. **E-Mail:** cdodd@lexingtonlegends.com.
Website: www.lexingtonlegends.com. **Years In League:** 2022-

OWNERSHIP MANAGEMENT
Operated By: Stands, LLC. **President/CEO:** Andy Shea. **VP Sales/Business Operations:** Colin Dodd. **VP Baseball Operations:** Michael Koltak. **Communications/Baseball Operations Assistant:** Ryan Schwalm. **VP/Facilities:** Chris Pearl. **Chief Brand Officer:** Kara Shepherd. **Ticket Sales Manager:** Ashley Grigsby. **Director of Fan Engagement:** Mike Allison. **Food & Beverage Manager:** Jordan Duncan. **Director of Merchandise:** Sidney Laughlin. **Senior Corporate Sales Executive:** Adam Vrzal. **Account Executives:** Kade Sord, Savannah Stephenson. **Luxury Suite Manager:** Taylor Retinger. **Promotions & Special Projects Manager:** Madison Spencer. **Facility Specialist:** Drew Fagaly.

FIELD STAFF
Manager: Mark Minicozzi. **Pitching Coach:** TBA. **Hitting Coach:** TBA. **Bench Coach:** Michael Koltak. **Trainer:** Joe Holstedt. **Clubhouse Manager:** Brady Woods.

GAME INFORMATION
Radio Announcer: Michael Watkins. **Ballpark:** Wild Health Field. **Location:** 207 Legends Lane, Lexington.

LANCASTER BARNSTORMERS

Address: 650 North Prince Street, Lancaster, PA. 17603.
Telephone: (717) 509-4487. **E-Mail:** info@lancasterbarnstormers.com.
Website: www.LancasterBarnstormers.com. **Years In League:** 2005-

OWNERSHIP MANAGEMENT
Operated By: Lancaster Baseball Club, LLC.
Partners: Bob Zuckerman, Ian Ruzow, Steve Zuckerman, Rob Liss. **President/GM:** Michael Reynolds. **VP, Sales/Marketing:** Kristen Simon. **VP, Operations:** Mike Logan. **CFO:** Pam Raffensberger. **Box Office Manager/Ticket Sales:** Adam Smith. **Corporate Sponsorships:** Melissa Tucker. **Promotions:** Alex Bunn. **Community Relations:** Maureen Wheeler. **Marketing:** Ronnie Ramone. **Special Events:** Sarah Weisenfluh. **Fan Engagement:** Ryan Cortazzo. **Concessions:** Jim Cardone. **Social Media Director:** Laura AlFaridzi.

FIELD STAFF
Manager: Ross Peeples. **Hitting Coach:** Jeff Bianchi. **Bench Coach:** Troy Steffy. **Trainer:** Anya Holmberg. **Clubhouse**

Manager: Blake Glass.

GAME INFORMATION

Radio Announcer: Dave Collins. **Flagship Station/Streaming Platform:** YouTube.com/York Revolution. **Ballpark:** Clipper Magazine Stadium. **Location:** 650 N. Prince St, Lancaster, PA.

LEXINGTON LEGENDS

Address: 207 Legends Lane, Lexington, KY 40505.
Telephone: (859) 252-4487. **E-Mail Address:** cdodd@lexingtonlegends.com.
Website: www.lexingtonlegends.com. **Years In League:** 2021-

OWNERSHIP MANAGEMENT

Operated By: Stands, LLC.
President/CEO: Andy Shea. **VP Sales/Business Operations:** Colin Dodd. **VP Baseball Operations:** Michael Koltak. **VP/Facilities:** Chris Pearl. **Chief Brand Officer:** Kara Shepherd. **Communications/Baseball Operations Assistant:** Ryan Schwalm. **Ticket Sales Manager:** Ashley Grigsby. **Director of Fan Engagement:** Mike Allison. **Food & Beverage Manager:** Jordan Duncan. **Director of Merchandise:** Sidney Laughlin. **Senior Corporate Sales Executive:** Adam Vrzal. **Account Executives:** Kade Sord, Savannah Stephenson. **Luxury Suite Manager:** Taylor Retinger. **Promotions & Special Projects Manager:** Madison Spencer.

FIELD STAFF

Manager: P.J. Phillips. **Pitching Coach:** J.J. Hoover. **Hitting Coach:** Jeremy Moore. **Bench Coach:** Cip Garza. **Team Medical Director:** Joe Holstedt. **Clubhouse Manager:** Brady Woods.

GAME INFORMATION

Radio Announcer: Michael Watkins. **Flagship Station/Streaming Platform:** YouTube.com/Lexington Legends. **Ballpark:** Wild Health Field. **Location:** 207 Legends, Lane, Lexington, KY.

LONG ISLAND DUCKS

Address: Fairfield Properties Ballpark, 3 Court House Dr, Central Islip, NY 11722.
Telephone: (631) 940-3825. **E-Mail:** info@liducks.com. **Website:** www.liducks.com.
Years In League: 2000-

OWNERSHIP MANAGEMENT

Operated By: Long Island Ducks Professional Baseball Club, LLC.
Founder/CEO: Frank Boulton. **Owner/Chairman:** Seth Waugh. **President/General Manager:** Michael Pfaff. **Assistant GM/Senior VP, Sales:** Doug Cohen. **VP, Box Office:** Brad Kallman. **VP, Communications:** Michael Polak. **Staff Accountant:** Annmarie DeMasi. **Dir., Group Sales:** Sean Smith. **Dir., Stadium Operations:** Anthony Polito. **Stadium Operations Manager:** Anthony Fiorelli. **Human Resources/Office Manager:** Christine Blumenauer. **Merchandise Manager:** Michelle Jensen. **Promotions & Community Relations Manager:** Tom Policastro. **Account Executives:** Matt Heilbrunn, Matt Markowski, Harrison Nolan, Yadiel Corporan. **Head Groundskeeper:** Dakota Smothergill. **Administrative Coordinator:** Christian Petrucci. **GM, Food & Beverage:** Alan Goodman. **Director, Catering, Suites & Restaurant:** Dave Jagsarran.

FIELD STAFF

Manager: Wally Backman. **Hitting Coach:** Lew Ford. **Pitching Coach:** Rick Tomlin. **Director, Sports Medicine:** Tony Amin. **Head Athletic Trainer:** Deanna Reynolds. **Clubhouse Manager:** Emil Coccaro.

GAME INFORMATION

Radio Announcers: Michael Polak, Michael Mohr, Chris King, David Weiss. **Flagship Station/Streaming Platform:** LIDucks.com; Facebook.com/liducks; YouTube.com/ducksbaseball. **Ballpark:** Fairfield Properties Ballpark. **Location:** 3 Court House Dr, Central Islip, NY.

SOUTHERN MARYLAND BLUE CRABS

Address: 11765 St. Linus Drive, Waldorf, Maryland 20602.
Telephone: (301) 638-9788. **E-Mail:** info@somdbluecrabs.com.
Website: www.somdbluecrabs.com. **Years In League:** 2008-

OWNERSHIP MANAGEMENT

Operated By: Crabs On Deck, LLC.
General Manager: Courtney Knichel. **Senior Director, Marketing & Broadcasting:** Andrew Bandstra. **Box Office Manager:** Abby Quirk. **Group Sales:** Omar Saulters. **Marketing/Broadcast Coordinator:** Stevie Bowen. **Stadium Operations:** Sheila Wilkerson. **Concessions:** United Food and Beverage. **Groundskeeper:** Ben Baker.

FIELD STAFF

Manager: Stan Cliburn. **Bench Coach:** Joe Walsh. **Pitching Coach:** Daryl Thompson. **Hitting Coach:** Ray Ortega. **Trainer:** Lauren Eck.

GAME INFORMATION

Radio Announcer: Andrew Bandstra. **Ballpark:** Regency Furniture Stadium. **Location:** 11765 St. Linus Drive, Waldorf, MD.

STATEN ISLAND FERRYHAWKS

Address: 75 Richmond Terrace, Staten Island, NY 10301. **E-Mail:** fun@ferryhawks.com. **Website:** www.ferryhawks.com. **Years In League:** 2022-

OWNERSHIP MANAGEMENT

Operated By: Staten Island Entertainment, LLC.

Owner: John Catsimatidis. **President/CEO:** Eric Shuffler. **Vice President/GM:** Gary Perone. **Player Personnel Director:** Eddie Medina. **Ticket Sales:** David Budash, Angelo Gradilone. **Fan Engagement & Ticket Sales:** Guy Zoda. **Corporate Sponsorships:** Joe Macchiarola. **Promotions:** Chelsea Ortiz. **Facility/Events Director:** Ray Irizarry. **Manager, Creative Services:** Trish Konczynski. **Director of Communications:** Joseph Langan

FIELD STAFF

Manager: Edgardo Alfonzo. **Hitting Coach:** TBA. **Pitching Coach:** TBA. **Trainer:** TBA

GAME INFORMATION

Ballpark: Ballpark by the Staten Island Ferry. **Location:** 75 Richmond Terrace, Staten Island, NY.

YORK REVOLUTION

Address: 5 Brooks Robinson Way, York, PA 17401.
Telephone: (717) 801-4487. **Email:** info@yorkrevolution.com.
Website: www.yorkrevolution.com. **Years In League:** 2007-

OWNERSHIP MANAGEMENT

Operated by: York Professional Baseball Club, LLC.

Owner: Bill Shipley. **President:** Eric Menzer. **General Manager/Vice President, Operations:** John Gibson. **VP, Business Development:** Nate Tile. **Director, Marketing/Communications:** Doug Eppler. **Director of Ticket & Retail Operations:** Cindy Brown. **Director of Group Sales:** Brandon Tesluk. **Marketing Manager:** Sarah Dailey. **Creative Director:** Cody Bannon. **Director of Operations:** David Dicce. **Director of Grounds & Field Operations:** Chris Carbaugh. **Creative Director:** Cody Bannon.

FIELD STAFF

Manager: Mark Mason. **Hitting/Third Base Coach:** Enohel Polanco. **Bench Coach:** Sandy DeLeon. **Trainer:** Meg Haas.

GAME INFORMATION

Radio Announcer: Darrell Henry Flagship Station/Streaming Platform: WOYK 98.9 FM/1350 AM; YouTube.com/York Revolution. **Ballpark:** PeoplesBank Park. **Location:** 5 Brooks Robinson Way, York, PA.

FRONTIER LEAGUE

Office Address: 2041 Goose Lake Rd Suite 2A, Sauget, IL 62206.
Telephone: (812) 437-8709. **Fax:** (708) 286-6481
Email Address:office@frontierleague.com. **Website:** www.frontierleague.com.
Year Founded: 1993.
CEO: Jon Danos
Commissioner Emeritus: Bill Lee.
Deputy Commissioners: Kevin Winn, Steve Tahsler.
President: Brian Lyter (Schaumburg). **Vice Presidents:** Al Dorso (Sussex County), Tom Kramig (Lake Erie), Michel Laplante (Quebec).
Board of Directors: David DelBello (Florence), Rich Sauget Jr. (Gateway), John Wilson (Joliet), Greg Lockard (New Jersey), Shawn Reilly (New York), Regan Katz (Ottawa), Rick Murphy (Tri-City), Rene Martin (Trois-Rivieres), Stu Williams (Washington), Mike VerSchave (Windy City).
Division Structure: East—New Jersey, New York, Ottawa, Quebec, Sussex County, Tri-City, Trois-Rivieres. **West**—Evansville, Florence, Gateway, Joliet, Lake Erie, Schaumburg, Washington, Windy City.
Regular Season: 96 games. **2021 Opening Date:** May 12. **Closing Date:** Sept 4.
Playoff Format: 2nd place team vs. 1st place team in best-of-five Divisional Series. Winners advance to best-of-five Championship Series.
Roster Limit: 24. **Eligibility Rule:** Minimum of ten Rookie 1/Rookie 2 players. Maximum of four players born before October 1, 1993. **Brand of Baseball:** Rawlings.
Statistician: PrestoSports

STADIUM INFORMATION

Club	Stadium	Opened	Dimensions LF	CF	RF	Capacity	2021 Att.
Evansville	Bosse Field	1915	315	415	315	5,110	76,482
Florence	UC Health Stadium	2004	325	395	325	4,200	83,217
Gateway	GCS Ballpark	2002	318	395	325	5,500	62,416
Joliet	DuPage Medical Group Field	2002	330	400	327	6,229	86,067
Lake Erie	Mercy Health Stadium	2009	325	400	325	5,000	70,062
New Jersey	Yogi Berra Stadium	1998	308	398	308	3,784	43,722
New York	Palisades Credit Union Park	2011	323	403	313	4,750	99,693
Ottawa	Ottawa Stadium	1993	325	404	325	10,332	n/a
Quebec	Stade Canac	1938	315	385	315	4,500	n/a
Schaumburg	Wintrust Field	1999	355	400	353	8,107	157,112
Sussex County	Skylands Stadium	1994	330	392	330	4,200	79,762
Tri-City	Joseph L. Bruno Stadium	2002	325	400	325	4,500	100,519
Trois-Rivieres	Stade Quillorama	1938	342	372	342	4,500	n/a
Washington	Wild Things Park	2002	325	400	325	3,200	82,420
Windy City	Ozinga Field	1999	335	390	335	2,598	65,022

EVANSVILLE OTTERS

Mailing Address: 23 Don Mattingly Way, Evansville, IN 47711.
Telephone: (812) 435-8686.
Website: www.evansvilleotters.com.
Facebook—Evansville Otters, **Twitter**—@EvilleOtters, **Instagram**—@evansvilleotters
Operated by: Evansville Baseball, LLC.
Owner: Bussing family. **President:** John Stanley. **Vice President, Sales:** Joel Padfield. **General Manager:** Travis Painter. **Director of Communications:** Preston Leinenbach. **Account Executive:** Keith Millikan. **Account Executive:** Nolan Vandergriff. **Director of Marketing/Community Relations:** Brittany Skinner. **PA Announcer:** Zane Clodfelter. **Field Manager:** Andy McCauley.

GAME INFORMATION

No. of Games Broadcast: Home-51, Away-45. **Radio/Video Stream:** evansvilleotters.com (Otters Digital Network). **Stadium Name:** Bosse Field (Opened in 1915). **Directions:** US 41 to Lloyd Expressway West (IN-62), Main St Exit, Right on Main St, ahead 1 mile to Bosse Field. **Standard Game Times:** Mon.-Sat., 6:35pm, Sun., **12:**35pm, - 5:05pm.
Doubleheaders: 5:35 p.m. **Visiting Club Hotel:** The Comfort Inn & Suites, 3901 Highway 41 North, Evansville, IN 47711. Phone 812-423-5818.

GATEWAY GRIZZLIES

Telephone: (618) 337-3000. **Email Address:** info@gatewaygrizzlies.com.
Website: www.gatewaygrizzlies.com.

Owner: Annie Sauget-Miller
General Manger: Steve Gomric. **Assistant General Manager:** James Caldwell. **Assistant General Manager:** Kurt Ringkamp. **Box Office & Graphics Marketing Manager:** Nate Owens. **Events & Sales Representatives:** Garret Murphy. **Director of Group Sales & Hospitality:** Nick Clemens. **Stadium Operations Assistant:** Sam Kehrer. **Marketing Assistant:** Bailey Redden. **Manager:** Steve Brook. **Pitching Coach:** Nick Kennedy. **Bench Coach:** Alex Ferguson. **Assistant Coach:** Dave Garcia.

GAME INFORMATION

No. of Games Broadcast: Home-48, Away-48. **PA Announcer:** Tom Calhoun. **Stadium Name:** GCS Credit Union Ballpark. **Location:** I-255 at exit 15 (Mousette Lane).

JOLIET SLAMMERS

Office Address: 1 Mayor Art Schultz Dr, Joliet, IL 60432
Telephone: (815) 722-2287
E-Mail Address: info@jolietslammers.com. **Website:** www.jolietslammers.com.
Owner: Joliet Community Baseball & Entertainment, LLC.
Chief Financial Officer: Heather Mills. **Executive Vice President of Baseball Operations/Chief Revenue Officer:** John Wilson. **Director of Food & Beverage:** Doug Clements. **Director of Community Relations:** Ken Miller. **Assistant General Manager:** Lauren Rhodes. **Marketing and Corporate Services Manager:** Lauren Baca. **Director of Promotions:** Brianna Avalos. **Box Office Manager:** Trey Wolters.
Field Manager: TBD

GAME INFORMATION

No. of Games Broadcast: 96. **Flagship Station:** www.jolietslammers.com. **Stadium Name:** DuPage Medical Group Field. **Location:** 1 Mayor Art Schultz Drive, Joliet, IL 60432. **Standard Game Times:** Mon.-Fri., 7:05 pm, Sat., 6:05 pm., Sun., 1:05 pm.

LAKE ERIE CRUSHERS

Address: 2009 Baseball Boulevard. Avon, Ohio 44011. **Telephone:** 440-934-3636.
Website: www.lakeeriecrushers.com.
Operated by: Blue Dog Baseball, LLC.
Managing Officer: Tom Kramig
Sr. Advisor: Ron Way. **Asst. GM/Director of Sales & Marketing:** Bryan Ralston. **Account Executives:** Andrew Fish, Jarrett Griebeler. **Box Office Manager:** Nathan Parker. **Corporate Sales Account Executives:** Brittany Valentine, Forrest Hage. **Director of Stadium Operations:** Wayne Loeblein. **Business Manager:** Brian Wentzel. **Director, Concessions/Catering:** OPEN . **Digital Marketing Manager:** Alyssa Bozin. **Promotions Manager:** Izzy Farmwald. **Director, Broadcasting:** Andy Barch. **Field Manager:** Camron Roth

GAME INFORMATION

Stadium Name: Mercy Health Stadium. **Location:** Intersection of I-90 and Colorado Ave in Avon, OH. **Standard Game Times:** Mon-Fri., 7:05 pm, Sat., 6:05 pm, Sun., 2:05 pm.

NEW JERSEY JACKALS

Office Address: 8 Yogi Berra Drive, Little Falls, NJ 07424. **Telephone:** (973) 746-7434.
Email Address: contact@jackals.com. **Website:** www.jackals.com.
Owner/President: Al Dorso. **President, Baseball Operations:** Gregory Lockard.
Sr. Vice President, Operations: Al Dorso Jr. **Vice President, Marketing:** Mike Dorso. **General Manager:** Gil Addeo. **Director, Creative Services:** William Romano. **Public Relations:** Chris Faust
Field Manager: Brooks Carey

GAME INFORMATION

No. of Games Broadcast: 96. **Webcast Address:** www.jackals.com. **Stadium Name:** Yogi Berra Stadium. **Location:** On the campus of Montclair State University; Route 80 or Garden State Parkway to Route 46, take Valley Road exit to Montclair State University. **Standard Game Times:** Mon.-Fri., 7:05 pm, Sat., 6:05 pm., Sun., 2:05 pm.

NEW YORK BOULDERS

Team President/GM: Shawn Reilly. **EVP:** Rob Janetschek.

Assistant GM, Digital Media: Megan Ciampo. **VP of Business Development:** Seth Cantor. **Director of Finance:** Michele Almash. **Director of Creative and Media Services:** Julie Trainor. **Promotions Director:** Jules Clyne. **Ticket Sales Manager:** Karen McCombs. **Box Office Manager:** Nicole Cartaino. **Account Executive:** Clayton Devries. **Media Relations:** Ken Kostik. **Facilities and Operations Coordinator:** Bobby Nodelman. **Educational Director:** Gail Gultz. **PR & Media Coordinator:** Steve Balsan. **Palisades Food Sevice Manager:** Brenda Richter.

Field Manager: TJ Stanton. **Player Procurement/Scouting:** Kevin Tuve.

GAME INFORMATION

Stadium Name: Clover Stadium. **Location:** 1 Palisades Credit Union Park Drive. **Standard Game Times:** Mon.-Fri. 7pm, Sat. 6:30pm. Sun. May/June. 1:30pm. July/August. 4 pm

OTTAWA TITANS

Mailing Address: 300 Coventry Road, Ottawa, ON, K1K 4P5. **Telephone:** (343) 633-2273. **Fax:** (343) 633-2274.

Website: www.ottawatitans.com. **E-Mail:** . contact@ottawatitans.com

Founded: 2020. **First Year In League:** 2022.

Operated by: Ottawa Titans Baseball Club Inc.

Principal Owner/President/CEO: Sam Katz

Co-Owners: Ottawa Sports & Entertainment Group, Jacques J.M. Shore

Vice President/COO: Regan Katz. **CFO:** Jason McRae-King. **General Manager:** Martin Boyce. **Assistant General Manager:** Sebastien Boucher. **Vice President of Sales and Operations:** Davyd Balloch.

Media Manager/Broadcaster: Davide Disipio. **Corporate Sales Executive:** Mike Beard. **Box Office Manager:** Matthew Rose. **Administrative & Merchandise Manager:** Jasmine Doobay-Joseph. **Business Development:** Melissa Schlichting. **IT & Misc.:** Jason Young, Ed Doiron. **Food & Beverage Manager:** AJ Scarcella. **Clubhouse Manager:** Marc Leduc.

Field Manager & Director of Baseball Operations: Bobby Brown.

GAME INFORMATION

Stadium: Ottawa Stadium. **Year Opened:** 1993. **Official Scorer:** Frank Calamatas

English Announcer: Davide Disipio. **Standard Game Times: M-F:** 6:30 p.m.; **Saturday:** 6:00 p.m.; **Sunday:** 1:00 pm.

QUEBEC CAPITALES

Owners: Jean Tremblay, Pierre Tremblay, Michel Laplante

President: Michel Laplante. **General Manager:** Charles Demers. **Assistant General Manager:** Jean Grignon-Francke. **Communications Director:** Dave Rouleau. **Sales Director:** Denis Desbiens

Ticketing Coordinator: Marie-Christine Rouette. **Promotions and Community Coordinator, Fondation of Capitales:** Janel Laplante. **Partnership Coordinator:** Francine Gendron. **Victoria Baseball Complex: Alexandre Harvey Graphic Consultant:** Frédéric Gariépy. **Graphic Designer:** Jade Harnish. **Gift Shop Manager:** Marc-André Langlois.

Field Manager: Patrick Scalabrini.

GAME INFORMATION

Stadium Name: Stade Canac. **Location:** 100 Cardinal Maurice-Roy, Quebec, QC, G1K 8Z1. **Standard Game Times:** Tue.-Fri., 7:05 pm, Sat., 7:05 pm, Sun., 5:05 pm.

SCHAUMBURG BOOMERS

Office Address: 1999 Springinsguth Road, Schaumburg, IL 60193

Email Address: info@boomersbaseball.com. **Website:** www.boomersbaseball.com.

Owned by: Pat and Lindy Salvi. **Vice President & General Manager:** Michael Larson.

Assistant GM: Hanna Olson. **Director of Facilities:** Mike Tlusty. **Director Food/Beverage:** Julia Fasiang. **Broadcaster:** Tim Calderwood. **Box Office Manager:** Christopher Salazar. **Director of Promotions:** Lexi Fiolka. **Director of Community Relations:** Peter Long. **Director of Marketing & Media:** Alyson Kobler. **Director of Baseball Operations:** Ricky Rapp. **Director of Stadium Operations:** Ryan Veith

Field Manager: Jamie Bennett.

GAME INFORMATION

Broadcaster: Tim Calderwood. **No. of Games Broadcast:** Home-48, Away-48. **Flagship Station:** WRMN 1410 AM Elgin. **Stadium:** Wintrust Field. **Location:** I-290 to Thorndale Ave Exit, head West on Elgin-O'Hare Expressway until Springinsguth Road Exit, second left at Springinsguth Road (shared parking lot with Schaumburg Metra Station). **Visiting Club Hotel:** SpringHill Suites 1550 McConnor Pkwy, Schaumburg, IL 60173

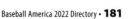

SUSSEX COUNTY MINERS

Owner, President: Al Dorso Sr. **Vice President, Operations:** Al Dorso Jr. **Vice President, Marketing:** Mike Dorso.
General Manager: Justin Ferrarella. **Director, Broadcasting and Media Relations:** Bret Leuthner. **Senior Graphic Design:** Will Romano. **Broadcasting, PXP, & Media Relations:** Sean Bretherick. **Manager, Stadium Operations:** William Darmstead. **Head Groundskeeper:** L.J. Black. **Group Sales:** Sergio Rivas-Ortiz.
Field Manager/Director of Baseball Operations: Bobby Jones.

GAME INFORMATION

Broadcaster: Bret Leuthner. **No. of Games Broadcast:** 100. **Webcast Address:** www.scminers.com.
Stadium Name: Skylands Stadium. **Location:** In New Jersey, I-80 to exit 34B (Route 15 North) to Route 565 North; From Pennsylvania, I-84 to Route 6 (Matamoras) to Route 206 North to Route 565 North. **Standard Game Times:** Mon.-Fri., 7:05 pm, Sat., 6:05 pm, Sun., 2:05 pm.

TRI-CITY VALLEYCATS

Office Address: Joseph L Bruno Stadium, 80 Vandenburgh Ave, Troy, NY 12180.
Mailing Address: PO Box 694, Troy, NY 12181.
Telephone: (518) 629-2287. **Fax:** (518) 629-2299.
E-Mail Address: info@tcvalleycats.com. **Website:** www.tcvalleycats.com

OWNERSHIP/MANAGEMENT

Operated By: Tri-City ValleyCats Inc. **Principal Owners:** Martin Barr, Jane Burton, Doug Gladstone, Rick Murphy, Stephen Siegel. **President:** Rick Murphy. **Vice President/General Manager:** Matt Callahan. **Assistant GM:** Michelle Skinner. **Ticket Sales and Operations Manager:** Jessica Guido. **Food & Beverage Manager:** Missy Henry. **Stadium Operations Manager:** Ed Krajewski. **Media Relations Coordinator:** Jacob LaChapelle. **Hospitality & Special Events Coordinator:** Maggie Stalter. **Account Executive:** Sam Kinum.

FIELD STAFF

Manager: Pete Incaviglia. **Bench Coach:** Thomas Incaviglia. **Pitching Coach:** Joe Gannon

GAME INFORMATION

Radio Announcer: Joe Mixie. **No. of Games Broadcast:** 53. **Flagship Station:** TBD. **PA Announcer:** Anthony Pettograsso. **Official Scorer:** Patrick Barry. **Stadium Name:** Joseph Bruno Stadium. **Location:** From north, I-87 to exit 7 (Route 7), go east 1 1⁄2 miles to I-787 South, to Route 378 East, go over bridge to Route 4, right to Route 4 South, one mile to Hudson Valley Community College campus on left; From south, I-87 to exit 23 (I-787), I-787 north six miles to exit for Route 378 east, over bridge to Route 4, right to Route 4 South, one mile to campus on left; From east, Massachusetts Turnpike to exit B-1 (I-90), nine miles to Exit 8 (Defreestville), left off ramp to Route 4 North, five miles to campus on right; From west, I-90 to exit 24 (I-90 East), I-90 East for six miles to I-787 North (Troy), 2.2 miles to exit for Route 378 East, over bridge to Route 4, right to Route 4 south for one mile to campus on left. **Standard Game Times:** Mon. - Thurs. 630pm, Fri. - Sat. 7pm. Sun. 5 pm. **Ticket Price Range:** $5.50-$13.50. **Visiting Club Hotel:** The Desmond Hotel Albany, 660 Albany-Shaker Road, Albany, NY 12211. **Telephone:** (518) 869-8100.

TROIS-RIVIÈRES AIGLES

Office Address: 1760 Avenue Gilles-Villeneuve, Trois-Rivières, QC G9A 5K8.
Telephone: (819) 379-0404. **Email Address:** info@lesaiglestr.com.
Website: www.lesaiglestr.com
Owners: Côté-Reco Group and Vertdure Group. **President:** René Martin. **General Manager:** Simon Laliberté.
Director, Marketing: Maxime Bordeleau. **Operations Director:** Frédérik Bélanger. **Advisor, Partnerships And Events:** Étienne Rivard. **Ticketing Coordinator:** Sylvie Dubé.
Field Manager: Matt Rusch. **Coaches:** Kyle Lafrenz.

GAME INFORMATION

No. of Games Broadcast: 51. **Webcast Address:** www.cfou.ca/direct.php.
Stadium Name: Stade Quillorama. **Location:** Take Hwy 40 West, exit Boul. des Forges/Centre-ville, keep right, turn right at light, turn right at stop sign.

WASHINGTON WILD THINGS

Office Address: One Washington Federal Way, Washington, PA 15301.
Telephone: (724) 250-9555. **Fax:** (724) 250-2333.
Email Address: info@washingtonwildthings.com
Website: washingtonwildthings.com.
Owned by: Sports Facility, LLC. **Operated by:** Washington Frontier League Baseball,
LLC. **Managing Partners:** Stu Williams, Francine W. Williams. **Executive Director, Sports Facility, LLC:** Steve Zavacky.
President/General Manager: Tony Buccilli. **Vice President:** Christine Blaine. **Vice President of Finance, Sports Facility,
LLC:** JJ Heider. **Broadcaster, Media Relations:** Kyle Dawson. **Operations Manager:** Travis Pettit. **Creative Services and
Production Manager:** Sean Seaman. **Community Relations Manager:** Stephanie Keller. **Account Executive:** Jesus Paez.
Account Executive: Erik Stouter.
Field Manager: Tom Vaeth.

GAME INFORMATION
Stadium Name: Wild Things Park. **Location:** I-70 to exit 15 (Chestnut Street), right on Chestnut Street to Washington
Crown Center Mall, right at mall entrance, right on to Mall Drive to stadium.
Standard Game Times: Mon.-Sat., 7:05 pm, Sun., 5:35 pm.

WINDY CITY THUNDERBOLTS

Office Address: 14011 South Kenton Avenue, Crestwood, IL 60418
Telephone: (708) 489-2255. **Fax:** (708) 489-2999.
Email Address: info@wcthunderbolts.com. **Website:** www.wcthunderbolts.com.
Owned by: Franchise Sports, LLC.
General Manager: Mike VerSchave. **Assistant GM:** Bill Waliewski. **Director, Community Relations:** Johnny Sole.
Director, Not-For-Profit Events: Karen Engel.
Field Manager: Brian Smith. **Hitting Coach:** Kevin Santiago.

GAME INFORMATION
No. of Games Broadcast: 96. **Flagship Station:** WXAV, 88.3 FM. **Official Scorer:** Chris Gbur. **Stadium Name:** Ozinga
Field. **Location:** I-294 to South Cicero Ave, exit (Route 50), south for 1 1/2 miles, left at Midlothian Turnpike, right on
Kenton Ave; I-57 to 147th Street, west on 147th to Cicero, north on Cicero, right on Midlothian Turnpike, right on Kenton.
Standard Game Times: Mon.-Fri., 7:05 pm, Sat., 6:05 pm, Sun., 2:05 pm.

PIONEER BASEBALL LEAGUE

Office Address: 1111 Diamond Valley Rd, Suite 105 Windsor, CO 80550.
Telephone: 509-456-7615.
E-Mail Address: fanmail@pioneerleague.com.
Website: www.pioneerleague.com.
Years League Active: 1939-42, 1946-
President: Mike Shapiro. **Commissioner:** Jim McCurdy. **Vice President:** Henry Hunter. **Director of League Administration:** Rachel Blackman. **Director of Business Operations:** Josh Gonzalez. **Director of New Media:** Jackson Shapiro.
Directors: Dave Baggott (Ogden), Peter C. Davis (Missoula), Chris Phillips (Rocky Mountain), Kevin Greene (Idaho Falls), Hal Roth (Grand Junction), Vinny Purpura (Great Falls), Dave Heller (Billings), Jeff Eiseman (Boise), Marty Kelly (Glacier) and Jeff Katofsky (Windsor).
Regular Season: 96 games (split schedule). **2022 Opening Date:** May 23. **Closing Date:** Sept. 10.
Playoff Format: Three-game divisional playoffs. Winners meet in best-of-three series for league championship. **Roster Limit:** 25 active, minimum of 22 dressed for each game. **Player Eligibility Rule:** The players on a Member Club's Active Roster may have played professional baseball for three (3) or fewer years.

STADIUM INFORMATION

Club	Stadium	Opened	LF	CF	RF	Capacity	2021 Att.
Billings	Dehler Park	2008	329	410	350	3,071	96,594
Boise	Memorial Stadium	1989	335	400	335	3,426	129,805
Grand Junction	Sam Suplizio Field	1949	302	400	333	7,014	102,015
Great Falls	Centene Stadium at Legion Park	1956	335	414	335	3,800	83,826
Idaho Falls	Melaleuca Field	1976	340	400	350	3,400	81,870
Missoula	Ogren Park at Allegiance Field	2004	309	398	287	3,500	87,981
Ogden	Lindquist Field	1997	335	396	334	5,000	88,751
Rocky Mountain	Security Service Field	1988	350	410	350	8,500	88,112
Glacier	Flathead Field	2022					
Windsor	Future Legends Complex	2022					

BILLINGS MUSTANGS

Office Address: Dehler Park, 2611 9th Avenue North, Billings, MT 59101.
Mailing Address: PO Box 1553, Billings, MT 59103-1553.
Telephone: (406) 252-1241. **Fax:** (406) 252-2968.
E-Mail Address: mustangs@billingsmustangs.com. **Website:** billingsmustangs.com.
Years in League: 1948-63, 1969-

OWNERSHIP/MANAGEMENT
Operated By: Mustangs Baseball LLC.
President/CEO: Dave Heller. **General Manager:** Gary Roller. **Director, Stadium Operations:** Matt Schoonover. **Director, Broadcasting/Media Relations:** TBA. **Director, Food and Beverage Services:** Curt Prchal. **Director, Field Operations:** Sam Sheets.

FIELD STAFF
Manager: TBA. **Hitting Coach:** TBA. **Pitching Coach:** TBA. **Bench Coach:** TBA. **Athletic Trainer:** TBA. **Strength & Conditioning Coach:** TBA.

GAME INFORMATION
Radio Broadcaster: TBA. **No. of Games Broadcast:** 96. **Flagship Station:** ESPN 910-AM KBLG. **PA Announcer:** Sarah Spangle. **Official Scorer:** Evan O'Kelly. **Stadium Name:** Dehler Park. **Location:** I-90 to Exit 450, north on 27th Street North to 9th Avenue North. **Standard Game Times:** Mon.–Sat., 6:35 pm, Sun., 1:05 pm. **Ticket Price Range:** $6-$12.

BOISE HAWKS

Address: 5600 N. Glenwood St. Boise, ID 83714.
Telephone: (208) 322-5000. **Fax:** (208) 322-6846.
Website: www.boisehawks.com **Years in League:** 1975-76, 1978, 1987-Present.

OWNERSHIP/MANAGEMENT
Operated by: Boise Professional Baseball LLC. **President:** Jeff Eiseman. **HR & Operations:** Missy Martin. **Vice President:** Bob Flannery. **General Manager:** Mike Van Hise. **Director, Stadium Ops/Food & Beverage:** Jake Lusk. **Manager, Accounting/Office:** Judy Peterson. **Ticket Sales Manager:** Matt Osbon. **Group Event Executive:** Colton Hampson. **Account Executive:** Kristi Croteau, Andrew Lee. **Assistant Director, Stadium Operations:** Christian Lomeli. **Media Relations/Marketing Manager:** Paige Plotzke. **Head Groundskeeper:** John Gides.

FIELD STAFF
   Manager: Gary Van Tol. **Hitting Coach:** TBD. **Pitching Coach:** Michiel van Kampen.

GAME INFORMATION
   Radio Announcer: Leonard Barry. **No. of Games Broadcast:** 96. **Flagship Station:** TBD. **PA Announcer:** Jeremy Peterson. **Official Scorer:** Curtis Haines. **Stadium Name:** Memorial Stadium. **Location:** I-84 to Cole Rd., north to Western Idaho Fairgrounds at 5600 North Glenwood St. **Standard Game Time:** 7:15 pm. **Ticket Price Range:** $8-35. **Visiting Club Hotel:** Simple Suites.

GLACIER RANGE RIDERS

Address: 75 McDermott Lane Kalispell, MT 59901
Website: gorangeriders.com
E-mail: information@gorangeriders.com. **Years in League:** 2022-

OWNERSHIP/MANAGEMENT
   Operated by: Ridge Run Enterprises, LLC. **Principal Owner:** Marty Kelly. **Vice President:** Chris Kelly. **GM:** Erik Moore. **Director of Baseball Operations:** Nick Hogan. **Marketing & Entertainment:** Taylor Huntman. **Sales & Marketing:** Leo Kelly.

FIELD STAFF
   Manager: Nick Hogan.

GAME INFORMATION
   No. of Games Broadcast: 96.

GRAND JUNCTION ROCKIES

Address: 1315 North Ave., Grand Junction, CO, 81501
Telephone: (970) 255-7625. **Fax:** (970) 241-2374
Email: mritter@gjrockies.com. **Website:** www.gjrockies.com
Years in League: 2001–

OWNERSHIP/MANAGEMENT
   Principal Owners/Operated by: GJR, LLC. **President:** Mick Ritter. **Assistant GM:** Matt Allen. **Director of Broadcasting and Sales:** Ethan Jordan.

FIELD STAFF
   Manager: TBA. **Hitting Coach:** TBA. **Pitching Coach:** TBA. **Supervisor:** TBA.

GAME INFORMATION
   Radio Announcer: Ethan Jordan. **No. of Games Broadcast:** 96. **Flagship Station:** TBA, gjrockies.com. **Television Announcer:** Ethan Jordan. **No. of Games Televised:** 48. **Flagship:** KGJT, My Network, Dish Network. **Produced by:** Colorado Mesa University. **PA Announcer:** Tim Ray. **Official Scorers:** Unknown. **Stadium Name:** Suplizio Field. **Location:** 1315 North Ave. Grand Junction, CO 81501. **Standard Game Times:** 6:40 pm. **Ticket Price Range:** $7-$12.

GREAT FALLS VOYAGERS

Address: 1015 25th St N, Great Falls, MT 59401.
Telephone: (406) 452-5311. **Fax:** (406) 454-0811.
E-Mail Address: voyagers@gfvoyagers.com. **Website:** www.gfvoyagers.com.
Years in League: 1948-1963, 1969-

OWNERSHIP/MANAGEMENT
   Operated By: Great Falls Baseball Club.
   Owner/CEO: Vinny Purpura. **President:** Scott Reasoner. **Assistant General Manager:** John Burks.

FIELD STAFF
   Manager: Tommy Thompson. **Hitting Coach:** TBD. **Pitching Coach:** TBD.

GAME INFORMATION
   Radio Announcer: Shawn Tiemann. **No. of Games Broadcast:** 96. **Flagship Station:** KXGF-1400 AM. **PA Announcer:** Chris Evans. **Official Scorer:** Mike Lewis. **Stadium Name:** Centene Stadium. **Location:** From I-15 to exit 281 (10th Ave S), left on 26th, left on Eighth Ave North, right on 25th, ballpark on right, past railroad tracks. **Ticket Price Range:** $8-15. **Visiting Club Hotel:** Days Inn, 101 14th Ave NW, Great Falls, MT 59404. **Telephone:** (406) 727-6565

IDAHO FALLS CHUKARS

Office Address: 900 Jim Garchow Way, Idaho Falls, ID 83402.
Mailing Address: PO 2183, Idaho, ID 83403. **Telephone:** (208) 522-8363. **Fax:** (208) 522-9858.
E-Mail Address: chukarsbaseball@gmail.com. **Website:** www.ifchukars.com.
Years in League: 1940-42, 1946-

OWNERSHIP/MANAGEMENT

Operated By: The Elmore Sports Group. **Principal Owner:** David Elmore. **President/General Manager:** Kevin Greene. **Vice President:** Paul Henderson. **Assistant GM:** Chris Hall. **Clubhouse Manager:** TBA. **Head Groundskeeper:** Tony McCarty.

FIELD STAFF

Manager: Billy Gardner Jr. **Hitting Coach:** TBA. **Pitching Coach:** Bob Milacki.

GAME INFORMATION

Radio Announcer: John Balginy. **No. of Games Broadcast:** 96. **Flagship Station:** ESPN 980-AM & 94.5 and 105.1FM. **PA Announcer:** Javier Hernandez. **Official Scorer:** John Balginy. **Stadium Name:** Melaleuca Field. **Location:** I-15 to West Broadway exit, left onto Memorial Drive, right on Mound Avenue, 1/4 mile to the stadium. **Standard Game Times:** Mon.-Sat., 7:15 pm, Sun., 4:00 pm. **Ticket Price Range:** $10-14. **Visiting Club Hotel:** Shilo Inn, 780 Lindsay Blvd, Idaho Falls, ID 83402. **Telephone:** (208) 523-0088.

MISSOULA PADDLEHEADS

Address: 140 N Higgins, Suite 201, Missoula, MT 59802. **Telephone:** (406) 543-3300. **E-Mail Address:** mellis@gopaddleheads.com. **Website:** www.gopaddleheads.com.
Years in League: 1956-60, 1999-

OWNERSHIP/MANAGEMENT

Operated By: Big Sky Professional Baseball LLC. **Co-Chairs:** Peter & Susan Crampton Davis.
President: Matt Ellis. **Senior Director of Sales and Retail:** Kim Klages Johns. **1st Impresssions Manager:** Halle Nurse. **Director of Creative Content Manager:** Wesley Harton. **Director of Wow:** Sam Boyd. **Retail Manager:** Dawna Kulaski. **Group Sales Manager:** Matt Zaleski. **Administration & eCommerce Specialist:** Jeanie Leidholt. **Accounting Director:** Rebecca Anciaux.

FIELD STAFF

Manager: Michael Schlact. **Hitting Coach:** TBA. **Pitching Coach:** TBA. **Bench Coach:** TBA. **Athletic Trainer:** TBA. **Strength & Conditioning Coach:** TBA.

GAME INFORMATION

Radio Announcer: TBA. **No. of Games Broadcast:** 98. **Flagship Station:** ESPN 102.9 FM. **PA Announcer:** TBA. **Official Scorer:** TBA. **Stadium Name:** Ogren Park Allegiance Field. **Location:** 700 Cregg Lane, Missoula MT 59801. **Directions:** Take Orange Street to Cregg Lane, west on Cregg Lane, stadium west of McCormick Park past railroad trestle. **Standard Game Times:** Mon.-Sat., 7:05 pm, Sun., 5:05 pm. **Ticket Price Range:** $9-$17.

NORTHERN COLORADO OWLZ

Address: 1801 Diamond Valley Drive Windsor, CO 80550. **Telephone:** 970-460-0151. **E-Mail Address:** info@futurelegendscomplex.com. **Website:** www.nocoowlz.com. **Years in League:** 2022-

OWNERSHIP/MANAGEMENT

Principal Owner: Jeff Katofsky. **President/GM:** Rosie Aguilera. **Executive Director of Operations:** Casey Katofksy. **Director of Marketing and Communications:** Damian Foley. **Digital Media Manager:** Nathan Martinez. **Associate General Manager:** Harrison Shapiro.

GAME INFORMATION

No. of Games Broadcast: 96.

OGDEN RAPTORS

Address: 2330 Lincoln Ave, Ogden, UT 84401. **Telephone:** (801) 393-2400. **Fax:** (801) 393-2473.
E-Mail Address: homerun@ogden-raptors.com. **Website:** www.ogden-raptors.com.
Years in League: 1939-42, 1946-55, 1966-74, 1994-Present

OWNERSHIP/MANAGEMENT

Operated By: Ogden Professional Baseball, Inc. **Principal Owners:** Dave Baggott, John Lindquist.

President/General Manager: Dave Baggott. **General Manager:** Trever Wilson. **Assistant Director of Game Day Operations:** Richard Armstrong. **Director, Social Media:** Kevin Johnson. **Director, Information Technology:** Chris Greene. **Groundskeeper:** Kenny Kopinski. **Official Scorer:** Dennis Kunimura.

FIELD STAFF

Manager: Kash Beauchump. **Hitting Coach:** TBA. **Pitching Coach:** Les Lancaster. **Clubhouse Manager:** Dave "MacGyver" Ackerman.

GAME INFORMATION

Radio Announcer: Andrew Haynes. No. **of Games Broadcast:** 96. **Flagship Station:** ogden-raptors.com. **PA Announcer:** Pete Diamond. **Official Scorer:** Dennis Kunimura. **Stadium Name:** Lindquist Field. **Location:** I-15 North to 21th Street exit, east to Lincoln Avenue, south three blocks to park. **Standard Game Times:** Mon.-Sat., 7 pm, Sun., 4pm. **Ticket Price Range:** $6-12. **Visiting Club Hotel:** Unavailable.

ROCKY MOUNTAIN VIBES

Address: 4385 Tutt Blvd., Colorado Springs, CO 80922.
Telephone: (719) 597-1449. **Fax:** (719) 597-2491.
E-Mail Address: info@vibesbaseball.com. **Website:** www.vibesbaseball.com.
Years in League: 2019-

OWNERSHIP/MANAGEMENT

Operated By: Rocky Mountain Vibes. **Principal Owner:** Dave Elmore. **President/General Manager:** Chris Jones. **Assistant GM:** Aaron Griffith. **Vice President:** Kyle Fritzke.

Director of Promotions: Cliff Cage. **Group Sales Manager:** Jake Hathaway. **Event Manager:** Brien Smith. **Clubhouse Manager:** Dan Ortiz

FIELD STAFF

Manager: Matías Carrillo García. **Pitching Coach:** Mike Garcia

GAME INFORMATION

No. **of Games Broadcast:** 96. **Flagship Station:** Tuneln. **PA Announcer:** TBD. **Official Scorer:** TBD. **Stadium Name:** UCHealth Park. **Location:** I-25 South to Woodmen Road exit, east on Woodmen to Powers Blvd., right on Powers to Barnes Road. **Standard Game Times:** Mon.-Fri., 6:40 pm, Sat., 6:00 pm, Sun., 1:30 pm. **Ticket Price Range:** $5-15..

INDEPENDENT LEAGUES

PECOS LEAGUE

Website: www.PecosLeague.com.
Address: PO Box 271489, Houston, TX 77277.
Telephone: (575) 680-2212.
E-mail: info@pecosleague.com.
Commissioner: Andrew Dunn.
All-Star Game: Santa Fe, July 10
Pacific Division: Santa Rosa Scuba Divers, Santa Rafael Pacifics, Santa Cruz Seaweed, Martinez Sturgeon, Monterey Amberjacks, Wasco Reserve, Bakersfield Train Robbers and Tucson Saguaros.
Mountain Division: Roswell Invaders, Alpine Cowboys, Austin Weirdos, Weimar Hormigas, Santa Fe Fuego, Trinidad Triggers, Garden City Wind and Colorado Springs Snow Sox.
Year Founded: 2010.
Regular Season: 50 games. **Start Date:** May 22. **Finish Date:** July 31.
Playoffs: Top two teams from each division beginning on Aug. 1.
Eligibility Rules: 25 and under.
Brand of Baseball: Rawlings.

UNITED SHORE PROFESSIONAL BASEBALL LEAGUE

Location: Jimmy Johns Field. 7171 Auburn Rd, Utica, MI. 48317
Telephone: (248) 601-2400
Email: baseballoperations@uspbl.com. **Website:** www.uspbl.com
Owner and CEO: Andy Appleby. **Chief Operating Officer:** Dana Schmitt.
Senior Vice President, Client Services: Jeremiah Hergott. **Executive Director of Baseball Operations:** Justin Orenduff. **Vice President, Tickets & Premium Sales:** Dan Griesbaum Jr. **Senior Director of Baseball Administration:** Mike Zielinski. **Director of Finance & Accounting:** Nick Cowles. **Finance Assistant:** Thomas Soma. **Corporate Partnership Services Manager:** Dan Veit. **Director of Food & Beverage:** Gabriela Kirkland. **Assistant Director of Food & Beverage:** Ronald Johnson. **Special Events & Suite Catering Manager:** Azaria Ali. **Senior Director of Ballpark Operations:** Dillon DuBois. **Merchandise Manager:** Abbey Robinson. **Senior Director of Marketing & Public Relations:** Katie Page. **Graphic Designer:** Courtney Allen. **Director of Premium Sales & Service:** Adam Lewis. **Senior Director of Ticket Operations:** Brian Piper.
Teams: Birmingham-Bloomfield Beavers, Eastside Diamond Hoppers, Utica Unicorns, Westside Woolly Mammoths.
Managers: Birmingham: Ed Campaniello. **Eastside:** Paul Noce. **Utica:** Jim Essian. **Westside:** John Dombrowski/Taylor Grzelakowski.
DVS Pitching: Shane McCatty. **Director of Player Development:** Willi Martin. **Scouting Consultant:** Ryan Pothakos. **Development Coach:** Scott Pickens. **Development Coach:** Doug Martin.
Roster Limit: 20. **Eligibility Rules:** Players must be between 18 and 26 years old.
2022 Start Date: May 20th. **End Date:** Sept. 3. **All-Star Game:** July 9. **Playoffs:** Sept. 9-11. **Season length:** 50 games per team. **Playoff Format:** Single-game elimination.

INTERNATIONAL

AMERICAS

MEXICO

MEXICAN LEAGUE

Address: Avenida Insurgentes Sur #797 Interior 3 y 4. Col. Nápoles. C.P. 03810, Benito Juárez, Ciudad de México. **Telephone:** 52-5557-1007. **E-Mail Address:** oficina@lmb. com.mx. **Website:** milb.com/mexican

Years League Active: 1955-

President: Horacio De la Vega Flores. **Director, Administration:** Oscar Neri Rojas Salazar.

Division Structure: North—Aguascalientes, Dos Laredos, Durango, Guadalajara, Laguna, Monclova, Monterrey, Saltillo, Tijuana. **South**—Campeche, Leon, Mexico City, Oaxaca, Puebla, Quintana Roo, Tabasco, Veracruz, Yucatan.

Regular Season: 90 games (split-schedule). **2022 Opening Date:** April 21. **Closing Date:** Aug. 7.

Playoff Format: Five teams from each division qualify for a four-round playoff. Championship round is best-of-seven series.

Roster Limit: 28. **Roster Limit, Imports:** 7.

AGUASCALIENTES RIELEROS

Office Address: Andador Manuel Madrigal 102 Héroes 20190 Aguascalientes. **Telephone:** 01 449 915 15 96 y 97. **E-Mail Address:** hola@rielerosags.com. **Website:** rielerosags.com

President: Tacho Alvarez. **General Manager:** Enrique Reyes. **Manager:** Luis Rivera.

CAMPECHE PIRATAS

Office Address: Calle Filiberto Qui Farfan No. 2, Col. Camino Real, CP 24020, Campeche. **Telephone:** (52) 981-827-4759. **E-Mail Address:** http://www.piratasdecampeche.mx/contacto/ **Website:** piratasdecampeche.mx.

President: Jorge Carlos Hurtado Montero. **General Manager:** Gabriel Lozano Berron.

Manager: Francisco Campos.

DOS LAREDOS TECOLOTES

Office Address: Reforma 4310, Col. México, Nuevo Laredo, Tamps. **Telephone:** (52) 1 867 279 8519. **E-Mail Address:** contacto@tecolotes2laredos.com. **Website:** tecolotes2laredos.com.

President/CEO: Chara Mansur Beltran. **General Manager:** Cuitlahuac Rodriguez Garza-Gongora.

Manager: Mark Weidemaier.

DURANGO GENERALES

Office Address: De Los Deportes, Unidad Deportiva, 98065_00 Zacatecas, ZAC. **Telephone:** (52) 618-196-4267. **E-Mail Address:** info@generalesdedurango. com. **Website:** generalesdedurango.com.

President: Virgilio Ruiz Isassi. **General Manager:** Enrique Couoh.

Manager: Alvaro Espinoza.

GUADALAJARA MARIACHIS

Office Address: Santa Lucia #373 Colonia Tepeyac, Zapopan, Jalisco C.P 45150. **Telephone:** (52) 333-037-7969. **Website:** mismariachis.com.mx.

President: Rafael Tejeda. **Manager:** Omar Gastelum.

LAGUNA ALGODONEROS

Office Address: Algodoneros Unión Laguna Juan Gutemberg s/n C.P. 27000 Torreón, Coah. Estadio Revolución. **Telephone:** (52) 871-718-5515. **E-Mail**

Address: info@unionlaguna.mx. **Website:** unionlaguna. mx.

President: Francisco Orozco Marín. **General Manager:** Jorge Luis Lechuga Torres.

Manager: Oscar Robles.

LEON BRAVES

Office Address: Estadio Domingo Santana Boulevard Congreso de Chilpancingo 803, Unidad Deportiva. León Guanajuato, México. CP 37237. **Telephone:** (52) 477-272-8675. **E-Mail Address:** contacto@bravosdeleon. mx. **Website:** bravosdeleon.com.

President: Arturo Blanco Díaz. **General Manager:** Daniel Espino. **Manager:** Eduardo Arredondo.

MEXICO CITY DIABLOS ROJOS

Office Address: Av río Churubusco #1001, Colonia ex-ejidos de la Magdalena Mixhuca, Alcaldía Iztacalco, C.P. 08010 CDMX. **Telephone:** (56) 91-28-72-92. **E-Mail Address:** contacto@diablos-rojos.com. **Website:** diablos.com.mx.

President: Alfredo Harp Helu. **General Manager:** Jorge Del Valle Mohar.

Manager: Miguel Ojeda.

MONCLOVA ACEREROS

Office Address: Cuauhtemoc #299, Col Ciudad Deportiva, CP 25750, Monclova, Coahuila. **Telephone:** (52) 866-636-2650. **E-Mail Address:** contacto@acereros. com.mx. **Website:** acereros.com.mx.

President: Gerardo Benavides Pape. **General Manager:** Miguel Valentin Gamez Mendoza.

Manager: Mickey Callaway.

MONTERREY SULTANES

Office Address: Estadio de Béisbol Monterrey, en Av. Manuel L. Barragán S/N, Col. Regina, CP. 64290 Monterrey, N.L. **Telephone:** (52) 81-2270-2000. **E-Mail Address:** info@ sultanes .com.mx. **Website:** sultanes.com.mx.

President: José Maiz Garcia. **General Manager:** Miguel Flores. **Manager:** Gerardo Alvarez.

OAXACA GUERREROS

Office Address: Calz. Héroes de Chapultepec S.N. esq calle de los Derechos Humanos Col. Centro, Oaxaca de Juárez. **Telephone:** (52) 951-515-5522. **E-Mail Address:** contacto@guerreros.mx. **Website:** guerreros.mx.

President: Lorenzo Peón Escalante.

General Manager: Jaime Brena Núñez.

Manager: Erick Rodriguez.

PUEBLA PERICOS

Office Address: Calz. Ignacio Zaragoza 666, Maravillas. 72220 Puebla, Mexico. **E-Mail Address:** contacto@pericosdepuebla.com. **Website:** pericosdepuebla. com.

President: Jose Miguel Bejos. **General Manager:** Mario Valenzuela.

Manager: Wilfredo Romero.

QUINTANA ROO TIGRES

Office Address: SM 21, 21, 77500 Cancún, Quintana Roo. Telephone: (52) 998-887-3108. **E-Mail Address:** medios@tigresqroo.com. **Website:** tigresqroo.com.

President: Fernando Valenzuela Burgos. **General Manager:** Francisco Minjarez Garcia.

Manager: Tony Rodriguez.

SALTILLO SARAPEROS

Office Address: Blvd. Nazario Ortiz S/N Col. Ciudad Deportiva CP. 25284 Saltillo, Coahulia. Telephone: (52) 844-

416-9455. **E-Mail Address:** contacto@saraperos.com.mx. **Website:** saraperos.com.mx.
President: Cesar H. Cantu Garcia. **General Manager:** Roberto Magdaleno.
Manager: Roberto Vizcarra.

TABASCO OLMECAS

Office Address: Avenida Velodromo de la Ciudad Deportiva S/N, Atasta, 86100 Villahermosa, Tabasco. Telephone: (52) 993-352-2787. **E-Mail Address:** hola@olmecastabasco.mx. **Website:** olmecastabasco.mx.
President: Juan Carlos Manzur Pérez. **General Manager:** Felix Zulueta García.
Manager: Pedro Mere.

TIJUANA TOROS

Office Address: Mision de Santo Tomas Rio Eufrates con, Col. Infonavit Capistrano, 22223 Tijuana, B.C., Mexico. **Telephone:** (52) 664-635-5600. **E-Mail Address:** contacto@torosdetijuana.com. **Website:** torosdetijuana.com.
President: Alberto Ignacio Uribe Maytorena. **General Manager:** Ricky Williamson.
Manager: Homar Rojas.

VERACRUZ AGUILA

Office Address: Paseo Jacarandas 224 B, Virginia, 94294, Boca del Río, Veracruz. **E-Mail Address:** contacto@elaguiladeveracruz.com. **Website:** elaguiladeveracruz.com.
President: Bernardo Pasquel. **General Manager:** Fernando Magro Soto.
Manager: Emmanuel Valdez.

YUCATAN LEONES

Office Address: Calle 6 Nº315 x 35, Col. Morelos Oriente, Mérida, Yucatán. C.P. 97174. **Telephone:** (52) 999-432-0655. **E-Mail Address:** contacto@leones.mx. **Website:** leones.mx.
President: Juan José Arellano. **General Manager:** Alejandro Orozco Garcia.
Manager: Luis Matos.

MEXICAN ACADEMY

Rookie Classification
Mailing Address: Ubicación: Av. El Fundador #100, Col. San Miguel, El Carmen N.L., C.P. 66550. **Telephone:** (81) 8158-7900. Fax: (52) 555-395-2454. **E-Mail Address:** pgarza@academia-lmb.com. **Website:** academia-lmb.com.

President: C.P. Plinio Escalante Bolio. **Director General:** Salvador Viera Higuera. **Communications:** Pablo Garza Garcia.
Regular Season: 50 games. **Opening Date:** Not available. **Closing Date:** Not available.

DOMINICAN REPUBLIC

DOMINICAN SUMMER LEAGUE

Member, National Association
Rookie Classification
Mailing Address: Calle Segunda No 64, Reparto Antilla, Santo Domingo, Dominican Republic. **Telephone:** (809) 532-3619. **Website:** dominicansummerleague.com. **E-Mail Address:** ligadeverano@codetel.net.do.
Years League Active: 1985-.
President: Orlando Diaz.
Member Clubs/Division Structure: North—Cubs Blue, Dodgers Shoemaker, Guardians Reds, Pirates Black, Rangers1, Rays2, Red Sox Blue, Royals White. **South**—Angels, Cardinals Blue, Mets1, Nationals, Phillies Reds, Rockies, Twins, Yankees1. **Northeast**—Brewers2, Colorado, D-backs2, Giants Orange, Mariners, Orioles2, Pirates Gold, Yankees2. **Northwest**—Astros, Athletics, Dodgers Bautista, Guardians Blue, Marlins, Rays1, Red Sox Red, Royals Blue. **Baseball City**—Blue Jays, D-backs1, Orioles1, Padres, Reds, White Sox. **San Pedro**—Brewers2, Cardinals Red, Cubs Red, Giants Black, Mets2, Phillies White, Rangers2, Tigers.
Regular Season: 72 games. **Opening Date:** Unavailable. **Closing Date:** Unavailable.
Playoff Format: Six teams qualify for playoffs, including four division winners and two wild-card teams. Teams with two best records receive a bye to the semifinals; four other playoff teams play best-of-three series. Winners advance to best-of-three semifinals. Winners advance to best-of-five championship series.
Roster Limit: 35 active. **Player Eligibility Rule:** No player may have four or more years of prior minor league service. No draft-eligible player from the U.S. or Canada (not including players from Puerto Rico) may participate in the DSL. No age limits apply.

JAPAN

Mailing Address: Mita Bellju Building, 11th Floor, 5-36-7 Shiba, Minato-ku, Tokyo 108-0014. **Telephone:** 03-6400-1189. **Fax:** 03-6400-1190.
Website: npb.or.jp, npb.or.jp/eng
Commissioner: Atsushi Saito.
Secretary General: Atsushi Ihara. **Executive Director, Baseball Operations:** Minoru Hata. **Executive Director, NPB Rules & Labor:** Nobuhisa "Nobby" Ito.
Executive Director, Central League Operations: Kazuhide Kinefuchi. **Executive Director, Pacific League Operations:** Kazuo Nakano.
Directors: Kenji Miyoshi, Tomoharu Inoue, Mitsuo Iida, Hoshi Harumi, Hidenori Ebata, Tatsuto Shimada, Kazuaki Mihara, Hiroyuki Kato, Shosaku Yokota, Osamu Tanimoto, Kiyoaki Suzuki, Mitsuro Owaki
Nippon Series: Best-of-seven series between Central and Pacific League champions, begins Oct. **22**.

All-Star Series: July 26 at Fukuoka PayPay Dome; Matsuyama Botchan Stadium.
Roster Limit: 70 per organization (one major league club, one minor league club). Major league club is permitted to register 28 players at a time, though just 25 may be available for each game.
Roster Limit, Imports: Four in majors (no more than three position players or pitchers); unlimited in minors.

CENTRAL LEAGUE

Regular Season: 143 games.
2022 Opening Date: March 25.
Playoff Format: Second-place team meets third-place team in best-of-three series. Winner meets first-place team in best-of-seven series to determine representative in Japan Series (first-place team has one-game advantage to begin series).

CHUNICHI DRAGONS
Mailing Address: Chunichi Bldg 6F, 4-1-1 Sakae, Naka-ku, Nagoya 460-0008. **Telephone:** 052-261-8811.
Field Manager: Kazuyoshi Tatsunami.

HANSHIN TIGERS
Mailing Address: 2-33 Koshien-cho, Nishinomiya-shi, Hyogo-ken 663-8152. **Telephone:** 0798-46-1515.
Field Manager: Akihiro Yano.

HIROSHIMA TOYO CARP
Mailing Address: 2-3-1 Minami Kaniya, Minami-ku, Hiroshima 732-8501. **Telephone:** 082-554-1000.
Field Manager: Shinji Sasaoka.

TOKYO YAKULT SWALLOWS
Mailing Address: Seizan Bldg, 4F, 2-12-28 Kita Aoyama, Minato-ku, Tokyo 107-0061. **Telephone:** 03-3405-8960.
Field Manager: Shingo Takatsu.

YOKOHAMA DENA BAYSTARS
Mailing Address: Kannai Arai Bldg, 7F, 1-8 Onoe-cho, Naka-ku, Yokohama 231-0015. **Telephone:** 045-681-0811.
Field Manager: Daisuke Miura.

YOMIURI GIANTS
Mailing Address: Yomiuri Shimbun Bldg, 26F, 1-7-1 Otemachi, Chiyoda-ku, Tokyo 100-8151. **Telephone:** 03-3246-7733. **Fax:** 03-3246-2726.
Manager: Tatsunori Hara.

PACIFIC LEAGUE
Regular Season: 143 games.
2022 Opening Date: March 26. **Closing Date:** Oct. 21.
Playoff Format: Second-place team meets third-place team in best-of-three series. Winner meets first-place team in best-of-seven series to determine league's representative in Japan Series (first-place team has one-game advantage to begin series).

CHIBA LOTTE MARINES
Mailing Address: 1 Mihama, Mihama-ku, Chiba-shi, Chiba-ken 261-8587. **Telephone:** 03-5682-6341.
Field Manager: Tadahito Iguchi.

FUKUOKA SOFTBANK HAWKS
Mailing Address: Fukuoka Yahuoku Japan Dome, Hawks Town, 2-2-2 Jigyohama, Chuo-ku, Fukuoka 810-0065. **Telephone:** 092-847-1006. **Owner:** Masayoshi Son.
Field Manager: Hiroshi Fujimoto.

HOKKAIDO NIPPON HAM FIGHTERS
Mailing Address: 1 Hitsujigaoka, Toyohira-ku, Sapporo 062-8655. **Telephone:** 011-857-3939.
Field Manager: Tsuyoshi Shinjo.

ORIX BUFFALOES
Mailing Address: 3-Kita-2-30 Chiyozaki, Nishi-ku, Osaka 550-0023. **Telephone:** 06-6586-0221. **Fax:** 06-6586-0240.
Field Manager: Satoshi Nakajima.

SAITAMA SEIBU LIONS
Mailing Address: 2135 Kami-Yamaguchi, Tokorozawa-shi, Saitama-ken 359-1189. **Telephone:** 04-2924-1155. **Fax:** 04-2928-1919.
Field Manager: Hatsuhiko Tsuji.

TOHOKU RAKUTEN GOLDEN EAGLES
Mailing Address: 2-11-6 Miyagino, Miyagino-ku, Sendai-shi, Miyagi-ken 983-0045. **Telephone:** 022-298-5300. **Fax:** 022-298-5360.
Field Manager: Kazuhisa Ishii.

KOREA

KOREA BASEBALL ORGANIZATION
Mailing Address: 946-16 Dokokdong, Kangnam-gu, Seoul, Korea. **Telephone:** (02) 3460-4600. **Fax:** (02) 3460-4639.
Years League Active: 1982-.
Website: koreabaseball.com.
Commissioner: Ji-Taek Ji. **Secretary General:** Yang Hae-Young.
Member Clubs: Doosan Bears, Hanwha Eagles, Kia Tigers, KT Wiz, LG Twins, Lotte Giants, NC Dinos, Kiwoom Heroes, Samsung Lions, SSG Landers.
Regular Season: 144 games. **2022 Opening Date:** April 2.
All-Star Game: July 16.
Playoffs: Third- and fourth-place teams meet in best-of-three series; winner advances to meet second-place team in best-of-five series; winner meets first-place team in best-of-seven Korean Series for league championship.
Roster Limit: 26 active through Sept 1, when rosters expand to 31. **Imports:** Two active.

TAIWAN

CHINESE PROFESSIONAL BASEBALL LEAGUE
Mailing Address: 2F, No 32, Pateh Road, Sec 3, Taipei, Taiwan 10559. **Telephone:** 886-2-2577-6992. **Fax:** 886-2-2577-2606. **Website:** cpbl.com.tw.
Years League Active: 1990-.
Commissioner: Chi-Chang Tsai.
Member Clubs: EDA Rhinos, Chinatrust Brothers, Lamigo Monkeys, Uni-President 7-Eleven Lions, Weichuan Dragons.
Regular Season: 120 games. Each team plays 60 games in the first and second halves of the season.
Player Limits: 25 active players. Three foreign players and no more than two foreign players on the field per team at any time.
2022 Opening Date: April 2. **All-Star Game:** July 30-31. **Postseason Start:** Oct. 29. **Playoffs:** Half-season winners are eligible for the postseason. If a non-half-season winner team possesses a higher overall winning percentage than any other half-season winner, then this team gains a wild card and will play a best-of-five series against the half-season winner with the lower winner percentage. The winner of the playoff series advances to Taiwan Series (best-of-seven). If the same team clinches both first- and second-half seasons, then that team is awarded one win to start the Taiwan Series.

EUROPE

NETHERLANDS

DUTCH MAJOR LEAGUE CLUBS

Mailing Address: Koninklijke Nederlandse Baseball en Softball Bond (Royal Dutch Baseball and Softball Association), Postbus 2650, 3430 GB Nieuwegein, Holland.Telephone: 31-30-202-0100..**Website:** www.knbsb.nl

QUICK AMERSFOORT
Mailing Address: Postbus 780, 3800 AT Amersfoort. **Telephone:** +31 (0) 33-461-1914. **Website:** www.bsc-quick.nl

L&D AMSTERDAM PIRATES
Mailing Address: Herman Bonpad 5, 1067 SN Amsterdam. **Telephone:** +31 (0) 20-616-2151. **Website:** www.amsterdampirates.nl

CURACAO NEPTUNE
Mailing Address: Abraham van Stolkweg 31, 3041 JA Rotterdam. **Telephone:** +31 (0) 10-737-5369. **Website:** neptunussport.com

DSS/KINHEIM
Mailing Address: Rijksstraatweg 206, 2022 DH Haarlem. **Telephone:** +31 (0) 23-527-2678. **Website:** www.dss-honksoftbal.nl

SILICON STORKS
Mailing Address: Postbus 53016, 2505 AA 'S-Gravenhage. **Telephone:** +31 (0) 70-323-4151. **Website:** www.storks.nl

HCAW
Mailing Address: Zanderijweg 4-6, 1403 XV Bussum. **Telephone:** +31 (0) 35-693-1430. **Website:** www.hcaw.nl

HOOFDDORP PIONIERS
Mailing Address: Postbus 475, 2130 AL Hoofddorp. **Telephone:** +31 (0) 23-561-3557. **Website:** www.hoofd-dorp-pioniers.nl

OOSTERHOUT TWINS
Mailing Address: Postbus 4085, 4900 CB Oosterhout NB. **Telephone:** +31 (0) 162-433-760. **Website:** www.twins-sc.com

RCH PINGUINS
Mailing Address: Ringvaartlaan 4 2103 XW Heemstede. **Telephone:** +31 (0) 023-528-4388. **Website:** www.rch-pinguins.nl

ITALY

ITALIAN BASEBALL LEAGUE CLUBS

Mailing Address: Federazione Italiana Baseball Softball, Viale Tiziano 74, 00196 Roma, Italy. **Telephone:** 39-06-32297201. **FAX:** 39-06-01902684. **Website:** www.fibs.it
President: Marco Landi.
Teams: Group A: Settimo Asd; Cagliari B.C. Asd; Ciemme Oltretorrente Bc; Ecotherm Brescia; Grizzlies Torino 48; Parmaclima; Platform-Tmc Poviglio; Senago Baseball. Group B: Asd Bas. Soft. Rovigo; Camec Collecchio Baseball; Metalco Dragons; New Black Panthers A.S.D.; Padova Bas. Soft. Club; Sultan Allestimenti Navali; Tecnovap Verona; Unipolsai Fortitudo. Group C: A.S.D. B.S.C. Godo; A.S.D. Longbridge 2000 B.C.; Csa Srl Torre Pedrera Falcons Sc Asd; Erba Vita New Rimini Baseball; Farma Crocetta B.C. Asd; Fontana Ermes Sala Baganza; S.S.D. Modena B.C.- Soc. Coop.; San Marino. Group D: Academy Of Nettuno Baseball Orange; Asd Nettuno B.C. 1945; Athletics Baseball; Big Mat B.S.C. Grosseto 1952; Hotsand Macerata; Jolly Roger; Paternò Red Sox Asd.

WINTER BASEBALL

CARIBBEAN BASEBALL CONFEDERATION

Mailing Address: Frank Feliz Miranda No 1 Naco, Santo Domingo, Dominican Republic. **Telephone:** (809) 381-2643. **Fax:** (809) 565-4654.
Commissioner: Juan Francisco Puello. **Secretary:** Benny Agosto.
Member Countries: Cuba, Colombia, Dominican Republic, Mexico, Nicaragua, Panama, Puerto Rico, Venezuela.
2023 Caribbean Series: Caracas, Venezuela, February.

DOMINICAN LEAGUE

Office Address: Ave. Tiradentes, Ensanche La Fé, Estadio Quisqueya, Santo Domingo, Dominican Republic. **Telephone:** (809) 567-6371. **Fax:** (809) 567-5720. **E-Mail Address:** ligadom@hotmail.com. **Website:** lidom.com.
Years League Active: 1951-.
President: Vitelio Mejía Ortiz. **Vice President:** Winston Llenas Davila.
Member Clubs: Aguilas Cibaenas, Estrellas de Oriente, Gigantes del Cibao, Leones del Escogido, Tigres del Licey, Toros del Este.

Regular Season: 50 games.
Playoff Format: Top four teams meet in 18-game round-robin. Top two teams advance to best-of-nine series for league championship. Winner advances to Caribbean Series.
Roster Limit: 30. **Imports:** 7.

MEXICAN PACIFIC LEAGUE

Mailing Address: Ave. Américas No. 1905, 5to. Piso, Col. Colomos Providencia, Guadalajara, Jalisco. **Telephone:** (52) 333-817-0768. **E-Mail Address:** medios@lmp.mx. **Website:** lmp.mx.
Years League Active: 1958-.
President: Omar Canizales Soto. **General Manager:** Christian Veliz Valencia.
Member Clubs: Culiacan Tomateros, Guasave Algodoneros, Hermosillo Naranjeros, Jalisco Charros, Los Mochis Cañeros,Mazatlan Venados, Mexicali Aguilas, Monterrey Sultanes, Navojoa Mayos, Obregon Yaquis.
Regular Season: 68 games.
Playoff Format: Six teams advance to best-of-seven quarterfinals. Three winners and losing team with best record advance to best-of-seven semifinals. Winners meet in best-of-seven series for league championship. Winner advances to Caribbean Series.
Roster Limit: 30. **Imports:** 5.

PUERTO RICAN LEAGUE

Office Address: Avenida Munoz Rivera 1056, Edificio First Federal, Suite 501, Rio Piedras, PR 00925. **Mailing Address:** PO Box 191852 San Juan, PR 00919--1852. **Telephone:** (786) 244-1146. **Website:** ligapr.com. **E-mail address:** info@ligapr.com
Years League Active: 1938-2007; 2008-
President: Juan Flores Galarza. **Operations Director:** Carlos J. Berroa Puertas. **Press Director:** Edna Garcia.
Member Clubs: Caguas Criollos, Carolina Gigantes, Mayaguez Indios, RA12, Santurce Cangrejeros.
Regular Season: 40 games.
Playoff Format: Top four teams meet in round robin series, with top two teams advancing to best-of-seven final. Winner advances to Caribbean Series.
Roster Limit: 30. **Imports:** 5.

VENEZUELAN LEAGUE

Mailing Address: Avenida Casanova, Centro Comercial "El Recreo," Torre Sur, Piso 3, Oficinas 6 y 7, Sabana Grande, Caracas, Venezuela. **Telephone:** (58) 212-761-6408. **Website:** lvbp.com.
Years League Active: 1946-.
President: Giuseppe Palmisano. **Vice Presidents:** Humberto Oropeza, Antonio Jose Herrera. **General Manager:** Domingo Alvarez.
Member Clubs: Anzoategui Caribes, Aragua Tigres, Caracas Leones, La Guaira Tiburones, Lara Cardenales, Magallanes Navegantes, Margarita Bravos, Zulia Aguilas.
Regular Season: 64 games.
Playoff Format: Top two teams in each division, plus a wild-card team, meet in 16-game round-robin series. Top two finishers in best-of-seven series for league championship. Winner advances to Caribbean Series.
Roster Limit: 26. **Imports:** 7.

COLOMBIAN LEAGUE

Office/Mailing Address: Hotel Eslait Cra 53 No. 72-27 2do piso, Baranquilla. **Telephone:** (57) 368-6561. **E-mail Address:** r.mendoza@diprobeisbol.com. **Website:** lpbcol.com.
President: Pedro Salzedo Salom. **Director, Operations:** Abdala Villa Eljach. **Director, Communications:** Ricardo Mendoza Puccini.
Member Clubs: Barranquilla Caimanes, Barranquilla Gigantes, Cartagena Tigres, Monteria Vaqueros, Santa Marta Leones, Sincelejo Toros.
Regular season: 42 games.
Playoff Format: Top three teams play 10-game round robin. Top two teams meet in best-of-seven finals for league championship.

AUSTRALIA

AUSTRALIAN BASEBALL LEAGUE

Address: Suite 3.03 (Level 3) 88 Albert Road South Melbourne, VIC 3205. **Telephone:** (61) 3 9915 9900. **E-Mail Address:** playbaseball@baseball.com.au. **Website:** theabl.com.au.
CEO: Glenn Williams. **General Manager:** Shane Tonkin. **Editor-In-Chief, Content Manager:** David Penrose.
Teams: Adelaide Giants, Auckland Tautara, Brisbane Bandits, Canberra Cavalry, Melbourne Aces, Perth Heat, Sydney Blue Sox.
Opening Date: Unavailable. Play usually opens in November with playoffs in February.
Playoff Format: The teams with the best four records qualify for the playoffs. Teams are seeded 1-4, with the top two seeds hosting all three games of the best-of-three semifinal series. Winners advance to a best-of-three championship series.

DOMESTIC LEAGUE

ARIZONA FALL LEAGUE

Mailing Address: Arizona Fall League C/O Salt River Fields - Centerfield Office 7555 North Pima Road Scottsdale, AZ 85258. **Telephone:** (480)-990-1005. **E-Mail Address:** arizonafallleague@mlb.com. **Website:** mlb.com/arizona-fall-league. **Years League Active:** 1992-.
Operated by: Major League Baseball.
Communications: Chuck Fox.
Teams: Glendale Desert Dogs, Mesa Solar Sox, Peoria Javelinas, Salt River Rafters, Scottsdale Scorpions, Surprise Saguaros.
Regular season: 32 games. **Opening Date:** Unavailable. Play in 2021 began on Oct. 13 with the championship game on Nov. 20. **Playoff Format:** Division champions meet in one-game championship.
Roster Limit: 35 players per team plus a "taxi squad" of reserve players. Each major-league organization is required to provide seven players. Triple-A and Double-A players are eligible provided they are on Double-A or Triple-A rosters no later than August 15. Each organization is permitted to send two high Class A level players and two players below high Class A. No players with more than one year active or two years total of credited major-league service as of August 31 (including major league disabled list time) are eligible. Each team is allotted 20 pitchers but only 15 are designated "active" each game day.

COLLEGES

COLLEGE ORGANIZATIONS

NATIONAL COLLEGIATE ATHLETIC ASSOCIATION

Mailing Address: 700 W. Washington Street, PO Box 6222, Indianapolis, IN 46206. **Telephone:** (317) 917-6222. **Fax:** (317) 917-6826 (championships), (317) 917-6710 (baseball).

E-mail Addresses: Division I Championship: aholman@ncaa.org (Anthony Holman), rlburhr@ncaa.org (Randy Buhr), ctolliver@ncaa.org (Chad Tolliver), thalpin@ncaa.org (Ty Halpin), kgiles@ncaa.org (Kim Giles). **Division II Championship:** ebreece@ncaa.org (Eric Breece). **Division III:** jpwilliams@ncaa.org (J.P. Williams).

Websites: www.ncaa.org, www.ncaa.com.

President: Dr. Mark Emmert. **Managing director, Division I Championships/Alliances:** Anthony Holman. **Director, Division I Championships/Alliances:** Randy Buhr. **Associate Director, Championships/Alliances:** Chad Tolliver. **Division II Assistant Director, Championships/Alliances:** Eric Breece. **Division III Assistant Director, Championships/Alliances:** J.P. Williams. **Media Contact, Division I Championships, Alliances/College World Series:** Jeff Williams. **Playing Rules Contact:** Ty Halpin. **Statistics Contacts:** Jeff Williams (Division I and RPI); Mark Bedics (Division II); Sean Straziscar (Division III).

Chairman, Division I Baseball Committee: Mike Buddie (Director of Athletics, Army).

Division I Baseball Committee: Jeff Altier (Director of Athletics, Stetson); Jay Artigues (Director of Athletics, Southeastern Louisiana); Sherard Clinkscales (Director of Athletics, Indiana State); Jennifer Cohen (Director of Athletics, Washington); John Cohen (Director of Athletics, Mississippi State); Kirby Hocutt (Director of Athletics, Texas Tech); Matthew Hogue (Director of Athletics, Coastal Carolina); Bob Moosburger (Director of Athletics, Bowling Green State); Eddie Nunez (Director of Athletics, New Mexico).

Chairman, Division II Baseball Committee: Todd Resser (Director of Athletics, Columbus State). **Chairman, Division III Baseball Committee:** Michael Lindberg (Director of Athletics, Wells, N.Y.).

2023 National Convention: Jan. 11-14 at San Antonio.

2022 CHAMPIONSHIP TOURNAMENTS

NCAA DIVISION I
College World Series: Omaha, June 17-26/27
Super Regionals (8): Campus sites, June 10-12
Regionals (16): Campus sites, June 3-6

NCAA DIVISION II
World Series: USA Baseball National Training Complex, Cary, N.C. June 4-11.

NCAA DIVISION III
World Series: Veterans Memorial Stadium, Cedar Rapids, Iowa, June 3-8

NATIONAL JUNIOR COLLEGE ATHLETIC ASSOCIATION

Mailing Address: 8801 JM Keynes Drive, Suite 450, Charlotte, NC 28262. **Telephone:** (719) 590-9788. **Fax:** (719) 590-7324. **E-Mail Address:** mgarrison@njcaa.org. **Website:** www.njcaa.org.

Executive Director: Christopher Parker. **Director, Division I Baseball Tournament:** Rod Lovett. **Director, Division II Baseball Tournament:** Angelo Maltese. **Director, Division III Baseball Tournament:** Antonio Cannavaro. **Director, Media Relations:** McKenzie Garrison.

2022 CHAMPIONSHIP TOURNAMENTS

DIVISION I
World Series: Grand Junction, CO, May 28-June 3/4.

DIVISION II
World Series: Enid, OK, May 28-June 3/4.

DIVISION III
World Series: Greeneville, TN, May 28-June 3/4.

CALIFORNIA COMMUNITY COLLEGE ATHLETIC ASSOCIATION

Mailing Address: 2017 O St., Sacramento, CA 95811. **Telephone:** (916) 444-1600. **Fax:** (916) 444-2616. **E-Mail Addresses:** ccarter@cccaasports.org, jboggs@cccaasports.org. **Website:** www.cccaasports.org.

Executive Director: Jennifer Cardone, Interim. **Director, Championships:** George Mategakis. **Administrative Assistant:** Rima Trotter, rtrotter@cccaasports.org.

2022 CHAMPIONSHIP TOURNAMENT

State Championship: TBD.

NORTHWEST ATHLETIC CONFERENCE

Mailing Address: Clark College TGB 121, 1933 Fort Vancouver Way, Vancouver, WA 98663. **Telephone:** (360) 992-2833. **Fax:** (360) 696-6210. **E-Mail Address:** nwaacc@clark.edu. **Website:** www.nwacsports.org.

Executive Director: Marco Azurdia. **Executive Assistant:** Donna Hays. **Sports Information Director:** Tracy Swisher. **Director, Operations:** Alli Young.

2022 CHAMPIONSHIP TOURNAMENT

NWAC Championship: TBD.

AMERICAN BASEBALL COACHES ASSOCIATION

Office Address: 4101 Piedmont Parkway, Suite C, Greensboro, NC 27410. **Telephone:** (336) 821-3140. **Fax:** (336) 886-0000. **E-Mail Address:** abca@abca.org. **Website:** www.abca.org.

Executive Director: Craig Keilitz. **Deputy Executive Director:** Jon Litchfield. **Asst. Executive Director, Trade Show:** Juahn Clark. **Asst. Executive Director, Convention/Marketing:** Zach Haile. **Asst. Executive Director, Coaching Outreach:** Ryan Brownlee.

Chairman: Keith Madison. **President:** Rick Hitt (South Florida State JC).

2023 National Convention: Jan. 5-8 in Nashville.

NCAA DIVISION I CONFERENCES

AMERICA EAST CONFERENCE

Mailing Address: 451 D Street, Suite 702, Boston, MA 02127. **Telephone:** (617) 695-6369. **Fax:** (617) 695-6380. **Website:** www.americaeast.com. **Baseball Members (First Year):** Albany (2002), Binghamton (2002), Hartford (1990), Maine (1990), Maryland-Baltimore County (2004), Massachusetts-Lowell (2014), New Jersey Tech (2021), Stony Brook (2002). **2022 Tournament:** Four teams, double-elimination, May 26-29 at Mahaney Diamond, Orono, Maine.

AMERICAN ATHLETIC CONFERENCE

Mailing Address: 545 E. John Carpenter Freeway, Third Floor, Irving, TX 75062. **Telephone:** (469) 284-5167. **E-Mail Address:** csullivan@theamerican.org. **Website:** www.theamerican.org. **Baseball Members:** (First Year): Central Florida (2014), Cincinnati (2014), East Carolina (2015), Houston (2014), Memphis (2014), South Florida (2014), Tulane (2015), Wichita State (2018). **Director, Communications:** Chuck Sullivan. **2022 Tournament:** Eight teams, double-elimination, May 24-29 at Spectrum Field, Clearwater, Fla.

ATLANTIC COAST CONFERENCE

Mailing Address: 4512 Weybridge Ln., Greensboro, NC 27407. **Telephone:** (336) 851-6062. **Fax:** (336) 854-8797. **E-Mail Address:** sphillips@theacc.org. **Website:** www. theacc.com. **Baseball Members (First Year):** Boston College (2006), Clemson (1954), Duke (1954), Florida State (1992), Georgia Tech (1980), Miami (2005), North Carolina (1954), North Carolina State (1954), Notre Dame (2014), Louisville (2015), Pittsburgh (2014), Virginia (1955), Virginia Tech (2005), Wake Forest (1954). **Associate Director, Communications:** Steve Phillips. **2022 Tournament:** 12 teams, group play followed by single-elimination semifinals and finals. May 24-29 at Truist Field, Charlotte.

ASUN CONFERENCE

Mailing Address: 3301 Windy Ridge Parkway SE, Suite 350, Atlanta, GA 30339. **E-Mail Addresses:** greg. mette@asunsports.org. **Website:** www.asunsports. org. **Baseball Members:** (First Year): Bellarmine (2021), Central Arkansas (2022), Eastern Kentucky (2022), Florida Gulf Coast (2008), Jacksonville (1999), Jacksonville State (2022), Kennesaw State (2006), Liberty (2019), Lipscomb (2004), North Alabama (2019), North Florida (2006), Stetson (1986). **Director, Sports Information:** Greg Mette. **2022 Tournament:** Eight teams, double-elimination, May 25-28 at Swanson Stadium and JetBlue Park, Fort Myers, Fla.

ATLANTIC 10 CONFERENCE

Mailing Address: 11827 Canon Blvd., Suite 200, Newport News, VA 23606. **Telephone:** (757) 706-3059. **Fax:** (757) 706-3042. **E-Mail Address:** ddickerson@ atlantic10.org. **Website:** www.atlantic10.com. **Baseball Members:** (First Year): Davidson (2015), Dayton (1996), Fordham (1996), George Mason (2014), George Washington (1977), Massachusetts (1977), Rhode Island (1981), Richmond (2002), St. Bonaventure (1980), Saint Joseph's (1983), Saint Louis (2006), Virginia Commonwealth (2013). **Commissioner:** Bernadette V. McGlade. **Director, Communications:** Drew Dickerson. **2022 Tournament:** Seven teams, double elimination. May 24-28 at Houlihan Park, Bronx, N.Y.

BIG EAST CONFERENCE

Mailing Address: BIG EAST Conference, 655 3rd Avenue, 7th Floor, New York, NY 10017. **Telephone:** (212) 969-3181. **Fax:** (212) 969-2900. **E-Mail Address:** kquinn@ bigeast.com. **Website:** www.bigeast.com. **Baseball Members:** (First Year): Butler (2014), Connecticut (1979-2013, 2021), Creighton (2014), Georgetown (1985), St. John's (1985), Seton Hall (1985), Villanova (1985), Xavier (2014). **Assistant Commissioner, Olympic Sports/ Marketing Communications:** Kristin Quinn. **2022 Tournament:** Four teams, modified double-elimination. May 26-29 at Prasco Park, Mason, Ohio.

BIG SOUTH CONFERENCE

Mailing Address: 7233 Pineville-Matthews Rd., Suite 100, Charlotte, NC 28226. **Telephone:** (704) 341-7990. **Fax:** (704) 341-7991. **E-Mail Address:** brandonm@big-south.org. **Website:** www.bigsouthsports.com. **Baseball Members (First Year):** Campbell (2012), Charleston Southern (1983), Gardner-Webb (2009), High Point (1999), Longwood (2013), North Carolina A&T (2022), UNC Asheville (1985), Presbyterian (2009), Radford (1983), South Carolina-Upstate (2019), Winthrop (1983). **Assistant Director, Public Relations/Baseball Contact:** Brandon McGinnis. **2022 Tournament:** Six teams, double-elimination. May 25-28, at Truist Point, High Point, N.C.

BIG TEN CONFERENCE

Mailing Address: 5440 Park Place, Rosemont, IL 60018. **Telephone:** (847) 696-1010. **Fax:** (847) 696-1110. **E-Mail Addresses:** kkane@bigten.org. **Website:** www. bigten.org. **Baseball Members (First Year):** Illinois (1896), Indiana (1906), Iowa (1906), Maryland (2015), Michigan (1896), Michigan State (1950), Minnesota (1906), Nebraska (2012), Northwestern (1898), Ohio State (1913), Penn State (1992), Purdue (1906), Rutgers (2015). **2022 Tournament:** Eight teams, double-elimination, May 25-29, Charles Schwab Field Omaha.

BIG 12 CONFERENCE

Mailing Address: 400 E. John Carpenter Freeway, Irving, TX 75062. **Telephone:** (469) 524-1009. **E-Mail Address:** russell@big12sports.com. **Website:** www. big12sports.com. **Baseball Members (First Year):** Baylor (1997), Kansas (1997), Kansas State (1997), Oklahoma (1997), Oklahoma State (1997), Texas Christian (2013), Texas (1997), Texas Tech (1997), West Virginia (2013). **Assistant Director, Media Relations:** Russell Luna. **2022 Tournament:** Eight teams, double-elimination. May 25-29 at Globe Life Field, Arlington, Texas.

BIG WEST CONFERENCE

Mailing Address: 2 Corporate Park, Suite 206, Irvine, CA 92606. **Telephone:** (949) 261-2525. **Fax:** (949) 261-2528. **E-Mail Address:** jstcyr@bigwest.org. **Website:** www.bigwest.org. **Baseball Members (First Year):** Cal Poly (1997), UC Davis (2008), UC Irvine (2002), UC Riverside (2002), UC San Diego (2021), UC Santa Barbara (1970), Cal State Bakersfield (2021), Cal State Fullerton (1975), Cal State Northridge (2001), Hawaii (2013), Long Beach State (1970). **Director, Communications:** Julie St. Cyr. **2022 Tournament:** None.

COLONIAL ATHLETIC ASSOCIATION

Mailing Address: 8625 Patterson Ave., Richmond, VA 23229. **Telephone:** (804) 754-1616. **Fax:** (804) 754-1973.

E-Mail Address: rwashburn@caasports.com. Website: www.caasports.com. Baseball Members (First Year): College of Charleston (2014), Delaware (2002), Elon (2015), Hofstra (2002), James Madison (1986), UNC Wilmington (1986), Northeastern (2006), Towson (2002), William & Mary (1986). Associate Commissioner/Communications: Rob Washburn. 2022 Tournament: Six teams, double-elimination. May 25-29 at Latham Park, Elon, NC.

CONFERENCE USA

Mailing Address: 5201 N. O'Connor Blvd., Suite 300, Irving, TX 75039. Telephone: (214) 774-1300. Fax: (214) 496-0055. E-Mail Address: jstepp@c-usa.org. Website: www.conferenceusa.com. Baseball Members (First Year): Alabama-Birmingham (1996), Charlotte (2014), Florida Atlantic (2014), Florida International (2014), Louisiana Tech (2014), Marshall (2006), Middle Tennessee State (2014), Old Dominion (2014), Rice (2006), Southern Mississippi (1996), Texas-San Antonio (2014), Western Kentucky (2015). Assistant Commissioner, Communications: Jordan Stepp. 2022 Tournament: Eight teams, double-elimination. May 25-29 at Pete Taylor Park, Hattiesburg, Miss.

HORIZON LEAGUE

Mailing Address: 129 E. Market Street, Suite 900, Indianapolis, IN 46204. Telephone: (317) 237-5622. Fax: (317) 237-5620. E-Mail Address: dgliot@horizonleague.org. Website: www.horizonleague.org. Baseball Members (First Year): Illinois-Chicago (1994), Northern Kentucky (2016), Oakland (2014), Purdue-Fort Wayne (2021), Wright State (1994), Wisconsin-Milwaukee (1994), Youngstown State (2002). Director, Communications and Digital Media Strategy: Dan Gliot. 2022 Tournament: Six teams, modified double-elimination. May 25-28, hosted by No. 1 seed.

IVY LEAGUE

Mailing Address: 228 Alexander Rd., Second Floor, Princeton, NJ 08544. Telephone: (609) 258-6426. Fax: (609) 258-1690. E-Mail Address: trevor@ivyleaguesports.com. Website: www ivyleaguesports.com. Baseball Members (First Year): Rolfe—Brown (1948), Dartmouth (1930), Harvard (1948), Yale (1930). Gehrig—Columbia (1930), Cornell (1930), Pennsylvania (1930), Princeton (1930). Assistant Executive Director, Communications/Championships: Trevor Rutledge-Leverenz. 2022 Tournament: Two teams, best-of-three series, May 21-22, hosted by No. 1 seed.

METRO ATLANTIC ATHLETIC CONFERENCE

Mailing Address: 712 Amboy Ave., Edison, NJ 08837. Telephone: (732) 738-5455. E-Mail Address: taylor.oconnor@maac.org. Website: www.maacsports.com. Baseball Members (First Year): Canisius (1990), Fairfield (1982), Iona (1982), Manhattan (1982), Marist (1998), Monmouth (2014), Niagara (1990), Quinnipiac (2014), Rider (1998), Saint Peter's (1982), Siena (1990). Director, New Media: Taylor O'Connor. 2022 Tournament: Six teams, double elimination, May 25-28 at Clover Stadium, Pomona, N.Y.

MID-AMERICAN CONFERENCE

Mailing Address: 24 Public Square, 15th Floor, Cleveland, OH 44113. Telephone: (216) 566-4622. Fax: (216) 858-9622. E-Mail Address: jguy@mac-sports.com. Website: www.getmesomemaction.com. Baseball Members (First Year): Akron (2020), Ball State (1973), Bowling Green State (1952), Central Michigan (1971), Eastern Michigan (1971), Kent State (1951), Miami (1947), Northern Illinois (1997), Ohio (1946), Toledo (1950), Western Michigan (1947). Assistant Commissioner, Communications and Social Media: Jeremy Guy. 2022 Tournament: Six teams, double-elimination, hosted by No. 1 seed.

MID-EASTERN ATHLETIC CONFERENCE

Mailing Address: 2730 Ellsmere Ave., Norfolk, VA 23513. Telephone: (757) 951-2055. Fax: (757) 951-2077. E-Mail Address: cunninghamj@themeac.com; porterp@themeac.com. Website: www.meacsports.com. Baseball Members (First Year): Coppin State (1985), Delaware State (1970), Maryland-Eastern Shore (1970), Norfolk State (1998). Assistant Director, Media Relations: Jeff Cunningham. 2022 Tournament: Four teams, double-elimination. May 18-21 at Miller Field, Norfolk, Va.

MISSOURI VALLEY CONFERENCE

Mailing Address: 1818 Chouteau Ave., St. Louis, MO 63103. Telephone: (314) 444-4300. Fax: (314) 444-4333. E-Mail Address: davis@mvc.org. Website: www.mvc-sports.com. Baseball Members (First Year): Bradley (1955), Dallas Baptist (2014), Evansville (1994), Illinois State (1980), Indiana State (1976), Missouri State (1990), Southern Illinois (1974), Valparaiso (2019). Assistant Commissioner, Communications: Ryan Davis. 2022 Tournament: Eight teams, double-elimination, May 24-28 at Hammons Field, Springfield, Mo.

MOUNTAIN WEST CONFERENCE

Mailing Address: 10807 New Allegiance Dr., Suite 250, Colorado Springs, CO 80921. Telephone: (719) 488-4052. Fax: (719) 487-7241. E-Mail Address: sbuchanan@themw.com. Website: www.themw.com. Baseball Members (First Year): Air Force (2000), Fresno State (2013), Nevada (2013), Nevada-Las Vegas (2000), New Mexico (2000), San Diego State (2000), San Jose State (2014). Director, Strategic Communication: Stuart Buchanan. 2022 Tournament: Four teams, double-elimination, May 26-29, Tony Gwynn Stadium, San Diego.

NORTHEAST CONFERENCE

Mailing Address: 200 Cottontail Lane, Vantage Court South, Somerset, NJ 08873. Telephone: (732) 469-0440. Fax: (732) 469-0744. E-Mail Address: rventre@northeast conference.org. Website: www.northeastconference.org. Baseball Members (First Year): Bryant (2010), Central Connecticut State (1999), Fairleigh Dickinson (1981), Long Island (1981), Merrimack (2020), Mount St. Mary's (1989), Sacred Heart (2000), Wagner (1981). Director, Communications/Social Media: Ralph Ventre. 2022 Tournament: Four teams, double-elimination. May 26-29 at TBD.

OHIO VALLEY CONFERENCE

Mailing Address: 215 Centerview Dr., Suite 115, Brentwood, TN 37027. Telephone: (615) 371-1698. Fax: (615) 891-1682. E-Mail Address: kschwartz@ovc.org. Website: www.ovcsports.com. Baseball Members (First Year): Austin Peay State (1962), Belmont (2013), Eastern Illinois (1996), Morehead State (1948), Murray State (1948), Southeast Missouri State (1991), Southern Illinois-Edwardsville (2012), Tennessee-Martin (1992), Tennessee Tech (1949). Assistant Commissioner: Kyle Schwartz. 2022 Tournament: Eight teams, double-elimination, May 25-28 at Lexington Legends Ballpark, Lexington, Ky.

PACIFIC-12 CONFERENCE

Mailing Address: Pac-12 Conference 360 3rd Street, 3rd Floor San Francisco, CA 94107. **Telephone:** (415) 580-4200. **Fax:** (415)549-2828. **E-Mail Address:** jolivero@pac-12.org. **Website:** www.pac-12.com. **Baseball Members (First Year):** Arizona (1979), Arizona State (1979), California (1916), UCLA (1928), Oregon (2009) Oregon State (1916), Southern California (1923), Stanford (1918), Utah (2012), Washington (1916), Washington State (1919). **Public Relations Contact:** Jon Olivero. **2022 Tournament:** Eight teams, double-elimination, May 25-29 at Scottsdale Stadium, Scottsdale, Ariz.

PATRIOT LEAGUE

Mailing Address: 3773 Corporate Pkwy., Suite 190, Center Valley, PA 18034. **Telephone:** (610) 289-1950. **Fax:** (610) 289-1951. **E-Mail Address:** rsakamoto@patriot-league.com. **Website:** www.patriotleague.org. **Baseball Members (First Year):** Army (1993), Bucknell (1991), Holy Cross (1991), Lafayette (1991), Lehigh (1991), Navy (1993). **Assistant Commissioner, Communications:** Ryan Sakamoto. **2022 Tournament:** four teams, two rounds of best-of-three series, hosted at campus sites, May 14-15, May 20-22.

SOUTHEASTERN CONFERENCE

Mailing Address: 2201 Richard Arrington Blvd. N., Birmingham, AL 35203. **Telephone:** (205) 458-3000. **Fax:** (205) 458-3030. **E-Mail Address:** scartell@sec.org. **Website:** www.secsports.com. **Baseball Members (First Year): East Division**—Florida (1933), Georgia (1933), Kentucky (1933), Missouri (2013), South Carolina (1992), Tennessee (1933), Vanderbilt (1933). **West Division**—Alabama (1933), Arkansas (1992), Auburn (1933), Louisiana State (1933), Mississippi (1933), Mississippi State (1933), Texas A&M (2013). **Director, Communications:** Chuck Dunlap. **2022 Tournament:** 12 teams, modified single/double-elimination. May 24-29 at Hoover Metropolitan Stadium, Hoover, Ala.

SOUTHERN CONFERENCE

Mailing Address: 702 N. Pine St., Spartanburg, SC 29303. **Telephone:** (864) 591-5100. **Fax:** (864) 591-3448. **E-Mail Address:** jwashington@socon.org. **Website:** www.soconsports.com. **Baseball Members (First Year):** The Citadel (1937), East Tennessee State (1979-2005, 2015), Furman (1937), Mercer (2015), UNC Greensboro (1998), Samford (2009), VMI (1925-2003, 2015), Western Carolina (1977), Wofford (1998). **Media Relations Assistant:** Jasmine Washington. **2022 Tournament:** Four teams, double-elimination, May 24-29 at Fluor Field, Greenville, S.C.

SOUTHLAND CONFERENCE

Mailing Address: 2600 Network Blvd, Suite 150, Frisco, Texas 75034. **Telephone:** (972) 422-9500. **Fax:** (972) 422-9225. **E-Mail Address:** jyonis@southland.org **Website:** southland.org. **Baseball Members (First Year):** Houston Baptist (2014), Incarnate Word (2014), McNeese State (1973), New Orleans (2014), Nicholls State (1992), Northwestern State (1988), Southeastern Louisiana (1998), Texas A&M-Corpus Christi (2007). **Assistant Communications Director:** Josh Yonis. **2022 Tournament:** Eight teams, pool play hosted by top two seeds leading to best-of-three series hosted by highest remaining seed. May 19-22, May 26-28.

SOUTHWESTERN ATHLETIC CONFERENCE

Mailing Address: 1101 22nd Street South, Birmingham, AL 35205. **Telephone:** (205) 251-7573. **Fax:** (205) 297-9820. **E-Mail Address:** a.roberts@swac.org. **Website:** www.swac.org. **Baseball Members (First Year): East Division**—Alabama A&M (2000), Alabama State (1982), Bethune-Cookman (2022), Florida A&M (2022), Jackson State (1958), Mississippi Valley State (1968). **West Division**— Alcorn State (1962), Arkansas-Pine Bluff (1999), Grambling State (1958), Prairie View A&M (1920), Southern (1934), Texas Southern (1954). **Asst. Commissioner, Communications:** Andrew Roberts. **2022 Tournament:** Eight teams, double-elimination. May 25-29 at Regions Field, Birmingham.

SUMMIT LEAGUE

Mailing Address: 340 W. Butterfield Rd., Suite 3D, Elmhurst, IL 60126. **Telephone:** (630) 516-0661. **Fax:** (630) 516-0673. **E-Mail Address:** powell@thesummitleague.org. **Website:** www.thesummitleague.org. **Baseball Members (First Year):** Nebraska-Omaha (2013), North Dakota State (2008), Northern Colorado (2022), Oral Roberts (1998), St. Thomas (2022), South Dakota State (2008), Western Illinois (1984). **Associate Commissioner, Communications:** Ryan Powell. **2022 Tournament:** Four teams, double-elimination. May 25-28 at J.L. Johnson Stadium, Tulsa.

SUN BELT CONFERENCE

Mailing Address: 1500 Sugar Bowl Dr., New Orleans, LA 70112. **Telephone:** (504) 556-0884. **Fax:** (504) 299-9068. **E-Mail Address:** nunez@sunbeltsports.org. **Website:** www.sunbeltsports.org. **Baseball Members (First Year): East Division**—Appalachian State (2015), Coastal Carolina (2017), Georgia Southern, (2015), Georgia State (2014), South Alabama (1976), Troy (2006). **West Division**—Arkansas-Little Rock (1991), Arkansas State (1991), Louisiana-Lafayette (1991), Louisiana-Monroe (2007), Texas-Arlington (2014), Texas State (2014). **Asst. Commissioner, Digital & Creative Services:** Keith Nunez. **2022 Tournament:** Eight teams, double-elimination. May 24-29 at Riverwalk Stadium, Montgomery, Ala.

WESTERN ATHLETIC CONFERENCE

Mailing Address: 9250 East Costilla Ave., Suite 300, Englewood, CO 80112. **Telephone:** (303) 799-9221. **Fax:** (303) 799-3888. **E-Mail Address:** cthompson@wac.org. **Website:** www.wacsports.com. **Baseball Members (First Year): Southwest Division**—Abilene Christian (2022), Lamar (2022), Sam Houston State (2022), Stephen F. Austin (2022), Tarleton State (2022), Texas-Rio Grande Valley (2014). **West Division**—California Baptist (2019), Grand Canyon (2014), Dixie State (2021), New Mexico State (2006), Sacramento State (2006), Seattle (2013), Utah Valley (2014). **Director, Media Relations:** Chris Thompson. **2022 Tournament:** Eight teams, double-elimination, May 25-28/29 at Hohokam Stadium, Mesa, Ariz.

WEST COAST CONFERENCE

Mailing Address: 951 Mariners Island Blvd., Third Floor, San Mateo, CA 94404. **Telephone:** (650) 873-8622. **E-Mail Addresses:** rmccrary@westcoast.org. **Website:** www.wccsports.com. **Baseball Members (First Year):** Brigham Young (2012), Gonzaga (1996), Loyola Marymount (1968), Pacific (2014), Pepperdine (1968), Portland (1996), Saint Mary's (1968), San Diego (1979), San Francisco (1968), Santa Clara (1968). **Asst. Commissioner, Communications:** Ryan McCrary. **2022 Tournament:** Four teams, double-elimination, May 26-28 at Banner Island Ballpark, Stockton, Calif.

NCAA DIVISION I TEAMS
* Denotes recruiting coordinator

ABILENE CHRISTIAN WILDCATS

Conference: Western Athletic. **Mailing Address:** 1600 Campus Ct., Abilene, TX 79601. **Website:** www.acusports.com. **Head Coach:** Rick McCarty. **Telephone:** (325) 674-2817. **Baseball SID:** Zach Carlyle. **Assistant Coaches:** Blaze Lambert, Craig Parry. **Telephone:** (325) 674-2817. **Home Field:** Crutcher Scott Field. **Seating Capacity:** 4,000. **Outfield Dimension: LF**—333, **CF**—381, **RF**—303.

AIR FORCE

Conference: Mountain West. **Mailing Address:** 2169 Field House Dr. Air Force Academy, CO 80840-9500. **Website:** www.goairforcefalcons.com. **Head Coach:** Mike Kazlausky. **Telephone:** (719) 333-0835. **Baseball SID:** Nick Cicere. **Telephone:** (719) 333-3950. **Assistant Coaches:** Ryan Forrest, Jimmy Roesinger. **Telephone:** (719) 333-7539. **Home Field:** Falcon Field. **Seating Capacity:** 1,000. **Outfield Dimension: LF**—349, **CF**—400, **RF**—316

AKRON

Conference: Mid-American. **Mailing Address:** The University of Akron Athletic Department, Infocision Stadium, 375 East Exchange St., Akron, OH 44325. **Website:** www.gozips.com. **Head Coach:** Chris Sabo. **Telephone:** (330) 972-5131. **Baseball SID:** Brian Dennison. **Telephone:** (330) 972-5131. **Assistant Coaches:** Cory Mee, Connor Faix. **Telephone:** (330) 972-5131. **Home Field:** Skeeles Field. **Seating Capacity:** 1,500. **Outfield Dimension: LF**—320, **CF**—390, **RF**—305.

ALABAMA

Conference: Southeastern. **Mailing Address:** 1201 Coliseum Drive, Tuscaloosa, AL 35401. **Website:** RollTide.com. **Head Coach:** Brad Bohannon. **Telephone:** (205) 348-4029. **Baseball SID:** Alex Thompson. **Telephone:** (205) 348-6084. **Assistant Coaches:** Matt Reida, Jason Jackson. **Telephone:** (205) 348-6084. **Home Field:** Sewell-Thomas Stadium. **Seating Capacity:** 5,867. **Outfield Dimension: LF**—320, **CF**—360, **RF**—320.

ALABAMA A&M

Conference: Southwestern. **Mailing Address:** 4900 Meridian Street, PO Box 1597, Normal, AL 35762. **Website:** www.aamusports.com. **Head Coach:** Elliott Jones. **Telephone:** (256) 372-7213. **Baseball SID:** Terissa Mark. **Telephone:** (256) 372-5880. **Assistant Coaches:** Corben Green, Ashanti Wheatley. **Home Field:** Bulldog Baseball Field. **Seating Capacity:** 500. **Outfield Dimension: LF**—330, **CF**—402, **RF**—318

ALABAMA STATE

Conference: Southwestern. **Mailing Address:** 915 S Jackson St., Montgomery, AL 36104. **Website:** www.bamastatesports.com. **Head Coach:** Jose Vazquez. **Telephone:** (334) 229-5600. **Baseball SID:** Travis Jarome. **Telephone:** (334) 229-2601. **Assistant Coaches:** Drew Clark, Matt Crane. **Telephone:** (334) 229-5601. **Home Field:** Wheeler-Watkins Complex. **Seating Capacity:** 500. **Outfield Dimension: LF**—330, **CF**—400, **RF**—300.

ALABAMA-BIRMINGHAM

Conference: Conference USA. **Mailing Address:** 1720 2nd Ave. S, Bartow Arena, Birmingham, AL 35294-1160. **Website:** www.uabsports.com. **Head Coach:** Casey Dunn. **Baseball SID:** Hailee Roe. **Telephone:** (205) 934-0722. **Assistant Coaches:** BJ Green, Alan Kunkel. **Home Field:** Regions Field. **Seating Capacity:** 8,500. **Outfield Dimension: LF**—320, **CF**—400, **RF**—325.

ALBANY

Conference: America East. **Mailing Address:** 1400 Washington Avenue Albany, NY 12222. **Website:** www.ualbanysports.com. **Head Coach:** Jon Mueller. **Baseball SID:** Taylor O'Connor. **Telephone:** (518) 442-3072. **Assistant Coaches:** Jeff Kaier, John Saviano. **Telephone:** (518) 442-3337. **Home Field:** Varsity Field.

ALCORN STATE

Conference: Southwestern. **Mailing Address:** 1000 ASU Drive #510 Lorman, MS 39096. **Website:** www.alcornsports.com. **Head Coach:** Reginald Williams. **Telephone:** (601) 877-4090. **Baseball SID:** Dahkeem Williams. **Assistant Coaches:** Kirt Cormier. **Home Field:** William "Bill" Foster Field at Willie E. "Rat" McGowan Stadium.

APPALACHIAN STATE

Conference: Sun Belt. **Mailing Address:** Bodenheimer Dr, ASU Box 32153, Boone, NC 28607. **Website:** www.appstatesports.com. **Head Coach:** Kermit Smith. **Baseball SID:** Shane Harvell. **Assistant Coaches:** Britt Johnson, Justin Aspegren. **Telephone:** (828) 262-8664. **Home Field:** Jim and Bettie Smith Stadium. **Seating Capacity:** 827. **Outfield Dimension: LF**—335, **CF**—400, **RF**—330.

ARIZONA

Conference: Pac-12. **Mailing Address:** McKale Center, 1 National Championship Drive, PO Box 210096, Tucson, AZ 85721-0096. **Website:** www.arizonawildcats.com. **Head Coach:** Chip Hale. **Telephone:** (520) 621-4102. **Baseball SID:** Brett Gleason. **Telephone:** (520) 621-0914. **Assistant Coaches:** Dave Lawn, Trip Couch. **Telephone:** (520) 621-4714. **Home Field:** Hi Corbett Field. **Seating Capacity:** 9,500. **Outfield Dimension: LF**—366, **CF**—392, **RF**—349.

ARIZONA STATE

Conference: Pac-12. **Mailing Address:** Carson Center, PO Box 872505, Tempe, AZ 85287-2505. **Website:** www.thesundevils.com. **Head Coach:** Willie Bloomquist. **Telephone:** (480)

965-3677. **Baseball SID:** Jeremy Hawkes. **Telephone:** (480) 965-9544.

Assistant Coaches: Sam Peraza, Mike Goff.
Home Field: Phoenix Municipal Stadium. **Seating Capacity:** 8,775. **Outfield Dimension:** LF—345, CF—410, RF—345.

ARKANSAS

Conference: Southeastern.
Mailing Address: 1255 S. Razorback Rd, Fayetteville, AR 72701. **Website:** www.arkansasrazorbacks.com.
Head Coach: Dave Van Horn. **Baseball SID:** Oliver Grigg.
Assistant Coaches: Nate Thompson, Matt Hobbs.
Home Field: Baum-Walker Stadium. **Seating Capacity:** 11,084. **Outfield Dimension:** LF—320, CF—400, RF—320.

ARKANSAS STATE

Conference: Sun Belt.
Mailing Address: 217 Olympic Drive, Jonesboro, AR 72401. **Website:** ww.astateredwolves.com.
Head Coach: Tommy Raffo. **Baseball SID:** Caleb Garner. **Telephone:** (870) 972-2707.
Assistant Coaches: Rick Guarno, Alan Dunn.
Home Field: Tomlinson Stadium-Kell Field. **Seating Capacity:** 1,200. **Outfield Dimension:** LF—335, CF—400, RF—335.

ARKANSAS-LITTLE ROCK

Conference: Sun Belt.
Mailing Address: 2801 South University Ave. Little Rock, AR 72204. **Website:** www.lrtrojans.com.
Head Coach: Chris Curry. **Baseball SID:** Rand Champion.
Assistant Coaches: Noah Sanders, James Leverton.
Home Field: Gary Hogan Field. **Seating Capacity:** 2,500. **Outfield Dimension:** LF—335, CF—390, RF—305.

ARKANSAS-PINE BLUFF

Conference: Southwestern.
Mailing Address: 1200 North University Drive, Mail Slot 4891, Pine Bluff, AR 71601. **Website:** www.uapblionsroar.com.
Head Coach: Carlos James. **Telephone:** (870) 575-8995. **Baseball SID:** Cameo Stokes. **Telephone:** (870) 575-7955.
Assistant Coaches: Roger Mallison. **Telephone:** (870) 575-8995.
Home Field: Torii Hunter Baseball Complex. **Seating Capacity:** 1,000. **Outfield Dimension:** LF—331, CF—401, RF—331

ARMY

Conference: Patriot League.
Mailing Address: United States Military Academy, Army West Point Athletics, 639 Howard Rd., West Point, NY 10996. **Website:** www.goarmywestpoint.com.
Head Coach: Jim Foster. **Telephone:** (845) 938-4938. **Baseball SID:** Meg Ellis. **Telephone:** (845) 938-4090.
Assistant Coaches: Matt Kinney, Anthony Spataro.
Home Field: Johnson Stadium at Doubleday Field. **Seating Capacity:** 880. **Outfield Dimension:** LF—327, CF—400, RF—327.

AUBURN

Conference: Southeastern.
Mailing Address: 351 S. Donahue Dr., Auburn, AL 36830. **Website:** www.auburntigers.com.
Head Coach: Butch Thompson. **Telephone:** (334) 844-4990. **Baseball SID:** George Nunnelley.
Assistant Coaches: Gabe Gross, Karl Nonemaker.
Home Field: Plainsman Park. **Seating Capacity:** 4,096. **Outfield Dimension:** LF—315, CF—385, RF—331.

AUSTIN PEAY STATE

Conference: Ohio Valley.
Mailing Address: Austin Peay State University, Box 4515, 601 College Street, Clarksville, TN 37044. **Website:** www.letsgopeay.com.
Head Coach: Travis Janssen. **Baseball SID:** Cody Bush.
Assistant Coaches: Shane Conlon, Trevor Fitts.
Home Field: Raymond C. Hand Park. **Seating Capacity:** 1,000. **Outfield Dimension:** LF—319, CF—392, RF—327.

BALL STATE

Conference: Mid-American.
Mailing Address: Ball State Athletics, HP 260, Muncie, IN 47306-0929. **Website:** www.ballstatesports.com.
Head Coach: Rich Maloney. **Telephone:** (765) 285-1425. **Baseball SID:** Chad Smith. **Telephone:** (765) 285-8242. **Assistant Coaches:** Blake Beemer, Larry Scully. **Telephone:** (765) 285-8226.
Home Field: Ball Diamond at First Merchants Ballpark Complex. **Seating Capacity:** 1,500. **Outfield Dimension:** LF—325, CF—400, RF—325.

BAYLOR

Conference: Big 12.
Mailing Address: 1500 South University Parks Dr., Waco, TX 76706. **Website:** www.baylorbears.com.
Head Coach: Steve Rodriguez. **Telephone:** (254) 710-3029. **Baseball SID:** Max Calderon. **Telephone:** (254) 710-3073. **Assistant Coaches:** Mike Taylor, Jon Strauss. **Telephone:** (254) 710-3041.
Home Field: Baylor Ballpark. **Seating Capacity:** 5,000. **Outfield Dimension:** LF—330, CF—400, RF—300.

BELLARMINE

Conference: ASUN.
Mailing Address: 2001 Newburg Road, Louisville, KY 40205. **Website:** www.athletics.bellarmine.edu.
Head Coach: Larry Owens. **Telephone:** (502) 272-8278. **Baseball SID:** Natalie Cousin. **Telephone:** (502) 272-8217.
Assistant Coaches: Nick Eversole, Chris Dominguez. **Telephone:** (502) 272-8278.
Home Field: Knights Field. **Outfield Dimension:** LF—335, CF—380, RF—335.

BELMONT

Conference: Ohio Valley.
Mailing Address: 1900 Belmont Blvd, Nashville, TN, 37212 . **Website:** www.belmontbruins.com.
Head Coach: Dave Jarvis. **Telephone:** (615) 460-6166. **Baseball SID:** Noah Syverson.
Assistant Coaches: Aaron Smith, AJ Gaura. **Telephone:** (615) 460-6165.
Home Field: E.S. Rose Park. **Outfield Dimension:** LF—330, CF—400, RF—330.

BETHUNE-COOKMAN

Conference: Southwestern.
Mailing Address: 640 Dr. Mary McLeod Bethune Boulevard, Daytona Beach, FL 32114. **Website:** www.bcuathletics.com.
Head Coach: Jonathan Hernandez. **Telephone:** (386) 481-2224. **Baseball SID:** Bryce Hoynoski. **Telephone:** (386) 481-2278.
Assistant Coaches: Jose Carballo, Joel Sanchez.
Home Field: Jackie Robinson Ballpark. **Seating Capacity:** 4,200. **Outfield Dimension: LF**—317, **CF**—400, **RF**—325.

BINGHAMTON

Conference: America East.
Mailing Address: 4400 Vestal Parkway East, Binghamton, NY 13902. **Website:** www.bubearcats.com.
Head Coach: Tim Sinicki. **Telephone:** (607) 777-2525. **Baseball SID:** John Hartrick. **Telephone:** (607) 777-6800.
Assistant Coaches: Ryan Hurba, Mike Folli. **Telephone:** (607) 777-5808.
Home Field: Bearcats Baseball Complex. **Seating Capacity:** 2,500. **Outfield Dimension: LF**—325, **CF**—390, **RF**—325.

BOSTON COLLEGE

Conference: Atlantic Coast.
Mailing Address: 140 Commonwealth Ave, Chestnut Hill, MA 02467. **Website:** www.bceagles.com.
Head Coach: Mike Gambino. **Baseball SID:** Brendan Flynn.
Assistant Coaches: Kevin Vance, Tyler Holt.
Home Field: Harrington Athletics Village. **Seating Capacity:** 1,000. **Outfield Dimension: LF**—330, **CF**—403, **RF**—330.

BOWLING GREEN STATE

Conference: Mid-American.
Mailing Address: 1600 Stadium Dr. Bowling Green, OH 43403. **Website:** www.bgsufalcons.com.
Head Coach: Kyle Hallock. **Baseball SID:** Kyle Edmond.
Assistant Coaches: Matt Rembielak, Joey Gamache.
Home Field: Stellar Field. **Seating Capacity:** 1,100. **Outfield Dimension: LF**—340, **CF**—400, **RF**—340.

BRADLEY

Conference: Missouri Valley.
Mailing Address: 1501 W. Bradley Avenue Renaissance Coliseum Peoria, IL 61625. **Website:** www.bradleybraves.com.
Head Coach: Elvis Dominguez. **Telephone:** (309) 677-2684. **Baseball SID:** Jason Veniskey. **Telephone:** (309) 677-4583.
Assistant Coaches: Kyle Trewyn, Andrew Werner. **Telephone:** (309) 677-3636.
Home Field: Dozer Park. **Seating Capacity:** 7,500. **Outfield Dimension: LF**—310, **CF**—400, **RF**—310.

BRIGHAM YOUNG

Conference: West Coast.
Mailing Address: 111 MLRP, Provo UT 84094. **Website:** www.byucougars.com.
Head Coach: Mike Littlewood. **Telephone:** (801) 422-5049. **Baseball SID:** Duff Tittle. **Telephone:** (801) 422-5048.

Assistant Coaches: Brent Haring, Trent Pratt. **Telephone:** (801) 422-4910.
Home Field: Miller Park. **Seating Capacity:** 2,200. **Outfield Dimension: LF**—347, **CF**—402, **RF**—343

BROWN

Conference: Ivy League.
Mailing Address: 233 Hope St Providence, RI 02912. **Website:** www.brownbears.com.
Head Coach: Grant Achilles. **Telephone:** (401) 863-3090. **Baseball SID:** Tim Geer. **Telephone:** (401) 863-7014.
Assistant Coaches: Christopher Tilton, Zach Hubbard.
Home Field: Attanasio Family Field at Murray Stadium. **Seating Capacity:** 1,000.

BRYANT

Conference: Northeast.
Mailing Address: 1150 Douglas Pike, Smithfield, R.I. 02917. **Website:** www.bryantbulldogs.com.
Head Coach: Ryan Klosterman. **Telephone:** (401) 232-6397. **Baseball SID:** Tristan Hobbes. **Telephone:** (401) 232-6558.
Assistant Coaches: Eric Pelletier, Ted Hurvul.
Home Field: Conaty Park. **Seating Capacity:** 500. **Outfield Dimension: LF**—330, **CF**—400, **RF**—330.

BUCKNELL

Conference: Patriot League.
Mailing Address: Kenneth Langone Athletics & Recreation Center, Bucknell University, One Dent Drive, Lewisburg, PA 17837. **Website:** www.bucknellbison.com.
Head Coach: Scott Heather. **Telephone:** (570) 577-3593. **Baseball SID:** Cole Cloonan. **Telephone:** (570) 577-1227.
Assistant Coaches: Jason Neitz, Kyle Norman. **Telephone:** (570) 577-1059.
Home Field: Depew Field. **Seating Capacity:** 1,000. **Outfield Dimension: LF**—330, **CF**—400, **RF**—330.

BUTLER

Conference: Big East.
Mailing Address: Butler University Athletics 510 W. 49th Street Indianapolis, IN 46208. **Website:** www.butlersports.com.
Head Coach: Dave Schrage. **Telephone:** (317) 940-9721. **Baseball SID:** Kit Stetzel. **Telephone:** (317) 940-9994.
Assistant Coaches: Ben Norton, Matt Kennedy. **Telephone:** (317) 940-6536.
Home Field: Bulldog Park. **Seating Capacity:** 500. **Outfield Dimension: LF**—330, **CF**—400, **RF**—330.

CALIFORNIA

Conference: Pac-12.
Mailing Address: Frank Schlessinger Way, Berkeley, CA 94720. **Website:** www.calbears.com.
Head Coach: Mike Neu. **Telephone:** (510) 642-9026. **Baseball SID:** Gerrit Van Genderen.
Assistant Coaches: Noah Jackson, Matt Flemer.
Home Field: Evans Diamond. **Seating Capacity:** 2,500. **Outfield Dimension: LF**—320, **CF**—395, **RF**—320.

CAL BAPTIST

Conference: Western Athletic.
Mailing Address: 8432 Magnolia Avenue, Riverside, Calif. 92503. **Website:** www.cbulancers.com.

Head Coach: Gary Adcock. **Telephone:** (951) 343-4382. **Baseball SID:** Andrew Shortall. **Telephone:** (951) 343-4779.

Assistant Coaches: Andrew Brasington, Tyler Hancock. **Telephone:** (951) 552-8577.

Home Field: Totman Stadium. **Seating Capacity:** 800. **Outfield Dimension:** LF—331, CF—406, RF—317.

CAL POLY

Conference: Big West.

Mailing Address: Cal Poly Athletics, 1 Grand Avenue, San Luis Obispo, CA 93407-0388. **Website:** www.gopoly.com.

Head Coach: Larry Lee. **Telephone:** (805) 756-6367. **Baseball SID:** Eric Burdick. **Telephone:** (805) 756-6550.

Assistant Coaches: Ben Greenspan, Jake Silverman. **Telephone:** (805) 756-2462.

Home Field: Baggett Stadium. **Seating Capacity:** 3,132. **Outfield Dimension:** LF—335, CF—405, RF—335.

CAL STATE BAKERSFIELD

Conference: Big West.

Mailing Address: 9001 Stockdale Hwy, 8 GYM, Bakersfield, CA 93311-1022. **Website:** www.gorunners.com.

Head Coach: Jeremy Beard. **Telephone:** (509) 430-5354. **Baseball SID:** Dan Sperl.

Assistant Coaches: Quinn Hawksworth, Justin Hixon. **Home Field:** Hardt Field. **Seating Capacity:** 1,500. **Outfield Dimension:** LF—325, CF—390, RF—325.

CAL STATE FULLERTON

Conference: Big West.

Mailing Address: PO Box 6810, Fullerton, Calif., 92834. **Website:** www.fullertontitans.com.

Head Coach: Jason Dietrich. **Telephone:** (657) 278-2200. **Baseball SID:** Bryant Freese.

Assistant Coaches: Josh Belovsky, Neil Walton. **Home Field:** Goodwin Field. **Seating Capacity:** 3,500. **Outfield Dimension:** LF—330, CF—400, RF—330.

CAL STATE NORTHRIDGE

Conference: Big West.

Mailing Address: 18111 Nordhoff St., Northridge, CA 91330. **Website:** www.gomatadors.com.

Head Coach: Dave Serrano. **Telephone:** (818) 677-7055. **Baseball SID:** Nick Bocanegra. **Telephone:** (818) 677-7188.

Assistant Coaches: Bobby Andrews, Eddie Cornejo. **Home Field:** Matador Field. **Seating Capacity:** 1,000. **Outfield Dimension:** LF—325, CF—390, RF—325.

CAMPBELL

Conference: Big South.

Mailing Address: 76 Upchurch Lane Lillington, NC 27546. **Website:** www.gocamels.com.

Head Coach: Justin Haire. **Baseball SID:** Davis Dupree.

Assistant Coaches: Joey Holcomb, Tyler Robinson. **Home Field:** Jim Perry Stadium. **Seating Capacity:** 1,250. **Outfield Dimension:** LF—337, CF—395, RF—328.

CANISIUS

Conference: Metro Atlantic.

Mailing Address: 2001 Main Street, Buffalo, N.Y., 14208. **Website:** www.gogriffs.com.

Head Coach: Matt Mazurek. **Baseball SID:** Marshall Haim.

Assistant Coaches: Jeremy Hileman, Garrett Cortright. **Home Field:** Demske Sports Complex.

CENTRAL ARKANSAS

Conference: ASUN.

Mailing Address: 201 Donaghey Ave., Bear Hall - 4th Floor, Conway, AR 72035. **Website:** www.ucasports.com.

Head Coach: Nick Harlan. **Telephone:** (402) 366-5948. **Baseball SID:** Steve East. **Telephone:** (501) 450-5743.

Assistant Coaches: Justin Cunningham, Hayden Simpson.

Home Field: Bear Stadium.

CENTRAL CONNECTICUT STATE

Conference: Northeast.

Mailing Address: 1615 Stanley Street, New Britain, CT 06051. **Website:** www.ccsubluedevils.com.

Head Coach: Charlie Hickey. **Telephone:** (860) 832-3074. **Baseball SID:** Jeff Mead.

Assistant Coaches: Patrick Hall, Rob Bono. **Home Field:** CCSU Baseball Field. **Seating Capacity:** 2,500. **Outfield Dimension:** LF—330, CF—400, RF—310.

CENTRAL FLORIDA

Conference: American Athletic.

Mailing Address: 4422 Knights Victory Way, Orlando, FL 32816. **Website:** www.ucfknights.com.

Head Coach: Greg Lovelady. **Baseball SID:** Dan Forcella.

Assistant Coaches: Ted Tom, Nick Otte. **Home Field:** John Euliano Park. **Seating Capacity:** 3,841. **Outfield Dimension:** LF—325, CF—390, RF—325.

CENTRAL MICHIGAN

Conference: Mid-American.

Mailing Address: 100 Rose Center, Mt. Pleasant, MI 48859. **Website:** www.cmuchippewas.com.

Head Coach: Jordan Bischel. **Telephone:** (920) 362-2329. **Baseball SID:** Andy Sneddon. **Telephone:** (231) 838-9188.

Assistant Coaches: Tony Jandron, Kyle Schroeder. **Telephone:** (906) 869-1446.

Home Field: Theunissen Stadium. **Seating Capacity:** 2,046. **Outfield Dimension:** LF—330, CF—400, RF—330.

CHARLESTON SOUTHERN

Conference: Big South.

Mailing Address: 9200 University Blvd., Charleston, S.C. 29406. **Website:** www.csusports.com.

Head Coach: Marc McMillan. **Baseball SID:** Taylor Chitwood. **Telephone:** (843) 863-7433.

Assistant Coaches: Anthony Izzio, Damon Lessler. **Home Field:** Nielsen Field at CSU Ballpark. **Seating Capacity:** 1,000. **Outfield Dimension:** LF—330, CF—400, RF—330.

CHARLOTTE

Conference: Conference USA.

Mailing Address: 8711 Phillips Rd. Charlotte, NC 28215. **Website:** www.charlotte49ers.com.

Head Coach: Robert Woodard. **Baseball SID:** Joe Templin.

Assistant Coaches: Toby Bicknell, Austin Meine. **Home Field:** Robert & Miriam Hayes Stadium. **Seating Capacity:** 3,000. **Outfield Dimension:** LF—335, CF—390, RF—315.

CINCINNATI

Conference: American Athletic.
Mailing Address: Richard E. Lindner Center 2751 O'Varsity Way, Cincinnati, Ohio 45221-0021. **Website:** www.gobearcats.com.
Head Coach: Scott Googins. **Telephone:** (513) 556-0566. **Baseball SID:** Alex Pepke. **Telephone:** (412) 996-5598.
Assistant Coaches: JD Heilmann, Kyle Sprague. **Telephone:** (513) 556-0565.
Home Field: UC Baseball Stadium. **Seating Capacity:** 3,085. **Outfield Dimension: LF**—325, **CF**—400, **RF**—325.

CITADEL

Conference: Southern.
Mailing Address: 171 Moultrie Street, Charleston, SC 29409. **Website:** www.citadelsports.com.
Head Coach: Tony Skole. **Baseball SID:** John Brush.
Assistant Coaches: Zach Lucas, Blake Cooper.
Home Field: Joe Riley Park. **Seating Capacity:** 7,500.
Outfield Dimension: LF—305, **CF**—398, **RF**—337.

CLEMSON

Conference: Atlantic Coast.
Mailing Address: 100 Perimeter Road; Clemson, SC 29633. **Website:** www.clemsontigers.com.
Head Coach: Monte Lee. **Telephone:** (864) 656-1947.
Baseball SID: Brain Hennessy. **Telephone:** (864) 656-1921.
Assistant Coaches: Bradley LeCroy, Andrew See.
Telephone: (864) 656-1950.
Home Field: Doug Kingsmore Stadium. **Seating Capacity:** 6,272. **Outfield Dimension: LF**—310, **CF**—390, **RF**—320.

COASTAL CAROLINA

Conference: Sun Belt.
Mailing Address: 965 One Landon Loop, Conway, S.C. 29526. **Website:** www.goccusports.com.
Head Coach: Gary Gilmore. **Telephone:** (843) 349-2524. **Baseball SID:** Kevin Davis. **Telephone:** (843) 349-2822.
Assistant Coaches: Kevin Schnall, Jason Beverlin. **Telephone:** (843) 349-3460.
Home Field: Springs Brooks Stadium. **Seating Capacity:** 2,500. **Outfield Dimension: LF**—320, **CF**—390, **RF**—320.

COLLEGE OF CHARLESTON

Conference: Colonial.
Mailing Address: 301 Meeting Street Charleston, SC 29401. **Website:** www.cofcsports.com.
Head Coach: Chad Holbrook. **Telephone:** (803) 622-0053. **Baseball SID:** Whitney Noble. **Telephone:** (843) 953-3683.
Assistant Coaches: Kevin Nichols, Will Dorton. **Telephone:** (843) 940-0868.
Home Field: Patriots Point. **Seating Capacity:** 2,000.
Outfield Dimension: LF—300, **CF**—400, **RF**—330.

COLUMBIA

Conference: Ivy League.
Mailing Address: Dodge Physical Fitness Center, 3030 Broadway, Mail Code 1900, New York, N.Y. 10027. **Website:** www.gocolumbialions.com.
Head Coach: Brett Boretti. **Telephone:** (212) 854-

8448. **Baseball SID:** Mike Kowalsky. **Telephone:** (212) 854-7064.
Assistant Coaches: Dan Tischler, Erik Supplee. **Telephone:** (212) 851-0105.
Home Field: Robertson Field at Satow Stadium.
Seating Capacity: 1,500.

CONNECTICUT

Conference: Big East.
Mailing Address: 2111 Hillside Rd., Storrs, CT 06268. **Website:** www.uconnhuskies.com.
Head Coach: Jim Penders. **Telephone:** (860) 208-9140. **Baseball SID:** Chris Jones. **Telephone:** (860) 938-6191.
Assistant Coaches: Joshua MacDonald, Jeffrey Hourigan. **Telephone:** (860) 465-6088.
Home Field: Elliot Ballpark. **Seating Capacity:** 2,000.
Outfield Dimension: LF—330, **CF**—400, **RF**—330.

COPPIN STATE

Conference: Mid-Eastern.
Mailing Address: 2500 West North Avenue Baltimore, MD 21217. **Website:** www.coppinstatesports.com.
Head Coach: Sherman Reed. **Telephone:** (410) 951-3723. **Baseball SID:** Steve Kramer. **Telephone:** (410) 951-3723.
Assistant Coaches: Sean Repay, Jovanny Zarzabal.
Home Field: Joe Cannon Stadium. **Seating Capacity:** 1,500. **Outfield Dimension: LF**—310, **CF**—425, **RF**—310.

CORNELL

Conference: Ivy League.
Mailing Address: Cornell University Athletics, Teagle Hall, 512 Campus Road, Ithaca, N.Y. 14853. **Website:** www.cornellbigred.com.
Head Coach: Dan Pepicelli. **Baseball SID:** Brandon Thomas. **Telephone:** (607) 255-5627.
Assistant Coaches: Tom Ford, Frank Hager. **Telephone:** (908) 868-1392.
Home Field: Hoy Field. **Seating Capacity:** 500.

CREIGHTON

Conference: Big East.
Mailing Address: 2500 California Plaza, Omaha NE, 68178. **Website:** www.gocreighton.edu.
Head Coach: Ed Servais. **Baseball SID:** Glen Sisk. **Telephone:** (402) 280-2433.
Assistant Coaches: Connor Gandossy, Mitch Mormann.
Home Field: Charles Schwab Field. **Seating Capacity:** 35,000. **Outfield Dimension: LF**—335, **CF**—408, **RF**—335.

DALLAS BAPTIST

Conference: Missouri Valley.
Mailing Address: 3000 Mountain Creek Parkway, Dallas, TX 75211. **Website:** www.dbupatriots.com.
Head Coach: Dan Heefner. **Telephone:** (214) 333-5324. **Baseball SID:** Reagan Ratcliff. **Telephone:** (214) 333-5942.
Assistant Coaches: Cliff Pennington, Micah Posey. **Telephone:** (214) 333-6987.
Home Field: Horner Ballpark. **Seating Capacity:** 2,000. **Outfield Dimension: LF**—330, **CF**—390, **RF**—330.

DARTMOUTH

Conference: Ivy League.
Mailing Address: Dartmouth Athletics, 6083 Alumni

Gym, Hanover, N.H. 03755. **Website:** dartmouthsports.com.

Head Coach: Bob Whalen. **Telephone:** (603) 646-2477. **Baseball SID:** Rick Bender. **Telephone:** (603) 646-1030.

Assistant Coaches: Blake McFadden, Mike Odenwaelder. **Telephone:** (603) 646-9775.

Home Field: Red Rolfe Field at Biondi Park. **Seating Capacity:** 1,000.

DAVIDSON

Conference: Atlantic 10.

Mailing Address: 200 Baker Drive, Davidson NC 28035. **Website:** www.davidsonwildcats.com.

Head Coach: Rucker Taylor. **Telephone:** (704) 894-2772. **Baseball SID:** Justin Parker. **Telephone:** (704) 894-2931.

Assistant Coaches: Ryan Munger, Parker Bangs. **Telephone:** (704) 894-2002.

Home Field: Wilson Field. **Seating Capacity:** 700. **Outfield Dimension: LF**—320, **CF**—385, **RF**—330.

DAYTON

Conference: Atlantic 10.

Mailing Address: University of Dayton, Baseball Office, 300 College Park, Dayton OH 45469. **Website:** www.daytonflyers.com.

Head Coach: Jayson King. **Telephone:** (603) 381-1279. **Baseball SID:** Eric Robinson. **Telephone:** (815) 325-0986.

Assistant Coaches: Travis Ferrick, Kyle Decker. **Telephone:** (540) 903-4967.

Home Field: Woerner Field at AES Ohio Stadium. **Seating Capacity:** 1,000. **Outfield Dimension: LF**—330, **CF**—400, **RF**—330.

DELAWARE

Conference: Colonial.

Mailing Address: 631 South College Avenue, Newark, DE 19716. **Website:** www.bluehens.com.

Head Coach: Jim Sherman. **Telephone:** (302) 831-8596. **Baseball SID:** Kevin Tritt. **Telephone:** (302) 831-8715.

Assistant Coaches: Jad Prachniak, Dan Hammer.

Home Field: Bob Hannah Stadium. **Seating Capacity:** 1,300. **Outfield Dimension: LF**—320, **CF**—400, **RF**—330.

DELAWARE STATE

Conference: Mid-Eastern.

Mailing Address: 1200 N. DuPont Highway, Dover, DE 19901. **Website:** www.dsuhornets.com.

Head Coach: JP Blandin. **Telephone:** (302) 857-6035. **Baseball SID:** Dennis Jones. **Telephone:** (302) 857-6068.

Assistant Coaches: Stephen Baughan, Jacob Ogurek. **Telephone:** (302) 857-7809.

Home Field: Soldier Field. **Seating Capacity:** 500.

DIXIE STATE

Conference: Western Athletic.

Mailing Address: 225 S. 700 E., St. George, UT 84770. **Website:** www.dixieathletics.com.

Head Coach: Chris Pfatenhauer. **Telephone:** (435) 652-7530. **Baseball SID:** Steve Johnson. **Telephone:** (435) 652-7524.

Assistant Coaches: Bobby Rinard, Zach Wilkins. **Telephone:** (435) 652-7530.

Home Field: Bruce Hurst Field. **Seating Capacity:** 2,500. **Outfield Dimension: LF**—325, **CF**—380, **RF**—335.

DUKE

Conference: Atlantic Coast.

Mailing Address: 101 Whitford Dr, Durham, NC 27708. **Website:** www.goduke.com.

Head Coach: Chris Pollard. **Baseball SID:** Jeff Friday. **Telephone:** (919) 684-6934.

Assistant Coaches: Josh Jordan, Jason Stein.

Home Field: Durham Bulls Athletic Park. **Seating Capacity:** 10,000. **Outfield Dimension: LF**—305, **CF**—400, **RF**—327.

EAST CAROLINA

Conference: American Athletic.

Mailing Address: 102 Clark-LeCLair Stadium East Carolina University Greenville, NC 27858. **Website:** www.ecupirates.com.

Head Coach: Cliff Godwin. **Telephone:** (252) 737-1985. **Baseball SID:** Malcolm Gray. **Telephone:** (252) 737-4523.

Assistant Coaches: Jeff Palumbo, Austin Knight. **Telephone:** (252) 737-1984.

Home Field: Lewis Field at Clark-LeClair Stadium. **Seating Capacity:** 5,800. **Outfield Dimension: LF**—320, **CF**—390, **RF**—320.

EAST TENNESSEE STATE

Conference: Southern.

Mailing Address: ETSU Athletics, PO Box 70707, Johnson City, TN 37614. **Website:** www.etsubucs.com.

Head Coach: Joe Pennucci. **Telephone:** (423) 439-4496. **Baseball SID:** Thomas Arteaga.

Assistant Coaches: Jamie Pinzino, Chad Marshall.

Home Field: Thomas Stadium. **Seating Capacity:** 1,000. **Outfield Dimension: LF**—325, **CF**—400, **RF**—325.

EASTERN ILLINOIS

Conference: Ohio Valley.

Mailing Address: Eastern Illinois Athletic Department, 600 Lincoln Avenue, Charleston, IL 61920. **Website:** www.eiupanthers.com.

Head Coach: Jason Anderson. **Baseball SID:** Rich Moser. **Telephone:** (217) 581-7480.

Assistant Coaches: Derek Francis, Tyler Shipley.

Home Field: Coaches Stadium at Monier Field. **Seating Capacity:** 500.

EASTERN KENTUCKY

Conference: ASUN.

Mailing Address: 521 Lancaster Avenue, 115 Alumni Coliseum, Richmond, KY 40475. **Website:** www.ekusports.com.

Head Coach: Chris Prothro. **Telephone:** (859) 622-2128. **Baseball SID:** Kevin Britton. **Telephone:** (859) 622-2006.

Assistant Coaches: Walt Jones, Cody Wofford. **Telephone:** (859) 622-8295.

Home Field: Turkey Hughes Field at Earle Combs Stadium. **Seating Capacity:** 1,000. **Outfield Dimension: LF**—340, **CF**—410, **RF**—330.

EASTERN MICHIGAN

Conference: Mid-American.

Mailing Address: 799 N Hewitt Rd Ypsilanti MI 48197. **Website:** www.emueagles.com.

Head Coach: Eric Roof. **Telephone:** (734) 487-1985. **Baseball SID:** Alex Jewell.

Assistant Coaches: Aaron Hilt, Jonathan Roof.
Home Field: Oestrike Stadium. **Seating Capacity:** 2,500.

ELON

Conference: Colonial.
Mailing Address: 100 Campus Drive, Elon, N.C. 27244. **Website:** www.elonphoenix.com.
Head Coach: Mike Kennedy. **Telephone:** (336) 278-6741. **Baseball SID:** Pierce Yarberry. **Telephone:** (336) 278-6712.
Assistant Coaches: Robbie Huffstetler, Jerry Oakes. **Telephone:** (336) 278-6794.
Home Field: Walter C. Latham Park. **Seating Capacity:** 5,100. **Outfield Dimension: LF**—325, **CF**—385, **RF**—325.

EVANSVILLE

Conference: Missouri Valley.
Mailing Address: 1800 Lincoln Ave, Evansville,IN 47714. **Website:** www.gopurpleaces.com.
Head Coach: Wes Carroll. **Baseball SID:** Michael Robertson.
Assistant Coaches: Keirce Kimbel, Jared Morton. **Telephone:** (812) 488-2764.
Home Field: German American Bank Field at Charles H. Braun Stadium. **Seating Capacity:** 1,200.

FAIRFIELD

Conference: Metro Atlantic.
Mailing Address: Fairfield University Athletics, Walsh Athletic Center, 1073 N. Benson Road, Fairfield, CT 06824. **Website:** www.fairfieldstags.com.
Head Coach: Bill Currier. **Telephone:** (203) 254-4000. **Baseball SID:** Ivey Speight. **Telephone:** (203) 254-4000.
Assistant Coaches: Brian Fay, Jordan Tabakman.
Home Field: Alumni Baseball Diamond. **Seating Capacity:** 350. **Outfield Dimension: LF**—330, **CF**—400, **RF**—330.

FAIRLEIGH DICKINSON

Conference: Northeast.
Mailing Address: 1000 River Rd, Teaneck, NJ 07666. **Website:** www.fduknights.com.
Head Coach: Rob DiToma. **Telephone:** (201) 692-2245. **Baseball SID:** Chelsea Ellis.
Assistant Coaches: Manny Roman, Andrew Romanella. **Telephone:** (201) 692-2245.
Home Field: Naimoli Family Baseball Complex. **Seating Capacity:** 500. **Outfield Dimension: LF**—318, **CF**—380, **RF**—315.

FLORIDA

Conference: Southeastern.
Mailing Address: University of Florida, 2800 Citrus Rd, Gainesville, FL 32608. **Website:** www.floridagators.com.
Head Coach: Kevin O'Sullivan. **Baseball SID:** Sullivan Bortner. **Telephone:** (352) 318-6680.
Assistant Coaches: Craig Bell, Chuck Jeroloman.
Home Field: Florida Ballpark. **Seating Capacity:** 7,000. **Outfield Dimension: LF**—330, **CF**—400, **RF**—330.

FLORIDA ATLANTIC

Conference: Conference USA.
Mailing Address: 777 Glades Road, Boca Raton FL, 33431. **Website:** www.fausports.com.
Head Coach: John McCormack. **Baseball SID:** Jonathan Fraysure.

Assistant Coaches: Greg Mamula, Brady Kirkpatrick.
Home Field: FAU Baseball Stadium. **Seating Capacity:** 1,718. **Outfield Dimension: LF**—330, **CF**—400, **RF**—330.

FLORIDA GULF COAST

Conference: ASUN.
Mailing Address: 10501 FGCU Boulevard South, Fort Myers, FL 33965. **Website:** www.fgcuathletics.com.
Head Coach: Dave Tollett. **Telephone:** (239) 590-7051. **Baseball SID:** Adam Grossman.
Assistant Coaches: Brandon Romans, Matt Reid.
Home Field: Swanson Stadium. **Seating Capacity:** 1,500. **Outfield Dimension: LF**—325, **CF**—400, **RF**—325.

FLORIDA INTERNATIONAL

Conference: Conference USA.
Mailing Address: FIU Athletics, 11200 SW 8th Street, Miami, FL 33199. **Website:** www.fiusports.com.
Head Coach: Mervyl Melendez. **Baseball SID:** Tyler Brain. **Telephone:** (305) 348-2084.
Assistant Coaches: Jeff Conine, Willie Collazo. **Telephone:** (305) 348-7403.
Home Field: FIU Baseball Stadium. **Seating Capacity:** 2,000. **Outfield Dimension:** LF-325, **CF**—400, **RF**—325.

FLORIDA STATE

Conference: Atlantic Coast.
Mailing Address: 403 W. Stadium Dr., Tallahassee, FL, 32306. **Website:** www.seminoles.com.
Head Coach: Mike Martin, Jr. **Baseball SID:** Steven McCartney.
Assistant Coaches: Mike Metcalf, Jimmy Belanger.
Home Field: Mike Martin Field at Dick Howser Stadium. **Seating Capacity:** 6,700. **Outfield Dimension: LF**—340, **CF**—400, **RF**—320.

FORDHAM

Conference: Atlantic 10.
Mailing Address: Rose Hill Gym, 441 East Fordham Road, Bronx, N.Y. 10458. **Website:** www.fordhamsports.com.
Head Coach: Kevin Leighton. **Telephone:** (718) 817-4292. **Baseball SID:** Scott Kwaitkowski. **Telephone:** (718) 817-4219.
Assistant Coaches: Elliot Glynn, Pat Porter. **Telephone:** (718) 817-4295.
Home Field: Houlihan Park. **Seating Capacity:** 1,000.

FRESNO STATE

Conference: Mountain West.
Mailing Address: 1620 East Bulldog Lane OF 87 Fresno, CA 93740. **Website:** www.gobulldogs.com.
Head Coach: Mike Batesole. **Telephone:** (559) 278-2178. **Baseball SID:** Travis Blanshan.
Assistant Coaches: Ryan Overland, Greg Gonzalez. **Telephone:** (559) 278-2178.
Home Field: Pete Beiden Field at Bob Bennett Stadium. **Seating Capacity:** 5,757. **Outfield Dimension: LF**—330, **CF**—400, **RF**—330.

GARDNER-WEBB

Conference: Big South.
Mailing Address: 110 South Main Street, Boiling Springs, NC 28017. **Website:** www.gwusports.com.
Head Coach: Jim Chester. **Telephone:** (704) 406-4421. **Baseball SID:** Marc Rabb. **Telephone:** (704) 406-4355.
Assistant Coaches: Conner Scarborough, Anthony

Marks. **Telephone:** (704) 406-3557.
Home Field: Bill Masters Field at John Henry Moss Stadium. **Seating Capacity:** 600. **Outfield Dimension:** **LF**—330, **CF**—385, **RF**—330.

GEORGE MASON

Conference: Atlantic 10.
Mailing Address: 4400 University Dr. Fairfax Va, 22030. **Website:** www.gomason.com.
Head Coach: Bill Brown. **Baseball SID:** Steve Kolbe.
Assistant Coaches: Ryan Terrill, Shawn Camp.
Home Field: Raymond "Hap" Spuhler Field. **Outfield Dimension: LF**—320, **CF**—400, **RF**—320.

GEORGE WASHINGTON

Conference: Atlantic 10.
Mailing Address: 4200 S Four Mile Run Dr, Arlington, VA 22206. **Website:** www.gwsports.com.
Head Coach: Gregory Ritchie. **Telephone:** (202) 994-7399. **Baseball SID:** Julian Coltre. **Telephone:** (202) 994-8604.
Assistant Coaches: Tyler Kavanaugh, Ryan Gaynor. **Telephone:** (202) 994-7399.
Home Field: Tucker Field. **Seating Capacity:** 500. **Outfield Dimension: LF**—330, **CF**—380, **RF**—330.

GEORGETOWN

Conference: Big East.
Mailing Address: McDonough Arena Washington, DC 20057. **Website:** www.gohoyas.com.
Head Coach: Edwin Thompson. **Baseball SID:** Dylan Smith.
Assistant Coaches: Julius McDougal, George Capen.
Home Field: Shirley Povich Field. **Seating Capacity:** 1,500. **Outfield Dimension: LF**—330, **CF**—375, **RF**—330.

GEORGIA

Conference: Southeastern.
Mailing Address: P.O. Box 1472, Athens, Ga. 30603.
Website: www.georgiadogs.com.
Head Coach: Scott Stricklin. **Telephone:** (706) 542-7971. **Baseball SID:** Christopher Lakos. **Telephone:** (706) 542-7994.
Assistant Coaches: Scott Daeley, Sean Kenny. **Telephone:** (706) 542-7971.
Home Field: Foley Field. **Seating Capacity:** 2,760. **Outfield Dimension: LF**—350, **CF**—404, **RF**—314.

GEORGIA SOUTHERN

Conference: Sun Belt.
Mailing Address: P.O. Box 8086, Statesboro, GA 30460. **Website:** www.gseagles.com.
Head Coach: Rodney Hennon. **Telephone:** (912) 478-1350. **Baseball SID:** Aaron Socha.
Assistant Coaches: Alan Beck, AJ Battisto. **Telephone:** (912) 478-1350.
Home Field: JI Clements Stadium. **Seating Capacity:** 3,500. **Outfield Dimension: LF**—335, **CF**—390, **RF**—329.

GEORGIA STATE

Conference: Sun Belt.
Mailing Address: 2819 Clifton Springs Road Decatur, Georgia 30034. **Website:** www.georgiastatesports.com.
Head Coach: Brad Stromdahl. **Baseball SID:** Allison George.
Assistant Coaches: Matt Taylor, Lars Davis.
Home Field: GSU Baseball Complex. **Seating**

Capacity: 2,000. **Outfield Dimension: LF**—330, **CF**—385, **RF**—330.

GEORGIA TECH

Conference: Atlantic Coast.
Mailing Address: 150 Bobby Dodd Way, Atlanta, GA 30332. **Website:** www.ramblinwreck.com.
Head Coach: Danny Hall. **Baseball SID:** Andrew Clausen.
Assistant Coaches: James Ramsey, Danny Borrell.
Home Field: Mac Nease Baseball Park at Russ Chandler Stadium. **Seating Capacity:** 3,600. **Outfield Dimension: LF**—328, **CF**—400, **RF**—334.

GONZAGA

Conference: West Coast.
Mailing Address: 502 E. Boone Ave; Spokane, WA 99258. **Website:** www.gozags.com.
Head Coach: Mark Machtolf. **Baseball SID:** Connor Gilbert. **Telephone:** (509) 313-6373.
Assistant Coaches: Danny Evans, Brandon Harmon.
Home Field: Patterson Ballpark and Steve Hertz Field. **Seating Capacity:** 2,000. **Outfield Dimension: LF**—328, **CF**—390, **RF**—328.

GRAMBLING STATE

Conference: Southwestern.
Mailing Address: 100 North Stadium Drive, Hobdy Assembly Center, Grambling, LA 71245. **Website:** www. gsutigers.com.
Head Coach: Davin Pierre. **Telephone:** (318) 274-2416. **Baseball SID:** Curtis Ford.
Assistant Coaches: Adrian Turner, Phil Adams. **Telephone:** (520) 858-9765.
Home Field: Wilbert Ellis Field at R.W.E. Jones Park. **Seating Capacity:** 1,100. **Outfield Dimension: LF**—315, **CF**—400, **RF**—350.

GRAND CANYON

Conference: Western Athletic.
Mailing Address: 3300 W Camelback Road, Phoenix, AZ 85017. **Website:** www.gculopes.com.
Head Coach: Andy Stankiewicz. **Telephone:** (602) 639-6042. **Baseball SID:** Josh Hauser. **Telephone:** (602) 639-8328.
Assistant Coaches: Gregg Wallis, Jon Wente. **Telephone:** (602) 639-7676.
Home Field: GCU Ballpark. **Seating Capacity:** 4,000. **Outfield Dimension: LF**—320, **CF**—375, **RF**—330.

HARTFORD

Conference: America East.
Mailing Address: 200 Bloomfield Avenue West Hartford CT, 06117. **Website:** www.hartfordhawks.com.
Head Coach: Steve Malinowski. **Telephone:** (860) 768-4656. **Baseball SID:** Dan Szewczak. **Telephone:** (860) 768-7785.
Assistant Coaches: TJ Ward, John Slusarz. **Telephone:** (860) 768-4972.
Home Field: Fiondella Field. **Seating Capacity:** 1,200. **Outfield Dimension: LF**—325, **CF**—400, **RF**—325.

HARVARD

Conference: Ivy League.
Mailing Address: 65 North Harvard St., Boston, MA 02163. **Website:** www.gocrimson.com.
Head Coach: Bill Decker. **Telephone:** (617) 496-2629.

Baseball SID: Nick Dow. **Telephone:** (617) 496-1379.
Assistant Coaches: Bryan Stark, Nate Cole.
Telephone: (617) 496-1435.
Home Field: O'Donnell Field. **Seating Capacity:**
1,600. **Outfield Dimension: LF**—335, **CF**—415, **RF**—335.

HAWAII

Conference: Big West.
Mailing Address: 1337 Lower Campus Road,
Honolulu, HI 96822. **Website:** www.hawaiiathletics.com.
Head Coach: Rich Hill. **Telephone:** (808) 956-6247.
Baseball SID: Eric Mathews. **Telephone:** (808) 956-9748.
Assistant Coaches: Dan Cox, Dave Nakama.
Telephone: (808) 956-6247.
Home Field: Les Murakami Stadium. **Seating
Capacity:** 4,312. **Outfield Dimension: LF**—325,
CF—385, **RF**—325

HIGH POINT

Conference: Big South.
Mailing Address: One University Parkway, High Point,
N.C. 27268. **Website:** www.highpointpanthers.com.
Head Coach: Joey Hammond. **Baseball SID:** Sarah
Duysen. **Telephone:** (336) 841-4638.
Assistant Coaches: Miles Miller, Mickey Williard.
Home Field: Williard Stadium. **Seating Capacity:** 501.

HOFSTRA

Conference: Colonial.
Mailing Address: 230 Hofstra University, PFC 232,
Hempstead NY 11549. **Website:** www.gohofstra.com.
Head Coach: Frank Catalanotto. **Telephone:** (516)
463-3759. **Baseball SID:** Len Skoros. **Telephone:** (516)
463-4602.
Assistant Coaches: Matt Wessinger, Chris Rojas.
Telephone: (516) 463-5065.
Home Field: University Field. **Seating Capacity:** 600.
Outfield Dimension: LF—322, **CF**—382, **RF**—337.

HOLY CROSS

Conference: Patriot League.
Mailing Address: 1 College St. Worcester, MA 01610.
Website: www.goholycross.com.
Head Coach: Ed Kahovec. **Telephone:** (508) 793-2753.
Baseball SID: Sarah Kirkpatrick. **Telephone:** (508) 793-
2780.
Assistant Coaches: Sam Tinkham, Ryan O'Rourke.
Telephone: (508) 793-3406.
Home Field: Hanover Insurance Park at Fitton Field.
Seating Capacity: 3,000. **Outfield Dimension: LF**—332,
CF—385, **RF**—313.

HOUSTON

Conference: American Athletic.
Mailing Address: 3204 Cullen Blvd., Houston, TX
77004. **Website:** www.uhcougars.com.
Head Coach: Todd Whitting. **Baseball SID:** Andrew
Pate.
Assistant Coaches: Ross Kivett, Kyle Bunn.
Home Field: Darryl & Lori Schroeder Park. **Seating
Capacity:** 3,500. **Outfield Dimension: LF**—330,
CF—390, **RF**—330.

HOUSTON BAPTIST

Conference: Southland.
Mailing Address: 7502 Fondren Blvd. Houston, Tx
77074. **Website:** www.hbuhuskies.com.

Head Coach: Lance Berkman. **Telephone:** (281)
649-3000. **Baseball SID:** Russ Reneau. **Telephone:** (281)
649-3098.
Assistant Coaches: Tyler Bremer, Clayton VanderLaan.
Telephone: (281) 649-3000.
Home Field: Husky Field. **Seating Capacity:** 500.
Outfield Dimension: LF—330, **CF**—406, **RF**—330.

ILLINOIS

Conference: Big Ten.
Mailing Address: 601 E. Kirby Avenue Champaign, Ill.,
61820. **Website:** www.fightingillini.com.
Head Coach: Dan Hartleb. **Baseball SID:** John
Peterson.
Assistant Coaches: Adam Christ, Mark Allen.
Home Field: Illinois Field. **Seating Capacity:** 1,500.
Outfield Dimension: LF—330, **CF**—400, **RF**—330.

ILLINOIS-CHICAGO

Conference: Horizon League.
Mailing Address: 839 West Roosevelt Road, Chicago,
IL 60608. **Website:** www.uicflames.com.
Head Coach: Sean McDermott. **Telephone:** (312)
355-1757. **Baseball SID:** Dan Wallace. **Telephone:** (312)
355-3139.
Assistant Coaches: John Flood, Brendon Hayden.
Telephone: (312) 355-2973.
Home Field: Les Miller Field at Curtis Granderson
Stadium. **Seating Capacity:** 1,800. **Outfield Dimension:**
LF—325, **CF**—400, **RF**—325.

ILLINOIS STATE

Conference: Missouri Valley.
Mailing Address: 100 North University St. Normal, IL
61761. **Website:** www.goredbirds.com.
Head Coach: Steve Holm. **Baseball SID:** Scott Beaton.
Assistant Coaches: Wally Crancer, RD Spiehs.
Home Field: Duffy Bass Field. **Seating Capacity:**
2,500. **Outfield Dimension: LF**—330, **CF**—400, **RF**—330.

INCARNATE WORD

Conference: Southland.
Mailing Address: 4301 Broadway, CPO 288, San
Antonio, TX 78209. **Website:** www.uiwcardinals.com.
Head Coach: Ryan Shotzberger. **Baseball SID:** Alexa
Low. **Telephone:** (210) 829-6048.
Assistant Coaches: Greg Evans, Kyle Simonds.
Home Field: Daniel Sullivan Field. **Seating Capacity:**
1,000. **Outfield Dimension: LF**—335, **CF**—407, **RF**—335

INDIANA

Conference: Big Ten.
Mailing Address: Simon Skjodt Assembly Hall, 1001
East 17th Street, Bloomington, IN 47408-1590. **Website:**
www.iuhoosiers.com.
Head Coach: Jeff Mercer. **Baseball SID:** Greg
Campbell.
Assistant Coaches: Derek Simmons, Dustin Glant.
Home Field: Bart Kaufman Field. **Seating Capacity:**
4,000. **Outfield Dimension: LF**—330, **CF**—400, **RF**—340.

INDIANA STATE

Conference: Missouri Valley.
Mailing Address: 401 North 4th Street, Terre Haute,
IN, 47809. **Website:** www.gosycamores.com.
Head Coach: Mitch Hannahs. **Telephone:** (812) 237-
4051. **Baseball SID:** Seth Montgomery. **Telephone:** (812)

237-4073.
Assistant Coaches: Brian Smiley, Justin Hancock.
Home Field: Bob Warn Field. **Seating Capacity:** 2,500.
Outfield Dimension: LF—340, **CF**—402, **RF**—340.

IONA

Conference: Metro Atlantic.
Mailing Address: 715 North Ave, New Rochelle NY,
10801. **Website:** www.icgaels.com.
Head Coach: Conor Burke. **Baseball SID:** Jack Ravitz.
Assistant Coaches: Mike Sciamanico, Cameron Curler.
Home Field: City Park. **Outfield Dimension: LF**—355,
CF—385, **RF**—330.

IOWA

Conference: Big Ten.
Mailing Address: S300 Carver Hawkeye Arena, Iowa
City, IA 52242-1020. **Website:** www.hawkeyesports.com.
Head Coach: Rick Heller. **Telephone:** (319) 335-9390.
Baseball SID: James Allan. **Telephone:** (319) 335-6439.
Assistant Coaches: Marty Sutherland, Robin Lund.
Telephone: (319) 335-9329.
Home Field: Duane Banks Field. **Seating Capacity:**
1,500. **Outfield Dimension: LF**—329, **CF**—395, **RF**—329.

JACKSON STATE

Conference: Southwestern.
Mailing Address: 1400 N Lynch Street Jackson, MS
39217. **Website:** www.gojsutigers.com.
Head Coach: Omar Johnson. **Telephone:** (601)
979-3930. **Baseball SID:** Evan Murry. **Telephone:** (601)
979-0849.
Assistant Coaches: Kevin Whiteside, Chadwick Hall.
Home Field: Braddy Field. **Seating Capacity:** 800.

JACKSONVILLE

Conference: ASUN.
Mailing Address: 2800 University Blvd N, Jacksonville,
FL, 32211. **Website:** www.judolphins.com.
Head Coach: Chris Hayes. **Baseball SID:** Scott Manze.
Telephone: (904) 256-7402.
Assistant Coaches: Brad Wilkerson, Jerry Edwards.
Home Field: John Sessions Stadium. **Seating
Capacity:** 1,750. **Outfield Dimension: LF**—340,
CF—405, **RF**—340.

JACKSONVILLE STATE

Conference: ASUN.
Mailing Address: 700 Pelham Rd N Jacksonville, AL
36265. **Website:** www.jsugamecocksports.com.
Head Coach: Jim Case. **Baseball SID:** Tony Schmidt.
Telephone: (256) 782-5377.
Assistant Coaches: Mike Murphree, Evan Bush.
Home Field: Rudy Abbott Field at Jim Case Stadium.
Seating Capacity: 2,020. **Outfield Dimension: LF**—330,
CF—403, **RF**—335.

JAMES MADISON

Conference: Colonial.
Mailing Address: 800 S Main St, Harrisonburg, VA
22807. **Website:** www.jmusports.com.
Head Coach: Marlin Ikenberry. **Telephone:** (540) 568-
3932. **Baseball SID:** Christian Howe. **Telephone:** (540)
568-6155.
Assistant Coaches: Alex Guerra, Jimmy Jackson.
Telephone: (540) 568-6516.
Home Field: Eagle Field at Veterans Memorial Park.

Seating Capacity: 1,200. **Outfield Dimension: LF**—330,
CF—400, **RF**—320.

KANSAS

Conference: Big 12.
Mailing Address: 1651 Naismith Dr Lawrence, KS
66045. **Website:** www.kuathletics.com.
Head Coach: Ritch Price. **Baseball SID:** Brandon Perel.
Assistant Coaches: Ritchie Price, Ryan Graves.
Home Field: Hoglund Ballpark. **Seating Capacity:**
2,500. **Outfield Dimension: LF**–330, **CF**—400, **RF**—330.

KANSAS STATE

Conference: Big 12.
Mailing Address: 1800 College Ave. Manhattan KS
66502. **Website:** www.kstatesports.com.
Head Coach: Pete Hughes. **Baseball SID:** Christopher
Brown.
Assistant Coaches: Ryan Connolly, Austin Wates.
Home Field: Tointon Family Stadium. **Seating
Capacity:** 2,344. **Outfield Dimension: LF**—325,
CF—390, **RF**—320.

KENNESAW STATE

Conference: ASUN.
Mailing Address: 590 Cobb Avenue, Kennesaw, GA,
30144. **Website:** www.ksuowls.com.
Head Coach: Ryan Coe. **Telephone:** (470) 578-6264.
Baseball SID: Matteen Zibanejadrad. **Telephone:** (470)
578-7792.
Assistant Coaches: Derrick Tucker, Matthew Passauer.
Telephone: (470) 578-2098.
Home Field: Stillwell Stadium. **Seating Capacity:**
1,200. **Outfield Dimension: LF**—331, **CF**—400, **RF**—330.

KENT STATE

Conference: Mid-American.
Mailing Address: MAC Center, PO Box 5190, Kent, OH
44242. **Website:** www.kentstatesports.com.
Head Coach: Jeff Duncan. **Telephone:** (330) 672-8432.
Baseball SID: Dan Griffin. **Telephone:** (330) 672-8468.
Assistant Coaches: Mike Birkbeck, Barrett Serrato.
Telephone: (330) 672-8433.
Home Field: Olga A. Mural Field at Schoonover
Stadium. **Seating Capacity:** 500.

KENTUCKY

Conference: Southeastern.
Mailing Address: 510 Wildcat Court, Lexington, Ky,
40506. **Website:** www.ukathletics.com.
Head Coach: Nick Mingione. **Telephone:** (859)
257-8052. **Baseball SID:** Matt May. **Telephone:** (859)
257-8504.
Assistant Coaches: Will Coggin, Dan Roszel.
Telephone: (859) 257-8052.
Home Field: Kentucky Proud Park. **Seating Capacity:**
5,000. **Outfield Dimension: LF**—335, **CF**—400, **RF**—320.

LAFAYETTE

Conference: Patriot League.
Mailing Address: 700 W Pierce Street 307A Easton PA
18042. **Website:** www.goleopards.com.
Head Coach: Tim Reilly. **Telephone:** (610) 330-5945.
Baseball SID: Hannah Simmons. **Telephone:** (610) 330-
5518.
Assistant Coaches: John Lyons-Harrison, Ryan Ricci.
Telephone: (610) 330-3257.

Home Field: Kamine Stadium. **Seating Capacity:** 500. **Outfield Dimension: LF**—332, **CF**—403, **RF**—335.

LAMAR

Conference: Western Athletics.
Mailing Address: 211 Redbird Lane Beaumont, TX 77710. **Website:** www.lamarcardinals.com.
Head Coach: Will Davis. **Telephone:** (225) 802-3784. **Baseball SID:** James Dixon.
Assistant Coaches: Scott Hatten, Sean Snedeker.
Home Field: Vincent-Beck Stadium. **Seating Capacity:** 3,500. **Outfield Dimension: LF**—325, **CF**—380, **RF**—325.

LEHIGH

Conference: Patriot League.
Mailing Address: 27 Memorial Dr W, Bethlehem, PA 18015. **Website:** www.lehighsports.com.
Head Coach: Sean Leary. **Telephone:** (610) 758-4315. **Baseball SID:** Josh Liddick.
Assistant Coaches: AJ Miller, Sean Buchanan. **Telephone:** (610) 758-4315.
Home Field: J. David Walker Field. **Outfield Dimension: LF**—320, **CF**—400, **RF**—320.

LIBERTY

Conference: ASUN.
Mailing Address: 1971 University Blvd. Lynchburg VA 24515. **Website:** www.libertyflames.com.
Head Coach: Scott Jackson. **Telephone:** (434) 582-2305. **Baseball SID:** Ryan Bomberger.
Assistant Coaches: Matt Williams, Tyler Cannon.
Home Field: Worthington Field at Liberty Baseball Stadium. **Seating Capacity:** 4,500. **Outfield Dimension: LF**—325, **CF**—395, **RF**—325.

LIPSCOMB

Conference: ASUN.
Mailing Address: One University Park Drive, Nashville, TN 37204-3951. **Website:** www.lipscombsports.com.
Head Coach: Jeff Forehand. **Telephone:** (615) 966-5716. **Baseball SID:** Hannah Jo Riley. **Telephone:** (270) 227-6485.
Assistant Coaches: Ryan Price, Matt Myers.
Home Field: Ken Dugan Field at Stephen Lee Marsh Stadium. **Seating Capacity:** 1,500. **Outfield Dimension: LF**—330, **CF**—405, **RF**—330.

LONG BEACH STATE

Conference: Big West.
Mailing Address: 1250 Bellflower Blvd Long Beach, CA 90840. **Website:** www.longbeachstate.com.
Head Coach: Eric Valenzuela. **Telephone:** (562) 985-8215. **Baseball SID:** Collin Robinson. **Telephone:** (562) 985-7797.
Assistant Coaches: Daniel Costanza, Bryan Peters.
Home Field: Bohl Diamond at Blair Field. **Seating Capacity:** 3,000. **Outfield Dimension: LF**—335, **CF**—395, **RF**—330.

LONG ISLAND

Conference: Northeast.
Mailing Address: 720 Northern Blvd., Brookville, N.Y. 11548. **Website:** www.liuathletics.com.
Head Coach: Dan Pirillo. **Telephone:** (516) 299-2939. **Baseball SID:** Casey Snedecor. **Telephone:** (718) 488-1307.

Assistant Coaches: Tom Carty, Paul Gehring.
Telephone: (516) 299-3985.
Home Field: LIU Baseball Stadium. **Outfield Dimension: LF**—330, **CF**—400, **RF**—330.

LONGWOOD

Conference: Big South.
Mailing Address: 201 High Street Farmville, VA 23909. **Website:** www.longwoodlancers.com.
Head Coach: Chad Oxendine. **Baseball SID:** Sam Hovan. **Telephone:** (434) 395-2345.
Assistant Coaches: Brad Mincey, Mickey Beach. **Telephone:** (434) 395-2351.
Home Field: Buddy Bolding Stadium. **Seating Capacity:** 500. **Outfield Dimension: LF**—330, **CF**—390, **RF**—330.

LOUISIANA-LAFAYETTE

Conference: Sun Belt.
Mailing Address: 201 Reinhardt Drive, Lafayette, LA, 70506. **Website:** www. ragincajuns.com
Head Coach: Matt Deggs. **Baseball SID:** Matt Sullivan. **Telephone:** (337) 482-6331.
Assistant Coaches: Jake Wells, Seth Thibodeaux.
Home Field: M.L. "Tigue" Moore Field at Russo Park. **Seating Capacity:** 6,015. **Outfield Dimension: LF**—330, **CF**—400, **RF**—330.

LOUISIANA-MONROE

Conference: Sun Belt.
Mailing Address: 308 Warhawk Way, Monroe, La., 71203. **Website:** www.ulmwarhawks.com.
Head Coach: Michael Federico. **Telephone:** (318) 342-3591. **Baseball SID:** Mike Hammett. **Telephone:** (318) 342-7925.
Assistant Coaches: Jake Carlson, Matt Collins. **Telephone:** (318) 342-5396.
Home Field: Warhawk Field. **Seating Capacity:** 1,800. **Outfield Dimension: LF**—330, **CF**—400, **RF**—330.

LOUISIANA STATE

Conference: Southeastern.
Mailing Address: Nicholson Dr. at N. Stadium Dr., Baton Rouge, LA 70803. **Website:** www.lsusports.net.
Head Coach: Jay Johnson. **Telephone:** (225) 578-4148. **Baseball SID:** Bill Franques. **Telephone:** (225) 578-8226.
Assistant Coaches: Dan Fitzgerald, Jason Kelly. **Telephone:** (225) 578-4148.
Home Field: Alex Box Stadium. **Seating Capacity:** 10,326. **Outfield Dimension: LF**—330, **CF**—405, **RF**—330.

LOUISIANA TECH

Conference: Conference USA.
Mailing Address: Thomas Assembly Center 1650 West Alabama Ruston, La. 71270. **Website:** www.latechsports.com.
Head Coach: Lane Burroughs. **Baseball SID:** Patrick Davis. **Telephone:** (318) 257-5071.
Assistant Coaches: Cooper Fouts, Matt Miller.
Home Field: J.C. Love Field at Pat Patterson Park. **Seating Capacity:** 2,100. **Outfield Dimension: LF**—315, **CF**—380, **RF**—325.

LOUISVILLE

Conference: Atlantic Coast.
Mailing Address: 215 Central Ave, Louisville, KY 40292. **Website:** www.gocards.com.
Head Coach: Dan McDonnell. **Telephone:** (502) 852-0103. **Baseball SID:** Stephen Williams. **Telephone:** (502) 852-4857.
Assistant Coaches: Eric Snider, Roger Williams. **Telephone:** (502) 852-8145.
Home Field: Jim Patterson Stadium. **Seating Capacity:** 4,000. **Outfield Dimension: LF**—330, **CF**—402, **RF**—330.

LOYOLA MARYMOUNT

Conference: West Coast.
Mailing Address: 1 LMU Drive, Los Angeles CA, 90045. **Website:** www.lmulions.com.
Head Coach: Nathan Choate. **Telephone:** (310) 338-2949. **Baseball SID:** Matthew Lerman. **Telephone:** (310) 338-7768. **Assistant Coaches:** Tony Asaro, Mitch Karraker. **Telephone:** (310) 338-4533.
Home Field: George C. Page Stadium. **Seating Capacity:** 600. **Outfield Dimension: LF**—326, **CF**—406, **RF**—321.

MAINE

Conference: America East.
Mailing Address: 5745 Mahaney Clubhouse Orono, ME 04469. **Website:** www.goblackbears.com.
Head Coach: Nick Derba. **Telephone:** (207) 581-1090. **Baseball SID:** Bryce Colbeth.
Assistant Coaches: Scott Heath, Ryan McClaran.
Home Field: Mahaney Diamond. **Seating Capacity:** 3,000. **Outfield Dimension: LF**—330, **CF**—400, **RF**—330.

MANHATTAN

Conference: Metro Atlantic.
Mailing Address: 4513 Manhattan College Parkway, Riverdale, N.Y. 10471. **Website:** www.gojaspers.com.
Head Coach: Mike Cole. **Telephone:** (718) 862-7821. **Baseball SID:** Phil Paquette.
Assistant Coaches: Chris Cody, David Vandercook. **Telephone:** (718) 862-7104.
Home Field: Van Cortlandt Park.

MARIST

Conference: Metro Atlantic.
Mailing Address: McCann Center, 3399 North Road, Poughkeepsie, N.Y. 12601. **Website:** www.goredfoxes. com.
Head Coach: Chris Tracz. **Telephone:** (845) 575-3000. **Baseball SID:** Harrison Baker.
Assistant Coaches: Mike Coss, Adam Chase.
Home Field: McCann Baseball Field. **Seating Outfield Dimension: LF**—320, **CF**—390, **RF**—320.

MARSHALL

Conference: Conference USA.
Mailing Address: Marshall Athletics Department. **Website:** www.herdzone.com.
Head Coach: Jeff Waggoner. **Telephone:** (304) 696-6454. **Baseball SID:** Cody Linn. **Telephone:** (304) 696-2418.
Assistant Coaches: Joe Renner, Brian Karlet. **Telephone:** (304) 696-7146.
Home Field: Kennedy Center YMCA.

MARYLAND

Conference: Big Ten.
Mailing Address: XFINITY Center, 8500 Paint Branch Drive, College Park, MD 20742. **Website:** www.umterps. com.
Head Coach: Rob Vaughn. **Baseball SID:** Matt Gilpin.
Assistant Coaches: Matt Swope, Anthony Papio.
Home Field: Bob "Turtle" Smith Stadium. **Seating Capacity:** 2,500. **Outfield Dimension: LF**—320, **CF**—380, **RF**—325.

MARYLAND-BALTIMORE COUNTY

Conference: America East.
Mailing Address: 1000 Hilltop Cir, Baltimore, MD 21250. **Website:** www.umbcretrievers.com.
Head Coach: Liam Bowen. **Baseball SID:** Gavin Prather.
Assistant Coaches: Phil Disher, Matt Marsh.
Home Field: Alumni Field. **Seating Capacity:** 1,000. **Outfield Dimension: LF**—340, **CF**—360, **RF**—340.

MARYLAND-EASTERN SHORE

Conference: Mid-Eastern.
Mailing Address: 1 Backbone Road, Princess Anne, MD 21853. **Website:** www.easternshorehawks.com.
Head Coach: Brian Hollamon. **Telephone:** (410) 651-7864. **Baseball SID:** Shawn Yonker. **Telephone:** (410) 651-6289.
Assistant Coaches: Shawn Phillips, Dave Johnson. **Telephone:** (410) 651-8620.
Home Field: Arthur W. Perdue Stadium. **Seating Capacity:** 5,200. **Outfield Dimension: LF**—309, **CF**—402, **RF**—309.

MASSACHUSETTS

Conference: Atlantic 10.
Mailing Address: 200 Commonwealth Avenue, 3rd Floor, Amherst, MA 01003. **Website:** www.umassathletics.com.
Head Coach: Matt Reynolds. **Telephone:** (413) 545-3120. **Baseball SID:** Hana Johnson.
Assistant Coaches: Mark Royer, Steve Adkins. **Telephone:** (703) 346-8571.
Home Field: Earl Lorden Field. **Outfield Dimension: LF**—330, **CF**—400, **RF**—330.

MASSACHUSETTS-LOWELL

Conference: America East.
Mailing Address: 1 University Ave, Lowell, MA 01854. **Website:** www.goriverhawks.com.
Head Coach: Ken Harring. **Telephone:** (978) 934-2344. **Baseball SID:** Dan Kastner. **Telephone:** (978) 934-6685.
Assistant Coaches: Nick Barese, Joe Consolmagno.
Home Field: LeLacheur Park. **Seating Capacity:** 4,797. **Outfield Dimension: LF**—337, **CF**—400, **RF**—301.

MCNEESE STATE

Conference: Southland.
Mailing Address: 700 E. McNeese Street - Lake Charles, LA 70609. **Website:** www.mcneesesports.com.
Head Coach: Justin Hill. **Baseball SID:** Jared Morris. **Telephone:** (337) 475-5207.
Assistant Coaches: Nick Zaleski, Jim Ricklefsen.
Home Field: Joe Miller Ballpark. **Seating Capacity:** 2,000. **Outfield Dimension: LF**—330, **CF**—400, **RF**—330.

MEMPHIS

Conference: American Athletic.
Mailing Address: Park Avenue Campus, Memphis, TN, 38111. **Website:** www.gotigersgo.com.
Head Coach: Daron Schoenrock. **Baseball SID:** Mike Weisman.
Assistant Coaches: Clay Greene, Russ McNickle.
Home Field: FedEx Park at Avron Fogelman Field.
Seating Capacity: 2,000. **Outfield Dimension:** LF—318, CF—380, RF—317.

MERCER

Conference: Southern.
Mailing Address: 1501 Mercer University Drive, Macon, GA 31207. **Website:** www.mercerbears.com.
Head Coach: Craig Gibson. **Telephone:** (478) 301-2396. **Baseball SID:** Zach Durkee. **Telephone:** (478) 301-5219.
Assistant Coaches: Willie Stewart, Cory Barton.
Home Field: OrthoGeorgia Park. **Seating Capacity:** 1,500. **Outfield Dimension:** LF—320, CF—400, RF—320.

MERRIMACK

Conference: Northeast.
Mailing Address: 315 Turnpike Street, North Andover, MA 01845. **Website:** www.merrimackathletics.com.
Head Coach: Brian Murphy. **Baseball SID:** Nick Penkala. **Telephone:** (978) 837-5053.
Assistant Coaches: Patrick McKenna, Charlie Fletcher.
Home Field: Warrior Baseball Diamond. **Outfield Dimension:** LF—335, CF—390, RF—335.

MIAMI

Conference: Atlantic Coast.
Mailing Address: 5821 San Amaro Drive, Coral Gables, FL, 33146. **Website:** www.miamihurricanes.com.
Head Coach: Gino DiMare. **Telephone:** (305) 284-4171. **Baseball SID:** Josh White. **Telephone:** (305) 284-6656.
Assistant Coaches: Norberto Lopez, JD Arteaga. **Telephone:** (305) 284-4171.
Home Field: Alex Rodriguez Park at Mark Light Field.
Seating Capacity: 3,500. **Outfield Dimension:** LF—330, CF—400, RF—330.

MIAMI (OHIO)

Conference: Mid-American.
Mailing Address: 550 E Withrow Street, Oxford, OH 45056. **Website:** www.miamiredhawks.com.
Head Coach: Danny Hayden. **Baseball SID:** Cole Neelon. **Telephone:** (513) 529-0402.
Assistant Coaches: Bailey Montgomery, Jeff Opalewski.
Home Field: McKie Field at Hayden Park. **Seating Capacity:** 600. **Outfield Dimension:** LF—332, CF—400, RF—341.

MICHIGAN

Conference: Big Ten.
Mailing Address: 1000 South State Street, Ann Arbor, MI 48109. **Website:** www.mgoblue.com.
Head Coach: Erik Bakich. **Baseball SID:** Kurt Svoboda. **Telephone:** (734) 615-0331.
Assistant Coaches: Nick Schnabel, Steve Merriman.
Home Field: Ray Fisher Stadium. **Seating Capacity:** 4,000. **Outfield Dimension:** LF—330, CF—400, RF—330.

MICHIGAN STATE

Conference: Big Ten.
Mailing Address: Room 304, Jenison Field House, 223 Kalamazoo Street, East Lansing, MI 48824-1025. **Website:** www.msuspartans.com.
Head Coach: Jake Boss. **Telephone:** (517) 355-4486. **Baseball SID:** Zach Fisher. **Telephone:** (517) 355-2271.
Assistant Coaches: Mark Van Ameyde, Graham Sikes. **Telephone:** (517) 355-3419.
Home Field: McLane Baseball Stadium at Kobs Field. **Seating Capacity:** 2,500.

MIDDLE TENNESSEE STATE

Conference: Conference USA.
Mailing Address: 1672 Greenland Drive, Murfreesboro, TN 37132. **Website:** www.goblueraiders.com.
Head Coach: Jim Toman. **Telephone:** (615) 898-2961. **Baseball SID:** Carson Herbert. **Telephone:** (615) 898-8209.
Assistant Coaches: Jerry Meyers, Jordan Getzelman.
Home Field: Reese Smith, Jr. Field. **Seating Capacity:** 2,600. **Outfield Dimension:** LF—330, CF—390, RF—330.

MINNESOTA

Conference: Big Ten.
Mailing Address: 516 15th Ave. SE, Minneapolis, MN 55455. **Website:** www.gophersports.com.
Head Coach: John Anderson. **Telephone:** (612) 625-1060. **Baseball SID:** EJ Stevens.
Assistant Coaches: Patrick Casey, Ty McDevitt. **Telephone:** (612) 625-3568.
Home Field: Siebert Field. **Seating Capacity:** 1,420. **Outfield Dimension:** LF—330, CF—390, RF—330.

MISSISSIPPI

Conference: Southeastern.
Mailing Address: South Oxford Campus, 5th Floor, PO Box 1848, Oxford, MS 38677 . **Website:** www.olemisssports.com.
Head Coach: Mike Bianco. **Baseball SID:** Mitch Praxl. **Telephone:** (662) 915-7896.
Assistant Coaches: Carl Lafferty, Mike Clement. **Telephone:** (662) 915-6643.
Home Field: Swayze Field. **Seating Capacity:** 10,715. **Outfield Dimension:** LF—330, CF—390, RF—330.

MISSISSIPPI STATE

Conference: Southeastern.
Mailing Address: 288 Lakeview Drive, Mississippi State, MS 39762. **Website:** www.hailstate.com.
Head Coach: Chris Lemonis. **Telephone:** (662) 325-3597. **Baseball SID:** Anna Claire Thomas. **Telephone:** (662) 325-0972.
Assistant Coaches: Jake Gautreau, Scott Foxhall. **Telephone:** (662) 325-3597.
Home Field: Dudy Noble Field at Poke-DeMent Stadium. **Seating Capacity:** 15,000. **Outfield Dimension:** LF—330, CF—400, RF—305.

MISSISSIPPI VALLEY STATE

Conference: Southwestern.
Mailing Address: 14000 Highway 82 West, Box 7246, Itta Bena, MS 38941. **Website:** www.mvsusports.com.
Head Coach: Stanley E. Stubbs. **Baseball SID:** Brian Baublitz, Jr. **Telephone:** (662) 254-3011.

Assistant Coaches: Jaylan Bledsoe, Matt Ribera.
Home Field: Magnolia Field. **Seating Capacity:** 120.
Outfield Dimension: LF—313, **CF**—394, **RF**—315.

MISSOURI

Conference: Southeastern.
Mailing Address: 1 Champions Drive, Suite 200,
Columbia, MO 65211. **Website:** www.mutigers.com.
Head Coach: Steve Bieser. **Baseball SID:** Jacob Bell.
Assistant Coaches: Jason Hagerty, Mitch Plassmeyer.
Home Field: Taylor Stadium. **Seating Capacity:** 3,031.
Outfield Dimension: LF—340, **CF**—400, **RF**—340.

MISSOURI STATE

Conference: Missouri Valley.
Mailing Address: 901 S. National Avenue, Springfield,
MO 65897. **Website:** www.missouristatebears.com.
Head Coach: Keith Guttin. **Telephone:** (417) 836-4497.
Baseball SID: Ben Adamson. **Telephone:** (417) 836-4584.
Assistant Coaches: Paul Evans, Joey Hawkins.
Telephone: (417) 836-4496.
Home Field: Hammons Field. **Seating Capacity:**
8,000. **Outfield Dimension:** LF—315, **CF**—400, **RF**—330.

MONMOUTH

Conference: Metro Atlantic.
Mailing Address: 400 Cedar Ave, West Long Branch,
NJ 07764. **Website:** www.monmouthhawks.com.
Head Coach: Dean Ehehalt. **Baseball SID:** Gary Kowal.
Assistant Coaches: Chris Collazo, Sean Thompson.
Home Field: Monmouth Baseball Field. **Seating
Capacity:** 1,000. **Outfield Dimension:** LF—330,
CF—400, **RF**—330.

MOREHEAD STATE

Conference: Ohio Valley.
Mailing Address: 111 Playforth Pl, Morehead, KY
40351. **Website:** www.msueagles.com.
Head Coach: Mik Aoki. **Baseball SID:** Matthew
Schabert.
Assistant Coaches: Braeden Ward, Tyler Jackson.
Home Field: Allen Field. **Seating Capacity:** 1,200.

MOUNT ST. MARY'S

Conference: Northeast.
Mailing Address: 16300 Old Emmitsburg Road,
Emmitsburg, MD 21727. **Website:** mountathletics.com.
Head Coach: Frank Leoni. **Telephone:** (301) 447-3806.
Baseball SID: Matt McCann. **Telephone:** (301) 447-5384.
Assistant Coaches: Cullen Moore, Aaron Tarr.
Telephone: (301) 447-3806.
Home Field: E.T. Straw Family Stadium. **Seating
Capacity:** 500. **Outfield Dimension:** LF—325, **CF**—385,
RF—325.

MURRAY STATE

Conference: Ohio Valley.
Mailing Address: 217 Stewart Stadium, Murray, KY,
42071. **Website:** www.goracers.com.
Head Coach: Dan Skirka. **Telephone:** (270) 809-4892.
Baseball SID: Clay Wagoner. **Telephone:** (270) 809-7051.
Assistant Coaches: Tanner Gordon, Cooper Goen.
Home Field: Johnny Reagan. **Outfield Dimension:**
LF—330, **CF**—400, **RF**—330.

NAVY

Conference: Patriot League.
Mailing Address: 121 Blake Road, Annapolis, Md.,
21402. **Website:** www.navysports.com.
Head Coach: Paul Kostacopoulos. **Telephone:** (410)
293-5571. **Baseball SID:** Ryan Sargent. **Telephone:** (410)
293-8787.
Assistant Coaches: Jeff Kane, Mike Trapasso.
Telephone: (410) 293-5428.
Home Field: Terwilliger Brothers Field at Max Bishop
Stadium. **Seating Capacity:** 1,500. **Outfield Dimension:**
LF—318, **CF**—390, **RF**—300.

NEBRASKA

Conference: Big Ten.
Mailing Address: 403 Line Dr Cir, Lincoln, NE 68508.
Website: www.huskers.com.
Head Coach: Will Bolt. **Baseball SID:** Keith Mann.
Assistant Coaches: Lance Harvell, Jeff Christy.
Home Field: Haymarket Park. **Seating Capacity:**
8,757. **Outfield Dimension:** LF—335, **CF**—403, **RF**—325.

NEBRASKA-OMAHA

Conference: Summit League.
Mailing Address: 6001 Dodge Street, Omaha, NE,
68182. **Website:** www.omavs.com.
Head Coach: Evan Porter. **Baseball SID:** Tony Boone.
Assistant Coaches: Brian Strawn, Payton Kinney.
Home Field: Tal Anderson Field. **Seating Capacity:**
1,500. **Outfield Dimension:** LF—330, **CF**—410, **RF**—330.

NEVADA

Conference: Mountain West.
Mailing Address: 1664 N. VIrginia Street, Legacy Hall/
MS 232, Reno, NV 89557-0232. **Website:** www.nevada-
wolfpack.com.
Head Coach: TJ Bruce. **Telephone:** (775) 682-6978.
Baseball SID: Grace Tafolla. **Telephone:** (319) 310-4576.
Assistant Coaches: Troy Buckley, Abe Alvarez.
Home Field: Don Weir Field at Peccole Park. **Seating
Capacity:** 3,000. **Outfield Dimension:** LF—340,
CF—401, **RF**—340.

NEVADA-LAS VEGAS

Conference: Mountain West.
Mailing Address: 4505 South Maryland Parkway. Las
Vegas, NV 89154. **Website:** www.unlvrebels.com.
Head Coach: Stan Stolte. **Telephone:** (702) 895-3402.
Baseball SID: Kelsey Olsen.
Assistant Coaches: Cory Vanderhook, Kevin Higgins.
Telephone: (702) 449-9309.
Home Field: Earl E. Wilson Stadium. **Seating
Capacity:** 3,000. **Outfield Dimension:** LF—335,
CF—400, **RF**—335.

NEW JERSEY TECH

Conference: America East.
Mailing Address: 100 Lock Street Newark, NJ 07102.
Website: www.njithighlanders.com.
Head Coach: Robert McClellan. **Baseball SID:** Myles
Rudnick.
Assistant Coaches: Giuseppe Papaccio, Anthony
Deleo.
Home Field: Jim Hynes Stadium. **Seating Capacity:**
700.

NEW MEXICO

Conference: Mountain West.
Mailing Address: 1414 University Drive Albuquerque, N.M. 87106. **Website:** www.golobos.com.
Head Coach: Tod Brown. **Telephone:** (505) 925-5500.
Baseball SID: Alma Solis.
Assistant Coaches: Jon Coyne, Michael Lopez.
Telephone: (505) 925-5500.
Home Field: Santa Ana Star Field. **Seating Capacity:** 1,000. **Outfield Dimension: LF**—338, **CF**—420, **RF**—338.

NEW MEXICO STATE

Conference: Western Athletic.
Mailing Address: Fulton Center, 1815 Wells Street, Las Cruces, N.M. 88003-8001. **Website:** www.nmstatesports.com.
Head Coach: Mike Kirby. **Telephone:** (575) 646-7693.
Baseball SID: Charlie Hurley. **Telephone:** (575) 646-4120.
Assistant Coaches: Michael Pritchard, Keith Zuniva.
Telephone: (575) 646-2739.
Home Field: Presley Askew Field. **Seating Capacity:** 1,000. **Outfield Dimension: LF**—345, **CF**—400, **RF**—345.

NEW ORLEANS

Conference: Southland.
Mailing Address: 2000 Lakeshore Dr. New Orleans, LA 70148. **Website:** www.unoprivateers.com.
Head Coach: Blake Dean. **Baseball SID:** Emanuel Pepis.
Assistant Coaches: Brett Stewart, Dax Norris.
Home Field: Maestri Field at Privateer Park. **Seating Capacity:** 2,900. **Outfield Dimension: LF**—330, **CF**—405, **RF**—330.

NIAGARA

Conference: Metro Atlantic.
Mailing Address: Upper Level Gallagher Center, PO Box 2009, Niagara University, N.Y., 14109. **Website:** www.purpleeagles.com.
Head Coach: Rob McCoy. **Telephone:** (716) 286-7361.
Baseball SID: Breanna Jacobs. **Telephone:** (716) 286-8586.
Assistant Coaches: Matt Spatafora, Alex Zuia.
Telephone: (716) 286-8624.
Home Field: Bobo Field. **Outfield Dimension: LF**—327, **CF**—394, **RF**—315.

NICHOLLS STATE

Conference: Southland.
Mailing Address: PO Box 2032, Thibodaux, LA 70310. **Website:** www.geauxcolonels.com.
Head Coach: Mike Silva. **Baseball SID:** Jamie Bustos.
Telephone: (985) 448-4281.
Assistant Coaches: Ladd Rhodes, Cody Livingston.
Home Field: Ben Meyer Diamond at Ray E. Didier Field. **Seating Capacity:** 3,200. **Outfield Dimension: LF**—331, **CF**—400, **RF**—331.

NORFOLK STATE

Conference: Mid-Eastern.
Mailing Address: 700 Park Avenue, Norfolk, VA 23504. **Website:** www.nsuspartans.com.
Head Coach: Keith Shumate. **Telephone:** (757) 823-8196. **Baseball SID:** Matt Michalec. **Telephone:** (757) 823-2628.
Assistant Coaches: Matt Rein, Matt Blevins.

Telephone: (757) 823-8196.
Home Field: Marty L. Miller Field. **Seating Capacity:** 1,500. **Outfield Dimension: LF**—330, **CF**—402, **RF**—318.

NORTH CAROLINA

Conference: Atlantic Coast.
Mailing Address: PO Box 2126 Chapel Hill, NC 27515. **Website:** www.goheels.com.
Head Coach: Scott Forbes. **Telephone:** (919) 962-2351. **Baseball SID:** Jody Jones.
Assistant Coaches: Bryant Gaines, Jesse Wierzbicki.
Telephone: (919) 962-2351.
Home Field: Boshamer Stadium. **Seating Capacity:** 4,100. **Outfield Dimension: LF**—335, **CF**—400, **RF**—340.

NORTH CAROLINA A&T

Conference: Big South.
Mailing Address: 1601 E. Market Street, Greensboro, N.C. 27411. **Website:** www.ncataggies.com.
Head Coach: Ben Hall. **Telephone:** (336) 285-4272.
Baseball SID: Brian Holloway. **Telephone:** (336) 285-3608.
Assistant Coaches: Jamie Serber, Elliott McCummings. **Telephone:** (336) 285-2434.
Home Field: World War Memorial Stadium. **Seating Capacity:** 7,500. **Outfield Dimension: LF**—327, **CF**—401, **RF**—327.

NORTH CAROLINA STATE

Conference: Atlantic Coast.
Mailing Address: 1081 Varsity Drive Raleigh, NC 27607. **Website:** www.gopack.com.
Head Coach: Elliott Avent. **Telephone:** (919) 515-3613. **Baseball SID:** Lizzie Hattrich.
Assistant Coaches: Chris Hart, Clint Chrysler.
Telephone: (919) 513-0093.
Home Field: Doak Field at Dail Park. **Seating Capacity:** 3,100. **Outfield Dimension: LF**—325, **CF**—400, **RF**—330.

NORTH DAKOTA STATE

Conference: Summit League.
Mailing Address: Dept 1200 PO BOX 6050 Fargo, ND 58108. **Website:** www.gobison.com.
Head Coach: Tyler Oakes. **Baseball SID:** Myles Johnson.
Assistant Coaches: Brandon Hunt, Tanner Neale.
Home Field: Newman Outdoor Field. **Seating Capacity:** 5,000. **Outfield Dimension: LF**—318, **CF**—408, **RF**—314.

NORTH FLORIDA

Conference: ASUN.
Mailing Address: 1 UNF Dr, Jacksonville, FL 32224. **Website:** www.unfospreys.com.
Head Coach: Tim Parenton. **Telephone:** (904) 620-1556. **Baseball SID:** Brock Borgeson. **Telephone:** (904) 620-2586.
Assistant Coaches: Tommy Boss, Andrew Hannon.
Telephone: (904) 620-2586.
Home Field: Harmon Stadium. **Seating Capacity:** 1,000. **Outfield Dimension: LF**—335, **CF**—400, **RF**—335.

NORTHEASTERN

Conference: Colonial.
Mailing Address: 360 Huntington Avenue, Boston MA 02115. **Website:** www.nuhuskies.com.

Head Coach: Mike Glavine. Telephone: (617) 373-3657. Baseball SID: Brandon Poli.

Assistant Coaches: Kevin Cobb, Nick Puccio. Telephone: (617) 373-5256.

Home Field: Friedman Diamond. Seating Capacity: 2,000. Outfield Dimension: LF—326, CF—400, RF—342.

NORTHERN COLORADO

Conference: Summit League.

Mailing Address: 270D Butler-Hancock Athletic Center. Website: www.uncbears.com.

Head Coach: Carl Iwasaki. Telephone: (970) 351-1714. Baseball SID: Thomas Hoffman. Telephone: (970) 351-1056.

Assistant Coaches: Pat Jolley, Dan Martony. Telephone: (970) 351-1203.

Home Field: Jackson Field. Seating Capacity: 1,500. Outfield Dimension: LF—349, CF—416, RF—356.

NORTHERN ILLINOIS

Conference: Mid-American.

Mailing Address: Intercollegiate Athletics, Convocation Center (CV), DeKalb, IL 60115. Website: www.niuhuskies.com.

Head Coach: Mike Kunigonis. Telephone: (815) 753-0147. Baseball SID: Mike Haase. Telephone: (815) 753-9538.

Assistant Coaches: Luke Stewart, Josh Pethoud. Telephone: (815) 753-0147.

Home Field: Ralph McKinzie Field. Seating Capacity: 1,500. Outfield Dimension: LF—312, CF—395, RF—322.

NORTHERN KENTUCKY

Conference: Horizon League.

Mailing Address: 500 Nunn Drive Highland Heights, KY 41099. Website: www.nkunorse.com.

Head Coach: Dizzy Peyton. Telephone: (859) 572-5940. Baseball SID: Devon Lucal. Telephone: (859) 572-7659.

Assistant Coaches: Connor Walsh, Steve Dintaman. Home Field: Bill Aker Baseball Complex. Seating Capacity: 500. Outfield Dimension: LF—320, CF—365, RF—320.

NORTHWESTERN

Conference: Big Ten.

Mailing Address: 1501 Central Street, Evanston, IL 60208. Website: www.nusports.com.

Head Coach: Josh Reynolds. Baseball SID: Amit Malik.

Assistant Coaches: Dusty Napoleon, Brad Hill.

Home Field: Rocky & Berenice Miller Park. Seating Capacity: 1,500. Outfield Dimension: LF—326, CF—401, RF—310.

NORTHWESTERN STATE

Conference: Southland.

Mailing Address: 468 Caspari Drive, Natchitoches, LA 71497. Website: www.nsudemons.com.

Head Coach: Bobby Barbier. Telephone: (318) 357-4139. Baseball SID: Jason Pugh. Telephone: (318) 357-6468.

Assistant Coaches: Spencer Goodwin, Chris Bertrand. Telephone: (318) 357-4134.

Home Field: Brown-Stroud Field. Seating Capacity: 1,200. Outfield Dimension: LF—320, CF—400, RF—325.

NOTRE DAME

Conference: Atlantic Coast.

Mailing Address: University of Notre Dame Notre Dame, IN 46556. Website: www.und.com.

Head Coach: Link Jarrett. Baseball SID: Matt Paras.

Assistant Coaches: Rich Wallace, Chuck Ristano.

Home Field: Frank Eck Stadium. Seating Capacity: 2,500. Outfield Dimension: LF—330, CF—405, RF—330.

OAKLAND

Conference: Horizon League.

Mailing Address: 318 Meadow Brook Road, Rochester, MI 48309. Website: www.goldengrizzlies.com.

Head Coach: Jordon Banfield. Baseball SID: John Ciszewski.

Assistant Coaches: Brian Nelson, Ian Sanderson. Telephone: (512) 468-7540.

Home Field: Oakland Baseball Field. Seating Capacity: 500. Outfield Dimension: LF—333, CF—380, RF—320.

OHIO

Conference: Mid-American.

Mailing Address: 95 Richland Ave, Athens, OH 45701. Website: www.ohiobobcats.com.

Head Coach: Craig Moore. Baseball SID: Sarah Newgarde.

Assistant Coaches: Kirby McGuire, Tim Brown.

Home Field: Bob Wren Field. Seating Capacity: 4,000. Outfield Dimension: LF—340, CF—405, RF—340.

OHIO STATE

Conference: Big Ten.

Mailing Address: 2400 Olentangy River Road, Columbus, OH 43210. Website: www.ohiostatebuckeyes.com.

Head Coach: Greg Beals. Telephone: (614) 292-1075. Baseball SID: Gary Petit. Telephone: (614) 292-3270

Assistant Coaches: Dan DeLucia, Matt Angle.

Home Field: Bill Davis Stadium. Seating Capacity: 4,450. Outfield Dimension: LF—330, CF—400, RF—330.

OKLAHOMA

Conference: Big 12.

Mailing Address: 401 Imhoff Rd, Norman, OK 73072. Website: www.soonersports.com.

Head Coach: Skip Johnson. Telephone: (405) 325-8354. Baseball SID: Eric Hollier.

Assistant Coaches: Clay Overcash, Clay Van Hook.

Home Field: L. Dale Mitchell Park. Seating Capacity: 3,180. Outfield Dimension: LF—335, CF—411, RF—335.

OKLAHOMA STATE

Conference: Big 12.

Mailing Address: O'Brate Stadium, OSU Baseball, 103 N. Bellis St., Stillwater, OK 74078. Website: www.okstate.com.

Head Coach: Josh Holliday. Baseball SID: Wade McWhorter. Telephone: (405) 744-7853.

Assistant Coaches: Rob Walton, Justin Seely.

Home Field: O'Brate Stadium. Seating Capacity: 8,000. Outfield Dimension: LF—330, CF—402, RF—320.

OLD DOMINION

Conference: Conference USA.

Mailing Address: 4500 Parker Ave, Norfolk VA 23508.

Website: www.odusports.com.
Head Coach: Chris Finwood. **Telephone:** (757) 683-4230. **Baseball SID:** Matt Wurzburger. **Telephone:** (757) 683-3395.
Assistant Coaches: Logan Robbins, Mike Marron. **Telephone:** (757) 683-4230.
Home Field: Bud Metheny Baseball Complex.
Seating Capacity: 2,500. **Outfield Dimension: LF**—325, **CF**—395, **RF**—325.

ORAL ROBERTS

Conference: Summit League.
Mailing Address: 7777 S. Lewis Ave. Tulsa, OK 74171. **Website:** www.oruathletics.com.
Head Coach: Ryan Folmar. **Telephone:** (918) 495-7639. **Baseball SID:** Jon Opiela. **Telephone:** (915) 495-6616.
Assistant Coaches: Ryan Neill, Wes Davis. **Telephone:** (918) 495-7132.
Home Field: J.L Johnson Stadium. **Seating Capacity:** 2,418. **Outfield Dimension: LF**—330, **CF**—400, **RF**—330.

OREGON

Conference: Pac-12.
Mailing Address: 2727 Leo Harris Pkwy, Eugene OR 97401. **Website:** www.goducks.com.
Head Coach: Mark Wasikowski. **Telephone:** (541) 346-5235. **Baseball SID:** Todd Miles. **Telephone:** (541) 346-0962.
Assistant Coaches: Jake Angier, Jack Marder.
Home Field: PK Park. **Seating Capacity:** 4,000.
Outfield Dimension: LF—335, **CF**—390, **RF**—325.

OREGON STATE

Conference: Pac-12.
Mailing Address: 104 Gill Coliseum, Corvallis, OR 97333. **Website:** www.osubeavers.com.
Head Coach: Mitch Canham. **Baseball SID:** Hank Hager.
Assistant Coaches: Ryan Gipson, Rich Dorman.
Home Field: Goss Stadium. **Seating Capacity:** 4,000.
Outfield Dimension: LF—330, **CF**—400, **RF**—330.

PACIFIC

Conference: West Coast.
Mailing Address: 3601 Pacific Ave, Stockton, CA 95211. **Website:** www.pacifictigers.com.
Head Coach: Chris Rodriguez. **Telephone:** (209) 946-2163. **Baseball SID:** Zachary Karbach. **Telephone:** (209) 946-2479.
Assistant Coaches: Dan Jaffe, Ben Buechner.
Home Field: Klein Family Field. **Seating Capacity:** 2,500. **Outfield Dimension: LF**—317, **CF**—405, **RF**—325.

PENN STATE

Conference: Big Ten.
Mailing Address: Bryce Jordan Center, University Park, PA 16802. **Website:** www.gopsusports.com.
Head Coach: Rob Cooper. **Baseball SID:** Paul Marboe. **Telephone:** (814) 777-7604.
Assistant Coaches: Dallas Burke, Josh Newman. **Telephone:** (814) 865-8605.
Home Field: Medlar Field at Lubrano Park. **Seating Capacity:** 5,406. **Outfield Dimension: LF**—325, **CF**—410, **RF**—320.

PENNSYLVANIA

Conference: Ivy League.
Mailing Address: Weightman Hall, 235 S. 33rd Street, Philadelphia, PA 19104. **Website:** www.pennathletics.com.
Head Coach: John Yurkow. **Telephone:** (215) 898-6282. **Baseball SID:** Adam Reiter. **Telephone:** (215) 898-6128.
Assistant Coaches: Mike Santello, Josh Schwartz. **Telephone:** (215) 746-2325.
Home Field: Meiklejohn Stadium. **Seating Capacity:** 856. **Outfield Dimension: LF**—330, **CF**—380, **RF**—330.

PEPPERDINE

Conference: West Coast.
Mailing Address: 24255 Pacific Coast Highway Malibu, CA 90263. **Website:** www.pepperdinewaves.com.
Head Coach: Rick Hirtensteiner. **Telephone:** (310) 506-4404. **Baseball SID:** Kaitlyn Amaral. **Telephone:** (310) 406-4333.
Assistant Coaches: Danny Worth, Cameron Rowland. **Telephone:** (310) 506-4199.
Home Field: Eddy D. Field Stadium. **Seating Capacity:** 1,800. **Outfield Dimension: LF**—330, **CF**—400, **RF**—330.

PITTSBURGH

Conference: Atlantic Coast.
Mailing Address: 4200 Fifth Ave., Pittsburgh, PA 15260. **Website:** www.pittsburghpanthers.com.
Head Coach: Mike Bell. **Baseball SID:** Korey Blucas. **Telephone:** (412) 648-8240.
Assistant Coaches: Ty Megahee, Joe Mercadante.
Home Field: Charles L. Cost Field. **Seating Capacity:** 900. **Outfield Dimension: LF**—325, **CF**—405, **RF**—330.

PORTLAND

Conference: West Coast.
Mailing Address: 5000 N. Willamette Blvd., Portland, OR 97203-5798. **Website:** www.portlandpilots.com.
Head Coach: Geoff Loomis. **Telephone:** (503) 943-7707. **Baseball SID:** Kyle Garcia.
Assistant Coaches: Jake Valentine, Connor Lambert. **Telephone:** (503) 943-7732.
Home Field: Joe Etzel Field. **Seating Capacity:** 1,300.
Outfield Dimension: LF—325, **CF**—388, **RF**—325.

PRAIRIE VIEW A&M

Conference: Southwestern.
Mailing Address: P.O.Box 519, MS 1500, Prairie View, TX 77446. **Website:** www.pvpanthers.com.
Head Coach: Auntwan Riggins. **Telephone:** (936) 261-3955. **Baseball SID:** La Tonia Thirston.
Assistant Coaches: Brian White, Anthony Macon. **Telephone:** (936) 261-3955.
Home Field: Tankersley Field. **Seating Capacity:** 800.
Outfield Dimension: LF—327, **CF**—400, **RF**—327.

PRESBYTERIAN

Conference: Big South.
Mailing Address: 105 Ashland Ave. Clinton, S.C. 29325. **Website:** www.gobluehose.com.
Head Coach: Elton Pollock. **Telephone:** (864) 833-8236. **Baseball SID:** Greg Hartlage. **Telephone:** (864) 833-7095.
Assistant Coaches: John O'Neil, Blake Miller.

Telephone: (864) 833-7093.
Home Field: Elton Pollock Field at PC Baseball Complex. **Seating Capacity:** 500. **Outfield Dimension:** LF—325, CF—400, RF—325.

PRINCETON

Conference: Ivy League.
Mailing Address: Bill Clarke Field, Princeton University, Princeton, N.J. 08544. **Website:** www.goprincetontigers.com.
Head Coach: Scott Bradley. **Baseball SID:** Warren Croxton.
Assistant Coaches: Mike Russo, Alex Jurczynski.
Home Field: Bill Clarke Field. **Seating Capacity:** 850.
Outfield Dimension: LF—325, CF—400, RF—315.

PURDUE

Conference: Big Ten.
Mailing Address: Mollenkopf Athletic Center, 1225 Northwestern Ave., West Lafayette, IN 47907. **Website:** www.purduesports.com.
Head Coach: Greg Goff. **Telephone:** (765) 494-7639.
Baseball SID: Ben Turner. **Telephone:** (765) 494-3198.
Assistant Coaches: Terry Rooney, Chris Marx.
Telephone: (765) 494-3960.
Home Field: Alexander Field. **Seating Capacity:** 2,000. **Outfield Dimension:** LF—340, CF—408, RF—330.

PURDUE-FORT WAYNE

Conference: Horizon League.
Mailing Address: 2101 E. Coliseum Blvd., Fort Wayne, IN 46805-1499. **Website:** www.gomastodons.com.
Head Coach: Doug Schreiber. **Baseball SID:** Derrick Sloboda. **Telephone:** (260) 481-0729.
Assistant Coaches: Brent McNeil, Ken Jones.
Telephone: (260) 481-5455.
Home Field: Mastodon Field. **Seating Capacity:** 200.
Outfield Dimension: LF—330, CF—400, RF—330.

QUINNIPIAC

Conference: Metro Atlantic.
Mailing Address: 275 Mt Carmel Ave. Hamden CT 06518. **Website:** www.gobobcats.com.
Head Coach: John Delaney. **Baseball SID:** Nick Sczerbinski. **Telephone:** (203) 582-7655.
Assistant Coaches: Pat Egan, Corey Keane.
Telephone: (203) 582-6571.
Home Field: Bobcats Field. **Outfield Dimension:** LF—315, CF—405, RF—310.

RADFORD

Conference: Big South.
Mailing Address: 801 E Main St, Radford, VA 24142.
Website: www.radfordathletics.com.
Head Coach: Karl Kuhn. **Baseball SID:** Shelton Moss.
Telephone: (540) 831-5726.
Assistant Coaches: Damian Stambersky, Shelton Moss. **Telephone:** (540) 831-6513.
Home Field: Sherman Carter Memorial Stadium.
Seating Capacity: 800. **Outfield Dimension:** LF—330, CF—400, RF—330.

RHODE ISLAND

Conference: Atlantic 10.
Mailing Address: 3 Keaney Rd Suite 1, Kingston, R.I. 02881. **Website:** www.gorhody.com.
Head Coach: Raphael Cerrato. **Baseball SID:** Jodi

Pontibrand.
Assistant Coaches: Sean O'Brien, David Fischer.
Home Field: Bill Beck Field. **Outfield Dimension:** LF—330, CF—400, RF—330.

RICE

Conference: Conference USA.
Mailing Address: Department of Athletics, MS 548, 6100 Main Street, Houston, TX 77005. **Website:** www.riceowls.com.
Head Coach: Jose Cruz, Jr.. **Baseball SID:** Chuck Pool.
Telephone: (713) 348-5775.
Assistant Coaches: Paul Janish, Colter Bostick.
Telephone: (713) 348-8859.
Home Field: Reckling Park. **Seating Capacity:** 7,000.
Outfield Dimension: LF—330, CF—400, RF—330.

RICHMOND

Conference: Atlantic 10.
Mailing Address: University of Richmond Robins Center 365 College Road Richmond, VA 23173. **Website:** www.richmondspiders.com.
Head Coach: Tracy Woodson. **Telephone:** (804) 289-8391. **Baseball SID:** Bridgette Robles. **Telephone:** (804) 287-6455.
Assistant Coaches: Nate Mulberg, Josh Epstein.
Telephone: (804) 289-8391.
Home Field: Pitt Field. **Seating Capacity:** 600.
Outfield Dimension: LF—328, CF—380, RF—328.

RIDER

Conference: Metro Atlantic.
Mailing Address: 2083 Lawrenceville Rd. Lawrenceville NJ, 08536. **Website:** www.gobroncs.com.
Head Coach: Dr. Barry Davis. **Telephone:** (609) 896-5055. **Baseball SID:** Norm Yacko. **Telephone:** (609) 896-5135.
Assistant Coaches: Lee Lipinski, Mike Petrowski.
Home Field: Sonny Pittaro Field. **Seating Capacity:** 2,500. **Outfield Dimension:** LF—330, CF—410, RF—330.

RUTGERS

Conference: Big Ten.
Mailing Address: 83 Rockafeller Road, Piscataway, NJ 08854. **Website:** www.scarletknights.com.
Head Coach: Steve Owens. **Telephone:** (732) 445-7834. **Baseball SID:** Jimmy Gill. **Telephone:** (732) 445-8103.
Assistant Coaches: Brendan Monaghan, Kyle Pettoruto. **Telephone:** (732) 445-7746.
Home Field: Bainton Field. **Seating Capacity:** 1,500.
Outfield Dimension: LF—329, CF—392, RF—324.

SACRAMENTO STATE

Conference: Western Athletic.
Mailing Address: 6000 J St., Sacramento, CA 95819.
Website: www.hornetsports.com.
Head Coach: Reggie Christiansen. **Telephone:** (916) 278-4036. **Baseball SID:** Robert Barsanti. **Telephone:** (916) 278-6896.
Assistant Coaches: Tyler LaTorre, David Flores.
Telephone: (916) 278-2017.
Home Field: John Smith Field. **Seating Capacity:** 1,200. **Outfield Dimension:** LF—333, CF—400, RF—333.

SACRED HEART

Conference: Northeast.
Mailing Address: William H. Pitt Center, 5151 Park Avenue, Fairfield, CT 06825. **Website:** www.sacredheart-pioneers.com.
Head Coach: Nick Restaino. **Telephone:** (203) 365-7632. **Baseball SID:** Shaina Blakesley. **Telephone:** (203) 396-8127.
Assistant Coaches: Wayne Mazzoni, PJ DeFilippo. **Telephone:** (203) 260-4932.
Home Field: Veteran's Park. **Seating Capacity:** 500.

ST. BONAVENTURE

Conference: Atlantic 10.
Mailing Address: PO Box G, Reilly Center, St. Bonaventure, N.Y. 14778. **Website:** www.gobonnies.com.
Head Coach: B.J. Salerno. **Telephone:** (716) 375-2641. **Baseball SID:** Scott Eddy. **Telephone:** (716) 375-4019.
Assistant Coaches: Donovan Moffat. **Telephone:** (716) 375-2699.
Home Field: Handler Park at McGraw-Jennings Field. **Outfield Dimension: LF**—330, **CF**—403, **RF**—330.

ST. JOHN'S

Conference: Big East.
Mailing Address: 8000 Utopia Pkwy., Jamaica, NY 11439. **Website:** www.redstormsports.com.
Head Coach: Mike Hampton. **Telephone:** (718) 990-6148. **Baseball SID:** Andrew O'Connell. **Telephone:** (718) 990-1522.
Assistant Coaches: Danny Bethea, George Brown.
Home Field: Jack Kaiser Stadium. **Seating Capacity:** 3,500. **Outfield Dimension: LF**—325, **CF**—390, **RF**—325.

ST. JOSEPH'S

Conference: Atlantic 10.
Mailing Address: 5600 City Avenue, Philadelphia, PA 19131. **Website:** www.sjuhawks.com.
Head Coach: Fritz Hamburg. **Telephone:** (610) 660-1718. **Baseball SID:** Joe Greenwich. **Telephone:** (610) 660-1738.
Assistant Coaches: Ryan Wheeler, Pat Brown. **Telephone:** (610) 660-2592.
Home Field: John W. Smithson Field. **Seating Capacity:** 400. **Outfield Dimension: LF**—327, **CF**—400, **RF**—330.

ST. PETER'S

Conference: Metro Atlantic.
Mailing Address: 2641 John F. Kennedy Blvd., Jersey City, N.J. 07306. **Website:** www.saintpeterspeacocks.com.
Head Coach: Lou Proietti. **Telephone:** (201) 761-7319. **Baseball SID:** Trevor Clifton. **Telephone:** (201) 761-7322.
Assistant Coaches: Jacob Tobin.
Home Field: Joseph J. Jaroschak Field. **Seating Capacity:** 500.

SAINT LOUIS

Conference: Atlantic 10.
Mailing Address: 3330 Laclede Avenue, St. Louis, MO 63102. **Website:** www.slubillikens.com.
Head Coach: Darin Hendrickson. **Telephone:** (314) 977-3172. **Baseball SID:** Nick Rettig. **Telephone:** (314) 977-2524.
Assistant Coaches: Logan Moon, Josh Turnock. **Telephone:** (314) 977-3260.

Home Field: Billiken Sports Center. **Seating Capacity:** 500. **Outfield Dimension: LF**—330, **CF**—403, **RF**—330.

SAINT MARY'S

Conference: West Coast.
Mailing Address: 1928 St. Mary's Road, Moraga, CA 94575. **Website:** www.smcgaels.com.
Head Coach: Greg Moore. **Baseball SID:** Tim Fitzgerald. **Telephone:** (925) 631-4383.
Assistant Coaches: Jordon Twohig, Max Shupe.
Home Field: Louis Guisto Field. **Seating Capacity:** 1,100. **Outfield Dimension: LF**—330, **CF**—400, **RF**—330.

ST. THOMAS

Conference: Summit League.
Mailing Address: 2115 Summit Ave, St. Paul, MN, 55105. **Website:** www.tommiesports.com.
Head Coach: Chris Olean. **Telephone:** (651) 962-5924. **Baseball SID:** Gene McGivern.
Assistant Coaches: Tanner Vavra, Neal Kunik.
Home Field: Koch Diamond. **Seating Capacity:** 400. **Outfield Dimension: LF**—315, **CF**—455, **RF**—330.

SAM HOUSTON STATE

Conference: Western Athletic.
Mailing Address: 600 Bowers Blvd; Huntsville, TX 77340. **Website:** www.gobearkats.com.
Head Coach: Jay Sirianni. **Telephone:** (936) 294-2580. **Baseball SID:** Ben Rikard. **Telephone:** (936) 294-1764.
Assistant Coaches: Fuller Smith, Shane Wedd. **Telephone:** (936) 294-4435.
Home Field: Don Sanders Stadium. **Seating Capacity:** 1,163. **Outfield Dimension: LF**—330, **CF**—400, **RF**—330.

SAMFORD

Conference: Southern.
Mailing Address: 800 Lakeshore Drive, Birmingham, AL 35229. **Website:** www.samfordsports.com.
Head Coach: Tony David. **Telephone:** (205) 726-4294. **Baseball SID:** Joey Mullins. **Telephone:** (205) 726-2799.
Assistant Coaches: Tyler Shrout, Brad Moss. **Telephone:** (205) 726-4095.
Home Field: Joe Lee Griffin Field. **Seating Capacity:** 1,000. **Outfield Dimension: LF**—330, **CF**—399, **RF**—335.

SAN DIEGO

Conference: West Coast.
Mailing Address: 5998 Alcala Park, San Diego, CA 92110. **Website:** www.usdtoreros.com.
Head Coach: Brock Ungricht. **Baseball SID:** Anderson Haigler. **Telephone:** (619) 260-8845.
Assistant Coaches: Matt Florer, Erich Pfohl.
Home Field: Fowler Park. **Seating Capacity:** 2,000. **Outfield Dimension: LF**—312, **CF**—395, **RF**—327.

SAN DIEGO STATE

Conference: Mountain West.
Mailing Address: 5500 Campanile Dr. San Diego, CA 92182. **Website:** www.goaztecs.com.
Head Coach: Mark Martinez. **Telephone:** (619) 594-1818. **Baseball SID:** Jim Solien. **Telephone:** (619) 594-2576. **Assistant Coaches:** Sergio Brown, Shaun Cole. **Telephone:** (619) 594-6889.
Home Field: Tony Gwynn Stadium. **Seating Capacity:** 3,000. **Outfield Dimension: LF**—340, **CF**—410, **RF**—340.

SAN FRANCISCO

Conference: West Coast.
Mailing Address: 2130 Fulton St. San Francisco, CA 94117. **Website:** www.usfdons.com.
Head Coach: Nino Giarratano. **Telephone:** (415) 422-2934. **Baseball SID:** Alec Hendon.
Assistant Coaches: Mat Keplinger, Allen Smoot.
Home Field: Benedetti Diamond. **Seating Capacity:** 1,500. **Outfield Dimension:** LF—330, **CF**—425, **RF**—300.

SAN JOSE STATE

Conference: Mountain West.
Mailing Address: 1 Washington Sq, San Jose, CA 95192. **Website:** www.sjsuspartans.com.
Head Coach: Brad Sanfilippo. **Baseball SID:** Sky Kerstein.
Assistant Coaches: Thomas Walker, Seth Moir.
Home Field: Excite Ballpark. **Seating Capacity:** 4,200. **Outfield Dimension:** LF—320, **CF**—390, **RF**—320.

SANTA CLARA

Conference: West Coast.
Mailing Address: 500 El Camino Real Santa Clara, CA 95053. **Website:** www.santaclarabroncos.com.
Head Coach: Rusty Filter. **Telephone:** (408) 554-4882. **Baseball SID:** Dean Obara. **Telephone:** (408) 554-4690.
Assistant Coaches: Jon Karcich, Jay Brossman. **Telephone:** (408) 554-4680.
Home Field: Stephen Schott Stadium. **Seating Capacity:** 1,500. **Outfield Dimension:** LF—340, **CF**—402, **RF**—335.

SEATTLE

Conference: Western Athletic.
Mailing Address: 901 12th Avenue, PO Box 222000, Seattle, WA 98122. **Website:** www.goseattleu.com.
Head Coach: Donny Harrel. **Telephone:** (206) 398-4399. **Baseball SID:** Russell Brown.
Assistant Coaches: Millard Dawson, Carter Capps.
Home Field: Bannerwood Park. **Seating Capacity:** 300.

SETON HALL

Conference: Big East.
Mailing Address: 400 South Orange Ave, South Orange, NJ 07079. **Website:** www.shupirates.com.
Head Coach: Robert Sheppard. **Telephone:** (973) 761-9557. **Baseball SID:** Peter Long. **Telephone:** (973) 761-9493.
Assistant Coaches: Mark Pappas, Pat Pinkman. **Telephone:** (732) 757-9534.
Home Field: Mike Sheppard Stadium. **Seating Capacity:** 1,000. **Outfield Dimension:** LF—315, **CF**—380, **RF**—330.

SIENA

Conference: Metro Atlantic.
Mailing Address: 515 Loudon Rd., Loudonville, NY 12211. **Website:** www.sienasaints.com.
Head Coach: Tony Rossi. **Telephone:** (518) 786-5044. **Baseball SID:** Mike Demos. **Telephone:** (518) 783-2377.
Assistant Coaches: Joe Sheridan
Home Field: Connors Park. **Seating Capacity:** 1,000. **Outfield Dimension:** LF—300, **CF**—400, **RF**—325.

SOUTH ALABAMA

Conference: Sun Belt.
Mailing Address: 300 Joseph E. Gottfried Drive, Mobile, AL 36688. **Website:** www.usajaguars.com.
Head Coach: Mark Calvi. **Telephone:** (251) 414-8243. **Baseball SID:** Charlie Nichols. **Telephone:** (251) 414-8017.
Assistant Coaches: Alan Luckie, Nick Magnifico. **Telephone:** (251) 460-6876.
Home Field: Stanky Field. **Seating Capacity:** 3,775. **Outfield Dimension:** LF—330, **CF**—400, **RF**—330.

SOUTH CAROLINA

Conference: Southeast.
Mailing Address: 1304 Heyward St. Columbia, SC 29208. **Website:** www.gamecocksonline.com.
Head Coach: Mark Kingston. **Telephone:** (803) 777-7808. **Baseball SID:** Kent Reichert. **Telephone:** (803) 777-5257.
Assistant Coaches: Chad Caillet, Justin Parker. **Telephone:** (803) 777-7808.
Home Field: Founders Park. **Seating Capacity:** 8,242. **Outfield Dimension:** LF—325, **CF**—400, **RF**—325.

SOUTH CAROLINA-UPSTATE

Conference: Big South.
Mailing Address: 800 University Way, Spartanburg, SC 29303. **Website:** www.upstatespartans.com.
Head Coach: Mike McGuire. **Telephone:** (803) 629-5093. **Baseball SID:** Ryan Fry. **Telephone:** (864) 503-5129.
Assistant Coaches: Adam Brown, Kane Sweeney. **Telephone:** (864) 503-5176.
Home Field: Cleveland S. Harley Park. **Seating Capacity:** 800. **Outfield Dimension:** LF—335, **CF**—402, **RF**—335.

SOUTH DAKOTA STATE

Conference: Summit League.
Mailing Address: 2820 Marshall Center Brookings, SD. 57007. **Website:** www.gojacks.com.
Head Coach: Rob Bishop. **Telephone:** (605) 688-5625. **Baseball SID:** Jason Hove. **Telephone:** (605) 688-4623.
Assistant Coaches: Brian Grunzke, Kirk Clark. **Telephone:** (605) 688-5625.
Home Field: Erv Huether Field. **Seating Capacity:** 600. **Outfield Dimension:** LF—330, **CF**—390, **RF**—330.

SOUTH FLORIDA

Conference: American Athletic.
Mailing Address: 4202 E. Fowler Ave Tampa FL 33620. **Website:** www.gousfbulls.com.
Head Coach: Billy Mohl. **Telephone:** (813) 974-2504. **Baseball SID:** Dave Albrecht.
Assistant Coaches: Bo Durkac, Karsten Whitson.
Home Field: USF Baseball Stadium. **Seating Capacity:** 3,211. **Outfield Dimension:** LF—325, **CF**—400, **RF**—330.

SOUTHEAST MISSOURI STATE

Conference: Ohio Valley.
Mailing Address: 1 University Plaza, Cape Girardeau, MO 63701. **Website:** www.semoredhawks.com.
Head Coach: Andy Sawyers. **Baseball SID:** Jeff Honza. **Telephone:** (573) 651-2933.
Assistant Coaches: Dan McKinney, Trevor Ezell.
Home Field: Capaha Park. **Seating Capacity:** 2,000. **Outfield Dimension:** LF—330, **CF**—400, **RF**—300.

SOUTHEASTERN LOUISIANA

Conference: Southland.
Mailing Address: SLU 10309, Hammond, LA 70402.
Website: www.lionsports.net.
Head Coach: Matt Riser. **Telephone:** (985) 549-5130.
Baseball SID: Damon Sunde. **Telephone:** (985) 549-3774.
Assistant Coaches: Andrew Gipson, Gerry Salisbury.
Home Field: Pat Kenelly Diamond at Alumni Field.
Outfield Dimension: LF—330, **CF**—400, **RF**—330.

SOUTHERN

Conference: Southwestern.
Mailing Address: A.W. Mumford Fieldhouse, PO Box 9942, Baton Rouge, LA 70813. **Website:** www.gojag-sports.com.
Head Coach: Chris Crenshaw. **Telephone:** (225) 771-3882. **Baseball SID:** Rodney Kirschner. **Telephone:** (225) 771-5609.
Assistant Coaches: Daniel Dulin, TJ Perkins.
Home Field: Lee-Hines Field. **Seating Capacity:** 1,500.

SOUTHERN CALIFORNIA

Conference: Pac-12.
Mailing Address: 3501 Watt Way, Los Angeles, CA 90089. **Website:** www.usctrojans.com.
Head Coach: Jason Gill. **Telephone:** (213) 740-8446.
Baseball SID: Jacob Breems. **Telephone:** (213) 740-3809.
Assistant Coaches: Ted Silva, Matt Fonteno.
Telephone: (213) 740-8447.
Home Field: Dedeaux Field. **Seating Capacity:** 2,500.
Outfield Dimension: LF—335, **CF**—395, **RF**—335.

SOUTHERN ILLINOIS

Conference: Missouri Valley.
Mailing Address: 1490 Douglas Dr. Carbondale, IL 62901. **Website:** www.siusalukis.com.
Head Coach: Lance Rhodes. **Baseball SID:** John Lock.
Assistant Coaches: Brett Peel, Tim Jamieson.
Home Field: Itchy Jones Stadium. **Seating Capacity:** 3,500. **Outfield Dimension: LF**—329, **CF**—390, **RF**—329.

SOUTHERN ILLINOIS-EDWARDSVILLE

Conference: Ohio Valley.
Mailing Address: 1 Hairpin Dr, Edwardsville, IL 62026.
Website: www.siuecougars.com.
Head Coach: Sean Lyons. **Telephone:** (618) 650-2032.
Baseball SID: Joe Pott. **Telephone:** (618) 650-2860.
Assistant Coaches: Brandon Scott, Alex Maloney.
Telephone: (618) 650-2032.
Home Field: Roy E. Lee Field at Simmons Baseball Complex. **Seating Capacity:** 1,000. **Outfield Dimension: LF**—330, **CF**—390, **RF**—330.

SOUTHERN MISSISSIPPI

Conference: Conference USA.
Mailing Address: 18 College Dr. Hattiesburg, MS 39406. **Website:** www.southernmiss.com.
Head Coach: Scott Berry. **Baseball SID:** Jack Duggan.
Assistant Coaches: Travis Creel, Christian Ostrander.
Home Field: Pete Taylor Park. **Seating Capacity:** 3,266. **Outfield Dimension: LF**—340, **CF**—400, **RF**—340.

STANFORD

Conference: Pac-12.
Mailing Address: 641 Campus Drive, Stanford, CA 94305. **Website:** www.gostanford.com.

Head Coach: David Esquer. **Telephone:** (650) 723-4528. **Baseball SID:** Tyler Geivett.
Assistant Coaches: Thomas Eager, Steve Rodriguez.
Telephone: (650) 725-2373.
Home Field: Klein Field at Sunken Diamond. **Seating Capacity:** 4,000. **Outfield Dimension: LF**—335, **CF**—400, **RF**—335.

STEPHEN F. AUSTIN

Conference: Western Athletic.
Mailing Address: PO BOx 13010, SFA Station, Nacogdoches, TX 75962. **Website:** www.sfajacks.com.
Head Coach: Johnny Cardenas. **Baseball SID:** Chelsea Groves. **Telephone:** (936) 468-2606.
Assistant Coaches: Mike Haynes, Caleb Clowers.
Telephone: (936) 468-7796.
Home Field: Jaycees Field. **Seating Capacity:** 740.
Outfield Dimension: LF—320, **CF**—390, **RF**—320.

STETSON

Conference: ASUN.
Mailing Address: 421 N. Woodland Blvd., Unit 8359, DeLand, FL 32723. **Website:** www.gohatters.com.
Head Coach: Steve Trimper. **Telephone:** (386) 822-8106. **Baseball SID:** Ricky Hazel. **Telephone:** (386) 822-8130.
Assistant Coaches: Shane Gierke, Dave Therneau.
Telephone: (386) 822-8730.
Home Field: Melching Field at Conrad Park. **Seating Capacity:** 2,500. **Outfield Dimension: LF**—335, **CF**—403, **RF**—335.

STONY BROOK

Conference: America East.
Mailing Address: 100 Nicolls Road, Stony Brook, NY 11794. **Website:** www.stonybrookathletics.com.
Head Coach: Matt Senk. **Telephone:** (631) 632-9226.
Baseball SID: Cameron Boon. **Telephone:** (631) 632-7289. **Assistant Coaches:** Jim Martin, Alex Brosnan.
Telephone: (631) 632-9226.
Home Field: Joe Nathan Field. **Seating Capacity:** 1,500. **Outfield Dimension: LF**—330, **CF**—390, **RF**—330.

TARLETON STATE

Conference: Western Athletic.
Mailing Address: 1333 W Washington St. Stephenville, TX 76402. **Website:** www.tarletonsports.com.
Head Coach: Aaron Meade. **Telephone:** (254) 968-1666. **Baseball SID:** Nate Bural. **Telephone:** (254) 968-1802. **Assistant Coaches:** Dallas Reed, Jon Ubbenga.
Telephone: (254) 968-9563.
Home Field: Tarleton Baseball Complex. **Seating Capacity:** 750. **Outfield Dimension: LF**—320, **CF**—400, **RF**—320.

TENNESSEE

Conference: Southeastern.
Mailing Address: 1551 Lake Loudoun Blvd, Knoxville, TN 37996. **Website:** www.utsports.com.
Head Coach: Tony Vitello. **Telephone:** (865) 974-2057.
Baseball SID: Sean Barows. **Telephone:** (865) 974-7478.
Assistant Coaches: Frank Anderson, Josh Elander.
Telephone: (865) 974-2057.
Home Field: Lindsey Nelson Stadium. **Seating Capacity:** 4,283. **Outfield Dimension: LF**—320, **CF**—390, **RF**—320.

TENNESSEE-MARTIN

Conference: Ohio Valley.
Mailing Address: 554 University Street, Martin, TN, 38237. **Website:** www.utmsports.com.
Head Coach: Ryan Jenkins. **Telephone:** (731) 881-3691. **Baseball SID:** Brandon Burke. **Telephone:** (731) 881-7694.
Assistant Coaches: Bill White, Pat Cottrell.
Home Field: Skyhawk Baseball Field. **Seating Capacity:** 500. **Outfield Dimension: LF**—330, **CF**—385, **RF**—330.

TENNESSEE TECH

Conference: Ohio Valley.
Mailing Address: 1100 McGee Blvd. Cookeville TN 38501. **Website:** www.ttusports.com.
Head Coach: Matt Bragga. **Telephone:** (931) 372-3853. **Baseball SID:** Mike Lehman. **Telephone:** (931) 372-3088.
Assistant Coaches: Todd Miller, Blake Beck.
Telephone: (931) 372-3853.
Home Field: Quillen Field at Bush Stadium at the Averitt Express Baseball Complex. **Seating Capacity:** 1,100. **Outfield Dimension: LF**—329, **CF**—405, **RF**—330.

TEXAS

Conference: Big 12.
Mailing Address: PO Box 7399, Austin, TX 78713-7399. **Website:** www.texassports.com.
Head Coach: David Pierce. **Telephone:** (512) 471-5732. **Baseball SID:** Kevin Rodriguez. **Telephone:** (512) 471-2078.
Assistant Coaches: Sean Allen, Philip Miller.
Home Field: UFCU Disch-Falk Field. **Seating Capacity:** 6,649. **Outfield Dimension: LF**—340, **CF**—400, **RF**—325.

TEXAS A&M

Conference: Southeastern.
Mailing Address: Texas A&M Athletics, 1228 TAMU, College Station, TX 77843-1228. **Website:** www.12thman.com.
Head Coach: Jim Schlossnagle. **Baseball SID:** Thomas Dick.
Assistant Coaches: Nate Yeskie, Nolan Cain.
Home Field: Blue Bell Park. **Seating Capacity:** 6,100. **Outfield Dimension: LF**—330, **CF**—400, **RF**—330.

TEXAS A&M-CORPUS CHRISTI

Conference: Southland.
Mailing Address: 6300 Ocean Drive, Unit 5719, Corpus Christi, TX 78412. **Website:** www.goislanders.com.
Head Coach: Scott Malone. **Telephone:** (361) 825-3413. **Baseball SID:** Robbie Kleinmuntz. **Telephone:** (361) 825-3410.
Assistant Coaches: Marty Smith, Seth LaRue.
Telephone: (361) 825-3252.
Home Field: Chapman Field. **Seating Capacity:** 500. **Outfield Dimension: LF**—330, **CF**—404, **RF**—330.

TEXAS-ARLINGTON

Conference: Sun Belt.
Mailing Address: Gilstrap Athletic Center, 1309 W. Mitchell Street, Arlington, TX 76019-0079. **Website:** www.utamavs.com.
Head Coach: Darin Thomas. **Telephone:** (817) 272-9744. **Baseball SID:** Ian Applegate. **Telephone:** (817)

272-9610.
Assistant Coaches: Taylor Dugas, Brady Cox.
Telephone: (817) 272-7170.
Home Field: Clay Gould Ballpark. **Seating Capacity:** 1,600. **Outfield Dimension: LF**—330, **CF**—400, **RF**—330.

TEXAS-RIO GRANDE VALLEY

Conference: Western Athletic.
Mailing Address: 1201 W. University Dr. Edinburg, TX 78539. **Website:** www.goutrgv.com.
Head Coach: Derek Matlock. **Telephone:** (956) 665-2235. **Baseball SID:** Jonah Goldberg. **Telephone:** (956) 665-2240.
Assistant Coaches: Rob Martinez, Russell Raley.
Telephone: (956) 665-2891.
Home Field: UTRGV Baseball Stadium. **Seating Capacity:** 5,000. **Outfield Dimension: LF**—325, **CF**—410, **RF**—325.

TEXAS-SAN ANTONIO

Conference: Conference USA.
Mailing Address: One UTSA Circle, San Antonio, TX 78249-0691. **Website:** www.goutsa.com.
Head Coach: Patrick Hallmark. **Telephone:** (210) 458-8339. **Baseball SID:** Brady Meister. **Telephone:** (712) 870-3423.
Assistant Coaches: Ryan Aguayo, Zach Butler.
Telephone: (562) 665-8714.
Home Field: Roadrunner Field. **Seating Capacity:** 800.

TEXAS CHRISTIAN

Conference: Big 12.
Mailing Address: TCU Athletics Department, TCU Box 297600, Fort Worth, TX 76129. **Website:** www.gofrogs.com.
Head Coach: Kirk Saarloos. **Baseball SID:** Brandie Davidson. **Telephone:** (817) 257-7479.
Assistant Coaches: Bill Mosiello, John DiLaura.
Home Field: Charlie and Marie Lupton Baseball Stadium at Williams-Reilly Field. **Seating Capacity:** 4,500. **Outfield Dimension: LF**—330, **CF**—400, **RF**—330.

TEXAS SOUTHERN

Conference: Southwestern.
Mailing Address: Texas Southern Athletics, 3100 Cleburne Street, Houston, TX 77004. **Website:** www.tsusports.com.
Head Coach: Michael Robertson. **Telephone:** (713) 313-4315. **Baseball SID:** Ryan McGinty. **Telephone:** (713) 313-6829.
Assistant Coaches: Ricky Urbano.
Home Field: MacGregor Park.

TEXAS STATE

Conference: Sun Belt.
Mailing Address: Texas State University Department of Athletics Darren B. Casey Athletic Administration Complex 601 University Drive San Marcos Texas 78666. **Website:** www.txstatebobcats.com.
Head Coach: Steven Trout. **Telephone:** (512) 245-3383. **Baseball SID:** Phillip Pongratz. **Telephone:** (512) 245-4692.
Assistant Coaches: Josh Blakley, Chad Massengale.
Telephone: (512) 245-3383.
Home Field: Bobcat Ballpark. **Seating Capacity:** 2,500. **Outfield Dimension: LF**—330, **CF**—405, **RF**—330.

TEXAS TECH

Conference: Big 12.
Mailing Address: 2901 Drive of Champions Ste. 200 Lubbock, TX 79409. **Website:** www.texastech.com.
Head Coach: Tim Tadlock. **Telephone:** (806) 834-4646.
Baseball SID: Matt Burkholder.
Assistant Coaches: J-Bob Thomas, Matt Gardner.
Home Field: Dan Law Field at Rip Griffin Park.
Seating Capacity: 4,432. **Outfield Dimension:** LF—327, CF—402, RF—327.

TOLEDO

Conference: Mid-American.
Mailing Address: 2801 W. Bancroft Street - MS 408, Toledo, OH 43606. **Website:** www.utrockets.com.
Head Coach: Rob Reinstetle. **Baseball SID:** Chris Cullum. **Telephone:** (419) 530-6263. **Telephone:** (419) 530-4913.
Assistant Coaches: Nick McIntyre, John Sheehan. **Telephone:** (419) 530-3097.
Home Field: Scott Park. **Seating Capacity:** 1,000. **Outfield Dimension:** LF—330, CF—400, RF—330.

TOWSON

Conference: Colonial.
Mailing Address: John B. Schuerholz Park - 8000 York Road - Towson, MD 21204. **Website:** www.towsontigers.com.
Head Coach: Matt Tyner. **Telephone:** (410) 704-2646.
Baseball SID: David Vatz. **Telephone:** (410) 704-3102.
Assistant Coaches: Tanner Biagini, Blake Nation. **Telephone:** (410) 704-2646.
Home Field: John B. Schuerholz Park. **Seating Capacity:** 1,000. **Outfield Dimension:** LF—312, CF—424, RF—301.

TROY

Conference: Sun Belt.
Mailing Address: 5000 Veterans Memorial Drive Troy , AL 36082. **Website:** www.troytrojans.com.
Head Coach: Skylar Meade. **Baseball SID:** Brandon Mostyn.
Assistant Coaches: Ben Wolgamot, Adam Godwin. **Telephone:** (217) 260-2069.
Home Field: Riddle-Pace Field. **Seating Capacity:** 2,500. **Outfield Dimension:** LF—340, CF—400, RF—310.

TULANE

Conference: American Athletic.
Mailing Address: 333 Ben Weiner Drive, New Orleans, LA 70118. **Website:** www.tulanegreenwave.com.
Head Coach: Travis Jewett. **Telephone:** (504) 862-8216. **Baseball SID:** Tom Symonds. **Telephone:** (504) 862-8249.
Assistant Coaches: Daniel Latham, Jay Uhlman. **Telephone:** (504) 314-7203.
Home Field: Greer Field at Turchin Stadium. **Seating Capacity:** 5,000. **Outfield Dimension:** LF—325, CF—400, RF—325.

UC DAVIS

Conference: Big West.
Mailing Address: Hickey Gym 264, One Shields Ave., Davis, CA 95616. **Website:** www.ucdavisaggies.com.
Head Coach: Tommy Nicholson. **Baseball SID:** Matt Murphy. **Telephone:** (530) 752-8050.

Assistant Coaches: Andrew Ayers, Zack Thornton.
Home Field: Phil Swimley Field at Dobbins Stadium.
Seating Capacity: 3,500. **Outfield Dimension:** LF—310, CF—410, RF—310.

UC IRVINE

Conference: Big West.
Mailing Address: UC Irvine Athletics, Intercollegiate Athletics Building, Irvine, CA 92697-4500. **Website:** www.ucirvinesports.com.
Head Coach: Ben Orloff. **Baseball SID:** Alex Croteau.
Assistant Coaches: JT Bloodworth, Danny Bibona.
Home Field: Cicerone Field. **Seating Capacity:** 1,500. **Outfield Dimension:** LF—335, CF—408, RF—335.

UCLA

Conference: Pac-12.
Mailing Address: 405 Hilgaard Ave, Los Angeles, CA 90095. **Website:** www.uclabruins.com.
Head Coach: John Savage. **Baseball SID:** Andrew Wagner. **Telephone:** (310) 206-4008.
Assistant Coaches: Bryant Ward, Niko Gallego.
Home Field: Jackie Robinson Stadium. **Seating Capacity:** 1,820. **Outfield Dimension:** LF—330, CF—390, RF—330.

UC RIVERSIDE

Conference: Big West.
Mailing Address: 900 University Avenue, Riverside, CA 92521. **Website:** www.gohighlanders.com.
Head Coach: Justin Johnson. **Baseball SID:** Chelsea Pfohl.
Assistant Coaches: Curtis Smith, Mike Burns.
Home Field: Riverside Sports Complex. **Outfield Dimension:** LF—330, CF—400, RF—330.

UC SAN DIEGO

Conference: Big West.
Mailing Address: 9500 Gilman Drive, RIMAC 4th Floor, La Jolla, CA 92093-0531. **Website:** www.ucsdtritons.com.
Head Coach: Eric Newman. **Telephone:** (858) 534-8162. **Baseball SID:** Kendrick Mooney. **Telephone:** (858) 534-8451.
Assistant Coaches: Bryson LeBlanc, Matt Harvey. **Telephone:** (858) 246-1648.
Home Field: Triton Ballpark. **Seating Capacity:** 500. **Outfield Dimension:** LF—330, CF—400, RF—330.

UC SANTA BARBARA

Conference: Big West.
Mailing Address: ICA Building Santa Barbara, CA 93106-5200. **Website:** www.ucsbgauchos.com.
Head Coach: Andrew Checketts. **Telephone:** (805) 893-3690. **Baseball SID:** Daniel Moebus-Bowles. **Telephone:** (805) 893-8603.
Assistant Coaches: Dylan Jones, Donegal Fergus. **Telephone:** (805) 893-3690.
Home Field: Caesar Uyesaka Stadium. **Seating Capacity:** 1,000. **Outfield Dimension:** LF—335, CF—400, RF—335.

UNC ASHEVILLE

Conference: Big South.
Mailing Address: 1 University Heights, Asheville, NC 28804. **Website:** www.uncabulldogs.com.
Head Coach: Scott Friedholm. **Telephone:** (828) 251-6920. **Baseball SID:** Andy Fisher. **Telephone:** (828)

251-6931.
Assistant Coaches: Chris Bresnahan, Kyle Ward.
Telephone: (828) 250-2309.
Home Field: Greenwood Field. **Seating Capacity:** 1,000. **Outfield Dimension: LF**—320, **CF**—390, **RF**—330.

UNC GREENSBORO

Conference: Southern.
Mailing Address: 1400 Spring Garden St, Greensboro, NC 27412. **Website:** www.uncgspartans.com.
Head Coach: Billy Godwin. **Baseball SID:** Jesika Moore. **Assistant Coaches:** Greg Starbuck, Hunter Allen.
Home Field: UNCG Baseball Stadium. **Seating Capacity:** 3,500. **Outfield Dimension: LF**—340, **CF**—405, **RF**—340.

UNC WILMINGTON

Conference: Colonial.
Mailing Address: 610 S. College Road, Wilmington, NC 28403. **Website:** www.uncwsports.com.
Head Coach: Randy Hood. **Baseball SID:** Tom Riordan.
Assistant Coaches: Chris Moore, Kelly Secrest.
Home Field: Brooks Field. **Seating Capacity:** 3,500. **Outfield Dimension: LF**—340, **CF**—390, **RF**—340.

UTAH

Conference: Pac-12.
Mailing Address: 1825 E South Campus Drive, Salt Lake City UT, 84112. **Website:** www.utahutes.com.
Head Coach: Gary Henderson. **Baseball SID:** Ryan Gallant.
Assistant Coaches: Mike Brown, Todd Guilliams.
Home Field: Smith's Ballpark. **Seating Capacity:** 14,511. **Outfield Dimension: LF**—345, **CF**—420, **RF**—315.

UTAH VALLEY

Conference: Western Athletic.
Mailing Address: 800 W University Pkwy, Orem, UT 84058. **Website:** www.gouvu.com.
Head Coach: Eddie Smith. **Baseball SID:** James Warnick. **Telephone:** (801) 863-6231.
Assistant Coaches: Nate Rasmussen, Grant Kukuk.
Home Field: UCCU Ballpark. **Seating Capacity:** 5,000. **Outfield Dimension: LF**—306, **CF**—426, **RF**—309.

VALPARAISO

Conference: Missouri Valley.
Mailing Address: 1700 Chapel Dr, Valparaiso, IN 46383. **Website:** www.valpoathletics.com.
Head Coach: Brian Schmack. **Baseball SID:** Brandon Vickrey.
Assistant Coaches: Kory Winter, Mitch Boe.
Home Field: Emory G. Bauer Field. **Seating Capacity:** 700. **Outfield Dimension: LF**—330, **CF**—400, **RF**—330.

VANDERBILT

Conference: Southeastern.
Mailing Address: 2601 Jess Neely Drive, Nashville,TN 37212. **Website:** www.vucommodores.com.
Head Coach: Tim Corbin. **Telephone:** (615) 322-3716.
Baseball SID: Josh Foster. **Telephone:** (615) 322-3716.
Assistant Coaches: Scott Brown, Mike Baxter.
Telephone: (615) 322-3716.
Home Field: Hawkins Field. **Seating Capacity:** 3,700. **Outfield Dimension: LF**—310, **CF**—400, **RF**—330.

VILLANOVA

Conference: Big East.
Mailing Address: 800 Lancaster Avenue, Villanova, PA 19085. **Website:** www.villanova.com.
Head Coach: Kevin Mulvey. **Baseball SID:** Drew McDonald.
Assistant Coaches: Eddie Brown, Jabin Weaver.
Home Field: Villanova Ballpark at Plymouth. **Seating Capacity:** 750. **Outfield Dimension: LF**—320, **CF**—400, **RF**—320.

VIRGINIA

Conference: Atlantic Coast.
Mailing Address: Disharoon Park - PO Box 400839 - Charlottesville, Va., 22904-4839. **Website:** www.virginiasports.com.
Head Coach: Brian O'Connor. **Telephone:** (434) 243-5114. **Baseball SID:** Scott Fitzgerald.
Assistant Coaches: Kevin McMullan, Drew Dickinson. **Telephone:** (434) 243-5114.
Home Field: Disharoon Park. **Seating Capacity:** 5,359. **Outfield Dimension: LF**—332, **CF**—404, **RF**—332.

VIRGINIA COMMONWEALTH

Conference: Atlantic 10.
Mailing Address: 1300 W. Broad St. Box 842003 Richmond, Va. 23284. **Website:** www.vcuathletics.com.
Head Coach: Shawn Stiffler. **Baseball SID:** Andy Lohman.
Assistant Coaches: Rich Witten, Sean Cutler-Voltz.
Home Field: The Diamond. **Seating Capacity:** 9,560. **Outfield Dimension: LF**—330, **CF**—402, **RF**—330.

VIRGINIA MILITARY INSTITUTE

Conference: Southern.
Mailing Address: 401 N Main Street Lexington, VA 24450. **Website:** www.vmikeydets.com.
Head Coach: Jonathan Hadra. **Telephone:** (540) 464-7601. **Baseball SID:** Mike Carpenter. **Telephone:** (540) 464-7015. **Assistant Coaches:** Sam Roberts, Ray Noe. **Telephone:** (540) 464-7605.
Home Field: Gray-Minor Stadium. **Seating Capacity:** 1,400. **Outfield Dimension: LF**—320, **CF**—380, **RF**—330.

VIRGINIA TECH

Conference: Atlantic Coast.
Mailing Address: 25 Beamer Way, Virginia Tech (0502), Blacksburg, VA, 24061. **Website:** www.hokiesports.com.
Head Coach: John Szefc. **Telephone:** (540) 231-5906.
Baseball SID: Mike Skovan. **Telephone:** (845) 204-1777.
Assistant Coaches: Kurt Elbin, Ryan Fecteau.
Telephone: (540) 231-5906.
Home Field: English Field at Atlantic Union Bank Park. **Seating Capacity:** 4,000. **Outfield Dimension: LF**—330, **CF**—400, **RF**—330.

WAGNER

Conference: Northeast.
Mailing Address: One Campus Road, Staten Island, NY, 10301. **Website:** www.wagnerathletics.com.
Head Coach: Craig Noto. **Telephone:** (718) 420-4121.
Baseball SID: Brian Morales. **Telephone:** (718) 320-3215.
Assistant Coaches: Devin Burke, Andrew Turner.
Home Field: Richmond County Bank Ballpark.
Seating Capacity: 6,500. **Outfield Dimension: LF**—318, **CF**—390, **RF**—322.

WAKE FOREST

Conference: Atlantic Coast.
Mailing Address: 1834 Wake Forest Rd., Winston-Salem, N.C. 27106. **Website:** www.godeacs.com.
Head Coach: Tom Walter. **Baseball SID:** Ryan Sosic.
Assistant Coaches: Bill Cilento, Corey Muscara.
Home Field: David F. Couch Ballpark. **Seating Capacity:** 3,823. **Outfield Dimension: LF**—310, **CF**—400, **RF**—300.

WASHINGTON

Conference: Pac-12.
Mailing Address: Box 354070, Graves Building, Seattle, WA 98195. **Website:** www.gohuskies.com.
Head Coach: Lindsay Meggs. **Telephone:** (206) 616-4335. **Baseball SID:** Griffin Whitmer. **Telephone:** (908) 447-0783.
Assistant Coaches: Elliott Cribby, Andy Jenkins.
Home Field: Husky Ballpark. **Seating Capacity:** 2,200.
Outfield Dimension: LF—327, **CF**—395, **RF**—317.

WASHINGTON STATE

Conference: Pac-12.
Mailing Address: Cougar Baseball Complex, Pullman, WA, 99163. **Website:** www.wsucougars.com.
Head Coach: Brian Green. **Telephone:** (509) 335-0250. **Baseball SID:** Bobby Alworth. **Telephone:** (509) 335-5785.
Assistant Coaches: Terry Davis, Anthony Claggett. **Telephone:** (509) 335-0211.
Home Field: Bailey-Brayton Field. **Seating Capacity:** 3,500. **Outfield Dimension: LF**—335, **CF**—400, **RF**—335.

WEST VIRGINIA

Conference: Big 12.
Mailing Address: 1 Waterfront Place, Morgantown, WV 26501. **Website:** www.wvusports.com.
Head Coach: Randy Mazey. **Baseball SID:** Joe Mitchin.
Assistant Coaches: Steve Sabins, Mark Ginther.
Home Field: Wagener Field at Monongalia County Ballpark. **Seating Capacity:** 3,500. **Outfield Dimension: LF**—325, **CF**—400, **RF**—325.

WESTERN CAROLINA

Conference: Southern.
Mailing Address: Ramsey Center - Athletics; 92 Catamount Road, Cullowhee, N.C. 28723. **Website:** www.catamountsport.com.
Head Coach: Bobby Moranda. **Telephone:** (828) 227-2021. **Baseball SID:** Daniel Hooker. **Telephone:** (828) 227-2339.
Assistant Coaches: Taylor Sandefur, Andrew Cox. **Telephone:** (828) 227-2022.
Home Field: Ronnie G. Childress Field at Hennon Stadium. **Seating Capacity:** 1,500. **Outfield Dimension: LF**—325, **CF**—395, **RF**—325.

WESTERN ILLINOIS

Conference: Summit League.
Mailing Address: 1 University Circle Macomb, Illinois 61455. **Website:** www.goleathernecks.com.
Head Coach: Andy Pascoe. **Telephone:** (309) 298-1521. **Baseball SID:** Keion Robinson. **Telephone:** (309) 298-1133.
Assistant Coaches: Taylor Sheriff, Jared Morton. **Telephone:** (814) 525-8881.

Home Field: Alfred D. Boyer Stadium. **Seating Capacity:** 500. **Outfield Dimension: LF**—330, **CF**—400, **RF**—330.

WESTERN KENTUCKY

Conference: Conference USA.
Mailing Address: 1605 Champions Ave, Bowling Green, KY 42101. **Website:** www.wkusports.com.
Head Coach: John Pawlowski. **Baseball SID:** Matt Keenan.
Assistant Coaches: Adam Pavkovich, Tim Donnelly.
Home Field: Nick Denes Field. **Seating Capacity:** 1,500. **Outfield Dimension: LF**—330, **CF**—400, **RF**—330.

WESTERN MICHIGAN

Conference: Mid-American.
Mailing Address: 1903 W. Michigan Ave, Kalamazoo, MI 49008. **Website:** www.wmubroncos.com.
Head Coach: Billy Gernon. **Baseball SID:** Rob Low. **Telephone:** (269) 387-4122.
Assistant Coaches: Adam Piotrowicz, Jordan Keur.
Home Field: Robert J. Bobb Stadium at Hyames Field. **Seating Capacity:** 2,500. **Outfield Dimension: LF**—310, **CF**—395, **RF**—335.

WICHITA STATE

Conference: American Athletic.
Mailing Address: 1845 Fairmount Street, Wichita, KS, 67260. **Website:** www.goshockers.com.
Head Coach: Eric Wedge. **Telephone:** (316) 978-3636. **Baseball SID:** Denning Gerig. **Telephone:** (316) 978-5461.
Assistant Coaches: Mike Sirianni, Mike Pelfrey. **Telephone:** (316) 978-3636.
Home Field: Eck Stadium. **Seating Capacity:** 8,153. **Outfield Dimension: LF**—330, **CF**—390, **RF**—330.

WILLIAM & MARY

Conference: Colonial.
Mailing Address: PO Box 399, Williamsburg, VA 23187. **Website:** www.tribeathletics.com.
Head Coach: Mike McRae. **Telephone:** (757) 221-3492.
Assistant Coaches: Daniel Sweeney, Paul Panik.
Home Field: Plumeri Park. **Seating Capacity:** 1,000.

WINTHROP

Conference: Big South.
Mailing Address: 1162 Eden Terrace. Rock Hill, SC 29733. **Website:** www.winthropeagles.com.
Head Coach: Tim Riginos. **Telephone:** (864) 903-9796. **Baseball SID:** Preston Elwell.
Assistant Coaches: Austin Hill, Robbie Monday.
Home Field: Winthrop Ballpark. **Seating Capacity:** 2,000. **Outfield Dimension: LF**—325, **CF**—400, **RF**—325.

WISCONSIN-MILWAUKEE

Conference: Horizon League.
Mailing Address: 3409 N Downer Ave. Milwaukee, WI 53211. **Website:** www.mkepanthers.com.
Head Coach: Scott Doffek. **Telephone:** (414) 750-4738. **Baseball SID:** Chris Zills. **Telephone:** (414) 750-2090.
Assistant Coaches: Shaun Wagner, Cory Bigler. **Telephone:** (414) 265-8346.
Home Field: Franklin Field. **Seating Capacity:** 4,000. **Outfield Dimension: LF**—330, **CF**—408, **RF**—330.

WOFFORD

Conference: Southern.
Mailing Address: 429 N. Church Street, Spartanburg, SC 29303. **Website:** www.woffordterriers.com.
Head Coach: Todd Interdonato. **Telephone:** (864) 597-4497. **Baseball SID:** Wyatt Streett. **Telephone:** (864) 597-4098. **Assistant Coaches:** JJ Edwards, Josh Schulman. **Telephone:** (864) 597-4099.
Home Field: Russell C. King Field. **Seating Capacity:** 2,500. **Outfield Dimension: LF**—325, **CF**—395, **RF**—325.

WRIGHT STATE

Conference: Horizon League.
Mailing Address: 3640 Colonel Glenn Hwy, Dayton, OH 45435. **Website:** www.wsuraiders.com.
Head Coach: Alex Sogard. **Baseball SID:** Nick Phillips.
Assistant Coaches: Nate Metzger, Chase Stone.
Home Field: Nischwitz Stadium. **Seating Capacity:** 1,500. **Outfield Dimension: LF**—330, **CF**—400, **RF**—330.

XAVIER

Conference: Big East.
Mailing Address: 3800 Victory Pkwy Cincinnati OH 45207. **Website:** www.goxavier.com.
Head Coach: Billy O'Conner. **Telephone:** (513) 745-2890. **Baseball SID:** Hayley Schletker.
Assistant Coaches: Brian Furlong, Joey Bellini.
Home Field: Hayden Field. **Seating Capacity:** 500.
Outfield Dimension: LF—310, **CF**—380, **RF**—310.

YALE

Conference: Ivy League.
Mailing Address: PO Box 208216, New Haven, CT 06520-8216. **Website:** www.yalebulldogs.com.
Head Coach: John Stuper. **Telephone:** (203) 432-1466. **Baseball SID:** Sam Rubin. **Telephone:** (203) 432-1456.
Assistant Coaches: Andrew Dickson, Corey Keane.
Home Field: George H.W. Bush Field. **Seating Capacity:** 6,200. **Outfield Dimension: LF**—330, **CF**—405, **RF**—330.

YOUNGSTOWN STATE

Conference: Horizon League.
Mailing Address: 1 University Plaza, Youngstown, Ohio 44555. **Website:** www.ysusports.com.
Head Coach: Dan Bertolini. **Baseball SID:** Drae Smith. **Telephone:** (330) 941-8359.
Assistant Coaches: Eric Bunnell, Shane Davis.
Home Field: Eastwood Field. **Seating Capacity:** 6,000.
Outfield Dimension: LF—335, **CF**—405, **RF**—335.

AMATEUR & YOUTH

INTERNATIONAL ORGANIZATIONS

WORLD BASEBALL SOFTBALL CONFEDERATION

Headquarters: Maison du Sport International—54, Avenue de Rhodanie, 1007 Lausanne, Switzerland.
Telephone: (+41-21) 318-82-40. **Fax:** (41-21) 318-82-41.
Website: www.wbsc.org. **E-Mail:** office@wbsc.org.
Year Founded: 1938.
President: Riccardo Fraccari (Italy). **Secretary General:** Beng Choo Low (Japan). **Vice President Baseball:** Willi Kaltschmitt Luján (Guam). **Vice President Softball:** Beatrice Allen (Gambia). **Softball Executive VP:** Craig Cress (USA). **Baseball Executive VP:** Tom Peng (Taiwan). **Treasurer:** Angelo Vicini (San Marino). **Members At-Large:** Ron Finlay (Australia), Paul Seiler (USA). Taeki Utsugi (Japan), Tommy Velázquez (Puerto Rico). **Athlete Representative For Baseball:** Justin Huber (Australia). **Athlete Representative For Softball:** María Soto (Venezuela). **Global Ambassador:** Andrés Manuel Lopez Obrador (Mexico) Antonio Castro Soto del Valle (Cuba), Meliton Sanchez (Panama). **Executive Director:** Michael Schmidt. **Softball Director:** Ron Radigonda. **Assistant to the President:** Giovanni Pantaleoni. **Marketing/Tournament Manager:** Masaru Yokoo, Laurie Gouthro. **Public Relations Officer:** Oscar Lopez, Lori Nolan. **National Federation Relations:** Francesca Fabretto, Brian Glauser, Aki Huang, Amy Park. **Antidoping Officer:** Victor Isola. **Administration/Finance:** Sandrine Pennone, Laetitia Barbey.

CONTINENTAL ASSOCIATIONS

CONFEDERATION PAN AMERICANA DE BEISBOL (COPABE)

Mailing Address: Calle 3, Francisco Filos, Vista Hermosa, Edificio 74, Planta Baja Local No. 1, Panama City, Panama. **Telephone:** (507) 229-8684. **Website:** en.copabe.org. **E-Mail:** emayorgab@yahoo.com
Chairman: Eduardo De Bello (Panama). **Secretary General:** Hector Pereyra (Dominican Republic).

AFRICA BASEBALL SOFTBALL ASSOCIATION (ABSA)

Office Address: Paiko Road, Chanchaga, Minna, Niger State, Nigeria.
Mailing Address: P.M.B. 150, Minna, Niger State, Nigeria.
Telephone: (234) 8037188491. **E-mail:** absasecretariat @yahoo.com
President: Sabeur Jlajla. **Vice President Baseball:** Etienne N'Guessan. **Vice President Softball:** Fridah Shiroya. **Secretary General:** Ibrahim N'Diaye. **Treasurer:** Moira Dempsey. **Executive Director:** Lieutenant Colonel (rtd) Friday Ichide. **Deputy Executive Director:** Francoise Kameni-Lele.

BASEBALL FEDERATION OF ASIA

Mailing Address: 9F. -3, No. 288, Sec 6 Civic Blvd.,Xinyi Dist., Taipei City, Taiwan (R.O.C.). **Telephone:** 886-227910336. **E-Mail Address:** bfa@baseballasia.org
Presidents: Tom Peng, Beng Choo Low. **Vice Presidents:** Suzuki Yoshinobu, Chen Xu, Susan Zhang Xuan. **Secretary General:** Hua-Wei Lin, Sallw Lim Swee Gaik. **Members At Large:** Allan Mak, Alfonso Martin Eizmendi, Pervaiz Shah Khawar. **Directors:** Richard Lin, Yi Chuan Pan, Kazuhiro Tawa, Chang Chia Hsing.

EUROPEAN BASEBALL CONFEDERATION

Mailing Address: Savska cesta 137, 10 000 Zagreb, Croatia. **Telephone:** 43-17744114. **E-Mail Address:** office@wbsceurope.org . **Website:** www.wbsceurope.org/en
Presidents: Didier Seminet (France), Gabriel Waage (Czech Republic). **Secretary General:** Krunoslav Karin. **Treasurer:** Eddy Van Straelen. **Members At Large:** Petr Ditrich, Marco Manucci, Roderick Balk, Youri Alkalay, Kristian Palvia, Mette Nissen Jakobsen.

BASEBALL CONFEDERATION OF OCEANIA

Mailing Address: 48 Partridge Way, Mooroolbark, Victoria 3138, Australia. **Telephone:** +61-394170022. **E-Mail Address:** office@wbscoceania.org
Secretary General: Chet Gray. **Vice Presidents:** Laurent Cassier, Rex Capil. **Members At Large:** Inoke Niubalavu, Ralph Tarasomo, Hynes David, Vaughan Wyber.

ISG BASEBALL

Mailing Address: 3829 S Oakbrook Dr. Greenfield, WI 53228. **Telephone:** 414-704-5467. **E-Mail Address:** isgbaseball14@gmail.com. **Website:** isgbaseball.com. **President:** Tom O'Connell. **Vice President:** Peter Caliendo. **Secretary/Treasurer:** Randy Town. **Board Members:** Jim Jones, John Casey, Ron Maestri, Pat Doyle, John Vodenlich.

NATIONAL ORGANIZATIONS

USA BASEBALL

Mailing Address, Corporate Headquarters: 2933 South Miami Blvd, Suite 119, Durham, NC 27703.
Telephone: (919) 474-8721.
Fax: (855) 420-5910.
E-mail Address: info@usabaseball.com.
Website: usabaseball.com.
President: Mike Gaski. **Treasurer:** Jason Dobis.
Board of Directors: Mike Gaski (President), Jason Dobis (Treasurer), Elliot Hopkins (Secretary); **Members:** Veronica Alvarez, Jenny Dalton-Hill, Willie Bloomquist, John Gall, George Grande, Steve Keener, Chris Marinak, Jacob May, Tony Reagins, Wes Skelton, Derek Topik, Ernie Young.

National Members Organizations: Amateur Athletic Union (AAU); American Amateur Baseball Congress (AABC); American Baseball Coaches Association (ABCA); American Legion Baseball, Babe Ruth Baseball; Dixie Baseball; Little League Baseball; National Amateur Baseball Federation (NABF); National Assocaition of Intercollegiate Athletics (NAIA); National Baseball Congress (NBC); National Collegiate Athletic Association (NCAA); National Federation of State High School Athletic Associations (NFHS); National High School Baseball Coaches Associatin (BCA); National Junior College Athletic Association (NJCAA); Police Athletic League (PAL); PONY Baseball; T-Ball USA; United States Specialty Sports Association (USSSA).

STAFF

Executive Director/CEO: Paul Seiler. **Coordinator, Sport Performance:** Jake Barnes. **Director, Coaching Development:** Andrew Bartman. **General Manager, 18U National Team:** Ashley Bratcher. **Assistant Director, Athlete Safety:** Lisa Braxton. **General Manager, National Teams:** Eric Campbell. **Assistant Director, Youth Programs:** Anthony Cangelosi. **Director, Youth Programs:** Tyler Collins. **Director, Baseball Operations:** Brett Curll. **Chief Finance Officer:** Ray Darwin. **Director, Media Relations:** Emily Fedewa. **Assistant Director, Accounting & Finance:** Matt Forslund. **General Manager, Sports Properties:** Jimmy Frush. **Director, Travel Services:** Monica Garza. **Director, Baseball Administration:** Allison Gupton. **Senior Director, Technology:** Russell Hartford. **Director, Baseball Operations:** Carter Hicks. **Assistant Director, Creative Services:** Jenna Hiscock. **Assistant Director, Creative Services:** Mark Jenkins. **Director, Creative Services:** Kevin Jones. **Director, Baseball Operations:** Ben Kelley. **Director, Player Development:** Jim Koerner. **Director, Baseball Operations:** Charles Lane. **Director, Accounting & Finance:** Cicely McLaughlin. **Coordinator, Retail & Travel Services:** Alexandra Morin. **Senior Director, Retail:** Carrington Nicholson. **Assistant Director, Creative Services:** Colin Pelosi. **Chief Operating Officer:** David Perkins. **Coordinator, National Training Complex Operations:** Dylan Pfingst. **Director, Sport Performance:** Drew Pomeroy. **Social Media Coordinator:** Jackie Regruth. **Senior Director, Athlete Safety & Education:** Lauren Rhyne. **Assistant Director, Baseball Operations:** Ann Claire Robinson. **Director, 12U National Team Program:** Will Schworer. **Coordinator, Media Relations:** Josh Spitz. **Senior Director, National Training Complex Operations:** James Vick. **Assistant Director, Education:** Sarah Wood. **Senior Director, Media Relations:** Brad Young.

BASEBALL CANADA

Mailing Address: 2212 Gladwin Cres., Suite A7, Ottawa, Ontario K1B 5N1. **Telephone:** (613) 748-5606.
Fax: (613) 748-5767. **E-mail Address:** info@baseball.ca.
Website: baseball.ca.
President & CEO: Jason Dickson. **Head Coach/Director, National Teams:** Greg Hamilton. **Business/Sport Development Director/Women's National Team Manager:** Andre Lachance. **Media/PR Coordinator:** Adam Morissette. **Project Coordinator/Safe Sport Liaison:** June Sterling. **Administrative Assistant:** Penny Baba. **Coach & Umpire Service Coordinator:** Michel Landriault. **Administrative Coordinator, Men's National Teams:** Nancy Dunbar.

NATIONAL BASEBALL CONGRESS

Mailing Address: 300 N. Mead, Ste 109 Wichita, KS 67202. **Telephone:** (316) 265-6236. **Website:** nbcbaseball.com.
Year Founded: 1931.

ATHLETES IN ACTION

Mailing Address: 651 Taylor Dr., Xenia, OH 45385.
Telephone: (937) 352-1000. **E-mail Address:** baseball@athletesinaction.org. **Website:** aiabaseball.org. **Baseball Director of Operations/GM:** Chris Beck. **Xenia Scouts Program Director:** Dave Gnau. **International Teams Director:** John McLaughlin. **Baseball Staff:** Jason Lester.

SUMMER COLLEGE LEAGUES

NATIONAL ALLIANCE OF COLLEGE SUMMER BASEBALL

Telephone: (321) 696-6995. **E-Mail Address:** sfoggi@FloridaLeague.com. **Website:** nacsb.pointstreaksites.com

Executive Director: Stefano Foggi (Florida League). **Assistant Executive Director:** Bobby Bennett (Sunbelt Baseball League), Jeff Carter (Southern Collegiate Baseball League). **Treasurer:** Jason Woodward (Cal Ripken Collegiate Baseball League). **Director, Public Relations:** Henry Bramwell (Hamptons Collegiate Baseball League). **Compliance Officer:** Sean McGrath (New England Collegiate Baseball League).

Member Leagues: Atlantic Collegiate Baseball League, California Collegiate League, Cal Ripken Collegiate Baseball League, Cape Cod Baseball League, Florida Collegiate Summer League, Great Lakes Summer Collegiate League, New England Collegiate Baseball League, New York Collegiate Baseball League, Southern Collegiate Baseball League, Sunbelt Baseball League, Valley Baseball League, Hamptons Collegiate Baseball League.

ALASKA BASEBALL LEAGUE

League Mailing Address: P.O. Box 2690 Palmer, AK 99645. **President:** Chris Beck. **Email:** Chris.beck@athletesinaction.org.

MAT-SU MINERS

General Manager: Pete Christopher.
Mailing Address: P.O. Box 2690 Palmer, AK 99645.
Telephone: 907-746-4914/907-745-6401. **Fax:** 907-746-5068. **E-Mail:** gmminers@gci.net. **Fax:** 907-561-2920. **Website:** matsuminers.org.
Head Coach: Tyler LeBrun
Field: Hermon Brothers, Grass, No Lights.

ANCHORAGE BUCS

General Manager: Shawn Maltby
Mailing Address: 435 W. 10th Avenue Suite B, Anchorage, AK 99501. **Office:** 907-561-2827. **Fax:** 907-561-2920. **E-Mail:** shawn@anchoragebucs.com.
Website: anchoragebucs.com
Head Coach: Grant Palmer
Field: Mulcahy Field -Turf Infield, Grass Outfield, Lights

ANCHORAGE GLACIER PILOTS

General Manager: Mike Hinshaw
Mailing Address: 435 W. 10th Avenue, Suite A, Anchorage, Alaska 99501. **Office:** 907-274-3627. **Fax:** 907-274-3628. **E-Mail:** gpilots@alaska.net.
Website: glacierpilots.com.
Head Coach: Mike Cordero.
Field: Mulcahy Field -Turf Infield, Grass Outfield, Lights

CHUGIAK-EAGLE RIVER CHINOOKS

General Manager: Chris Beck
Mailing Address: 651 Taylor Drive, Xenia, Ohio 45385. **Office:** 937-352-1000. **Fax:** 937-352-1001.
E-Mail: Chris.beck@athletesinaction.org.
Website: cerchinooks.com.
Head Coach: Jon Groth.
Field: Lee Jordan Field-Turf Infield, Grass Outfield, No Lights

PENINSULA OILERS

General Manager: Kyle Brown.
Mailing Address: 601 S. Main St., Kenai, Alaska 99611.
Office: 907-283-7133. **Fax:** 907-283-3390.
E-Mail: tory@oilersbaseball.com.
Website: oilersbaseball.com
Head Coach: Larry McCann.
Field: Coral Seymour Memorial Park-Grass , No Lights

ATLANTIC COLLEGIATE BASEBALL LEAGUE

Mailing Address: 8 Millbrook Drive, Middletown, NJ 07748.
Telephone: (215) 536-5777. **Fax:** (215) 536-5777.
Website: acbl-online.com.
Year Founded: 1967.
Commissioner: Angelo Fiore.
President: Joe Mazza.
Secretary: Mike Kalb. **Executive Vice President:** Doug Cinella. **Treasurer:** Bob Hoffman.

ALLENTOWN RAILERS

Mailing Address: Suite 202, 1801 Union Blvd, Allentown, PA 18109. **E-Mail Address:** ddando@lehighvalleybaseballacademy.com. **Field Manager:** Dylan Dando.

JERSEY PILOTS

Mailing Address: 11 Danemar Drive, Middletown, NJ 07748. **Telephone:** (732) 939-0627. **E-Mail Address:** baseball@jerseypilots.com. **General Manager:** Mike Kalb.

NEW YORK PHENOMS

General Manager: Rob Bass. **Telephone:** (646) 296-1720. **E-Mail Address:** radbyrob@aol.com. **Field Manager:** Anthony Ferrante. **Field:** College of Staten Island Baseball Complex, Staten Island, NY.

NORTH JERSEY EAGLES

Mailing Address: 12 Wright Way, Oakland NJ 07436. **General Manager:** Brian Casey.

OCEAN GULLS

General Manager: Angelo Fiore, afiore@fioreservicegroup.com. **Telephone:** 904-237-1468.

QUAKERTOWN BLAZERS

Telephone: (215) 679-5072.
Website: quakertownblazers.com. **Field Manager:** Chris Ray.

TRENTON GENERALS

E-Mail Address: mrolsh@msn.com.
General Manager: Michael Olshin.

CALIFORNIA COLLEGIATE LEAGUE

Mailing Address: 11756 Chestnut Ridge Street, Moorpark, CA 93021. **Telephone:** (805) 680-1047. **Fax:** (805) 684-8596. **E-Mail Address:** burns@calsummerball. com. **Website:** calsummerball.com.
Founded: 1993. **Executive Director:** Aaron Millman.

ACADEMY BARONS

Address: 901 E. Artesia Blvd, Compton, CA 90221. **Telephone:** (424) 209-5727. **Website:** calsummerball. com/academy-barons-roster. **E-Mail Address:** darrell. miller@mlb.com. **Contact:** Natalia Reynoso. **Field manager:** Kenny Landreaux.

ARROYO SECO SAINTS

Telephone: (626) 695-6903. **Website:** arroyoseco-saints.com. **E-mail Address:** amilam@arroyosecobase-ball.com. **General Manager:** Aaron Milam/Nicholas Gorman. **Field Manager:** Aaron Milam.

CONEJO OAKS

Address: 1710 N. Moorpark Rd., #106, Thousand Oaks, CA 91360. **Telephone:** 805-304-0126.
Website: calsummerball.com/conejo-oaks-roster/. com. **E-Mail Address:** oaksbaseball@yahoo.com. **Field Manager:** David Soliz. **General Manager:** Randy Riley.

HEALDSBURG PRUNE PACKERS

Address: Rec Park 515 Piper St. Healdsburg, Calif. 95448. **Mailing Address:** PO Box 1543 Healdsburg CA 95448. **Telephone:** 707-280-6693. **Email Address:** JGG21@aol.com. **GM/Field Manager:** Joey Gomes.

LINCOLN POTTERS

Address: 436 Lincoln Blvd., Ste. 104, Lincoln, CA 95648. **Telephone:** (916) 752-8986. **Website:** lincolnpot-ters.com. **E-Mail Address:** ryan.stevens@slugger.com. **Field Manager:** Ryan Stevens. **General Manager:** Moe Geohagen. **Head Coach:** Clemente Bonilla.

ORANGE COUNTY RIPTIDE

Address: 14 Calendula Rancho, Santa Margarita, CA 92688. **Telephone:** (949) 228-7676. **Website:** ocriptide. com. **E-Mail Address:** ocriptidebaseball@gmail.com. **Field Manager:** Mitch LeVier. **General Manager:** Matt Lundgren.

SAN LUIS OBISPO BLUES

Address: 3195 McMillan Ave, Ste. B2, San Luis Obispo, CA 93401. **Telephone:** 805-512-9996. **Website:** blues-baseball.com. **E-Mail Address:** adam@bluesbaseball. com. **GM:** Adam Stowe. **Field Manager:** Clay Cederquist.

SANTA BARBARA FORESTERS

Address: 4299 Carpinteria Ave., Suite 201, Carpinteria, CA 93013. **Telephone:** (805) 684-0657. **Website:** sbforest-ers.org. **E-Mail Address:** pintard@earthlink.net. **General Manager and Field Manager:** Bill Pintard.

SOLANO MUDCATS

Address: 508 Stonewood Dr., Vacaville, CA 95687. **Website:** solanomudcats.org. **E-mail Address (GM):** solanomudcats@gmail.com. **General Manager:** Ben Crombie.

SONOMA STOMPERS

Address: 117 W. Napa St., Suite A, Sonoma, CA 95476. **Website:** stompersbaseball.com. **E-mail Address:** info@stompersbaseball.com. **General Manager:** Eddie Mora-Loera. **Field Manager:** Zack Pace.

WALNUT CREEK CRAWDADS

Address: 1630 Challenge Dr., Concord, CA 94607. **Website:** crawdadsbaseball.com. **E-mail Address (GM):** bcummings@walnutcreekcrawdads.com. **Field Manager:** Brant Cummings.

CAL RIPKEN COLLEGIATE LEAGUE

Address: 24219 Hawkins Landing Drive, Gaithersburg, MD 20882. **Telephone:** (301) 693-2577. **E-Mail:** jason_d_woodward@mcpsmd.org. **Website:** calripkenleague.org.
Year Founded: 2005.
Commissioner: Jason Woodward. **League President:** Brad Rifkin. **Deputy Commissioner:** Jerry Wargo.
Regular Season: 36 games. **Playoff Format:** Top two teams from each division plus two remaining teams with best records qualify. Teams play best of three series, winners advance to best of three series for league championship. **Roster Limit:** 35 (college-eligible players 22 and under).

ALEXANDRIA ACES

Address: 221 9th Street, S.E. Washington, DC 20003. **Telephone:** (202) 255-1683. **E-Mail:** cberset21@gmail. com. **Website:** alexandriaaces.org. **Chairman/CEO:** Donald Dinan. **General Manager:** TBD. **Head Coach:** Chris Berset. **Ballpark:** Frank Mann Field at Four Mile Run Park.

BALTIMORE DODGERS

Address: 17 Sunrise Court Randallstown, MD 21133. **Telephone:** (443) 834-3500. **Email:** juan.waters@verizon. net. **Website:** baltimoredodgers.org. **President:** Juan Waters. **Head Coach:** Derek Brown. **Ballpark:** Joe Cannon Stadium at Harmans Park.

BETHESDA BIG TRAIN

Address: 6400 Goldsboro Road Suite 220 Bethesda, MD 20817. **Telephone:** 301-229-1854. **Fax:** 301-229-8362. **E-Mail:** faninfo@bigtrain.org. **Website:** bigtrain.org. **General Manager:** David Schneider. **Head Coach:** Sal Colangelo. **Ballpark:** Shirley Povich Field.

D.C. GRAYS

Address: 1800 M Street NW, 500 South Tower, Washington, DC 20036. **Telephone:** (202) 492-6226. **Website:** dcgrays.com. **E-Mail Address:** barbera@acg-consultants.com. **President:** Mike Barbera. **General Manager:** Antonio Scott. **Head Coach:** Reggie Terry. **Ballpark:** Washington Nationals Youth Academy.

FCA BRAVES

Address: 8925 Leesburg Pike, Vienna, VA 22182. **Telephone:** (702) 909-2750. **Fax:** (703) 783-1319. **E-Mail:** fcabraves@gmail.com. **Website:** fcabraves.com. **President/General Manager:** Todd Burger. **Head Coach:** Chris Warren. **Ballpark:** Annandale High School.

GAITHERSBURG GIANTS

Address: 18221A Flower Hill Way, Gaithersburg, MD 20879. **Telephone:** (240) 793-3367. **E-Mail:** gaithersburggiants@gmail.com. **Website:** gaithersburggiants.org. **General Manager:** Matt Cangas. **Head Coach:** Jeff Rabberman. **Ballpark:** Criswell Automotive Field.

SILVER SPRING-TAKOMA T-BOLTS

Address: 906 Glaizewood Court, Takoma Park, MD 20912. **Telephone**: 301-983-1358. **E-Mail:** tboltsbaseball@gmail.com. **Website:** tbolts.org. **General Manager**: Brian Brewer. **Head Coach:** Doug Remer. **Ballpark:** Blair Stadium at Montgomery Blair High School.

CAPE COD BASEBALL LEAGUE

Mailing Address: PO Box 266, Harwich Port, MA 02646. **Telephone:** (508) 432-6909.
E-Mail: info@capecodbaseball.org.
Website: capecodbaseball.org.
Year Founded: 1885.
Commissioner: Eric Zmuda. **President:** Chuck Sturtevant. **Treasurer:** Paul Logan. **Secretary:** Paula Tufts. **Senior VP:** Bill Bussiere. **VP:** Tom Gay, Paul Galop. **Senior Deputy Commissioner/Director of Officiating:** Sol Yas. **Deputy Commissioner:** Mike Carrier, Peter Hall. **Director Public Relations:** Ben Brink. **Director Broadcasting:** John Garner. **Director, Communications:** Jim McGonigle. **Division Structure:** East—Brewster, Chatham, Harwich, Orleans, Yarmouth-Dennis. **West**—Bourne, Cotuit, Falmouth, Hyannis, Wareham.
Regular Season: 40 games. **All-Star Game and Home Run Contest:** July 24. **Playoff Format:** Top four teams in each division qualify for three rounds of best-of-three series.

BOURNE BRAVES

Mailing Address: PO Box 895, Monument Beach, MA 02553. **Telephone:** (508) 868-8378. **E-Mail Address:** nnorkevicius@yahoo.com. **Website:** bournebraves.org. **President:** Nicole Norkevicius. **General Manager:** Darin Weeks. **Head Coach:** Scott Landers.

BREWSTER WHITECAPS

Mailing Address: PO Box 2349, Brewster, MA 02631. **Telephone:** (508) 896-8500, ext. 147. **Fax:** (508) 896-9845. **E-Mail Address:** ckenney@brewsterwhitecaps.com. **Website:** brewsterwhitecaps.com. **President:** Chris Kenney. **General Manager:** Ned Monthie. **Head Coach:** Jamie Shevchik.

CHATHAM ANGLERS

Mailing Address: PO Box 428, Chatham, MA 02633. **Website:** chathamas.com. **President:** Steve West. **General Manager:** Mike Geylin. **Email:** mgeylin@kgpr.com. **Head Coach:** Tom Holliday.

COTUIT KETTLEERS

Mailing Address: PO Box 411, Cotuit, MA 02635. **Telephone:** (508) 428-3358. **E-Mail Address:** bmurpfcape@aol.com. **Website:** kettleers.org. **President:** Andy Bonacker. **General Manager:** Bruce Murphy. **Head Coach:** Mike Roberts.

FALMOUTH COMMODORES

Mailing Address: PO Box 808 Falmouth, MA 02541. **Telephone:** (508) 566-4988. **Website:** falmouthcommodores.org. **President:** Mark Kasprzyk. **General Manager:** Chris Fitzgerald. **Head Coach:** Jeff Trundy.

HARWICH MARINERS

Mailing Address: PO Box 201, Harwich Port, MA 02646. **Telephone:** (508) 432-2000. **Fax:** (508) 432-5357. **E-Mail Address:** mehendy@comcast.net. **Website:** harwichmariners.org.
President: Mary Henderson. **General Manager:** Ben Layton. **Head Coach:** Steve Englert.

HYANNIS HARBOR HAWKS

Mailing Address: PO Box 832, West Hyannis Port, MA 02672. **Telephone:** (508) 737-5890. **Fax:** (877) 822-2703. **E-Mail Address:** brpfeifer@aol.com. **Website:** harborhawks.org.
President: Brad Pfeifer. **General Manager:** Brian Guiney. **Head Coach:** Gary Calhoun.

ORLEANS FIREBIRDS

Mailing Address: PO Box 504, Orleans, MA 02653. **Telephone:** (508) 255-0793. **Fax:** (508) 255-2237. **E-Mail Address:** bodonnell15@gmail.com. **Website:** orleansfirebirds.com. **President:** Bob O'Donnell. **General Manager:** Sue Horton. **Head Coach:** Kelly Nicholson.

WAREHAM GATEMEN

Mailing Address: PO Box 287, Wareham, MA 02571. **Telephone:** (508) 748-0287. **Fax:** (508) 880-2602. **E-Mail Address:** alang.gatemen@gmail.com.
Website: gatemen.org. **President:** Tom Gay. **General Manager:** Andrew Lang. **Head Coach:** Harvey Shapiro.

YARMOUTH-DENNIS RED SOX

Mailing Address: PO Box 78 Yarmouth Port, MA 02675. **Telephone:** (508) 889-8721. **E-Mail Address:** sfaucher64@gmail.com. **Website:** ydredsox.org. **President:** James DeMaria. **General Manager:** Steve Faucher. **Head Coach:** Scott Pickler.

COASTAL PLAIN LEAGUE

Mailing Address: 117 Thomas Mill Road, Holly Springs, NC 27540. **Telephone:** (919) 852-1960. **Email Address:** justins@coastalplain.com. **Website:** coastalplain.com. **Year Founded:** 1997. **Chairman/CEO:** Jerry Petitt. **COO/Commissioner:** Justin Sellers. **Director of Media & Content Development:** Shelby Hilliard.

Division Structure: North—Peninsula Pilots, Tri-City Chili Peppers, Wilson Tobs. **East**—Florence RedWolves, Holly Springs Salamanders, Morehead City Marlins, Wilmington Sharks. **South**—Lexington County Blowfish, Macon Bacon, Spartanburgers, Savannah Bananas. **West**—Asheboro Copperheads, Forest City Owls, High Point-Thomasville HiToms, Martinsville Mustangs. **Regular Season:** 52 games. **Playoff Format:** Three rounds. **Rd 1/2:** One game. **Rd 3:** Best of three.

ASHEBORO ZOOKEEPERS

Mailing Address: PO Box 4036, Asheboro, NC 27204. **Telephone:** (336) 460-7018. **Fax:** (336) 523-1220. **E-Mail Address:** info@zkbaseball.com. **Website:** zkbaseball.com. **Owners:** Ronnie Pugh, Steve Pugh, Doug Pugh, Mike Pugh. **General Managers:** Dennis Garcia, Jeremy Knight. **Head Coach:** Jeremy Knight.

FLORENCE FLAMINGOS

Mailing Address: 520 Francis Marion Rd., Florence, S.C. 29503. **Telephone:** (843) 629-0700. **E-Mail Address:** info@florenceflamingos.com. **Website:** www.florence-flamingos.com. **Managing Partner:** Steve DeLay. **Head Coach:** Lane Harvey.

FOREST CITY OWLS

Mailing Address: 214 McNair Field Drive, Forest City, NC 28043. **Telephone:** (828) 245-0000. **E-Mail Address:** info@forestcitybaseball.com. **Website:** www.forestcity-baseball.com. **Owners:** Phil & Becky Dangel. **General Manager:** Kiva Fuller. **Head Coach:** Connor Dailey.

HIGH POINT-THOMASVILLE HI-TOMS

Mailing Address: 7003 Ballpark Road, Thomasville, NC 27360. **Telephone:** (336) 472-8667. **Fax:** (336) 472-7198. **E-Mail Address:** info@hitoms.com. **Website:** hitoms.com. **Owner:** Richard Holland. **President:** Greg Suire. **Head Coach:** Douglas Russ.

HOLLY SPRINGS SALAMANDERS

Mailing Address: 101 Tennis Court, Holly Springs, NC 27540. **Telephone:** 919-249-7322. **Email Address:** info@salamandersbaseball.com. **Website:** salamandersbaseball.com. **Owner:** Capital Broadcast Company. **General Manager:** Chip Hutchinson. **Head Coach:** Brian Rountree.

LEXINGTON COUNTY BLOWFISH

Mailing Address: 474 Ball Park Road, Lexington, SC 29072. **Telephone:** (803) 254-3474. **E-Mail Address:** info@blowfishbaseball.com. **Website:** goblowfishbaseball.com. **Owner:** Bill & Vicki Shanahan. **Head Coach:** Fico Kondla.

MACON BACON

Mailing Address: 225 Willie Smokey Glover Drive, Macon, GA. **Telephone:** 478-803-1795. **E-Mail Address:** info@maconbaconbaseball.com. **Website:** macon baconbaseball.com. **Owner:** SRO Partners (Jon Spoelstra & Steve DeLay). **President:** Brandon Raphael. **Head Coach:** Keith Soine.

MARTINSVILLE MUSTANGS

Mailing Address: 450 Commonwealth Blvd E Martinsville, VA 24112. **Telephone:** (276) 403-5250. **E-Mail Address:** info@martinsvillemustangs.com. **Website:** www.martinsvillemustangs.com. **President:** Greg Suire. **General Manager:** Ruthanne Duffy. **Head Coach:** Brandon Nania.

MOREHEAD CITY MARLINS

Mailing Address: PO Box 460, New Bern, NC 28563. **Telephone:** (252) 269-9767. **Fax:** (252) 637-2721. **E-Mail Address:** mcmarlins@gmail.com. **Website:** mhc marlins.com. **General Manager:** Buddy Bengel. **Head Coach:** Sam Carel.

PENINSULA PILOTS

Mailing Address: 1889 W. Pembroke Ave., Hampton, VA 23661. **Telephone:** (757) 245-2222. **Fax:** (757) 245-8030. **E-Mail Address:** info@peninsulapilots.com. **Website:** peninsulapilots.com. **Owner:** Henry Morgan. **General Manager:** Alex Ahl. **Head Coach/Vice President:** Hank Morgan.

SAVANNAH BANANAS

Mailing Address: 1401 E. Victory Drive, Savannah, GA 31404. **Telephone:** 912-712-2482. **E-Mail Address:** jared@thesavannahbananas.com. **Website:** the savannahbananas.com. **Owner:** Fans First Entertainment (Jesse & Emily Cole). **President:** Jared Orton. **Head Coach:** Tyler Gillum.

SPARTANBURGERS

Mailing Address: 1000 Duncan Park Dr, Spartanburg, SC 29302. **Telephone:** (864) 754-3556. **E-Mail Address:** info@spartanburgers.com. **Website:** spartanburgers.com. **Owner:** Matt Perry. **General Manager:** Claudia Padgett. **Head Coach:** Wesley Brown.

TRI-CITY CHILI PEPPERS

Mailing Address: 901 Meridian Ave, Colonial Heights, VA 23834. **Telephone:** (804) 499-3104. **E-Mail Address:** info@chilipeppersbaseball.com. **Website:** www.chili-peppersbaseball.com. **Owner:** Chris Martin. **General Manager:** Steve Taggart. **Head Coach:** James Bierlein.

WILMINGTON SHARKS

Mailing Address: 2149 Carolina Beach Road, Wilmington, NC 28401. **Telephone:** (910) 343-5621. **Fax:** (910) 343-8932. **E-Mail Address:** media@wilmingtonsharks.com. **Website:** wilmingtonsharks.com. **Owners:** National Sports Services. **General Manager:** Carson Bowen. **Head Coach:** Russ Burroughs.

WILSON TOBS

Mailing Address: 300 Stadium St. SW., Wilson, NC 27893. **Telephone:** (252) 291-8627. **Fax:** (252) 291-1224. **E-Mail Address:** mike@wilsontobs.com. **Website:** wilsontobs.com. **Owner:** Richard Holland. **President:** Greg Suire. **General Manager:** Mike Bell. **Head Coach:** Harry Markotay.

FLORIDA COLLEGIATE SUMMER LEAGUE

Mailing Address: 250 National Place, Unit #152, Longwood, FL 32750. **Telephone:** (321) 206-9174. **Fax:** (407) 574-7926. **E-Mail Address:** info@floridaleague.com. **Website:** floridaleague.com.

Year Founded: 2004.

President: Stefano Foggi. **League Operations Director:** Phil Chinnery.

Regular Season: 45 games. **Playoff Format:** Five teams qualify; No. 4 and No. 5 seeds meet in one-game playoff. Remaining four teams play best-of-three series. Winners play best-of-three series for league championship.

DELAND SUNS

Operated by the league office. **E-Mail Address:** suns@floridaleague.com. **Head Coach:** Rick Hall.

LEESBURG LIGHTNING

E-Mail Address: lightning@floridaleague.com. **Head Coach:** Rich Billings.

SANFORD RIVER RATS

Operated by the league office. **E-Mail Address:** rats@floridaleague.com. **Head Coach:** Josh Montero.

SEMINOLE COUNTY SCORPIONS

Operated by the league office. **E-Mail Address:** scorpions@floridaleague.com. **Head Coach:** Bob Rikeman.

WINTER GARDEN SQUEEZE

Operated by the league office. **Email Address:** squeeze@floridaleague.com. **Head Coach:** Terry Abbott. **General Manager:** Adam Bates.

WINTER PARK DIAMOND DAWGS

E-Mail Address: dawgs@floridaleague.com. **Head Coach:** Chuck Schall.

FUTURES COLLEGIATE LEAGUE OF NEW ENGLAND

Mailing Address: 46 Chestnut Hill Rd, Chelmsford, MA 01824. **Telephone:** (617) 593-2112. **E-Mail Address:** futuresleague@yahoo.com

Website: thefuturesleague.com.

Year Founded: 2010.

Commissioner: Joe Paolucci.

Teams (Contact): Bristol Blues (www.bristolbluesbaseball.com) (**Brian Rooney:** gm@bristolblues.com); Brockton Rox (**Todd Marlin:** tmarlin@brocktonrox.com); Martha's Vineyard Sharks (**Russ Curran:** russ.curran@mvsharks.com); Nashua Silver Knights (**Rick Muntean:** rick@nashuasilverknights.com); North Shore Navigators (**Bill Terlecky:** navigatorsgm@gmail.com); Pittsfield Suns (**Kristen Huss:** kristen@pittsfieldsuns.com); Worcester Bravehearts (**Dave Peterson:** dave@worcesterbravehearts.com)

Regular Season: 56 games; 28 home, 28 away. **Playoff Format:** Six teams qualify. First round consists of two single elimination play-in games (3 seed vs. 6 seed and 4 seed vs 5 seed), two remaining teams play a best of three semifinal round followed by a best-of- three championship round to determine league champion. Extra-inning Games are determined by Home Run Derby!!

Roster Limit: 35. 10 must be from New England or play collegiately at a New England college.

GREAT LAKES SUMMER COLLEGIATE LEAGUE

Mailing Address: PO Box 666, Troy, OH 45373. **Telephone:** (937) 308-1536. **E-Mail:** glsclcommish@gmail.com.

Website: greatlakesleague.org.

Year Founded: 1986.

President: Jim DeSana. **Commissioner:** Deron Brown.

Regular Season: 42 games. **Playoff Format:** Top six teams meet in playoffs. **Roster Limit:** 30 (college-eligible players only).

Teams: (15 Teams)—Cincinnati Steam (Cincinnati, OH); Galion Graders (Galion, OH); Grand Lake Mariners (Celina, OH); Grand River Loggers (Grand Haven, MI); Hamilton Joes (Hamilton, OH); Lake Erie Monarchs (Flat Rock, MI); Licking County Settlers (Newark, OH); Lima Locos (Lima, OH); Lorain County Ironmen (Lorain, OH); Muskegon Clippers (Muskegon, MI); Richmond Jazz (Richmond, IN); Saint Clair Green Giants (Tecumseh, ON); Southern Ohio Copperheads (Athens, OH); Xenia Scouts (Xenia, OH).

METROPOLITAN COLLEGIATE BASEBALL LEAGUE

Mailing Address: 78 Knollwood Drive, Paramus NJ 07652

President: Brian Casey 374-545-1991

Website: metropolitanbaseball.com

Email: mcbl@metropolitanbaseball.com

MIDWEST COLLEGIATE LEAGUE

Mailing Address: 1500 119th Street Whiting IN 46394. **E-Mail Address:** commissioner@midwestcollegiateleague.com. **Website:** midwestcollegiateleague.com.

Year Founded: 2010.

President/Commissioner: Don Popravak.

Regular Season: 52 games. **Playoff Format:** Top four teams meet in best of three series. Winners meet in best of three championship series.

Roster Limit: 30

Teams: Bloomington Bobcats, Crestwood Panthers, DuPage County Hounds, Joliet Admirals, NWI Oilmen, Southland Vikings.

M.I.N.K. LEAGUE

(Missouri, Iowa, Nebraska, Kansas)

Mailing Address: PO Box 367, Nevada, MO 64772. **Telephone:** (417) 667-6159. Fax: (417) 667- 4210. **Email Address:** jpost@morrisonpost.com. **Website:** minkleaguebaseball.com

Year Founded: 1995.

Commissioner: Bob Steinkamp. **President:** Jeff Post. **Vice President:** Jud Kindle. **Secretary:** Edwina Rains.

Regular season: 44 games.

Playoff Format: The top three teams from each division will qualify for the playoffs. The second and third place finishers in each division will play a "Wild Card" one-game playoff. The winner of those games will play the regular season division winner from each division in a one game playoff. The winner of each division will then play a two out of three series to determine the MINK League Champion. Championship starts on July 25.

Opening day: June 1st. **All-Star Game:** June 26th.

CHILLICOTHE MUDCATS

Mailing Address: 11 E 2nd Street, Chillicothe, MO 64601. **Telephone:** (660) 247-1504. **Fax:** (660) 646-6933. **E-Mail Address:** doughty@greenhills.net. **Website:** chillicothemudcats.com. **General Manager:** Doug Doughty.

CLARINDA A'S

Mailing Address: 225 East Lincoln, Clarinda, IA 51632. **Telephone:** (712) 542-4272. **E-Mail Address:** m.everly@mchsi.com. **Website:** clarindaiowa-as-baseball.org. **General Managers:** Ryan Eberly, Rodney J. Eberly. **Head Coach:** Ryan Eberly.

JOPLIN OUTLAWS

Mailing Address: 5860 North Pearl, Joplin, MO 64801. **Telephone:** (417) 825-4218. **E-Mail Address:** merains@mchsi.com. **Website:** joplinoutlaws.com. **President/General Manager:** Mark Rains.

NEVADA GRIFFONS

Mailing Address: PO Box 601, Nevada, MO 64772. **Telephone:** (417) 667-6159. **E-Mail Address:** Ryan.Mansfield@mcckc.edu. **Website:** nevadagriffons.org. **President:** Dan Keller. **General Manager:** Ryan Mansfield. **Head Coach:** Ryan Mansfield.

OZARK GENERALS

Mailing Address: 1336 W Farm Road 182, Springfield, MO 65810. **Telephone:** (417) 832-8830. **Fax:** (417) 877-4625. **E-Mail Address:** rda160@yahoo.com. **Website:** generalsbaseballclub.com. **General Manager/Head Coach:** Rusty Aton.

ST. JOSEPH MUSTANGS

Mailing Address: 2600 SW Parkway, St. Joseph, MO 64503. **Telephone:** (816) 279-7856. **Fax:** (816) 749-4082. **E-Mail Address:** kyturner@stjoemustangs.com. **Website:** stjoemustangs.com. **President:** Dan Gerson. **General Manager:** Ky Turner. **Manager/Director, Player Personnel:** Johnny Coy.

SEDALIA BOMBERS

Mailing Address: 2205 S Grand, Sedalia, MO 65301. **Telephone:** (660) 287-4722. **E-Mail Address:** eric@sedaliabombers.com. **Website:** sedaliabombers.com. **President/General Manager/Head Coach:** Jud Kindle. **Vice President:** Ross Dey.

JEFFERSON CITY RENEGADES

Telephone: 630-781-7247 **E-Mail Address:** jcrenegades@gmail.com. **Website:** jcrenenegades.com. **President/General Manager:** Steve Dullard. **Head Coach:** Mike DeMilia.

NEW ENGLAND COLLEGIATE LEAGUE

Mailing Address: 122 Mass Moca Way, North Adams, MA 01247. **Telephone:** (413) 652-1031. **Fax:** (413) 473-0012. **E-Mail Address:** smcgrath@necbl.com. **Website:** necbl.com. **Year founded:** 1993. **President:** John DeRosa. **Commissioner:** Sean McGrath. **Deputy Commissioner:** Gregg Hunt. **Secretary:** Max Pinto. **Treasurer:** Tim Porter. **Regular Season:** 44 games.

DANBURY WESTERNERS

Mailing Address: PO Box 3828, Danbury, CT 06813. **Telephone:** (203) 502-9167. **E-Mail Address:** jspitser@msn.com. **Website:** danburywesterners.com. **President:** Jon Pitser. **General Manager:** Chris Nathanson. **Field Manager:** Ian Ratchford.

VALLEY BLUE SOX

Mailing Address: 100 Congress St, Springfield, MA 01104. **Telephone:** 860-305-1684. **E-Mail Address:** hunter@valleybluesox.com. **Website:** valleybluesox.com. **President:** Clark Eckhoff. **General Manager:** Hunter Golden. **Field Manager:** John Raiola.

KEENE SWAMP BATS

Mailing Address: 303 Park Ave., Keene, NH 03431. **Telephone:** 603-731-5240. **E-Mail Address:** swampbatsribby@gmail.com. **Website:** swampbats.com. **President:** Kevin Watterson. **Field Manager:** Unavailable.

WINNIPESAUKEE MUSKRATS

Mailing Address: 97 Ashley Drive, Laconia, NH 03246. **Telephone:** 603-303-7806. **E-Mail Address:** kristian@muskratsbaseball.com. **Website:** winnipesaukeemuskrats.com. **President:** Mike Smith. **General Manager:** Kristian Svindland. **Field Manager:** Mike Miller.

MYSTIC SCHOONERS

Mailing Address: PO Box 432, Mystic, CT 06355. **Telephone:** (860) 608-3287. **E-Mail Address:** dlong@mysticbaseball.org. **Website:** mysticbaseball.org. **Executive Director:** Don Benoit. **General Manager:** Dennis Long. **Field Manager:** Phil Orbe.

NEW BEDFORD BAY SOX

Mailing Address: 309 Princeton St., New Bedford, MA 02740. **Telephone:** 508-985-3052. **E-Mail Address:** tsilveira17@gmail.com. **Website:** nbbaysox.com. **President:** Stephen King. **General Manager:** Tammy Silveira. **Field Manager:** Chris Cabe.

NEWPORT GULLS

Mailing Address: PO Box 777, Newport, RI 02840. **Telephone:** (401) 845-6832. **E-Mail Address:** gm@newportgulls.com. **Website:** newportgulls.com. **President/General Manager:** Chuck Paiva. **Executive VP of Baseball Operations:** Chris Patsos. **Director of Baseball Operations:** Mike Falcone. **Field Manager:** Kevin Winterrowd.

NORTH ADAMS STEEPLECATS

Mailing Address: PO Box 540, North Adams, MA 01247. **Telephone:** 413-896-3153. **E-Mail Address:** matt.tora@steeplecats.org. **Website:** steeplecats.org. **President:** Matt Tora. **General Manager:** Matt Tora. **Field Manager:** Mike Dailey.

OCEAN STATE WAVES

Mailing Address: 875 Kingstown Rd, Wakefield, RI 02879. **Telephone:** (401) 360-2977. **E-Mail Address:** eric@oceanstatewaves.com. **Website:** oceanstatewaves.com. **President/General Manager:** Eric Hirschbein-Bodnar. **Field Manager:** Eric Hirschbein-Bodnar.

PLYMOUTH PILGRIMS

Mailing Address: 111 Camelot Drive, Plymouth, MA 02360. **Telephone:** 617-694-2658. **E-Mail Address:** KPlant@pilgrimsbaseball.com. **Website:** pilgrimsbaseball.com. **President:** Peter Plant. **General Manager:** Kevin Plant. **Field Manager:** Greg Zackrison.

SANFORD MARINERS

Field Address: Goodall Park, 38 Roberts Street, Sanford, ME 04073. **Telephone:** (207) 650-1902. **E-Mail:** aizaryk@bridgtonacademy.org. **General Manager:** Aaron Izaryk. **Field Manager:** Cejar Suarez.

VERMONT MOUNTAINEERS

Mailing Address: PO Box 57, East Montpelier, VT 05651. **Telephone:** (802) 272-8728. **E-Mail Address:** gmvtm@comcast.net. **Website:** thevermontmountaineers.com. **General Manager:** Brian Gallagher. **Field Manager:** Charlie Barbieri.

UPPER VALLEY NIGHTHAWKS

Mailing Address: 134 Stevens Road Lebanon, NH 03766. **Telephone:** 864-380-2873 **E-Mail Address:** noah@uppervalleynighthawks.com. **Website:** uppervalleybaseball.pointstreaksites.com. **President:** Noah Crane. **General Manager:** Phil Chaput. **Field Manager:** TBA.

NEW YORK COLLEGIATE BASEBALL LEAGUE

Mailing Address: 398 East Dyke St. Wellsville, NY 14895. **Telephone:** (585) 455-2345. **Website:** nycbl.com. **Year founded:** 1978. **President:** Bill McConnell. **Commissioner:** Joe Brown. **Email Address:** joebrown.nycbl@gmail.com. **Vice President:** Brian McConnell Jr. **Senior Marketing Director:** Dave Meluni. **Treasurer:** Dennis Duffy. **Secretary:** Steven Ackley. **Franchises: Eastern Division:** Cortland Crush, Onondaga Flames, Rome Generals, Sherrill Silversmiths, Syracuse Spartans, Saratoga Revolution. **Western Division:** Genesee Rapids, Hornell Dodgers, Niagara Power, Olean Oilers, Rochester Ridgemen, Wellsville Nitros. **Playoff Format:** six teams qualify and play a 1 game playoff and then two rounds of best of three series. **Roster Limit:** Unlimited (college-eligible players only).

CORTLAND CRUSH

Mailing Address: 2745 Summer Ridge Rd, LaFayette, NY 13084. **Telephone:** 315-391-8167. **Email Address:** wmmac4@aol.com. **Website:** cortlandcrush.com. **President:** Gary VanGorder. **Field Manager:** Bill McConnell.

GENESEE RAPIDS

Mailing Address: 9726 Rt. 19 Houghton, NY 14474. **Telephone:** 716-969-0688. **Email Address:** rkerr@frontiernet.net. **President:** Ralph Kerr. **Field Manager:** Joe Mesa.

HORNELL DODGERS

Mailing Address: PO Box 235, Hornell, NY 14843. **Telephone:** (607) 661-4173. **Fax:** (607) 661-4173. **E-Mail Address:** gm@hornelldodgers.com. **Website:** hornelldodgers.com. **General Manager:** Paul Welker. **Field Manager:** Justin Oney.

MANSFIELD DESTROYERS

Mailing Address: Mansfield Destroyers, 508 Gaines Street, Elmira, NY 14901. **Telephone:** (570) 335-9575. **E-Mail Address:** info@mansfielddestroyers.com. **President:** Don Lewis. **General Manager:** TBA. **Field Manager:** Brian Hill.

NIAGARA POWER

Mailing Address: P.O. Box 2012, Niagara University, NY 14109. **Telephone:** (716) 286-8653. **E-Mail Address:** ptutka@niagara.edu. **Website:** niagarapowerbaseball.com. **President:** Dr. Patrick Tutka. **Field Manager:** Stu Pederson.

OLEAN OILERS

Mailing Address: 126 N 10th, Olean, NY 14760. **Telephone:** 716-378-0641. **E-Mail Address:** Brian@oconnelllaw.net. **President:** Brian O'Connell. **Field Manager:** Unavailable.

ROCHESTER RIDGEMEN

Mailing Address: 651 Taylor Dr, Xenia, OH 45385. **Telephone:** (937) 352-1225. **E-Mail Address:** baseball@athletesinaction.org. **Website:** rochesterridgemen.org. **President:** Jason Jipson. **Field Manager:** John Byington.

ROME GENERALS

Email Address: Romegenerals@gmail.com. **Telephone:** (315) 542-0675. **Website:** romegenerals.com. **Baseball Director:** Ray DiBrango. **Field Manager:** Unavailable.

SHERRILL SILVERSMITHS

Mailing Address: 3 VanWoert Ave Unit 12, Oneonta, NY 13820. **Telephone:** (401)-935-1352. **E-Mail Address:** Djduffy316@gmail.com. **Website:** leaguelineup.com/silversmiths. **President:** Dennis Duffy & Mike Sherlock. **Field Manager:** Tim Bailey.

SYRACUSE SALT CATS

Mailing Address: 208 Lakeland Ave, Syracuse, NY 13209. **Telephone:** (315) 727-9220. **Fax:** (315) 488-1750. **E-Mail Address:** mmarti6044@yahoo.com. **Website:** leaguelineup.com/saltcats. **President:** Mike Martinez. **Field Manager:** Mike Martinez.

SYRACUSE SPARTANS

Mailing Address: 208 Lakeland Ave, Syracuse, NY 13209. **Telephone:** (315) 727-9220. **Fax:** (315) 488-1750. **E-Mail Address:** mmarti6044@yahoo.com. **General Manager:** JJ Potrikus. **Field Manager:** Brian Burns.

WELLSVILLE NITROS

Mailing Address: 2848 O'Donnell Rd, Wellsville, NY 14895. **Telephone:** 585-596-9523. **Fax:** 585-593-5260. **E-Mail Address:** nitros04@gmail.com. **Website:** nitrosbaseball.com. **President:** Steven J. Ackley. **Field Manager:** Tucker Hughes.

NORTHWOODS LEAGUE

Office Address: 2900 4th St SW, Rochester, MN 55902. **Telephone:** (507) 536-4579. **Fax:** (507) 536-4597. **E-Mail Address:** info@northwoodsleague.com.
Website: northwoodsleague.com.
Year Founded: 1994.
Chairman: Dick Radatz, Jr. **President:** Gary Hoover. **Vice President, Business Development:** Matt Bomberg. **Vice President, Operations:** Glen Showalter. **Vice President, Licensing/Technology:** Tina Coil. **Vice President, Technology Development:** Greg Goodwin. **Division Structure: Great Lakes**—Battle Creek Battle Jacks, Fond du Lac Dock Spiders, Green Bay Rockers, Kalamazoo Growlers, Kenosha Kingfish, Kokomo Jackrabbits, Lakeshore Chinooks, Madison Mallards, Rockford Rivets, Traverse City Pit Spitters, Wisconsin Woodchucks, Wisconsin Rapids Rafters. **Great Plains**—Bismarck Larks, Duluth Huskies, Eau Claire Express, La Crosse Loggers, Mankato MoonDogs, Rochester Honkers, St. Cloud Rox, Thunder Bay Border Cats, Waterloo Bucks, Wilmar Stingers.

BATTLE CREEK BATTLEJACKS

Mailing Address: 189 Bridge Street, Battle Creek, MI 49017. **Telephone:** (269) 962-0735. **Fax:** (269) 962-0741. **Email Address:** info@battlecreekbombers.com. **Website:** battlecreekbombers.com. **General Manager:** Tyler Shore. **Field Manager:** Josh Rebandt. **Field:** C.O. Brown Stadium**.**

BISMARCK LARKS

Mailing Address: 300 N 4th Street, Suite 103, Bismarck, ND 58501. **Telephone:** (701) 557-7600. **Email Address:** info@larksbaseball.com. **Website:** larks baseball.com. **General Manager:** John Bollinger. **Field Manager:** Will Flynt. **Field:** Bismarck Municipal.

DULUTH HUSKIES

Mailing Address: PO Box 16231, Duluth, MN 55816. **Telephone:** (218) 786-9909.
Fax: (218) 786-9001. **E-Mail Address:** huskies@duluth huskies.com. **Website:** duluthhuskies.com. **Owner:** Michael Rosenzweig. **General Manager:** Greg Culver. **Field Manager:** Marcus Pointer. **Field:** Wade Stadium.

EAU CLAIRE EXPRESS

Mailing Address: 108 E Grand Ave, Eau Claire, WI 54701. **Telephone:** (715) 839-7788. **Fax:** (715) 839-7676. **E-Mail Address:** info@eauclaireexpress.com. **Website:** eauclaireexpress.com. **Owner:** Bill Rowlett. **Assistant Managing Director:** Andy Neborak. **General Manager:** Jacob Servais. **Director of Operations/Field Manager:** Dale Varsho. **Field:** Carson Park.

FOND DU LAC DOCK SPIDERS

Mailing Address: 980 E Division St., Fond du Lac, WI 54935. **Telephone:** (920) 907-9833. **Email Address:** info@ dockspiders.com. **Website:** dockspiders.com. **President:**

Rob Zerjav. **General Manager:** Chris Ward. **Field Manager:** Zac Charbonneau. **Field:** Herr-Baker Field

GREEN BAY ROCKERS

Mailing Address: 2325 Holgrem Way Suite, Green Bay, WI 54303. **Telephone:** (920) 497-7225. **Fax:** (920) 437-3551. **Email Address:** info@booyahbaseball.com. **Website:** booyahbaseball.com. **General Manager:** Sieeria Vieaux. **Field Manager:** TBA. **Field:** Capital Credit Union Park.

KALAMAZOO GROWLERS

Mailing Address: 251 Mills St, Kalamazoo, MI 49048. **Telephone:** (269) 492-9966.
Website: growlersbaseball.com. **General Manager:** Brian Colopy. **Field Manager:** Cody Piechocki. **Field:** Homer Stryker Field.

KENOSHA KINGFISH

Mailing Address: 7817 Sheridan Rd, Kenosha, WI 53143. **Telephone:** (262) 653-0900. **Website:** king fishbaseball.com. **General Manager:** Doug Cole. **Field Manager:** Duffy Dyer. **Field:** Simmons Field.

LA CROSSE LOGGERS

Mailing Address: 1225 Caledonia St, La Crosse, WI 54603. **Telephone:** (608) 796-9553. **Fax:** (608) 796-9032. **E-Mail Address:** info@lacrosseloggers.com. **Website:** lacrosseloggers.com. **Owner:** Dan Kapanke. **General Manager:** Chris Goodell. **Assistant General Manager:** Ben Kapanke. **Field Manager:** Brian Lewis. **Field:** Copeland Park.

LAKESHORE CHINOOKS

Mailing Address: 983 Badger Circle, Grafton, WI 53024. **Telephone:** (262) 618-4659. **Fax:** (262) 618-4362. **E-Mail Address:** info@lakeshorechinooks.com. **Website:** lakeshorechinooks.com. **Owner:** Jim Kacmarcik. **General Manager:** Eric Snodgrass. **Field Manager:** Travis Akre. **Field:** Kapco Park.

MADISON MALLARDS

Mailing Address: 2920 N Sherman Ave, Madison, WI 53704. **Telephone:** (608) 246-4277. **Fax:** (608) 246-4163. **E-Mail Address:** info@mallardsbaseball.com. **Website:** mallardsbaseball.com. **Owner:** Steve Schmitt. **President:** Vern Stenman. **General Manager:** Tyler Isham. **Field Manager:** Donnie Scott. **Field:** Warner Park.

MANKATO MOONDOGS

Mailing Address: 1221 Caledonia Street, Mankato, MN 56001. **Telephone:** (507) 625-7047. **Fax:** (507) 625-7059. **E-Mail Address:** office@mankatomoondogs.com. **Website:** mankatomoondogs.com. **General Manager:** Austin Link. **Field Manager:** Matt Wollenzin. **Field:** Franklin Rogers Park.

ROCHESTER HONKERS

Mailing Address: 307 E Center St, Rochester, MN 55904. **Telephone:** (507) 289-1170. **Fax:** (507) 289-1866. **E-Mail Address:** honkersbaseball@gmail.com. **Website:** rochesterhonkers.com. **General Manager:** Jeremy aagard. **Field Manager:** Deskaeh Bomberry. **Field:** Mayo Field.

ROCKFORD RIVETS

Mailing Address: 4503 Interstate Blvd., Loves Park, IL 61111. **Telephone:** 815-240-4159. **E-Mail Address:** info@rockfordrivets.com **Website:** rockfordrivets.com. **General Manager:** Chad Bauer. **Field Manager:** Josh Keim. **Field:** Rivets Stadium.

ST. CLOUD ROX

Mailing Address: 5001 8th St N, St. Cloud, MN 56303. **Telephone:** (320) 240-9798. **Fax:** (320) 255-5228. **E-Mail Address:** info@stcloudrox.com. **Website:** stcloudrox.com. **President:** Gary Posch. **Vice President:** Scott Schreiner. **General Manager:** Mike Johnson. **Field Manager:** Augie Rodriguez. **Field:** Joe Faber Field.

THUNDER BAY BORDER CATS

Mailing Address: PO Box 29105 Thunder Bay, Ontario P7B 6P9. **Telephone:** (807) 766-2287. **General Manager:** Dan Grant. **Field Manager:** Eric Vasquez. **Field:** Port Arthur Stadium.

TRAVERSE CITY PIT SPITTERS

E-Mail Address: info@traversecitybaseball.com. **General Manager:** Mickey Graham. **Field Manager:** Josh Rebandt.

WATERLOO BUCKS

Mailing Address: PO Box 4124, Waterloo, IA 50704. **Telephone:** (319) 232-0500. **Fax:** (319) 232-0700. **E-Mail Address:** waterloobucks@waterloobucks.com. **Website:** waterloobucks.com. **General Manager:** Dan Corbin. **Field Manager:** Casey Harms. **Field:** Riverfront Stadium.

WILLMAR STINGERS

Mailing Address: PO Box 201, Willmar, MN, 56201. **Telephone:** (320) 222-2010. **E-Mail Address:** ryan@willmarstingers.com. **Website:** willmarstingers.com. **Owners:** Marc Jerzak, Ryan Voz. **General Manager:** Nick McCallum. **Field Manager:** Bo Henning. **Field:** Taunton Stadium.

WISCONSIN RAPIDS RAFTERS

Mailing Address: 521 Lincoln St, Wisconsin Rapids, WI 54494. **Telephone:** (715) 424-5400. **E-Mail Address:** info@raftersbaseball.com. **Website:** raftersbaseball.com. **Owner:** Vern Stenman. **General Manager:** Andy Francis. **Field Manager:** Craig Noto. **Field:** Witter Field.

WISCONSIN WOODCHUCKS

Mailing Address: 2401 N 3rd St, Wausau, WI 54403. **Telephone:** (715) 845-5055. **Fax:** (715) 845-5015. **E-Mail Address:** info@woodchucks.com. **Website:** woodchucks.com. **Owner:** Mark Macdonald. **General Manager:** Ryan Treu. **Field Manager:** Ronnie Richardson. **Field:** Athletic Park.

PERFECT GAME COLLEGIATE LEAGUE

Mailing Address: 8 Michaels Lane, Old Brookville, NY 11545. **Telephone:** (516) 521-0206. **Fax:** (516) 801-0818. **E-Mail Address:** valkun@aol.com. **Website:** pgcbl.com. **Year Founded:** 2010. **President:** Jeffrey Kunion. **Director of Communications:** Travis Larner **Executive Committee:** Bob Ohmann (Newark Pilots), Paul Samulski (Albany Dutchmen). Robbie Nichols (Elmira Pioneers), George Deak (Utica Blue Sox), Kevin Hinchey (Saugerties Stallions)

Teams: East—Albany Dutchmen, Amsterdam Mohawks, Glens Falls Dragons, Mohawk Valley DiamondDawgs, Oneonta Outlaws, Saugerties Stallions, Utica Blue Sox. **West**—Adirondack Trail Blazers, Elmira Pioneers, Geneva Red Wings, Jamestown Jammers, Newark Pilots, Onondaga Flames

Regular Season: 50. **Playoff Format:** Top four teams in each division qualify for one-game playoff; next two series are best of three. **Roster Limit:** 35 (maximum of two graduated high school players per team).

ADIRONDACK TRAIL BLAZERS

President: Bobby Miller. **General Manager:** Matt Burns. **Head Coach:** Michael Fauvelle. **Telephone:** (315) 542-0675. **Field:** Robert Smith Sports Complex. **Email Address:** adirondacktrailblazers@rocketmail.com.

ALBANY DUTCHMEN

Mailing Address: PO Box 72, Saratoga Springs, N.Y. 12866. **President:** Paul Samulski. **General Manager:** Jason Brinkman. **E-Mail:** jbrinkma@gmail.com. **Telephone:** 518-210-8383. **Head Coach:** Nick Davey. **Field:** Siena Field.

AMSTERDAM MOHAWKS

Mailing Address: P.O. Box 334, Amsterdam, N.Y., 12010. **President:** Brian Spagnola. **Vice President:** Dave Dittman. **Head Coach:** Keith Griffin. **E-Mail Address:** gm@amsterdammohawks.com. **Telephone:** (518)791-7546. **Field:** Shuttlesworth Park.

ELMIRA PIONEERS

Mailing Address: 546 Luce Street, Elmira, N.Y. 14904. **Owners:** Nellie Franco-Nichols, Donald Lewis, Robbie Nichols. **Head Coach**: Matt Burch. **Telephone:** (607) 734-2690. **E-Mail Address**: donspioneers@gmail.com. **Field:** Dunn Field.

GENEVA RED WINGS

Mailing Address: N/A. **Owners:** Bob Ohmann, Lesilie Ohmann. **Head Coach:** Sean O'Connor. **Email:** info@genevaredwings.com. **Telephone:** (919) 422-4323. **Field:** McDonough Park.

GLENS FALLS DRAGONS

Mailing Address: PO Box 897, Glens Falls, N.Y. 12801. **President:** Ben Bernard. **Head Coach:** Cameron Curler. **Telephone:** (518) 361-5316. **E-Mail Address**: ben bernard1@yahoo.com. **Field:** East Field Stadium.

JAMESTOWN TARP SKUNKS

Owner: Mike Zimmerman. **President:** Dan Kuenzi. **Head Coach:** Anthony Barone. **Telephone:** (716) 720-4465. **E-Mail Address**: dkuenzi@mkesports.com. **Field:** Russell E. Diethrick Jr. Park.

MOHAWK VALLEY DIAMONDDAWGS

Mailing Address: PO Box 902, Little Falls, N.Y. 13365. **Owner:** Travis Heiser. **Head Coach:** Cory Haggerty. **Telephone:** (315) 985-0692. **E-Mail Address**: travis@mydiamonddawgs.com. **Field**: Veterans Memorial Park.

NEWARK PILOTS

Mailing Address: 65 Williams Street, Lyons, N.Y. 14489. **Owner**: Bob Ohmann, Leslie Ohmann. **Head Coach**: Matt Colbert. **Telephone**: (315) 576-6710. **E-Mail Address**: newarkpilots@gmail.com. **Field**: Colburn Park.

ONEONTA OUTLAWS

Mailing Address: 291 Chestnut Street, Oneonta, N.Y., 13280. **Owner**: Gary Laing. **General Manager**: Joe Hughes. **Head Coach**: Joe Hughes. **Telephone**: (607) 432-6326. **E-Mail Address**: joehughes@oneontaoutlaws.com. **Field**: Damaschke Field.

ONONDAGA FLAMES

Mailing Address: 285 Pinehurst Trace Drive, Pinehurst, NC 28374. **Owners**: Wayne Walker & Alyce Lee-Walker. **Head Coach:** Ryan Stevens. **Telephone:** (315) 308-0889. **E-Mail Address:** wayne@onondagaflames.com. **Stadium:** Onondaga Community College Baseball Complex.

SAUGERTIES STALLIONS

Mailing Address: 645 Rte 212, Saugerties, NY 12477. **Owner**: Kevin Hinchey. **Head Coach**: Collin Martin. **Telephone**: (845) 707-0265. **E-Mail Address**: the saugertiesstallions@gmail.com. **Field**: Cantine Field.

UTICA BLUE SOX

Mailing Address: 7179 County Highway 18, West Winfield, N.Y. 13491. **Owner**: George Deak. **General Manager**: George Deak. **Head Coach**: Doug Delett. **Telephone**: (315) 855-5013. **E-Mail Address**: George@ globalgraphicsny.com. **Field**: Donovan Stadium at Murnane Field.

WATERTOWN RAPIDS

Mailing Address: PO Box 6250, Watertown, N.Y. 13601. **Owners**: Michael Schell, Paul Velte. **General Manager**: Brandon Noble. **Field Manager**: Dave Anderson. **Telephone**: (315) 836-1545. **E-Mail Address**: rapidsgm@gmail.com. **Field**: Alex T. Duffy Fairgrounds.

PROSPECT LEAGUE

Mailing Address: PO Box 84, Elkville, IL 62932. **Telephone:** (618) 559-1343. **E-Mail Address:** commissioner@prospectleague.com. **Website:** prospectleague.com.
Year Founded: 1963 as Central Illinois Collegiate League; known as Prospect League since 2009.
Commissioner: Dennis Bastien.

CHAMPION CITY KINGS

Mailing Address: 1301 Mitchell Blvd., Springfield, OH 45503. **Telephone:** (937) 342-0320. **Fax:** (937) 342-0320. **E-Mail Address:** cckings@gmail.com. **Website:** championcitykings.com. **General Manager:** Ginger Fulton. **Field Manager:** John Jeanes.

CHILLICOTHE PAINTS

Mailing Address: 59 North Paint Street, Chillicothe, OH 45601. **Telephone:** (740) 773-8326. **Fax:** (740) 773-8338. **E-Mail Address:** paints@bright.net. **Website:** chillicothepaints.com. **General Manager:** Bryan Wickline. **Field Manager:** Brian Bigam.

DANVILLE DANS

Mailing Address: 4 Maywood, Danville, IL 61832. **Telephone:** (217) 918-3401. **Fax:** (217) 446-9995. **E-Mail Address:** danvilledans@comcast.net. **Website:** danvilledans.com. **League Director:** Jeanie Cooke. **General Manager:** Jeanie Cooke. **Field Manager:** Eric Coleman.

O'FALLON HOOTS

Telephone: Unavailable. **Email Address:** ofallon@ prospectleague.com. **General Manager:** David Schmoll. **Field Manager:** Joe Lincoln. **Stadium:** CarShield Field.

DUPAGE PISTOL SHRIMP

E-Mail Address: info@dupagepistolshrimp.com. **Telephone:** 855-748-2457. **General Manager & Field Manager:** John Jakiemiec. **Field:** BenU Baseball Field (Village of Lisle-Benedictine University Sports Complex).

LAFAYETTE AVIATORS

Mailing Address: PO Box 6494, Lafayette, IN 47904. **Telephone:** (414) 224-9283. **Fax:** (414) 224-9290. **E-Mail Address:** zchartrand@lafayettebaseball.com. **Website:** lafayettebaseball.com. **President:** Sean Churchill. **General Manager:** Zach Chartrand. **League Director:** Dan Kuenzi. **Field Manager:** Brent McNeil.

QUINCY GEMS

Mailing Address: 1400 N. 30th St., Suite 1, Quincy, IL 62301. **Telephone:** (217) 214-7436. **Fax:** (217) 214-7436. **E-Mail Address:** quincygems@yahoo.com. **Website:** quincygems.com. **League Director/General Manager:** Jimmie/Julie Louthan. **Field Manager:** Pat Robles.

SPRINGFIELD SLIDERS

Mailing Address: 1415 North Grand Avenue East, Suite B, Springfield, IL 62702. **Telephone:** (217) 679-3511. **Fax:** (217) 679-3512. **E-Mail Address:** slidersfun@spring fieldsliders.com. **Website:** springfieldsliders.com. **League Director/General Manager:** Todd Miller. **Field Manager:** Chris Holke.

TERRE HAUTE REX

Mailing Address:111 North 3rd St, Terre Haute, IN 47807. **Telephone:** (812) 478-3817. **Fax:** (812) 232-5353. **E-mail Address:** frontoffice@rexbaseball.com. **Website:** rexbaseball.com. **League Director/General Manager:** Bruce Rosselli. **Field Manager:**Tyler Wampler.

WEST VIRGINIA MINERS

Mailing Address: 476 Ragland Road, Suite 2, Beckley, WV 25801. **Telephone:** (304) 252-7233. **Fax:** (304) 253-1998. **E-mail Address:** wvminers@wvminersbaseball.com. **Website:** wvminersbaseball.com. **President:** Doug Epling. **League Director/General Manager/Field Manager:** Tim Epling.

SOUTHERN COLLEGIATE BASEBALL LEAGUE

Mailing Address: 9723 Northcross Center Court, Huntersville, NC 28078. **Telephone:** (704) 635-7126. **Cell:** (704) 906-7776. **E-Mail Address:** hhampton@scbl.org. **Website:** scbl.org.

Year Founded: 1999.

Chairman: Bill Capps, **Commissioner:** Jamie Billings. **President:** Jeff Carter. **Treasurer:** Brenda Templin. **Umpire in Chief:** Gary Swanson.

Regular Season: 42 games. **Playoff Format:** Six-team single-elimination tournament with best of three championship series between final two teams.

Roster Limit: 35 (College-eligible players only).

CHARLOTTE GALAXY

Mailing Address: 7209 East WT Harris Blvd, Suite J #245, Charlotte, NC 28227. **Telephone:** (704) 668-9167. **Email Address:** baseballnbeyond@aol.com. **General Manager:** David "Doc" Booth. **Head Coach:** Addison Rouse.

CONCORD ATHLETICS

Mailing Address: 366 George Lyles Parkway, Suite 125, Concord, NC 28027. **Telephone:** (704) 786-2255. **Email Address:** playconcordathletics@gmail.com. **General Manager:** David Darwin. **Head Coach:** Charles Weber

LAKE NORMAN COPPERHEADS

Mailing Address: 16405 Northcross Drive, Suite A Huntersville, NC 28078. **Telephone:** (704) 305-3649. **Email Address:** dshoe@copperheadsports.org. **General Manager:** Derek Shoe. **Head Coach:** Jeremy Johnson.

PIEDMONT PRIDE

Mailing Address: 1524 Summit View Drive, Rock Hill, SC 29732. **Telephone:** (803) 412-7982. **E-Mail Address:** joe@pridebaseball.net. **General Manager:** Logan Hudak. **Head Coach:** Joe Hudak.

CAROLINA VIPERS

Mailing Address: 12104 Copper Way, Suite 200, Charlotte NC 28277. **Telephone:** 980-256-5346. **E-Mail Address:** bnichols@goviperbaseball.com. **President:** Mike Polito. **General Manager:** Blaine Nichols. **Head Coach:** Aaron Bray.

MOORSVILLE SPINNERS

Mailing Address: 2643 N Hwy 16 Denver, NC 28037. **Telephone:** (704) 491-4112. **E-Mail Address:** ploftin@mooresvillespinners.com. **General Manager:** Phillip Loftin. **Head Coach:** Tripp Hamrick.

LINOIRE OILERS

Mailing Address: PO Box 1113 Icard NC 28666. **Telephone:** 828-455-1289. **E-Mail Address:** LenoirOilers@gmail.com. **General Manager:** Sara Wert. **Head Coach:** Ivan Acuna.

TEXAS COLLEGIATE LEAGUE

Mailing Address: 735 Plaza Blvd, Suite 200, Coppell, TX 75019. **Telephone:** (979) 985-5198. **Fax:** (979) 779-2398. **E-Mail Address:** info@tclbaseball.com. **Website:** texascollegiateleague.com.

Year Founded: 2004.
President: Uri Geva.
Roster Limit: 30 (College-eligible players only)

ACADIANA CANE CUTTERS

Mailing Address: 221 La Neuville, Youngsville, LA 70592. **Telephone:** (337) 451-6582. **E-Mail Address:** info@cane cuttersbaseball.com. **Website:** canecuttersbaseball.com. **Owners:** Richard Chalmers, Sandi Chalmers. **General Manager:** Richard Haifley.

BRAZOS VALLEY BOMBERS

Mailing Address: 405 Mitchell St, Bryan, TX 77801. **Telephone:** (979) 799-7529. **Fax:** (979) 779-2398. **E-Mail Address:** info@bvbombers.com. **Website:** bv bombers.com. **Owners:** Uri Geva. **General Manger:** Chris Clark. **Field Manager:** Curt Dixon.

TEXAS MARSHALS

Mailing Address: 7920 Beltline Rd, 8th Floor Suite 860 Dallas, TX 75254. **Telephone:** (855) 808-7529. **E-Mail Address:** info@texasmarshals.com. **Website:** texas marshals.com. **Owner:** Marc Landry. **General Manager:** Kenderick Moore. **Field Manager:** Brent Lavallee.

TEXARKANA TWINS

Ballpark: George Dobson Field, 4303 N Park Rd, Texarkana, TX 75503. **Telephone:** (903) 294-7529. **Head Coach:** Bill Clay.

VICTORIA GENERALS

Mailing Address: 1307 E Airline Road, Suite H, Victoria, TX 77901. **Telephone:** (361) 485-9522. **Fax:** (361) 485-0936. **E-Mail Address:** info@baseballinvictoria.com, tkyoung@victoriagenerals.com. **Website:** victoria generals.com. **President:** Tracy Young. **VP/General Manager:** Mike Yokum.

VALLEY BASEBALL LEAGUE

Mailing Address: Valley Baseball League, PO Box 1127, New Market, VA 22844. **Telephone:** (540) 810-9194. **Fax:** (540) 435-8453. **E-Mail Address:** cbalger@shentel. net. **Website:** valleyleaguebaseball.com.

Year Founded: 1897. **President:** C. Bruce Alger. **Executive Vice President:** Jay Neal. **Media Relations Director:** John Leonard. **Secretary:** Stacy Locke. **Treasurer:** Ed Yoder. **Regular Season:** 42 games. **Playoff Format:** Eight teams qualify; play three rounds of best of three series. **Roster Limit:** 30 (college-eligible only)

COVINGTON LUMBERJACKS

Mailing Address: PO Box 30, Covington, VA 24426. **Telephone:** (540) 969-9923, (540) 962-1155. **Fax:** (540) 962-7153. **E-Mail Address:** covingtonlumberjacks@valley leaguebaseball.com. **Website:** lumberjacksbase ball.com. **President:** Dizzy Garten. **Head Coach:** Alex Kotheimer.

PURCELLVILLE CANNONS

Mailing Address: P.O. Box 114, Purcellville, VA 20132. **Telephone:** (540) 303-9673. **Fax:** (304) 856-1619. **E-Mail Address:** info@purcellvillecannons.com. **Website:** purcellvillecannons.com. **President/Recruiting Coordinator/Head Coach:** Brett Fuller. **General Manager:** Ridge Fuller.

CHARLOTTESVILLE TOM SOX

Mailing Address: P. O. Box 4836, Virginia 22905. **Telephone:** (540)471-0799. **E-Mail:** mpad71@gmail.com. **Website:** TomSox.com. **President/General Manager:** Mike Paduano. **Head Coach:** Kory Koehler.

FRONT ROYAL CARDINALS

Mailing Address: 382 Morgans Ridge Road, Front Royal, VA 22630. **Telephone:** (703) 244-6662, (540) 631-9201. **E-Mail Address:** DonnaSettle@centurylink.net. frontroyalcardinals@valleyleaguebaseball.com. **Website:** valleyleaguebaseball.com. **President:** Donna Settle. **Head Coach:** Zeke Mitchem.

HARRISONBURG TURKS

Mailing Address: 1489 S Main St, Harrisonburg, VA 22801. **Telephone:** (540) 434-5919. **Fax:** (540) 434-5919. **E-Mail Address:** turksbaseball@hotmail.com. **Website:** harrisonburgturks.com. **Operations Manager:** Teresa Wease. **General Manager/Head Coach:** Bob Wease.

NEW MARKET REBELS

Mailing Address: PO Box 902, New Market, VA 22844. **Telephone:** (540) 435-8453. **Fax:** (540) 740-9486. **E-Mail Address:** nmrebels@shentel.net. **Website:** new marketrebels.com. **President/General Manager:** Bruce Alger. **Head Coach:** Arthur E. Stenberg IV.

STAUNTON BRAVES

Mailing Address: PO Box 428, Stuarts Draft, VA 24447. **Telephone:** (540) 886-0987. **Fax:** (540) 886-0905. **E-Mail Address:** sbraves@hotmail.com. **Website:** staunton-bravesbaseball.com. **General Manager:** Steve Cox. **Head Coach:** Lukas Ray.

STRASBURG EXPRESS

Mailing Address: PO Box 417, Strasburg, VA 22657. **Telephone:** (540) 325-5677, (540) 459-4041. **Fax:** (540) 459-3398. **E-Mail Address:** neallaw@shentel.net, strasburgxpress@gmail.com. **Website:** strasburg express.com. **General Manager:** Jay Neal. **Head Coach:** Anthony Goncalves.

WAYNESBORO GENERALS

Mailing Address: 3144 Village Drive, Waynesboro, VA 22980. **Telephone:** (540) 835-6312. **Fax:** (540) 932-2322. **E-Mail Address:** contact@waynesborogenerals.net. **Website:** waynesborogenerals.com. **Chairman:** Kathleen Kellett-Ward. **General Manager:** Tyler Hoffman. **Head Coach:** Zac Cole.

WINCHESTER ROYALS

Mailing Address: PO Box 2485, Winchester, VA 22604. **Telephone:** (540) 974-4104, (540) 664-3978. **Fax:** (540) 662-1434. **E-Mail Addresses:** winchesterroyals@gmail.com, info@winchesterroyals.org. **Website:** winchesterroyals.com. **President:** Donna Turrill. **Operations Director:** Jimmie Shipp. **Coach:** Mike Smith.

WOODSTOCK RIVER BANDITS

Mailing Address: P.O. Box 227, Woodstock, VA 22664. **Telephone:** (540) 481-0525. **Fax:** (540) 459-2093. **E-Mail Address:** woodstockriverbandits@valleyleaguebaseball. com. **Website:** woodstockriverbandits.org. **General Manager:** Robert "porky" Bowman. **Head Coach:** Mike Bocock. **Assistant Head Coach:** Paul Ackerman.

WEST COAST LEAGUE

Mailing Address: PO Box 10771, Portland OR 97296. **Telephone:** 503-233-2490. **E-Mail Address:** info@west coastleague.com. **Website:** westcoastleague.com.

Year Founded: 2005. **Commissioner:** Rob Neyer. **President:** Tony Bonacci. **Vice President:** Glenn Kirkpatrick. **Secretary:** Jose Oglesby. **Treasurer:** Dan Segel. **Supervisor, Umpires:** Dave Perez. **Division Structure: South**—Bend Elks, Corvallis Knights, Cowlitz Black Bears, Ridgefield Raptors, Walla Walla Sweets. **North**—Bellingham Bells, Kelowna Falcons, Port Angeles Lefties, Victoria Harbourcats, Wenatchee Applesox, Yakima Valley Pippins. **2022 Opening Date:** June 5. **Closing Date:** August 9. **Playoff Format:** Four-team tournament. **Roster Limit:** 35 (college-eligible players only).

BELLINGHAM BELLS

Mailing Address: 1221 Potter Street, Bellingham, WA 98229. **Telephone:** (360) 527-1035. **E-Mail Address:** stephanie@bellinghambells.com. **Website:** bellinghambells.com. **Owner:** Glenn Kirkpatrick. **General Manager:** Stephanie Morrell. **Head Coach:** Bob Geaslen. **Assistant Coaches:** Jim Clem, Jake Whisler, Boog Leach.

BEND ELKS

Mailing Address: 70 SW Century Dr Suite 100-373 Bend, Oregon 97702. **Telephone:** (541) 312-9259. **Website:** bendelks.com. **Owners:** John and Tami Marick. **Marketing and Sales:** Kelsie Hirko. **General Manager:** Michael Hirko. **Head Coach:** Alan Embree. **Assistant Coaches:** Dylan Jones, Blake Woosley.

CORVALLIS KNIGHTS

Mailing Address: PO Box 1356, Corvallis, OR 97339. **Telephone:** (541) 752-5656. **E-Mail Address:** dan.segel@ corvallisknights.com. **Website:** corvallisknights.com. **President:** Dan Segel. **General Manager:** Bre Miller. **Head Coach:** Brooke Knight. **Associate Head Coach/ Pitching Coach:** Ed Knaggs. **Assistant Coach:** Youngjin Yoon, Jacob Kopra.

COWLITZ BLACK BEARS

Mailing Address: PO Box 1255, Longview, WA 98632. **Telephone:** (360) 703-3195. **Website:** cowlitzblac kbears.com. **Owner/President:** Tony Bonacci. **General Manager:** Jim Appleby. **Head Coach:** Grady Tweit. **Assistant Coaches:** Jason Mackey, Michael Forgione.

KELOWNA FALCONS

Mailing Address: 201-1014 Glenmore Dr, Kelowna, BC, V1Y 4P2. **Telephone:** (250) 763-4100. **Website:** kelownafalcons.com. **Owner:** Dan Nonis. **General Manager:** Mark Nonis. **Head Coach:** Bryan Donohue.

PORT ANGELES LEFTIES

Mailing Address: PO Box 2204, Port Angeles, WA 98362. **Phone:** (360) 701-1087. **Website:** lefties baseball.com. **E-Mail Address:** matt@leftiesbaseball.com. **Owners:** Matt Acker, Jacob Oppelt, Eric Traut, Connor Traut. **General Manager:** Ryan Hickey. **Head Coach:** Matt Acker. **Assistant Coach:** Earl Smith, Anthony Murillo.

PORTLAND PICKLES

Address: 5308 SE 92nd Ave. Portland, OR 97266. **Phone:** (503)775-3080. **Owners:** Alan Miller, Jon Ryan, Scott Barchus. **Head Coach:** Justin Barchus. **Hitting Coach:** Mark Magdaleno. **Pitching Coach:** Jim Lawler. **Bench Coach:** Jim Hoppel.

RIDGEFIELD RAPTORS

Owner: Tony Bonacci. **Partner:** Wade Siegel. **E-Mail Address:** info@ridgefieldraptors.com. **General Manager:** Gus Farah. **Head Coach:** Chris Cota.

VICTORIA HARBOURCATS

Mailing Address: 101-1814 Vancouver Street, Victoria, BC, Canada, V8T 5E3. **Telephone:** (778) 265-0327. **Website:** harbourcats.com. **Owners:** Rich Harder, Jim Swanson, Ken Swanson, John Wilson. **Managing Partner:** Jim Swanson. **General Manager:** Brad Norris-Jones. **Head Coach:** Brian McRae. **Assistant Coaches:** Ian Sanderson, Todd Haney, Troy Birtwistle, Jason Leone, Curtis Pelletier.

WALLA WALLA SWEETS

Mailing Address: 109 E Main Street, Walla Walla, WA 99362. **Telephone:** (509) 522-2255. **E-Mail Address:** info@wallawallasweets.com. **Website:** wallawallasweets.com. **Owner:** Pacific Baseball Ventures, LLC. **President/COO:** Zachary Fraser. **General Manager:** Dan Ferguson. **Head Coach:** Frank Mutz. **Assistant Coaches:** Raul Camacho, Kyle Wilkerson.

WENATCHEE APPLESOX

Mailing Address: 610 N. Mission St. #204, Wenatchee, WA 98801. **Telephone:** (509) 665-6900. **E-Mail Address:** info@applesox.com. **Website:** applesox.com. **Owner/General Manager:** Jose Oglesby. **Owner/Assistant General Manager:** Ken Osborne. **Head Coach:** Ian Sanderson.

YAKIMA VALLEY PIPPINS

Mailing Address: PO Box 2397, Yakima, WA 98907. **Telephone:** (509) 575-4487. **E-Mail Address:** info@pippinsbaseball.com. **Website:** pippinsbaseball.com. **Owner:** Pacific Baseball Ventures, LLC. **President/COO:** Zachary Fraser. **General Manager:** Jeff Garretson. **Head Coach:** Kyle Krustangel. **Pitching Coach:** Cash Ulrich.

APPALACHIAN LEAGUE

Mailing Address: 1340 Environ Way, Chapel Hill, NC 27517. **Telephone:** 919-913-4590. **E-Mail Address:** dan@appyleague.com. **Website:** www.appyleague.com.

President: Dan Moushon. **Director of Communications and Media Relations:** Brad Young. **Baseball Chapel Representative:** Craig Stout (Princeton) **Steering Committee:** Chris Allen, Ashley Bratcher, Eric Campbell, Tim Corbin, John D'Angelo, Dan Hartleb, Gil Kim, Bryan Minniti, Dan Moushon, Jalen Phillips, Steve Sanders, John Savage, Bill Schmidt, Edwin Thompson.

Division Structure: East—Bluefield, Burlington, Danville, Princeton, Pulaski.

West—Bristol, Elizabethton, Greeneville, Johnson City, Kingsport.

Regular Season: 54 games. **2022 Opening Date:** June 3. **Closing Date:** August 7. **All-Star Game:** July 27 **Roster Limit:** 32 active.

BLUEFIELD RIDGE RUNNERS

Office Address: 2003 Stadium Dr. Bluefield WV 24701. **Mailing Address:** P.O. Box 356 Bluefield WV. 24701. **Telephone:** 304-324-1326. Fax 304-324-1318. **Email address:** bluefieldridgerunners@gmail.com. **Website:** www.bluefieldridgerunners.com.

Ownership/management: Bluefield Baseball Club **President:** George McGonagle. **Counsel:** Brian Cochran. **General Manager:** Rocky Malamisura **Manager:** Joe Oliver. **Hitting Coach:** Angel Sanchez. **Pitching coach:** Dennis Rasmussen. **Bench coach/ Tech Coach:** Garrett Schilling. **Head Groundskeeper:** Mike White.

Stadium Name: Bowen Field. **Location:** I-77 to Bluefield exit 1, Route 290 to Route 460 West, fourth light right onto Leatherwood Lane, left at first light, past Hometown Shell station and turn right, stadium quarter-mile on left. **Ticket Price Range:** $6.

BRISTOL STATE LINERS

Office Address: 1501 Euclid Ave, Bristol, VA 24201. **Mailing Address:** PO Box 1434, Bristol, VA 24203. **Telephone:** (276) 206-9946. **Fax:** (423)-968-2636. **E-Mail Address:** gm@bristolbaseball.com. **Website:** www.bristolstateliners.com.

Owned by: Bristol Baseball Inc.. **Operated by:** Bristol Baseball Inc. **President/General Manager:** Mahlon Luttrell. **Vice President:** Craig Adams, Mark Young. **General Council:** Lucas Hobbs. **Treasurer:** Delma Luttrell. **Secretary:** Connie Kinkead.

Manager: TBA. **Hitting Coach:** TBA. **Pitching Coach:** TBA. **Athletic Trainer:** TBA. **Strength & Conditioning Coach:** TBA.

Stadium: DeVault Memorial Stadium. **Standard Game Times:** Mon.-Sat., 7 pm, Sun., 6 pm. **Ticket Price Range:** $4-$8.

BURLINGTON SOCK PUPPETS

Office Address: 1450 Graham St, Burlington, NC 27217. **Mailing Address:** PO Box 1143, Burlington, NC 27216. **Telephone:** (336) 222-0223. **E-Mail Address:** info@gosockpuppets.com. **Website:** www.gosockpuppets.com

Owner: Knuckleball Entertainment, LLC. **President:** Ryan Keur. **General Manager:** Anderson Rathbun. **Assistant GM:** Thomas Vickers.

Manager: Jack McDowell. **Stadium:** Burlington Athletic Stadium. **Standard Game Time:** 7:00 pm. **Ticket Price Range:** $8-15.

DANVILLE OTTERBOTS

Office Address: Dan Daniel Memorial Park, 302 River Park Dr, Danville, VA 24540. **Mailing Address:** PO Box 330, Danville, VA 24543. **Telephone:** (434) 554-4487. **E-Mail Address:** danvillebaseball21@gmail.com. **Website:** www.mlb.com/appalachian-league/danville.

Operated by: Danville Baseball Club LLC. **Owners:** Ryan Keur, Brittany Keur. **General Manager:** Austin Scher. **Head Groundskeeper:** Ryan Brown. **Manager:** Desi Relaford. **Hitting Coach:** Angel Berroa. **Pitching Coach:** TBA. **Bench Coach:** TBA. **Athletic Trainer:** TBA. **Strength & Conditioning Coach:** TBA.

Stadium: American Legion Post 325 Field at Dan Daniel Memorial Park. **Standard Game Times:** Mon.-Sat., 7:00 pm, Sun. 5:00 pm. **Ticket Price Range:** $5-11.

ELIZABETHTON RIVER RIDERS

Address: 804 Holly Lane, Elizabethton, TN 37643. **Telephone:** (423) 547-6443.
Owned/Operated by: Boyd Sports LLC. **President:** Chris Allen. **Vice President:** Jeremy Boler. **General Manager:** Brice Ballentine.
Manager: Kevin Riggs. **Hitting Coach:** Jeremy Owens. **Pitching Coach:** TBD. **Athletic Trainer:** TBD. **Strength & Conditioning Coach:** TBD
Stadium: Northeast Community Credit Union Ballpark. **Standard Game Times:** 7:00 pm. **Ticket Price Range:** $5-7.

GREENEVILLE FLYBOYS

Address: 135 Shiloh Road, Greeneville, TN 37745. **Telephone:** (423) 609-7400. **E-Mail Address:** contact@flyboysbaseball.com. **Website:** https://www.mlb.com/appalachian-league/greeneville.
Owned by: Boyd Sports, LLC. **General Manager:** Kat Foster. **Assistant General Manager:** Brandon Bouschart. **Manager:** Alan Regier. **Hitting Coach:** TBD. **Pitching Coach/Assistant to the Pitching Coordinator:** TBD. **Bench Coach:** TBD. **Athletic Trainer:** TBD. **Strength & Conditioning Coach:** TBD
Stadium: Pioneer Park. **Standard Game Time:** Mon-Sat., 7:00 pm, Sun., 5:30 pm. **Ticket Price Range:** $5 group discount, $7 reserved, $8 premium.

JOHNSON CITY DOUGHBOYS

Office Address: 510 Bert St., Johnson City, TN 37601. **Mailing Address:** PO Box 179, Johnson City, TN 37605. **Telephone:** (423) 461-4866. **E-Mail Address:** zclark@jcdoughboys.com. **Website:** www.jcdoughboys.com.
Operated by: Boyd Sports, LLC. **President:** Chris Allen. **Vice President:** Jeremy Boler. **General Manager:** Zac Clark.
Manager: Rick Magnante. **Hitting Coach:** Cody Gabella. **Pitching Coach:** Cody Stull. **Athletic Trainer:** NA. **Strength and Conditioning Coordinator:** NA.
Stadium: TVA Credit Union Ballpark. **Standard Game Time:** Mon.-Sat. 7 pm, Sun. 5:30 pm. **Ticket Price Range:** $6-$9.

KINGSPORT AXMEN

Address: 800 Granby Rd, Kingsport, TN 37660. **Telephone:** (423) 224-2626. **Fax:** (423) 224-2625. **Website:** www.kingsportaxmen.com
Owner: Boyd Sports, LLC. **General Manager:** TBD. **Clubhouse Manager:** TBD
Manager: TBD. **Hitting Coach:** TBD. **Pitching Coach:** TBD. **Bench Coach:** TBD. **Athletic Trainer:** TBD. **Performance Coach:** TBD
Stadium: Hunter Wright Stadium. **Standard Game Times:** Mon-Sat., 7pm, Sun., 5:30pm. **Doubleheaders—** Mon-Sat. TBD, Sun: TBD. **Ticket Price Range:** $6 -$8.

PRINCETON WHISTLEPIGS

Office Address: 345 Old Bluefield Road, Princeton, WV 24739. **Mailing Address:** PO Box 5646, Princeton, WV 24740. **Telephone:** 304-487-2000. **Email Address:** gm@whistlepigsbaseball.com. **Website:** www.whistlepigs-baseball.com
Operated By: Princeton Baseball Association, Inc. **President:** Dewey Russell. **General Manager:** Danny Shingleton. **Director Stadium Operations:** Adam Sarver, Rusty Sarver. **Chaplain:** Craig Stout.

Field Manager: TBD.
Stadium: Hunnicutt Field. **Standard Game Time:** Mon.-Sat., 7 pm, Sun., 6 pm. **Ticket Price Range:** $5-8.

PULASKI RIVER TURTLES

Office Address: 529 Pierce Avenue, Pulaski, VA 24301. **Mailing Address:** PO Box 852, Pulaski, VA 24301. **Telephone:** (540) 980-1070. **Email Address:** info@pulaskiriverturtles.com
Operated By: Calfee Park Baseball Inc. **Park Owners:** David Hagan, Larry Shelor. **General Manager:** JW Martin. **Field Manager:** TBD.
Stadium: Historic Calfee Park. **Ticket Price Range:** $5-11.

MLB DRAFT LEAGUE

Website: www.mlb.com/mlb-draft-league. **Email:** draftleague@prepbaseballreport.com.
Founded: 2021.
Operated By: Prep Baseball Report.
President, Draft League: Kerrick Jackson.
Schedule: 80 games. **Start Date:** June 2. **Closing Date:** Sept. 4. **Playoffs:** Championship game, Sept. 6.

FREDERICK KEYS

Mailing Address: 21 Stadium Drive, Frederick, MD 21703. **Email:** info@frederickkeys.com. **Telephone:** 301-662-0013. **Website:** https://www.milb.com/frederick
General Manager: Andrew Klein.

MAHONING VALLEY SCRAPPERS

Address: 111 Eastwood Mall Blvd., Niles, OH 44446-1357. **Email:** info@mvscrappers.com. **Telephone:** (330) 505-0000. **Website:** www.milb.com/mahoning-valley.
General Manager: Jordan Taylor.

STATE COLLEGE SPIKES

Address: 112 Medlar Field at Lubrano Park, University Park, PA 16802. **Email:** frontoffice@statecollegespikes.com. **Telephone:** (814) 272-1711
Website: www.milb.com/state-college.
General Manager: Scott Walker.

TRENTON THUNDER

Mailing Address: 1 Thunder Road, Trenton, N.J. 08611. **Email:** fun@trentonthunder.com. **Telephone:** 609-394-3300. **Website:** www.milb.com/trenton
General Manager: Jeff Hurley.

WEST VIRGINIA BLACK BEARS

Address: 2040 Gyorko Drive, Granville, WV 26534. **Telephone:** (304) 293-7910. **Website:** https://www.milb.com/west-virginia-black-bears.
General Manager: TBD.

WILLIAMSPORT CROSSCUTTERS

Address: 1700 West Fourth St, Williamsport, PA 17701. **Email: Telephone:** (570) 326-3389. **Website:** https://www.milb.com/williamsport.
General Manager: Doug Estes.

HIGH SCHOOL BASEBALL

NATIONAL FEDERATION OF STATE HIGH SCHOOL ASSOCIATIONS

Mailing Address: PO Box 690, Indianapolis, IN 46206. **Telephone:** (317) 972-6900. **E-Mail Address:** baseball@nfhs.org. **Website:** nfhs.org.

Executive Director: Karissa Niehoff. **Chief Operating Officer:** Davis Whitfield. **Director of Sports, Sanctioning and Student Services:** B. Elliot Hopkins. **Director, Publications/Communications:** Bruce Howard.

NATIONAL HIGH SCHOOL BASEBALL COACHES ASSOCIATION

Mailing Address: PO Box 1038, Dublin, OH 43017. **Telephone:** (614) 578-1864. **E-Mail Address:** tsaunders@baseballcoaches.org. **Website:** baseballcoaches.org.
Executive Director: Tim Saunders (Dublin Coffman HS, Ohio). **Assistant Executive Director:** Ty Whittaker (Eastern Technical HS, Md.). **Associate Executive Director:** Ray Benjamin (St. Charles HS, Ohio). **Associate Exect[sic]ive Director:** Paul Twenge (Minnetonka HS, Minn.). **Executive Secretary:** Robert Colburn. **President:** Tony Perkins (Francis Howell HS, Mo.). **1st VP:** Tim Bordenet (Lafayette Central Catholic HS, Ind.). **2nd VP:** Scott Manahan (Bishop Watterson HS, Ohio).

2022 National Convention: Fort Myers, Fla.

NATIONAL TOURNAMENTS
IN-SEASON

INTERNATIONAL PAPER CLASSIC
Mailing Address: 4775 Johnson Rd., Georgetown, SC 29440. **Telephone:** (843) 527-9606. **Fax:** (843) 546-8521. Website: ipclassic.com.
Tournament Director: Alicia Johnson.
2022 Tournament: March 3-6.

47TH ANNUAL ANAHEIM LIONS CLUB BASEBALL TOURNAMENT
Mailing Address: 8281 Walker Street, La Palma, CA 90623. **Telephone:** (714) 220-4101x27502. **Fax:** (714) 995-1833. **Email:** Pascal_C@AUHSD.US. **Website:** www.e-clubhouse.org/sites/anaheim/.
Tournament Director: Chris Pascal.

NATIONAL CLASSIC BASEBALL TOURNAMENT
Mailing Address: 1651 Valencia Ave, Placentia, CA 92870. **Telephone:** (714) 993-2838. **Fax:** (714) 993-5350. **E-Mail Address:** mlucas@pylusd.org.
Website: www.nationalclassicbaseball.com
Tournament Director: Matt Lucas.
2022 Tournament: April 4-7.

USA BASEBALL NATIONAL HIGH SCHOOL INVITATIONAL
Mailing Address: 2933 South Miami Blvd, Suite 119, Durham, NC 27703. **Telephone:** (919) 474-8721.
Email: carterhicks@usabaseball.com.
Website: usabaseball.com.
2022 Tournament: April 6-9 at USA Baseball National Training Complex, Cary, N.C. (16 teams).

POSTSEASON

ALL-STAR GAMES/AWARDS
PERFECT GAME ALL-AMERICAN CLASSIC
Mailing Address: 850 Twixt Town Rd. NE, Cedar Rapids, IA 52402. **Telephone:** (319) 298-2923. **Fax:** (319) 298-2924. **Event Organizer:** Blue Ridge Sports & Entertainment. **VP, Showcases/Scouting:** Greg Sabers.
2022 Game: Summer, TBD.

BASEBALL FACTORY ALL-STAR CLASSIC
Mailing Address: 9212 Berger Rd., Suite 200, Columbia, MD 21046. **Telephone:** (410) 715-5080. **E-mail Address:** jason@factoryathletics.com. **Website:** baseballfactory.com/AllAmerica. **Event Organizers:** Baseball Factory, Team One Baseball.
2022 Game: Summer, TBD.

GATORADE CIRCLE OF CHAMPIONS
(National HS Player of the Year Award)
Mailing Address: The Gatorade Company, 321 N. Clark St., Suite 24-3, Chicago, IL, 60610. **Telephone:** (312) 821-1000. **Website:** gatorade.com.

SHOWCASE EVENTS

AREA CODE BASEBALL GAMES PRESENTED BY NEW BALANCE
Mailing Address: 23954 Madison Street, Torrance, CA 90505. **Telephone:** (310) 791-1142 x 4426. **E-Mail:** baseball@studentsports.com. **Website:** AreaCodeBaseball.com.
Event Organizer: Kirsten Leetch.
2022 Area Code Games: Summer, TBA.

AREA CODE BASEBALL UNDERCLASS GAMES PRESENTED BY NEW BALANCE
Event Organizer: Kirsten Leetch.
2022 Area Code Games: Summer, TBA.

ARIZONA FALL CLASSIC
Mailing Address: 9962 W. Villa Hermosa, Peoria, AZ 85383. **Telephone:** (602) 228-1592.
E-mail Address: azfallclassic@gmail.com.
Website: azfallclassic.com.
President: Tracy Heid
Event Director: Trevor Heid,
Information Directors: Tiffini Robinson, Tiana Eves

2022 EVENTS

Four Corner Classic . . . . Peoria/Maryvale, AZ, June 2-5

AZ Freshman

Fall Classic (class of 2026) . . . . Peoria, AZ, Oct. 16-16

AZ Sophomore

Fall Classic (class of 2025) . . . . Peoria, AZ, Oct. 6-9

AZ Senior

Fall Classic (class of 2023) . . . . . . Peoria, AZ, Sept. 29-Oct.2

Senior All Academic Game . . . . Sept. 29

AZ Junior

Fall Classic (class of 2024) . . . . Peoria, AZ , Sept. 22-25

Junior All Academic Tryout & Game . . . . Sept. 22

Easton Fall Classic . . . . Peoria, AZ, Oct. 20-23

BASEBALL FACTORY
Office Address: 9212 Berger Rd., Suite 200, Columbia, MD 21046. **Telephone:** (800) 641-4487, (410) 715-5080. **Fax:** (410) 715-1975. **E-mail Address:** info@baseballfactory.com. **Website:** baseballfactory.com.
Chief Executive Officer/Founder: Steve Sclafani. **President:** Rob Naddelman. **Chief Baseball Officer:** Steve Bernhardt. **Senior VP of Player Development:** Dan Forest. **Chief Program Officer:** Jim Gemler. **Executive Player Development Coordinator, VP of Business Development:** Dave Packer.
Regional Player Development Coordinators: Chris Brown, Matt Clementoni, Adam Darvick, Matt Deslonde, Matt Eckler, Stephen Gronowski, Rob Onolfi, John Perko, Matt Sammarco, Patrick Wuebben.
Baseball Factory National Tryout & Evaluation: Sam Carmel, Patrick Lawrence, Jordan Patterson, Gabe Vertucci, TJ Schaff.
Baseball Operations: Chad Addison, Pete Buck, Mark Daniels, Scott Demetral, Nick Dorazio, Josh Eldridge,

Randy Hodge, Don Jamerson, Chris Kievit, Mike Landis, Ryan Liddle, Trace Meyer, Talmadge Nunnari, David Sitton.
College Recruiting: Bernadette Bechta, Dan Mooney, Matt Richter.
Baseball Consultants: Rick Sofield, Mike Toomey.
Creative Team: Deen Adelakun Jr., Amanda Beck, Cameron Esposito, Brian Johnson, Tom Kreft, Lauren Peck, Wei Xue.
Financial Team: Michael Lardieri, Tripp Norton.

2022 Baseball Factory National Tryouts/College PREP Recruiting Program: Year round at various locations across the country. Open to high school players, ages 14–18, with a separate division for middle school players, ages 12–14. **Full schedule:** www.baseballfactory.com/tryouts.

EAST COAST PROFESSIONAL SHOWCASE
Website: www.eastcoastpro.org. **Mailing Address:** Hoover Met Complex, 100 Ben Chapman Dr, Hoover, AL 25244. **E-mail Address:** info@eastcoastpro.org
Tournament Directors: John Castleberry, Rich Sparks, Sean Gibbs, Arthur McConnehead, Lori Bridges.
2022 Showcase: Summer, TBA.

IMPACT BASEBALL
Mailing Address: P.O. Box 47, Sedalia, NC 27342.
E-mail Address: impactbaseballstaff@gmail.com.
Website: impactbaseball.com. **Founder/CEO:** Andy Partin. **2022 Events:** Various dates, June-Aug.

NORTHWEST CHAMPIONSHIPS
Mailing Address: 545 Tillicum Drive, Silverton OR 97381. **Telephone:** (503) 302-7117. **E-mail Address:** info@baseballnorthwest.com . **Website:** baseballnorthwest.com. **Tournament Organizer:** Josh Warner.

PERFECT GAME USA
(A Division of Perfect Game USA)
Mailing Address: 850 Twixt Town Rd. NE, Cedar Rapids, IA 52402. **Telephone:** (319) 298-2923. **Fax:** (319) 298-2924. **E-mail Address:** pgba@perfectgame.org. **Website:** perfectgame.org.
Year Founded: 1995.
President: Jerry Ford. **VP, Operations:** Taylor McCollough. **VP, Showcases/Scouting:** Greg Sabers.

PREP BASEBALL REPORT
Mailing Address: 4750 S. Vernon Ave, McCook, IL 60525. **Telephone:** 708-387-0500.
President: Sean Duncan. **Vice President of Operations and Multimedia:** Matt Yarber. **National Crosschecker:** Shooter Hunt. **National Supervisor:** Nathan Rode. **Director of College Scouting:** David Seifert. **Managing Director:** Cullen McGowan.

PROFESSIONAL BASEBALL INSTRUCTION—BATTERY INVITATIONAL

(for top high school pitchers and catchers)
Mailing Address: 1300 Route 17, North, Ramsey NJ 07446.
Telephone: (800) 282-4638. **Fax:** (201) 760-8820.
E-mail Address: info@baseballclinics.com.
Website: baseballclinics.com
President: Doug Cinnella.
Director of PR/Marketing: Jim Monaghan.

SELECTFEST BASEBALL

Mailing Address: P.O. Box 852, Morris Plains, NJ 07950. **E-mail Address:** selectfest@selectfestbaseball.org.
Website: selectfestbaseball.org. **Camp Directors:** Bruce Shatel, Robert Maida. **2022 Showcase:** TBD.

TEAM ONE BASEBALL

(A division of Baseball Factory)
Office Address: 220 Newport Center Drive, 11418, Newport Beach, CA 92660. **Telephone:** (800) 621-5452.
Fax: (949) 209-1829. **E-Mail Address:** jroswell@teamone-baseball.com. **Website:** teamonebaseball.com.
Executive Director: Justin Roswell. **Chief Program Officer:** Jim Gemler. **Executive VP:** Steve Bernhardt.
Senior VP, Player Development: Dan Forester.

2022 Showcases:

For a full listing of showcases visit: www.teamone-baseball.com/showcases.

2022 Tournaments:

Memorial Day Classic East	May 27-30
	Roger Dean Complex, Jupiter, Fla.
Memorial Day Classic West	May 27-30
	APU/ELAC, Southern California
Las Vegas Summer Classic	June 3-6
	Desert Diamond Complex, Las Vegas, NV
Father's Day Classic	June 24- 28
	Orange County Great Park, Irvine, CA
Firecracker Classic West	June 24-28
	University of La Verne / APU, Southern California
Firecracker Classic East	July 5-9
	Roger Dean Complex, Jupiter, FL
Southwest Championships 15U	July 15-19
	University of La Verne, La Verne, CA
Southwest Championships 16U	July 22-26
	University of La Verne, La Verne, CA
Southwest Championships 17U	July 29-Aug. 2
	OC Great Park, Irvine, CA
Jupiter Fall Classic	Sept. 24-26
	Roger Dean Complex, Jupiter, FL
SoCal Classic	Oct. 15-17
	APU/East LA College, Monterey Park, CA
Best of the West	Oct. 29-31
	OC Great Park, Irvine, CA
Texas Fall Classic	TBA
	Cy-Fair Sports, Cypress, TX

For a full listing of tournaments visit:
www.teamonebaseball.com/tournaments.

TOP 96 COLLEGE COACHES CLINICS

Mailing Address: 2639 Connecticut Avenue NW, Suite 250, Washington, DC 20008. **Telephone:** (202) 313-7385.
Emaiil Address: info@top96.com. **Website:** top96.com.
Directors: Doug Henson, Dave Callum.

YOUTH BASEBALL

ALL AMERICAN AMATEUR BASEBALL ASSOCIATION

Mailing Address: 1101 Flamingo Drive, APT 3106, Altoona, PA 16602.

Cell: (814) 931-8698.

E-Mail Address: aaabaprez@atlanticbb.net.

Website: aaabajohnstown.org

President: Mike Gossner

Executive Director: John Austin

2022 Events: aaabajohnstown.org/tournaments/

AMATEUR ATHLETIC UNION OF THE UNITED STATES, INC.

Mailing Address: P.O. Box 22409, Lake Buena Vista, FL 32830. **Telephone:** (407) 828-3459. **Fax:** (407) 934-7242. **E-mail Address:** oldpro77@msn.com. **Website:** aaubaseball.org.

Year Founded: 1982. **National Baseball Chairperson:** Ed Skovron.

AMERICAN AMATEUR BASEBALL CONGRESS

National Headquarters: 100 West Broadway, Farmington, NM 87401. **Telephone:** (505) 327-3120. **Fax:** (505) 327-3132. **E-mail Address:** info@aabc.us. **Website:** aabc.us.

Year Founded: 1935.

President: Richard Neely.

AMERICAN AMATEUR YOUTH BASEBALL ALLIANCE

Mailing Address: 3851 Iris Lane, Bonne Terre, MO 63628. **Telephone:** (314) 971-0028. **E-mail Address:** info@aayba.com. **Website:** aayba.com.

President, Baseball Operations: Carroll Wood.

President, Business Operations: Greg Moore.

AMERICAN LEGION BASEBALL

National Headquarters: American Legion Baseball, 700 N Pennsylvania St., Indianapolis, IN 46204. **Telephone:** (317) 630-1213. **Fax:** (317) 630-1369. **E-mail Address:** baseball@legion.org. **Website:** legion.org/baseball.

Year Founded: 1925.

Program Coordinator: Steve Cloud.

2022 World Series (19 and under): americanlegion.sportngin.com/2021alws

BABE RUTH LEAGUE

International Headquarters: 1670 Whitehorse-Mercerville Rd., Hamilton, NJ 08619. **Telephone:** (800) 880-3142. **E-mail Address:** info@baberuthleague.org. **Website:** baberuthleague.org.

Year Founded: 1951.

President/Chief Executive Officer: Steven Tellefsen.

BASEBALL FOR ALL

Mailing Address: 30745 Pacific Coast Hwy #328 Los Angeles, CA 90265. **E-mail Address:** girlsbaseball@baseballforall.com. **Website:** BaseballForAll.com

Providing baseball programming for girls.

CALIFORNIA COMPETITIVE YOUTH BASEBALL

Mailing Address: P.O. Box 338, Placentia, CA 92870. **Telephone:** (714) 993-2838. **E-mail Address:** ccybnet@gmail.com. **Website:** ccyb.net.

Tournament Director: Todd Rogers.

COCOA EXPO SPORTS CENTER

Mailing Address: 500 Friday Road, Cocoa, FL 32926. **Telephone:** (321) 639-3976. **E-mail Address:** brad@cocoaexpo.com. **Website:** cocoaexpo.com.

Activities: Spring training program, spring & fall leagues, instructional camps, team training camps, youth tournaments.

CONTINENTAL AMATEUR BASEBALL ASSOCIATION

Mailing Address: P.O. Box 1684 Mt. Pleasant, SC 29465. **Telephone:** (843) 860-1568. **E-mail Address:** Diamonddevils@aol.com. **Website:** cababaseball.com.

Year Founded: 1984.

Chief Executive Officer: Larry Redwine. **President/COO:** John Rhodes. **Executive Vice President:** Fran Pell.

COOPERSTOWN BASEBALL WORLD

Mailing Address: P.O. Box 646, Allenwood, NJ 08720. **Telephone:** (888) CBW-8750. **Fax:** (888) CBW-8720. **E-mail:** cbw@cooperstownbaseballworld.com.

Website: cooperstownbaseballworld.com.

Complex Address: Cooperstown Baseball World, SUNY-Oneonta, Ravine Parkway, Oneonta, NY 13820.

President: Debra Sirianni.

2022 Tournaments (15 Teams Per Week): Open to 12U, 13U, 14U, 15U, 16U

COOPERSTOWN DREAMS PARK

Mailing Address: 330 S. Main St., Salisbury, NC 28144. **Telephone:** (704) 630-0050. **Fax:** (704) 630-0737. **E-mail Address:** info@cooperstowndreamspark.com. **Website:** cooperstowndreamspark.com.

Complex Address: 4550 State Highway 28, Milford, NY 13807.

Chief Operating Officer: Mike Walter. **Director, Baseball Operations:** Geoff Davis.

2022 Tournaments: May 29-Aug. 21.

COOPERSTOWN ALL STAR VILLAGE

Mailing Address: P.O. Box 670, Cooperstown, NY 13326. **Telephone:** (800) 327-6790. **Fax:** (607) 432-1076. **E-mail Address:** info@cooperstownallstarvillage.com. **Website:** cooperstownallstarvillage.com.

Team Registrations: Hunter Grace. **Hotel Room Reservations:** Tracie Jones. **Presidents:** Martin and Brenda Patton.

DIXIE YOUTH BASEBALL

Mailing Address: P.O. Box 877, Marshall, TX 75671. **Telephone:** (903) 927-2255. **E-mail Address:** dyb@dixie.org. **Website:** youth.dixie.org. **Year Founded:** 1955.

Commissioner: William Wade.

DIXIE BOYS BASEBALL

Mailing Address: P.O. Box 8263, Dothan, AL 36304. **Telephone:** (334) 793-3331. **E-mail Address:** jjones29@sw.rr.com. **Website:** baseball.dixie.org.
Commissioner/Chief Executive Officer: Sandy Jones.

DIZZY DEAN BASEBALL

Mailing Address: P.O. Box 856, Hernando, MS 38632. **Telephone:** (662) 429-4365. **E-mail Address:** dannyphillips637@gmail.com. **Website:** dizzydeanbbinc.org.
Year Founded: 1962.
Commissioner: Danny Phillips. **President:** Joe Chandler. **VP:** Brent Frey. **Secretary:** John Gravet. **Treasurer:** Jim Dunn.

HAP DUMONT YOUTH BASEBALL

(A Division of the National Baseball Congress)
E-mail Address: hapdumontbaseball@gmail.com.
Year Founded: 1974.
President: Bruce Pinkall

KC SPORTS TOURNAMENTS

Mailing Address: KC Sports, 6324 N. Chatham Ave., No. 136, Kansas City, MO 64151.
Telephone: (816) 587-4545. **Fax:** (816) 587-4549.
E-mail Address: info@kcsports.org.
Website: kcsports.org.
Activities: USSSA Youth tournaments (ages 6-18).

LITTLE LEAGUE BASEBALL

International Headquarters: 539 US Route 15 Hwy, P.O. Box 3485, Williamsport, PA 17701-0485. **Telephone:** (570) 326-1921. **Fax:** (570) 326-1074. **E-Mail Address:** media@littleleague.org. **Website:** littleleague.org.
Year Founded: 1939.
Chairman: Hugh E. Tanner.
President and Chief Executive Officer: Stephen D. Keener. **Senior Vice President and Chief Financial Officer:** David Houseknecht. **Vice President, Operations:** Patrick Wilson. **Senior Vice President and Chief Marketing Officer:** Liz DiLullo Brown. **Senior Vice President and Chief Legal Officer:** Karl Eckweiler.

NATIONS BASEBALL-ARIZONA

Mailing Address: 7436 E. Kilarea Ave, Mesa AZ 85209. **Telephone:** 480-528-9911. **Website:** playballaz.com. **E-Mail:** playballaz@q.com.

NATIONAL AMATEUR BASEBALL FEDERATION

Mailing Address: P.O. Box 4099 Brandon, MS 29047. **Telephone:** 769-251-5158.
E-mail Address: nabfexecdirector@gmail.com.
Website: nabf.com. **Year Founded:** 1914.
Executive Director: Derek J. Topik.

INSTRUCTIONAL SCHOOLS/ PRIVATE CAMPS

ALL-STAR BASEBALL ACADEMY

Mailing Address: 1475 Phoenixville Pike, Suite 12, West Chester, PA 19380. **Telephone:** (484) 770-8325. **Fax:** (484) 770-8336. **E-mail Address:** basba@allstarbaseballacademy.com. **Website:** allstarbaseballacademy.com.
President/CEO: Jim Freeman. **Executive Director:** Mike Manning.

AMERICAN BASEBALL FOUNDATION

Mailing Address: 833 Saint Vincent's Drive Suite 205A, Birmingham, AL 35205. **Telephone:** (205) 558-4235. **Fax:** (205) 918-0800. **E-mail Address:** abf@asmi.org. **Website:** americanbaseballfoundation.com.
Executive Director: David Osinski.

ABC BASEBALL CAMPS

Mailing Address: 1353 Lake Shore Dr, Branson, MO 65616. **E-mail Address:** support@abcsportscamps.com. **Website:** abcsportscamps.com.

CHAMPIONS BASEBALL ACADEMY

Mailing Address: 5994 Linneman Street, Cincinnati, OH 45230. **Telephone:** (513) 831-8873. **Fax:** (513) 247-0040. **E-mail Address:** championsbaseball@ymail.com. **Website:** championsbaseball.net. **Director:** Mike Bricker.

ELEV8 SPORTS INSTITUTE

Mailing Address: 490 Dotterel Road, Delray Beach, FL 33444. **Telephone:** (800) 970-5896. **Fax:** (561) 865-7358. **E-mail Address:** info@elev8si.com. **Website:** elev8sportsinstitute.com/

FROZEN ROPES TRAINING CENTERS

Mailing Address: 24 Old Black Meadow Rd., Chester, NY 10918. **Telephone:** (845) 469-7331. **Fax:** (845) 469-6742. **E-mail Address:** info@frozenropes.com. **Website:** frozenropes.com.

IMG ACADEMY

Mailing Address: 5650 Bollettieri Blvd, Bradenton, FL 34210. **Telephone:** 1-800-872-6425. **E-mail Address:** info@imgacademy.com. **Website:** imgacademy.com

MARK CRESSE BASEBALL SCHOOL

Mailing Address: P.O. Box 1596 Newport Beach, CA 92659. **Telephone:** (714) 892-6145. **Fax:** (714) 890-7017. **E-mail Address:** info@markcresse.com.
Website: markcresse.com.
Owner/Founder: Mark Cresse.

US SPORTS CAMPS/NIKE BASEBALL CAMPS

Mailing Address: US Sports Camps, Inc. 1010 B Street, Suite 450 San Rafael, CA 94901. **Telephone:** (415) 479-6060. **Fax:** (415) 479-6061. **E-mail Address:** baseball@ussportscamps.com. **Website:** ussportscamps.com/baseball/.

MOUNTAIN WEST BASEBALL ACADEMY

Mailing Address: 389 West 10000 South, South Jordan, UT 84095. **Telephone:** (801) 561-1700. **E-mail Address:** kent@utahbaseballacademy.com. **Website:** mountainwestbaseball.com. **Director:** Bob Keyes

NORTH CAROLINA BASEBALL ACADEMY

Mailing Address: 1137 Pleasant Ridge Road, Greensboro, NC 27409. **Telephone:** (336) 931-1118. **E-mail Address:** info@ncbaseball.com. **Website:** ncbaseball.com.
Owner/Director: Scott Bankhead.

PENNSYLVANIA DIAMOND BUCKS

Mailing Address: 2320 Whitetail Court, Hellertown, PA 18055. **Telephone:** (610) 838-1219, (610) 442-6998. **E-mail Address:** janciganick@yahoo.com. **Camp Director:** Jan Ciganick. **Head of Instruction:** Chuck Ciganick.

PROFESSIONAL BASEBALL INSTRUCTION

Mailing Address: 1300 Route 17 North, Ramsey Square Shopping Center, Ramsey, NJ 07446. **Telephone:** (800) 282-4638. **Fax:** (201) 760-8820. **E-mail Address:** info@baseballclinics.com. **Website:** baseballclinics.com. **President:** Doug Cinnella.

RIPKEN BASEBALL CAMPS

Mailing Address: 873 Long Drive, Averdeen, MD 21209. **Telephone:** (410) 306-7575. **E-mail Address:** information@ripkenbaseball.com. **Website:** ripkenbaseball.com.

SHO-ME BASEBALL CAMP

Mailing Address: P.O. Box 2270, Branson West, MO 65737. **Telephone:** (417) 338-5838. **Fax:** (417) 338-2610. **E-mail Address:** info@shomebaseball.com. **Website:** shomebaseball.com.

COLLEGE CAMPS

Almost all of the elite college baseball programs have summer/holiday instructional camps. Please consult the college section for listings.

SENIOR BASEBALL

MEN'S SENIOR BASEBALL LEAGUE

(18+, 25+, 35+, 45+, 55+, 65+)
Mailing Address: One Huntington Quadrangle, Suite 3N07, Melville, NY 11747. **Telephone:** (631) 753-6725.
President: Steve Sigler. **Vice President:** Gary D'Ambrisi.
E-Mail Address: info@msblnational.com.
Website: msblnational.com.

NATIONAL ADULT BASEBALL ASSOCIATION

Mailing Address: 5944 S. Kipling St., Suite 200, Littleton, CO 80127. **Telephone:** (800) 621-6479. **E-Mail:** nabanational@aol.com. **Website:** dugout.org.
President: Shane Fugita.

NATIONAL AMATEUR BASEBALL FEDERATION

Mailing Address: P.O. Box 705, Bowie, MD 20718. **Telephone:** (410) 721-4727. **Fax:** (410) 721-4940.
Email Address: nabf1914@aol.com.
Website: nabf.com.
Year Founded: 1914.
Executive Director: Charles Blackburn.

ROY HOBBS BASEBALL

Veterans (30 or 35 and Over), Masters (45 and Over), Legends (53 and Over); Classics (60 and Over), Vintage (65 and Over), Timeless (70 and Over), Forever Young (75 and Over).
Mailing Address: 4301-100 Edison Ave., Fort Myers, FL 33916. **Telephone:** (330) 923-3400. **E-Mail Address:** teammatesupport@royhobbs.com.
Website: royhobbs.com.
CEO: Tom Giffen. **President:** Rob Giffen.

INDEX

INDEX

ED WOLFSTEIN

MAJOR LEAGUE TEAMS

Team	Page	Team	Page
Arizona Diamondbacks	16	Milwaukee Brewers	46
Atlanta Braves	18	Minnesota Twins	48
Baltimore Orioles	20	New York Mets	50
Boston Red Sox	22	New York Yankees	52
Chicago Cubs	24	Oakland Athletics	54
Chicago White Sox	26	Philadelphia Phillies	56
Cincinnati Reds	28	Pittsburgh Pirates	58
Cleveland Guardians	30	St. Louis Cardinals	60
Colorado Rockies	32	San Diego Padres	62
Detroit Tigers	34	San Francisco Giants	64
Houston Astros	36	Seattle Mariners	66
Kansas City Royals	38	Tampa Bay Rays	68
Los Angeles Angels	40	Texas Rangers	70
Los Angeles Dodgers	42	Toronto Blue Jays	72
Miami Marlins	44	Washington Nationals	74

MINOR LEAGUE TEAMS

Team (League)	Page		Page
Aberdeen (High-A East)	124	Columbus (Triple-A East)	88
Akron (Double-A Northeast)	103	Corpus Christi (Double-A Central)	114
Albuquerque (Triple-A West)	97	Dayton (High-A Central)	119
Altoona (Double-A Northeast)	103	Daytona (Low-A Southeast)	142
Amarillo (Double-A Central)	113	Delmarva (Low-A East)	137
Arkansas (Double-A Central)	113	Down East (Low-A East)	138
Asheville (High-A East)	124	Dunedin (Low-A Southeast)	142
Augusta (Low-A East)	136	Durham (Triple-A East)	89
Beloit (High-A Central)	118	El Paso (Triple-A West)	97
Biloxi (Double-A South)	109	Erie (Double-A Northeast)	105
Binghamton (Double-A Northeast)	104	Eugene (High-A West)	129
Birmingham (Double-A South)	109	Everett (High-A West)	129
Bowie (Double-A Northeast)	104	Fayetteville (Low-A East)	138
Bowling Green (High-A East)	125	Fort Myers (Low-A Southeast)	142
Bradenton (Low-A Southeast)	141	Fort Wayne (High-A Central)	119
Brooklyn (High-A East)	125	Fredericksburg (Low-A East)	139
Buffalo (Triple-A East)	87	Fresno (Low-A West)	132
Carolina (Low-A East)	136	Frisco (Double-A Central)	114
Cedar Rapids (High-A Central)	118	Great Lakes (High-A Central)	120
Charleston (Low-A East)	137	Greensboro (High-A East)	125
Charlotte (Triple-A East)	87	Greenville (High-A East)	126
Chattanooga (Double-A South)	110	Gwinnett (Triple-A East)	89
Clearwater (Low-A Southeast)	141	Harrisburg (Double-A Northeast)	105
Columbia (Low-A East)	137	Hartford (Double-A Northeast)	105
		Hickory (High-A East)	127

San Antonio (Double-A Central)	115
San Jose (Low-A West)	134
Scranton/Wilkes-Barre (Triple-A East)	95
Somerset (Double-A Northeast)	108
South Bend (High-A Central)	122
Spokane (High-A West)	130
Springfield (Double-A Central)	116
St. Lucie (Low-A Southeast)	144
St. Paul (Triple-A East)	94
Stockton (Low-A West)	134
Sugar Land (Triple-A West)	101
Syracuse (Triple-A East)	95
Tacoma (Triple-A West)	101
Tampa (Low-A Southeast)	144
Tennessee (Double-A South)	112
Toledo (Triple-A East)	96
Tri-City (High-A West)	130
Tulsa (Double-A Central)	116
Vancouver (High-A West)	131
Visalia (Low-A West)	135
West Michigan (High-A Central)	122
Wichita (Double-A Central)	117
Wilmington (High-A East)	128
Winston-Salem (High-A East)	128
Wisconsin (High-A Central)	123
Worcester (Triple-A East)	96

MLB PARTNER TEAMS

Team (League)	Page
Billings (Pioneer)	184
Boise (Pioneer)	184
Charleston (Atlantic)	175
Chicago (American)	171
Cleburne (American)	171
Evansville (Frontier)	179
Fargo-Moorhead (American)	172
Gary Southshore (American)	172
Gastonia (Atlantic)	175
Gateway (Frontier)	179
Glacier Range (Pioneer)	185
Grand Junction (Pioneer)	185
Great Falls (Pioneer)	185
High Point (Atlantic)	176
Idaho Falls (Pioneer)	185
Joliet (Frontier)	180
Kane County (American)	172
Kansas City (American)	173
Lake Country (American)	173
Lake Erie (Frontier)	180
Lancaster (Atlantic)	176
Lexington (Atlantic)	177
Lincoln (American)	173
Long Island (Atlantic)	177
Milwaukee (American)	174
Missoula (Pioneer)	186
New Jersey (Frontier)	180
New York (Frontier)	180

Team (League)	Page
Northern Colorado (Pioneer)	186
Ogden (Pioneer)	186
Ottawa (Frontier)	181
Quebec (Frontier)	181
Schaumburg (Frontier)	181
Sioux City (American)	174
Sioux Falls (American)	174
Southern Maryland (Atlantic)	177
Staten Island (Atlantic)	178
Sussex County (Frontier)	182
Tri-City (Frontier)	182
Trois-Rivieres (Frontier)	182
Washington (Frontier)	182
Wild Health (Atlantic)	176
Windy City (Frontier)	183
Winnipeg (American)	174
York (Atlantic)	178

Hillsboro (High-A West)	129
Hudson Valley (High-A East)	126
Indianapolis (Triple-A East)	90
Inland Empire (Low-A West)	132
Iowa (Triple-A East)	90
Jacksonville (Triple-A East)	91
Jersey Shore (High-A East)	127
Jupiter (Low-A Southeast)	143
Kannapolis (Low-A East)	139
Lake County (High-A Central)	120
Lake Elsinore (Low-A West)	133
Lakeland (Low-A Southeast)	143
Lansing (High-A Central)	121
Las Vegas (Triple-A West)	98
Lehigh Valley (Triple-A East)	91
Louisville (Triple-A East)	92
Lynchburg (Low-A East)	139
Memphis (Triple-A East)	92
Midland (Double-A Central)	115
Mississippi (Double-A South)	110
Modesto (Low-A West)	133
Montgomery (Double-A South)	110
Myrtle Beach (Low-A East)	140
Nashville (Triple-A East)	92
New Hampshire (Double-A Northeast)	106
Norfolk (Triple-A East)	93
Northwest Arkansas (Double-A Central)	115
Oklahoma City (Triple-A West)	98
Omaha (Triple-A East)	93
Palm Beach (Low-A Southeast)	143
Pensacola (Double-A South)	111
Peoria (High-A Central)	121
Portland (Double-A Northeast)	106
Quad Cities (High-A Central)	121
Rancho Cucamonga (Low-A West)	133
Reading (Double-A Northeast)	107
Reno (Triple-A West)	99
Richmond (Double-A Northeast)	107
Rochester (Triple-A East)	94
Rocket City (Double-A South)	111
Rome (High-A East)	128
Round Rock (Triple-A West)	99
Sacramento (Triple-A West)	100
Salem (Low-A East)	140
Salt Lake (Triple-A West)	100

OTHER ORGANIZATIONS

Organization	Page
Africa Baseball/Softball Association	226
Alaska Baseball League	228
All American Amateur Baseball Association	245
Amateur Athletic Union of the USA	245
America East Conference	196
American Baseball Coaches Association	195
American Amateur Baseball Congress	245
American Amateur Youth Baseball Alliance	245
American Athletic Conference	196
American Legion Baseball	245
Appalachian League	240
Area Code Games	243
Arizona Fall Classic	243
Arizona Fall League	193
Athletes In Action	227
Atlantic Coast Conference	196

Organization	Page
Atlantic Collegiate Baseball League	228
Atlantic Sun Conference	196
Atlantic 10 Conference	196
Australian Baseball League	193
Babe Ruth Baseball	245
Baseball Assistance Team	80
Baseball Canada	227
Baseball Chapel	80
Baseball Confederation of Oceania	226
Baseball Factory	243
Baseball Federation of Asia	226
Baseball For All	245
Baseball Trade Show	80
Baseball Winter Meetings	80

Organization	Page
Big East Conference	196
Big South Conference	196
Big Ten Conference	196
Big 12 Conference	196
Big West Conference	196
Cal Ripken Collegiate League	229
California Collegiate League	229
California Community College Athletic Association	195
California Competitive Youth Baseball	245
Cape Cod League	230
Catholic Athletes For Christ	80
Coastal Plain League	231
Cocoa Expo Sports Center	245
Colonial Athletic Association	196
Confederation Pan Americana De Beisbol	226
Continental Amateur Baseball Association	245
Conference USA	197
Cooperstown Baseball World	245
Cooperstown Dreams Park	245
Cooperstown All-Star Village	245
Dixie Boys Baseball	246
Dixie Youth Baseball	245
Dizzy Dean Baseball	246
Dominican League	192
Dominican Summer League	190
Dutch Major League	192
East Coast Professional Showcase	243
European Baseball Confederation	226
Florida Collegiate Summer League	232
Futures Collegiate League of New England	232
Great Lakes Summer Collegiate League	232
Hap Dumont Youth Baseball	246
Horizon League	197
Impact Baseball	243
International Sports Group	226
Italian Baseball League	192
Ivy League	197
KC Youth Baseball	246
Korea Baseball Organization	191
Little League Baseball	246

Organization	Page
M.I.N.K. League	232
MLB Players Alumni Association	80
MLB Draft League	241
Metro Atlantic Athletic Conference	197
Metropolitan Collegiate Baseball League	232
Mexican League	189
Mexican Pacific League	193
Mid-American Conference	197
Mid-Eastern Athletic Conference	197
Midwest Collegiate League	232
M.I.N.K. League	232
Missouri Valley Conference	197

Organization	Page
Mountain West Conference	197
National Alliance of College Summer Baseball	228
National Amateur Baseball Federation	246
National Baseball Congress	227
National Baseball Hall of Fame	79
National Collegiate Athletic Association	195
National Federation of State High School Associations	242
National High School Baseball Coaches Association	242
National Junior College Athletic Association	195
Nations Baseball—Arizona	246
Negro Leagues Baseball Museum	79
New England Collegiate League	233
New York Collegiate Baseball League	234
Nippon Professional Baseball	190
Northwest Championships	243
Northeast Conference	197
Northwoods League	235
Ohio Valley Conference	197
Pacific-12 Conference	198
Patriot League	198
Pecos League	187
Perfect Game Collegiate Baseball League	236
Perfect Game USA	243
Prep Baseball Report	243
Professional Baseball Instruction	244
Professional Baseball Scouts Foundation	79
Prospect League	237
Puerto Rican League	193
Reviving Baseball in Inner Cities	80
Scout of the Year Foundation	79
Selectfest Baseball	244
Society for American Baseball Research	79
Southeastern Conference	198
Southern Collegiate Baseball League	237
Southern Conference	198
Southland Conference	198
Southwestern Athletic Conference	198
Summit League	198
Sun Belt Conference	198
Team One Baseball	244
Texas Collegiate League	238
Top 96 College Coaches Clinic	244
United Shore Professional Baseball League	187
USA Baseball	227
Valley Baseball League	238
Venezuelan League	193
West Coast Conference	198
West Coast League	239
Western Athletic Conference	198
World Baseball Softball Confederation	226